# Indian Cultural Diplomacy: Celebrating Pluralism in a Globalised World

# Indian Cultural Diplomacy: Celebrating Pluralism in a Globalised World

*Paramjit Sahai*

**Vij Books India Pvt Ltd**
New Delhi (India)

**Indian Council of World Affairs**
Sapru House, New Delhi

*Published by*

**Vij Books India Pvt Ltd**
(Publishers, Distributors & Importers)
2/19, Ansari Road
Delhi – 110 002
Phones: 91-11-43596460, 91-11-47340674
Fax: 91-11-47340674
e-mail: vijbooks@rediffmail.com
web : www.vijbooks.com



ISBN: 978-93-88161-07-7 (Hardback)

ISBN: 978-93-88161-09-1 (ebook)

## *Dedication*

To my Parents, who inculcated basic human values in me and taught me respect for Others

and

To my Foreign Service colleagues, my fellow travellers and partners in Cultural Diplomacy

# Contents

# Foreword

I am happy that my friend Paramjit Sahai has written a book titled, ***"Indian Cultural Diplomacy: Celebrating Pluralism in a Globalised World"*** where the author expounds both the history of cultural diplomacy of India and also highlights the importance of cultural diplomacy in the wider context of emerging power equations in the world. The author provides a fascinating tour of ideas and institutions in the realm of cultural diplomacy within India and outside in this book that he came across within India and abroad during his distinguished diplomatic career of 37 years.

Paramjit Sahai approvingly quotes the definition of cultural diplomacy provided by the Institute for Culture Diplomacy, Washington D.C. It says that; "*Cultural Diplomacy may best be described as a course of actions, which are based on and utilize the exchange of ideas, values, traditions and other aspects of culture or identity, whether to strengthen relationships, enhance socio-cultural cooperation, promote national interests and beyond; Cultural diplomacy can be practiced by either the public sector, private sector or civil society" (ICD).* The author then goes on to ask relevant questions: How central is cultural diplomacy in the diplomatic arena? Where does it find its place in the diplomatic architecture? How does it manifest itself as an important instrument in furthering foreign policy, commercial and other interests? Is there an intrinsic link between culture and commerce? Does culture precede commerce or it is the other way around? Discussing about cultural diplomacy in the Indian context in particular the author asks: What is the policy framework and structures created to pursue the policy objectives? In what manner they interplay and coordinate their roles, both at the policy and implementation levels? What role is played by cultural agreements and the cultural exchange programmes (CEPs) created there under?

In 1998, I had opined that the role of culture has increased in global affairs in the modern world. I had then written: "*in the last decade of the 20th century culture emerged as a third factor in determining the status of a nation in the world after market and military strength, the market having replaced military strength from its position of supremacy in the post-Cold War World"*.

As expressed through language and art, philosophy and religion, education and science, films and newspapers, radio and television, social habits and customs, political institutions and economic organizations, culture heightens the skills of an individual and a society in its totality in all walks of life because it is by culture that a man or a society gets an insight into the whole. Culture includes not only art, music, dance, and drama, but a whole way of life. In fact, culture is '*sanskriti*', or a process of refinement. It is in this broader sense that culture has to be viewed.

We often use civilization and culture in an interchangeable manner. But there is a vital difference between the two. Civilization is much bigger and may contain in its fold several cultural expressions and values.Culture and civilization have, however, a close relationship. Civilizations are actually large cultural spheres containing many nations. In short, civilization in which someone lives is that person's broadest cultural identity. Like all human creations, civilizations also experience cycles of birth, life, decline and death but the basic tenets of culture are somewhat indestructible.

India, Egypt, Iraq, Greece, and China have been recognized as the five cradles of human civilization. By the year AD 1, India was a highly developed culture. India's culture which blossomed more than 5000 years ago, has given successive generations of Indians a mind-set, a value system, and a way of life, which has been retained with remarkable continuity despite the passage of time, repeated foreign invasions, and the enormous growth in population. It gives to Indians as well as to people of Indian origin a unique personality today, as it has done in the past. In fact, these constitute enduring imprints on Indian consciousness.

Over the ages, there has gradually developed a composite Indian culture with its own unbroken history. The story of Indian culture is a story of unity and synthesis, of reconciliation and development, of harmony and assimilation, of fusion of old traditions with new values. One example of assimilation could be that of the ants that carry particles of foodstuff from different places and deposit them all at one place, yet each particle is distinct and identifiable. The process of assimilation in Indian culture, however, is different and is more comparable to '*bee activity*' rather than to '*ant activity*'. Bees move from one flower to the next, collect nectar, and then assimilate it so that it ultimately becomes honey. The essential feature of honey is that, while the nectar of each flower cannot be separated, the honey from each place will have its own distinctive taste depending on the season, the climate, and the flowers visited by the bees. Similarly, Indian culture is the honey prepared from the nectar of cultural activities from various parts of the country.

One of the striking features of Indian culture over the millennia has been that peace and empathy have always been a part of public discourse. For example, the most frequently quoted is the concept of the world as one family – '***VasudhaivaKutumbakam***' is a floating verse, often quoted to express the harmony of human relations and associated with the Vedic world view. My enquiries revealed that this particular verse does not flow from the Vedas and the Upanishads and its authorship is not known. This verse is also found mentioned in the *Hitopadesah* along with other floating verses.

In several significant ways cultural diplomacy emanated from India. The phenomenon acquired prominence since the reign of Asoka (304 B.C. - 232 BCE). Asoka adopted *dhamma* as an instrument of state policy and renounced warfare. He approached the question of effecting harmony among people and coordinating relations with neighbouring countries and beyond, in accordance with dhamma. Purely from the angle of governance, Asoka's genius lies in making dhamma amenable to implementation in day-to-day life. Towards this an elaborate administrative machinery was created. Asoka introduced the officer of dhamma known as the dhamma-mahamattas. They were also posted in other countries.

The world has changed enormously since Asoka's times. Today thanks to technology, the world is well connected. People, ideas and goods move much faster. In this globalised world, culture has moved from the periphery of foreign relations to the central place. As Sahai writes: "*to understand Indian approach on cultural diplomacy, it is essential to appreciate how culture has become an integral part of the life of the people and the nation. Indian approach to the world is through its acceptance of the philosophy that the whole world is a family ('VasudhaivaKutumbakam'). It is defined by the 'Idea of India', which means the acceptance of a composite culture that is inclusive. It has been nurtured and enriched over the years, through a process of acculturation. It has its ethos in its pluralistic society, secularism and democracy, which are also enshrined in the Indian Constitution*".

Paramjit Sahai goes on to provide an in-depth discussion on the roles of Ministry of Culture, Indian Council of Cultural Relations (ICCR), three national academies (i.e. Sahitya Akademi, Sangeet Natak Akademi and Lalit Kala Akademi) and national museums. He also talks about functions of IIC, IGNCA and INTACH in promotion of India's culture. He rightly identifies Bollywood and Yoga as significant vehicles of cultural diplomacy. The author also attaches great value to the role of Indian Diaspora in this behalf.

The tragic events that took place in the United States on 11 September 2011,encouraged me to contemplate on this theme with a view to explore an enduring framework for a global public policy – a policy for harmony among different peoples and societies in the post 9/11 world as seen through the lens of India's civilizational experience. I would like to call the approach I am suggesting *Bahudhā.* This comes from my personal attachment to an attitude that has greatly contributed to the enrichment of harmonious life in India: '*respect for another person's view of truth with hope and belief that he or she may be right'*. This is best expressed in the Rigvedic hymn that enjoined more than three millennia ago.

*Ekam Sad VipraBahudhā Vadanti*

*(The Real is one, the learned speak of it variously)*

Pluralism is the closest equivalent of Bahudha in English. But Bahudha denotes much more than pluralism as *dharma* conveys more than religion. Pluralist societies are necessarily multi-ethnic, multi-religious, and multilingual societies. In such societies, there are various boundaries: racial, linguistic, religious, and at times even ideological. The *Bahudha* approach does not believe in annexation or transgression of boundaries or assimilation of identities and propagation of a simplistic world view. It merely facilitates dialogue and thereby promotes understanding of the collective good. The *Bahudha* approach is conscious of the fact that societies without boundaries are not possible.

The culture of *Bahudha*'s deeply rooted in the inculcation of a special attitude from an early age. Dialogue requires a state of mind where one can strongly believe in one's own way of looking at issues while simultaneously accommodating another's point of view. It is this mental discipline that makes one willing to consider the validity of other person's view point. In short, the *Bahudhā* approach is both a celebration of diversity and an attitude of mind that respects another person's point of view. Democracy and dialogue are central to this approach.

Paramjit Sahai highlights the significance of '*idea of India*' which rests on Democracy, Secularism, Diversity and Pluralism. India's cultural diplomacy has to abide by its belief in "*idea of India*" and this need to be "*insulated from political winds that blow from time to time*". Cultural Diplomacy must support empathy, self-control, morality and reason. It is imperative to have a new vision and a fresh approach to mobilise the voices of leaders and nations and redefine moral and social concepts to meet the challenges of today. To maintain and strengthen that process, dialogue between the world's leading civilisations is essential. The Bahudha approach could be consciously pursued as a part of India's Cultural Diplomacy.

Paramjit Sahai's effort is indeed laudable. ***Indian Cultural Diplomacy: Celebrating Pluralismin a Globalised World*** is a well organised book neatly divided into sections and chapters that provides a comprehensive analysis of almost every facet of cultural diplomacy in India in theory and practice. The book will be consulted for long by students and teachers, scholars and diplomats concerned with India's culture and its values and their usefulness and relevance in diplomacy.

**Balmiki Prasad Singh***

* He is Former Governor of Sikkim and Home Secretary and Culture Secretary of Government of the Republic of India. Author of widely acclaimed book *Bahudha and the Post 9/11 World.*

# Preface

I got my exposure to cultural diplomacy, which is the heart of diplomacy during my first posting to Moscow and wanted to learn more about this diplomatic vehicle, which helps in bringing about connectivity among peoples. It was on 10 December 1964 in Moscow, my first place of diplomatic assignment that my interest in cultural diplomacy got kindled. I arrived in Moscow on 9 December 1964 and was staying at Hotel Leningradsky. I leisurely sauntered to the restaurant by myself and was stunned and shocked not by awe but by surprise and happiness, when the orchestra greeted me with the tune 'Mera Joota Hai Japani, Yeh Patloon Englishtani, Sar Pe Laal Topi Roosi, Phir Bhi Dil Hai Hindustan' – a song from the film 'Awaara', sung by Raj Kapoor, not only a legendary actor in India, but a household name in the then Soviet Union, from Moscow to Almaty; Tbilisi to Tashkent or Baku to Bokhara.

I was easily recognized as an Indian, being a Sikh, as those were the days of cultural connectivity, when different identities were celebrated. We have come a long way since then, as in the present days, there is more dissent and discord and cultural disconnect; where identities, real or mistaken, divide 'us' from 'them', be it among nations, big or small; or among individuals, be it, Blacks or Whites; Sikhs or Hindus; Christians or Muslims; Shias or Sunnis and Arabs or Jews.

The playing of the Raj Kapoor tune was an honour to India, as those were the days of 'Druzhba' (Friendship) between India and the then Soviet Union (USSR), with Indo-Soviet Friendship Society, having its presence across the length and the breadth of the Soviet Union, where India-Soviet Friendship 'Mantra' was chanted. It was much more than that, as the wordings of the song beautifully captured the essence of cultural diplomacy in a globalised world, where people could have multiple identities or don different identities, but could live together in an atmosphere of understanding.

Raj Kapoor, as a vagrant (Awaara) gave us Nobel Laureate Rabindranath Tagore's message of a 'Universal Man'; while you maintain your separate identities, yet could live in a comradely spirit, endowed with human feelings, be it you were wearing Japanese shoes, Russian red cap, British Pants, but were an Indian at heart. It is a kind of accepting other individuals as human beings, while you still maintained your core identity. It is akin to Amartya Sen's concept of multiple identities, which acquires relevance for over 258 million migrants across the globe. If we view Diaspora in such a context then only we can expect it to play the role of a bridge builder, while it connects with the host state yet it stays connected with the home state.

At Moscow, I also learnt about the nitty-gritty of cultural diplomacy, as I was charged with the responsibility of looking after cultural work. I got involved with the drafting of the Cultural Exchange Program (CEP) and its implementation. India had an all pervasive and multifaceted CEP, which covered all the fields that dealt with connectivity, be it media, sports, education, exchange of visits at the leadership level, youth exchanges etc.

A goodwill visit by a Parliamentary delegation led by the Minister for Parliamentary Affairs Satya Narain Sinha in 1965 provided an opportunity to learn on the importance of such exchanges and how these could be used in promoting understanding. Visit by Prime Minister Lal Bahadur Shastri in January 1966 which resulted in the signing of the Tashkent Declaration, gave an opportunity to connect with the media, as senior correspondents and editors had accompanied him.

After the split of the Soviet Union in 1991, I was involved with the process that led to the establishment of diplomatic relations, including signing of cultural agreements with countries in Central Asia. This provided an opportunity to draft such agreements.

Over the years, my postings took me to different places in the globe, to big or small countries; to the developed or the developing world; to different cultures, be it the Western, African or Asian. Each posting was a learning experience and honing of skills in the use of cultural diplomacy.

We have to remember that there is no 'one-size fit' cultural diplomacy approach nor one type even for the same country, nor the same for all its peoples. This has to be in tune with the changing requirements and the target audience and has to be regularly calibrated. The approach in the Soviet Union or Russia was different from that in Zambia and Malawi or between Sweden and Malaysia. All these aspects would be narrated, based on personal experiences.

For easier understanding of the phenomenon of cultural diplomacy and its various facets and dimensions, the book has been divided into eight sections, with each section having two chapters, with interconnected themes. It is a mix of theory and practice; a combination of theoretical concepts with practical experiences, distilled from personal experiences and that of other colleagues in the Foreign Service.

For me, I completed full circle of cultural diplomacy in Malaysia, a multicultural society, which had adopted 'Malaysia, Truly Asia' as it's Brand, for not only promoting tourism, but also observed it in real practice. It is a confluence of three cultures – Malay, Chinese and Indian. There was both symbolism and substance, when people celebrated national days, like 'Hari Raya' (Eid), Chinese New Year or Deepavali. At the popular level, Bollywood had also permeated among all peoples, be it royalty or commoners. Indian customs, like serving of 'Pan' (Beetle Leaves) had also become an integral part of a Malay marriage. Indian prayers or 'Shlokas' (verses) in Sanskrit at the Coronation Ceremonies of the Kings imparted a touch of grace and solemnity.

I would, therefore, like to conclude my introductory remarks with a Bollywood song, 'kuch kuch hota hai', which was often sung at the King's Birthday, when I was posted there. Bollywood does connect, but cultural diplomacy is 'Beyond Bollywood'. It is not 'kuch kuch' (something), but 'sub kuch' (everything) about promoting 'understanding with everyone'. Cultural Diplomacy is the heart of 'Diplomacy'. How does it connect with 'Soft Power' and 'Public Diplomacy', with which it is interchangeably used? Let me whet your appetite to learn more about cultural diplomacy, and hopefully, you would find some answers, as you wade through the pages of this Book. We need more 'Connectivity Bridges' than 'Strategic Partnerships', as we seek dialogue through the medium of Cultural Diplomacy.

–Paramjit Sahai

# Acknowledgements

First of all, let me convey my thanks to the Indian Council of World Affairs (ICWA), which entrusted me with this Book Project. The process started with former Director General Rajiv Bhatia roping me in and continued with Nalin Surie, who was patient enough, to let me go ahead at my pace, given some setback in my health. Publication of the Book takes place under another Director General TCA Raghavan.

My special thanks go to Piyush Srivastava, Joint Secretary, ICWA, with whom I liaised on a regular basis. I would also like to thank Pankaj Jha, former Director (Research) ICWA with whom I was involved at the time of conceptualization of this book project and the present Director Nivedita Ray, who helped me in giving finishing touches to the book.

This Book is not only based on the study of Primary and Secondary sources, but it also draws heavily on my practical experience and that of my other colleagues and other stakeholders like former civil servants, academicians, journalists, artists, curators, and administrators in the cultural arena in India and abroad. It is not possible to name everyone but I will mention a few prominent ones.

First of all, let me thank my friend, batchmate and mentor Lalit Mansingh, former Foreign Secretary and Director General, ICCR, who was my sounding board and gave me sound advice in clearing my thoughts on some of the theoretical concepts that agitated my mind and offered valuable inputs after going through the draft manuscript on some chapters. My thanks are also to former Foreign Secretary Shyam Saran for his insights into cultural diplomacy and cross cultural communications. I am thankful to C Rajasekhar, former ICCR Director General, for going through the draft manuscript and offering valuable comments/suggestions. My thanks are also due to Yogesh Tiwari, for giving his critical inputs and suggestions.

My profuse thanks to ICCR and its numerous officers and staff, in particular, Director Generals, who were extremely helpful in letting me have access to the relevant material and use the Library. Thanks to the present DG, ICCR, Riva Ganguly Das and former DGs, Niranjan Desai, Suryakanthi Tripathi, Dr. Suresh Goel, Satish Mehta and Amarendra Khatua, with whom I interacted regularly and who provided meaningful inputs. My thanks to all officers and staff in ICCR, in particular to Namrata Kumar and Padmaja, DDGs; Pankaj Vohra, Sanjay Vedi, Mahmood Akhtar, Kamaljit and Mrs. Nalini Singhal, for rendering support to this book project.

I am also indebted to the Ministry of Culture and in particular to K.K. Mittal, Additional Secretary for briefing me with the current thinking of the Ministry. My thanks are also to Ashok Vajpayee, writer and poet and former Joint Secretary, who shared his experiences with me, as a practitioner and administrator.

Media plays an important role which is dealt with in a separate chapter on 'Media and Foreign Policy in a Globalised World' in the Book. A questionnaire was developed to draw upon the experience of leading journalists, who happily shared their experiences. My special thanks are to stalwarts like H.K. Dua, S. Nihal Singh, Mahendra Vaid and Vijay Naik for their erudite comments.

My thanks to my colleagues in the PD and XP Divisions; this is presently known as XPD Division. My thanks to Pinak Chakravarty, Amit Dasgupta, Navdeep Suri, Syed Akbaruddin, Vikas Swarup and Riva Ganguly Das.

I owe a lot to a number of foreign diplomats posted in India, who willingly and candidly shared their experiences with me, as practitioners of cultural diplomacy in India. To name a few at Chandigarh, these are David Elliott, Deputy British High Commissioner, Tanisha Thiara, Head, British Council, Dr. Christopher Gibbins, Consul General of Canada and Mr. Dominique Waag, Director, Alliance Francaise. In Delhi, these included, Ms. Mayu Hagiwara, First Secretary, (Culture) at the Japanese Embassy; Mr. Walter Douglas, Minister Counsellor Public Affairs and David Mees, Cultural Counsellor at US Embassy and Mr. Fyodor A R Rozovskiy, Counsellor and Regional Director of the Russian Centre of Science and Culture.

My thanks are also due to a number of cultural personalities, curators and administrators in the United States. I would like to name a few, Ms. Liz Tunick, International Department, Smithsonian Institution; Ms. Debra Daimond, Curator, Freer Gallery; Dr. James Early, Director, Centre for Folk Life and Heritage; Ms. Sameen Piracha, Asia Pacific Centre; Ms.

Masum Momaya, Curator, 'Beyond Bollywood' Exhibition; Dr. Paul Taylor, Curator, 'Sikhs: Heritage of Punjab' Exhibition; Dr. Ausef Sayeed, Consul General of India at Chicago and Sreedharan, Minister (Press, Information and Culture), Embassy of India.

My profuse thanks are to my former colleagues and our High Commissioners and Ambassadors, who apprised me of the ground reality on the working of cultural diplomacy in present times. My special thanks are to Y.K. Sinha, Vijay Gokhale, Gurjit Singh, Gautam Bambawale, Amar Sinha, Ashok Sharma, Manjeev Puri, Navdeep Suri, R.K. Singh, Somnath Ghosh, Sunil Lal, Dr. Ausef Sayeed and Viraj Singh. My thanks to all the Cultural Attaches and other diplomats in these diplomatic missions, who helped me in this book project.

My thanks to my wife Neena and my daughters, Sonia and Tania, for keeping their hawk eyes on me, whenever I went astray from the central theme of the Book. They were also my sounding boards and gave me candid advice and comments. Luckily, I received encouragement from my sons-in-law, Adesh and Justin and my grandsons, Aryaman and Shayan, who wanted me to continue with this endeavour.

I have no words to express my thanks to Balmiki Prasad Singh, Former Governor of Sikkim and Home Secretary and Culture Secretary of India for agreeing to write the Foreword. It enhances the value of the Book through its sheer illumination, as it places it in the broader context of culture and civilisation.

My thanks are also to my publishers, the father and the son duo, Pradip and Rohan Vij, for all the help and guidance in shaping this book to its present state.

Finally, my thanks to Dr. Rashpal Malhotra, Executive Vice Chairman, CRRID and other colleagues at the Centre, with whom I have been academically involved. My thanks are also due to Rajan Thomas, Sohan Lal Sharma and Rubinder Kaur, for providing quality secretarial assistance.

# Introduction

The Book is divided into eight sections, with each one having two chapters. The sections group chapters that have similar themes. In the first section, we would have a look at the theoretical framework of cultural diplomacy and as it has evolved over the years in India. The second section deals with the cultural policy framework, structures and instrumentalities, as we look at the role of the Ministry of Culture and the Indian Council for Cultural Relations (ICCR).

In the third section, we look at the role of Other Bodies in promoting cultural diplomacy and direction of India's cultural diplomacy in Southeast and Central Asia. In the fourth section, we look at vehicles of cultural diplomacy. One chapter exclusively deals with education, while the other chapter looks at other vehicles, like Bollywood, Yoga, Art and Literature, Music and Sports. In the fifth section, we view the role of Diaspora and Media, as 'Connectivity Bridges'.

In the sixth section, we have a look at cultural diplomacy as it works at the global level (Smithsonian Institute) and at the grassroots level (Chandigarh). In the seventh section, we move to the diplomatic missions at the operational level. We look at the role of the Indian diplomatic missions in a select number of countries from different regions as well as at some foreign countries and diplomatic missions as they carry out cultural diplomacy in India.

In the concluding chapter (Chapter XV) in the eighth section, we travel the path, which we have covered in various chapters. We make 'Concluding Observations' and then come to the final part, 'The Way Ahead', which is in the nature of suggestions and recommendations for India's cultural diplomacy, in terms of policy, programmes, thrust areas and structures, keeping in view our own experience and looking at the best practices developed in some countries. A brief description of the contents in each chapter is given below.

**Chapter I** provides a window to the understanding of 'Cultural Diplomacy in a Globalised World'. It looks at the definition in the traditional and modern contexts of cultural diplomacy and its role, while attempting to understand the context in which the word 'culture' is used in this Book. An attempt is made to grasp various contours of this globalised world, in so far these would have relevance for the understanding of cultural diplomacy.

How does cultural diplomacy find and traverse its path and what are its essential features? Is it about promoting understanding among peoples and nations or about influencing their actions? Our search results in our finding that the nations also have a personality, as we realize the importance of cross cultural communication in any successful dealing with other nations.

Is cultural diplomacy a component of 'soft power' as everything is being viewed in the power paradigm; be it 'hard or soft'? How does cultural diplomacy fit in with other concepts like public diplomacy? Could we view cultural diplomacy as a 'Friendship Bridge' that helps us in promoting civilizational dialogue against the disruptive forces that are overtaking us?

We are driven to understand that Cultural Diplomacy is about understanding 'others' as we would like them to understand us. It is about 'acceptance' of others as they are and not about conversion of them to our viewpoint. If this is so, then cultural diplomacy cannot be considered a constituent part of 'soft power' as defined by Joseph Nye Jr., even though he treats culture as one component in his definition of 'soft power'. Cultural Diplomacy does not involve imposition of one's views unto others. An effective cultural diplomacy would need an open environment, where there is free flow of ideas in an atmosphere that is devoid of hatred and intolerance.

At the operational level, cultural diplomacy need not be restricted to official diplomatic initiatives. Non-official stakeholders have emerged as important players, as they are better placed to provide understanding, as they do not carry any official baggage. Ultimately, Cultural Diplomacy performs the role of a 'Connectivity Bridge' that promotes communication, leading to conversation and connectivity, which paves way for cooperation among stakeholders.

While pursuing the path of cultural diplomacy, we have to ensure that we are not dragged into 'cultural nationalism' and should avoid the path of cultural hegemony. We have, however, to realize that the benefits of cultural diplomacy are not easily measurable and it is a long drawn out process that needs patience. It involves all the stakeholders, as government alone cannot deliver.

**Chapter II** presents an overview of India's cultural diplomacy, tracing its origins and evolution since India's Independence. It traces how the cultural diplomacy has evolved over the years under the leadership of different Prime Ministers, with each leader leaving his/her imprint. The chapter looks at the global thrust of India's cultural diplomacy; in keeping with the Indian ethos of 'Vasudhaiva Kutumbakam' (The whole world is a family). The chapter looks into the direction of cultural diplomacy, noting how it is evolving in different regions and the likely thrust areas.

The chapter notes that India has not delineated a formal policy on cultural diplomacy. India has, however, enunciated policy guidelines and created framework and structures to ensure its implementation. The respective roles, of the Ministries of Culture and External Affairs, which oversee cultural diplomacy, are discussed. The mandate of the Indian Council of Cultural Relations (ICCR), which is the nodal implementing agency, is described.

Two case studies on France and Australia look at the impact of VVIP visits on cultural connectivity and the role played by leaders. While in another case study on India and Pakistan, impact of political climate on cultural connectivity is explored.

India recognizes the importance of the role of cultural diplomacy, as it is in its DNA. Cultural connectivity has thus emerged as an important component of VVIP visits. India's cultural diplomacy finds resonance in other countries, as its composite culture promotes understanding, by respecting diversity and pluralism. The need for preserving this composite culture is regularly stressed by Indian leaders including the President, the Vice-President and the Prime Minister.

Efforts that are afoot, to move cultural diplomacy in the genre of power; be it 'soft power', are viewed. Do such moves defeat the raisin d'être of cultural diplomacy which is to promote understanding and not to resort to conversion and empowerment. For the author, any move in that direction would be antithetical to the essence of cultural diplomacy.

**Chapter III** focuses on the 'Role of the Ministry of Culture (MOC) in Cultural Diplomacy' and looks at how it is fulfilling its mandate to disseminate Indian culture and developing 'cultural relations between India and various countries'. It achieves its objectives directly and through statutory and specialized bodies created under it. MOC relies on two principal instrumentalities – Cultural Agreements and Festivals of India.

There is an in-depth discussion on the history and evolution of India's cultural agreements, with India having signed 130 cultural agreements across the globe. A mismatch between the signing of cultural agreements and their implementation is noted, as the effective rate of implementation is fifty percent; this is generally considered reasonable in the global context.

It is noted that India was a late starter in launching Festivals of India, with the first festival launched in UK in 1982. The underlying philosophy in holding these festivals is spelt out. After a lull period during the 1990s and the first decade of the 21st century, India is now aggressively mounting Festivals of India.

Sufficient funding is being provided since 2014, resulting in India focusing on a large number of countries. ICCR has developed its own Brand 'Namaste India' and it organizes festivals under this banner. It entered into a MOU with the Ministry of Culture in 2016, acquiring formal stature as one organization, to mount festivals on their behalf.

A section of the chapter deals with the role of the Foreign Cultural Associations and the nature of assistance provided by the Ministry of Culture. The unmistakable conclusion is that the Ministry of Culture has to be optimally involved and move out of its silo, as it connects with the Ministry of External Affairs and other stakeholders and becomes a driving force in pushing its statutory bodies and subordinate offices to play a pro-active role.

**Chapter IV** deals with the 'Indian Council for Cultural Relations (ICCR) and its Instrumentalities'. ICCR is the designated nodal implementing agency, which was set up in 1950 and that now works under the administrative control of the Ministry of External Affairs (MEA). The chapter looks at its mandate and its global reach and provides an overall picture of the working of ICCR. Its responsibilities that are broadly divided under three heads, 'Academic and Intellectual', 'Arts and Culture' and 'Other Activities', are evaluated.

Administration of Scholarships is the main activity of ICCR, as over 60 per cent of its budget is spent on this activity. ICCR disperses 3000 scholarships annually under its own scheme and that of the Ministry of External Affairs and other Bodies. One-third of the scholarships are awarded to Afghan scholars, while another 1000 scholarships are awarded to students from Africa. The entire focus is on developing countries. ICCR now plans to focus on developed countries also.

The other major activity is the establishment and management of 'Chairs of Indian Studies'. The chapter looks at the distribution of the Chairs and their areas of focus. Around 1/3$^{rd}$ of the Chairs are for the study of Hindi. The trend is to set up these 'Chairs' in the developed countries. The Years 2010 and 2011 were the growth period, when the number peaked to over 100 Chairs. It has now stabilized at 65 Chairs.

ICCR's other main activity is the running of cultural centres abroad, which stood at 36 in 2016. This is not a large number, given the fact that India is a global player. The centres are largely located in the developing countries and mainly in Asia. How effective are these centres and how professionally are these manned, has been the question that has bogged practically all the former Director Generals of ICCR and the Ministry of External Affairs and the Parliamentary Committees? How do we make these centres as 'cultural hubs'? This is the moot point and emerges as a matter of critical importance?

A section in this chapter dissects the budget, to get a picture on ICCR's priorities, while noting its inadequacy and low level of funding. Over 70% of the budget is spent on administrative matters, while only 30% is left for cultural activities. There is a constant struggle between programming and funding. It also comes out that greater professionalism needs to be imparted to the running of these centres.

Despite these handicaps and limitations, ICCR has delivered. Its role has come up for a sharper focus, as Cultural Diplomacy is on the high table for the new government. ICCR, therefore, is working towards promoting Brand India, with the emphasis on traditional Indian culture and scientific research, yoga, Ayurveda and study of Sanskrit and Indology.

**Chapter V** focuses on the 'Role of Other Cultural Bodies' in the arena of cultural diplomacy. Indian Government sees a role for such Bodies, as these play the role of facilitators, realizing its limits in becoming the sole functionary. In keeping with this approach, it created certain Statutory, Specialized Bodies and Subordinate Institutions, and vested them with independent authority. It is also letting other Cultural Bodies emerge in the Private Sector.

In this chapter, we look at three sets of Bodies. Firstly, at those that were created by the government but were specifically involved in culture-related activities, such as the three central Akademies and National Museums. We also look at other Bodies, which were also created or supported by the government, but had a mixed mandate, which went beyond culture.

These include IIC, IGNCA and INTACH. In the third category we cover Cultural Organizations in the private sector, but those that are involved in promoting cultural diplomacy in one or another way. In this would fall the Prasiddha Foundation, Teamwork Arts etc.

The chapter looks at the structure and functioning of the three central Academies of Arts- Sahitya Akademi, Sangeet Natak Akademi and Lalit Kala Akademi- set up during 1953 and 1954. Their activities are reviewed in terms of their mandate. The picture does not look rosy, whatever may be their constraints. We also review the working of other Bodies as well their connectivity with ICCR.

While MOC has been active in promoting cultural diplomacy, yet the same is not the case with its statutory and specialized Bodies that work under it. The concluding part comes out with some suggestions in optimizing the role of these Bodies in promoting cultural diplomacy.

**Chapter VI**: deals with the 'Direction of Indian Cultural Diplomacy'. It is in the nature of a case study on India's Extended Neighbourhood, dealing with Central and Southeast Asia. The chapter notes the similarities and dissimilarities in India's cultural diplomacy profile in these two regions as well as in individual countries.

The chapter also touches upon specific periods, when India laid special focus on developing cultural links with these regions. In the case of Central Asia, it was through the launching of 'CIS Focus Year 2002', when special programmes/schemes were put in place. In the case of Southeast Asia, it was at the time of the India-ASEAN Commemorative Summit 2012, which celebrated the Silver Jubilee of India-ASEAN Partnership. Specific programmes launched on these occasions are briefly described.

The chapter also reviews the present status of connectivity under different vehicles of cultural diplomacy between India and these countries. While there is an upswing in India's connectivity with countries in Southeast Asia, yet the same is not true in the case of countries in Central Asia, in the absence of direct land route connectivity between India and Central Asia. Nonetheless a common strand that emerges is that of warmth in the relationship, based on respect for pluralism.

**Chapter VII** looks at 'Education as a Vehicle of Cultural Diplomacy'. Education has provided the connectivity among peoples and nations since times immemorial. Adam Gilchrist, Australia's Goodwill Ambassador to India on Education, aptly described its significance in the language of cricket as 'Education hits every boundary'. In the olden times, India had been known through its universities at Taxila and Nalanda. In the modern days, the United States has emerged as an important educational hub, with the government spurring up connectivity through its world-renowned Fulbright Scheme and other programmes.

The primary focus is on student exchanges that serve tripartite purpose – assist in learning, facilitate exchange of ideas and help in building long term friendship. Connectivity through education was the first goal of the British Council, when it was set up in 1934. Coincidentally President Roosevelt announced the commencement of cultural exchange programme with the Americas in the same year. The magnitude of such connectivity could be visualized, as it involved 4.5 million students in 2012 and whose number is expected to go up to 8 million in 2025 (OECD).

The chapter maps out the global scenario in education, starting with the purpose and role of education diplomacy. It looks at two case studies – USA as the global hub and Australia as the emerging new destination. This is followed up with a review of innovative programmes in education diplomacy mounted by some other countries.

Where does India figure in worldwide student mobility? India has a share of 4.6% in total numbers, with 4% outgoing and 0.6% incoming. India is a minor player as a destination. India has even failed to attract students from South Asian countries. India's efforts to emerge as a destination are noted, including the setting up of new educational institutions, like the Nalanda University and the South Asian University.

Education is emerging as an important agenda item during the VVIP visits. India has entered into bilateral agreements with many countries; so are the educational links that are growing among educational institutions. The nature and magnitude of such cooperation is covered in this chapter. Higher Education is emerging as an important area. So are the efforts of the Developed Countries to promote Reverse Education Diplomacy by launching schemes that facilitate studying by students from EU, UK, Australia and USA in India.

How could India emerge as a major destination is the question that exercises the mind of Indian leaders? To do so, it would need a concerted effort by all stakeholders. Is it ready to launch a new Education Policy, which paves way for India emerging, as a place of top class universities that offers world class quality education at competitive tuition fees? Could we draw upon the Australian experience to make India one such new destination in the near future?

**Chapter VIII** deals with "Primary Vehicles of Cultural Diplomacy', such as Bollywood and Yoga; Art and Literature; Music and Dance and Sports. Bollywood and Yoga are being viewed as components of India's soft power. These cultural vehicles receive support from governmental organizations including ICCR. In most cases, they are moving of their own, as the flow is dictated by commercial considerations, as many cultural products have become commercially viable. Local cultural groups have come up in many cities, which are running on a self-sustaining basis.

Bollywood automatically comes to everyone's mind, as it has connected India globally all over the world. It is not only Indian Diaspora, but even local population that is getting interested in Bollywood. Interest in Bollywood is growing among foreign governments, as it is helping in their tourism promotion, as Bollywood films have been shot in over 51 countries. Bollywood is seen as India's soft power window.

Unlike Bollywood, Yoga is receiving maximum promotional support from the government and ICCR, since the UN Declaration designating June 21 as the International Yoga Day (IYD) from 2015. ICCR has supported Diplomatic Missions in organizing activities to celebrate IYD. Yoga teachers are deputed to cultural centres and support is being provided to Ayush cells.

The chapter looks at how Music-classical and popular-is connecting India culturally. Literary Festivals have also emerged on the cultural scene. India gets connected through its cuisine, as it is becoming popular through its 'Chicken Tikka Massala' and growing trend towards vegetarianism.

The chapter also looks at sports connectivity, as this is emerging as a new area. Even though India is not a sporting nation, yet the government is giving attention, as it results in connecting with the youth. The role of Cricket in providing connectivity is also looked at.

Finally, a view has to be taken as to the nature and the level of governmental support that is required to promote these vehicles. Would it be better to let them move on their own steam, wherever they have taken off, as in the case of Bollywood?

**Chapter IX** enters a Greenfield area, as it looks at 'Diaspora: Strategic Asset on Foreign Policy'. Diaspora has been generally viewed as a connecting bridge between the home and the host states. Such a role is generally acceptable in non-political areas of culture and commerce. How would this play out in the case of foreign policy related issues when the place of Diaspora itself is coming under scanner.

In this chapter, we start with a conceptual framework, as we attempt to define concepts and issues. Diaspora cannot be considered as a strategic asset, although it could play a role in non-political and non-strategic foreign policy related issues. In this chapter, we also largely draw upon the country experiences of USA and Canada, while briefly reviewing practice in some other countries.

The above issue is discussed in the context of overall policies of Diaspora Engagement adopted by India and many other countries. We also draw upon a case study of Tamilian Diaspora in UK and Canada, which presents different results, as the outcome is dictated by the foreign policy contours set by the host state.

In this chapter, India's engagement with its Diaspora is discussed in its historical context as well as how it has evolved over the years. The engagement has been largely to meet the cultural needs of Diaspora, while seeking its involvements in the commercial arena; be it trade or investment. Diaspora involvement has been minimal in foreign policy related issues.

Indian Diaspora's involvement in the India-USA Civil Nuclear Cooperation Agreement in 2008 was a rare case. The success of such involvement leads us to a discussion, whether this could become a role model. The answer turns out to be in the negative, as one country approach cannot be replicated for others.

This issue is also discussed from another perspective. If India, as a home state would like to use Diaspora to promote its foreign policy interests; would it be willing to allow other states to use their Diaspora in promoting their foreign policy interests in India? The answer is likely to be in the negative. The considered view for India would be to adopt a cautionary approach and that too for each country, on a case by case basis for specific issues.

**Chapter X** deals with the important issue of the connectivity between 'Media and Foreign Policy in the Globalised World'. This assumes importance in the present-day world, where there is more disconnect than connect. Furthermore, the role of the media has also come under strain, not only from within (print media, TV, Radio) but also from the social media. Emergence of 'citizen journalists' further challenges the traditional reporters.

The Fourth Estate is also losing its credibility, as the rhetoric on 'Fake News' and 'Alternative Facts' grips us, resulting in a post-truth phenomenon, where facts are fiction and fiction becomes facts. There is a tendency by the leaders to bypass the Media, as they try to reach out directly to people through Tweets or Facebook and their success is measured as to the number of Tweets they make or Facebook entries they get. Will Twiplomacy overtake Traditional Diplomacy?

It is against the above backdrop that we look at Media and Foreign Policy Connectivity. This is viewed in the overall context of how media generates images, which are powerful enough to impact the mind of its readers and viewers. The role of technology in obliterating the distinction between the foreign and domestic news is noted, as it simultaneously brings the news within the reach of everyone.

What role media has played as a bridge builder or destroyer; each perspective is supported by specific examples. Other subjects that are covered in the chapter include, 'the Media Scene in India, 'Coverage of International Scene in the Indian Media' and a case study on the coverage of the inaugural address of the US President Donald Trump in January 2017.

A section in the chapter is devoted to the views of a representative section of the Media on a number of inter-related issues, such as the nature and level of coverage, level of priority to international news and interconnectivity between the Media and the Ministry of External Affairs. The overall impression is that it stands well connected through the Joint Secretary (External Publicity and Public Diplomacy Division (XPD).

The concluding remarks lead us to view an ideal situation. This would be to avoid mismatch between the Message (MEA) and the Messenger (Media). How to create a healthy environment, where they could work as partners, without trespassing on one another; the Foreign Policy Establishment providing the 'Text" and the Media delivering the "Message", while retaining its independence and integrity?

**Chapter XI** provides an insight into the Smithsonian Institution in Washington DC, which is a 'Global Cultural Hub' and the nature and the extent of its involvement with India. It is the world's largest Museum and Research complex, which provides free entry to its 19 Museums, with an annual flow of around 1 million visitors. It is the Mecca for every visitor to Washington DC. It also reaches out to a larger audience through its websites. It is driven by its tripartite functions of 'dissemination of education, culture and research internationally'.

In this chapter, we explore Smithsonian's history and its vision and mandate. We look at how Smithsonian is involved in the world cultural space, as it works with UNESCO and foreign countries. Some of the key areas are 'Integrating Heritage into Modern Education Systems', 'Transforming Museums into Educational Hubs', 'Redesigning Exhibits to provide Holistic Experience' and 'Museum Manpower Development and Skills'.

We learn how Smithsonian is also working with the State Department in a unique project, called 'American Spaces' which is 'to enhance the physical and programmatic environment of the State Department's public diplomacy venues abroad in support of foreign policy priorities'. Such experiences should provide useful information and data to optimize the working of Indian cultural centres.

In this chapter, we also look at how India connects with the Smithsonian. It stays permanently connected with the Smithsonian through two of its Art Galleries – The Freer Gallery of Art and Arthur Sackler Gallery – which are like Museums, where Indian Object d'Arts along with others from Asia are on permanent display. Apart from this, these Galleries also mount special Indian exhibitions that are covered in the chapter. This results in getting another window on India.

The Smithsonian introduced India to the American public through the Festival of India in 1985, when 'Mela: An Indian Fair' was a part of the celebrations at the Mall, which was a star attraction at the Annual Folk Life Festival.

The chapter provides detailed information on the two important exhibitions organized at the Smithsonian Museum of Natural History – 'Sikhs: Legacy of the Punjab' during 2004-07 and 'Beyond Bollywood: Indo-Americans Shape the Nation' during 2014-15.

Where does India stand with the Smithsonian? The chapter concludes with a number of suggestions that could help in India gaining from better connectivity through a number of ways. The most important would be for ICCR to enter into MoU with Smithsonian as well as consider setting up India-Smithsonian Institution Endowment.

**Chapter XII** takes us to another journey, as we move away from global cultural space at the Smithsonian to the local, so as to understand how Cultural Diplomacy operates at the grassroots level. There is a growing recognition all over that cultural diplomacy-related activities have to move beyond the capitals and move to other destinations, if the aim is to create an overall impact among people across any country. India has also awakened to this necessity, as it is making States its partners in cultural activities abroad.

In this chapter, we look at the working of cultural diplomacy through case studies of Chandigarh in India and Chicago in USA, which have emerged as cultural hubs at the city level. The review takes place, keeping in view the policy guidelines and approach adopted by the Indian government. There is a new thrust on the establishment of state to state and city to city relationship. At the Indian end, Chandigarh was selected as it is one of the Regional Offices set up by ICCR and serves the northern region.

The Regional Office plays an important role as an outpost of ICCR and facilitates in organizing cultural programmes. It also maintains connectivity with the Chandigarh Administration as well as connects with the diplomatic missions that are based in Chandigarh. Chandigarh is blessed with excellent infrastructure, by way of performance halls, Academies of Art, Literature, Music and Dance and is home to well-known artists and has receptive audience.

A review of the activities, undertaken by the Regional Office helps in getting a good insight on how cultural diplomacy operates at the grassroots level. A segment in this Chapter also provides useful information and data on how diplomatic missions in Chandigarh are launching cultural diplomacy-related activities.

The study of Chicago, on the other hand, provides us with interesting glimpses on how Chicago has become people friendly cultural hub, as it caters to the needs of the local population as well as diversity of foreign visitors. It also provides an interesting insight into the working of sister-cities relationship, even though Delhi-Chicago city to city relationship is on a low key. We also get a picture of how Chicago is culturally connected with India, as it was here that Swami Vivekananda gave his message of accepting other faiths in 1893.

How do we connect Chandigarh and Chicago? A number of suggestions are made in the last section. Chicago could provide useful inputs on the ongoing debate on 'Smart vs Better Cities', as Chandigarh moves in the direction of a Smart City. Chandigarh could learn how to make its parks people-friendly and establish connectivity between the Panjab University and world-renowned Universities located at Chicago.

**Chapter XIII** deals with the role played by Indian Diplomatic Missions at the operational level, as driving force and implementing agencies in the countries, where they are located. This chapter is in the nature of a field study, as it is based on responses to a questionnaire to our Heads of Missions (HOMs) and further interaction with them. It also provides an indication on the nature and level of interest taken by them in the area of cultural diplomacy. It also helps us in gauging whether there is a common strand that runs or we see any variations in the approaches of different missions.

Luckily for us, the response from our HOMs turned out to be representative in nature, as we were able to cover all the regions. In Europe, the response was from Austria, Belgium, Estonia, Finland and Germany; in Asia, the response was from Afghanistan, Australia, China, Malaysia, Maldives, Mongolia, Pakistan, Qatar and Sri Lanka; in the Americas, the response was from Brazil and USA (Washington DC and Chicago).

This chapter, therefore, turns out to be a mine of information on cultural diplomacy in action in the field. Prima facie, we get to gauge the level of interest that is in the area of cultural diplomacy, which was hitherto a low priority field of work among diplomats. Generally speaking, the common refrain has been that cultural diplomacy has arrived and the diplomatic missions have become more proactive. They are also playing an important role in enabling India to connect with the world, as an emerging power. Overall, we get a positive picture, but with a proviso that it is the leadership of the Head of the Mission (HOM) that sets the tone and the direction.

The last section in the chapter provides a broad overall picture. Each country has its own story to narrate, which depends upon a number of factors, as listed out in the text. There is also a variation in response from countries in the same region. A common strand, however, is of wider acceptance of India, as it is not perceived to be a cultural hegemon. Bollywood has been instrumental in connecting with people. Diaspora has also played an important role, both as a consumer of Indian culture as well as its promoter.

Indian basket of vehicles of cultural diplomacy remains largely restricted to its traditional ware of teaching classical dances and music, yoga and Hindi. The challenge would be to link cultural heritage with modernity.

The ultimate challenge, however, would be to develop country-specific initiatives, as we cannot have one omnibus cultural diplomacy approach that fits all sizes.

**Chapter XIV** is a companion to Chapter XIII, as we look at the policy framework and programmes initiated under the aegis of cultural diplomacy by foreign diplomatic missions in India. It is divided into two parts; Part I deals with the theoretical policy framework, while Part II looks at how this is being put into action in India. In this chapter, we not only look at the role of well-known and major players, but also other countries that are emerging as important players in the field of cultural diplomacy.

In Part I, we look at the policies and practices of certain countries, such as the United States, Russia, China, Japan, South Korea, Mexico and South Africa. In Part II, we peep into cultural diplomacy as practiced in India by some countries, such as the United States, Russia, and Japan, based on interaction with the representatives of diplomatic missions. This is both, in the global and the Indian contexts. Such evaluation is done, keeping in view certain parameters as are relevant for this examination.

What are the trends that emerge, which would be relevant for India? A common strand is the primary role played by the Ministry of Foreign Affairs, which is supplemented by other Ministries, keeping in view their policies, priorities and areas of focus. Image Building remains an important concern, with each country adopting different strategies to project the right kind of image.

Cultural Centres play an important role, while countries use different types of centres to suit their needs. Country Festivals are also considered an important vehicle to promote cultural connectivity. Sister-Cities relationships are considered an important vehicle, in particular by China, Japan and South Korea, as these join hands in working together on 'East Asia City of Culture' Project, under the aegis of UNESCO's 'Creative Cities Network'.

The above perspectives on the operation of their cultural diplomacy in India would be helpful in devising our own programmes. There is a growing recognition to view cultural diplomacy as a two-way channel to build relationship through reciprocal cultural exchange, albeit not in the same fields.

Education, Youth Exchanges and learning of Languages emerge as important areas of cultural connectivity between India and these countries.

While efforts could be made to build on these; yet new steps could be taken to learn from their experiences in Image Building; converting cultural exchange into cultural creativity and cultural trade and promoting linkages at the grassroots level among our cities.

**Chapter XV** is the concluding chapter of the Book**.** It takes us through various stages, till we reach the final stage of making recommendations, which is one sub-head of this chapter, 'The Way Ahead'. We start with a hard look at 'The Present Day Global Environment'. This presents a dismal picture as walls are getting erected to bar the entry of migrants and the chasm between 'us' and 'them' is growing. We are not able to 'Walk the Talk' on an 'Inclusive Society' and are witnessing an increase in hate crimes. All communities and places are becoming vulnerable. The world is heading for more polarization, as dialogue takes a back seat.

Above is the global environment in which Cultural Diplomacy has to operate. It is here that cultural diplomacy triggers in, as people realize the importance of connectivity and through that of promoting understanding. We notice how cultural diplomacy plays its part; while avoiding being drawn in to the genre of power, even if it is categorized as soft power.

Next, we have a good look at the issue of identity that is getting politicized with the rise of nationalistic forces, bordering on xenophobia. Immigrants are required to take the loyalty test. Preservation of diversity is coming under stress and is facing pressure for acceptance of local values. We, however, see a ray of hope, when we see 'Pluralism' being celebrated and the examples from different parts of the world are given in the text.

From here, we move to the next section that deals with the ground realities of Indian cultural diplomacy. We take a good look at its working, its success stories and its shortcomings. We then move forward to the next stage as to what is the core of India's cultural diplomacy. It is unmistakably the 'Idea of India', which rests on Democracy, Secularism, Diversity and Pluralism. This has become India's Brand, by which it is known and respected. This would and should, therefore, remain the core of any future pursuits in cultural diplomacy. What ultimately count are the perceptions in the host states.

There is discussion on the role of Bollywood and India Diaspora that connect India with other countries. A separate section deals with the issue of insulating cultural diplomacy from political winds and limitations under which Diaspora operates. In another section of this chapter, we look at the final picture that emerges, which deals with the centrality of cultural diplomacy.

Finally, we come to the concluding section, 'The Way Ahead'. This deals with a set of specific recommendations at the macro and micro levels. At the policy level, we need to give a shape to broad contours of our cultural diplomacy. We need to set up a Joint Policy Mechanism that could synergize the Ministries of External Affairs and Culture, to work as strategic partners rather than working in silos.

Furthermore, suggestions are made for mechanisms that need to be built to provide for greater connectivity among various stakeholders, so as to create greater synergy and thrust in our efforts. DG, ICCR has to be empowered to enable him to provide effective leadership.

What is the 'Way Ahead' then? India's cultural diplomacy that is built on the ethos of 'Vasudhaiva Kutumbakam' and is well placed to play a meaningful role in this globalised world. India has to abide by its belief in the "Idea of India", which is the core of its cultural diplomacy. The same has to be insulated from political winds that blow from time to time.

Cultural Diplomacy is essentially a people-centric process and should remain so in the future also. A process that could help reaching out directly to people across the globe, as Prime Minister Modi wanted to speak directly on the theme of 'Joint Cooperation on Poverty Alleviation'.

**Overall Observations:** The writing of a Book is both a pleasant and a challenging exercise. I was glad to accept the challenge from ICWA to delve into a subject, which has become a cliché as it is oft repeated by leaders and diplomats alike but not many have ventured to explore this in depth.

Cultural Diplomacy is interchangeably used with Public Diplomacy and Soft Power, which have grown as disciplines for study. Mine was, therefore, an exploratory effort as a student. I have learnt about many splendours of cultural diplomacy, which I had an occasion to implement in various diplomatic missions. Each Mission presented a unique opportunity and experience, given the dissimilarity of cultural backgrounds and the nature and level of India's diplomatic relations with those countries.

The writing of the Book, therefore, became more challenging as I delved deeper into some of the aspects. I have attempted to distil the knowledge that I have acquired both in theoretical and practical terms, in the shape of this Book. Hopefully this would whet the appetite of other diplomats and scholars to go into greater depth into some of the areas covered and explore new ones. For me, the biggest challenge has been whether to view 'Cultural Diplomacy' as 'Soft Power' or not. The Author would like 'Cultural Diplomacy' to remain outside the 'Power Paradigm', even if it is considered Soft Power.

For me 'Cultural Diplomacy' is the 'Mother of all Diplomacies', as it lays the foundation stone, over which the diplomatic structures are built. Cultural diplomacy promotes dialogue among different cultures. It is to bring change in perceptions, by converting negative vibes into positive ones. A successful Cultural Diplomacy initiative has to be a win-win situation for all, both 'us' and 'them'.

Cultural Diplomacy plays a larger role, as a 'Connectivity Bridge' in enhancing 'Understanding' among peoples and nations, as it does not push in the direction of converting others into one's viewpoint. Hope that the Book results in generating more light than heat, as we further explore this topic in depth.

# Section – I

# Understanding Indian Cultural Diplomacy in a Globalised World

## Chapter – 1

# Cultural Diplomacy in a Globalised World

---

### Introduction

The first chapter sets the stage for understanding cultural diplomacy in a globalised world. What is cultural diplomacy and its purpose? Is it to promote understanding among peoples and nations through understanding of different cultures?

How central is cultural diplomacy in the diplomatic arena? Where does it find its place in the diplomatic architecture? How does it manifest itself as an important instrument in furthering foreign policy, commercial and other interests? Is there an intrinsic link between culture and commerce? Does culture precede commerce or is it the other way around?

How do we define culture, when using it as a diplomatic tool? Do we view culture in a broader or narrower construct? Is it restricted to promotion of cultural relations only or does it go beyond this? Are we restricting the conduct of cultural diplomacy to only official sources or are we going to expand our horizon and include non-governmental players?

What are the features of globalisation that we need to understand in the context of cultural diplomacy? Do we look at the demographic profile of the countries, given the present day migratory flows? Has it resulted in changing the demographic character of the countries and how does this become relevant for cultural diplomacy?

How has the population in different parts of the world become diversified? A large-scale migration requires adaptation of the migrants into the host state. How have the governments addressed the issues of 'Identity and Diversity' in a transnational world, as the same compete with one another? Is it through pursuing policies of assimilation or multiculturalism? Do we see a clash of civilizations, as per the Huntington thesis, where identities clash with one another? Does globalisation lead to cultural homogenization or hegemony?

How does understanding of culture help in promoting connectivity? Does it result in tearing down, real or perceived barriers, between the foreigners and the locals and the majority and the minority communities? Do we see imposition of local values on the immigrants, be it Australian, British or French? Are we seeing the emergence of cultural nationalism? Are we becoming sensitive or insensitive to the views of others?

What is the shape of a globalised world as it is emerging? Is it getting more connected or disconnected, in so far it relates to peoples' connectivity? What are the fault lines, if disconnected? What are the factors that bring about connectivity? What role does culture play in bringing about connectivity? Is connectivity the heart of cultural diplomacy?

How are cultural diplomacy and public diplomacy interconnected? Does cultural diplomacy get submerged in public diplomacy, which has become a vehicle of public policy for all the foreign ministries, as they are required to relate to foreign audiences? How does cultural diplomacy fit in with public diplomacy, which uses culture as one of its vehicles in achieving its objectives? Do we view cultural diplomacy as 'soft power', in converting other's to one's view point, as per terminology used by Joseph Nye Jr.

## Understanding Cultural Diplomacy

Cultural diplomacy is an important diplomatic tool in enhancing connectivity among peoples. In this globalised world, it has assumed a greater role, as we strive to build a world on understanding, while accepting its diversity. The need for such an understanding has assumed criticality as we are witnessing the emergence of a conflict situation. It is not only a clash of civilizations as envisaged by Samuel Huntington but also among peoples belonging to the same faith. We are coming under pressure from state and non-state actors, who are promoting terrorism, whose primary purpose is to create cleavages among different groups in a society.

We live in a world that is dominated by the 'Power' narrative. From 'Hard Power', we have shifted our focus to 'Soft Power' and we are now turning our eye to 'Smart Power'-another terminology created by Joseph Nye Jr. We also categorize countries in terms of their strength, by calling them 'Super Powers' or 'Major Powers'.

In the context of globalisation, we have also tended to divide countries, keeping in view their level of development, such as 'First World', 'Second World' or 'Third World'. We also view nations as 'developed', 'developing' or 'least developed', as we try to apportion responsibilities and benefits, in terms of their capacity to pay or absorb level of assistance. In the cultural context, we view nations, as 'high' or 'low' context, depending over their style of communication.

Definitional issues confront both, theoreticians and practitioners of diplomacy. The matter gets complicated, as new diplomatic vocabulary, like public diplomacy, soft power and smart power are added to confound the situation. At times, this is on account of differing understanding or perceptions of the topic as seen from one's perspective; while in other cases it is purely for tactical reasons.

Cultural diplomacy is a combination of two words. In the traditional sense, it simply means using 'culture' in the pursuit of national interests through diplomatic channels by the State. The word 'diplomacy' implies government's involvement. In the context of modern diplomacy, however, what becomes important is the role that culture plays in bringing about connectivity and this need not be spearheaded by the government.

It would be pertinent to state that Alliance Françoise, which is not a government organization, has better advanced the French interest rather than some other organizations, which are publicly funded. Cultural diplomacy could also be directly promoted by private groups, such as concerts by Zubin Mehta in Vienna or India or supported by the state agency, like ICCR, when Teamwork Arts mounts an exhibition 'Eye on India' in Chicago or organizes Festival of India in Australia.

How do scholars and experts define cultural diplomacy? Let us first look at the traditional approach, where Richard Arndt has defined it as follows:

> "Cultural relations grow naturally and organically, without government intervention- the transactions of trade and tourism, student flows, communications, books circulation, migration, media access, intermarriage-millions of daily cross-cultural encounters. If that is correct, cultural diplomacy be said to take place when formal diplomats, serving national governments, try to shape and channel this natural flow to advance national interests"(Arndt).

It has two components-natural and organic growth of cultural relations and the involvement of diplomats to channelize these relations to advance national interests. This was true in the twentieth century, but it does not stand the test the way cultural diplomacy is pursued in the twenty-first century, where diplomats and non-diplomats criss-cross in using culture in promoting national interests, be it individually or jointly or with the support of the government, moral or financial. Diplomatic touch can be provided in myriad ways and forms, as we are treating students, academia, cultural personalities, sports persons and Diaspora, as our Ambassadors, notionally speaking.

Two commonly held definitions of cultural diplomacy in the modern context, which cater to the role of non-diplomatic players, are as follows:

- "Exchange of ideas, information, and other aspects of culture among nations and their peoples to foster mutual understanding" (Milton Cummings, 2009).
- "The use of creative expression and exchange of ideas, information and people to increase mutual understanding" (Walter Lacquer, 1994).

At the functional level, a former Director General, ICCR defined it in these words, "Cultural diplomacy is the use of culture in establishing effective communication and understanding between different societies" (Goel, Suresh, 2015).[1]

A former Indian Ambassador also views cultural diplomacy playing an important role 'in creating awareness of a nation state's cultural achievements and thereby to create better understanding amongst the target nations and peoples' (Yogesh Tiwari, 2007).

Let us also look at it from the perspective of a dancer, choreographer and art administrator Pratibha Prahlad and organizer of Delhi International Arts Festival (DIAF), who recognizes that 'cultural diplomacy is of extreme importance'. For her,"Culture is all about understanding people, value system, art, languages and the way people transact their life" (Cited in Geeta Sahai, 2016).

All the above definitions have convergence on two points; the heart of cultural diplomacy is promoting understanding among peoples and nations, through using culture as a vehicle of communication and connectivity. This view gets endorsed by another academic, who opines that cultural diplomacy 'can be helpful in bridging difference and in opening new avenues of communication' (Goff, Patricia, 2013).

The above interpretation assumes importance if we view the whole world as a family, which was the aim in creating institutions, like 'The League of Nations' or the 'United Nations', even though these have not come up to their expectations. Cultural diplomacy does not fall in the 'Power' genre, as it is not to be played like a game of poker, chess or bridge. It is also not about victory of 'A' over 'B', but about connecting 'A' with 'B', generating understanding about each other; resulting in building mutual trust and paving way for promotion of relationship.

The ultimate thing to keep in mind is that cultural diplomacy is about 'Understanding'. It is not about soft power, as it is people-centric and its aim is to create an atmosphere of trust. Of course, it is through trust that relationship could be further advanced. It would, therefore, be better not to describe cultural diplomacy as a tool but as a vehicle, which helps in building a conducive atmosphere, which paves way for fostering friendly relations over which ties could be built. For me, cultural diplomacy should be aptly described as a 'Connectivity Bridge' that connects peoples and nations.

Cultural diplomacy, to simply put it, is promoting understanding among peoples and nations through communications by using the medium of culture. I would view it as 4C's, as 'Culture, Connectivity, Communication and Cooperation', where communication is a key element of cultural diplomacy. It is 'Culture' that provides the 'Connectivity Bridge'; while it is 'Communication' that leads to 'Cooperation'. The need for such an understanding becomes more pronounced in a globalised world. It thus becomes a 5-C's Process- 'Culture, Connectivity, Communication, Conversation, and Cooperation'. It is through communication of culture that you connect to converse, which results in cooperation.

The history of cultural diplomacy can be traced to early travellers, traders, religious preachers and sea-farers, artists and teachers, who could be placed in the category of 'Cultural Ambassadors'. Nalanda University was a living example, which facilitated such cultural interactions. The Institute for Cultural Diplomacy (ICD) treats any form of cultural exchange as cultural diplomacy, if it takes place 'in fields such as art, sports, literature, music, science, business & economy and beyond'. ICD defines cultural diplomacy in the present day context as follows:

> "Cultural Diplomacy may best be described as a course of actions, which are based on and utilize the exchange of ideas, values, traditions and other aspects of culture or identity, whether

> to strengthen relationships, enhance socio-cultural cooperation, promote national interests and beyond; Cultural diplomacy can be practiced by either the public sector, private sector or civil society" (ICD, 2017).

In this Book, we are following this broad definition. Each country chooses its own diplomatic tools to promote its own national interests. The choice, however, varies both in terms of time and space, as we are living in a dynamic world. Cultural diplomacy has a greater role to play across the globe, given the chasm that separates nations and peoples, as cultural divide among them is increasing.

We are also witnessing a plethora of new diplomatic terminologies, as leaders of the world recognise the need of connectivity, working individually, bilaterally or globally, to find solutions to intricate problems. We often hear of new terms, like Pressure Diplomacy, Coercive Diplomacy, Twitter Diplomacy, Cowshed Diplomacy, Birthday Diplomacy, Yoga Diplomacy, Golf Diplomacy, Muscular Diplomacy, Sports Diplomacy, Spiritual Diplomacy, Mango Diplomacy, Airdrop Diplomacy, Shrine Diplomacy, Faith Diplomacy, Smart Diplomacy and Cohesive Diplomacy.

We all need to understand each other, be it as individuals or nations. Cultural diplomacy is about understanding 'others' as we would like them to understand us. Vice President Hamid Ansari (Vice President, 2010) beautifully captured this thought in a Persian Couplet, which reads:

"*Tafawut ast ma'ani shanidan man-o-tu*
*Tu bastan-e-dar, o man fateh-bab mi shawam*

What you and I hear are different. You hear the sound
Of closing doors but I of doors that open".

Cultural diplomacy is about perceptions; 'it is not how we perceive ourselves, but how we are perceived by others' (Tharoor, Shashi, 2011). It is about listening and appreciating the view point of others, as it is not my way or highway. A former Australian Ambassador put it that it is more about hearing and listening before talking (Malone, David). Cultural diplomacy has the formidable task of creating understanding, as it aims at changing the mind set. It helps in building trust, results in the opening of doors and thus creates an environment that is conducive for promoting peace and friendship.

It is, therefore, not surprising to see the Report of an Advisory Group to the US State Department assigning a seminal role to cultural diplomacy as 'a lynchpin of public diplomacy'. It believes that through culture, we can 'understand the role of a nation, which could help in enhancing our national security in subtle, wide ranging and sustainable ways' (US State Department 2005). At the operational level, Americans make a distinction between the functions performed by cultural diplomacy, which deals with cultural relations, while public diplomacy deals with the 'Image Building' of the Nation-State.

Cultural diplomacy helps in generating positive ethos and empathy about one another and thus directly impacts on minds. It is in the minds that wars are fought as per the preamble of UNESCO. It helps in creating 'positivity in the minds of people' (Goel, Suresh)[1]. Therefore, there should be no hesitation in characterizing it as positive diplomacy.

India's then Foreign Minister M.C. Chagla recognized the role of culture, as a unifying force in promoting understanding among peoples and nations, thereby giving enhanced role to cultural diplomacy. He saw culture providing an everlasting intellectual bond among people and observed: "Culture has greater influence over minds than science and technology or industrial growth and if there is that cultural bond that brings minds together that is the more lasting bond than any other" (Cited in Sarkar, Bidyut, 1968).

How true, as we try to bridge trust deficit on a daily basis among peoples and nations?

How does this bond take place? It is through a two-layered operation. Cultural diplomacy would, therefore, imply a two-pronged action – the vanguard action, which would be to "create a cultural presence" and the rear-guard impact that would be to "ensure how the other person or nation would recognize and understand the projecting nation" (Banerjee, Utpal, 1973). Ultimately, it is not only about the message or the best India story, but also how it is understood and received by the target audience in a particular destination.

Dr. Karan Singh, former President of the Indian Council for Cultural Relations (ICCR) has an interesting take on cultural diplomacy. He likens diplomacy to 'the Ganga-Jamuna-Saraswati Triveni' in these words:

> "There are three streams of diplomacy. There is the traditional diplomacy or the classical diplomacy, which has been practiced for thousands of years. It is akin to the Ganga. There is a growing stream which has become dominant in the last 10 to 15 years.

> That is economic diplomacy. I call it the Yamuna. The third is the invisible stream like the Saraswati of the Triveni. That is cultural diplomacy. It is very different from the other two" (Cited in Misra, Satish, 2006).

Cultural diplomacy can thus be viewed as a latent force that is lying dormant and invisible. Its strength, however, is measured in terms of its potency.

Cultural factors are acquiring pre-eminence, as these help in creating an appropriate climate or environment for development of ties among 'Nation-States'. Cultures become the unifying force, if properly understood and used. An ultimate outcome of such an understanding is the creation of friendly environment for promotion of bilateral economic and political links.

While pursuing our goals we, however, need to keep in view Prime Minister Nehru's golden words, 'on the need for adopting an open, correct and friendly approach' which he uttered at the time of the launch of the Indian Council for Cultural Relations (ICCR) in 1950. He added:

> "It becomes essential that one must try to understand each other in the right way. The right way is important. That right approach, friendly approach is important, because friendly approach brings a friendly response" (Nehru).

How prophetic and pragmatic were those words that are valid and applicable even now?

Cultural diplomacy thus becomes important as it "has the power to penetrate our common humanity" (Clinton, 2000). Cultural diplomacy thus enthuse us with a positive approach in dealing with humanity in the international arena. Madeline Albright, then US Secretary of State, who is herself a product of varied cultural influences, said that "Culture is not marginal but central to our diplomacy". She saw an important role for cultural diplomacy "to project abroad a richer image of America, preserve cultural diversity worldwide and promote universal values of democracy and mutual respect among nations and peoples". She said, "Foreign Policy development has to have culture on the table" (The White House Conference, 2000).

All the above are laudable goals to achieve. The Modi Government is putting culture at the centre of the table during all VVIP visits to India and foreign visits abroad.

Cultural diplomacy, therefore, is not only promoting cultural exchanges, but the process also results in promoting the image of the Nation-State. It is, therefore, both a vehicle as well as an end product as seen in projecting the image of a country. A natural by product and result is that it ultimately leads to promoting diplomatic relations in commercial, political, strategic and other fields

## Centrality of Cultural Diplomacy

Connectivity is the buzz word as nations strive to connect with one another, in an effort to build bridges of friendship. Recognizing the important role of culture diplomacy, President Clinton took the initiative to organize the First International Conference on 'Culture and Diplomacy' in November 2000, as a way to mark its importance, when the world was at the portals of the 21st century.

A similar message was echoed by the then External Affairs Minister Pranab Mukherjee, when he opened the cultural centre in Kolkata on June 1, 2008. He said, "Today cultural diplomacy has assumed even greater importance as we seek to strengthen and reinforce people-to-people contacts transcending political boundaries" (EAM, 2008).

Reference to people-to-people connectivity has become a salient feature of Joint Statements. This remained one of the main focus areas during the visit of Prime Minister Sheikh Hasina to India in April, 2017 as the two leaders decided 'to make the year 2018 as the Year of India in Bangladesh and 2019 as the Year of Bangladesh in India (Joint Statement, 2017).

Cultural diplomacy is thus central for the understanding of people, as the so called 'McWorld' (Barber, Benjamin, 1995) has not erased distinction between 'us' and 'them'. Furthermore, despite the presence of 258 million migrants across the globe, it has failed to usher in 'multiculturalism' in real practice, as old divides have continued to exist, while new ones are emerging. In this so called Flat World of Friedman (Friedman, 2002), we still do not have the 'Universal Man', as envisioned by Rabindranath Tagore.

The importance and role of cultural diplomacy depends on the role "Culture" is expected to play in shaping international relations. Its role has been viewed differently at different times in different societies. In the olden times culture followed trade in some cases, like the Silk Route, while in other cases, trade followed culture, like spread of Buddhism in South East Asia. President Xi of China is dexterously weaving culture and commerce in his initiative on 'One Belt, One Road' (OBOR).

The heart of cultural diplomacy is to promote understanding among people, who come from different backgrounds and hold different values, through the medium of culture. Dr. Karan Singh, the then President, ICCR stated, 'Culture has no boundaries and using it as a way to interact with the masses has been the most effective way to win hearts in the era of globalisation' (The Tribune, 2010). Culture in the context of cultural diplomacy looks at a broader spectrum and is not limited to performing arts only. It embraces both 'high culture' and 'low culture' activities and a host of other activities.

Where does cultural diplomacy find its place in the diplomatic architecture? Traditionally speaking, it was the political work that attracted diplomats. In the post-cold war scenario, the economic strength of a country as measured in terms of its share in international trade has emerged as the preponderant factor, replacing the military muscle as the most important factor for a global power. There is now a worldwide recognition of the importance of cultural diplomacy, as 'Nation-States' have woken up to the important role of culture as a factor in not only understanding and promotion but also building and sustaining relationship among them.

B P Singh, former Secretary of Culture, placed culture as the third most important factor in determining the status of a country in a community of nations. It is the "cultural strength of a country that gives it cohesiveness, endurance and a memory to carry the country forward as a civilization in the world" (Singh, B P, 1998).

Unlike BP Singh, Richard Arndt, US diplomat-cum-scholar, describes cultural diplomacy as the 'First Resort of the Kings' in a book that bears the same title, in these words: "Reflecting on human kind as a cultural diplomat, I came to understand that war in Hugo Grotius' phrase was "the last resort of kings" (ultima ratio regum)-then cultural was surely the first" (Arndt, 2005).

The Author is prepared to go along with Arndt and place cultural diplomacy on a higher pedestal, as it is akin to 'Foundation Stone' for the diplomatic structure, as it helps in connecting, before they start communicating and conducting business with one another.

## What Defines 'Culture' in 'Cultural Diplomacy'?

How do we define the word 'culture' in the context of cultural diplomacy? The word culture has both a narrow and a broader construct. To understand the role of Cultural Diplomacy, it is essential to classify the context in which the term 'culture' is used. In a narrow context, it means performing arts; while in a broader context, it means a whole way of life of a society.

For the purpose of this book, we are accepting broader definition of culture that was adopted by UNESCO in 1982. It reads, 'Culture comprises the whole complex of distinctive spiritual, material, intellectual and emotional features that characterize a society or social group. It includes not only the arts and letters, but also modes of life; the fundamental rights of the human being, value systems, traditions and beliefs' (UNESCO, 1982). It is this holistic definition of culture, as a way of life, traditions and beliefs and value systems that we are adopting.

In India, we also view culture in a broader context. B.P. Singh states that 'culture' embraces'a whole way of life and it is "Sanskriti" or process of refinement. Culture concerns the entire gamut of human activity and its achievements' (Singh, BP). An Indian expert sees its essence in values that are embodied in the beliefs of people and value orientation patterns thus become the essential feature of culture (Alexander, 1992). Another Indian expert also views culture as 'an integrated whole, a living phenomenon and dynamic in nature' (Atal, Yogesh, 1991).

Interaction among different cultures results in acculturation, as 'no culture is either rigid enough not to allow the change or docile to allow itself to be submerged' (Atal, Yogesh). Interaction among different cultures, therefore, gives rise to acculturation. This propounds the philosophy of co-existence and give and take among different cultures.

India is a living example of such acculturation, as it was able to successfully weave tapestry of a composite culture, which is blending of diverse cultures through its interaction with different cultures. India has not only accepted a broader definition of culture, but it has also accepted that dialogue is essential for enrichment of culture, as embodied in its philosophy of 'Vasudhaiva Kutumbakam' (The whole world is a family).

In short, culture is a total social heritage acquired by man as a member of the society. Culture is shared and has distinctive forms (patterns) and shapes of human behaviour. Its essence is the values embodied in the beliefs of people and value orientation patterns become the essential features of 'Culture' (Alexander). It is the 'summation of material and creative resources of a people living within identifiable geographical frontiers' (Laksmi Reddy, 2001).

Culture is an integrated whole and is not merely a sum total of its parts. Culture, as a totality of way of life of a people, includes among others, economy of a society. Cultural development, therefore, refers to 'development of all aspects of a society's life. Gunnar Myrdal's thesis in 'Asian Drama' that traditional societies could not modernize without giving up their beliefs and values is no more valid. Culture constitutes 'a balancing and a driving force for development and an objective of development itself' (Singh, B P).

Culture identifies us as an "entire people and eras in terms of the ways in which we think they see or saw the world". It helps us to place them viz.-a-viz. one another, usually with ourselves at the centre of the world and at the end of time. It is, in short, 'a way of organizing the world in time and space' (Mazumdar, T K, 1969).

## Cultural Personality of States

Culture, in the context of 'Nation-States', results in their acquiring a 'Personality' of their own. The Culture of a 'Nation' finds its manifestation through language and art, philosophy and religion, education and science, films and newspapers, radio and television, social habits and customs, political institutions and economic organizations.

Each Nation thus acquires a distinct personality and a national stereotype. At times, such stereotypes are at variance with reality as it is the perceptions that matter. Cultural factors are acquiring pre-eminence, as these help in creating an appropriate climate or environment for development of ties among 'Nation-States'. Cultures become the unifying force, if properly understood.

This results in 'Nations' getting branded, as per the national stereotypes, as they or others perceive them. Such images linger, like American Hegemon, Indian Elephant, Chinese Dragon or ASEAN Tigers. We have seen how ASEAN countries coordinate their approaches through 'ASEAN Way', which rests on two pillars – 'mushwara' (consultation) and 'muwafakat' (consensus) [Kaul, T N, 1982]. Cross Cultural Communications are essential for promoting better understanding, as illustrated by former foreign secretary Shyam Saran from his experiences in China and Nepal (Shyam Saran)[2].

Prime Minister Modi has ushered in new Brand Images for India, like 'Make in India', 'Digital India', 'Start up India' and 'Swatchh Bharat' (Clean India). It is the same, when Prime Minister Modi describes India-Bhutan relations, using a new imagery of 'B4B', Bhutan for Bharat (India) and Bharat for Bhutan, during his visit to Bhutan in June 2014, which was the first prime ministerial visit abroad by Modi. Prime Minister Modi has come out with a new brand for India, 'New India', which has not been fully spelt out.

Furthermore, understanding cultural behaviour of the states is also essential, as this is helpful in ensuring better results, when they communicate with one another. Raymond Cohen, an authority on 'Culture and Negotiations', places States under two labels. 'High Context States' with interdependent societies, like China, India, Japan and Mexico, which reflect predominantly non-verbal and implicit communication style. 'Low Context States' with individualistic societies like USA and West Europe, which adopt predominantly verbal and explicit style (Cohen, Raymond). This is a useful definition in the context of cultural diplomacy, even though we notice that there are variations in the behaviour pattern among nations belonging to the same group, as other factors are also at play, such as in the case of India and Pakistan.

Such an understanding of the cultural traits of States does help in providing a smooth process for negotiations. Raymond Cohen fully illustrates with examples drawn from the experience of USA with India, Mexico, Egypt, as to how an understanding of cultural traits or its lack, has helped or hindered the negotiating process. Could we ascribe the recent problems between India and Nepal since 2015, to this non-verbal and implicit communication style? It is, thus, by triggering in cultural diplomacy, we are able to understand how people and nations behave. It helps in changing perceptions and removing ignorance through dialogue and interaction.

Lee Kuan Yew, former Prime Minister of Singapore, also commented in his book on such 'Cultural Stereotypes' when he said that 'The Tunku's simple belief was that 'politics was for Malays and business for the Chinese. This might have been so in his father's time, but was not realistic in 1962' (Lee Kuan Yew, 1998).

This would mean projecting Brand Equity of a Nation after discovering its Unique Selling Point (USP) to inject phraseology from the commercial world. The task of cultural diplomacy would be "to produce understanding that goes beyond stereotyped images and to mould perceptions in a favourable way" (Kishan Rana, 2014). It is the 'Idea of India' that is the USP for India.

At times, such stereotypes are politically motivated to promote particular interests of the State. At times, an effort is made to put across ideas which are in tune with different cultures. George Bush's war against terrorism was later categorized 'Operation Freedom', replacing the use of original epithet 'Operation Justice', when it became known that under Islam, only God can mete out justice. His references to Iraq, Iran and North Korea, as 'an Axis of Evil' were also couched in cultural terms, even though it created some murmurs among Europeans. Leaders still have not given up their fascination for the use of the term 'Axis of Evil', although the composition of the Axis has changed.

## Globalisation and Cultural Diplomacy

Globalisation is not only about flow of currency, but it is equally about movement of humans, flow of ideas and their cultures, understanding of which has relevance for this Book. In this section, we would look at and understand certain trends and facets of globalisation that would determine the environment under which cultural diplomacy operates. These would relate to the issues of 'Mobility, Homogenization, Identity, Diversity, Pluralism and Multiculturalism'.

### *Mobility*

We all live in a globalised world, which means a world that is well connected among nations and peoples. How does it impact on Mobility? While we see greater connectivity in terms of flow of capital and means of communication, yet this is restricted, as far as movement of people is concerned. While there is a right to leave one's country under the Human Rights Conventions, yet there is no complementary right to enter another country.

This right to entry is regulated by individual countries, which is dictated by their national interests. It is the same, whether it is fixing H1B Visa by the US President Trump or abolishing of Category 427 Visa by the Australian Prime Minister Turnbull or the inclusion of student visas in the overall immigration limits by the United Kingdom. Even if there are no open borders, yet movement of people does take place; some voluntary, some forced. As per the current data, globally 258 million people were international migrants in 2017, which was about 3.4 per cent of the then total population. This represented an increase of 49 % since 2000 (International Migrants Report, 2017).

So far, no effective international regime governing the movement of people has emerged. There are ineffective conventions on the movement of people. WTO has not been able to find an effective answer on facilitating the movement of people, who provide services. At the regional level, some conventions do provide for movement of service providers. Movement of peoples is, therefore, largely governed by the nation-states; in keeping with their domestic requirements to sub serve their national interest.

Nonetheless, there is a movement across the national borders. The presence of more than 258 million international migrants, who are living in foreign lands, has changed the demographic character of a large number of countries. This has resulted in diversity of populations. Have these societies become multicultural, is debatable? It all depends upon how open are those countries and how migrants negotiate their identities in the host states, while maintaining their links with the home state.

How compatible are the cultures in the home and the host states; greater the compatibility, faster is the process of adaptation. Issues of such compatibility come into the forefront in situations, when migrants are not perceived to observe local norms and traditions. A recent case that typified such behaviour was when immigrants misbehaved with locals in Cologne (Germany) at the time of celebrations, marking the New Year in 2016. This resulted in the rise of shrill voices for preservation of local cultures and traditions.

International migrants are spread across the world, even their percentage share as a component of the local population varies, from country to country. International migrants comprised more than 10 percent of the resident population, in most of the countries in Europe and Northern America. The percentage share of foreign-born vis-à-vis the total population is given in brackets in respect of major countries, such as USA (15.3 %), Canada (21.5%), United Kingdom (13.4%), Germany (14.8%), France (12.2%) and Russia (8.1%). In respect of other European countries, Switzerland topped the list with a share of 29.6%; it was followed by Luxembourg (21.9%), Austria (19%), Sweden (17.8%), Spain (12.8%), Netherlands (12.1%) and Italy (10%) (International Migrants Report, 2017).

In Asia, the countries with a significant number of international migrants included Singapore (46%), followed by Australia (28.8%), New Zealand (22.7%) and Kazakhstan (20%). In Africa, South Africa had a share of 7.1%; while in the case of Gabon, Libya and Congo, it was 13.8%, 12.4% and 7.2% respectively. West Asia presented a different picture all together, as in most of the countries it exceeded more than the local resident population. UAE topped the list with an amazing share of 88.4%, followed by Kuwait (75.5%), Qatar (65.2%), Bahrain (48.4%), Oman (44.7%), Saudi Arabia (37%), Jordan (33.3), Lebanon (31.9%) and Israel (23.6%).

On the other hand, we also get an interesting picture in respect of those countries, which have a minimal presence of international migrants, as a percentage of their total population. China tops the list, with a share of 0.1%; followed by Sri Lanka (0.2%), India (0.4%),Nigeria (0.6%), Zambia (0.9%), Pakistan (1.7%), Japan (1.8%), Kenya (2.2%), Republic of Korea (2.3%) and Zimbabwe (2.4%). (International Migrants Report, 2017)

Against the above backdrop, what are the trends we notice? Demographically, the picture has changed, as diversity in population is a fact of life. Voices are heard in many countries to restrict the entry of new immigrants. The US President Donald Trump would like to ban the entry of fresh immigrants from certain Muslim countries.

Some EU countries would like to even restrict the free movement of people within EU countries against the letter of the Schengen Agreement and the spirit of EU, as this is one of its core principles. Leaders in Hungary and Poland would like to seal their borders, while the Prime Minister of Denmark would like to take possession of gold and money brought in by the immigrants to provide for their social security benefits. Concerns over immigration resulted in voters favouring Brexit from EU, under a referendum on June 23, 2016.

On the other hand, the Chancellor of Germany Angela Merkel stayed committed to bringing in 1 million immigrants in 2015, but is facing challenges from conservative or nationalist parties that are against the entry of fresh immigrants. UK is commencing its exit process from EU, consequent to the Brexit vote. It is a paradox that while President Obama and Prime Minister David Cameron competed to attract 'the best and the brightest' immigrants, yet they moaned the outsourcing of jobs to India and China and were worried being 'Bangalored', even though their countries' economies gained from the contribution of migrants.

### *Homogenization*

In the cultural arena, globalisation is largely taken to mean homogenization. We often hear about 'MacWorld', a word coined by Benjamin Barber that symbolically employs the simile of a hamburger, which has been popularized globally by McDonald. Benjamin Barber describes,

> "MacWorld as the onrush of economic and ecological forces that demand integration and uniformity and that mesmerize the world with fast music, fast computers, and fast food – with MTV, Macintosh and McDonald's, pressing nations into one commercially homogenous global network: one MacWorld

> tied together with technology, ecology, communications, and commerce" (Barber, Benjamin, 1999).

This homogenization of culture is largely associated with the global onslaught of the American culture. What is American culture is, however, debatable. It is seen primarily as consumer culture. Seen in this context, it invites backlash of "all those millions of people who detest the way globalisation homogenizes people, puts Israeli-made banana cream pie on the face of a Jordanian Muslim, brings strangers into your home with strange ways, erases the distinctiveness of cultures and mercilessly uproots the olive trees that locate and anchor you in the world" (Friedman, Thomas, 1999).

While a number of people are prepared to adapt to "Americanized-globalised consumer culture", yet some are not prepared to give up local for global, giving rise to another phenomenon called G-Local. At one level, we witness protests against McDonald's in India for cultural and political reasons. We also, at another level, see McDonald adapting itself to Indian culture through introduction of Veggie-Burgers and even in France changing its trademark of blue flag in France.

While there is a slow acceptance of American consumer culture, yet it invites strong reaction, when American culture is projected as representing the best in terms of values. This formed the conclusion of the book – '*The Lexus and the Olive Tree*' – authored by Thomas Friedman, when he imparts the American culture "a spiritual value and role model".

The above raises questions on the 'spiritual and role model' character of the American culture. Friedman concluded:

> "A healthy global society is one that can balance the Lexus and the olive tree all the time, and there is no better model for this on earth today than America. And that's why I believe so strongly that for globalisation to be sustainable America must be at its best – today, tomorrow, all the time. It not only can be, it must be, a beacon for the whole world. Let us not squander this precious legacy"(Friedman, Thomas, 1999).

The above certainly invites comments, as America is not always at its best and can lay claim to permanency on its superior status, howsoever, justifiable it may be. Steps taken by the US President Trump are a pointer in this direction that America is not at its best as it targets immigrants from certain Muslim countries and pushes to promote American interests, while shunning American values, under the garb of 'Making America Great

Again' or "America First', which is tantamount to jettisoning globalisation, as it closes its doors to immigrants from certain categories and countries. A cartoon appropriately captured this, as it showed the blackened face of the Statute of Liberty.

Even if we accept homogenisation in consumer culture but that does not result in homogenisation of ideas or their acceptance. These vary, as it depends upo the context and the locale. Terrorists may eat hamburgers or relish their cokes, yet they happily shoot from their guns or throw hand grenades at innocent Americans. The huge 'popularity of Bollywood in Pakistan has scarcely reduced anti-Indian sentiments among sections of the Pakistani establishment' (Thussu, Daya, 2013). Love of Bollywood films by the Chinese President Xi Jinping does not result in preventing the Peoples Liberation Army (PLA) from taking adversarial position on India.

Another important trend is the relationship of commerce and culture, which works against homogenization. Commercial impulses are becoming the driving force. We are seeing a clash of interests in this regard. Motion Pictures Association of America (MPAA) had played an important role in pushing American commercial interests in Germany, France and India. Countries like France would like to preserve their policy of 'cultural exceptionalisn". French-American cultural clash was the subject matter of a number of French books, such as Emanuel Todd's "*Apres e empire*' (More to life than America) and Philippe Rogers' '*L'ennemi Americaine*' (The American Enemy)". UNESCO stands fully committed to preserving and promoting cultural diversity.

Modern Information and Communication Technologies (ICTs) have reduced the effectiveness of the state control of its territory, resulting thereby in reducing its "capacities for cultural control and homogenization". Pakistanis can now see Indian films, while Indians can see Pakistani plays on TV and this is not being affected in anyway by the status of bilateral relationship between the two neighbours. Intermediaries, like YouTube, are bringing connectivity in their own way. Coke Studios in Pakistan and India are an example in promoting cultural connectivity through music.

### *Identity*

We all have an identity, be it as an individual, a group or a nation. It is, therefore, natural to think in terms of 'us' and 'them'. At the human level also, there is reluctance to accept others, even though there is a certain level of tolerance. The aim of cultural diplomacy is to promote 'understanding' among ourselves, by accepting and respecting those differences that are identity related.

Cultural diplomacy has to primarily grapple with the issue of identity, per se. It is both at the level of individuals and nations, as even the latter have also acquired their own identities. At global level, we all are connected and differences tend to disappear, as we watch the same programmes and wear similar dresses. In fact, the jean has become the biggest leveller, not only among the genders, but also among people across the world.

At the national level, we tend to equate our identities, with the home or the host state, to suit our convenience. At the local level, we opt for our distinct identity, as we are nurtured by similar values and traditions, which result in our acquiring certain social and cultural traits. It is, here that we start identifying with the group as 'we'; we thus see ourselves as different from another group, called 'they'.

With globalisation and free movement of people, we are witnessing two contradictory trends. Firstly, there is a desire towards accommodation and the host states have put in place certain programmes to help the immigrants get better integrated with the local population. Civil Society also plays a participatory role in facilitating integration, even though the level and nature of such integration would vary from place to place.

At the same time, there is another trend, leading to accentuation of such differences, when local values are being imposed on the immigrants at the altar of politics. This is a universal phenomenon, which is clubbed under the word 'Ethnicity', which is an umbrella term used for interpreting differences in class, colour, creed, caste, religion or even gender.

In India also, we are faced with identity politics, as the same challenge the cherished values of democracy, pluralism and secularism, which has come to be defined as the 'Idea of India'. It is the strength of these cherished values, which have resulted in India remaining on an even keel, despite attempts made by vested interests to destabilize Indian polity. Such challenges arise, when the society grapples with the issue of protection of minorities (Christians, Sikhs and Muslims) or regional groups (residents from North-eastern States) or addressing gender disparities or discriminations based on race or caste.

Similar kind of perceptions are held abroad, be it UK over being overrun by non-whites or USA being overrun by the Mexicans. Most of the countries are not immune from identity politics, which gets more pronounced at the time of elections. At times, we also encounter another phenomenon of 'Mistaken Identity', when the Sikhs become victim of hate crimes.

Identity politics was a hot topic during the US Presidential Elections in 2016. It also prominently figured during the elections of the Mayor of London in May 2015. The election results, however, were a vote for multiculturalism, with the victory of Sadiq Khan, a British Muslim of Pakistani origin. On the other hand, the results of the election of Mayor of Jakarta in April 2017 were a vote against multiculturalism. We saw identity politics being played, during the elections of the President of India in July 2017.

Simultaneously, we are seeing another phenomenon of transnationalism or multiple identities. According to Amartya Sen, globalisation has also resulted in obliteration of national identities and given rise to acceptance of multiple identities, especially in the urban centres, which are emerging as congregation of people from across the globe, as a result of migration. Baroness Helena Kennedy, the then Chair of the British Foreign Policy Council described this trend in her own way, when she said that there 'will be conundrums about what it means to be British, German or Italian or Kazakh. Every nation is a community of nations' (Keith Phillip Lepor, 1997). In the United States, we also see hyphenated identities, like India-Americans, Italian-Americans, and Black-Americans.

On the other hand, migratory flows have stoked nationalist feelings among local population, which feels economically deprived. This takes the form of preservation of values or culture. In the case of the United Kingdom, the then Prime Minister Cameron had harped on British values, making it incumbent on immigrants to have sufficient knowledge of the English language and British traditional values (The Tribune, 2016: 1& 2). In the case of France, it disallows use of cultural symbols, be it 'hizab' or cross, skull cap or turban in public places, like schools, to preserve France's secular identity (The Times of India, 2003). In Switzerland, it takes the form of ban for the construction of minarets (prayer towers) of mosques (NYT, 2009).In the case of Germany; they have announced ban on the wearing of 'hizab' by officials.

Former President of USSR Mikhail Gorbachev fully captured the essence of this trend at the level of nation-states, which is about promoting understanding, while retaining their identity, as they forged partnerships in a global world. He described this phenomenon in the following words:

> "Globalisation manifesting itself as an intense interaction of all nations with each one retaining its own identity; what is needed is understanding, solidarity, sensitivity and of course effective support – and where necessary direct assistance of a kind that helps each nation to exercise its free choice as its right" (Keith Phillip Lepor, 1997).

### *Cultural Diversity*

Close to the issue of homogenization of culture, is the question of 'Cultural Diversity'. For a country like India, cultural diversity, like bio-diversity, is essential for a sustainable world. This is true and is a matter of faith and fact in the case of India, which sees strength in cultural diversity. It is embedded in its ethos and has become an integral part of its social fabric. Many other countries, like USA, Canada, Australia, New Zealand and the United Kingdom also recognize the strength of diversity and have made it a part of their legislation or declared policy.

It was Mahatma Gandhi, who spoke on the need of understanding other cultures while retaining one's own moorings. He said,

> "I do not want my house to be walled and my windows to be stuffed. I want the culture of all lands to be blown about my house as freely as possible, but I refuse to be blown off my feet by anyone".

The Sikh Golden Temple at Amritsar is a living embodiment of such openness, as the entry to the holy temple is open through its four doors, representing the four directions-North, East, West and the South. President Clinton also saw globalisation as 'a force for diversity and not uniformity' (Clinton, 2000). The crux of cultural diplomacy is to view different cultures in a neutral stance, while we respect ours and imbibe positive elements from other cultures.

Prime Minister Vajpayee on the other hand went a step further, as he saw strength in diversity. He said:

> "This religious, cultural and civilization diversity need not divide us. Rather it can become a powerful basis for unity, if we adhere to the principle of tolerance and equal respect for all faiths and cultural traditions – even as we remain suitably proud of our own" (Vajpayee, 2002).

His message is appropriate and timely in the present day. India's newly elected President Kovind's first message on July 25 2017 was on the strength of India's 'Diversity'.

The desire to preserve this cultural diversity manifests regularly at the national and regional levels. We get a glimpse of diversity in 'Brahddesi Sangeet Mahotsav' (Festival and Seminar on 'Regional Music Traditions of Northern India'), which has become an annual feature at the Kala Bhavan, Chandigarh. This is also seen at the Annual Jazz Festivals organized by ICCR against the backdrop of light and sound effect at the Purana Qila (Old Fort), Delhi. It again gets reiterated at the International Sufi Conference in 2016, with a message of pluralism from Prime Minister Modi.

A similar feeling echoes, when we watch Sufi Dancers from Iran, Egypt, Azerbaijan or Morocco, whirling at the Kamani Auditorium at the invitation of ICCR. It is also seen when Indian festival, Diwali, is celebrated abroad in many countries or India celebrates Eid or Christmas.

Malaysia has developed its own unique style as leaders, representing three cultures-Malay, Chinese and Indian- hold open door functions for all the communities when they celebrate their own festivals, be it Hari Raya, Chinese New Year or Diwali.

Vice President Hamid Ansari, however, adds a cautionary note, on the need to bridge the gap between theory and practice. He said, 'This distinction between description and prescription is critical to the accommodation of diversity. Most states in the modern world would meet the first criterion; a far lesser number, however, qualify for the second' (Vice President, 2010). It is for us to respect pluralism and preserve our diversities, as these are the strength of a nation.

***Pluralism***

Another important trend in the context of globalisation's impact on culture is the growth of pluralistic cultures in nation-states as a result of migration of people. This phenomenon is more dominant in the case of large urban centres, where the population mix is from diverse national groups.

A lively debate has ensued in India on the meaning of 'tolerance', 'nationalism' and the 'Idea of India' among political parties, the academia, the thinkers, students, the writers and even the Bollywood stars. Each one is vociferously supporting one's own narrative, as they pit themselves against one another, generating more heat than light. The strength, however, lies in the diversity of views, which is the hallmark of Indian polity.

Growth of pluralistic cultures within the nation-state is leading to the acceptance of different cultures. Malaysia can confidently promote a tourist slogan of 'Malaysia, Truly Asia', being the home of three civilizations – Chinese, Indian and Malay. Nation-states are seeing themselves as 'mosaics' and not 'melting pots', as national cultures are losing their specificity and it is becoming one among many cultures, even though it may retain its national character.

### *Multiculturalism*

This issue received greater attention after the 1960s, when the United States rescinded its 'All Whites Immigration Policy' in 1965 and Australia in the 1970s. Globally two models were available – multiculturalism and assimilation- for negotiating identity-related issues. Multiculturalism, which is followed by the United Kingdom and its erstwhile colonies, Canada, Australia and New Zealand, favoured acceptance of multiple identities in the hope that this would provide for co-existence. The United States also opted for multiculturalism. The other process – assimilation – was favoured by France, which favoured the emergence of a single identity, centred around citizenship and not on caste, colour, creed or faith.

Views of experts differ as to which is the preferred approach – multiculturalism or assimilation – to facilitate integration of the migrants. Furthermore, the term multiculturalism has come to define both 'a society that is particularly diverse, usually as a result of immigration and the policies that are necessary to manage such a society' (Malik, Kenan, 2015). In other words, it embodies both, 'a description of society and a prescription' for dealing with it (Malik, Kenan). While pursuing multicultural policies, different governments have taken different routes. In the case of the United Kingdom, it is through offer of political stakes to the immigrants, while in the case of Germany, by treating immigrants as 'guest workers' and the Turks, the largest community, was encouraged to preserve their own culture, language and life style, with a view to avoiding the creation of a common inclusive culture.

It is also linked to the issue of social identity, as to how individuals view themselves in a society. It is identification with a particular community and in the process becoming distinct from others. In the present day, culture and not class has become an increasingly central medium through which people perceive their social differences and hence 'social solidarity is defined not in political terms but rather in terms of ethnicity, culture or faith', as 'the politics of ideology have given way to the politics of identity' (Malik, Kenan, 2015).

## Cultural Connect and Disconnect

We are now living in a global world, which is in greater flux. Movement of people has not generated understanding, but created greater chasm among them, as we are becoming more intolerant of the 'other'. It is a conflict of values, tradition vs. modernity; breaking the barriers of social stratification, be it on the basis of colour, gender, caste or race; conflict between different faiths and between the same faiths themselves. We are seeing a trend towards greater dis-connectivity, as cross-cultural communication is missing, resulting in lack of understanding of one another.

The way the visit of the Iranian President Rouhani to France and Italy was handled in January 2016, provides us with a glimpse into cultural sensitivities that are ignored or respected, as we see below in these two instances:

- Cancellation of a luncheon engagement between the French President Hollande and the visiting Iranian President Hassan Rouhani at a restaurant, as the Iranians requested 'a halal, alcohol free meal', while the French officials said that making a meal Iran friendly went against 'their Republican values' (Caroline Mortimer, 2016).
- Covering of nude statues in Rome's Capitoline Museum, keeping in view the cultural sensitivities of the delegation of the Iranian President Rouhani. This 'cultural kowtow' did not go down well with some Europeans, as it was perceived a concession to the values of immigrants (Vardarajan, Tunku, 2016). It is, therefore, not surprising for the writer Nayantara Sehgal suggesting to the Cultural Minister to consider draping saris on the figures at the Khajuraho temples.

Cultural sensitivity is also respected in another way, when world leaders make a special effort to offer vegetarian meal to the visiting Indian Prime Minister Modi. This gesture was accorded to him by the Singapore Prime Minister when he took him to a vegetarian meal at the 'Komla Vilas' restaurant in Singapore in November 2015. A similar gesture was also extended to him by President Nieto of Mexico when he himself drove the Indian Prime Minister for a vegetarian meal at a restaurant in Mexico City in June 2016. The Prime Minister of Portugal Antonio Costa went a step further when he gave a full Gujarati vegetarian meal to the visiting Indian

Prime Minister in June 2017. Prime Minister of Israel Netanyahu arranged an Indian meal cooked by Indian chefs during Prime Minister Modi's visit in July 2017. The Japanese Prime Minister Shinzo Abe and his wife dressed themselves in 'Modi Vest' and 'Salwar Kamiz' respectively, during their visit to India in September 2017. The Canadian Prime Minister Trudeau and his family dressed themselves in ethnic Indian dresses during their visit to India in February 2018.

Let us now observe that on a daily basis, we come across many situations and incidents, which are pointers towards disconnect. Some of these are narrated below, by way of illustration:

- The Sikh Gurdwara Prabhandak Committee (SGPC) refusing to honour the visiting Premier of the Ontario Province (Canada) Kathleen Wynne with 'Siropa' (robe of honour) during her visit to the Golden Temple, Amritsar on January 31, 2016, in keeping with the traditions of the Sikh religion, which were against the same sex marriage (Aseem Bassi and Usmeet Kaur, 2016). Kathleen Wynne was generous enough to accept this in her stride, as she was used to 'homophobia'.

- Amazon Japan facing criticism, when it allowed an advertiser to offer 'Obosin bin' (Mr. Monk Delivery), to help find a Buddhist monk on line to perform rituals or other services like funeral. This was considered as disrespect to the religion by the Japan Buddhist Association (The Hindustan Times, 2016:1).

- Coldplay Band showcasing India's myriad colours in their latest video song 'Hymn for the Weekend' with Beyonce, sporting ethnic outfit and jewellery, with henna on her hands, received critical comments from certain circles, being 'stereotypical portrayal of the country' (The Sunday Times, 2016).

- Politicising the absence of the Sikh Regiment from the 2016 Republic Day Parade in Delhi by the Akal Takht and criticising Prime Minister Modi for not taking up with the French President the issue of the Sikhs not allowed to wear turbans (The Hindustan Times, 2016:3).

- Arising of controversy over the participation of Ghulam Ali, Pakistani Ghazal Singer to attend the launch of 'Ghar Wapsi', a movie, in which he had sung a patriotic song apart from acting (The Hindu, 2016:1).

- Charging of Umar Draz, a Pakistani fan of Indian cricketer Virat Kohli for hoisting Indian flag (Omar Farooq Khan, 2016).

- Covering some artwork with white sheet of paper at the Dhaka Art Summit in Feb. 2016 by the Bangladesh Shilpkala Academy and the organizers Samdeni Art Foundation, under pressure of the Chinese Ambassador to Bangladesh. Art works were the creation of film makers, Ritu Sarin and Tenzing Sonam, titled 'Last Words', comprising letters of five Tibetans, who self-immolated themselves, as these portrayed the struggle of the Tibetans (Pallavi Pundir and Vandana Kalra, 2016).

- Refusal to shake hands with the male officials by an Algerian woman married to a French citizen at a naturalization ceremony in France in April 2018. This results in denial of French Citizenship to her on the grounds that such refusal was "in a place and at a moment that is symbolic; reveals a lack of assimilation"(Aurelian Breeden, 2018).

On the other hand, we also see a celebration of cultural connectivity, as evidenced through some of the recent developments, which are described below:

- Paying of tribute by Google to the Indian artist Amrita Sher-Gill on her 103rd birthday, showing her famous painting 'Three Girls' and the world renowned Bharatanatyam dancer Rukmini Devi on her 112th Birthday. The Indian Premier League Cricket Matches, with doodles also find a place on its homepage during the month of April 2016. The Google doodles would be seen in Argentina, Iceland, Portugal, Lithuania, Serbia, Slovenia, Israel, Kenya, Kazakhstan, Indonesia and Japan besides India (The Hindustan Times, 2016:2).

- Scattering of the ashes of the legendary singer, David Bowie on the Indonesian Island of Bali as per the Buddhist traditions, as per the will of the singer. He was seen dressed in 'sarong' and had versions of many of his songs in 'Bahasa Indonesia'. His last wish did not come as a surprise 'as the artist had been fascinated by the religion and even studied it in London' (Sandhu, Serina, 2016).

- Planning to add a cultural aspect to the French parade on the Bastille Day, as the French President Hollande was impressed with the cultural floats, camels and dances from different states, which were a part of the Indian Republic Day Parade (Coomi Kapoor, 2016).

- Participation by a French Regiment in the Republic Day Parade on 26 January 2016, which became the first foreign contingent to earn this honour. India had sent a regiment for participation at the Bastille Day Parade in Paris in 2009 and to Russia in 2015 to mark its 70$^{th}$ Anniversary of Victory in the World War II.

- Hiking of funds for the celebration of 'Diwali', the festival of lights, at Leicester (UK), a poster town for multiculturalism in Britain and Europe, with the largest concentration of Gujaratis from India. The allocation reached one-third of its annual budget of 384, 500 pounds for cultural events, given its popularity across faith groups (Prasun Sonwalkar, 2016).

- Pooling of resources by the governments to ensure the return of heritage objects that were stolen or smuggled in the past. In a recent case, France helped Cambodia in receiving the Head of the stone sculpture 'Harihara', which combines the features of 'Vishnu' and 'Shiva'. Later, the returned head was attached to the Body lying at the National Museum at Pnom Penh in January 2016 (The Hindu, 2016).

- Celebrating Indian festival of Diwali at the White House and the Parliaments in the United Kingdom and Canada, which have become an annual feature of their activities.

- Jointly honouring the Nobel Laureate Rabindranath Tagore by India, Bangladesh and the United Kingdom at a landmark function held at the British Parliament on April 4, 2014 (Kounteya Sinha, 2014).

- Using of a scarf by the then President of South Korea to cover her head during her meeting with the Iranian President Rouhani in Tehran in May, 2016 (The San Diego Union-Tribune, 2016).

- Placing of the sculpture of the Hindu Goddess 'Saraswati' at the entrance of the Indonesian Embassy at Washington DC, symbolizing the pluralist culture of Indonesia and its long standing cultural links with India (The Hindu, 2013).

- Issuing of silver coins in April 2016 by a Canadian Bank, to mark the Sikh festival of Baisakhi; symbolically honouring the community. Canada and India jointly issued a postage stamp on September 22, 2017, to mark the festival of Diwali.

- Issuing of a postage stamp by the Government of Fiji, showing the face of a Sikh, as celebration of its diversity.
- Declaration of the month of April as 'Sikh Awareness and Appreciation Month' by the US State of New Jersey. Earlier, the States of Indiana and Delaware had declared April as the 'Sikh Heritage' and 'Sikh Awareness' Month respectively (The Tribune, 2018).

## Cultural Diplomacy, Public Diplomacy and Soft Power

Any discussion on cultural diplomacy would necessitate our understanding how it is placed vis-à-vis similar concepts like 'soft power' and 'public diplomacy', which are glitzy terms and are in vogue these days? Are these synonymous? If not, how do these relate to one another? Has the world of cultural diplomacy been subsumed into these catchy frameworks? Is cultural diplomacy being reincarnated as soft power?

Invariably, in common parlance, the above terms are used interchangeably with 'cultural diplomacy', as these employ 'culture' as a resource. To understand the full import of these terms, we would have to look at not only the contexts in which these were created, but also the desired outcomes or objectives, which these were required to achieve.

Cultural diplomacy in the modern day context appeared in the 1930s, when the US President Roosevelt was wooing the States in the Americas. Public diplomacy appeared on the scene in the 1960s, whose guiding spirit was Edward Murrow, Director of USIA (United States Information Agency), but theoretical framework was provided by Edmund Gullion, Dean of the Fletcher School of Law and Diplomacy, Tufts University in 1965. The concept of 'soft power' was ushered in by Joseph Nye Jr. in 1990.

President Roosevelt found inherent strength in cultural diplomacy, in connecting with people through cultural exchanges; he wanted to send a message of friendship and brotherhood to them. The birth of public diplomacy, also called 'people's diplomacy' was in response to changing international environment; to reach out/communicate directly to foreign publics to mould opinion, as their voice in foreign policy-related issues was growing.

Soft power concept grew out of conviction and necessity that 'hard power' alone could not arbiter growing complexity of post-cold war international relations. As there were limitations to what soft power could achieve, Nye unleashed another term, 'smart power', which was to be a judicious mix of 'hard power' and 'soft power'. Smart power was developed by him 'to counter the misperception that soft power alone can produce effective foreign policy' (Nye, 2009).

How does then cultural diplomacy relate to public diplomacy, which has become the buzz word, as image building has become larger than life for nations and leaders. Prima facie, 'Cultural Diplomacy' is a 'Connectivity Bridge' that promotes understanding among peoples and nations. Public diplomacy is essentially to promote 'the national interest through understanding, informing and influencing foreign audiences' (US State Department 2005). Joseph Nye defined it as 'an instrument that governments use to mobilize these resources to communicate with and attract the publics of other countries, rather than merely their governments' (Nye 2008).

Public diplomacy aims at building 'Images' and then seeking 'Rapid Results'. It uses a three stage process of Communications- Daily Communications; Strategic Communications and Long Term Communications. Governments hire public relations firms to build up right images or correct wrong images. Indian Embassy in the United States is also using public relations agencies to promote its image.

Cultural diplomacy cannot be equated with public diplomacy; even though in practice it is used interchangeably with it, which is the most 'in thing' these days. Public diplomacy is definitely about influencing foreign publics by using the appropriate communication strategy. Its focus, therefore, is on the academia, think tanks, pressure groups, businessmen and other influential elite, which have a say in the formulation of foreign policy and conduct of international relations. Public diplomacy is 'a direct onslaught on the brain (intellect), while cultural diplomacy softly plays on the heart' (Sahai, 2002).

The following points would give you a picture as to how cultural diplomacy differs from public diplomacy:

- Cultural diplomacy aims at connecting nations and peoples; while public diplomacy has a narrower focus of projecting the national interests, as perceived by the government of the day.

- Culture diplomacy is people-centric, while public diplomacy is government-centric. Thus the focus in the case of cultural diplomacy is on people per se; in the case of public diplomacy, the focus is on decision makers, either directly or indirectly.
- Cultural diplomacy is for promoting understanding, per se, and accepting others as they are. Public diplomacy, on the other hand, is for bringing about an attitudinal change among the target groups.
- Cultural diplomacy accepts diversity, while public diplomacy aims at seeking alignment of views.
- Cultural diplomacy is about winning the hearts by generating empathy, while public diplomacy is about convincing the heads through rationalization of arguments.
- Cultural diplomacy is for generating friendship and is holistic in nature; while public diplomacy is issue-based and its focus is on specific issues, be it anti-terrorism, India Pak relations, nuclear disarmament etc.
- Results from cultural diplomacy are intangible and flow over a longer time frame. In the case of public diplomacy, these could be immediately visible; like the outcome of VVIP visits, signing of Agreements etc., assurance of support on candidatures or issues of importance.
- Cultural diplomacy is "decidedly more 'idealistic' and 'qualitative', as it seeks to develop mutual understanding and combat ethnocentrism and stereotyping.
- Cultural diplomacy operates on a two-way channel, as it values mutual exchanges, wherein lies its strength.

There is, however, some overlapping between cultural and public diplomacy, as the latter also uses culture as a resource. It is this that makes Nye view 'Cultural diplomacy as an instrument of public diplomacy'. Some countries accord cultural diplomacy a higher status, when they view it as 'the lynchpin of public diplomacy'. We, however, have to note that similarity only extends to the use of 'culture' as 'the means' and does not extend to 'the ends', as both are geared to attaining different objectives.

How does then cultural diplomacy relate to 'soft power'? Joseph Nye Jr., who expounded this concept in 1990, described it as follows:

> "Soft power occurs when 'one country gets other countries to want what it wants- might be called co-optive or soft power in contrast with hard power or command power of ordering others to do what it wants'. It tends to be associated with 'intangible power resources such as culture, ideology, and institutions" (Nye, 1990).

Nye further expounded that "One can affect others' behavior in three main ways: threats of coercion ("sticks"), inducements and payments ("carrots"), and attraction that makes others want what you want' (Nye, 2008). He also talked about resources of soft power in these words:

> "The soft power of a country rests primarily on three resources; its culture (in places where it is attractive to others); its political values (when it lives up to them at home and abroad); and its foreign policies (when these are seen as legitimate and having moral authority)" (Nye, 2008).

What is of significance to note is the emphasis placed 'to live those ideals' and also acquiring their legitimacy through acceptance by others? It only shows that soft power is hard to achieve.

Former Minister of State for External Affairs Shashi Throor has a different take on soft power; for him, it is 'not about conquering others but about being yourself', it is not about display or exhibition, it is rather how others see what we are and 'what is important is the values and principles for which India stands' (Tharoor, Shashi, 2011). This apparently is a hybrid between soft power and cultural diplomacy and not in consonance with the views of Joseph Nye; it is closer to our definition of cultural diplomacy, which aims at 'Connectivity' and not 'Conversion'. This also partially explains why these terms are used interchangeably, because many scholars and practitioners loosely interpret the same.

From the above, it should be clearly understood that cultural diplomacy cannot be equated with 'soft power', as coined by Joseph Nye. It has to be remembered and reiterated that the primary focus of 'soft power' is to convert and co-opt through means other than military. In the case of cultural diplomacy, it is about 'dialogue' and through dialogue to promote understanding.

Could we still equate cultural diplomacy with soft power? The answer, would be both 'No' and 'Yes'. It is 'No', as the primary purpose or the vanguard action of cultural diplomacy is not conversion to one's viewpoint, as per Joseph Nye's definition. But it is also 'Yes', as its rear-guard action results in removing cobwebs from the minds of individuals and it helps in creating a conducive atmosphere, which paves way for building friendly relations.

In practice, however, Cultural diplomacy is beginning to be equated with soft power, as the term is loosely used and it accepts culture as its component that ultimately results in promoting a country's interests. The word 'soft power' is flogged often, over and over again, as it sells as an attractive and convenient terminology for pushing one's ideas. Some Indian leaders and experts view cultural diplomacy, as a part of India's soft power.

We will, therefore, have to continue grappling with this perception, as it happens with many other situations that cannot be unequivocally defined. In short, we have to remember that cultural diplomacy is about 'connectivity'; while public diplomacy is about out-reach/communication with foreign audiences and soft power is to covert or co-opt others to one's view point. We would, however, have to live through this definitional jungle on cultural diplomacy being interchangeably used with public diplomacy or soft power; while we stick to our definition of 'Cultural Diplomacy' as a 'Connectivity Bridge' in this Book.

## Features, Trends and Perceptions on Cultural Diplomacy

Cultural diplomacy has emerged as an important area for the study of diplomacy. All over the world, the governments recognize its centrality, as this is becoming an important vehicle in the diplomatic arsenal of various countries. Its importance is increasing in proportion to dis-connectivity, which is emerging among nations and peoples, although efforts are continuing towards 'cultural connectivity', as seen from various examples in the text of this chapter.

It is now generally getting accepted by think tanks, like DEMOS that 'culture has a vital role to play in international relations', as it has 'wider, connective and human values' and it is 'both the means by which we come to understand others, and an aspect of life with innate worth that we enjoy and seek out' (Demos, 2007).

We are seeing a growing recognition and emergence of a number of narratives on cultural diplomacy on the part of the governments and diplomatic missions, regarding its relevance and importance. The common refrain that emerges from our interaction with the Indian Heads of Missions is their commitment to cultural diplomacy and their willingness to promote and pursue its objectives, unlike in the past when there was preference for political work only.

When we talk of cultural diplomacy, we view it as a diplomatic activity. This was the traditional view held by theoretician-cum –practitioner Arndt and some others. This view has changed in the context of modern day diplomacy. What is important is the use of the vehicle of 'culture' in the pursuit of our goals? Diplomatic touch can be provided in myriad ways and forms, as we are treating artists, students, academia, cultural personalities, sportspersons and Diaspora, as our Ambassadors, notionally speaking.

We have adopted a broader construct of the word 'culture' in the definition of cultural diplomacy in this Book. It is a whole gamut of life, as defined by UNESCO. In practice also, we have adopted this broader construct in our Cultural Agreements, which are comprehensive in nature.

Cultural diplomacy is not only about peoples, but it also about nations. They also have a cultural personality. Awareness of such traits helps in cross-cultural conversations, which help the process of conduct of diplomacy.

Cultural diplomacy operates in a globalised world, as peoples and nations connect one another. Cultural diplomacy starts from the hypothesis that the whole world is a family, which is in tune with Indian ethos of 'Vasudhaiva Kutumbakam'. The mere presence of 258 million migrants has changed the demographic character of practically every country in the world. This has brought into focus identity-related issues, adaptation in their new homes and acceptance of new values.

How do migrants make an adjustment between their identities in the home state with that in the host states? It is not a question of mere physical adjustment, but more so, a case of psychological adjustment as they grapple with the values of the host state. This necessitates their adapting to those new values. The issues of identity get addressed, depending upon the nature of acceptance of diversity and pluralism in the host states. India stands out in this as a shining example, where its composite culture has made this process easier.

A natural corollary to this would be a desire to live together peacefully and harmoniously. How do we do that when we realize that all the members, like the five fingers in a hand, are not equal and do not have similar aspirations and goals. It takes different routes, be it multiculturalism or assimilation. We have seen how different processes have made it easier or difficult. This, ipso facto, means that we have to recognize 'Diversity'. In the global world, this translates into acceptance of diversity and acceptance of 'others' as 'us', as we would like them to accept us.

Cultural diplomacy is to empower people and generate awareness in them to appreciate 'others' as they would like to be known 'themselves'. It is only through accepting others that one feels empowered to influence them. The strength of cultural diplomacy lies 'in accepting the influences of others, so as to get the freedom to claim influences of Indian thought elsewhere'. We need to remember 'this axiomatic double entry book keeping of culture – the giving and the receiving – is perhaps the challenge of our all too shrill times' (Keerthik Sisidharan, 2017).

It is not only about understanding 'the other', but also how you are perceived by them. It is 'more listening and less talking'. Images and perception, therefore, become important, as these are difficult to change, as the same are not always based on hard facts. This results in Branding, with each leader and nation building or promoting their own images, through their respective USP (Unique Selling Power).

Having accepted these basics, we move to the next stage. How do we promote understanding? This can come through communication and interaction. This would require an environment that is conducive; where there is free flow of people and ideas across the nations. It is here that the cultural diplomacy triggers in. Addressing the Indian community at The Hague during his visit to the Netherlands on June 28, 2017, Prime Minister Modi said that 'India is federal in true spirit' and diversity was its 'specialty' (The Hindustan Times, 2017).

Cultural diplomacy should be viewed as 'Connectivity Bridge'- A Bridge that is in the mutual interest of all the partners/stakeholders. It is not to be seen as a unilateral step but has to be built on an exchange mechanism. Its relevance has not to be seen as an adjunct to 'soft power' or its component, as it is not about seeking power through influence. It is not about scoring points but winning friends, by generating awareness about one and another, in the true Indian spirit of treating guests as gods.

We will have to also remember that cultural diplomacy is about 'connectivity'; while public diplomacy is about out-reach/communication with foreign audiences and soft power is to covert or co-opt others to one's viewpoint, even though these terms may continue to be used interchangeably. While 'culture' is a common resource, yet the end objectives are different; it is a story of using same 'means' but for different 'ends'.

What are the features of a successful cultural diplomacy? It is about interaction and dialogue and changing the mindset. It is also about building bridges of friendship and not erecting walls, as Pope Francis would state. The raison d'être of cultural diplomacy is to open doors and not to shut these, where they are already open. We need to open minds and not to partition them. It is to act as a catalyst and help in changing the mindset at all levels across the board.

It has to be linked to free flow of ideas and peoples and would necessitate adopting a liberal visa regime, as Joseph Nye Jr. subtly observed, 'in an effort to exclude a dangerous few, we are keeping out the helpful many' (Joseph Nye: 2). This is the problem between India and Pakistan, which EAM Sushma Swaraj tried to correct during her visit to Pakistan in November, 2015. Sohail Mahmood, Pakistani High Commissioner harped on easing visa processes, during his visit to Chandigarh in April, 2018. We need to see 'more walk and less talk' and liberalise the current visa regime, if we want results.

Culture and politics do not gel. What people need is a positive mental attitude, to bring about transformation and develop basic human values, which Dalai Lama calls "secular ethics", since they 'do not depend on religious faith'.

Cultural diplomacy is not a one-shot affair. It also requires long term commitment and acceptance, as some of 'the fundamental goals of cultural diplomacy appear to be like the values of art' (Sablosky, 2003). It is not easy to measure success of cultural diplomacy, as it is intangible. It is a slow process and the results are unobtrusive. It, therefore, requires long term commitment and investment (Centre for Arts and Culture, 2004).

We have noticed that cultural diplomacy is most successful, when government's involvement is at an arm's length. Successful structures, like BBC and Alliance Françoise, have been based on these principles. ICCR is also structured as an autonomous body; it is debatable how autonomous it is in practice.

Furthermore, 'Cultural exchange gives us the chance to appreciate points of commonality and, where there are differences, to understand the motivations and humanity that underline them' (Demos, 2007). Its strength comes from 'its independence, its freedom and the fact that it represents and connects people, rather than necessarily governments or policy positions' (ibid).

Shashi Tharoor's simile of 'Katories (Bowls) and Thali (Plate or Tray)' helps in defining the present-day phenomenon of 'Identity', as it captures the concept of 'Unity in Diversity'. Can we go beyond this and learn to eat from the same 'Thali', as the Arabs do? What we need is to learn to share and move beyond mere survival to that of co-existence.

Cultural diplomacy operates like the cardinal philosophy and spirit of '*Bhagwad Gita*' for a 'Karma Yogi', which is 'We have control over actions, but not results'. It has to be pursued in the right manner and with good intentions. The results would eventually follow, which would be a win-win position for 'us' and 'them'.

The ultimate test of cultural diplomacy would be if we can also see a global man in this so called global village. Nobel Laureate Rabindranath Tagore had such a vision and we would be paying a fitting tribute to him, if we work towards realization of his dreams, as we invoke his poetic words:

> "Deep is my desire
> In country after country to identify
> Myself with all men; to be born
> As an Arab child in the desert, fearless and free,
> Raised on camel's milk; to explore
> Cold Stone mansions, Buddhist monasteries
> On Tibet's plateau; to drink grape-wine
> As a Persian in a rose-garden; to ride
> Horses as an intrepid Tartar; to toil
> With dedication, as in the ancient Chinese land;
> To be polite and vigorous as a Japanese;
> To experience, existence in all homes".

## Endnotes

1. Goel, Suresh, Former Director General, ICCR. Based on a response to a Questionnaire on May 27, 2015 and subsequent conversations on a number of occasions in Delhi.

2. Shyam Saran, Former Foreign Secretary, MEA. Based on interaction on May 12, 2015 in Delhi.

## References

Alexander, K. C. and K. P. Kumaran, 1992, *Culture and Development: Cultural Patterns in Areas of Uneven Development*.

Amarjot Kaur, 2016, 'No horsing around!', *The Tribune*, March 9.

Arndt, Richard M, 2005, *The First Resort of Kings, American Cultural Diplomacy in the Twentieth Century*, Potomac Books Inc., Washington DC.

Aseem Bassi and Usmeet Kaur. 2016, Ontario premier at Golden Temple today amid gay row', The *Hindustan Times*, Jan. 31.

Atal, Yogesh (ed.), 1991, *Culture-Development Interface*, Vikas Publishing House.

Aurelian Breeden, 2018, 'No handshake, no citizenship, French court tells Algerian woman' *The Hindu,* April 23.

Bandopadhyay, Krishnaidu, 2016, 'Hindu gods forgotten in India revered in Japan', *The Times of India*, January 11.

Bandopadhyaya, J, 1973, *The Making of India's Foreign Policy*; Allied Publishers, New Delhi.

Banerjee, Utpal K, 1973, 'Role of Cultural Diplomacy' *in Indian Democracy: Agenda for the 21st Century*, Foreign Services Institute, New Delhi, Konark Publications Ltd.

Barber, Benjamin R, 1992, 'Jihad Vs McWorld', *The Atlantic Monthly*, March.

Ben Shapiro, 2016, 'Pope Says Building Walls Is "Not Christian". So, What Does The Bible Say About Walls?' *Daily Wire*, February 19.

Caroline Mortimer, 2016, 'Wine on menu ruins Rouhani – Hollande lunch', *The Times of India*, January 29.

Centre for Arts and Culture, 2004, 'Recommendations and Research',

July. www.interarts.net/descargas/interarts687.pdf, (Accessed on December 16, 2017).

Clinton, 2000, The While House Conference: Address of President Clinton, at the conference on 'Culture and Diplomacy', The White House, Washington DC, November 28.

Cohen, Raymond, 2005, *Negotiating Across Cultures*, United States Institute of Peace Press, Washington DC, Revised Edition.

Coomi Kapoor, 2016, 'Inside Track', *The Sunday Express*, January 31.

Dasgupta, Arun, 1996, *Intellectual and Academic Cooperation between India and Southeast Asia in 'India and Southeast Asia – Challenges and Opportunities* (ed. Baladas Ghoshal), IIC, New Delhi.

Demos, Kirsten Bound, Rachel Briggs, John Holden, Samuel Jones, 2007, Cultural Diplomacy, DEMOS, London. https://www.demos.co.uk/files/Cultural_diplomacy_-_web.pdf (Accessed on December 16, 2017).

Dutt, Barkha, 2016, 'Stand up for our rights', *The Hindustan Times*, March 12.

EAM, 2008, Address of External Affairs Minister, Pranab Mukherjee at the inauguration of the Rabindranath Tagore Centre, Kolkata, June 1.

Engineer, Asghar Ali (Ed.), 2002, *Islam in India: The Impact of Civilizations*, Shipra, Delhi.

Friedman, Thomas, 1999, *The Lexus and the Olive Trees*, Farrar Streams, Guns, New York.

Friedman, Thomas, 2002, 'Globalisation, Above and Well', *New York Times,* September 22.

Geeta Sahai, 2016, 'Making India a cultural power', The Governance Now, May 14.www.governancenow.com/views/.../making-india-a-cultural-power-pratibha-prahlad (Accessed on December 16, 2017).

Goel, Suresh, 2013, 'Message from Dr. Suresh Goel, DG, ICCR and Special Secretary, MEA' in Sharma, Anjana (ed.), *Civilizational Dialogue, Asian Inter-connections and Cross-cultural Exchanges*, ICCR & Manohar.

Goff, Patricia, 2013, 'Cultural Diplomacy' in *The Oxford Handbook of Modern Diplomacy,* Oxford University Press, UK.

Gujral, I K, 1998, *A Foreign Policy for India*, External Publicity Division, Ministry of External Affairs, New Delhi.

Gupta, Vivek and Aseem Bassi, 2016, 'SGPC not to offer "Siropa" to lesbian Canadian premier', *The Hindustan Times*, January 30.

Hart, Justin, 2013, *Empire of Ideas*, Oxford University Press, New York.

Huntington, Samuel, 1997, *The Clash of Civilization and the Remaking of the World Order*, Simons & Schuster.

ICD, 2018, Institute for Cultural Diplomacy, http://www.culturaldiplomacy.org/index.php?en_culturaldiplomacy (Accessed on 24-05-18).

Inaugural Address by M C Chagla, 1968, President of ICCR as quoted in Bidyut Sarkar, ed., *India and Southeast Asia*, Proceedings of a Seminar on India and Southeast Asia, ICCR.

International Migrants Report, 2017, https://www.un.org/development/desa/publications/ international-migration-report-2017.html (Accessed on January 7, 2018).

Jasmine Singh, 2016, 'Punjabi Dholl, the Brazilian Way', *The Tribune*, February 15.

Joel Brinkley and Ian Fisher, 2006, 'US says it also finds cartoons of Muhammad offensive', *The New York Times*, February 4.

Joint Statement, 2017, India - Bangladesh Joint Statement during the State Visit of Prime Minister of Bangladesh to India, April 8.

Joseph S. Nye, Jr., 2003, 'Propaganda Isn't the Way: Soft Power', *The International Herald Tribune*, January 10.

Joseph Nye, 2004, 'You Can't Get From There', *The New York Times*, November 29.

Kaiser, Ejaz, 2016, 'Peace Unity ensure nations growth: PM', *The Hindustan Times*, January 12.

Karlekar, Hiranmay, 1998, *Independent India: The First Fifty Years*, ICCR, Oxford University Press.

Kaul, TN, 1982, *Reminiscences, Discreet and Indiscreet*, Lancers Publishers, New Delhi.

Keerthik Sasidharan, 2017, "Every Culture gives and receives', *The Hindu*, April 9.

Keith Phillip Lepor (ed.), 1997, *After the Cold War: Essays on the Emerging New World Order, University of Texas*, Austin, Foreword by Gorbachev.

Kishan Rana, 2014, 'How to Brand India', *Business Standard*, November 15.

Kounteya Sinha, 2014, 'Rabindranath Tagore honoured at UK's Palace of Westminster', *The Times of India*, April 4.

Lakshmi Reddy, 2001, 'Malaysia: Perspectives on Culture' – Paper presented at an International Conference on India Malaysia Relations, Hyderabad, December.

Lee Kuan Yew, 1998, *The Singapore Story: Memories of Lee Kuan Yew, Times Edition*, Singapore.

*Lok Sabha Report*, 1997, Second Report, Standing Committee on External Affairs, 1996-97, Eleventh Lok Sabha, April.

Luke Harding, 2006, 'Cartoons that rocked the World', *The Guardian*, London, February 6.

Malik Kenan, 2015 , 'The Failure of Multiculturalism', *The Foreign Affairs*, March-April.

Malone, David M, 2013 'The Modern Diplomatic Mission' in *The Oxford Handbook of Modern Diplomacy*, Oxford University Press, UK.

Mazumdar, T, K., 1969, 'Indian Development: Viewed Culturally' in *Culture-Development Interface,* Yogesh Atal (ed.), New Delhi.

*Media Briefing*, 2013, Transcript of Joint Media Interaction of External Affairs Minister and US Secretary of State Mr. John Kerry, New Delhi, June 24.

*Media Transcript*, 2013, Chairman's Statement of the 3rd East Asia Foreign Ministers' Meeting, Brunei Darussalam, July 3.

Milton Cummings, 2009, 'Cultural Diplomacy and the United States Government: A Survey', Centre for Arts and Culture, Washington DC. https://www.americansforthearts.org/sites/default/files/MCCpaper.pdf (Accessed on December 16, 2017).

Misra, Satish, 2006, 'Karan Singh, Cultural diplomacy needs a big thrust', *The Tribune*, November 24.

Nadim, Farrukh, 2013, 'Nalanda University deserves place in World

Heritage Sites: Salman Khurshid, *The Tribune*, February 13.

*NDTV,* 2012, 'Shashi Tharoor: Soft power can make us a global power', December 4.

Nehru, 1950, Inaugural Address of Prime Minister Nehru in 1950 at the time of the inauguration of the Indian Council of Cultural Relations (ICCR), quoted in a *Pamphlet on ICCR*, New Delhi.

*New Delhi Times*, 2016, 'France mulls stripping terrorists of citizenship as Paris attack takes its toll', February 15.

Nye, 1990, Joseph S. Nye, Jr., 'Soft Power', *Foreign Policy, No. 80* (Autumn, 1990). http://www.jstor.org/stable/1148580 (Accessed: 09-05-2018).

Nye, 2008, Joseph S. Nye, Jr., 'Public Diplomacy and Soft Power',*The Annals of the American Academy of Political and Social Science, Vol. 616*, (March, 2008) http://www.jstor.org/stable/25097996 (Accessed: 09-05-2018).

Nye, 2009, Joseph S. Nye, Jr., 'Get Smart: Combining Hard and Soft Power', *Foreign Affairs, Vol. 88*, No. 4 (July/August 2009). http://www.jstor.org/stable/20699631 (Accessed: 09-05-2018).

NYT, 2009, Nick Cumming-Bruce and Steven Erlanger,'Swiss Ban Building of Minarets on Mosques', *New York Times*, November 29.

Obama, 2014, 'President Obama extends warmest greetings for Diwali'. (www.whitehouse.gov/blog (2014 1/22) (Accessed on December 16, 2017).

Omar Farooq Khan, 2016, 'Kohli's Pak fan held for hoisting Indian flag', *The Times of India*, Jan. 28.

Pallavi Pundir and Vandana Kalra, 2016, 'Dhaka art summit: Tibetan exhibit covered up after China protest', *Indian Express*, February 8

PBD, 2009, Inaugural Address of Prime Minister of India, Pravasi Bharatiya Divas (PBD), New Delhi, January 7.

PM, 2012, 'Remarks by Prime Miniter, Dr. Manmohan Singh at Flag Down of the ASEAN-India Car Rally', 21 December, New Delhi.

Prasun Sonwalkar, 2016, 'Fortunes Change for UK Indians as Leicester hikes Diwali budget', *The Hindustan Times*, Jan. 29.

Rugh, William A, 2014, *Front Line Public Diplomacy*, Palgrave Macmillan

Series, New York.

Sablosky, 2003, Julient Artunes, 'Recent Trends in Department of State for support for Cultural Diplomacy, 1993-2002', Centre for Arts and Culture, Washington DC. https://www.americansforthearts.org/sites/default/files/JASpaper.pdf (Accessed on December 16, 2017).

Sahai, P S, 2002, 'Globalisation, Cultural Diplomacy and the Indian Ocean: An Indian Perspective', Paper presented at the Panjab University, Chandigarh, Nov.

Sahai, P S, 2009, 'India's Cultural Diplomacy in Southeast Asia', HCMC University, May 16-19.

Sandhu, Serina, 2016, 'David Bowie requested his ashes be scattered in Bali in line with 'Buddhist rituals', *The Indepedent*, January 30.

Sarkar, Bidyut (ed.), 1968, *India and Southeast Asia*, Proceedings of a Seminar, ICCR.

Satyanarayanan, S. 2009, 'Bollywood magic in Southeast Asia', *The Hindu*, October 14.

Saxena, Shoban. 2009, 'How to be a cultural super power', *The Tribune*, Nov. 22.

Sharma, Anjana (ed.), 2013, *Civilizational Dialogue, Asian Inter-connections and Cross-cultural Exchanges*, ICCR & Manohar.

Simon, Mark, 2008, *A Comparative Study of Cultural Diplomacy of Canada, New Zealand and India*. Thesis submitted for the Ph. D. degree for The University of Auckland. https://researchspace.auckland.ac.nz/bitstream/handle/2292/2943/02whole.pdf (Accessed on December 16, 2017).

Singapore Lecture, 1994, Narasimha Rao, PV, 'India and the Asia Pacific: Forging a New Partnership', Institute of Southeast Asian Studies, Singapore.

Singh, B.P. 1998, *India's Culture, The State, The Arts and Beyond*, Oxford University Press.

Singh, Dr. Karan, 2013, Foreword in Sharma, Anjana (ed.), *Civilizational Dialogue, Asian Inter-connections and Cross-cultural Exchanges*, ICCR & Manohar.

State Department. 2005, 'Cultural Diplomacy, The Linchpin of Public Diplomacy', Report of the Advisory Committee on Cultural

Diplomacy (ACCD), US Department of State, Washington DC, September. https://www.state.gov/documents/organization/54374.pdf (Accessed on December 16, 2017).

Suryanarayana, P.S. 2006, 'Bridge chasm between the West and the Muslim World: Badawi', *The Hindu*, February 11.

Tharoor, Shashi, 2011, 'Indian Strategic Power: Soft', *The Huffington Post*, May 25. (http://www.huffingtonpost.com/entry/indian-strategic-powers-so b 207785.html? section=India (Accessed on December 16, 2017).

Tharoor, Shashi, 2012, *PAX INDICA: India and the World of the 21st Century*, Thomson Press India Ltd, New Delhi.

Tharoor, Shashi, 2017, 'Leveraging soft power needs hard work', *The Tribune*, February 18.

*The Chicago Tribune*, 2016, Kathleen Hennessy& Christi Parsons, 'Obama opens up about race', July 20.

The Dalai Lama, 2017, 'Secular ethics for our times', *The Indian Express*, July 1.

*The Hindu*, 2005, 'Cultural Diplomacy, not a luxury: Karan Singh', September 3.

*The Hindu*, 2013, 'Indonesia gifts US a Saraswati Statue', June 10.

*The Hindu*, 2016, 'France returns head of Hindu statue taken 130 years ago', January 22.

*The Hindu*, 2016:1, 'Ghulam Ali event in Mumbai cancelled', January 28.

*The Hindustan Times* 2016:2, 'Google pays tribute to Amrita Sher-Gill', January 31.

*The Hindustan Times*, 2016: 3, 'Akal Takht slams Centre for keeping Sikhs out of the parade', January 30.

*The Hindustan Times*, 2016:1, 'Amazon faces flak in Japan for delivering monks', January 31.

*The Hindustan Times*, 2017, 'Dutch nationals to get 5-year business, tourist visas: PM', June 29.

The President, 2017, 'Argument is acceptable, but not intolerance: President', *Sunday Tribune*, April 2.

*The San Deigo Tribune*, 2016, 'Iran leader urges for nuclear weapons-free Korean Peninsula', May 2.

*The Sunday Times*, 2016: 'Beyonce in desi garb stirs cultural appropriation row', January 31.

*The Tribune*, 2001, 'Cultural diplomacy wins over politics', Nov. 4.

*The Tribune*, 2010, 'From land of snake charmers, to global cultural hot spot', Nov, 12.

*The Tribune*, 2012, 'Shankar personified India's soft power', Dec. 13.

*The Tribune*, 2014: 'India sends drinking water to Maldives', December 5.

*The Tribune* 2016, 'Migrants who cannot speak English may have to leave Britain: UK PM Cameron', January 18.

*The Tribune* 2016:1, 'Cameron again says, he backs burqa ban', Jan. 20.

*Tribune* 2016*:2*, 'Obama cites Sikhs to talk about strength of faith', February 6.

*The Tribune*, 2018, 'New Jersey declares April as "Sikh Awareness" Month', March 30.

The While House Conference, 2000, Address of Madeline Albright, at the conference on 'Culture and Diplomacy', The White House, Washington DC, November 28. http://www.presidency.ucsb.edu/ws/?pid=975 (Accessed on December 16, 2017).

Thussu, Daya, 2013. *Communicating India's Soft Power: Buddha to Bollywood*, Palgrave Macmillan.

*Times of India*, 2003, 'French-edict betrays anti-Muslim bias, December 25.

UNESCO, 1982, UNESCO Conference at Mexico.

US Department of State. 2005, 'Cultural Diplomacy: The Linchpin of Public Diplomacy' (Report of the Advisory Committee on Cultural Diplomacy, September.https://www.state.gov/documents/organization/54374.pdf (Accessed on December 16, 2017).

Vajpayee, 2002, Statement by Indian Prime Minister Atal Behari Vajpayee, at the CICA Summit', Almaty (Kazakhstan), June 4.

Vardarajan, Tunku, 2016, 'Europe's cultural nightmare', *The Sunday Express*, January 31.

Varma, Pavan, 2006, 'Soft Power', *The Tribune*, Oct. 7.

Vatsayan, Kapila, 2007, 'Culture: The crafting of Institutions in Independent India' in *Indian Democracy: Agenda for 21st Century*, Foreign Service Institute, New Delhi.

Vice President, 2010, Vice President Hamid Ansari's Inaugural Address at an International Seminar on 'Indian Culture in a Globalised World, , New Delhi, November 11.

Vice President, 2016, Remarks by Vice President Hamid Ansari at the inauguration of Interfaith Conference at Malappuram, Kerala, January 12.

Vishavjeet Chaudhry, 2016, 'Varsities have a pivotal role', *The Tribune*, March 9.

*Vision Statement*, 2012, 'Vision Statement ASEAN-India Commemorative Summit', December 20, New Delhi.

Walter Lacquer, 1994, 'Save Public Diplomacy: Broadcasting America's Message Matters', *Foreign Affairs,* 73: 5, September-October.

Yaswant Raj, 'Trump dominates Trumpless debate', *The Hindustan Times*, Jan. 30, 2016.

Yogesh Tiwari, 2007, 'Cultural Diplomacy: Creating awareness and understanding', http://www.merinews.com/article/cultural-diplo macy-creating-awareness-and-understanding/126569.shtml (Accessed on May 22, 2018).

# Chapter – II

# India's Cultural Diplomacy-An Overview

## Introduction

In this chapter, it is proposed to look at Indian approach to cultural diplomacy, its origins and evolution since India's Independence. Does India have a policy on cultural diplomacy? If so, what are the thrust areas and the direction of the policy? Is there any regional or country focus?

What is the policy framework and structures created to pursue the policy objectives? How do we view the role of the Ministries of External Affairs and Culture? In what manner they interplay and coordinate their roles, both at the policy and implementation levels? What role is played by Cultural Agreements and the Cultural Exchange Programmes (CEPs) created there under?

Is there a designated nodal agency that oversees cultural diplomacy? What is the nature of its connectivity, with other state-created organizations and cultural bodies in the private sector? Is there a place for other stakeholders; what is the extent and the nature of such involvement?

What are the main instrumentalities used to promote cultural diplomacy–Cultural Centres, Festivals of India and Chairs of Indian Studies? How successful are these? What are the other tools that are used to conduct cultural diplomacy? What are the vehicles of cultural diplomacy that have been used successfully by India? How important is the role of the Youth and Sports in the context of cultural diplomacy.

In this chapter, we would also look at the direction of India's cultural diplomacy. Do VVIP visits give a push to cultural diplomacy; we would learn about it through two case studies on the impact of VVIP visits – France and Australia. There is another case study on India-Pakistan to fathom the impact of political climate on cultural diplomacy.

In this chapter, we would also have a look at the innovative programmes mounted by India and other countries, which have created an impact and could be usefully adapted as best practices by us. These would include programmes initiated by India and our diplomatic missions as well as India-specific programmes launched in other countries that have an India focus.

What role should be played by the government? Do we see a change in the focus of the Modi government; if so, then in what direction? In a separate section, we would look at how Prime Minister Modi is giving a new thrust to our cultural diplomacy.

## Indian Approach on Cultural Diplomacy

To understand Indian approach on cultural diplomacy, it is essential to appreciate how culture has become an integral part of the life of the people and the nation. Indian approach to the world is through its acceptance of the philosophy that the whole world is a family ('Vasudhaiva Kutumbakam'). It is defined by the 'Idea of India', which means the acceptance of a composite culture that is inclusive. It has been nurtured and enriched over the years, through a process of acculturation. It has its ethos in its pluralistic society, secularism and democracy, which are also enshrined in the Indian Constitution.

Indian cultural diplomacy is embedded in its history, as King Ashoka resorted to spreading the message of peace and friendship through the teachings of Lord Buddha in 260 BC. In the modern age, its philosophical underpinnings were laid down by Swami Vivekananda. He captivated his audience at the World Parliament of Religions at Chicago in 1893 when he addressed them. His message was for 'understanding and not conversion' across the globe, when he stated that what was required was 'acceptance and not toleration' of other religions. His message underscored the need to view peoples and situations in a complementary and not a comparative perspective. His inimitable words at Chicago were:

> "I am proud to belong to a religion which has taught the world both tolerance and universal acceptance. We believe not only in universal toleration, but we accept all religions as true. I am proud to belong to a nation which has sheltered the persecuted and the refugees of all religions and all nations".

Swami Vivekananda also gave his concept of a 'Universal Religion' in these words: 'It will be a religion which will have no place for persecution or intolerance in its polity, which will recognize divinity in every man and woman, and whose whole scope, whose whole force, will be created in aiding humanity to realise its own true, divine nature' (Swami Vivekananda).

Swami Vivekananda narrated how India had accepted with open arms at different times, both Israelites and Zoroastrians, when they came as refugees. To support his argument, he narrated a hymn,

> "As the different streams having their sources in different places and mingle their water in the sea, so, O Lord, the different paths which men take through different tendencies, various though they appear, crooked or straight, all lead to thee".

A similar message of acceptance of diversity was echoed by the national poet Subramanya Bharathi, who sang that "Mother India spoke in eighteen languages. It is the very essence of our culture, and is an inseparable part of our outlook" (Karlekar, Hiranmay, 1998). It is only now that we have started talking of multiple identities.

Two things that thus immediately strike about Indian Culture are its pluralistic nature and its composite character. Indian Culture is not seen in a segmented way, either in terms of language, region, or religion. We do not hear of a Hindu or Muslim or Christian view of Indian Culture nor do we hear of it being an Assamese or Bengali, or Punjabi or Tamilian.

Indian leaders over the years have stressed these aspects in their own way. Mahatma Gandhi expressed the idea in these words, "There is in Hinduism room enough for Jesus, as there is for Mohammed, Zoroaster and Moses".

His prayer song, 'Allah Ishwar Tere Nam' (Allah and Ishwar are the names of the same Entity) still captivates the hearts of all persons. This makes India 'a unity in diversity', where unity represents truth, which is many faceted.

Our present-day leaders have echoed similar messages, from time to time. Our then Vice President Krishan Kant beautifully summed up Indian Culture's pluralistic character, when he stated,

> "Indian Constitution embodies the spirit of Indian Civilization, which visualizes the one in the many and the many in the one. India has always been a land of many religions, many ethnic strains and many languages" (Karlekar).

Acceptance of diversity or tolerance with us is more than what is usually connected by the concept of secularism.

At the first India-Arab Foreign Ministers meeting in Jeddah in January 2016, External Affairs Minister Sushma Swaraj stated that:

> "Our Constitution is committed to the fundamental principle of faith-equality: the equality of all faiths not just before the law but also in daily behaviour. In every corner of my country, the music of the azaan welcomes the dawn, followed by the chime of a Hanuman temple's bells, followed by the melody of the Guru Granth Sahib being recited by priests in a gurdwara, followed by the peal of church bells every Sunday. Acceptance of diversity is not only enshrined in the Indian Constitution, but forms an integral part of societal values".

A similar message was given by Vice President Hamid Ansari in his inaugural address at an Interfaith Conference in Mallapuram (Kerala), when he stated, "Accepting and understanding of religions along with tolerance was necessary to build an inclusive and pluralistic society" (Vice President, 2016).

Indian scholars have also held a similar view of India's pluralistic culture. Asghar Ali Engineer in an article 'Minorities: Many-splendoured Contributions' highlighted the fact that 'no single community can claim the entire credit for the richness of its culture and traditions' and how it has inherited a 'composite culture'. He concluded that 'the strength of Indian democracy lies in its plurality. Historically we have a pluralist society and the more we recognize the role of pluralism in our country, the better it will be for its future' (Karlekar).

Under Articles 25 to 30 of the Constitution of India, religious as well as cultural and linguistic minorities are protected. In the olden times, cultural pluralism and its protection were accepted as the duty of the king. His protection of 'dharma' was not a narrow one; limited to religion only, but it enveloped the 'entire range of social obligations of which religious ritual was a part' (Thapar, Romila, 1998).

The four basic wheels of Indian Culture are family; religion; arts, music and drama; and literature and philosophy. These all have remained functional and have been renewed by successive generations, giving "continuity to India as a civilizational force" (Singh, B P, 1998).

## The Origins and Thrust of Indian Cultural Diplomacy

The seed for Indian Cultural Diplomacy was planted by Jawaharlal Nehru at the Asian Relations Conference held in April 1947 in New Delhi, before India gained Independence. The conference was held at his initiative and he underscored the importance of cultural diplomacy in bringing about understanding among people. In his inaugural address at the setting up of the Indian Council for Cultural Relations (ICCR) in 1950, Prime Minister Jawaharlal Nehru stated that the heart of the activities of ICCR would be to promote understanding of each other in this interdependent world. He also emphasized the importance of 'the right way' and 'the right approach' that evoked 'a friendly response' (Pamphlet).

A similar message was reiterated by Prime Minister Narasimha Rao, when he delivered the 1994 Singapore Lecture on Indian Cultural Heritage. What Nehru said in 1950, Prime Minister P.V. Narasimha Rao put it in his own words that Indian Cultural Heritage would survive 'all onslaughts from outside, integrating healthy influences and also influencing external factors in the process'. For him, Information Revolution should have, 'as its natural corollary, an enlightened understanding of our cultural affinities and differences.' He further stated, "The more we know of each other, the better we understand each other. Geographical, linguistic and legal barriers must come down" (Singapore Lecture, 1994).

This still remains the main goal, as reiterated by Dr. Suresh Goel, the then Director General, Indian Council for Cultural Relations (ICCR). He stated that cultural diplomacy aims at creating 'understanding among people, not to view others as enemies' and help in creating 'space where we can talk without being challenged or threatened; both at the level of peoples and nations'. While pursuing its objectives, "India has adopted a 'Partnership Approach', as it promoted two-channel cultural diplomacy" (Goel, Suresh),[1] which has been commended by many experts.

Over the years, cultural diplomacy is acquiring a new dimension, as it is being viewed as 'the soft power of a country to reinforce the strategic foreign policy interests of a country' (Varma, Pavan, 2006). Prime Minister Manmohan Singh saw India's soft power as "an increasingly important element in our expanding global footprint" (PBD, 2011).

The initial focus of Indian cultural diplomacy was on Asia. This was clearly stated at the Asian Relations Conference, as the aim was on 'strengthening the ties of cultural cooperation and exchange between India and other

Asian countries'. Later, the scope was widened at the behest of Prime Minister Nehru and Education Minister Maulana Abul Kalam Azad.

The principal body, Indian Council for Cultural Relations (ICCR), was thus mandated to oversee cultural diplomacy globally. There is no change in this direction, as the whole world remains the focus of the Modi Government. An eventual consequence of this global mandate has lead to ICCR in not developing a strategic depth in areas of importance to India's cultural diplomacy.

ICCR has given a new dimension to its approach on cultural diplomacy through a scheme of Institution of Awards, which suitably recognizes important persons, who have been instrumental in promoting connectivity. During the years 2015 and 2016, it instituted three Awards, namely 'Distinguished Indologist Award', 'World Sanskrit Award', and 'Distinguished Alumni Award'.

We, however, need to remember that over the years, Indian culture has been sustained by the artists themselves, as the earlier patronage they received from the princely states was not available anymore. Classical Dance traditions of Bharatnatyam, Kathak and Odissi were revived by legendary persons, like Krishna Iyer, Rukmini Devi at Kalakshetra in the 1960s and 1970s and Sattria Dance in Orissa in the 1980s.

Classical Music survived under the patronage of Maharajas, who supported – various Gharanas-Jaipur, Gwalior and Patiala. Revival of Classical Music was also seen at Maihar, through legendary personalities, like Allauddin Khan, Ali Akbar Khan and Ravi Shankar. Recognition was given to Instruments like Shenai and Sarangi, which were used for wedding and performed by low caste performers, and these moved into high culture.

All India Radio also played an important role in the revival, through the recording of classical music (70 RPM). Door Darshan played an equally important part by showing performances of famous dancers who had acclaimed international fame, like Mulani Sar, Damayanti Joshi, Indrani Rahman. The then Minister of Information and Broadcasting B V Keskar played an important role. The present day India thus has a composite culture that is inclusive and has prospered.

## Evolution of India's Cultural Diplomacy

How has India's cultural diplomacy evolved over the years under various Prime Ministers? Do we see continuity or change, if any? Let us start with the beginning, going prior to India's independence. It was King Ashoka in 260 BC, who spread the message of peace by sending emissaries to neighbouring countries that resulted in spreading Buddhism.

Buddhism still connects India with many countries and Prime Minister Modi is refocusing on these links, as he connects with Sri Lanka, China and Southeast Asian countries during his foreign visits. Sri Lankan President Sirisena acknowledged this connectivity during his visit to India in February 2015, when he stated that 'the philosophy of the Buddha and the philosophy of Hinduism have a very close relationship' (MFA, Sri Lanka, 2015).

Later, we move to another phase, where it was commerce that connected India with countries in Southeast Asia in the Eleventh Century AD. It resulted in the movement of Hinduism and Buddhism to those countries. India's cultural footprints are still visible in those countries. India, on its part also, came under the Muslim influence through trade exchanges with the Arabs in West Asia. We saw the beginnings of those linkages in the Malabar Coast in the State of Kerala. This linkage between commerce and culture is, however missing in India's present day cultural diplomacy.

The British Period in India also contributed through architecture, Archeological Discoveries, like Sanchi Stupa, setting up of Theosophical Societies by Annie Besant, and establishment of infrastructure and communication links through the English language. Revival of Indian Culture took place in the 20th century.

It was Jawahar Lal Nehru, who set the ball rolling for India's cultural diplomacy. He outlined his approach at the Asian Relations Conference in April, 1947, which was even prior to India's Independence. He saw cultural diplomacy as a vehicle for promoting understanding among peoples and nations, and wanted India to adopt a friendly approach. It was here that the foundations of India's present day cultural diplomacy were laid.

Prime Minister Nehru as an internationalist had a global and intellectual approach to cultural diplomacy, as he was not seeped into traditional culture. For him, it was the 'Idea of India' that mattered. He adopted a detached, secular and non-religious perspective, when he viewed phenomenon, like Kumbh Mela, Buddhism. In this, he was helped by Maulana Azad, the then India's Education and Culture Minister, who also respected India's 'Composite Culture', which was turned into 'India Brand'. He fine tuned this approach and was responsible for implementation of cultural diplomacy in its early phase.

Prime Minister Indira Gandhi, on the other hand focused on the vehicles of Art and Dance, as projected through festivals and concerts, as she was captivated by Indian classical dances in her childhood. She started the process of Festivals of India – the first one was held in UK in 1982 and the focus was primarily on art and not commerce. Indira Gandhi saw the Festival of India in Great Britain as 'the commencement of a major people to people dialogue'. She felt that it was necessary to stretch out the hand of friendship 'to reach beyond the leaders and touch the minds of people, in a world, where the minds of leaders were closed' (Jayakar, Pupul). She created cultural infrastructure, like the setting up of a separate Directorate of Festivals of India, which functioned independently under Pupul Jayakar, who was nicknamed 'Cultural Czarina'.

Rajiv Gandhi continued with the tradition of Festivals of India. A two-year long Festival of India was organized in USA during 1985-86, which projected a modern India, sending a message of 'India in the 21st Century'. The Youth leader was the star attraction. Later such festivals were mounted in other countries, such as France, USSR and Sweden. He also saw festivals as a vehicle for promoting integration within India. He started the process of setting up Zonal Cultural Centres in India. These Centres are still involved in providing cultural connectivity. Is it symbolic or real? The jury is still to be out and it remains a matter of individual opinion.

Prime Minister Atal Behari Vajpayee, although coming from different background and ideology, was also wedded to India's composite culture. Under his leadership, India's approach to cultural diplomacy remained largely unchanged. Message of composite culture continued to remain relevant.

Later, two Prime Ministers of India, P V Narasimharao and Manmohan Singh, continued with the Nehruvian approach. Prime Minister Manmohan Singh recognised the importance of cultural diplomacy, when he said that "India's classical traditions and the colour and vibrancy of contemporary Indian culture are making waves around the world". He also saw a role for Diaspora and Education Diplomacy. For him the salient features were as follows:

> "India has a message for the world. It is the message of pluralism, of tolerance, of the balance between individual rights

> and collective responsibilities. ….India is a symbol of that great idea 'unity in diversity' that India represents". (PBD, 2011).

Prime Minister Narendra Modi brings in a new vigour to the pursuit of India's cultural diplomacy. Culture is at the centre table and finds its manifestation in diverse forms during his foreign trips abroad. His foreign trips have been high on symbolism, while he also tries to achieve substantive results during those visits. We see this in his performing 'Ganga Aarti' with the Japanese Prime Minister Abe at Varanasi or sitting with President Xi in the traditional Gujarati 'Jhoola' (swing); gifting of saplings of Bodhi Tree to foreign leaders; signing of cultural exchange programmes with Sri Lanka or receiving a stolen idol from the Prime Minister of Australia. He would like India to use its cultural strength to project its greatness, harking back to India's cultural heritage, as he believes that 'Culture and people breathe life into a relationship' (Modi, 2015).

'Composite Culture' of India, which has evolved over the years, was influenced by different streams, flowing from many sources at different periods of its history. Indian soil has been hospitable to all, be it Jews, Christians, Zoroastrians (Parsis) and Muslims from all denominations. India is also the land of the birth of Hinduism and Buddhism, Jainism and Sikhism. It has syncretised all cultural influences, welding these into its unique 'Composite Culture'. India is also the land of religious and spiritual movements; be it 'Sufism' among Muslims (Amir Khusro, Bulle Shah) or 'Bhakti Movement' among Hindus (Kabir, Guru Nanak).

Indian 'Composite Culture', therefore, represents the synthesis of different cultures, as it weaves the essence of these into an exquisite tapestry. This is seen in all forms of art and architecture; be it dance, music, paintings, frescoes, literature. There is continuity in India's approach to cultural diplomacy, although there is greater visibility at the present juncture under Modi. It is also carried through by persons, who belong to different denominations, which represents India's hallmark of 'Unity in Diversity'.

## Framework of Indian Cultural Diplomacy

The Ministry of External Affairs (MEA) is the nodal Ministry that oversees India's cultural diplomacy. This responsibility is shared with the Ministry of Culture (MOC). MEA is involved both with the formulation and execution of cultural diplomacy. It does this through the Indian Council for Cultural Relations (ICCR), a nodal agency set up by the Indian government in 1950. Another Division, called, Public Diplomacy (PD) Division, set up in 2006, performed functions, some of which also fell in the realm of cultural diplomacy. This Division was merged with the External Publicity Division in 2014 and is renamed External Publicity and Public Diplomacy (XPD) Division.

MOC is concerned with 'disseminating Indian culture' and developing 'cultural relations between India and various countries' (MOC, 2011-12). There is no change in its mandate. To achieve these objectives, it uses the instrumentality of Cultural Agreements and Cultural Exchange Programmes (CEPs) that are developed there under. MOC also works with other Ministries and Bodies, when it formulates and implements the CEPs. It is also charged with the responsibility of organizing Festivals of India abroad. In 2016, it entered into an agreement with ICCR to function as an implementing agency in organizing such festivals (MOC, 2016-17).

Cultural Agreements provide the framework for the pursuit of cultural relations. These basically convey intent of concerned countries, to cooperate in the agreed fields and disciplines. Cultural Agreements are, however, not a necessary prerequisite to carry out cultural relations. Broadly speaking, cultural agreements cover areas, such as cultural exchanges, sports, education, mass-media, youth affairs, etc. As on November 2016, India had signed 130 Cultural Agreements/Memorandum of Understanding.

It is through CEPs, which are in the nature of annual programmes of activities in different fields, as mutually agreed upon between the two countries; different facets of cultural diplomacy get executed. As against 130 Agreements, there were only 59 CEPs that were in place; 15 of these were signed during 2015-16 (MOC, 2015-16). In the absence of CEP's, cultural agreements only remain a reference point. This, however, does not reflect any diminution of cultural relations; such relations continue to be conducted, while CEPs are being finalized on a periodic basis.

In keeping with Indian government's broad policy, it established three national academies – Sangeet Natak Akademi (Music and Dance Academy) in 1953; Lalit Kala Akademi (Fine Arts Academy) in 1954 and the Sahitya Akademi (Academy of Literature) in 1954. These academies also promote cooperation in respective disciplines under their charge, at the national, regional and international levels. Other Bodies, which help in supplementing cultural activities, include the National School of Drama, National Museum, Modern Gallery of Art, Archeological Survey of India and National Archives. All these Bodies help in providing cultural connectivity with their counterparts in foreign countries.

As stated earlier, Public Diplomacy Division of MEA, through its outreach programme also performed functions which fell under the ambit of cultural diplomacy. Some of its recent activities included generating awareness on India through Indian Films and Bollywood Music, hosting visits of Indian diaspora parliamentarians and journalists.

An innovative programme of Public Diplomacy Division included a live telecast on CNBC Awaz on 6 July, 2013, called 'Foreign Policy Class – Diplomacy ka Mahakumbh', which was a three and a half hours' programme in Hindi, involving discussion on various facets of foreign policy, which included participation from the then External Affairs Minister Salman Khurshid and other practitioners of diplomacy. One segment called, 'Har ek friend jaroori hota hai' (Every friend is essential), captured the essence of cultural diplomacy, as it conveyed the message, similar to that of Nehru's, in a Bollywood style theme song (MEA website).

## Direction of India's Cultural Diplomacy

Is India's Cultural Diplomacy globally oriented or do we see a regional or country focus? When ICCR was created, the initial focus was on Asia. Later, it was decided to adopt a global approach. ICCR has followed its global mandate. How has it been translated in practice? India has followed four broad patterns, as indicated below in respect of different Regions and Country-Groups:

- **Russia and Central Asia**, where cultural diplomacy is conducted directly by the respective governments, under Cultural Agreements and is government-centric.
- **Southeast Asia,** is the region, where cultural connectivity is rooted in our close historical and cultural ties. Cultural relations are fostered with the support of the respective governments and are conducted by the State and non-State organisations.
- **South Asia,** where we share cultural heritage and infrastructure, like SAARC Cultural Centre, but we do not have optimal level of cultural activity. Cultural Connectivity is largely guided by the respective governments. It is buffeted by the prevailing political climate, in particular, in the case of Pakistan.
- **Europe and North America,** where it is largely left to the initiative of the private sector.

India's cultural connectivity is more intense with countries in Southeast Asia, given close historical, cultural and civilization links; presence of large Diaspora communities and existence of a number of India-specific cultural associations. In the case of Russia and Central Asia, it has not reached the level of the erstwhile Soviet Union, as it is largely government-centric and lacks adequate financial support. In the case of North America and USA, it is nurtured by private groups, where culture and commerce gel together. This has resulted in well known artists finding a cultural space in prestigious halls. In the case of South Asia, it is minimal, as it has become the handmaiden of political vicissitudes, even though it had the natural advantage, given the similarity of cultural backgrounds.

Russia is gaining importance with increased cultural exchange programmes, including celebration of Festivals of India and Russia in respective countries. It is China that has emerged as an important star on India's cultural horizon, given multifaceted cooperation in diverse cultural activities, be it Bollywood, Yoga or Education. Joint production of Films has taken place. In May 2016, China released the first ever Chinese translations of the collective works of Nobel Laureate Rabindranath Tagore, 'a rare honour to the famed poet, who enjoys iconic status among generations of Chinese people' (Tagore, 2016). There are plans to create the theatre version of Raj Kapoor's film 'Awaara'.

Bollywood received a big boost from the Chinese President Xi, when he said that he had personally seen 'Dangal' of Amir Khan, which was playing in over 6000 screens across China. It was also commercially successful; having raked in over Rs 11000 million, becoming the 33rd film to cross one billion yuans ($147 million) mark (Indian Express, 2017). During their meeting at Istana on the sidelines of the SCO Summit, President Xi and Prime Minister Modi deliberated on enhancing cultural cooperation, including the planned Yoga Day celebrations in China (The Hindustan Times, 2017).

India's cultural connection with UK falls in a special category; India started with the first Festival of India in 1982 and another Festival is ongoing in 2017. In Europe, cultural links are strong with Germany and Austria, being centres for the study of Indology; while these are growing with Belgium, which is the seat of the European Union, as witnessed through the holding of Europalia in 2013, which was a Festival of India in a number of European countries. Indian focus in Europe has also been on the setting up of Chairs of Indian Studies, while in Asia, it is through the setting up of Cultural Centres.

## Visit of French President to India and Cultural Connectivity: A Case Study

This visit of President Hollande of France to India during January 24-26, 2016, as the chief guest at the Republic Day parade, had a number of cultural aspects to it. The visit started at Chandigarh on January 24, was a celebration of the French architect Le Corbusier who planned the city, with Hollande speaking for the grant of heritage status to the city (Yadav, Deepak, 2016). The visit to the Rock Garden was recognition of the innovative spirit of its architect, Nek Chand, who had created beautiful art objects from waste materials, but was also seen as a signal to the unleashing of the innovative spirit of India and France (Kanwal, Shemina, 2016) as they collaborate on Modi's favourite project, 'Start up India', which was launched on January 19. The talk was not only about heritage but also about converting Chandigarh into a smart city, as an MOU was signed during this visit with France committing to connect three cities in India – Puduchery, Nagpur and Chandigarh. It committed to spending $ US 1 billion every year in India for urban development (Yadav, Deepak: 1, 2016).

During the State Visit of the French President Hollande to India, a number of initiatives were taken as announced in the Joint Statement issued on January 25, 2016. These are enumerated below:

- To hold a Festival of India: 'Namaste France' in France during September 15-November 30, 2016 and 'Bonjour India' by France in 2017.
- To set up a new Indian Cultural Centre in France by 2017; Alliance Françoise to open up new centres in Varanasi and Lucknow during 2016-17.
- To host the Regional Hindi Conference in Paris in 2016.
- To offer 5 scholarships for French citizens to learn Sanskrit.
- To strengthen sport linkages through steps, such as reinforcing the strength of the Academies set up in Delhi and Bangalore in 2014, by the Paris Saint-Germain Football Club, with a view to developing 'grassroots football in India'.

- To enhance cooperation and links between the Sports Federations- Francaise de Hockey and Hockey India.
- To twine two iconic Indian and French monuments – India Gate, New Delhi and Arc de Triumph, Paris;
- To honour the sacrifices made by Indian and French soldiers during World War I.

The two leaders also welcomed the joint efforts made in archaeological discovery of human existence near Chandigarh, dating back to 2.6 million years. They also welcomed the launch of the book 'Shadows of God' by the Institute Francoise de Pondicherry, cataloguing Indian Object de Arts and Cultural Heritage, while recognizing the Institute's contribution 'to the preservation and recovery of stolen art'.

France is contributing indirectly to the preservation of Indian cultural heritage, as it was helping in identifying stolen Indian artefacts through its collection of rare photographs of the Chola era temples that are catalogued at the French Institute of Pondicherry (IFP) [Prasad, S, 2016]. Hollande received a book on the photo archives from IFP.

Another significant aspect of the visit was the participation of a contingent of 56 personnel of the 35th Infantry Regiment of the 7th Armoured Division of the French Army at the Republic Day Parade, earning the distinction of becoming the first foreign contingent to participate in the Republic Day Celebrations in 2016 (*The Indian Express,* 2016). The Republic Day Parade inspired the French President to state that he would plan to add a cultural component to the Bastille Day Parade.

***Bonjour India, 2017***

It was launched on November, 2017 by the French Ambassador Alexandre Ziegler on November 8 in Delhi. 'Bonjour India 2017 – 2018' was 'a four-month-long voyage across India' during November 2017 to February 2018. It celebrated Indo-French partnership, as it aimed at shaping the next decade of people-to-people contacts between the two countries. It covered 100 programmes and projects in 33 cities across 20 states and union territories. Its focus was to promote collaboration in the areas of 'innovation, education, research, science and technology, art and culture'. This was the third edition of Bonjour India; the earlier ones were held in 2009 and 2013 respectively. Ambassdor Ziegler described this as connectivity between minds and hearts and highlighted its importance in these words:

"The third edition thus focuses on partnership, innovation and creativity, and is oriented in good measure towards the youth, for they renew and perpetuate our ties. Nothing can better uphold and create enduring relations than strengthening the partnership of hearts between our peoples" (Bonjour India, 2017).

## Prime Ministerial Visits: India and Australia Cultural Connectivity: A Case Study

Prime Minister Modi visited Australia in November 2014, which was significant as it also provided cultural connectivity at the people to people level. In his address to the Australian Parliament, Prime Minister Modi directly connected with the Australians by recalling sacrifices of Indian and Australian soldiers, at the battle of Gallipoli during the World War I. He also celebrated 'the legend of Bradman and class of Tendulkar' (Australia: I, 2014). He described cricket and hockey as 'natural glue between our two people', and noted the popularity of yoga and stressed the need for connecting our people more' (Australia: 2, 2014).

During his official visit to Australia in November 2014, Prime Minister Modi unveiled the statue of Mahatma Gandhi in Brisbane, which was his first engagement in the country. He said that Gandhi's statue was "A symbol of values we share, the ideas we aspire to and the world we wish to build".

Modi also spoke on involving the States in international relations and said, 'We truly welcome the engagement between states and cities.' He also said that it was natural for Brisbane and Hyderabad to have sisterly relationship. He saw great opportunities for collaboration in joint agriculture research and tourism with the state of Queensland. He had laudatory words for Indian Diaspora, for 'They breed friendship and understanding' (The Hindu, 2014).

During his visit, a new Cultural Exchange Programme was signed and the setting up of a Cultural Centre in Sydney and holding of a Festival of India in Australia in 2015 were announced. The Festival was held in 2016.

The Joint Statement issued in November referred to a number of areas, where the two countries could cooperate (Australia: 3, 2014). These included the signing of MOUs in Arts and Culture, and Tourism; deepening educational links through cooperation between Indian and Australian Universities; strengthening of sporting links with the establishment of world class Sports University; holding of a Festival of India in 2015 to showcase the dynamism and diversity of contemporary Indian culture and production of a film on Gallipoli, jointly by National Broadcasters, the Prasar Bharti and the Australian Broadcasting Corporation (ABC).

India-Australia cultural connectivity was taken forward during the visit of the Australian Prime Minister Turnbull to India in April 2017. Cooperation in the education sector was the highlight of the visit, as this was one of the main areas of focus. Turnbull was accompanied by Vice Chancellors from Australia's highest-ranking universities, the Group of Eight. The visit took note of the existing bilateral collaborative research arrangements in the fields of agriculture, science and technology. The visit led to the signing of a number of arrangements between various educational institutes.

India has already emerged as an important destination for Indian students; with 60000 students in 2016, it ranks second after USA. Prime Minister Modi wanted this relationship to move forward to a different level, where Australian Universities could build world class institutes (Press Statement). The visit thus presents a unique opportunity 'to think beyond student enrolment and establish higher sustainable partnership' (Amit Dasgupta, 2017).

The visit also had its people friendly lighter moments, as both the leaders connected with the common man through a ride in the Delhi Metro, where they were seen taking selfies (James Campbell). Cultural component was also not missing, as Prime Minister Modi gave a personal tour of the Lakshminarayan Temple to the visiting dignitary. Holding of the Festival of India in Australia in September 2016 has taken further this cultural connectivity. The Inaugural event at the Sydney Opera House brought 'together best of both cultures', where Australian Aboriginal dancers shared the stage with the Pung Cholon dancers from Manipur in India (Nath, Damini, 2016).

## Political Clouds and Cultural Diplomacy: A Case Study on India-Pakistan

How does India's cultural diplomacy operate with Pakistan? Do we see free flow of cultural linkages, given the common and shared civilization links that we have with each other? Do these get tempered by the prevailing political atmospherics? Does the cultural connectivity help in opening closed political doors?

We have often heard how ping pong diplomacy helped in opening US-China ties. Similarly, how Jazz and Bolshoi Ballet helped in thawing relations at the people to people level between the United States and the then Soviet Union, during the cold war period. We have seen this happening again with North Korea participating at the Winter Olympics in South Korea in March 2018.

Have Bollywood Films and Songs changed the course of the events or these have themselves become victim to the then prevailing political climate? In this part, it is proposed to answer these and other allied questions, as we have a look at the political clouds that have determined cultural flows between India and Pakistan.

We are starting with the preposition that political clouds have been regularly meandering over cultural flows between India and Pakistan. While doing so, we have to also remember that at the people to people level there is a strong urge to connect culturally and at the personal level. We have seen this happening, as Indians and Pakistanis are invariably drawn to one another when abroad, as they share strong cultural links in terms of language, dress, cuisine, music and dance.

The problem comes in connecting people living in India and Pakistan, as they are subjected to political dictates. Here a restricted visa regime and inadequate communication links hinder such connectivity. Such connectivity gets further restricted in times of tension. This was the case after the 26/11 Terrorist Attack in Mumbai in 2008. A fierce debate ensued then, whether cultural flows, such as that of the Ajoka Theatre Group from Pakistan should be allowed. The die was cast negatively, as nationalist frenzy had gripped the country.

Such a posture during times of emergencies is understandable; but how has culture-political connectivity played out during normal times. In the olden days, Pakistani Theatre and Bollywood provided the connectivity, despite restrictions on screening or telecasting. Pakistani plays like, 'Dhoop Kinarey', had a tremendous following in India and so were the Bollywood films in Pakistan. The passion for Sufi music and cricket also provided connectivity among peoples.

However, regular flow of cultural products and movement of people have been disrupted from time to time. Agreements on liberalization of visa have not been fully implemented. Religious tourism has fallen victim to political expediency. Cricket matches have also met with a similar fate. It is now happening in the case of hockey and wrestling, when a Pakistani Team was denied visa in May 2017 to participate in an Asian Wrestling Tournament, much to the chagrin of Pakistani officials.

Let us look at some recent incidents in four different areas – academics, cricket, music, and the Bollywood. The first related to the release of book, "Neither Dove Nor Hawk" by Muhammed Kasuri, former Foreign Minister of Pakistan, which provided contrasting images. The release of the book at Delhi in October 2015 was a smooth affair and was attended by former Prime Minister Manmohan Singh and former Deputy Prime Minister LK Advani along with other dignitaries. Similar was the position over its release at the Khushwant Singh Literary Festival of Mussoorie in October 2015. A different fate awaited its release at Mumbai, where the organizer Sudheendra Kulkarni from the Observers Research Foundation (ORF), got his face blackened by the activists of Shiv Sena, as they blew the trumpet of nationalism, resulting in getting India's image mired, as an intolerant society.

In the case of cricket, despite an initial agreement between the Pakistan Cricket Board and the BCCI to resume bilateral cricket matches in 2015, which had been suspended since 2007, could not be resumed in 2016. Even impleading by Imran Khan with Prime Minister Modi during his visit to India in December 2015 did not cut much ice. He tweeted, 'When I told Modi that India & Pak should play cricket, he gave a smile; I can't decipher that further'.

India and Pakistan have a see-saw relationship, as far as Bollywood is concerned. Pakistanis like viewing Indian films, but have to depend upon clearance from the Pakistani authorities. At present 16 films are banned; on the other hand, films like 'Sholay' are a great hit, as it has acquired an iconic status. Pakistani playback singers have rendered songs in Bollywood films. The door was opened to Pakistani Artists to act; but the same was closed under pressure from certain nationalist groups. Screening of Bollywood films was banned in Pakistan in 2016, which was later resumed, keeping in view commercial interests.

Another incidence was the cancellation of the musical concert by Pakistani ghazal maestro Ghulam Ali in Mumbai in October 2015, which was threatened with disruption by the supporters of Shiva Sena. We saw certain course correction in this case, as he returned to India for another performance at Kolkata on January 12, 2016, under the patronage of Chief Minister Mamta Banerjee. He expressed his thanks to her as he openly acknowledged that 'his days of sadness were over'. Mamta Banerjee scored a political point, when she quoted Vivekananda, by stating, "How would we survive with intolerance? An artist has no borders. Music has no boundaries. An artist belongs to the whole world" (Deccan Chronicle, 2016).

The above may be true for the whole world but this does not hold good in the case of India-Pakistan, as political barometer determines the flow of cultural connectivity.

## Other Organizations Promoting Cultural Diplomacy

While promoting the role of Indian cultural diplomacy, Indian leaders recognized the limits of the State becoming the sole promoter. India, therefore, left a window open for the involvement of other Public Bodies and non-official players, recognizing that cultural diplomacy has to be people oriented.

India's Education Minister Abdul Kalam Azad, set the guidelines, which still hold good. He stated:

> "In a democratic regime, the acts can derive their sustenance, only from people and the state – as the organized manifestation of the people's will – must, therefore, undertake its maintenance and development as one of its first responsibilities" (Website of Sangeet Natak Akademi) .

India was thus far ahead of others, as it did not want to constrict cultural diplomacy in a tight official jacket only.

Later, the Haksar Committee further clarified that the government's role would be in 'creating and maintaining a useful infrastructure for cultural activities rather than organizing cultural events'. What is true of the role of the government in the promotion of cultural activities in the domestic arena equally holds for cultural diplomacy (Lada Guruden Singh, 2017).

'Cultural Diplomacy' was thus not meant to remain the handmaiden of ICCR only, given the budgetary and other administrative constraints. A number of new players have emerged, which can be classified as 'cultural operators', as they use 'culture' in promoting connectivity and understanding among peoples, not only within India but also with foreign countries.

There is enough room for participation by non-official organizations, as ICCR performs the role of principal promoter and facilitator. This space is occupied by a number of organizations, which have mushroomed in India. This topic is discussed, in details, in a separate Chapter V in this Book.

## Primary Vehicles of Cultural Diplomacy

Art and Literature; Dance and Music; Films and Photos; Sports and Yoga have brought about connectivity among peoples over the years, as culture has not only resulted in generating awareness, but also led to promoting understanding among them. We have often heard of Jazz Diplomacy of Duke Wellington in the Soviet Union; Bolshoi Ballet in USA; Indian Classical Music and Dance of Ravi Shankar and Uday Shankar in USA; Dance Performances by Mrinalini Sarabhai in Latin America and Beatles in India and Ping Pong Diplomacy in China and our own Cricket Diplomacy as launched by Prime Minister Modi, in the garb of 'SAARC Yatra' in 2014. We will discuss this later in Chapter VIII. In this chapter, we would, however, have a look at the role of Youth and Sports in cultural diplomacy.

## Youth and Sports as an Emerging Area

India is not an active player in the areas of youth and sports exchanges, even though our leaders often talk of demographic dividend, having the largest number of young population in the world. The Ministry of Youth and Sports is the nodal Ministry. Its aim is 'to create an international perspective on various youth issues, promoting exchange of youth delegations on a reciprocal basis, to promote peace and understanding' and to provide for opportunities for foreign exposures through coaching and training abroad and from foreign coaches in India (MYS, 2013-14).

India has youth exchanges with a limited number of countries. It commenced such exchanges with two countries in 2006, China and South Korea, providing for exchange of 100-member and 20-member delegations respectively. From 2015, the number was increased to 2000-member and 500-member delegations. In 2011, which was declared the Year of India-China Exchanges, 500-member youth delegations were exchanged (MYS, 2014-15).

India started receiving a 100-member delegation from Bangladesh since 2012. It is not clear from the Ministry's Annual Report for 2013-14 whether a reciprocal visit was made by an Indian delegation. India signed MOUs with Vietnam, Nepal, Sri Lanka and Maldives to promote youth exchanges. Youth exchanges have commenced with these countries and it received a 50-members youth delegation from Nepal.

India also sends and receives youth delegations on an ad hoc basis to participate in specific events. A 12-member Indian youth delegation visited Cambodia in April 2015 to participate in International Youth

Cultural Festival. Another 55-member Indian delegation went to Russia to attend BRICS Youth Summit in July 2015 (MYS, 2015-16).

Strangely, cooperation in the field of sports gets triggered in only during the VVIP visits. A Memorandum of Understanding (MOU) was signed with Hungary on October 17, 2013 during the visit of the Hungarian Prime Minister to India, which inter alia provides for cooperation between the Olympic committees, sports federations, universities, sports scientific bodies etc (MYS, 2013-14). Another MOU was signed with Netherlands on January 30, 2014 during the visit of Sports Minister to India. Another MOU was signed with Australia on September 5, 2014 during the visit of Prime Minister of India, while one with Colombia was signed on November 21, 2014 in Bogota (MYS, 2014-15).

The year 2015-16 was prolific in sports diplomacy, as four MOUs were signed during that financial year. The year started with the signing of MOU with France on April 9, 2015 during Prime Minister Modi's visit to France. Two more MOUs were signed with Kazakhstan and Turkmenistan on July 8, 2015 and July 11, 2015 respectively during Prime Minister's visit to these countries. Another MOU was signed on October 11, 2015 with Maldives.

## Trends and Success Stories

In this part, we are narrating some of the recent trends and success stories achieved by India in the arena of cultural diplomacy with some countries. We are looking at the programmes that are innovative in nature and have created a greater impact. These include programmes initiated by India and our diplomatic missions; programmes jointly created; India-specific programmes launched by countries that have an India focus and programmes launched by other countries, which may have relevance for us. These are only illustrative and do not fully reflect the success stories across the globe. These are covered below under specific categories.

## Joint Projects

### *Flamenco India, Spain*

It was performed in Spain on October 20, 2015 and in September in India to mark the 60$^{th}$ anniversary of the establishment of diplomatic relations, represented 'a vibrant cultural coming together of India and Spain.' It was created and directed by Spanish filmmaker Calos Saura and was performed by 28 artists, 14 from each country. The stage was shared by Bharatnatyam,

Kathak and Flamenco Dancers. It turned out to be a great treat for the audience to see 'two cultures meet, where Flamenco goes its way and Indian dance forms go their own way, but it surprising mixes well', as observed by Carlos Saura (Flamenco India, 2016). ICCR helped organize 'Flamenco India' in India and performance was dubbed as "tour de force" that brought out the unique essence of both the art forms. Teamwork Arts was also one of the organizers, whose CEO Sonjoy Roy said that a film version of the show was also planned.

***MGC Asian Traditional Textile Museum, Cambodia***

The soft launch of the MGC Asian Traditional Textile Museum in Siem Reap was presided over by the Cambodian Deputy Prime Minister and Minister in charge of Council of Ministers Sok An and Secretary(East) Anil Wadhwa on 07 April 2014.

***India-China Women Artists Residency***

This residency, christened 'Maitri' (Friendship) was organized at Jaipur during November 5-9, 2014. Nine artists from China and ten from India participated (ICCR, 2014-15). A reciprocal programme was arranged in China with ten Indian women artists participating at Shanghai during October 24-30, 2015. The Works of Art created at the Jaipur Residency were displayed at a number of cities in India (MEA, 2015-16).

***7th Annual Kingston Multicultural Arts Festival (KMAF), Canada 2017***

High Commission of India partnered with Kingston Immigration Partnership, Kingston Community Health Centre and Kingston Economic Development Cooperation to celebrate the 7th Annual Kingston Multicultural Arts Festival (KMAF) 2016 on 11th September, 2016 at Confederation Park. This was for the first time that a foreign embassy partnered for such an event in Kingston (KMAF 2016). The festival showcased diversity of Canada and propagated the ethos of co-existence of Canadians of diverse nationalities in Kingston. It was also a unique opportunity to convey the message of India's unity in diversity.

***Vietnam***

At a seminar on 'Indo-Vietnam cultural relations: Retrospect and Prospect', organized by ICCR in Delhi on February 20-21, 2016, Vietnamese Ambassador Ton Sinh Thanh suggested adding a new dimension to age old links by exploring new areas of cultural connectivity through 'exchange of movies and promoting film shooting in each other's countries (Odisha Sun Times, 2016). Inaugurating the seminar, DG ICCR Rajasekhar[2] said that the seminar focussed on 'centuries old cultural bonding'; while President of ICCR Lokesh Chandra spoke on the Cham (Hindu) Kingdom in Central Vietnam. Ambassador Wadhwa Secretary (East) MEA touched upon 'the uniqueness in its civilization foundation' of the Mekong Ganga Cooperation Initiative.

### *Helping Maldives to Overcome Water Crisis*

India helped Maldives to meet its drinking water crisis in December, 2014, by airlifting drinking water through two of its C-17 heavy transporters and three of the IL-76 transporters from Chandigarh, carrying 60 tonnes of water on December 5, 2014. India also sent 'INS Sukanya' to Maldives; the ship had two reverse osmosis on board that could produce 40 tonnes of drinking water (NDTV, 2014).

### *Remembering Indian Soldiers*

Many countries organised programmes recognising the valour of Indian soldiers during World War I by paying tribute to them; it was a fine example of connectivity. A function was organized by the UK government in collaboration with the United Service Institution of India (USI) at the UK High Commission on October 30, 2014. This was a part of the celebrations organised by the UK Government, praising the valour of 1.1 million Indian servicemen, who took part in the war, resulting in 70,000 fatalities. Six of them were awarded Victoria Cross – the highest British Gallantry Honours (The Tribune, 2014).

Similar programmes were planned in other countries, such as France, Australia, Canada and New Zealand. In a similar vein, Prime Minister of Bangladesh honoured Indian soldiers, who participated in Bangladesh's War for Independence, during her visit to India in April, 2017.

### *Celebration of Diwali*

Diwali, the festival of lights has been celebrated at the White House by President Obama since 2009, served the purpose of connecting with Indians. It also honours the rich traditions that 'define American family and America as a great and diverse nation', strengthened by 'the contributions of all our people' (Obama, 2014). Diwali is celebrated in many countries. On this Day, the Canadian Prime Minister Trudeau also gave a message on 'Celebration of Diversity' in India and Canada.

***Bloco Bollywood, Brazil***

The first Indian street Party, called Bloco Bollywood was hosted at the Brazilian carnival in 2016; it was themed on Bhangra dance and music in Brazil. 500 Indians and Brazilians danced to the tune. Bloco is a theme party and Bloco Bollywood is expected to become a permanent feature in the calendar of Brazil. This has generated interest among Brazilians to learn about Bhangra at the Indian cultural centre (Singh, Jasmine, 2016).

***Unveiling Joint Diwali Stamp by India and Canada***

The stamp was unveiled on September 21, 2017 in Toronto by Deepak Chopra, President and CEO of Canada Post in the presence of Indian High Commissioner Vikas Swarup. A similar function was held in Delhi. The stamp features 'diyas' (traditional Diwali lamps), with fireworks. For Chopra, the Diwali stamp expressed "our pride in Canada being a land of diverse faiths, customs and celebrations" (Bhattacharya, Anirudh, 2017).

***8th Theatre Olympics, February-March, 2018***

It was the first time that an international theatre festival of such a magnitude was organized in India. The opening of the 8th Theatre Olympics on the grand stage with historic Lal Qila as its backdrop on February 17, 2018 was 'in tune with great heritage of Indian theatre, music with multiple genres, forms and underlying philosophical currents' (Diwan Singh Bajeli, 2018).

The Theatre Olympics was established in 1993 in Greece. It is a kind of autonomous body that has acquired the status of the foremost platform for presenting plays by leading theatre practitioners across the world. The 51-day festival was not only held in Delhi but also in various cities in the country 'aiming at uniting theatre practitioners and to transform it into mega event'. 30 countries participated to showcase their best productions.

According to Prof. Waman Kendre, Director of the National School of Drama (NSD), India hosted Theatre Olympics "to showcase the richness of Indian theatre, its multiple genres and presentational styles and rich content with universal appeal to foreign directors, playwrights, performers and technicians". Prof. Kendre felt that

> "This Mahakumbh of world theatre will foster the feeling of togetherness among theatre practitioners; encourage them to explore new vistas to create truly an artistic theatre which has contemporary relevance in a fast changing world. We hope the

historic event will keep the flag (dhwaj) of friendship flying high".

It was a ten-day event in Chandigarh during March 2018 and each show was fully packed, as there was tremendous response from the local audience. I saw a number of plays at Chandigarh, the response and the enthusiasm of the audience were on those lines and the Theatre Olympics turned out to be a connectivity bridge.

### *Consecration of 164 year old Singapore Temple*

Prime Minister Lee Hsien Loong along with four Cabinet Ministers led some 40,000 devotees to the consecration ceremony at 'The Sri Srinavasa Perumal Temple in the Little India in April 2018. The restoration work cost $ 3.4 million. According to the Minister of Trade and Industry, this reflected 'diversity in Singapore community'. This was the first time that the Prime Minster led this ceremony since he took over office in 2004 (The Hindu: 1, 2018).

### *Turban Day at Times Square, New York*

Sikhs of New York, a non-profit organization, has made 'Turban Day', an annual feature of their activities in April, during Baisakhi celebrations. At the last function on April 7, 2018, 9000 turbans were tied in eight hours, establishing a Guinness record. It is an effort 'to spread awareness about their culture and religion'. Non-Sikhs, men and women, donning turbans and turbaned Sikhs from the New York Police Force, were not only good for optics, but sent a message on cultural connectivity (Ruchi Varshnav, 2018).

## India-Specific Foreign Initiatives

### *Promotion of Indian Classical Music in China*

A cultural group called 'Chaiti' was set up by Indian expat music lovers, corporate houses and diplomatic missions in China in Beijing four years ago, to promote Indian classical music among Chinese by holding annual music shows in China. 'Chaiti' relates to the Hindu calendar month 'Chait' and is associated with light Hindustani classical music. Chaiti Art Foundation promotes all Indian classical music. Its first festival in May 2016 was well attended, predominantly by the Chinese. The Foundation enjoys the support of the Indian Embassy and the Consulate General at Shanghai (The Times of India, 2016).

### *Japan floats House League for Yoga*

Japan got the distinction of becoming the first in launching a first of its kind group, a Parliamentary League for Promotion of Yoga by 42 members of the Japanese Parliament in April 2017. The League was launched by Ambassador Sujan Chinoi in the presence of Sri Sri Ravi Shankar, and would be headed by former Minister for Education, Culture and Sports Hakubun Shimomura. Launching of this League is opportune at this juncture, as 2017 has been declared as the Year of India-Japan Friendly Exchanges (Economic Times, 2017).

### *Niagara Falls Draped in Indian Tricolour, Canada*

Canada's famous waterfalls, the Niagara Falls were illuminated on August 15, 2017 in saffron, white and green. Vikas Swaroop, Indian High Commissioner marked this event on his Twitter, 'Niagara Falls becomes Freedom Falls, being draped in Indian flag colours' (The Financial Express, 2017). Earlier Indian tri color had lighted the Niagara Falls, to mark India's Independence Day on August 15, 2014. It was through the efforts of the India-American Physicians of Rajasthan Medical Alumni Association of North America (RAJMAAI), which held its annual convocation at the Niagara Falls in Ontario, Canada (Asian Tribune, 2014).

### *France returns Head of Hindu statue taken 130 years ago*

The Head of a Hindu deity's statue from the 7th century was returned by France, more than 130 years after it was spirited away. The Head was reattached after a ceremony at the National Museum in Phnom Penh, Cambodia. The stone sculpture is of 'Harihara', a deity that combines aspects of Vishnu and Shiva, the two most important gods in the Hindu pantheon who represent the creation of the universe and its destruction.

### *Cricket Museum in Durban*

Three South African historians of Indian-origin opened the KwaZulu Nataional Cricket Union (KZNCU) Museum in December 2016. These three Indians – Krit Reddy, Goolam Vahad and Prof. Ashwin Desai – are passionate about cricket. The Museum showcases, 'an array of literature, artifacts and memorabilia spanning over 100 years including the Apartheid era' (The Tribune, 2016). This province is home to two-thirds of 1.4 million persons of Indian origin in South Africa. Cricket like any other sports was segregated on racial lines until 1990.

### *UAE's Emergence as Neutral Territory for Sports Diplomacy*

UAE has emerged as an important Neutral Cultural Centre in facilitating sports events among countries. It acquired this role, when it constructed the Sharjah Cricket Stadium in 1982, as a private initiative of two UAE citizens, who had an exposure to India (Sultan Sooud Al Qassemi, 2017).

Since then, UAE has offered venue for holding cricket matches between India and Pakistan. UAE has thus provided this cultural connectivity, while it has also commercially gained from this venture. It has turned out to be a good venue, given the presence of large expatriate communities from India and Pakistan. The Asian Cricket Council has taken a decision to shift the 50-over Asia Cup to UAE from India, because of its inability to host Pakistan (The Hindu, 2018). It will be held during September 13-28, 2018. UAE has also emerged an important destination for holding Bollywood Extravaganzas.

### *Launch of Book on Mahatma Gandhi by Japanese Professor, 2017*

Ambassador C. Rajasekhar, Director General of ICCR launched the Book, 'How Relevant is Gandhi Today? A Japanese Perspective', written by Japanese Professor Yamaguchi Hirochi on February 26, 2017 at the India International Centre, Delhi. Other speakers included Ambassador Alan Nazareth, whose book on Gandhi has been translated into Mandarin in China. The Book is a reflection of growing Japanese interest in Gandhi.

### *Spanish Sanskrit Directory Project*

Spain is actively involved in promoting cultural links with India. Oscar Pujol, dynamic Director of Instituto Cervantes, a formidable scholar had been associated with the Spanish Sanskrit Directory project. In 2012, it organized a dazzling exhibition of the late Mario Miranda's cartoons and sketches, done after a visit to Spain and equally stunning exhibition on Pablo Picasso (Pande, Ira, 2012).

### *Intercultural Exchanges promoted by American Field Services (AFS)*

A group of teenagers from various parts of the globe spent a year in India under an exchange programme arranged by the American Field Services (AFS). This is a culture–cum–education programme, where teenagers stay with the families. The aim of the programme is to promote 'peace and global understanding through intercultural exchanges'. AFS has organized more than 14000 exchanges per year in more than 54 countries. AFS has been present in India since 2005 in 27 cities with a pool of 750 volunteers. All the participants left with a message that India is such 'a diverse country with so much to offer and so many different cultures integrated together'. The ultimate message was, 'We all have but the same roots' (Spectrum, 2017).

### *Inclusive Blind Cricket Exhibition Match*

The Australian High Commission organized the above match in April 2018, as part of its 'Development 4 All' Programme. The two teams featured a mix of players from the World Cup winning India Blind Cricket Squad and diplomats from Australia, New Zealand and UK. The Australian High Commission has future plans to organize a tournament with four teams and enlarged diplomatic representation (Smita Sharma, 2018).

### *Football for Peace (FFP)*

It is a unique initiative and movement that aims at 'using the power of sports to harness its potential to unite and create greater understanding between people, communities and governments' and aims at achieving 'integration among people from diverse background' (New Delhi Times, 2017). FFP works with schools to put up educational workshops in the areas of peace, conflict resolution, equality and empowerment. It launched a 'City for Peace' initiative in Kozhikode (Kerala) in India in 2015. The movement was launched by British Pakistani Footballer Kashif Siddiqi along with Chilean soccer legend Ilias Figuerva.

### *Bangladesh Film Festival, Kolkata*

A Four-day Bangladesh Film Festival was held in Kolkata during January 5-8, 2018. On show were 28 documentary, feature and short films. The original plan was to hold the festival on 'Vijay Divas' on December 16, 2017 and most of the films were to centre on the Bangladesh War of Liberation. In view of change in the dates, some more films on other themes were added. The significance of the festival is that it was the first time in recent public memory that a film festival was being organized officially between Bangladesh and West Bengal. West Bengal is expected to hold a similar festival in Dhaka (Singh, Shiv Sahay, 2018).

### *The United States Postal Service Issuing Diwali Stamp*

The United States Postal Service (UPS) issued a Diwali Stamp in 2016, which was an outcome of a successful 6 years of campaigning by an activist Ranju Batra. According to her, 'the stamp is not about the celebration of a religion or even of a nation. It is about universal values of inclusiveness'.

On day one, the Campaign sold stamps worth $ 1,70,000, breaking all records of first day sale' (Varghese K George, 2017).

### *Two Halves, One Whole: Punjabi-Mexican Dance*

It is a unique effort to preserve the history of the two cultures-Punjabi and Mexican- through music and dance. They were brought together face to face in the State of California in the early 20th Century. The groups intermarried, with their children calling themselves "half and half". The succeeding generations were getting assimilated into the American culture. It brought together San Francisco's *Duniya Dance and Drum Company* and *the Ensambles Ballet Folklorico de San Francisco*, to create the dance series *Half and Halves*, by merging traditional Punjabi 'Bhangra' with Mexican Folklorico. This 'syncretism is reflected across the project's twelve pieces, all of which incorporate singers and musicians from both cultures, as well as testimonials from the original "half and half" generation' (USC, 2016).

### *Connecting Youth through Project Khwahish (Wish), Singapore*

This is a unique project; which connects the Youth from Singapore to Punjab, its culture and people. Khwahish, an initiative of the Young Sikh Association (YSA), a non-profit organization, which was founded by Satwant Singh in Singapore. It is open to Indian-origin youth and not restricted to Punjabis alone. Each year, a group of around 20 students, visit Punjab during school vacations in December. The last group visit was for three weeks in December 2017 to Rattoke village in the Sangrur District. They stayed with the families and in free time involved themselves in undertaking social activities, such as renovating the buildings of the Government Primary School (Singh, Avtar, 2017). This was the best way to provide connectivity among people, in particular the youth.

### *NRI Endowment for Kennedy Centre, Washington DC*

Ranvir and Adarsh Trehan, donated $ 1 million to create an 'India Fund' at the Kennedy Centre, a top American Centre for Performing Arts at Washington DC. This Fund would be exclusively used to present 'performing arts, artistic exhibits and festivals showcasing the history, traditions, literature, music, dance and culture of India'.

This country focused Fund is for artists, who are either citizens of India or whose ancestors are from India. This Fund could be used for 'several events every year or even a mini-festival or a substantial festival like Maximum India' (The Times of India, 2017).

### *Asian Food Festival, South Korea*

The Asian Food Festival was organized on the margins of the Asian Games 2014 in Incheon during September 19-October 4. Renowned chefs and restaurants from 10 Asian countries participated. They showed their culinary talents with cooking competitions and food display. From India, chefs from Crown Plaza participated. India Day was observed at the Festival on September 25, when Indian and Korean artists from Indian Cultural Centre (ICC) presented vibrant and colourful, Kathak and Bollywood dance performances (Indian Embassy, 2014).

### *US-India Dosti (Friendship) Initiative*

The US Embassy in Delhi launched a unique initiative in India called 'US India Dosti' Initiative in September 2017. Under this initiative, the Embassy officials showcased 'the appreciation, fascination and respect', which the US diplomatic community has for 'Indian culture, traditions and languages'. Gauri Seetharaman, Assistant Information Officer, US Embassy, New Delhi stated that it was to recognise that people to people ties 'serve as the bedrock of the US-India relationship and that is expressed through our mutual respect and appreciation for each others' culture and traditions'.

Under this initiative, US diplomats showcased their respect by 'reciting Indian poems and taking social trips'. The Embassy posted three short videos of poetry on the Facebook – Hindi poetry of Sohan Lal Dwivedi sung by Major Smocks on the Hindi Divas; recitation of a Punjabi poem by Bulle Shah and recitation of Urdu poems of Ghalib and Dagh by diplomats, Alaine and Nate. The three videos received overwhelming response and crossed over 100,000 views (Wire, AB, 2017).

### *Canada 150 to India 70 Moving Mural*

An international project 'Canada 150 to India 70 Moving Mural' celebrated Canada-India relations, which are built on shared commitment to 'democracy, pluralism and people to people links'. This 150 feet X 5 feet moving mural tells the story of Canada from indigenous cultures to connection with India and the common traditions which both the countries share. These are shared through 70 panels of paintings from three Canadian artists (CanIndia). Prime Minister Justin Trudeau inaugurated the function at Toronto on August 17, 2017. The exhibit was showcased at the Bikaner House, New Delhi in October 2017. 'Vibrant panels at "The Moving Mural" exhibition showcased Indian and Canadian contributions in varied spheres of life'. It was only through art and culture that 'such special occasions and human relations' could be celebrated (S Ravi, 2017).

### *Global Diversity Award 2017*

Filmstar Salman Khan was honoured with the Global Diversity Award 2017 on September 15, 2017 at the British Parliament House. The Award was given to him as a role model and a philanthropist. Previous Awardees included Amitabh Bachan, Aishwarya Rai, Shah Rukh Khan and Jackie Chan and Bangladesh Prime Minister Sheikh Hasina (Deccan Chronicle, 2017).

### *The 2nd Silk Road International Film Festival 2015*

India produced film 'Let the Heart Beat' premiered at the opening ceremony at Fuzhou (China). India was the guest of honour. According to the Director Zoya Akhtar, the appeal of the film lay in the story, which is based on human emotions, to which people from all countries relate (China Daily, 2015).

### *Spirit of India Run, 2016*

Pat Farmer, former Australian Minister, came on a mission to promote closer cultural and sports relations between the two countries. Under his 'Spirit of India Run' banner, he covered 4600 km between Kanyakumari and Srinagar in over two months, starting at Kanyakumari on January 26, 2017. His run also celebrated multiculturalism in India (Ahlawat, Bijendra, 2017).

### *OZ Haat Mela*

The Australian High Commission has been organizing 'OZ Haat Mela' since 2000, on the lines of 'Delhi Haat'. It is a part of its Direct Aid Programme that supports Non-Governmental Organizations (NGOs). The 17th such event was held in the premises of the High Commission on November 2017. 40 NGOs, which are the recipient of the grant, participated in this Mela that had a footfall of 3000 persons. The display included tribal art, textiles, home-use items, clothes, jewellery, accessories and Christmas decorations.

The occasion had a festive look; Australian food and wine, children's games and a dance performance by differently- abled children added a new dimension. John McCarthy, Australia's High Commissioner to India described the DAP program as "a mechanism for the High Commission to play some part in the Indian community. We fund various groups across India and Bhutan, to undertake development activities, with a special focus on the needs of women and children" (Prasad, KV, 2017).

### *Uzbek Artists Regale Indian Audience with Bollywood Songs*

The visiting artists from the Havas Group of Uzbekistan regaled the invited guests at the Embassy, with Bollywood songs of Yesteryears. At that function, Ambassador Farhod Arzeiv reminisced about India's cultural diversity and recalled how Bollywood was cementing existing traditional ties between the two countries. Uzbekistan is keen to welcome Bollywood to shoot films, as this could lead to generating tourism (Smita Sharma, 2018:1).

## Foreign Initiatives

### *Celebrating Ping Pong Diplomacy September 2017*

US celebrated the 45 years of Ping Pong Diplomacy of 1971-72, which led to the historic visit of President Nixon to China in February 1972, resulting in the opening of diplomatic relationship between USA and China. This reunity of surviving sports persons took place at the University of Michigan in Ann Arbor, which was the first stop on the Chinese Table Tennis team's visit to the US in 1972. Former World Champions, Liang Geliang and Zhen Huaiying, acknowledged the role played by the Ping Pong Diplomacy 'helping to break the ice between the two nations' (ECNS, 2017).

### *Korean-ASEAN Cinema Week 2017*

The Film Week was jointly launched in Indonesia by the Permanent Missions of Korea and Cambodia to ASEAN, ASEAN Secretariat and the Indonesian Ministry of Foreign Affairs. Under this initiative, films from ASEAN countries were screened in Jakarta from September 28 to October 1 and October 6-8, 2017 at Surabaya, East Java. The week was launched as the films are 'one of the most powerful ways to connect people', that help in developing 'deeper connections and, on a common level, you can feel something that you share' (Antara News, 2017).

### *Refugee Olympic Team (ROT) to shine spotlight on worldwide Refugee Crisis*

Ten refugee athletes acted as a symbol of hope for refugees worldwide and brought global attention to the magnitude of the refugee crisis when they took part in the Rio Olympic Games Rio in 2016. The athletes competed for the Refugee Olympic Team (ROT) – the first of its kind – and marched with the Olympic flag immediately before the host nation Brazil at the Opening Ceremony. The athletes were named to the ROT by the Executive Board (EB) of the International Olympic Committee (IOC).

***Korean Wave best tool for public diplomacy***

The Regional Public Diplomacy Division at the South Korean Ministry of Foreign Affairs runs a diplomat exchange program with the United States since 2011. Peterson was the fifth US diplomat posted to South Korea for this one year programme, which focuses on cultural connectivity, "as the best thing Koreans have going for them in foreign countries is the Korean Wave" (The Korea Herald, 2016). Peterson said that South Korea's popular music, dramas and movies have started to make their presence felt among the US audience.

***Mexican Telenovelas***

Exhibitions and literature are considered to be two 'pillars of cultural diplomacy'. Mexico is increasingly using its vibrant film and television industry, in particular "telenovelas" in projecting itself and generating commercial revenues, in particular in South America and USA, catering to the Mexican population. Translation of Books is considered useful in connecting to the outside world, with increasing focus on translation of books in to European languages.

***Global Youth Ambassadors Leadership Summit***

The City of Chicago has been hosting this Summit annually since 2016. This is a part of its activities under the rubric of 'Sisterly-Cities Relationships', which it has built with 38 International cities across the globe, including Delhi. This Programme aims at building 'the next generation of global women leaders', by focusing on teenage girls and help them becoming 'socially active leaders in their communities', as they strive to become 'agents of positive change in the world'. The Third Summit was organized by the City Council in collaboration with the University of Illinois at Chicago in July 2018. This was attended by 25 girl participants; 15 from abroad and 10 from Chicago. There was a participant from Lahore (Pakistan), but none from Delhi. The author attended the Closing Ceremony on July 27.

## Indian Initiatives

### *Helping Build Afghan Cricket Team*

During his term, Ambassador Amar Sinha has been instrumental in getting high-value projects completed in Afghanistan, such as Salma Dam, Afghan Parliament. One of his other initiatives was to support the emerging Afghan Cricket Team by extending India's support to some of the projects. These included getting a home ground for Afghanistan team in Greater Noida; helping Afghanistan in joining ICC (International Cricket Council) and getting Afghan players to play in the IPL (Indian Premier League). The sport is 'spreading like wild fire around the country and the spectacular performance of the Afghan football and cricket teams is a major unifier of the country and gives them a sense of pride like nothing else' (Amar Sinha).[3]

### *Celebrating Indian Festivals at the Embassy Residence*

Ambassador Lalit Mansingh arranged hosting of Indian festivals in London and Washington DC during his tenure. This resulted in bringing better connectivity with Indian Diaspora in these countries, such as US, USA and Canada where local groups celebrate such festivals in particular, Diwali. (Lalit Mansingh).[4]

### *Zee Production Company in Canada*

Zee Entertainment Enterprises (ZEE) became the first Indian broadcaster to set up a production unit in Vancouver (Canada) in September 2017. Zee considers itself as "a cultural ambassador of India, taking its rich and engaging content across the world', as stated by Amit Goenka, CEO of International Broadcasting (Bylykobashi, Kathrene).

### *WW I Expo Bringing Subcontinent Together*

On March 8, 2015, Indian Army organized World War I Expo to mark 100 years of the war as it showcased the role of men from the subcontinent – India, Pakistan, Nepal and Bangladesh'. The Exhibition was 'to pay respect and commemorate the contribution of all those who died irrespective of which modern-day country their progeny now live in'.

Exhibition was inaugurated by the President of India on March 10. Earlier, on March 9, the President laid a wreath at India Gate, which was attended by diplomats from Pakistan, Nepal, Bhutan, Bangladesh, UK and France. It was the first time that a Pakistani diplomat was invited to 'an Indian military function at the iconic India Gate' (Banerjee, Ajay, 2015).

### *Nepal-Bharat Library Connecting with Nepalese*

The Embassy of India took a new initiative, in association with the BP Koirala Nepal-India Foundation to connect with Nepalese people by providing opportunity at the Nepal-Bharat Library in Kathmandu through a series of monthly programems to promote Nepalese art, literature, music and films.

The first of the series called 'Conversation' began in January 2013 that provided forum for writers. The second called 'Poemandu', a poetry recitation programme was launched in March 2013. The third 'Cinemandu' was a screening of Nepalese films. The fourth, 'Voices' provided space for sharing of views and interaction to young and upcoming journalists, thinkers, scholars.

These programmes are increasingly popular and have been regularly held every month and are well attended with the hall brimming to its full capacity of 100 persons. The programmes have become a 'Brand' in themselves for preservation and promotion of cultural and intellectual heritage between the nations (Abhey).

### *Cha com Letras (Tea with Words), Brazil*

The $19^{th}$ edition of 'Cha' was held in Brasilia in December 2017 in conjunction with the Festival of India. This programme provides a unique literary space, where you mix tea with literary words. This is a new initiative taken by K Abhay, India's Deputy Chief of Mission to Brazil. He had earlier taken similar initiatives, like 'Poetry at Monument' in Delhi and 'Poemandu' in Kathmandu (Nepal). On this occasion, homage was paid to well known Brazilian Poet Cecilia Meireles, who is remembered as 'a Brazilian with an Indian Soul' and is credited with the finest translation of Tagore's Poetry into Portuguese.

### *Distinguished Lecture Series*

It is one of the flagship programmes, initiated by the Public Diplomacy Division. The objective is to reach out to University campuses and beyond, where MEA could contribute to a more informed and nuanced debate on foreign policy. The ideal template included 'an engagement between our distinguished speaker and faculty and students at the university, an interaction with local media and a meeting with the leadership of the city (state) where the university is located' (Suri, Navdeep, 2017).

The aim is 'to engage if not influence, with domestic debates on key foreign policy issues'. Retired Ambassadors are motivated to visit universities in different corners of India. It is a highly successful venture that many PD practitioners in UK, Germany, Australia and elsewhere were fascinated by this initiative and had explored ways to replicate it in their countries (ibid).

***Artists in Residence at the Rashtrapati Bhavan***

President Pranab Mukherjee launched this unique programme in December 2013. Under this programme artist and writers stay in the Rashtrapati Bhavan for a month or so and become a part of its life. It is aimed at inspiring 'creative thinking and rejuvenating artistic impulses' while honouring established and talented young artists and writers (The Hindustan Times, 2017:1).

## Initiative of Indian Diplomatic Missions

Given below are some of the programmes organized by our diplomatic missions during the last two years or so. These are only illustrative and not exhaustive:

- Holding of a joint Yoga – Tai Chi Event at the Temple of Heaven in Beijing during the visit of Prime Minister Modi to China in May 2015 was a symbol of civilizational connectivity between India and China.
- Holding of International Yoga Day in 2015 in front of Heritage buildings in Cambodia and Indonesia.
- Involving locals with the Indian Cultural Centres, which could take varied forms. In, Ulaanbaatar (Mongolia), the Cultural Centre was set up by Mongol citizens. In San Paulo (Brazil) all the teachers are Brazilian, while ICC in Colombo (Sri Lanka) draws upon the resources of local teachers.
- Organization of Film shows by screening Bollywood films for social purposes. This included 'Taare Zamin Paar' in partnership with the Brazilian Association of Dyslexia (ABD) to generate awareness on children with special ability.
- Performance by the Rhubab Troupe led by Humayoun Barkhi at the Rashtrapati Bhawan in November 2014, in the presence of the President and former Afghan President Hamid Karzai.

- Organisation of 'A passage to India Festival' by the local Indian community in November 2013 and March 2015 by the Indian Association in Doha, Qatar.

- Holding of a 'Paintings Exhibition', called 'Cultural Confluence – United Colours' at the National Art Gallery on January 26, 2015. The paintings were created by Indian, Maldivian and South Asian Artists.

- Focusing on 'Hinduism' as a theme at the 2015 Salzburg Music Festival. It included Ensemble Nepathya in Kutiyattam, Dhrupad, Khayal and Bharatnatyam.

- Belgium government commemorating the centenary of the World War I, honouring 130,000 Indian soldiers, who fought at the Flanders Fields in Belgium, with 9000 losing their lives.

- Bringing out a Comic on India-Indonesia Bilateral relations in the 'Panchtantra' Format by the then Indian Ambassador Gurjit Singh.

## Prime Minister Modi and Cultural Connectivity

Prime Minister Modi's foreign trips have been high on symbolism, while he also tries to achieve substantive results during those visits. Similarly, he also relies on culture and acronyms as he connects with his host in Bhutan, through catchy alliterations, such as B4B (Bharat to Bhutan, Bhutan to Bharat) in June 2014; Chalen Saath Saath' (Walking Together), a joint Oped with President Obama in the Washington Post in September 2014; Joint Radio Programme 'Man Ki Baat' with President Obama in January 2015.

Culture has thus become an important component of Prime Minister Modi's visits abroad. During his visit to Canada on April 16-17, 2015, Prime Minister Stephen Harper returned a 12$^{th}$ century old statue of 'Parrot Lady', which had been smuggled into Canada. Prime Minister Modi presented a miniature painting of Guru Nanak and his two disciples – Bala and Mardana, sending a message of secularism and inclusiveness of Indian society to the Canadians and as a gesture to the Sikh diaspora in Canada, which is the largest component of Indian Diaspora

Modi also does not miss the opportunity to add cultural props to his foreign visits, as he described his visit to Jaffna in Sri Lanka as 'TriveniYatra'. This included three events, such as laying the foundation stone for the cultural centre, handing over of houses built with Indian assistance to war-widows and launching of train service to Talaimanar that was built with Indian assistance. A photo caption, 'Ties on Track' (The Hindustan Times, March 15, 2015), showing Modi flagging off train from Madhu Road to Talaimanar in Sri Lanka, fully conveyed the message.

Modi also announced the setting up of a 'world class' Cultural Centre in Jaffna, as 'a symbol of shared strong historical and cultural links' and a library, whose importance he described in these words, 'While roads, airports and ports link people, library links generations of people and their histories' (The Hindu, 2015).

Modi has emerged as a Fashion Icon, as he was adjudged as one of the five global leaders in Fashion Diplomacy. The other four included Michelle Obama; Peng Liyuan, First Lady of China; Kate Middleton, Duchess of Cambridge and Evo Morales, President of Bolivia. Modi's traditional kurta (a loose collarless shirt) paired with a vest or scarf has made waves and has earned its own hash tag, Modi Kurta (USC). During his visit to India in January 2015 President Obama remarked, in a lighter vein that Michelle had found a competitor in Modi. Visiting Heads of State/Government at the Africa Summit in October 2015 and the BRICS Summit in November 2016 also turned fashion icons as they donned Modi 'Kurta' and Vest respectively.

Modi has given us new Indian Brands, 'Start up India', 'Digital India' and 'Make in India'. India needs a new image 'Work for India'. The Government of India adopted the icon of Swami Vivekananda by declaring his birthday on January 12, as the Youth Day. The theme of the 20th National Youth Festival organized in Raipur (Chhatisgarh) in 2016 was 'Indian youth for skill development and harmony'. Prime Minister Modi reiterated his earlier message that growth and prosperity could be ascertained only through peace, unity and harmony (Kaiser, 2016).

Modi is aggressively pursuing the Buddhist connection, even though this initiative was initially taken by Prime Minister Manmohan Singh. He is using 'culture' to connect to people in Asia and found that Buddhist philosophy, which does not necessarily contradict Hinduism, connects all of Asia. Modi successfully outlined this link during his visit to Sri Lanka in 2015, when he reminded them of old civilasational links established during the times of King Ashoka, when he tried to connect Gaya in India with Anirudhapuram in Sri Lanka (Kadir Pethiyagoda, 2015). Modi has vested this with greater symbolism, as he has carried saplings of original Bodhi tree during his visits abroad – Nepal in November 2014; China,

Mangolia, South Korea in May 2014. President Pranab Mukherjee had also carried a sapling to Vietnam in September 2014.

The Modi government has recognized the importance of taking the States on board in pursuance of its 'Cooperative Federalism' policy. One of its planks is to promote engagement of the States with foreign countries in the areas of business and culture. This initiative was unveiled during the visit of EAM Sushma Swaraj to Singapore in August 2014 (Prashar, Sachin, 2014). Modi himself reiterated the same during his visit to Australia in November 2014. To achieve this objective, a new Division, called the States Division was created in the Ministry of External Affairs, which acts as a nodal point.

Modi fully realizes the importance of tapping into the strength of Diaspora. Diaspora is the Centre of attraction for Prime Minister Modi in all his foreign visits. He earned the title of 'Rock Star' at his appearance at the Madison Square Garden (MSG) in New York in September 2014. The same opulent welcome was accorded to him by the Indian community at Toronto (Canada) in April 2015, where he was joined by Prime Minister Harper.

## Indian Cultural Diplomacy Pivoted to the 'Idea of India'

India is not new to cultural diplomacy, given its ancient civilization links, where culture has played an important role. It has effectively used it since the days of King Ashoka since 260 BC; in keeping with its ethos of 'Vasudhaiva Kutumbakam' (The whole world is a family).

Indian cultural diplomacy is, however, not enshrined in a theoretical framework. It is also not declaratory in character. It is, however, a living document, that has manifested itself since ages. It has well adapted itself, in response to various developments and has remained on course.

Cultural diplomacy is in India's DNA. It practiced cultural diplomacy, before the term gained currency in the West. It has reaped benefits from the pursuit of tenets of cultural diplomacy since the days of King Ashoka. This is manifested in the adoption of Buddha religion in many countries in Asia, where it still has large following.

India's pursuit of cultural diplomacy rests on two basic tenets – 'Vasudhaiva Kutumbakam' – (The Whole World is a Family) and 'One Truth and Many Paths'. It is tantamount to acceptance and pursuit of pluralism and diversity in international cultural relations. It would have to traverse the same path, in future also.

India has recognized the dynamic nature of cultural diplomacy. It has, therefore, allowed it to evolve, suitably responding to changing times. The core of India's cultural diplomacy is pivoted to the 'Idea of India' that rests on its 'composite culture', which is the product of acculturation, as it was open to whiffs of fresh air from other civilizations. While addressing a community gathering at the Bhai Ganga Singh Sabha Gurdwara in Tehran in April 2016, Prime Minster Modi reiterated that "We Indians have a specialty. We accept everyone and assimilate with everyone."

Unlike many other countries, India has viewed cultural diplomacy as a two-way channel to promote understanding among peoples from different countries. It is not elitist in its approach and embraces all people. It equally uses classical and popular culture in its outreach programmes. It also ensures that fruits of cultural exchanges are shared all over India by involving its Regional Offices that are located in various states.

India has created adequate framework to pursue its goals of cultural diplomacy. The Ministry of External Affairs (MEA) is the nodal Ministry. The Ministry of Culture (MOC) has an assigned role in certain fields, which are connected with cultural diplomacy, such as concluding Cultural Agreements and holding of Festivals of India. The Government has also created a number of other Bodies to promote cultural linkages; it realizes the limitations on its part, both in terms of funding and its reach.

Indian Council for Cultural Relations (ICCR), which is an independent body, working under the aegis of MEA, is declared as the nodal organisation to pursue cultural diplomacy. It uses a number of instrumentalities to achieve its objectives. It works in coordination with MOC and other Governmental Bodies and NGOs in promoting international cultural cooperation.

ICCR, since its inception in 1950, has followed its original mandate of inclusivity, by focusing its programmes on a global basis. India's cultural connectivity is more intense with countries in Southeast Asia, given close historical, cultural and civilization links; presence of large Diaspora communities and existence of a number of India-specific cultural associations.

The leaders continue to harp on the 'inclusive' nature of India's culture. The same message is being given during the visits of Prime Minister Modi abroad. During his visit to Iran in April 2016, Modi gave a message of connectivity between cultures, between these two civilizations and conveyed respect for the Persian language and saw congruity between 'Sufism' and 'Vasudhaiva Kutumbakam'.

India has successfully used various vehicles of cultural diplomacy as it connects with the world. Bollywood has been in the forefront, while Yoga is coming on the horizon in a big way, as concerted efforts are being made by the government since the declaration of June 21 as International Yoga Day (IYD) in 2015 by the UN General Assembly. Prime Minister Modi has emrged as an image builder; so has the Indian Diaspora.

There is a broad continuity in India's pursuit of cultural diplomacy, which is at the diplomatic centre table. Of course, there have been marginal differences in terms of programmes or direction, depending upon on individual proclivities and preferences. There is, however, a greater thrust on cultural content and people to people connectivity in India's pursuit of international relations.

Cultural diplomacy is now at the central table during VVIP visits, which have cultural connectivity as an important takeaway, as seen from two case studies on Australia and France in this chapter. Similarly a greater symbolism is attached to such visits.

In the past, India had not used cultural diplomacy to push its foreign policy agenda. Attempts are afoot to shift its focus and a new narrative is being written. Steps are being taken to project this as a symbol of soft power and use it in building relationship on the strength of India's cultural heritage and its past glories. Consequently, a new thrust is being given with the introduction of new features and programmes, which have been described in this chapter.

The success of Indian 'Cultural Diplomacy' would depend upon its retaining its original intent of being a 'Connectivity Bridge' rather than becoming a tool of 'Soft Power', so as not to deflect from its original intent. It is, therefore, not surprising that the mandate of ICCR has remained unchanged, since its inception in 1950.

## Endnotes

1. Goel, Suresh, Former Director General, ICCR. Based on written response on May 27, 2015 and subsequent interaction in Delhi.
2. C. Rajasekhar, Director General, ICCR. Based on interaction on March 12, 2016 and a continuing dialogue on a number of other subsequent occasions.
3. Amar Sinha, Former Ambassador to Afghanistan and Secretary, MEA. Based on interaction and response from him on October 6, 2017.
4. Lalit Mansingh, Former Foreign Secretary, MEA and Director General, ICCR. Based on initial interaction on December 17, 2015 and many subsequent sessions, the last one on September 7, 2017.

## References

Abhay K., 2013, 'Innovations in Public Diplomacy', *GPP Blog*, 6 November. https://uscpublicdiplomacy.org/blog/innovations-public-diplomacy (Accessed on December 17, 2017).

Ahlawat, Bijendra, 2017, 'From Kanya Kumari to Srinagar', former Oz MP on a mission', *The Tribune,* March 13.

Amit Dasgupta and Shaun Star, 2017, 'India-Australia relations: Education as the tipping point', *The Hindustan Times*, April 12.

*Antara News* 2017,'Strengthening people-to-people relations in ASEAN through movies', September 21, 2017. https://en.antaranews.com/news/112719/strengthening-people-to-people-relations-in-asean-through-movies (Accessed on December 17, 2017).

*Asian Tribune*, 2014,'Indian tri color lights up Niagara Falls', August 28. http://asiantribune.com/node/85295 (Accessed on December 17, 2017).

Australia: I, 2014, Prime Minister Modi's Address to the Australian Parliament, Canberra, November 18.

Australia: 2, 2014, Prime Minister Modi's Statement, Canberra, November 18.

Australia: 3, 2014, Joint Statement issued at Canberra, November 18.

Banerjee, Ajay, 2015, 'WW I Expo to bring subcontinent together; opens in Delhi Tomorrow', *The Tribune,* March 9.

Bhattacharya, Anirudh, 2017, 'India Canada Unveil Joint Diwali Stamp', *The Hindustan Times*, September 23.

Bonjour India, 2017, Available at https://in.ambafrance.org/Bonjour-India-2017-2018 (Accessed on May 9, 2018).

Bylykobashi, Kathrene, 2017 'India's ZEE sets up prodco in Canada', *TBI Vision*, September 22.

*China Daily*, 2015, 'The 2nd Silk Road International Film Festival kicks off', September 23.

Dasgupta, Arun, 1996, 'Intellectual and Academic Cooperation between India and Southeast Asia' in *India and Southeast Asia – Challenges and Opportunities* (ed. Baladas Ghoshal), IIC, New Delhi.

Diwan Singh Bajeli, 2018, 'Theatre Olympics sets off a splendid stage', *The Hindu*, Feb 17, http://www.thehindu.com/entertainment/music/on-a-musical-note/article22804885.ece (Accessed on December 16, 2017).

*Deccan Chronicle*, 2016, 'Ghulam Ali concert can be hosted in Kolkata: Mamata Banerjee', January 10. http://www.deccanchronicle.com/151008/nation-current-affairs/article/ghulam-ali-concert-can-be-hosted-kolkata-mamata-banerjee (Accessed on December 16, 2017).

*Deccan Chronicle.* 2017, 'Salman Khan honoured by British Parliament House with Global Diversity Award', September 16. www.deccanchronicle.com/.../salman-khan-honoured-with-global-diversity-award-by. (Accessed on December 16, 2017).

*ECNS,* 2017, 'Ping Pong diplomats reunite', September 19, www.ecns.cn/2017/09-19/274224.shtml (Accessed on December 16, 2017).

*Economic Times*, 2017, Dipangan Roy Choudhury, 'In a first Japan floats home league for promotion of Yoga', April 6.

*Financial Express*, 2017, 'Niagara falls lit up in tricolour to mark India's 71st Independence Day', August 17. https://timesofindia.indiatimes.com/city/kochi/on-i-day-niagara-to-fall-in-tricolor/articleshowprint/60006053.cms (Accessed on December 16, 2017).

Flamenco India, 2016, 'Dancing to the rhythm of India-Spain ties',*The Statesman*, March 8.

*ICCR,* 2014-15, Annual Report of the Indian Council for Cultural Relations, New Delhi.

Igrouanne, Youssef, 2016, 'Marrakech, Bombay..... A Love Story', Consolidates Cultural Ties between Morocco and India, February 20. https://www.moroccoworldnews.com/2016/02/180254/marrakech-bombay-a-love-story-consolidates-cultural-ties-between-morocco-and-india/ (Accessed on December 16, 2017).

Inaugural Address of M.C. Chagla, 1968, President of ICCR as quoted in Bidyut Sarkar, ed., *India and Southeast Asia: Proceedings of a Seminar on India and Southeast Asia*, ICCR.

Inaugural Address of Prime Minister Nehru in 1950 at the time of the inauguration of the Indian Council of Cultural Relations (ICCR), quoted in a *Pamphlet on ICCR*, New Delhi.

Indian Embassy, 2014, *Press Release* of the Indian Embassy in Seoul, September 26.

James Campbell, 2017, 'Prime Minister Malcolm Turnbull shares train with India's "rock star"PM Narendra Modi', *Herald Sun*, April 10.

Jayakar, Pupul, 1992, *Indira Gandhi, A Biography*, Viking, Penguin Books India (P) Ltd.

Kadir Pethiyagoda, 2015, 'Modi deploys his cultural skills in Asia, Brrokings Institutions', June 1. Available at https://www.brookings.edu/opinions/modi-deploys-his-culture-skills-in-asia-2/ (Accessed on 12 December 2017).

Kaiser, Ejaz, 2016, 'Peace Unity ensure nations growth: PM', *The Hindustan Times*, January 12.

Kanwal, Shemina, Chaman, Vishaka, 2016, 'Rock on: French Prez was all questions', *The Times of India,* Chandigarh, January 25.

Karlekar, Hiranmay, 1998, *Independent India: The First Fifty Years,* ICCR, Oxford University Press.

Kasturi, Charu Sudan, 2015, 'Modi government plans Buddhism blitz in cultural diplomacy focus', *The Telegraph*, August 31.

KMAF, 2016, Kingston Multicultural Arts Festival 2016. Available at http://www.kipcouncil.ca/kingston-multicultural-art-festival- (Accessed on December 16, 2017).

Lada Guruden Singh, 'Haksar revisited: overhaul the Akademis'. www.narthaki.com/info/articles/art138.html (Accessed on December 20, 2017).

*Lok Sabha Report*, 1997, Second Report, Standing Committee on External Affairs, 1996-97, Eleventh Lok Sabha, April.

Madhumati, D.S., 2017, 'India launches satellite to help South Asian nations', *The Hindu*, May 5.

Maldives, Available at http://www.ndtv.com/india-news/maldives-water-crisis-india-transports-1-000-tonnes-of-fresh-water-to-male-709771 (Accessed on December 16, 2017).

MOC, 2011-12, Annual Report of the Ministry of Culture, New Delhi.

MOC, 2015-16, Annual Report of the Ministry of Culture, New Delhi.

MOC, 2016-17, Annual Report of the Ministry of Culture, New Delhi.

MEA 2015-16, Annual Report of the Ministry of External Affairs, New Delhi.

MEA Website, www.mea.gov.in (Accessed on December 16, 2017).

MFA, Sri Lanka, 2015, 'President returns after successful visit to India: 15-18 Feb.', February 18. Available at www.mfa.gov.lk/.../visits/...visits/5972-president-returns-after-successful-visit-to-india (Accessed on December 16, 2017).

Modi, 2015, Media Statement by Prime Minister with Japanese Prime Minister, New Delhi, December 12.

Modi, Chintan Girish, 2016, 'A new prescription for peace from India', *The Hindu*, January 18.

MYS, 2013-14, Annual Report of the Ministry of Youth and Sports.

MYS, 2014-15, Annual Report of the Ministry of Youth and Sports.

MYS, 2015-16, Annual Report of the Ministry of Youth and Sports.

Nadim, Farrukh, 2013, 'Nalanda University deserves place in World Heritage Sites: Salman Khurshid', *The Tribune*, February 13.

Nath, Damini, 2016, 'Indian and Australian Artistes collaborate for Sydney show', *The Hindu*, October 10.

*NDTV,* 2012: 'Shashi Tharoor: Soft power can make us a global power', December 4.

*NDTV*, 2014, 'Maldives Water Crisis: India Transports 1,000 Tonnes of Fresh Water to Male', December 7.

*New Delhi Times*, 2017, 'Football for Peace, Using Sports to Create a Better World', January 9.

Obama, 2014, 'President Obama extends warmest greetings for Diwali', October 22. Available at https://obamawhitehouse.archives.gov/.../2014/.../president-obama-extends-warmest-.. (Accessed on December 12, 2017).

*Odisha Sun Times*, 2016, 'Short Indian movies on Vietnam', February 21.

Pamphlet, ICCR, New Delhi.

Pande, Ira, 2012, 'Hard Power of Soft Diplomacy', *The Tribune*, July 1.

Pant, S B, 2017, 'Carrying forward the Koirala legacy', *ECS*, January 13.

Prashar, Sachin, 2014, 'Focus on States in Modi's diplomatic road map', *The Hindu*, August 17.

Patranobis, Sutirtho, 2016, 'India China need to strengthen people to people ties: Xi Jinping', *The Hindustan Times*, January 16.

*PBD,* 2009, Inaugural Address of Prime Minister of India, Pravasi Bharatiya Divas (PBD), New Delhi, January 7.

*PBD,* 2011, Inaugural Address of Prime Minister of India, Pravasi Bharatiya Divas (PBD), New Delhi, January 7.

Pillmarri, Akhilesh, 2016, '5 ways India can become a soft power', *The Diplomat*, July 6. https://thediplomat.com/2016/07/5-ways-india-can-become-a-soft-power-superpower/ (Accessed on 16 December 2017).

Prasad, KV, 2017, 'Oz charity — the Haat Mela way', *The Tribune*, December 4.

Prasad, S, 2016, 'Chola era idols in US custody belong to Villupuram Temple', *The Hindu*, January 23.

Prasar Bharti, 2017, 'Prasar Bharti hosts International Dance Festival in Hyderabad', *Asia News International (ANI)*, January 15.

Press Statement, 2017, Prime Minister Modi's Statement during the State Visit of Prime Minister of Australia to India, April 10.

Ruchi Varshnav, 2018, 'Sikhs of New York create Guinness record on Turban Day in Times Square', *India Times*, April 10.

Sahai, P S, 2002, 'Globalisation, Cultural Diplomacy and the Indian Ocean: An Indian Perspective', Paper presented at the Panjab University, Chandigarh, Nov.

Sahai, P S, 2009, 'India's Cultural Diplomacy in Southeast Asia', HCMC University, May 16-19.

Sarkar, Bidyut (ed.), 1968, *India and Southeast Asia*, Proceedings of a Seminar, ICCR.

S Ravi. 'Celebrating affinities and ties' *The Hindu*, October 23, 2017.

Satyanarayanan, S., 1968, 'Bollywood magic in Southeast Asia', *The Hindu*, October 14.

Saxena, Shoban, 2009, 'How to be a cultural super power', *The Tribune*, November 22.

Sharma, Anjana (ed.), 2013, *Civilizational Dialogue, Asian Inter-connections and Cross-cultural Exchanges*, ICCR & Manohar.

Shelly Bhoil, 2017, 'Indian metre, Brazilian echoes', Spectrum, *The Tribune,* December 10.

Shikoh, Dara, 2017, 'Conference on Dara Shikoh draws experts from 6 countries', *Business Standard*, April 25.

*Singapore Lecture*, 1994, Narasimha Rao, PV, 'India and the Asia Pacific: Forging a New Partnership', Institute of Southeast Asian Studies, Singapore.

Singh, Avtar, 2017, 'Singapore Youths renovating Singapore School', *The Hindustan Times,* December 11.

Singh, B P, 1998, *India's Culture: The State, The Arts and Beyond*, Oxford University Press.

Singh, Dr. Karan, 2013, Foreword in Sharma, Anjana (ed.), *Civilizational Dialogue, Asian Inter-connections and Cross-cultural Exchanges*, ICCR & Manohar.

Singh, Gurmukh, 2012, 'India's Soft Power Spreads', *The Tribune,* October 2.

Singh, Jasmine, 2016, 'Punjabi Dholl, the Brazilian Way', *The Tribune*, February 15.

Singh, Karan, 2006, 'Cultural diplomacy needs a big thrust, says Karan Singh', *The Tribune* September 24.

Singh, Rao Jaswant, 2016, 'Haryana govt to sign an MoU with ICCR to boost culture and tourism', *The Times of India*, January 29.

Singh, Shiv Sahay, 2018, 'Bangladeshi film festival begins in Kolkata', *The Hindu*, January 6.

Smita Sharma, 2018, 'Gentleman's game for a social cause', *The Tribune*, April 23.

Smita Sharma, 2018: 1, 'Slice of Uzbekistan in India', *The Tribune,* April 2.

Spectrum, 2017, 'Exchange values culture-education, *The Tribune*, May 28.

Sultan Sooud Al Qassemi, 2017, 'UAE's soft diplomacy brings nations together', *Gulf News,* March 7.

*Sunday Tribune*, 2017, 'Argument is acceptable, but not intolerance: President', April 2.

Suri, Navdeep, Recollecting Launch of Distinguished Lecture Series, Availablr at https://www.google.co.in/search?q=Navdeep+Suri%2C +Recollecting+Launch+of+Distinguished+Lecture+Series&oq=Nav deep+Suri%2C+Recollecting+Launch+of+Distinguished+Lecture+ Series&aqs=chrome..69i57.5740j0j8&sourceid=chrome&ie=UTF-8 (Accessed on 12 December 2017).

Swami Vivekanand, http://chicagovedanta.org/1893.html (Accessed on December 21, 2017).

Tagore, 2016, 'China releases first translations of Rabindranath Tagore's collective works', *Business Standard*, May 5.

Thapar, Romila (Ed.) 2000, *India – Another Millennium,*Penguin Books, New Delhi.

Thapar, Romila, 1998, 'Secularism: The Importance of Democracy' in

Karlekar, Hiranmay (ed.), *Independent India: The First Fifty Years*, ICCR, Oxford University Press.

Tharoor, Shashi, 2007, 'Leveraging soft power needs hard work', *The Tribune*, February 18.

Tharoor, Shashi. 2011, 'Indian Strategic Power: Soft', The Huffington Post, May 25. (http://www.huffingtonpost.com/entry/indian-strategic-powers-so b 207785. html? section=India. (Accessed on May 7, 2016).

*The Chicago Tribune*, 2013, Kathleen Hennessy& Christi Parsons, 'Obama opens up about race', July 20.

*The Financial Express*, 2017, 'Niagara Falls lit up in tricolor to mark India's 71st Independence Day', August 17.

*The Hindu*, 2005, 'Cultural Diplomacy, not a luxury: Karan Singh', Sept. 3.

*The Hindu*, 2013, 'Indonesia gifts US a Saraswati Statue', *The Hindu*, June, 10.

*The Hindu*, 2014, India, Australia share spaecial bond, Modi', November 16.

*The Hindu,* 2014:1, 'Modi raises Mansarovar Yatra route with Xi', July 11.

*The Hindu*, 2015, 'Peace, unity, reconciliation key to development: Modi', March 15.

*The Hindu*, 2018, 'Presence of Pakistan prompts Asia Cup to shift from India to UAE', April 11.

*The Hindu*, 2018: 1, '164-year-old Singapore temple reconsecrated', April 24.

*The Hindustan Times*, 2017: 1, 'Subodh Gupta, Bharti stay at Rashtrapti Bhavan', March 4.

*The Hindustan Times,* 2017, 'I watched Dangal, and liked it: Chinese President Xi Jinping to PM Modi', June 10.

*The Indian Express,* 2013, 'MEA parliamentary panel talks culture diplomacy', February 19.

*The Indian Express,* 2016, 'All for better ties: China-India Tourism year launched' Jan 13.

*The Indian Express,* 2016:1, 'French soldiers become first foreign military contingent at R-day parade', January 27.

*The Indian Express,* 2017. 'India-Pakistan Cultural exchanges should not fall prey to political relations', says Parliamentary panel', August 12. http://www.newindianexpress.com/nation/2017/aug/12/india-pakistan-cultural-exchanges-should-not-fall-prey-to-political-relations-says-parliamentary-pa-1641925.html (Accessed on December 12, 2017).

*The Indian Express*, 2017:1, 'I watched Dangal, liked the actors as well as the movie: Chinese President Xi Jinping tells PM Narendra Modi', June 10.

*The Korea Herald*, 2016, 'Korean Wave best tool for public diplomacy with US: diplomat', September 4.

*The Outlook,* 2017, '7th Delhi International Jazz Festival to kick off from Sept. 23', September 9.

*The Times of India* 2016, 'Indians in China form body to promote classical music', May 29.

*The Times of India, 2017*, 'Kennedy Centre receives $ 1 Million aid for Indian Cultural performances', November 26.

*The Tribune*, 2012, 'Shankar personified India's soft power', Dec. 13.

*The Tribune*, 2014. 'Grateful Britain recalls valour, sacrifices of Indian soldiers during World War-1', October 31.

*The Tribune*, 2014: 1, 'India sends drinking water to Maldives', December 5.

*The Tribune,* 2016, 'In Durban Cricket Museum by Indian-origin Historians', December 30.

*The Tribune* 2016: 1, 'Obama cites Sikhs to talk about strength of faith', February 6.

*The Tribune,* 2016: 2, 'Twitter helped Modi build tech-savvy image: Study', March 20.

Thussu, Daya & Ellen Frost, 2013, *Communicating India's Soft Power: Budha to Bollywood*, East-West Centre, Palgrave, MacMillan.

USC, https://uscpublicdiplomacy.org/story/five-global-leaders-fashion-diplomacy (Accessed on April 24, 2018).

USC, 2016,http://uscpublicdiplomacy.org/story/two-halves-one-whole-punjabi-mexican-dance (Accessed on April 26, 2018).

Varghese K George, 2017, 'The Diwali stamp has added to the charm'. *The Hindu*, October 18.

Varma, Pavan K, 2016, 'Global Village Is A Myth: Cultures still retain a stubborn opacity impenetrable to outsiders', *Times of India*, July 2.

Varma, Pavan, 2006, 'Soft Power', *The Tribune*, Oct. 7.

Vatsayan, Kapila, 2014, 'Culture: The crafting of Institutions in Independent India' in *Indian Democracy: Agenda for 21st Century*, Foreign Service Institute, New Delhi. Feb. 5.

Vice President 2016, Remarks by Vice President of India, Shri M. Hamid Ansari, at the inauguration of the Interfaith Conference at Malappuram, Kerala, January 12.

Website of Sangeet Natak Akademy. http://sangeetnatak.gov.in/sna/introduction/php (Accessed on December 20, 2017).

Wire, A B 2017, 'US diplomats sing Indian language poems to mark US-India friendship', September 22.

Xinhua, 2016: 'Xi congratulates on launch of 'Visit China Year' in India', Jan. 16.

Yadav, Deepak, 2016, 'Corbusier marvel vows Hollande' *The Times of Chandigarh*, January 25.

Yadav, Deepak, 2016:1, '$ 1 billion investment every year for India, Hollande', *The Chandigarh Times*, January 25.

# Section – II

# Framework, Structures and Instrumentalities of Indian Cultural Diplomacy

# Chapter – III

# Ministry of Culture's Role in Cultural Diplomacy

## Introduction

In this chapter, we would look at the assigned role of the Ministry of Culture (MOC) in cultural diplomacy. One of the mandates of this Ministry is 'promotion of international cultural relations.' International cultural relations mean the following (MOC 2014-15):

- Cultural Agreements and Cultural Exchange Programmes.
- Organisation of Festivals of India Abroad.
- Grant-in-aid to Indo-Foreign Friendship Cultural Societies.
- Schemes on International Cultural Relations.

MOC is mandated with the primary responsibility of 'preservation and conservation of the country's rich cultural heritage and promotion of art and culture.' The Ministry is also responsible for 'implementation of various UNESCO conventions in the field of culture and for inscribing world heritage sites.' The Ministry is also responsible for 'the protection, development and promotion of both tangible and intangible heritage and culture and also manages several knowledge resource centres.' It functions through two attached offices, six subordinate offices and thirty five autonomous organizations.

In this chapter, we would look at those areas, where it makes its direct presence in international cultural relations, namely Cultural Agreements, Festivals of India, Support to Indo-Foreign Friendship Cultural Societies and UNESCO. In another chapter, we would look at its Other Cultural

Bodies that are indirectly involved in areas impacting on cultural diplomacy.

The role and magnitude of Bilateral Cultural Agreements and Cultural Exchange Programmes (CEPs) would be studied and evaluated. How have cultural agreements and cultural exchange programmes made there under have operated?

What is our philosophy and approach on the organization of Festivals of India? Are these sporadically arranged or is there a pattern? Are there any variations in terms of content and organizational structure? What have been the results of such festivals and how do we evaluate their success?

## Cultural Agreements

### *An Overall Picture on Cultural Agreements*

India is of the view that cultural agreements perform a tripartite role as 'these help in the establishment of new relations, strengthening of old and historical relations and even for reorienting the relationship' (MOC 1985-86). India had signed 130 cultural agreements till July 12, 2015; the first agreement was signed with Turkey on June 29, 1951 and the last agreement was signed with Kyrgyzstan in 2015.

During the 1950s, India signed 8 agreements and another 9 agreements during the 1960s. 21 cultural agreements were signed until 1970; the number went up to 73 in 1985 (MOC 1985-86). At present, India has cultural agreements with 130 countries. There is, however, no pattern in the signing of the agreements, which could reflect India's preference for any country or region.

The largest numbers of agreements were signed during the 1950s and the 1960s, with the East European countries, namely, Poland (1957), Romania (1957), Czech Republic (1959), Hungary (1962) and Bulgaria (1963). Indonesia became the first country in Southeast Asia with which India signed the agreement in 1955. In South Asia, the distinction was achieved by Afghanistan, with which the agreement was signed in 1963.

In West Europe, the first such agreement was signed with Greece (1960), followed by France (1966), Metropolitan France (1966) and Germany (1969). In the Arab World, it was Egypt (1958), which was followed by Tunisia (1969). Other countries, with which cultural agreements were signed during the 1950s and the 1960s, include Japan (1956), Iran (1956) and Brazil (1962).

### *India's First Cultural Agreement with Turkey, 1951*

India signed the first cultural agreement with Turkey on June 29, 1951(Turkey, 1951). This Agreement was signed by Maulana Abul Kalam Azad, Education Minister. This has a preamble and 12 articles. The Preamble invokes the spirit of UNESCO. This Preamble formed a part of some of the later agreements, but has been largely missing in others. The emphasis was to promote relationship especially in the realm of science and education.

Article 1 deals with academic exchanges; Article 2 with student exchanges and Article 3 with training in the scientific, technical and industrial institutions. Article 4 deals with the establishment of cultural institutions; what is of significance is that it also defined cultural institutions, so as to avoid ambiguity on its interpretation. It defines these as 'educational centres, libraries, scientific institutions of an educational nature, and institutes for the promotion of art, such as art galleries and centres and societies and film libraries.'

Article 5 deals with cultural and intellectual exchanges and Art. 6 focuses on sports exchanges. Article 7 is an important article and is aimed at promoting understanding, with a view to ensuring that the text books did 'not contain any errors or misrepresentations about each other's country.' This is an important clause, as distorted presentation of history for political or other reasons, results in introducing biases in the minds of people, in particular the youth, which would stand in the way of promoting understanding. Article 8 provides for determination of equivalence of diplomas and degrees through periodical reviews. This is an essential prerequisite for any meaningful exchange of students and researchers.

Articles 9-12 deal with implementation. Article 9 mandates the authorities to ensure implementation; Article 10 provides for the Implementation Authority; Article 11 deals with ratification and Article 12 provides for automatic continuation of the Agreement, after its initial period of 10 years, unless any of the Parties gave a notice for its termination.

Article 10 is significant, as it provides for a unique implementation authority of a Special Commission in Turkey, comprising the Minister of Foreign Affairs and the Indian Ambassador and a similar one in Delhi, comprising the Minister of Education and the Turkish Ambassador. Such a provision exists only in India's Agreement with Indonesia. Was such a Body set up and how functional it was, is a matter for detailed scrutiny, as much is not known in the public domain.

### *Evolutionary Process of Cultural Agreements: Commonalties and Differences*

Do we see any pattern in the evolution of cultural agreements signed over the years? Are there any regional variations in respect of different regions, like South Asia, Western Europe, Central Asia or Southeast Asia? Does a common strain flow throughout these agreements or is there a country specific thrust?

Over the years, Cultural Agreements and Cultural Exchange Programmes (CEPs) have widened in scope and are 'exploring new avenues and are not restricted to the standard pattern of student, teacher, art exchanges' (MOC 1986-87). Many more areas of cooperation have been included, which include education, scientific cooperation, archaeology, heritage, mass media, sports etc.

To start with, a comparison with the agreement signed with Turkey in 1951 and with Kyrgyzstan, which is the latest agreement signed on July 12, 2015, would be appropriate. This agreement (Kyrgyzstan, 2015) is significantly different from that with Turkey; its points of congruency and differences are described below:

- In the preamble, role of the UNESCO is not recalled. The thrust, on the other hand, is on mutual recognition of 'the equal value of the national cultures'; facilitating 'mutual cultural enrichment', based on respect for 'ethno-cultural distinctiveness of each of them.' It thus seeks to promote 'cultural enrichment', while accepting 'cultural identity' and 'cultural diversity.' In fact, it is the heart and the soul of cultural diplomacy.
- It embraces a broader definition of culture, to comprise of 'culture, arts, youth, sports and mass media.'
- In the case of Agreement with Kyrgyzstan, the focus is on cooperation in protection, preservation and restoration of cultural heritage (Article 5) and return of cultural property (Article 4), which is missing in the case of Turkey.
- There is greater emphasis on cooperation among the youth in the Agreement with Kyrgyzstan.
- A significant departure is that there is no reference on the establishment of cultural institutions or ensuring the correctness of the materials in the text book or equivalence of degrees.

Similarly, there is no mention of an Implementation Machinery, unlike the high powered Joint Body comprising Minister and Ambassador as in the case of Turkey. Implementation, therefore, is left to the individual countries, which perhaps explains, why there is a low rate of implementation as commented by Ashok Vajpaye, former Joint Secretary in the Ministry of Culture (Ashok Vajpaye)[1].

***Is there a Common Template for Cultural Agreements?***

From the above we notice that India has not adopted a common template for a cultural agreement. It has broadly followed a country specific approach. An examination of a number of cultural agreements, however, reveals that these, however, still follow certain common norms and parameters. Some of these are listed below:

- Acceptance of a broader definition of culture, which would include 'art, culture, education, sports, public health and mass media (including films, TV, radio and press)' (Uganda, 1981).
- Facilitating the setting up of cultural institutions in the respective territories, which would mean 'educational centres, libraries, scientific institutions of an educational nature and institution for the promotion of art, such as art galleries, art centres, aid societies, film libraries and literary societies' (Iran, 1956).
- Setting up of an Implementing and Review Mechanism.
- Facilitating the setting up of Cultural Centres (Pakistan, 1998).
- Facilitating academic and youth exchanges and training.
- Ensuring that there is no misrepresentation of facts in the text books that could hurt other countries (Afghanistan, 1963).

There are, however, certain peculiar articles, which are either region or country specific. Some of these are enumerated below:

- To establish chairs in universities or other higher educational institutes and promote translation of books from Persian to Indian languages and vice versa (Iran, 1956).
- To show due deference to the respective Heads of each other's countries (ibid). This is an unusual clause, as it does not find place in other agreements.

- To ensure free movement of books through customs, with a caveat that such facility would not be extended to 'undesirable literature of an obscene, subversive or otherwise objectionable nature' (ibid). Implementation of this article could generate controversy, in case of differing interpretations, as the ultimate say would lie with the receiving State.
- To facilitate the setting up of cultural centres, through negotiation of an additional protocol (Pakistan, 1998).
- The Mass Media to help in contributing towards 'a better knowledge of their respective cultures and activities, by presenting 'different facets of the life and culture of the other party.' (Uganda, 1981)

***Review of Cultural Agreements with South Asian Countries***

In South Asia, India signed the first cultural agreement with Afghanistan in 1963. It has also cultural agreements with other countries; Bangladesh (1972); Sri Lanka (1977); Maldives (1983) Pakistan (1988) and Nepal (2004). India has no bilateral cultural agreement with Bhutan. Regarding Cultural Exchange Programmes (CEP), India has one with Sri Lanka for the years 2015-18, which was signed on 16 February 2015.

India signed two other agreements with Maldives on October 11, 2015. These relate to cooperation between the Foreign Service Institutes and the Ministries of Youth and Sports. The cooperation between the Foreign Service Institutes would help in significantly bridging the information gap, as diplomats are brought into contact with one another. Similarly, the Agreement on Youth Exchanges and Sports, although it is more in the sports arena, would help in bringing the new generation into contact with one another.

With Pakistan, India also has a Memorandum of Understanding between the Indian Council of Cultural Relations (ICCR) and the Pakistan National Council of the Arts (PNCA), which was signed on 31 December 1988. In the case of Pakistan, it is unusual to have a separate agreement between ICCR (India) and PNCA (Pakistan), where even normal flow through existing channels faces stumbling blocks.

There is no common template in these cultural agreements, although these, more or less, follow similar clauses for cooperation in the fields of art, culture and science. There is, however, difference of emphasis in the preamble. In the case of Afghanistan, it is on the age old cultural relations, while in the case of Bangladesh and Sri Lanka it is on the pursuit of the ideals of the Constitution of UNESCO. No such laudable objective is mentioned in the preamble to the Agreement with Pakistan.

All the agreements, however, embrace the broader definition of culture, which is more explicitly spelt out in the agreement with Pakistan, such as 'in the realms of art, culture, archaeology, education, mass media and sports.' These are permeated with the common desire to establish and develop closer cultural relations aimed at contributing towards a better knowledge of their respective cultures and activities in these fields.

A significant article is on avoidance of misrepresentation of facts in the text books, which first appeared in the agreement with Afghanistan and finds mention in agreements with other countries, more or less in similar language. Article 5 with Afghanistan reads: 'The two governments will encourage, as far as it has within their power, to ensure that textbooks prescribed for teaching institutions do not contain any errors or misrepresentations about each other's country.' It is a laudable objective, but difficult to realise in the absence of any joint credible implementation machinery. This, has, however, remained only on paper and a hollow commitment, as biases continue to exist in the text books.

### *Cultural Exchange Programmes with Sri Lanka and Bangladesh*

Cultural Agreements provide the umbrella for the pursuit of cultural exchanges. It is through Cultural Exchange Programmes (CEPs) that their implementation is ensured. Currently, we have one such CEP with Sri Lanka. It provides for cooperation under four broad heads – Performing Arts; Visual Art; Exhibitions, Museums, Libraries, Archives and Cultural Documentation; Archaeology and Publications and Professional Exchanges. What is of special significance is the emphasis on the teaching of Hindi and compilation of two anthologies of contemporary literature in Sinhalese and Tamil in Sri Lanka, to be translated and published in Hindi in India and contemporary Indian literature to be translated into Sinhalese.

India signed a Cultural Exchange Programme with Bangladesh on June 6, 2015 in Dhaka, for the Three Years' Period 2015-2017. It covers three broad areas: Part I (Art and Culture); Part II (Youth Affairs and Sports) and Part III (Media). Part I, which deals with Art and Culture, is the most comprehensive one. It has 23 operating paragraphs, which provide for exchange of 'dance, music, theatre, Jatra groups, art exhibitions, archaeological photographic exhibitions, mime shows, performing art groups, exhibitions and other cultural events' (Bangladesh, 2015). It thus provides for everything under the Sun, as far as Arts and Culture go.

Specific clauses deal with visits of scholars/academicians, joint research and archaeological conservation. Specific clauses also deal with Bangladesh's participation in the Triennale in India and of India in the Asian Art Biennial in Bangladesh; exchange of handicrafts exhibitions and children's paintings. Cooperation is envisaged among National Schools of Drama, National Museums, National Public Libraries, National Archives Bodies, Archaeological Surveys and Indira Gandhi Centre for the Arts (IGNCA). A para deals with publishing of an anthology of poetry/short stories/juvenile literature in Bangladesh and India.

Part II deals with 'Youth Affairs and Sports'. It has only one omnibus operating clause that deals with 'exchanging sports teams/coaches/ sports administrators in diverse disciplines'. It has, however, left out the implementation to the operational authorities, as mutually agreed upon by them.

Part III dealing with 'Mass Media' has eight operational clauses, providing for exchange of Radio and TV programmes on 'various facets of life and culture' and facilitating visits of journalists, radio and TV personnel. Other clauses deal with participation in International Film Festivals, organization of Film Weeks and training at regular courses. Clause 32 provides for distribution of films and television programmes on commercial terms.

CEP has a huge menu, but in practice there is limited media connectivity between the two countries. It is largely due to the fact that commercial factors do not work in favour of Bangladesh, given limited demand for their programmes in India. In our interaction with them, Bangladeshi participants at the conferences have openly voiced their concerns on this account. It has to be seen how we can provide for greater flow of information and ensure implementation of the CEP in its true form.

## Festivals of India

### *Philosophy Underlying Holding Festivals of India*

India has been a late entrant in the field of organizing Festivals of India. The concept owes its origin to the drive of the then Prime Minister Indira Gandhi and the genius of Pupul Jayakar, who gave a practical shape to turn this idea into reality. The first Festival of India was organized in UK in 1982, followed by USA and France in 1985 and Russia in 1987. These were mammoth affairs and in USA, it was spread over a year.

Such festivals were to be organized in countries which were considered important to us 'economically, politically and strategically' (Lok Sabha

Report, 1997). This philosophy still holds good. It is, however, not been fully put in to practice, as a certain amount of ad hocism has prevailed in the selection of venues (Niranjan Desai)[2].

There is now a renewed emphasis to make Festivals as an integral part of India's soft power. The underlying objective is stated below by the Ministry of Culture:

> "To help integrate India's soft power avenues into its external interchange, particularly harnessing and focusing on its spiritual culture and philosophical dimension to promote connectivity" (MOC, 2014-15).

Pupul Jayakar saw these as 'floating oil lamps in tiny boats on a river, for an instant to illumine the ripples on the water and the rapt faces of those that participate in the launching' (Singh, BP). The focus of these Festivals has been to project both traditional and modern India and to remove the stereotype of India as 'a fossilized monolith, a romantic and exotic land of maharajas, tigers, snake charmers, the Taj-Mahal and of course, grinding poverty' (Singh, BP).

Concerns are expressed over gap between conceptualization and implementation of Festivals. There is also divergence of views over the intended message and the message received in the host countries. Following remarks of Shashi Tharoor are pertinent in this regard:

> "India is highly visible at cultural shows around the world and ICCR is good at mounting festivals of India in foreign cities. What is important is that the message that really gets through is that of 'Who we are, not what we want to show" (Tharoor, Shashi, 2011).

***India's First Festival in UK, 1982***

Indira Gandhi saw the Festival of India in Great Britain as "the commencement of a major people to people dialogue." She felt that it was necessary to stretch out the hand of friendship to reach beyond the leaders and touch the minds of people in a world, where the minds of leaders were closed, as in the final analysis it is they who are history's moving force' (Jayakar, Pupul). It was a clear recognition of cultural diplomacy's role in generating people's power in the international arena.

The Festival was 'a germination and a new beginning, the coming together of young creative minds from India and Great Britain to dialogue through mutual concerns; through music, dance and theatre, exhibition of ancient art and contemporary artifact.' It was an attempt to project the authentic face of India – 'an ancient people with young minds, capable of answering the challenges of science and technology, of social change and democracy' (Jayakar, Pupul).

The Festival was inaugurated on March 22, 1982 at a concert at the Royal Festival Hall in London in the presence of The Prince of Wales and the Joint Patrons of the Festival – Prime Ministers of the United Kingdom and India. The curtain rose to the beat of the Ranjit Drum and to the Indian Presidential Guard, sounding a fanfare of trumpets. M.S. Subbulakshmi sang Bhajans in Sanskrit, Telugu and Hindi, followed by Ragmala on Sitar by Ravi Shankar, with Zubin Mehta conducting the London Philharmonic Orchestra.

The Festival had beautifully combined art with science, including a splattering of commerce. There was a display of classical Indian Art at the Hayward Gallery, which presented a magnificent thematic display of stone sculptures, bronzes, and paintings that were selected to illustrate the image of Man. At the Science Museum, an Indian exhibition of science and technology provided a glimpse of science in India, from the earliest years of its civilization to contemporary application of science and technological artefacts. A special sale of Indian products was organized at the Selfridges.

### *Festival in USA, 1985-86*

The success of the Festival of India in UK paved the way for holding similar festivals in other countries. The seed for holding the Festival of India in the United States was planted during the visit of Prime Minister Indira Gandhi to the United States in late July 1982. Her first meeting was with important cultural figures at the Metropolitan Museum of Arts in New York. She spoke on the success of the Festival of India in the United Kingdom, as she germinated the idea of holding a similar Festival in the United States. For her, the festivals helped in creating 'a new atmosphere that would create bridges of understanding and friendship amongst ordinary citizens' (Jayakar, Pupul). The holding of the Festival of India in the United States in the summer of 1985 was announced in the Joint communiqué issued before her departure for India.

Recounting the philosophy behind holding the Festival in USA, Pupul Jayakar, the Festival's principal organizer and an adviser on cultural affairs to Mrs. Gandhi, said that 'The Festival is intended to bring India alive to the people of the United States.' Elaborating further, she said, 'India is a country with a very ancient tradition that is still alive. There are people today producing objects with the same techniques and skills that were used a couple thousand years ago' (Jayakar, Pupul).

The primary focus was to also emphasize the less-known modern India. 'Besides the village life', Mrs. Jayakar said, 'there is also a new India of doctors and scientists and researchers. We hope to present a picture that it is possible for the two to coexist, and to show that technological revolution does not mean the end of the whole past' (McGill, Douglas C).

### *Features of Initial Mega Festivals in UK, USA, France and USSR*

The Festivals of India organised in UK, USA, France and USSR had certain common features, although these also had features that differentiated one from the other. These were part of a policy conceived by the then Prime Minister Indira Gandhi, who wanted to use Indian Art and Heritage to project India. The push for the festivals came from the top leadership; Reagan and Mrs. Gandhi's meeting in 1982 in Washington DC and Mrs Gandhi's meetings with Mitterrand and Gorbachev, later on.

The striking resemblance was that these were Mega in nature, conceived and implemented in grand design and spread over from six months to two years. Simon Mark described this programme of festivals as 'arguably the leading example in the post World War Two period of a common manifestation of state cultural diplomacy' (Simon Mark).

These festivals were spread over major cities across the countries and were not restricted to the capital cities alone. A wide range of activities were organised to cater to local interests. They were not focussed on the elite alone, but had certain features to reach out to the common man, such as the 'Aditi' Exhibition, built around life cycle.

These were also aimed at projecting a modern and secular India along with its heritage and composite culture. The commercial aspect, however, was largely missing, even though there were some mini efforts in inserting this element. This included organising exhibitions in Department Stores, like Selfridges in London and Bloomingdales in New York. All the Festivals received large attendance and good coverage in the local media.

Along with the above commonalities, there were marked differences also, in particular towards the focus of the festival in each country. The Festival in UK was nostalgic in nature, recreating the spirit of the 1947 Festival of India and celebration of joint bonds that existed between the two countries. It was also sharing of Art Objects, as British Museums and Galleries were flooded with India Art Objects acquired during the colonial days.

In the case of France, it was to remove misperceptions on India and also an effort on the part of India to become a part of its cultural milieu, as Paris is the cultural capital of the world. In the case of USA, it was about India Awareness and was intended 'to bring India alive to the people of the United States,' as stated by the then Prime Minister Rajiv Gandhi. In the case of USSR, it was a move to go beyond the friendship that existed between the governments and the people and move in the direction of development of commercial ties.

Furthermore, the Festival in USSR was the most opulent with a budget of US $ 20 million, as against USA, which had a budget of US $ 15 million, which included private contributions. In the case of USSR, it was a fully governmental venture; while in the case of other countries, it was in the nature of Public Private Partnership (PPP). Another factor that distinguished the Festival in USSR from others was the acceptance of the principle of reciprocity, as the USSR government agreed to launch its own Festival in India in 1988.

***Evolution and Growth of Festivals***

There is now a growing recognition in the Ministry of Culture (MOC) that these Festivals help in integrating 'India's soft power avenues into its external interchange,' particularly harnessing and focusing on its 'spiritual, cultural and philosophical dimensions' and promoting inbound tourism (MOC 2014-15).

The Ministry of Culture has now imparted a new vigour to the holding of Festivals of India (Mittal, KK)[3]. To give a thrust to holding these festivals it ensured adequacy of funds. The Standing Finance Committee of the Ministry approved budgetary estimates of Rs.430 million for holding such festivals for a period of three years from 2014-15 to 2016-17. FY 2016-17 can lay claim to be declared 'The Year of Festivals of India', as 23 Festivals were organised cutting across all the Continents; 11 in Asia, 7 in Africa and 5 in Europe.

Earlier, these Festivals had one-sided dimension. Now, these Festivals have acquired a two dimensional approach, with the focused countries/ regions, be it Russia, France, European Union, Australia, organizing Festivals in India also.

A number of countries are covered each year, as Festivals were organized in France, China, Canada, Spain and USA during 2010-11. In 2012-13, the primary focus was on Germany and the Festival was organized under the banner, 'Days of India in Germany 2012-13'. Mini Festivals were also organized in Brazil, Denmark, Iran, Kazakhstan, Russia and Saudi Arabia (MEA 2012-13).

'Namaste Festival' was organized in Belarus, Kazakhstan, Kyrgyzstan, Turkmenistan, Ukraine and Uzbekistan during 2014-15. Other Festivals organised in 2014-15 included '2nd Indo-Arab Cultural Festival' in Algeria and 'Celebrations of 180th Anniversary of Arrival of Indian Indentured Labour' in Mauritius. During, 2015-16, ICCR organized 'Namaste Russia'-a Festival of India in Russia and 'Year of India' in Nepal.

## Some Significant Festivals

In this part, we would briefly touch upon some festivals, which were either in the nature of entries into new territories or left an impact. These are narrated below:

### *Canada 2011*

The Year of India in Canada in 2011 did wonder as India came here in a big way to showcase 'its culture and traditional richness, treating Canadians to a surfeit of Indian classical music, folk traditions, food and what not' (Singh, Gurmukh 2010). Toronto also hosted the Indian Film Academy Awards (IIFA), an event that is Bollywood's biggest show held overseas. The Ministry of Overseas Indians (MOIA) also organized mini-Pravasi Bharatiya Divas (PBD) in Toronto.

The Indian bug also caught the Toronto International Film Festival (TIFF), which committed to focus itself on India. At its 37$^{th}$ film festival, it brought in a record number of 16 Indian or India-centric films. Sridevi's comeback film 'English Vinglish' was premiered at TIFF and she was hosted by the then Ontario Premier Dalton McGuinty, who is a fan of Bollywood (Singh, Gurmukh 2012).

### *Germany 2012-13*

'Days of India in Germany' Festival was organized in Germany from May 2012 – April 2013, marking both the anniversaries of the establishment of diplomatic relations. The Festival had four thematic strands – connecting cultures, connecting ideas, connecting minds and connecting capabilities.

### *Europalia 2013*

A tie-up between the Government of India and Europalia International culminated in Indian participation in Europalia Festivals. The India Festival was flagged off on 4 October, 2013. It was jointly inaugurated by the President of India Pranab Mukherjee along with The King and The

Queen of Belgium. The four-month long rich and diverse extravaganza showcased India's enormous and varied cultural wealth. Europalia is a major International Arts Festival, held every two years to celebrate one invited country's cultural heritage. During the 4-month Festival, ICCR sponsored 21 performing groups to showcase the diverse culture of India.

***Festivals of India in Peru and Cuba, 2013***

These festivals were held during October 25-31, 2013, in conjunction with the visit of the Vice President of India to these countries. These represented "major efforts for dissemination of Indian culture in Latin America" (MOC 2013-14). These Festivals comprised a Dance Festival, a Literary Festival, a Film Festival and a Food Festival. All the Festivals were inaugurated by the Vice President.

***Festival of India in China, 2014***

2014 was declared as the Year of India-China Friendly Exchanges. Programmes were organized in 14 cities under the banner, 'Glimpses of Indian Festivals'. A medley of events included classical dance performances, film festivals and food festivals. It was organized during 27 June to 13 July 2014 at Beijing, Kunming, Dali, Shenzhen and Shanghai. A key element was a Dance performance, 'Septakam', a septet of Indian Dances, showcasing seven major traditions, such as Bharatnatyam, Kathak, Kathakali, Odissi, Manipuri, Kuchipudi and Sattriya. It was choreographed by Madhavi Mudgal and music was composed by Madhup Mudgal.

***Australia 2016***

Confluence, Festival of India was held in Australia during August-November 2016. It consisted of 72 events performed by outstanding Indian cultural troupes and artists, across seven cities in Australia. Given its success and receptivity in Australia, it was decided to have its second edition during September-October 2017. Highlighting its importance, Dr. A M Gondane, Indian High Commissioner observed "Confluence essentially celebrates the vitality, credibility and the "soft power" of India's culture" (The Indian Down Under).

## Festivals of India Abroad in FY 2015-16

This year marks the beginning of a new stage, consequent to a policy shift in the approach of the Ministry of Culture (MOC), to refocus its attention on the holding Festivals of India abroad. It also looked more significant as attention was being paid to new destinations other than the normal beat, such as China, Russia, France or UK. These are briefly described below.

***Shahabat India-Indonesia***

The Festival of India was inaugurated on 13 March, 2015 at Prambanan Temple Complex, Yogjakarta. Indian artists from Charkula Art Academy, Mathura (India) performed the traditional folk dance on the theme of "Krishna and Radha", while the Indonesian artists performed the Ramayana ballet, which was enacted in the Ramayana International Festival in India in February 2015.

***Mauritius***

This Festival was launched at a gala inaugural ceremony on Friday 21 August, 2015 at the Indira Gandhi Centre for Indian Culture at Phoenix. Following the lighting of the ceremonial lamp and presentation of the Festival logo to the dignitaries, two very special inaugural performances kicked off the Festival of India - a Ramlila presentation by the famous Sri Ram Bharatiya Kala Kendra, Delhi and 'Nrityarupa', a composite presentation of classical dance forms, conceptualised by the prestigious Sangeet Natak Akademi.

The Festival of India in Mauritius, which continued till 1 November 2015, comprised a series of presentations of Indian performing arts by renowned artistes, including classical and folk dances & music, theatre, and even traditional puppetry. The Festival also included exhibitions on various cultural and educational themes, literary conferences and seminars, and film/documentary screenings. Besides showcasing Indian artists and performers, the Festival also presented artistic collaborations with Mauritian artists and organizations.

The 3rd World Urdu Conference was also organized under the umbrella of this Festival. A seven-member strong delegation of Urdu scholars/poets from the Sahitya Akademi took part in the Conference. The deliberations were followed by a cultural performance- Mehfil-e-Qawwali on 28th November, 2015.

***The Republic of Korea***

The Festival of India was inaugurated in Seoul at the Millennium Hilton on November 9, 2015. A 20-minute performance by the Drums of India group sponsored by the Ministry of Culture and a sponsor-supported Indian food festival was held at the inaugural event. The second performance in Seoul at Lotte Culture Hall, Yeongdongpo was held on November 10, 2015, where Drums of India Troupe was followed by an Odissi Dance Troupe, arranged by the Mission. The Drums of India Troupe also performed at the inauguration of India's first Cultural Centre in Busan on November 11, 2015 – India's Cultural Centre is the first standalone Cultural Centre in Korea's largest city.

### *Sri Lanka*

The Festival of India in Sri Lanka was launched on the 19th November 2015.The High Commission of India in Sri Lanka launched 'SANGAM' – the Logo for the Festival of India in Sri Lanka on 18 November 2015 in Colombo. It signified the confluence of cultures of India and Sri Lanka. The inaugural event of the Festival 'Nrityarupa' was organised at the most iconic venue in Colombo – the famed Neelum Pokuna Theatre, on 19 November 2015. Former President of Sri Lanka Chandrika Bandaranaike Kumaratunga was the chief guest at the inaugural event.

### *Mongolia*

The Festival of India in Mongolia was inaugurated in the Central Cultural Palace in Ulaanbaatar, capital of Mongolia on 7th November, 2015 coinciding with the celebration of the 60th anniversary of the establishment of diplomatic relations with Mongolia. The main event of the inauguration was "Drums of India" performed by a troupe of percussion artists from different parts of India. The function was very well attended and enjoyed with enthusiasm. The event received wide coverage in the print and electronic media.

### *Madgaskar*

The Festival of India was opened at Hotel Ibis in Antananarivo, Madagascar on 9 November, 2015. Around 300 invitees including high ranking officials in the local Govt, members of the Diplomatic Corps, members of the India Diaspora and persons of Malagasy and other nationalities attended the opening ceremony. The Festival continued till 15 November.

### *Egypt*

India by the Nile – Annual Indian Cultural Festival – March 30, 2015, MACIC, Cairo: The 3rd edition of this festival was launched by the Bollywood legend Amitabh Bachan at the India House. The event was organized by Teamwork Arts and supported by ICCR. This was followed by a screening of the film – Amar Akbar Athony and cultural event at the Pyramids – Return of the Legend.

### *Malaysia*

The Festival of India in Malaysia was inaugurated on 13 March 2015 by Datuk Dr. Ong Hong Peng, Secretary General of the Ministry of Tourism and Culture at the Petaling Jaya Civic Centre. 45 events were held in 100 days in all major cities during March-June 2015. A part of festivities was the Tamil Literary Festival held in Kuala Lumpur during April 3-5, 2015. The Festival showcased feast of Indian culture and art. The Festival culminated after the holding of the first ever International Yoga Day on June 21, 2015.

## Promotional Schemes under the Ministry of Culture

India is now placing increasing recognition on the role of cultural associations that exist abroad, which help in promoting cultural diplomacy. In fact, involvement of local associations has a multiplier effect in outreach, as they help in expanding and deepening contacts with local audiences and help in supplementing the work of officially sponsored programmes. To cite an example, note has to be taken of the exemplary role played by the Sutra Theatre in Malaysia, through its founder cum director, choreographer and dancer Ramli Ibrahim, a Malay Muslim, who has won worldwide acclaim for rendering Odissi Dance performances.

The Ministry of Culture promotes a number of schemes to provide connectivity with foreign countries through the medium of culture. Under its ***'Indo-Foreign Friendship Societies Scheme'***, it provides funding to Indian diplomatic missions to financially support local groups that are involved in promoting and holding Indian cultural activities in their respective countries. Under this scheme, each friendship society can be allocated funds annually up to a limit of Rs.5,00,000. The scheme was initially launched in the year 1981, but from 2011-12 onwards the funds are distributed through the diplomatic missions (MOC 2011-12). Since 2011, the Heads of Missions are the nodal points for disbursing grant. In special cases, this could be increased to Rs. 10,00,000. The annual grant amount has also increased over the years; so has been the spread of the scheme in various countries.

An amount of Rs. 29 million was disbursed during 2011-12 by 45 Indian Diplomatic Missions under this Scheme (MOC 2011-12,). A total amount of Rs. 115.59 million was sanctioned to 51 Diplomatic Missions as Grants-in-Aid during FY 2016-17. Although it is not a large amount, both cumulatively and individually, yet it has a tremendous psychological impact, in encouraging and spurring up the activities of local cultural associations. ICCR also has a similar scheme that supports local cultural associations.

Another scheme called, ***'Promoting International Cultural Relations'*** was launched in 2014-15, with the objective of 'disseminating and creating awareness, about various forms of Indian culture abroad' (MOC 2014-15). It has two components: firstly to financially assist Indian artists to showcase India's rich and diverse culture and secondly to encourage foreign artists to learn Indian culture in any form.

Another project called ***Indian Literature Abroad (ILA)*** was launched on January 16, 2010 by Prime Minister Manmohan Singh in Kolkata. This project focuses on translating Indian classics, contemporary writings and children's literature into six foreign languages viz, French, Chinese, Arabic, Spanish, English and Russian (MOC 2010-11).

## UNESCO and Cultural Diplomacy

UNESCO (United Nations Educational, Scientific and Cultural Organization) is the specialized agency of the United Nations. As its name suggests, it is charged with the responsibility for the maintenance of 'international peace and security', through 'wide diffusion of culture' and 'education of humanity for justice and liberty and peace' that are indispensable 'to the dignity of man and constitute a sacred duty, which all nations must fulfil in a spirit of mutual assistance and concern' as stated in the preamble to the UNESCO Charter.

India is a founder member of UNESCO and had been continuously elected to its Executive Board. The Ministry of Human Resource Development is the nodal Ministry, while India has a Permanent Representative based at the UNESCO headquarters at Paris. India subscribes to 19 Conventions of UNESCO that deal with natural and cultural heritage, education and intellectual property rights.

UNESCO plays an important role in the preservation of cultural heritage and promotion of pluralism that respects diversity. It is also a forum for promoting dialogue between different cultures and civilizations. The 'Idea of India' is, therefore, in line with the objectives of UNESCO. India also subscribes to the Convention for the Safeguarding of the Intangible Cultural

Heritage 2003 and the Convention on the Promotion and Protection of the Diversity of Cultural Expressions 2005.

UNESCO has also lent support to Indian institutions, like the Mahatma Gandhi Institute of Education for Peace and Development (Category I UNESCO Institute) and Regional Centre for Bio-technology (Category II UNESCO Institute), which have played an important role? UNESCO has also set up a group of 'Goodwill Ambassadors' to promote its objectives. In the past, Ambassador Madanjeet Singh was UNESCO's Goodwill Ambassador on Culture and he had authored a number of books.

## Ministry of Culture to be a Catalyst in International Cultural Cooperation

The Ministry of Culture (MOC) plays an important role in the arena of culture, but a limited role in cultural diplomacy. It primarily focuses on three areas: Cultural Agreements, Festivals of India and Grants-in-aid to Indo-Foreign friendship Societies. In this chapter, our primary focus was on two important instruments of cultural diplomacy: Culture Agreements and the Festivals of India.

Cultural Agreements are an important instrumentality, as these provide basic framework for the conduct of cultural diplomacy. The Agreements also serve another useful purpose, as these help in identifying not only areas ripe for cooperation, but also implementing agencies. It may, however, be mentioned that Cultural Agreements are not a prerequisite for cultural cooperation.

Cultural Agreements are broad in scope as these adopt a broader construct of the word 'Culture'. Our definition of 'Culture' in this Book is co-terminus with the same. The Agreements, thus, cover programmes under the areas of 'culture, arts, youth, sports and mass media'. These agreements do not follow a common template, as these are individually crafted, responding to the specific requirements of each country.

It is worth observing that India signed the first Cultural Agreement with Turkey in 1951 and in South Asia with Afghanistan in 1963. This is significant, as it reflected affirmation of India's desire to re-build and strengthen civilizational ties. As of 2016, India has 130 Cultural Agreements. These are spread all across the globe.

Around 50 percent of the Agreements lie dormant, as countries fail to timely sign a Cultural Exchange Programme (CEP) for administrative reasons or financial constraints. India is not alone, as globally speaking, fifty percent implementation rate is considered quite satisfactory. It is to fill these lacunae in implementation that MOC is now specifically focusing on the signing of CEPs and 15 such instruments were signed during 2015-2016.

Prime Minister Modi is paying special attention and has emerged as a catalyst in promoting cultural cooperation during his visits abroad. Cultural cooperation, therefore, emerges as an important component of Joint Statements issued during bilateral visits.

India was a late starter in launching Festivals of India abroad. The first one was in UK in 1982; followed by USA in 1985 and then in France in 1985 and USSR in 1987. These were Mega in nature, spread over a year or so and covered various types of activities. We are back in the festivals business with renewed vigour. A record number of 17 festivals were planned for 2016-17, five in Europe, seven in Africa and five in Asia.

Now Mini Festivals are being held in many countries and a number of such festivals were organized under the banner 'Namaste' in Belarus, Kazakhstan, Kyrgyzstan, Turkmenistan, Ukraine and Uzbekistan during 2014-15. 'Namaste' is the Brand that has been promoted by ICCR.

It is debatable whether the festivals succeeded in fulfilling their underlying philosophy of reaching out to people and taking the relationship beyond officials and the elite. They have been only partially successful in projecting a 'Modern India' along with glimpses of its cultural heritage. They create a splash, but the real ripple effect is missing, as there is no follow up. We still do not view festivals from a strategic perspective, although the Modi government would like these to emerge as instrumentalities of soft power.

The Ministry is also running a number of schemes to promote cultural connectivity with foreign countries. Under its 'Indo-Foreign Friendship Societies Scheme', it financially supports local groups that are involved in promoting Indian cultural activities through holding of events in their respective countries. The ambit of this scheme, which was launched in 1981, has been expanded; so has the package of financial assistance. It is still a paltry amount of Rs. five lakhs (US $ 8000) per annum per association.

An Annual Package of Rs. 115.59 million (US $ 2 million) for 51 countries is peanuts for India's outreach programme for global cultural connectivity and this needs to be enhanced. A positive feature of the Scheme is the involvement by the Ministry of Culture of the Head of Mission in this process, as they are our nodal points abroad. Apart from providing financial support, we have to consider how we can rope in these Bodies as our partners. We need to evolve suitable mechanism to build institutional level linkages, as such local involvement is essential for a successful cultural diplomacy initiative.

The Ministry of Culture may consider establishing Ambassador's Cultural Fund for mounting cultural activities by diplomatic missions, with the support of local cultural organizations. This is a practice followed by many countries. This would provide greater flexibility and speed in mounting cultural programmes locally. This could be tried on an experimental basis in some select Diplomatic Missions.

The Ministry has to be optimally involved in the area of cultural diplomacy. It needs to take a strategic view of the existing Cultural Agreements by reactivating existing Joint Review Mechanism. It also needs to evolve a strategic approach in selecting the sites for the holding of Festivals of India and could consider taking a leaf from Australia. Indian Diplomatic Missions need to be involved at the inception stages. Our cultural activities have to focus on sending a message of India's Diversity and Pluralism.

MOC has to energize various Cultural Bodies that are attached to it. This is the message that came out from the May 2014 Report of its High Powered Committee (HPC, 2014). This needs to be attended on a priority basis. While preparing Annual Action Plan for various Bodies, MOC should also include a component for international cultural cooperation.

There is also need for greater connectivity between the Ministries of External Affairs and Culture, rather than they working from their silos. Signing of a MOU between the Ministry of Culture and ICCR in 2016 was a step in the right direction, as this would bring about greater coordination and help in undertaking programmes on a cost-effective basis.

As stated earlier, International Cultural Cooperation is not a major part of MOC's activities. There are two options. It is for MOC to get more actively involved rather than playing a low key role and emerge as a 'Catalyst in International Cultural Cooperation'. If this is not possible for logistical or other reasons, then consider transferring this area of responsibility to the Ministry of External Affairs, as is the practice in many countries.

## Endnotes

1. Ashok Vajpaye, Author and Poet, Former Joint Secretary, Ministry of Culture, New Delhi. Response to a Questionnaire on September 24, 2015.
2. Niranjan Desai, Former Director General, ICCR, New Delhi. Interaction on December 15, 2015 in Delhi.
3. Mittal, KK, Additional Secretary, Ministry of Culture. Interaction on May 12, 2015 in Delhi.

## References


Afghanistan, 1963, India-Afghanistan Cultural Agreement, October 4. http://www.indiaculture.nic.in/sites/default/files/Cultural%20 Agreement/ 3.pdf (Accessed on 12 December 2017).

Bangladesh, Cultural Exchange Programme, 2015-2017, 2015, May 13. http://www.mofa.gov.bd/sites/default/files/Cultural%20Exchange %20Program%202015-2017.pdf (Accessed on 12 December 2017).

HPC, 2014, Report of the High Powered Committee on The Akademis and Other Institutions under The Ministry of Culture, May. http://www.indiaculture.nic.in/sites/default/files/hpc_report/HPC%20 REPORT%202014.pdf. (Accessed on 16 December 2017).

Iran,1956, India-Iran Cultural Agreement, December 1. http://www.indiaculture.nic.in/sites/default/files/Cultural%20Agreement/72.pdf (Accessed on 16 December 2017).

Jayakar, Pupul, 1992, *Indira Gandhi, A Biography*, Viking, Penguin Books India (P) Ltd.

Kyrgyzstan, 2015, India-Kyrgyzstan Cultural Agreement, July 12. http://www.indiaculture.nic.in/sites/default/files/Cultural%20Agreement/Agreement%20India%20and%20Kyrgyz.pdf (Accessed on 16 December 2017).

Lok Sabha Report, 1997, https://en.wikipedia.org/wiki/11th_Lok_Sabha, (Accessed on 12 December 2017).

*Lok Sabha Report,* 2016, Thirteenth Report of the Committee on External Affairs, November 23. 164.100.47.193/lsscommittee/External%20 Affairs/16_External_Affairs_13.pdf (Accessed on December 15, 2017).

McGill, Douglas C., 1984, "Festival of India' is set for the U.S. In 1985-86', *New York Times*, July 14.

MEA1985-86, Annual Report of the Ministry of External Affairs, New Delhi.

MEA 2012-13, Annual Report of the Ministry of External Affairs, New Delhi.

MOC 1985-86, Annual Report of the Ministry of Culture, New Delhi.

MOC 1986-87, Annual Report of the Ministry of Culture, New Delhi.

MOC 2010-11, Annual Report of the Ministry of Culture, New Delhi.

MOC 2011-12, Annual Report of the Ministry of Culture, New Delhi.

MOC 2013-14, Annual Report of the Ministry of Culture, New Delhi.

MOC 2014-15, Annual Report of the Ministry of Culture, New Delhi.

MOC 2015-16, Annual Report of the Ministry of Culture, New Delhi.

Pakistan, 1998, India-Pakistan Cultural Agreement, December 31. http://www.indiaculture.nic.in/sites/default/files/Cultural%20 Agreement/214.pdf (Accessed on 16 December 2017).

Simon Mark, 2008, 'A Comparative Study of the Cultural Diplomacy of Canada, New Zealand and India', The University of Auckland. https://researchspace.auckland.ac.nz/bitstream/handle/ 2292/ 2943/ 02 whole.pdf?sequence=9 (Accessed on 12 December 2017).

Singh, B.P., 1998, *India's Culture, The State, The Arts and Beyond*, Oxford University Press.

Singh, Gurmukh, 2010, 'India-Canada ties to see boost in 2011', *Two Circles*, December27.http://twocircles.net/2010dec27/232793.html (Accessed on April 24, 2018).

Singh, Gurmukh, 2012, 'India's Soft Power Spreads', *The Tribune*, October 2.

Tharoor, Shashi, 2011, 'Indian Strategic Power: Soft', *The Huffington Post*, May 25.

The Indian Down Under, http://www.indiandownunder.com.au/2017/09/back-again-confluence-a-festival-of-india-edition-2-from-september-23-to-october-29-2017/(Accessed on May 1, 2018).

Turkey, 1951, *India-Turkey Cultural Agreement*, June 29. http://www.indiaculture.nic.in/sites/default/files/Cultural%20Agreement/231.pdf (Accessed on 12 December 2017).

Uganda, 1981, India-Uganda Cultural Agreement 1981. November 24. http://www.indiaculture.nic.in/sites/default/files/Cultural%20Agreement/144.pdf (Accessed on 12 December 2017).

# Chapter – IV

# ICCR and its Instrumentalities

## Introduction

Indian Council for Cultural Relations (ICCR), set up in 1950, under the administrative control of the Ministry of External Affairs (MEA) has been designated as the nodal agency for the pursuit of India's cultural diplomacy. ICCR's objectives, as defined in the Memorandum of Association are as follows (ICCR):

- 'To participate in formulation and implementation of policies and programmes relating to India's cultural relations with other countries;
- To foster and strengthen cultural relations and mutual understanding between India and other countries;
- To promote cultural exchange with other countries and peoples;
- To establish and develop relations with the nationals and international organisations in the field of culture; and
- To take such measures as may be required to further these objectives'.

There has remained 'a strong connectivity between these four, unchanged, MOU objectives and the major part of the ICCR's activities' (Simon Mark). ICCR, therefore, has the "twin task of promoting and interpreting abroad Indian culture in its widest sense as well as establishing, reviving and strengthening cultural ties between India and other countries" (Bandhopadhyaya). The ultimate objective is to foster cultural connectivity between India and other countries and it adopts all such measures as may be required to further its objectives.

ICCR is, therefore, expected to play a role, both for the formulation and the implementation of cultural diplomacy, as it enhances mutual understanding through cultural exchanges. The formulation part, however, is largely missing, as there is no all-embracing policy on cultural diplomacy.

The activities of ICCR are broadly divided into 'Academic and Intellectual; Arts and Culture and Other Activities' (MEA 2015-16). Under the rubric of 'Academic and Intellectual' fall activities, such as administration of scholarships to foreign students; establishment of Chairs of Indian Studies; organization of seminars and conferences and award of fellowships.

Under the rubric of 'Art and Culture', are grouped the activities of cultural centres abroad, outgoing and incoming cultural troupes and holding of exhibitions abroad and India. Under the sub-head, 'Other Activities" are included diverse activities like the promotion and propagation of Hindi, publication of books and journals and presentation of artefacts, holding of annual memorial lectures. These are briefly described and covered under specific heads.

## International Scholarship Scheme

ICCR is the nodal point for administering various scholarship schemes for undergraduate, post graduate and doctoral programmes in various fields. These include not only art and culture and humanities, but are also available for professional courses in engineering, pharmacy, accountancy, business administration and management. It annually provides for around 3000 scholarships. Thrust of the Scholarship Scheme is towards developing countries, in particular, India's neighbours (ICCR 2011-12). There is no change in the mandate since then.

At any given time, therefore, around 6000 scholars are under the wings of ICCR. 35 per cent of the scholarships are offered under its own Scheme, while the remaining around 65 per cent are offered by MEA and other organisations. During 2015-16, ICCR operated 25 scholarship schemes, which it administers on behalf of other governmental agencies. ICCR offered 3339 scholarship slots for foreign students under various schemes during 2015-16 (MEA 2015-16). 50 foreign scholars are learning Indian dance and music in India under 'Guru-Shishya Parampara'.

How wide is the spread of foreign students into universities in India? In answer to a Parliament Question, Minister of State for External Affairs Gen V K Singh revealed that 6252 foreign students were studying in 51 educational institutions, under ICCR's scholarship schemes as on

December 4, 2014 (Business Standard, 2014). Full details are given in Annexure II, while the names of the institutions, where there were more than 100 students were as follows:

| | |
|---|---|
| JNTU, Anantpur | 199 |
| NIT Warangal | 129 |
| Osmania University | 970 |
| Panjab University | 262 |
| Gujarat University | 184 |
| NIT Silchar | 103 |

The offer in 2015-16 was twice the number of 1800 scholarships offered to 75 countries in 2000-01 (ICCR, 2000-01). 139 countries have now come under the sweep of this Scheme. As against 3339 slots, only 2308 were accepted, representing a utilization rate of 70 per cent, which has been the overall acceptance rate over a number of years.

Out of 3339 scholarships, 1000 are for Afghan nationals and 900 for students from African countries. Scholarships are also earmarked for South Asian countries under various schemes, with 200 reserved for Bangladesh, 64 for Nepal, 60 for Sri Lanka and 20 each for Maldives and Bhutan. ICCR also offers 100 scholarships annually for training in Music and Dance. It also operates around 70 scholarships for the study of Indian Traditional Medicinal Systems, which is a new area of study on offer (ICCR 2015-16).

A special scheme for Afghan students has been in operation since 2009, starting with an offer of 675 scholarships per annum (ICCR 2010-11). At present, these are in the range of 1000 scholarships for Afghanistan, which are fully availed of by the Afghanistan Government. The Presidents of Afghanistan have lauded India's support; the former President Hamid Karzai had himself studied at Shimla in India. ICCR also administers many other scholarship schemes on behalf of other governmental agencies. ICCR scholars are studying in 18 States in India in over 120 institutions, including in IITs and NITs.

ICCR is fully cognizant of the need to ensure that foreign students are not only provided academic facilities, but are also exposed to India and its culture and people. To achieve these, ICCR undertakes various welfare measures and also organises other activities and programmes, including lectures by eminent Indians. Cultural events, summer and winter camps are organised, to give foreign scholars an opportunity to explore and know India. All these activities help students in getting an understanding of India's rich and varied cultural heritage and its industrial and scientific capabilities. ICCR organized 12 summer camps during May-June 2015 and 12 winter camps during December 2015-February 2016. This is the pattern that is largely followed each year.

An International Students Festival was organised in Delhi in November 2015 on the occasion of Maulana Azad's birth anniversary. Students Festivals are also organised annually for foreign students in various cities by ICCR's Regional Offices, where foreign students present spectacles of their countries. The author has attended such festivals at Chandigarh. Interaction of foreign students is also organised with the External Affairs Minister and Governors in the respective States (Rajasekhar, C)[1]. Indian Missions abroad are encouraged to establish ICCR Alumni groups and many have already been established.

ICCR organized a conference on 'Higher Education in India for Foreign Students' on March 21-22, 2016. This was the first of its kind organized by ICCR, with a view to evaluating the existing scholarships schemes as well as to promote India as a destination for higher education. The participants included all the stakeholders in higher education. The author also participated in this conference at the invitation of ICCR. A number of Ambassadors also attended the inaugural session. The conference was inaugurated by the then Human Resource Development Minister Smriti Irani, who gave the message on India becoming a destination of higher education as it was in a position to offer quality education at competitive fees.

The conference was built around three main themes – Scope for Higher Education in India for foreign students; Challenges in administering scholarships and Foreign Students Welfare. How do we interest foreign students in undertaking post-graduate courses for study became the main point for discussion? Similarly, how foreign students from the developed countries could be motivated to study in India? The need for India taking steps in promoting itself as a 'Destination' was suggested. Suggestions were also made to sensitize students on India's cultural heritage. On the other hand, the concern of the Ambassadors was on the need of streamlining the procedures in administering scholarships.

## Cultural Centres

Like many other countries, ICCR has also taken resort to setting up Cultural Centres abroad. The focus of these Centres is 'to establish, revive and strengthen cultural relations and mutual understanding' and to 'promote awareness and appreciation of India's composite cultural heritage abroad' (ICCR 2011-12). This still remains the primary focus.

As on March 2016, ICCR had 35 full- fledged Cultural Centres and one sub-Centre abroad. ICCR opened two new Culture Centres – in Busan and Sydney in 2016. The number of Centres had more than doubled from 15 Centres in 2000-01. These Centres are actively promoting 'India's soft power abroad through a wide range of activities, including dance, music, theatre, yoga, Hindi language, talks, exhibitions, conferences and seminars' (MEA 2015-16).

What is important is not only the quantitative growth in numbers but the emphasis on bringing about a qualitative change in the functioning of these Centres. It is to project 'Modern India' and not only 'the rubric of exotica and mystique', associated with Indian culture, as former Director General Pavan Verma puts it, 'What is that makes India and Indians tick?' (Varma, Pavan, 2006).

For Dr. Suresh K. Goel, the then Director General of ICCR, the focus was to convert these Centres into 'hubs' of cultural activity, where India meets with other cultures and not to use these as 'islands of Indian culture alone'. Centres have started undertaking new activities like 'Fusion Music events, Book Launches, Kavi Sammelans etc. These Centres are seen as embodiment of India's soft power, in keeping with ICCR's efforts to turn these in to 'hubs for promoting Indian Culture' (MEA 2013-14).

The first Indian Cultural Centre was set up at Georgetown (Guyana) in 1972. This was followed by another in Paramaribo (Suriname) in 1978 and Suva in Fiji. India had only three Cultural Centres till the 1970s. Three more Centres were added in the 1980s. Nine were added in the 1990s. Till 2000, India had only fifteen Cultural Centres. 2010 can be called the 'Year of the Cultural Centres' as during that year alone eight new Centres were set up, followed by another 4 in 2011.

The primary focus of the initial Cultural Centres was to provide connectivity with the Indian Diaspora and meet their cultural needs on Indian classical dance and music. While Guyana and Suriname have India based teachers, Fiji has only local teachers. Yoga is also taught in all these Centres, while

Hindi is taught in Guyana and Fiji. It is, however, interesting to note that the Cultural Centre in Port Louis, Mauritius was opened only in 1988; the reasons for such a delay are not known. Surprisingly there is no Hindi teacher; Bhojpuri is the language of the vast majority of Indians, which supports Bhojpuri music and films.

It is strange that India was rather a late starter in setting up Cultural Centres in South and Southeast Asia, which should have been the areas of primary focus. Apparently, India was not politically at the same wave length and there were concerns over Indian connectivity till early 1980s. The first Cultural Centre was opened in Jakarta in 1988 and another in 2004 in Bali, Indonesia. Among the other Southeast Asian countries, India has Cultural Centres in Thailand (2009), Kuala Lumpur (2010) and Myanmar (2010). The author was not in favour of opening a Cultural Centre in Malaysia during his posting as High Commissioner, as it was more cost-effective to provide support to myriad cultural associations that were promoting Indian culture and heritage.

The first Cultural Centre in South Asia was set up in Colombo (Sri Lanka) in 1998. This was followed up with the setting up of Centres in Kabul (Afghanistan) in 2007. This was followed up with Centres in Kathmandu (Nepal) in 2008; Dhaka (Bangladesh) and Thimpu (Bhutan) in 2010; while the centre in Male (Maldives) was opened in 2011.

In East Asia, the first centre was set up in Beijing (China) in 2008, followed by Tokyo (Japan) in 2009 and also Seoul (South Korea) in 2009. In West Asia, there is only one Centre in Cairo (Egypt) which was set up in 1992. In Central Asia, the first two Centres were set up in Astana (Kazakhstan) and Tashkent (Uzbekistan) in 1994. Another centre was set up in Dushanbe (Tajikistan) in 2002.

In Africa, the first Centre was set up in Mauritius in 1988. This was followed up by the setting up two Centres in South Africa in 1993 at Durban and Johannesburg. Another centre was set up in Dar-e-Salaam in 2010.

In Western Europe, the first centre was set up in Berlin (Germany) in 1990. This was followed by another in London (United Kingdom) in 1998 and at The Hague (Netherlands) in 2011. In East Europe, the first centre was set up in Moscow (Russia) in 1989, followed by Budapest (Hungary) and Prague (Czechia) in 2010.

The first two Indian Centres were set up in the Americas at Georgetown (Guyana) in 1972 and Paramaribo (Suriname) in 1978 and the Port of Spain (Trinidad and Tobago) in 1994. In Latin America, the first centre was set up in Mexico City (Mexico) in 2010 and Sau Paulo (Brazil) in 2011.

The period during the years 2009-2011 was the most prolific in terms of setting up Centres, when 15 new Centres were opened, doubling the number that existed till 2000. This reflected a shift in India's approach to Cultural Diplomacy, resulting in increased focus on two major areas - Chairs of Indian Studies and Cultural Centres.

One of the priority for Karan Singh, when he took over as President in 2006 was to set up more Centres in Europe, as then there were only three Centres in Russia, Germany and UK (Misra, Satish). The focus thus shifted to Western Europe, as earlier it was left in the hands of private groups. Special funds were provided to ICCR by the government, which now stand frozen, resulting in standstill on the opening of new Centres or maintenance of old Centres. Lok Sabha's Standing Committee on External Affairs in its 13th Report highlighted the need for early opening of Cultural Centres in Paris and Washington DC (Lok Sabha, 2016).

The then President, ICCR, Karan Singh observed on the significance of these Centres in these words, "They are extremely popular with not only local population but also become links for the NRI children" (Misra, Satish). The focus, therefore, was on both-local population and Indian Diaspora.

Geographically speaking, there are 20 Cultural Centres in Asia, five in Europe, four in Africa and five in Latin America. A typical centre is rather small, headed by a Director, who belongs either to the ICCR cadre or is on deputation from MEA. There is very limited infusion at the level of professional experts. A Centre has a complement of three to four India-based teachers – in classical dance, music, Hindi and yoga.

Locally recruited teachers and staff are now being increasingly used to cut down on costs. Seventy per cent of the budget is used for administrative purposes and it therefore leaves a nominal budget of around 30% for the cultural activities. Unlike foreign Cultural Centres, Indian Cultural Centres do not raise funds from teaching or its other activities, like the British Council, Alliance Françoise.

Earlier, the focus of the Centres was on Indian Diaspora but now it is equally to reach out to the local persons. In programming also, there is a shift, as the focus is on combining 'heredity with modernity'. A partnership approach has also added another dimension, as it results in not only cutting the costs, but also helps in providing better outreach to the local audience. The Centres are, therefore, attempting to turn into 'cultural hubs', as they move out of the straight jacket of teaching classical music and dance.

## A Peep into the Activities of Cultural Centres

Data has been compiled from the regular monthly activities of some of these Centres, to provide you with a glimpse of their normal activities undertaken by some of these. It is still more of the same usual pattern. Occasionally, they break some new ground. Their activities for a typical month are as follows:

**South Korea.** South Korean students, along with dance teachers, presented a colourful reception in honour of EAM on December 28, 2014.

**The Nehru Centre, London.** An evening of ghazals and light classical music by Ms. Rita Ganguly was organized on 3 November 2014, to mark the birth centenary of the legendary Begum Akhtar.

**Maldives.** ICC Male organized a painting competition on the occasion of Children's Day on 14 Nov. 2014.

**Hungary.** Cultural Centre at Budapest organised ICCR Day on 18 November 2014. This Day falls on 11 November to commemorate the birth anniversary of Maulana Abul Kalam Azad. On this Day, Ambassador Malay Mishra launched the India Alumni Association for Hungary.

**China.** ICC China organized a Bollywood Performance at Lanzhou on 1 November 2014. This was jointly organised in collaboration with the Cultural Department of the Gangzu Province.

ICC Beijing organized Yoga Symposium on 13 March 2015 at the Embassy Auditorium, which was attended by 70 experts from 35 different yoga institutes. The aim was to encourage the yoga institutes to celebrate the first International Day of Yoga on 21 June 2015.

**Egypt.** The Centre organised Bollywood Extravaganza, 'A Tale of Love, Passion and Revenge', at the Cairo Opera House on April 1-3, 2015 and at the Syed Darwish Theatre, Alexandria from 6-8 April 2015.

**Surinam.** The Centre at the Port of Spain presented a Video Show on Yoga in collaboration with the Ashtang Yoga Society on 24 March 2015. This was edited by a local TV network Sankhya TV for telecast on local TV channels.

**Fiji.** Cultural Centre at Suva celebrated 'Holi' with gusto, with the multi-racial community in Fiji on 5 March 2015.

**Netherlands.** The Gandhi Centre at The Hague organized a cultural programme 'Rangras' on 13 March 2015.

**Tanzania.** ICC Dar-es-Salaam released two books – Tales of Panchatantra and Swami Vivekananda – authored by Gautam Ghosh at a ceremony held on 30 March 2015.

A number of cultural centres have mounted activities jointly with local bodies or other diplomatic missions in areas of mutual interest. Here is a bird's eye view on such activities in a particular month.

**Durban, South Africa.** An event to mark the 154th year of the arrival of Indians in South Africa was organized by ICC Durban on November 12-16, 2014. The function followed the unveiling of the Peace Pillars in Phoenix.

**International Tea Festival in Kazakhstan.** ICC Astana and Tea Board participated in the International Tea Festival at the Eurasian National University, Astana, which was held on 28 November, 2014. The Festival ended with a performance of Indian dance. This event was jointly organized by India, China, Turkey and South Korea to highlight 'the traditions of tea making and drinking in these countries'.

**South Korea.** Diplomatic Corps Charity Concert was held on December 16, 2014 at Seoul and was organized by the Ministry of Foreign Affairs (MFA) and the Diplomatic Corps. ICC dance teacher Dheerendra Tiwari showcased five Indian art forms.

**China.** Beijing International Film Festival was organized in March-June, 2015, which included the screening of Hindi movies NH10, Kannada movies Attchannu Mattu Kanaja, Titli, The Voyage Within (Bodhon), Elizabeth Pilgrimage (Elizabeth Ekadashi) and The Fort (Killa).

**Nepal.** Swami Fateh Krishna Sharma gave 'Raasleela' Performance on December 12, 2014. This function was jointly organised by the embassies of India, Russia, Bangladesh and Secretary General SAARC Arjun Bahadur Thapa.

## The Chairs of Indian Studies

ICCR had 70 Chairs of Indian Studies as on November 30, 2015. The purpose of the Chairs is 'not only educating foreign students abroad India, but also 'to become a milieu around which Indian Studies could develop in academic institutions abroad' (ICCR, 2011-12). These Chairs also 'develop scholarly interaction with the academics of that country and assist in disseminating information and a better appreciation of various India related issues' (ICCR 2014-15).

The Chairs are expected to contribute to connectivity on a long-term basis. 27 out of 70 Chairs are for the teaching of Indian languages (20 Hindi Chairs, 4 Sanskrit Chairs; 2 Tamil Chairs and 1 Bengali Chair). The remaining Chairs cover other India related subjects. 41 percent of the Chairs are for Language Studies, with 29 percent for the Study of Hindi.

Besides the Chairs abroad, ICCR also operates two Chairs in India. The Nelson Mandela Chair is permanently based at the Jawaharlal Nehru University (JNU), Delhi and is open to scholars from Africa. The second, The South Asian Association for Regional Cooperation (SAARC) Chair rotates between various universities in India. Scholars from SAARC countries are invited to hold this Chair. Presently, it is located at the Indian Council for Agricultural Research (ICAR), Delhi.

These Chairs are emerging as an important vehicle of cultural diplomacy. Here again there is also an increase in the number of Chairs, from 17 Chairs in 2000-01 to 91 in 2011-12. 30 new Chairs were created in 2010-11 and 17 additional in 2011-12. These Chairs cover languages and other aspects of Indian Studies in Universities abroad.

The Years 2011 and 2012 were the high growth period and could be dubbed as 'The Years of Indian Chairs'. Indian response was to a spurt of interest on India, at the level of governments and academic institutions. The number of Chairs touched a peak at 101 Chairs in November 2013. Later, ICCR had to abolish 24 Chairs due to budgetary constraints. Furthermore, 12 Hindi Chairs were transferred to the budget of the Hindi Section in MEA. The number thus came down to 65 by March 31, 2014. The number of Chairs stood at 70 in March 2016.

A noticeable feature in the case of location of such new Chairs was their preponderance in the developed countries, with 7 in Germany, 4 in UK,

4 in USA, 3 in Canada, 2 each in France, Denmark, Sweden and Japan. Among the other countries, China has 5 Chairs; while there are 3 in Poland, 2 each in Russia, Indonesia, Thailand and Trinidad and Tobago. Chairs on Tagore Studies were also established in Bangladesh and China during the year 2011-12.

The focus of the new Chairs was on contemporary Indian studies, although some continue to focus on Indian culture, Hindi and Sanskrit. Professors are also encouraged to perform 'outreach activities', by joining hands with local institutions in also organizing programmes, outside their Residence University/Institution.

## Connecting with Leadership and the Academia

ICCR runs a number of programmes; the most prominent and prestigious one is ***' Distinguished Visitors Programme'*** under which it hosts eminent personalities, distinguished writers, scholars, opinion-makers, academics, intellectuals and academics from abroad. Under this programme, leaders are invited to share their experiences and interact with their counterparts, which results in mutually beneficial exchange of views on topics of common interest.

During the Financial Year 2015-16, ICCR hosted seven distinguished visitors from Latvia, Tunisia, Nepal, Trinidad and Tobago and Namibia, which included former President Sam Nujoma. Under another programme, Academic Visitors Programme, it hosted 10 prominent academicians from Ethiopia, Greece, Kazakhstan, Japan, Germany, Poland, Malaysia and the United States. In 2013-14, ICCR hosted only 3 eminent personalities (ICCR 2015-16).

Under its ***'Outgoing Visitors Programme'*** in 2015-16, the Council sponsored/provided travel grant to 24 participants from India to Azerbaijan, Bhutan, , Canada, Mauritius, Spain, Thailand, UK, and USA. It sent 18 eminent scholars during 2014-15. During 2013-14, ICCR sponsored 15 visits.

ICCR also provides for Senior and Junior Fellowships. During 2015-16, it accepted four senior fellows (two from UK, one each from Russia and the Czech Republic) and two junior fellows, one each from Nepal and Russia. In 2013-14, 2 junior fellows from Iran and Slovenia and 2 senior fellows from Indonesia and Spain received grants. In 2013-14, it invited 5 academics also from Bangladesh.

Academic exchanges under ICCR are on a modest scale as Rs.25.77 lakhs was incurred and it formed an insignificant part of the ICCR's budget for FY 2015-16. In fact, even this paltry amount was less than Rs.28.49 lakhs for FY in 2013-14, although a marginal increase from Rs 20.20 lakhs in FY 2014-15.

## Conferences and Seminars

Organization of Conferences and Seminars has become another important part of the activity of ICCR. It achieves this objective through lending support to various academic institutes/universities in India, by encouraging them to organize conferences/seminars/ symposiums on culture and related subjects in India and abroad.

The year 2011 was the year of Tagore and Buddhism, as India strove to revive interest in the study of Tagore and Buddhism. Three conferences on Buddhism were organized in Singapore, Taiwan and Vietnam, while other three were on Tagore and held in Nepal, Russia and Vietnam.

The year 2013 was 'The Year of Swami Vivekananda' and conferences were held in Argentina and Australia. The year 2015 was the 'The Year of Yoga' and 2016 was the ' The Year of Ambedkar'.

ICCR also organizes a number of important international conferences in India on cultural diplomacy related themes. Some of the important conferences were as follows:

- Interfaith Conference on 'World Religions: Diversity Not Dissension' in New Delhi, March 7-9, 2013.
- 'The Relevance of Traditional Cultures for the Present and the Future' in New Delhi, March 24-26, 2014.

During the years, viz. 2014-16, ICCR paid special focus on organizing a number of conferences as well as extending support to universities/ other organizations that organized conferences on matters of interest to ICCR. During the last two years, viz. 2014-16, following conferences were organized by ICCR in India:

- International Conference on 'Shared Heritage as New Variables in the Indo-Korean Relations: Historicizing the Legend of Princess of Ayodhaya and Its Legacy', on July 14-15, 2015 at New Delhi. It was attended by seven delegates from South Korea and nine from India.

- Two other conferences- 'Gandhi and His Legacy: From Lawyer to Mahatma: How South Africa Shaped His Thought and Action' and 'Gandhi's Impact on Africa' were organised in South Africa.
- International Seminar on 'Indo-Vietnam Cultural Relations: Retrospect and Prospects', which was held on February 20-21, 2016 at Azad Bhawan, New Delhi.

ICCR also participated with a number of organizations in India and abroad in jointly organizing such conferences. Some of these were:

- 'Bhagwat Gita and its Contemporary Relevance' on September 24-25, 2015 at the Nehru Centre, London.
- 'Rishi Sufi Traditions of Kashmir' during October 25-27, 2015 at Srinagar. This was done in collaboration with the University of Kashmir and J&K Academy of Art, Culture and Language.
- 'Sanskrit and Indological Studies in India, Russia and Neighbouring Countries: Past, Present and Future' during October 28-29, 2015 at Moscow. This was done in collaboration with Russian State University for the Humanities (RSUH), Moscow.

## Annual Festivals

ICCR organizes a number of festivals in India annually, which are open for participation by foreign troupes. It is an important step that focuses on different themes and regions, such as South Asian Bands Festival, the Commonwealth Games Festival, The Africa Festival, World Percussion Festival, International Jazz Festival, Sufi International Festival and The International Dance & Music Festival.

Some of these festivals are arranged by ICCR itself; while in other cases it extends support to other organizers in the private sector. Foreign participation is from different corners of the world. These are normally held in the winter months during October and February. These groups normally perform in Delhi but some of these travel to other cities also.

Some of the main festivals organized during the 2015-16 financial year and participating countries are as follows:

*6th Edition of World Flute Festival*

ICCR assisted Krishna Prerna Charitable Trust in organizing this festival during September 11-13, 2015 at Delhi. Groups from Belarus, Hungary, Japan, Lithuania and Spain participated.

*9th Edition of Delhi International Arts Festival (DIAF) 2015*

ICCR collaborated with Prasiddha Foundation to hold the Festival during October 16-31 in New Delhi. International groups from China, Egypt, Indonesia, Israel, Kyrgyzstan, Portugal, Taiwan, Turkey and UK participated.

*2nd Edition of International Folk Dance and Music Festival*

It was organized during October 16-18, 2015. The participating countries included Hungary, Israel, Kyrgyzstan, Mauritius, Russia, Spain and Sri Lanka.

*2nd Edition of International Bhakti Festival*

ICCR collaborated with Krishna Prerna Charitable Trust and it was held during December 7-9, 2015. Groups from Bangladesh, Bhutan and Mauritius participated.

*6th Edition of International Dance & Music Festival*

It was held on December 7-9, 2015. Cultural Groups from Kyrgyzstan, Maldives, Malaysia, Mauritius, South Africa, Sri Lanka and Vietnam participated. The Council organized the 4th Festival of Contemporary and Folk-Dance Performances from groups from Kazakhstan, France, Malaysia, Russia, Mexico and China in different parts of India from 12 to 19 October 2013.

*3rd Edition of World Percussion Festival*

ICCR collaborated with Krishna Prerna Charitable Trust in organizing this festival on March 5-6, 2016. The participating groups were from Afghanistan, Belgium, Indonesia, Italy and Russia. At a festival organized on Feb 15-27, 2013, the participating countries included Brazil, South Africa, and Sri Lanka.

## ICCR Awards

ICCR instituted three Awards in 2015 (MEA 2015-16). These Awards were created to honour those, who have contributed in fostering connectivity with India. The details of the Awards and their recipients are given below.

### *Distinguished Indologist Award*

The Award was presented to Professor Heinrich Freiherr Von Steitencron from Germany by the President of India on November 21, 2015 after the inauguration of an 'International Conference of Indologists' at the Rashtrapati Bhawan. The conference was organized at the initiative of the President himself.

### *ICCR Distinguished Alumni Award*

The ceremony for the First Award was held on December 15, 2015 at New Delhi. Sushma Swaraj, External Affairs Minister presented the Awards. The three Awardees of 2015 were: Le Luong Minh (Vietnam), Secretary General of ASEAN; Zenebu Tadesse Woldetsadik (Ethiopia), Minister of Women and Youth Affairs and Mrs. Milena Salvini (France), Noted Kathakali Dancer and Founder of Centre Mandapa, Paris.

### *ICCR World Sanskrit Award*

Princess Maha Chakri Sirindhom of Thailand and Professor George Cardona from the Pennsylvania University (USA) were presented with the ICCR World Sanskrit Award for 2015 and 2016 respectively. The institution of the Award was announced by the External Affairs Minister Sushma Swaraj at the 16th World Sanskrit Conference in Bangkok in June 2015. The Awards were presented by Vice President Hamid Ansari on November 20, 2016. Accepting the Award, Princess Maha Chakri described Sanskrit "as the eternal legacy to mankind" and stated that it "is through Sanskrit that Indian values and ethos" have been embedded in Thai Culture (Business Standard).

## New Thrust Areas

Brief highlights of the focused areas are given below; some of these were briefly alluded to in the section dealing with conferences.

### *International Ramayana Mela, February 2015*

This was inaugurated by Prime Minister Modi at the FICCI Auditorium on 23 February 2015. He said that all countries that have Gautam Buddha, Ram and Ramayana 'as part of their culture have bond with India that transcends diplomatic ties'. He said that 'the message of Ramayana remains relevant today'. He saw the International Ramayana Mela (Festival) as 'a positive beginning' for connecting with small towns and cities in India, 'to savour the diversity of India'. Troupes from eight countries, including India, participated in this Mela that was held in 14 different cities in India from 14-27 February 2015. The participating countries included Cambodia, Fiji, Indonesia, Malaysia, Singapore, Thailand, and Trinidad and Tobago.

***Conferences on 'Indian Diaspora & Cultural Heritage: Past, Present and Future'***

It was organised at Delhi on February 11-13, 2015. This was the first of its kind organized by ICCR and was attended by 43 scholars from 13 countries, which included 19 scholars from abroad. In her inaugural address, EAM Sushma Swaraj appreciated the efforts made by Indian Diaspora 'to keep the Indian cultural heritage alive and vibrant'.

***International Conference on Indologists***

It was held on November 21-23, 2015 at the Rashtrapati Bhawan, New Delhi. It was attended by 21 scholars from abroad and 7 from India. This was at the initiative of Pranab Mukherjee, President of India, who also inaugurated the same.

The 2nd International Conference of Indologists was successfully held at Shenzhen from 11-13 November, 2016. The Conference saw participation of more than 75 Indologists from all over the world including China, Germany, Thailand, Chile and India. The Indologists presented papers in five broad areas namely: Indological Studies in China, Indological Studies all over the World, Buddhist Culture and World Culture, Indology and Indo-China Cultural Exchanges and Indian Literature and Grammar.

***International Roma Conference, February 12-14, 2016***

This was organized by ARSP (Antarashtriya Sahayog Parishad.) in collaboration with ICCR. It aimed at focusing on 'Roma roots with India' through re-establishing cultural relations with Roma communities across the globe. The conference was inaugurated by EAM Sushma Swaraj. 33 Scholars and 11 cultural performers from 14 countries participated. Roma have 'preserved Indian customs and traditions' through 'words in their languages and their own ways of living'.

In her inaugural address on February 12, EAM Sushma Swaraj, recognized Roma 'as the first flag bearers of the Indian culture overseas', as there is credible evidence of their migration from India towards the West in the 5$^{th}$ century. The 20 million strong Roma communities are spread over 30 countries and have been known by their different identities in each country. Sushma Swaraj assured them 'India's continuous and unstinted support' and welcomed them 'to contribute to Mother India's development and be active partners in this noble and exciting venture' (Dr. Bala, Shashi).

### *Buddhism*

ICCR is focusing on using Buddhism in its efforts in linking India culturally with China, East and Southeast Asian countries. ICCR's President Lokesh Chandra said that it was time that India invested 'in tapping Buddhism as a key arm of our cultural diplomacy'. Buddha has thus emerged as 'a new top cultural diplomat' (Kasturi Charu Sudan). ICCR held a large number of seminars on India's Buddhist links. It also hosted a Festival in Ladakh with participation from China, Mongolia and South Korea. Fudan University in Shanghai hosted a seminar on India-China Buddhist links in September 2015, which was the first of its kind.

### *Conference on Dara Shikoh*

ICCR organized an international conference on 'Dara Shikoh: Reclaiming Spiritual Legacy of India' on April 27-28, 2017 at Azad Bhavan, Delhi. Eminent scholars, academics and historians from Afghanistan, Kazakhstan, Iran, Uzbekistan, USA and India participated. The objective of the conference was 'to present Dara Shikoh's contribution and initiatives in bringing about homogenization of Hinduism and Islam and thereby building a cohesive social and cultural edifice of India' (Khandelwal, Heena, 2017)

### *Gala Cultural Events at Rashtrapati Bhavan*

ICCR has adopted another innovative approach, whereby it organizes cultural events to support regional meetings with a cultural programme not only by Indian artists, but also from the participating countries, such as at the ASEAN Summit Conference in 2012. A Cultural Evening was organized at the Rashtrapati Bhawan on December 20, in which artists from India and some ASEAN contries performed. In this way, ICCR celebrates not only Indian culture but also cultures of participating countries. A Gala Performance was held for leaders from Africa at the Rashtrapati Bhawan on October 24, 2015. Later, performances were also held in Guwahati and Vadodara where 100 artists from India and Bolivia, Egypt, Ethiopia, Ghana, Uganda and Zambia participated. It is a unique way to connect culturally with other countries.

### *7th Delhi International Jazz Festival*

ICCR organized a three day music festival at the Nehru Park, Chanakyapuri, New Delhi from September 23 to 25, 2017. This is one of the signature festivals organized annually by ICCR since 2011. Each year groups from different countries and India participate at the festival, which is considered to be 'a treat for Jazz lovers in India'. This year, the participating groups came from France, Israel, Korea, Mexico, Spain, Taiwan, South Africa and India. Riva Ganguly Das, Director General, ICCR said that ICCR played an important role in developing 'this genre within Indian boundaries'. Stating its importance, she added, "ICCR believes that music can play a role in engaging and creating dialogue with other nations. Festivals help us in understanding cultures of other countries" (The Outlook 2017).

### *ICCR-Meridian International Center (MIC) Collaboration*

ICCR signed an MOU with MIC in Washington DC on May 2, 2013. The MOU aims at promoting mutual understanding through holding of cultural programmes/events. This is an important initiative by ICCR to reach out to foreign cultural bodies, to promote cultural exchanges. MIC is a global leadership organization that works with the US government, foreign governments and embassies 'to create innovative cultural, leadership development, educational and policy programmes'. It organized a photographic exhibition on the theme 'A History of US-India Relations; 1790-1947', which provided a good glimpse into bilateral ties, prior to India's Independence. The exhibition was held at the American Cultural Centre, Delhi and other cities in India during 2016.

## Incoming and Outgoing Cultural Troupes

ICCR spends 14-15% of its annual budget on exchange of cultural troupes, which are in the neighbourhood of 200 troupes annually both ways. It is colossal in terms of the number of troupes, which is matched by the quality of performances. ICCR's aim is to 'showcase quality performance by Indian cultural troupes' and to project 'the richness and diversity of Indian Culture' (ICCR 2015-16).

During 2015-16, it sponsored 121 groups to 90 countries from 18 States of India. A number of these performances are linked to participation at prestigious international festivals organized abroad. During 2014-15, ICCR sponsored 86 cultural groups to 93 countries from 24 States of India; while in 2013-14 it sponsored only 61 groups. We notice an increase in the number of groups sponsored over the years.

ICCR is also involved in a two-way cultural diplomacy. It, therefore, actively supports visits by foreign troupes to India, as a part of reciprocal return visits to India's Festivals abroad or as a part of the ongoing cultural diplomacy of other countries. In this way, it helps in fulfilling its mandate 'in creating understanding through culture, by showcasing such performances, so that the people of India get to see and appreciate cultures from across the globe' (ICCR 2014-15). A number of foreign troupes participate in major annual festivals organized in India. During 2014-15, ICCR hosted 72 international groups.

## Exhibitions

Holding of Exhibitions of Indian arts and crafts is an important activity of ICCR. It sponsors exhibitions abroad and also receives the same in India under the bilateral Cultural Exchange Programmes. ICCR also organizes exhibitions as a part of its Festivals of India abroad. ICCR also owns 'a rich collection of 27 exhibitions (paintings, photographs and textiles), which are sent for display during art events abroad (ICCR 2014-15). ICCR also has an in-house Art Gallery at its premises at Azad Bhavan, where it mounts exhibitions by foreign artists and even Indian artists under its 'Horizon Series', which is to promote budding artists.

During 2013-14, the Council sponsored 25 artists/exhibitions, covering various subjects such as art, India's architecture, contemporary Indian art and miniature paintings. 13 of these exhibitions were from its own collections, including 6 sent to Belgium in connection with Europalia-India Festival and one at MGC Asian Traditional Textile Museum, Siem-Reap in Cambodia. The Council also hosted 2 exhibitions from Trinidad and Tobago and Peru (ICCR 2013-14).

During the period 2014-15, ICCR sent 36 exhibitions abroad. It also hosted 2 exhibitions from abroad and organized 39 exhibitions under its 'Horizon Series'. It also extended support to artists from Turkmenistan and Netherlands. During the period 2015-16, ICCR organized 18 exhibitions abroad, covering photographs, paintings and textiles. It also hosted 2 exhibitions from Moscow and Vietnam at its Azad Bhavan Gallery.

## Publications

ICCR is centrally located and has its own premises, which include a conference/performance hall and art gallery. It has its own Library, which is well stocked. It has over 60000 books, which form a part of four major collections – Azad Collection; Africa Collection; AVR Collection and ICCR Publications Collection. ICCR brings out six publications namely Indian Horizons, Africa Quarterly (both English Quarterlies), Gagananchal (Hindi Bimonthly), Papeles de la India (Spanish, Biannual), "Recontre Avec L' Inde (French Biannual), and "Thaqafat-ul-Hind" (Arabic Quarterly). The area where ICCR's premises are located has become congested, which makes access difficult to visitors and impacts on participation by the general public in its programmes.

## Review of the Working of ICCR

An evaluation of the role of the ICCR was undertaken by the Parliament in 1996-97 and it finds mention in the second report of the Standing Committee on External Affairs. The main thrust of the Report was on ICCR being given "real functional autonomy in pursuit of its objectives" as this would "at the same time confer on it greater credibility." It also talked about the "need for continuous reorientation of the activities of the Cultural Centers abroad not only to meet the cultural thrust which ICCR is supposed to emphasize but also to improve India's image and further our own policy objectives." It recognizes the importance of the ICCR projecting 'a holistic image of a vibrant India.' It talked of involvement of private sector and the need and desirability of more funds for cultural diplomacy.

The report also stressed the need for assessing the utility of Chairs on Indian Studies "in the context of contemporary needs and complaints" and recommended the need of "setting up new Chairs with the emphasis on the study of contemporary India in selected target countries." It wanted the ICCR to give added focus on activities other than Performing Arts, so as to avoid being unwittingly identified in public perception "as a kind of impresario organization." This emphasis on the directional change of the activities of ICCR would be of interest to the readers as Academic Institutions now can look for additional support from ICCR in conducting seminars and other activities (Lok Sabha Report, 1997).

**In its 'Performance Audit Report' of ICCR** for the Years 2007-2012 conducted in 2013, Comptroller and Auditor General noted that ICCR was established 'with the primary objective of establishing, reviving and strengthening cultural relations and mutual understanding between India and other countries'(CAG, Report No 16, 2013). He made following pertinent comments on its functioning:

- The Authorities of the Council, namely General Assembly, Governing Body and Finance Committee did not meet in accordance with the prescribed frequency, 'nor was any annual plan of action prepared.'

- Inadequate publicity to ICCR Scholarship Scheme resulting in 'sub-optimal utilization of slots and skewed representation of the countries under the Programme.'
- 25 per cent of the slots under the Scholarship Scheme were allocated to countries with which there was no Cultural Exchange Programme.
- Three Cultural Centres were opened and run without the approval of the Ministry of External Affairs.
- The posts of the Directors of the Centres were operated without the approval of the Ministry of Finance. The posts of the Directors were filled 'in an arbitrary manner' in the absence of guidelines for appointment.
- There were major deficiencies to the procurement process resulting in incurring of 'sufficient expenditure.'

The Comptroller and Auditor General made a number of recommendations. Some of the relevant ones for the functioning of ICCR are enumerated below:

- To hold the meetings of the statutory authorities according to prescribed periodicity.
- To devise a suitable mechanism to evaluate effectiveness of its programmes.
- To ensure effective implementation of Scholarship Schemes 'through enhanced communication with Indian Missions.'
- To make utilization of Scholarships more broad based and ensure adequate utilization of slots.
- To award Scholarships to students from countries with which 'valid agreements exists.'
- To open new Cultural Centres after seeking MEA's approval.
- To prepare guidelines for appointment and terms and conditions of Director of Cultural Centres.

- To devise suitable norms for selection of artists for international exhibitions.

**Parliamentary Standing Committee on External Affairs** presented its Thirteenth Report to Lok Sabha on November 23, 2016. It focused on 'India's Soft Power Diplomacy including Role of Indian Council for Cultural Relations (ICCR) and Indian Diaspora'. It placed ICCR's role in the context of soft power and made a detailed review of the functioning of ICCR in major areas of its activities. It recognized ICCR's role as

> "the nodal organization for the projection of India's soft power abroad, and ever since its establishment in 1950, it has emerged as the principal governmental organization for our cultural engagement with the world and for promoting our culture in all its magnificence through various activities" (Lok Sabha Report, 2016).

It found that the budgetary allocations were inadequate to meet the expanding mandate of ICCR. It recommended a sufficient increase in its budget, while simultaneously asking it to ramp up its institutional capacity for better utilization. It also batted for adequate human resource, while stressing the need for appointment of 'the most appropriate persons' to head the cultural centres overseas.

The Committee made certain pertinent recommendations to tone up its functioning. It recommended that ICCR/MEA and other Line Ministries should 'work together to strengthen the soft power diplomacy of the country.'It also recommended the acceleration of the process on the establishment of ICCR Alumni Groups abroad, while urging it to pay attention to 'the welfare and well-being of foreign scholars', to avoid repetition of incidents involving attacks on African students. It also recommended empanelment of artists representing 'unique art and dance forms on the verge of extinction.'

The Committee also wanted ICCR to increasingly adopt Public Private Partnerships (PPPs) in setting up cultural centres as well as enter into institutional partnerships with reputed cultural organizations abroad. It also suggested the need for setting up a cultural centre in the Gulf Region where none existed; while cautioning on the need for setting up Regional Cultural Centres, as these may not be viable.

The Committee also wanted ICCR to move in the direction of dissemination of ideas by 'showcasing India's democracy and diversity' and going beyond the realm of music and dance. It forcefully stated this in these words:

> "India's soft power should also embrace the attraction of words and ideas, including contemporary and classical literature, thereby projecting India to those wishing to know more in depth about the country and its culture." (Lok Sabha Report, 2016).

Where are we now, after a gap of twenty years since the 1997 Report of the Parliamentary Standing Committee on External Affairs and its new Report in 2016? ICCR is still grappling with the issues raised in these reports and the subsequent CAG's Audit Report of 2013. There is no regular review of the activities of ICCR; it has financial and administrative constraints. The diminishing cadre of ICCR is adding to administrative slothness and the remaining cadre is not professionally trained.

ICCR has not succeeded in giving a new orientation to its programmes, which still are largely concentrated on Performing Arts. It has not succeeded in veering towards greater academic programmes. Chairs of Indian Studies have not resulted in imparting dynamism to academic connectivity in the host countries.

Indian cultural centres still have a long way to go before becoming cultural hubs, which attract local youth. A Committee, under former DG, ICCR Veena Sikri, reviewed the activities of Cultural Centres in mid-2017; hopefully the report would come out with recommendations that could rejuvenate the working of these Centres.

There is merit in the suggestions made by the Committee, as these have been oft repeated. We, however, have to bear in mind the practicability in implementing these, given the perennial problem of manpower shortages and budgetary constraints.

We also need to keep in view that 'Cultural Diplomacy' is for 'Connectivity' and not 'Conversion' to one's view, as seen in the context of soft power. We, therefore, would have to restrain ourselves from efforts to place 'Cultural Diplomacy' in the genre of power.

## ICCR Priorities

ICCR's Budget Estimates provide a window to our understanding of its thrust areas. This also helps in measuring its performance, as the same have to be related to the adequacy of funds made available for its activities and their utilisation thereof. ICCR conducts a number of activities directly out of its allocated budget. It also does 'Agency Work' on behalf of the Ministry of External Affairs and other governmental organizations.

ICCR incurred an expenditure of Rs.16157.58 lacs (Rs.1616 million) during Fiscal Year 2015-16. Its annual direct expenditure has, however, remained static in rupee terms for the last three years. In fact, there is a marginal decline from F.Y 2013-14 when the expenditure stood at Rs.16580.96 lacs (Rs.1658 million). If we allow for inflation then there is a decline in funding by about 20 per cent during the last three years.

What are the focus areas, where the bulk of the expenditure is incurred? It is divided under two broad sub-heads – Expenditure incurred in India and Expenditure incurred Abroad. An expenditure of Rs.5721.11 lakhs (Rs.572 million) was incurred within India during the F.Y. 2013-14 under 15 sub-heads. Around 48 per cent of the expenditure was on International Students, followed by festivals (22 per cent); incoming and outgoing visitors and delegations (14 per cent) and cultural programmes (8 per cent).

It may be noticed that the funding declined to Rs.4547.79 lacs (Rs 455 million) during FY 2015-16, which represented a decline by around 18 per cent. An interesting feature was an increase in the percentage share of expenditure for international students, which went up to 55 per cent; while on incoming delegations it went up to 26 per cent. The primary reason for the overall decline was that a low level of expenditure of Rs.7.23 lakhs was incurred as against Rs.1297 lakhs incurred for festivals during FY 2013-14.

As against the above expenditure in India, ICCR incurred an expenditure of Rs.8712 lacs (Rs.871 million) abroad in F.Y. 2015-16. This was under three sub heads: Cultural Centres Abroad (Rs.6980.84 lacs); Chairs/Centres of Indian Studies (Rs.1486.91lacs) and grants to NGOs (Rs.245.02 lacs). It may be noticed that around 80% of the budget was spent on the Cultural Centres; while around 17% was earmarked for Chairs of Indian Studies.

There was, however, a marginal decline in the expenditure on cultural centres, as some of these were closed. There was an increase by 20 per cent for the Chairs of Indian Studies as more Chairs were established. There was, however, a substantial increase by 300 per cent towards grants to NGOs; it was a positive development, as more local organizations were getting involved culturally with India.

## ICCR gearing itself to fulfill its Mandate despite constraints

ICCR has the singular distinction of being the nodal agency for India's Cultural Diplomacy, since it was set up in 1950. It initially functioned under the Ministry of Education, but since 1970 it operates under the Ministry of External Affairs and is thus better placed to pursue cultural diplomacy related activities.

ICCR has a global mandate, but it has budgetary constraints. Even its limited budget was primarily used for paying for salaries of administrative staff, as the same accounted for over 70% of its total budget for ICCR and its cultural centres abroad. What is, however, disheartening to note is inefficient budget management, as funds had to be surrendered for a number of years, as pointed out by the Audit.

ICCR's biggest constraint, however, is manpower, as it lacks in adequate numbers and professionalism is largely missing, as it has limited trained manpower. There is not only staff shortage at ICCR, but its cadre of specialists has also been dwindling over the years, with the retirement of old hands. This was resulting in ICCR losing its institutional memory. ICCR was thus forced to use consultants, who were not able to deliver satisfactory results (Suryakanthi Tripathi)[2].

The administrative problem is further exacerbated, as adhocism prevails in the appointments and postings to cultural centres. MEA's use of ICCR 'for roles at the time of international conferences for arranging cultural performances also makes a further dent on its depleting manpower resources' (Lalit Mansingh)[3].

ICCR has a big task ahead, as it is challenged to fulfil its mandate with its limited resources. It has achieved a certain amount of success. Much, however, could be achieved, if it could review its functioning with regard to two of its signature programmes- Cultural Centres and Chairs of Indian Studies. It should not go in for the number of Centres or Chairs, but towards imparting quality to these institutional frameworks.

ICCR's cultural centres have to become 'Ideas Exchange', as they send out the message of pluralism and diversity through holding Seminars and Conferences. Cultural Centres have to become 'Cultural Hubs'. They need to place special focus on the Youth-related activities as well as integrating local festivals into their own programmes.

As far as Indian Chairs are concerned, we need to impart greater stability and continuity. Indian Chairs have to integrate into the educational institutes abroad. We have to move beyond tokenism and strive to evolve meaningful partnerships with appropriate institutions abroad.

Similarly, more dynamism has to be imparted to ICCR's Scholarship Schemes by attracting more students from the developed countries. ICCR is now focusing on students from developed countries. ICCR is also laying special emphasis on revitalizing the Scholarship Scheme. It deliberated over the scholarship-related schemes with all the stake-holders, including diplomatic missions, at a 'National Conference on Higher Education for Foreign Students organized in March 2016. The Recommendations need to be followed up. There is also a need for active involvement of Indian Diplomatic Missions, both as promoters and facilitators.

ICCR's Programme on Distinguished Visitors works on a paltry budget and that needs to be expanded. We need to build greater synergy into our Academic Programmes, both in terms of their outreach and quality of scholarship that we can attract. Deputy Director General Namrata Kumar informed the author that they planned to add 'an intellectual content to ICCR's programmes' (Namrata Kumar)[4]. Hope that concrete steps are taken to expand the Distinguished Visitors Programme. Our focus has to be equally on budding leaders, while we continue honouring old friends. It has to have futuristic agenda, as is the case with similar programmes run by other countries.

ICCR has made certain notable achievements in instituting three Awards in 2015 – Indology, Sanskrit and Alumni. It should help in providing greater connectivity with the 'Friends of India', as long term relationship is one of the objectives of cultural diplomacy. We will have to ensure that we go beyond their symbolic value, as we convert these into effective instruments for 'Connectivity'. At such Award-related conferences we have to ensure the participation of the Youth, which was missing, in particular, at the Indology Conference.

ICCR's aim is to 'showcase quality performance by Indian cultural troupes' and to project 'the richness and diversity of Indian Culture' (ICCR 2015-16). ICCR has to impart a new thrust to its activities, so as to wear the mantle of a 'Performing Arts Plus' Organisation and move beyond an 'impressario' to a 'directorial' role.

ICCR is gearing itself to meet the challenges of manpower and financial constraints, to fulfil its mandate. Amarendra Khatua, the then Director General of ICCR promised to impart a new vigour and thrust. His vision is to promote Brand India through emphasis on traditional Indian cultural and scientific research, yoga, Ayurveda, Sanskrit, Vedas, folk arts and culture, Puranic and historical cultural and philosophical linkage between India and the world (Manish Chand).

ICCR has plans to increase cultural centres from 36 to 50 in the next 15 years. It is also planned to take 'two-way cultural diplomacy' to second and third tier cities. To achieve all these objectives, Khatua planned to work in tandem with the territorial divisions, as India's footprints reached in Africa, Latin America and neighbouring countries (Simran Sodhi).

The newly appointed President of ICCR, Vijay Sahasrabuddhe, is more enthusiastic in meeting the challenges for ICCR, as he would like to give a new thrust to its functioning. In an interview in January 2018, he said that 'for strong diplomatic ties to evolve between countries, organisations like the ICCR are expected to provide sound, enduring foundations'. Citing his priorities for ICCR, he said that firstly, it would be 'creating a greater understanding about India and Indian civilization'. Secondly, it would be 'to further consolidate the institutional strength of ICCR.' The ultimate goal for him would be 'to work to translate popular global goodwill for India into a more vibrant diplomatic relationship' (Hebbar, Nistula, 2018).

All said and done, ICCR needs to be headed by a Director General, who is empowered, dedicated and knowledgeable and is well versed in the area of cultural diplomacy and has capacities to carry along other stakeholders as partners in this joint venture on cultural diplomacy.

ICCR's present premises are not suitable for students, visitors and audience, as the area has become congested and is not easily accessible. A move to 'Chanakyapuri' (Diplomatic Enclave) in New Delhi would be ideal. To start with, ICCR could be allowed to use the newly constructed premises of the 'Pravasi Kendra', which is located in the Diplomatic Enclave, to organise its programmes. This would also help ICCR in involving Diaspora in the range of its activities.

ICCR can thus meet the challenges of financial and manpower constraints through better coordination with Line Ministries, in particular, Ministry of Culture, various Divisions in the Ministry of External Affairs, State Governments and other stakeholders. Signing of MOUs by ICCR with the MOC and State Governments, are positive pointers in this joint approach. Every year, a State could be designated as ICCR's Partner and ICCR could focus on that State, in line with Government's policy of 'True Federalism', as it spreads the message of pluralism and diversity.

**Annexure I**

## Comparative Statement on Expenditure of ICCR's Activities during the (FYs) 2013-2016

**Table-I**

| Sr. No. | Appropriate Head | Expenditure (Figs in Lacs) | | |
|---|---|---|---|---|
| | | FY-2013-14 | FY-2014-15 | FY- 2015-16 |
| 1 | Incoming and Outgoing Visitors and Delegations | 850.60 | 1355.42 | 1280.45 |
| 2 | Cultural Performances of ICCR | 468.30 | 227.70 | 177.61 |
| 3 | Audio-Visual Recordings, Digitization, Website Designing | 0.50 | 4.14 | 0.00 |
| 4 | Seminars/Symposia/ Conferences/Lectures/SIS | 15.25 | 33.56 | 197.16 |
| 5 | International Students Divisions | 2743.86 | 3342.05 | 2502.83 |
| 6 | Exhibitions | 91.17 | 169.60 | 183.49 |
| 7 | Presentation of Books and Art Objects | 6.64 | 28.37 | 37.96 |
| 8 | Publications | 48.13 | 48.69 | 35.79 |
| 9 | Libraries | 9.87 | 15.37 | 11.74 |
| 10 | Multi Media | 23.92 | 24.12 | 4.17 |
| 11 | Hindi Activities | 90.05 | 30.91 | 54.63 |
| 12 | Festivals | 1297.97 | 121.98 | 7.23 |
| 13 | Fellowship | 28.49 | 20.20 | 25.77 |
| 14 | Anniversary Celebrations | 18.33 | 0.24 | 1.28 |
| 15 | Misc (Investment+ Deposits+GPF) | 28.03 | 25.85 | 27.68 |
| **Total** | | **5721.11** | **5466.20** | **4547.79** |

**Table-II**

**Projects Abroad**

| Sr. No. | Appropriate Head | Expenditure (Figs in Lacs) | | |
|---|---|---|---|---|
| | | **FY-2013-14** | **FY-2014-15** | **FY- 2015-16** |
| 1 | Cultural Centres Abroad | 7146.15 | 6677.90 | 6980.84 |
| 2 | Chairs/Centres of Indian Studies | 1203.23 | 1006.41 | 1486.91 |
| 3 | Grants to NGOs | 84.11 | 124.32 | 245.02 |
| **Total** | | **8433.49** | **7808.63** | **8712.77** |

**Annexure II**

**University/Institute-wise Break up of Students as on 2014**

| Sl. No. | Name of University/Institute | Number of Scholars |
|---|---|---|
| 1 | Assam University | 7 |
| 2 | Tejpur University | 3 |
| 3 | Dibrugarh University | 3 |
| 4 | NIT Silchar | 103 |
| 5 | IIT Guwahati | 7 |
| 6 | Assam Agricultural University | 3 |
| 7 | Ayurvedic College | 2 |
| 8 | Banaras Hindu University | 50 |
| 9 | Sampurnanad Sanskrit University | 2 |
| 10 | NIT Rourkela | 62 |
| 11 | University of Agriculturle, Bhuvneshwar | 7 |
| 12 | Ravenshaw University | 5 |
| 13 | SRJAN Institute | 4 |
| 14 | Calicut Univeristy | 40 |
| 15 | NIT Calicut | 12 |
| 16 | Kerala Agriculture University | 3 |
| 17 | MG University, Kottayam | 14 |
| 18 | Kerala University | 13 |
| 19 | Central University of Kerala | 2 |
| 20 | Central University of Science & Technology | 2 |
| 21 | Kerala Kalamandalam | 2 |
| 22 | Gujarat University | 184 |
| 23 | Gujarat Technological University | 202 |
| 24 | Sardar Patel University | 32 |
| 25 | Veer Narmad South Gujarat University | 34 |
| 26 | Central University of Gujarat | 6 |
| 27 | SVNIT Surat | 45 |
| 28 | M.S. University, Baroda | 9 |

| 29 | Ananad Agriculture University | 1 |
|---|---|---|
| 30 | Navsari Agriculture University | 4 |
| 31 | Junagadh Agriculture University | 1 |
| 32 | IIT Gandhinagar | 1 |
| 33 | Gujarat Ayurved University | 24 |
| 34 | Dance & Music (Kadamb Institute) | 1 |
| 35 | Punjab University | 262 |
| 36 | Kurukshetra University | 7 |
| 37 | NIT Kurukshetra | 42 |
| 38 | R. Gandhi Ayurved College | 3 |
| 39 | Dr. Y.S. Parmar University, Ludhiyana | 2 |
| 40 | Punjab Agriculture University | 7 |
| 41 | Guru Angad Vetenerary Sc. University | 1 |
| 42 | Punjabi University, Patiala | 3 |
| 43 | NIT Jalandhar | 7 |
| 44 | NIT Hamirpur | 1 |
| 45 | Guru Nanak Dev University | 3 |
| 46 | H.P. University, Shimla | 9 |
| 47 | Andhra University | 43 |
| 48 | Acharya N.G. Ranga Agriculture University | 9 |
| 49 | English & Foreign Language University | 20 |
| 50 | JNTU, Anantpur | 199 |
| 51 | NIT Warangal | 129 |
| 52 | Osmania University | 970 |
| 53 | JNTU, Hyderabad | |

## Endnotes

1 Rajasekhar, C, Director General, ICCR, New Delhi. Interaction on March 21, 2016 in Delhi.

2 Suryakanthi Tripathi, Former Director General, ICCR. Interaction on October 23, 2015 in Delhi.

3 Lalit Mansingh, Former Foreign Secretary and Director General, ICCR. Interaction on October 4, 2016 in Delhi.

4 Namrata Kumar, Deputy Director General, ICCR. Interaction on March 22, 2016 in Delhi.

## References

Bandopadhyaya, J., 1973, *The Making of India's Foreign Policy;* Allied Publishers, New Delhi.

*Business Standard,* 2014, 'Foreign Students Studying in Indian Universities and Institutions on Scholarship by ICCR' December 12. http://www.business-standard.com/article/government-press-release/foreign-students-studying-in-indian-universities-and-institutions-on-scholarship-by-114121000804_1.html.

*Business Standard*, 2016, 'Thai Princess, US Professor Conferred World Sanskrit Awards', November 21.

CAG, Report No. 16 of 2013 on the Performance Budget of ICCR. Available at https://cag.gov.in/sites/default/files/audit_report_files/Union_Performance_Civil_Autonomous_Bodies_16_2013_chapter_4.pdf (Accessed 12 December 2017).

Dr. Bala, Shashi, 2016, *ARSP Monthly Letter*, June.

Chand, Manish, 'Cultural Diplomatic Poised for a Bigger Role to Promote India Image: ICCR Chief Amarendra Khatua'. http://www.indiawrites.org/cultural-diplomacy-poised-bigger-role-promote-brand-india-iccr-chief-amarendra-khatua/ (Accessed 12 December 2017).

Hebbar, Nistula, 2018 'Homogeneity is inherent to most cultural traditions: Vinay Sahasrabuddhe', *The Hindu*, Jan 7.

EAM, 2016, Address of External Affairs Minister Sushma Swaraj at the Roma Conference, New Delhi, Feb 12.

ICCR, http://www.iccr.gov.in/content/constitution (Accessed on May 1, 2018).

ICCR 2000-01, Annual Report of the Indian Council of Cultural Relations, New Delhi.

ICCR 2010-11, Annual Report of the Indian Council of Cultural Relations, New Delhi.

ICCR 2011-12, Annual Report of the Indian Council of Cultural Relations, New Delhi.

ICCR 2013-14, Annual Report of the Indian Council of Cultural Relations, New Delhi.

ICCR 2014-15, Annual Report of the Indian Council of Cultural Relations, New Delhi.

ICCR 2015-16, Annual Report of the Indian Council of Cultural Relations, New Delhi.

Jayakar, Pupul, 1992, *Indira Gandhi, A Biography*, Viking, Penguin Books India (P) Ltd.

Kasturi, Charu Sudan, 2015, 'Modi government plans Buddhism blitz in cultural diplomacy focus' *The Telegraph*, August 31.

Khandelwal, Heena, 2017, 'Dara Shikoh was Founding Father of Secularism in India', *DNA*, April 30.

*Lok Sabha Report*, 1997, Second Report, Standing Committee on External Affairs, 1996-97, Eleventh Lok Sabha, April 1997.

*Lok Sabha Report,* 2016, Thirteenth Report of the Committee on External Affairs, November 23. 164.100.47.193/lsscommittee/External%20 Affairs/16_External_Affairs_13.pdf (Accessed on December15, 2017).

MEA 2011-12, Annual Report of the Ministry of External Affairs.

MEA 2013-14, Annual Report of the Ministry of External Affairs.

MEA 2015-16, Annual Report of the Ministry of External Affairs.

Misra, Satish, 2006, 'Cultural diplomacy needs a big thrust, says Karan

Singh', *The Tribune*, September 24.

Simon Mark, 'A Comparative Study of the Cultural Diplomacy of Canada, New Zealand and India', The University of Auckland, 2008. https://researchspace.auckland.ac.nz/bitstream/handle/ 2292/ 2943/02 whole.pdf?sequence=9 (Accessed on December 12, 2017).

Sodhi, Simran, 2017, 'Chandigarh to host global poetic event as soft power outreach', *The Tribune*, Feb. 4.

*The Outlook* 2017, '7th Delhi International Jazz Festivals to kick off from Sept. 23', September 9.

Varma, Pavan, 2006, 'Soft Power', *The Tribune*, Oct. 7.

# Section – III

# Role of Other Cultural Bodies and Direction of Indian Cultural Diplomacy

# Chapter – V

# Role of Other Cultural Bodies

## Introduction

While promoting the role of Indian cultural diplomacy, Indian leaders recognized the limits of the State becoming the sole promoter. India, therefore, left a window open for the involvement of other Public Bodies and non-official players, recognizing that cultural diplomacy have to be people oriented and there has to be an opening from the straight jacket of diplomacy.

India was, therefore, one of the few countries to realize the limits to the direct involvement of state in cultural matters. In his Inaugural Address at the setting up of the Sangeet Natak Akademi on January 28, 1953, Maulana Azad, the then Education Minister said,

> 'In a democratic regime, the arts can derive their sustenance only from the people. And the state as the organized manifestation of people's will must, therefore, undertake its maintenance and development, as one of its first responsibility' (Maulana Azad, 1953).

India sees government's primary role in 'creating and maintaining a useful infrastructure for cultural activities rather than organizing cultural events'. India was thus far ahead of others, as it did not want to constrict cultural diplomacy in a tight official jacket only.

Keeping in view, the above approach, the government set up a nodal agency, ICCR, to implement India's cultural diplomacy-related programmes and activities. This still left enough room for involvement of non-official organizations, with ICCR performing the role of principal promoter and facilitator.

In the olden times, cultural diplomacy was the preserve of the private sector, as promotion of art and culture, depended upon the patronage of princely states and promoters of art. In Independent India, the role of the government increased, as it became the primary source for institutional and financial support for art and culture.

This led to the creation of different sets of cultural operators. Firstly, those that were created by the government to specifically perform cultural activities, such as the three Akademis of Art and National Museums. Secondly, other independent organizations that were created and supported by the government but had a larger mandate, which also included cultural connectivity, such as India International Centre (IIC), Indira Gandhi National Centre for Arts (IGNCA) and Indian National Trust for Art and Cultural Heritage (INTACH).

At the regional level, we would look at the role envisaged for SAARC (South Asian Association for Regional Cooperation) in promoting cultural connectivity among the member states. How was the SAARC mandate on Culture implemented through SAARC Cultural Centre?

We would also be focusing on some other bodies that have emerged in the private sector for a variety of reasons, namely, interest in art and culture, per se; fulfillment of Corporate Social Responsibility (CSR) and encouraging involvement of the youth in cultural activities.

In this chapter, we would thus briefly touch upon a few prominent organizations and institutions, which are playing an important role in this regard. They play the twin role of facilitators, not only for India-sponsored activities but also for events promoted by other foreign countries in the arena of cultural diplomacy.

## Akademis of Art

Maulana Azad recognized the role of the government in the establishment of these Akademis, as similar institutions were established at the national level by a large number of countries in Europe (Maulana Azad, 1954:1). He, however, flagged governmemt's limitations, as he firmly believed that 'Art cannot really flourish until there are strong non-official agencies working for it', which had to be 'autonomous bodies without any interference from the Government in their activities' (Maulana Azad 1954:2).

The Ministry of Culture, therefore, set up three Akademis, which work as autonomous bodies. These Akademis deal with the promotion, preservation and development of Indian visual arts, literature, and performing arts (dance, music theatre). Maulana Azad wanted these Akademis to cherish and develop the precious heritage of dance, drama and music; not only 'for our own sake', but also as 'India's contribution to the cultural heritage of mankind' (Maulana Azad, 1953). He had a larger vision and the same global spirit was to guide the functioning of these Akademis.

Sangeet Natak Akademi (Academy of Music and Drama), an apex body in the field of performing arts, was the first one to be set up in 1953. Its mandate is 'to preserve and promote vast intangible heritage of India's diverse culture', expressed in the form of music, dance and drama. It is in the field of music that 'the essence of Indian civilization and culture' has always been 'a spirit of assimilation and synthesis' (Maulana Azad, 1953).

The Sahitya Akademi (The Academy of Literature) was set up on 12 March 1954 to 'educate public taste and advance the cause of literature' and 'encourage the development of creative literature in different Indian languages' (Maulana Azad, 1954:1). It is thus concerned with the development of Indian letters and aims at fostering and coordinating literary activities in all the Indian languages.

The third, Lalit Kala Akademi (National Academy of Art), was set up on 5 August 1954. It is the apex cultural body in the field of visual arts. This Akademi plays an important role in 'developing the finer aspects of personality through artistic education', whose utility is manifested through development of 'our manual skills and perceptive sensibilities' (Maulana Azad, 1954:2). In his Inaugural Address, Maulana Azad highlighted the primary objective of this Body was 'to preserve the glorious traditions of the past and enrich them by the work of our modern artists' (Maulana Azad, 5-4-1954).

The three Academies also focus on international cooperation in their respective fields, through organization of events in India and participation in programmes organized abroad. They also work through their regional centres and constituent units in India. In this part, we would briefly touch upon their significant activities that promoted international connectivity during the year 2015-16 (MOC 2015-16).

### *Sangeet Natak Akademi*

For it, the most significant item was the organization of the Festival of Yoga, called 'Yog Parv' held during June 21-27, 2015 in India, which included performing and visual arts, workshops and interactive sessions. 'Yog Chakra', a multimedia encounter on 'Tradition and Modernity' was launched on June 21, the International Yoga Day (IYD), which included exhibitions and performances in the context of yoga.

The Sangeet Natak Akademi was appointed as the nodal agency for the 2015 Festival of India-Mauritius – Phase II by the Ministry of Culture. It mounted a number of events, which included 'Mehandi Art Work' during October 14-19; Dance Choreography 'Krishna' by Dr. Sonal Mansingh on November 6-7; and Qawwali by Nizami Brothers during November 26-28.

Prior to 2015-16, Sangeet Natak Akademi had undertaken a number of activities during earlier years. It presented 'Nrityarupa', a Dance Festival, crafted under its artistic direction at the Festival of India in Latin America (Peru and Cuba) during October 26-30, 2013 (MOC 2013-14). It also presented 'Nrityarupa', a Mosaic of Indian Dances in Vietnam in March 2014, showcasing six major dance traditions. It also presented another Dance performance, 'Septakam', a septet of Indian Dances, showcasing seven major traditions (MOC 2014-15). Sangeet Natak Akademi, as the nodal agency for Intangible Cultural Heritage (ICH), organized a cultural show for an international delegation of UNESCO on October 22, 2013 at New Delhi (MOC 2013-14).

***Sahitya Akademi***

It is actively involved in promoting and implementing activities under the cultural exchange programmes that include literary meetings and translation activities. It sends Indian delegates abroad and arranges literary programmes for foreign writers. It also promotes translation from foreign to Indian languages and vice-versa and also awards fellowships. Prof. Jin Dinghan a renowned Indologist from China was awarded Honorary Fellowship on 27 August 2015. It organized a Poetry Session on February 11, 2015, in association with the Literature Translation Institute (LTI) of Korea on February 11, 2015. It also hosted the visit of a delegation from the Maldives Akademy on March 30, 2015. It sent a delegation of writers and scholars to participate in Indo-China Literacy Exchange Programmes in Beijing and Shanghai during August 27-September 1, 2015.

Sahitya Akademi also organized 'Sabad', World Poetry Festival on March 21-24, 2014 at Delhi, to mark the 150th Birth Anniversary of Swami Vivekanand and 100th Year of Gurudev Rabindranath Tagore's receiving the Nobel Prize. 23 poets from 21 countries participated, besides 21 Indian participants from different Indian languages. It also organized 'Waves' – Indian Ocean Rim Association (IORA) Poetry Festival on March 1-3,

2014, to which poets from all the 20 member states were invited. The Festival was supported by the Ministry of External Affairs (MOC 2014-15).

### *Lalit Kala Akademi*

Its main activity is the holding of Triennale exhibition to which international artists are invited. It has not performed in this regard, as the last Triennale was held in 2005; the one proposed to be held in November 2015 was postponed. It also holds Biennale with other partners and held one such with Kochi Biennale Foundation in 2016 on the theme, 'Peripheries of Globalisation: Re-Making the Global Contemporary'.

Another Biennale was held with the Chennai Chamber during July 27-August 6, 2015, where it showcased 122 paintings, which included participation of 10 Korean artists. This was one of the largest expositions of contemporary paintings from Korea in India. It also organized an exhibition in collaboration with the Museum of Sacred Art (MOSA) Belgium and Italy during March 21-26, 2015. The theme was 'Spiritual in Indian Arts'.

Lalit Kala Akadedmi is also involved in the promotion of other activities. It has some unique programmes, like 'Others on Art', under which it organized an Indonesian Dance programme on November 22, 2013 at Delhi. Under its 'Artists on Art' Lecture Series, it invited Terry Burrows to deliver a lecture on 9 January in New Delhi.

## Other Cultural Bodies

Here we will have a look at some 'Cultural Bodies' created and supported by the government. Unlike the Akademies of Art, they had a larger mandate, which goes beyond culture. In this section, we would discuss the role of a few of these bodies in the cultural arena. Their involvement is in keeping with changing definition of cultural diplomacy, which goes beyond strictly diplomatic acts. A number of new players have emerged, which can be classified as 'cultural operators', as they use 'culture' in promoting connectivity and understanding among peoples, not only within India but also with foreign countries. Some of the important organizations that we have selected for coverage are- India International Centre, (IIC), New Delhi; Indira Gandhi National Centre for Arts (IGNCA), New Delhi and Indian National Trust for Arts and Cultural Heritage (INTACH), New Delhi.

## India International Centre, (IIC), New Delhi

Out of all these Bodies, IIC plays an important role, given the nature of cultural activities undertaken by it, both in terms of quality and quantity. It was founded in 1958 and inaugurated in 1962. IIC, therefore, does not shy away from comparing itself to a 'Triveni', a confluence of three streams of activities – intellectual, cultural and social streams – facilitating activities 'where people meet and mingle together' (IIC Website).

ICCR has utilized the facilities available at IIC to mount some of its activities, either independently or in partnership with IIC. Foreign Diplomatic Missions have also fully availed of facilities available at IIC, in mounting cultural activities, be it musical performance or dance, art or literary activity, film shows or an academic and intellectual event. Every year, ICCR mounts a variety of programmes in partnership with diplomatic missions based in India.

***The IIC Experience*** is the flagship programme of IIC that has been held annually during October-November since 2004. It was initiated 'to celebrate the vision of the IIC as a space giving voice to diversity, freedom, innovation, creativity, learning and entertainment.' It also brings together 'the spectrum of its activities—dance, music (both Indian and global), theatre, exhibitions and cuisine—using both indoor and outdoor spaces' (IIC 2016-17). It helps in connecting India with other foreign countries through a range of activities. Let us look at its focus areas, during the last three years 2014-16.

In 2014, the focus was on North-East India and the First World War. A photographic exhibition on the Stillwell Road showed the journey that ran from Assam to the Yunan province in China. The readings from the 'The Great War: Poetry of the Trenches' took us to the period when the poetry was created during those years and came to be known as 'Trench Poetry'. An exhibition of paintings 'Jaisalmer Yellow' displayed the work of 25 leading artists from all the eight SAARC countries. A Koto recital by a Japanese artist; an 'Evening of Classical Jazz' and 'Folk Dance and Songs of the Cossack' presented by a Russian Troupe added to the 'Experience'. The cuisine at the Festival represented both local and international flavours-Smorgasbord (Buffet Meal) from Sweden; Tempura from Japan and Borsch from Russia (IIC 2014-15).

In 2015, the focus was on Literature and Poetry. It was a rendering of Sufi and Carnatic Music that was combined with an Exhibition on Thanjavur manuscripts and two performances based on the Mahabharta (Kathakali

Dance and a Dance Drama). The dramatic presentation, 'Don Quixote and his Epoch' and two feature films marked the 400th anniversary of Cervantes' Don Quixote. The music concerts included Jazz by Chrystal Farrell from Goa, and Baroque Music by the Haydn Baryton Trio of Hungary. The exhibitions included life-size sculptures by Christine Margotin; and Young German Photographers, curated by Max Mueller Bhavan. This year's Film Festival— 'When Comedy is King'—focused on classic films in the genre from India and abroad (IIC 2015-16).

In 2016, the 'IIC Experience' was inaugurated with 'Chaturvidh: Four Dances in the Odishi Marga' and a tribute to M.S. Subbulakshmi, as a person and a musician. A concert by the Lyric Ensemble and by the Accordion State Youth Orchestra of Baden-Wuerttemberg, where thirty accordion players, in the age group of 16 to 25 years, performed pieces, including two syncretic ones from famous Indian films. A special screening of a newly restored 1916 silent film Cenere (Italy) that was accompanied with live soundtrack (saxophone, piano and drums).

The festival presented two unique film festivals— 'Celebrating Six Decades of Spanish Cinema' and 'A Date with Shakespeare', to mark his 400th Birth Anniversary. The films screened were Throne of Blood, Akira Kurosawa's illuminating adaptation in Japanese of Macbeth; Grigori Kozintsev's Russian version of Hamlet; and Orson Welles' Othello. At the Festival, visitors could taste a variety of cuisines that included flavours of coastal Kerala, the eastern food of Bengal; flavours of the Doab (Punjab). They also had a taste of German, European and Continental fare (IIC 2016-17).

ICCR in collaboration with the India International Centre (IIC) organized an International Conference on 'The Relevance of Traditional Cultures for the Present and the Future', which was inaugurated by Vice President Hamid Ansari on 24 March, 2014. On an earlier occasion on March 4, 2014, the Vice President released a publication on the proceedings of the Interfaith Conference organized by ICCR from 7-9 March, 2013.

## Indira Gandhi National Centre for Arts (IGNCA), New Delhi

The Indira Gandhi National Centre for the Arts (IGNCA) is an autonomous body set up under the Ministry of Culture in 1985. It is a Centre 'for academic pursuit and research; and dissemination in the field of arts' (MOC: 2015-16). It plays an important role in the preservation of intangible heritage. It is predicated upon former Prime Minister Mrs. Indira Gandhi's recognition of the role of the arts as essential to the integral quality of a person, at home with himself and society, representing holistic worldview 'articulated throughout Indian tradition and emphasized by modern Indian leaders, from Mahatma Gandhi to Rabindranath Tagore' (IGCNA Website).

IGNCA's distinguishing feature is in holding 'multi-disciplinary and cross-cultural and multi-media exhibitions, seminars and publications' (Vatsayan, Kapila); in creating interest into the subtleties of culture among the new generation. In November 2010, IGNCA organized an International Cultural Festival, called 'Friendship Through Cultures' to commemorate 60 years of ICCR and 122nd Birth Anniversary of Maulana Abul Kalam Azad.

In 2015, IGNCA hosted an International Conference and Festival on 'Ramlila' – celebrating the masterpiece of intangible heritage of humanity during November 23-30. IGNCA organized a number of programmes in Hyderabad, Bhopal and Lucknow to celebrate the birth anniversary of the renowned vocalist Begum Akhtar.

IGCNA also hosted Kathakar-International Storytellers Festivals during Jan. 30 - Feb.1, 2015, in collaboration with the British Council. Seven storytellers participated; three from India; three from UK and one from Hungary. IGNCA has also documented 26 eminent artists of Hindustani classical Music.

In 2015, IGNCA in collaboration with the Embassy of France and Rolli Books hosted a photo exhibition, which paid homage to the bravery of Indian soldiers in World War I. The other activities included holding of silent films, audio clippings and original memorables of soldiers. The French Ambassador to India Francis Richier also released a book on 'India and the First War: Commemorating 100 years of the Great War'.

IGNCA also hosted an international conference on March 25-26, 2015, on Marc Aurel Stein, an eminent archaeologist and explorer. The theme of the conference was on his 'South and Central Asian Legacy: Recent Discoveries and Research'. An exhibition, 'Fascinated by the Orient: Sir Marc Aurel Stein (1862-1943)' was also organized during March 24-April 17, 2015 in collaboration with the Hungarian Academy of Sciences, Budapest. Stein was the first European to have studied and documented Kashmiri Culture and made significant contribution to the study of the Silk Route.

IGCNA is currently executing a prestigious multi volume project on various aspects of Rashtrapati Bhavan's archeological history, its making, its arts and cultural artefacts (IGNCA 2012). IGNCA is endeavouring to discover and reinvent new ways of establishing a creative and meaningful dialogue between different stakeholders and adding cultural dimensions to development debate.

Marking the Silver Jubilee Celebration of IGNCA on November 19, 2017, President Pranab Mukherjee highlighted the role of culture in these words, "Culture as a balancing factor between progress and the inner needs of an individual; between his spiritual quest and material aspiration".

The President said that institutes like IGNCA constantly needed to discover and re-invent new ways of establishing a creative and meaningful dialogue between different stakeholders and adding cultural dimensions to the development debate (The President, 2012).

## Indian National Trust for Art and Cultural Heritage (INTACH)

It was founded in 1984 in New Delhi to spearhead heritage awareness and conservation in India. It has emerged as one of the world's largest organizations. It has over 91 chapters across the country, with a membership of 8400 persons. INTACH's mission is conservation and preservation of 'not just our natural and built heritage, but intangible heritage as well' (INTACH Website). It operates through various Divisions. INTACH received UNESCO's Special Consultative status in 2007.

INTACH's mission is based on the belief that 'living in harmony with heritage enhances the quality of life.' Some of its stated objectives include the following:

- To sensitize the public about India's pluralistic legacy;
- To foster collaboration and partnership with national and international organizations;
- To undertake the documentation of natural and cultural heritage;
- To promote the preservation of traditional art and crafts.

To achieve some of these objectives, INTACH has entered into an arrangement with IGNCA, New Delhi to digitalize its archives. INTACH has been involved in the preservation of precious objects. Its Art and Material Heritage Division successfully completed the conservation of nine wall paintings and two textile paintings at the Rashtrapati Bhavan in

2016. It also completed conservation work on a collection of paintings in the Catholic Church of Redemption, located to the east of the Parliament House in New Delhi.

INTACH is also involved internationally. Some of its important activities and programmes during 2015-16 included the following:

- Holding of a four-day international conference in February 2016 at Shillong on the theme, 'Oral Traditions: Continuation and Transformation, North East and South East Asia'. 50 participants from Malaysia, Thailand, Netherlands, UK and India took part in this Conference.
- Offer of 3 Research Scholarships to UK citizens for study in the field of art and culture in India.
- Co-hosting of the 19th Asia Europe Foundation (ASEF) in August 2016 in Pune, in collaboration with the Ministry of External Affairs, ASEF and the Symbiosis University, Pune. Its theme was 'Sustainable Urbanization in Heritage Cities'. 48 participants from ASEM countries attended this workshop for one week.

## SAARC and Cultural Diplomacy

What role does SAARC play in cultural diplomacy and how has India performed its role in that framework? Culture is an important component in achieving SAARC's goal of connectivity among nations and peoples of the SAARC member countries. A major role was envisaged for it under the SAARC Charter. What role cultural diplomacy has played in the SAARC context, is neither fully known nor understood?

Connectivity at SAARC takes place at three different levels. Firstly, at the policy level, where a number of official frameworks exist, such as SAARC Cultural Ministers, SAARC Education Ministers and SAARC Information Ministers. Secondly, at the level of SAARC institutions, like the SAARC Cultural Centre, Colombo; SAARC Information Centre, Thimpu; SAARC Human Resource Development Centre, and SAARC Radio and TV. Thirdly, at the level of SAARC – Accredited groups, like SAARC Writers, SAARC Editors etc. There are other SAARC or South Asian Groups that are also loosely associated with SAARC, but have not played a meaningful role.

SAARC's existing structures have not become fully functional, as the Ministerial level meetings have been sporadic with inadequate follow up action. Furthermore infrastructures, like SAARC Cultural Centre have not worked to their optimum level. In many cases there is inadequate information on the working of various other centres.

A SAARC Cultural Ministers' meeting was held in Delhi in 2014, after a gap of eight years. At that meeting, it was decided to declare Bamiyan and Dhaka as the SAARC Cultural Capital for 2015-16 and 2016-17 respectively. Nobody knows what this honour entails. There is a lack of awareness, as hardly anyone knows that Dhaka was the SAARC Cultural Capital and which is the current capital for 2017-18. I would certainly fail the test.

Furthermore, it was decided to declare the year 2016-17 as the Cultural Heritage Year (Delhi Declaration). What has SAARC done in the context of preservation of heritage is not in public domain? On the other hand, we notice that rich cultural heritage is allowed to disappear.

Has SAARC advanced the agenda of cultural diplomacy? What are the success stories, what are the failures and what are the constraints? What needs to be done to make SAARC more action-oriented and play a meaningful and productive role in the arena of cultural diplomacy? What role India has played? There are more questions than answers, as SAARC has yet to emerge as an effective regional organization.

***South Asia Satellite***

The launch of South Asia Satellite by India on May 5, 2017 provides a glimpse into the working of SAARC. The project was initiated as a SAARC Project, when Prime Minister Modi made an announcement at the SAARC Summit in Kathmandu in August 2014. Later it was renamed South Asia Satellite, as Pakistan refused to be a part of the same. The launch was hailed by Prime Minister Modi as 'the beginning of the journey to build the most advanced frontier of our partnership'; a partnership, where 'even sky is not the limit'.

It was built by India at a cost of Rs. 230 crores (Rs. 2300 million) and is expected 'to touch the lives of people' in the areas of space technology applications in telecommunication and broadcasting, tele-medicine, tele-education, e-governance and networking of academic and research institute.

All the leaders, except from Pakistan, hailed the success through the Video Conference. It is a peoples-oriented project aimed at 'securing growth, development and peace for our people and communities'. The media hailed it with headlines, 'Regional diplomacy lifts off on India's South Asia Satellite' (Madhumati DS).

***SAARC Cultural Centre***

It was set up in Colombo (Sri Lanka) as a regional centre to project 'the distinct identity of South Asia' by bringing people together through promotion of cultural cooperation (SAARC). It aims at functioning as a major meeting point for artistic communities by catering to their needs in all forms of art, such as performing arts, visual art and literature, as per the mandate of the SAARC Agenda for Culture, which was launched in 2007.

The objectives of the Centre are:

- To promote regional unity through cultural integration and intercultural dialogue; and
- To contribute towards preservation, conservation and protection of South Asia's cultural heritage

SAARC Agenda for Culture recognized the "crucial role of culture in bringing the peoples of South Asia together", as the region "is heir to a profound civilization continuum of great antiquity – for such harmonious relations among South Asians" and South Asian culture "is a living expression of the creative impetus inherent in the peoples of the region in their daily lives" (SAARC: 1).

During the years 2011-17, SAARC Cultural Centre had mounted around 10 programmes every year; the maximum was 17 in 2012. These covered exhibitions of paintings and handicrafts; holding of film festivals, artistic and photographic camps, literary festivals; and celebration of International Women's Day and SAARC Charter Day. Since 2011, the Centre has organized Film Festivals every year, which provide a unique experience in diversity. The last Festival was held in Colombo in November 2017. Over fifty per cent of the functions were organized in Colombo; SAARC was thus not fully visible in many member-countries.

Following are the programmes that were organized by India during the years 2011-16.

- Exhibition and Workshop in Traditional Handloom, November 1-6, 2012.
- Cultural Festival: Traditional Dance; 26-28 September 2014.
- SAARC Literary Festival, Bangalore, 2-5 July, 2015.

No programme was organized in 2011, 2013, and 2015 in India.

## National Book Trust: New Delhi International Book Fair

Organization of Books Festivals in India and participation in Book Festivals abroad has also emerged as an important area of cultural connectivity. Participation in Book Fairs helps in achieving the objectives of cultural diplomacy through the vehicle of Books. Annual New Delhi Book Fair has become an important event in the calendar of many countries, including Pakistan, which regularly participates. Each year, a country is designated as Partner Country.

Similarly, India participates in International Book Fairs held in foreign countries. The most important such fair is the Frankfurt Book Fair and India was declared the Partner Country in 2013. Indian Minister of State for Human Resource Development (HRD) Jitin Prasada was the guest of honour at the Seoul International Book Fair held in June 2013.

The responsibility to promote Books through Book Fairs falls on the shoulders of the National Book Trust (NBT), an Apex Body that was established in 1957 by the Ministry of Human Resource Development. Following are the main objectives of NBT:

- To produce and encourage the production of good literature in English, Hindi and other Indian languages.
- To make such literature available at moderate prices to the public.
- To arrange Book Fairs/Exhibitions and Seminars in India.
- To participate in Major International Book Fairs annually and showcase Books from India.
- To translate Books in foreign languages to Indian languages.

NBT plays an important role in promoting books and the habit of reading. It does this through organizing Book Fairs/Exhibitions in India and participating in Fairs abroad. It has been designated the nodal for organization of Book Fairs. New Delhi World Book Fair, held annually at the Pragati Maidan is its signature event for participation by foreign countries. This is the largest Book Event in Afro-Asian countries. Indian Trade Promotion Organisation (ITPO) is NBT's partner in mounting this Fair, during January/February every year. The First Fair was organized in 1972.

At the World Book Fair each year, NBT has a partner country as well as a theme. This Fair not only provides an opportunity to promote and sell books, but it also facilitates discussion on themes of interest to the participating country. More than 1000 books in major Indian languages in philosophy, language and literature from ancient to contemporary times are available. The Book Fair is not only confined to books but it is also a venue for organization of other events, embracing education and cultural activities. These include panel discussion, dramas, classical and folk dances, workshops, discussion, authors meet, seminars and cultural programmes, which not only add an extra dimension to the Fair, but also provide an opportunity for greater interaction.

In 2012, Poland was the guest country and the theme of the 20th World Book Fair was 'Towards 100 years of Indian Cinema'. In 2013, France was the guest country and the theme was 'Indigenous Voices: Mapping India's Folk & Tribal Literature'. In 2014, Poland was the guest of honour and the theme was 'Kathasagara: Celebrating Children's Literature'. In 2015, the theme of the Fair was 'Suryodaya: Emerging voices from North East India'. The slogan of the Fair was 'Books opening the mind, Doors opening the future'. The guest of honour country was Singapore with Korea as the focus country. In 2016, China was the guest of honour and the theme was cultural diversity 'Vivid Bharat - Diverse India'. The message of India-China partnership was the connecting rainbow - "Renaissance of Civilizations- Understanding through Exchanges". In 2017, Japan was the guest of honour and the theme was 'Manushi - Books Written on and by Women', with focus on the 'Culture of Reading'.

***France as Guest Country, 2013***

We would now look at 2013, when France was the Guest Country. The French Pavilion was established in collaboration with Oxford Bookstore, where more than 1200 newly-released books as well as a great number of titles in translation were up for sale. Many interesting activities for the members of the publishing industry as well as the general public were organized at the French Pavilion, which included the following:

- Roundtable conference on French publishing industry: "Non-fiction and Graphic Novel: New Trends in France".
- Joint conference by the French and the German Book Offices: "Globalocal Talk".

- Presentation on Nusrat Fateh Ali Khan in Paris, based on the book 'Nusrat: The Voice of Faith' by Pierre-Alain Baud, in partnership with Harper Collins India, in the presence of the author, the translator and musican Dhruv Sangari.
- Book release: The Grace of Brigands by Véronique Ovaldé, in partnership with Full Circle, in the presence of the author, journalist-novelist Amrita Tripathi and novelist Mridula Koshy.

***China and World Book Fair, 2016***

Let us move to 2016, when China was the Guest Country. China was the country partner and the International World Book Fair held at Pragati Maidan, Delhi from January 9-17, 2016. This was the 24th edition of the Book Fair, organized by the National Book Trust of India. The Culture Heritage of India was the theme for 2016, which included participation from 30 countries across the globe, including China, Egypt, Germany, Malaysia, Nepal, Poland, Pakistan, Serbia, and Spain. There was also participation from International Organisations, like WHO and UNESCO. The Fair was inaugurated on January 9, 2016 by the Union Human Resource Development Minister, Smriti Irani, who said that both India and China sought to deepen their ties through cooperation in publishing. The Chinese are already involved in translating Indian books. At this Fair, China participated with 250 publications.

***Book Promotion Abroad***

NBT is also the nodal agency for the promotion of Books overseas. It participates in various International Book Fairs and puts up Exhibitions to display select titles of Books brought out by Indian publishers. NBT has been regularly participating at various Fairs every year since 1970. It has participated at Frankfurt, Bologna, Jerusalem, Seoul, Sharjah, Beijing, Colombo, Tokyo, Bangkok, Minsk, Kuala Lumpur, Singapore, Warsaw, Nigeria, Kathmandu, Manila, London, Karachi, Dhaka and Lahore. India was Guest of Honour at Frankfurt (2006), Moscow (2009), Beijing (2010) and Seoul (2013). NBT also coordinated many Literary Programmes, including Seminars, Discussions, Reading Sessions and Authors' Presentations.

Books and Book Reading habits are growing in India. Markus Dohle, CEO of Penguin Random House said that multiplying of literary festivals in India was 'an indication of how books are an important part of Indian dialogue and culture'. These brought 'writers closer to readers and encouraged conversations and debates around reading, writing and books' (The Times of India, 2018:1)

## Private Sector

It is not only the above Bodies, which are sponsored/supported by the government, but a number of other private players that have emerged as 'Cultural Operators' and we are seeing the emergence of Public and Private Partnership (PPP) in cultural diplomacy between ICCR and the Private Sector. Sufficient data, however, is not in public domain. Some efforts have been made to compile basic information on some of these Cultural Operators in the private sector, based on their involvement with ICCR and other Indian cultural organizations. This would need to be further collated, while information on some of these set-ups is given below, by way of illustration.

### *Teamwork Arts*

It has emerged as one of the important company in the private sector, which is involved directly as well as partner of ICCR and the Ministry of Culture (MOC). It is a versatile entertainment company, which has also roots in the Performing Arts. It has also developed expertise in 'the development of contemporary arts, visual arts and literary festivals across the world' (Teamwork). In India, it is famous for organizing Jaipur Literary Festival (JLF).

Since 2007, it has organized a festival, 'Shared History' in South Africa in collaboration with the High Commission of India in South Africa. Its focus is in the genre of music, dance, theater and literature, but has also branched out to other areas, such as yoga, food, handicrafts, textiles and comedy. It has organized 'India by the Nile' Festival in Egypt since 2013 and 'Eye on India' in the United States since 2012. The Ministry of Culture (MOC) also commissioned it to organize Festivals of India in Australia in 2016 and in UK in 2017.

### *The Prasiddha Foundation and Delhi International Arts Festival (DIAF)*

This Foundation is known for organization of the Delhi International Arts Festival (DIAF) annually in Delhi, which has been supported by ICCR. Its tenth edition was held at Purana Qila in November 2016. The Foundation was set up in 1991 to foster love and appreciation for all forms of art, with a view to promoting cultural connectivity at the national and international levels. Its two flagship festivals are 'Shared Vaibhava' and Eek Aneka'.

DIAF is a culmination of different forms of art, which include dance performances, musical recital, book and poetry reading sessions and film festivals. At DIAF 2016, 23 countries participated from all across the world. It has established its reputation internationally and many countries premier their new productions at this Festival. The Beijing Contemporary Dance Theatre had its international premier, while the Italian Flag Waves made their first appearance. The Festival also provided a platform for differently-abled artists (The Hindustan Times 2016).

***Yuvsatta and Global Youth Peace Festival (GYPF)***

It is a Chandigarh based organization, established in 2007. It is following Gandhian principles to promote peace in the world. It works towards creating a more just world by empowering young change makers, 'as the chasm and barriers of race, religions, nationalities, gender and economic divides are growing, and the hatred and distrust is growing more intense by the day' (Yuvsatta).

One of its signature programme is the organization of 'Global Youth Peace Festival' annually that attracts Youth from across the world to spread the 'message of peace and patriotism' (Behal, Aish, 2017). The $12^{th}$ Festival was held in early October at Chandigarh to coincide with the Birthday of Mahatma Gandhi. The delegates represented 'the proverbial cultural diversity', as they came from different parts of the world, such as Afghanistan, Bangladesh, Malaysia, Syria, Liberia, South Africa, Japan and Mongolia (Singh, Manpriya, 2017).

***South Asia Foundation (SAF)***

It was founded by former Indian Ambassador Madanjeet Singh, UNESCO Goodwill Ambassador in 2010. It is a secular, non-profit and non-political organization. It runs eight autonomous chapters in Afghanistan, Bangladesh, Bhutan, India, Maldives, Nepal, Pakistan and Sri Lanka. Its objective is to uphold its 'core values of regional cooperation and peace through education and cultural interaction between the eight SAARC countries: Afghanistan, Bangladesh, Bhutan, India, Maldives, Nepal, Pakistan, and Sri Lanka' (SAF Website).

SAF's core objective is to promote regional cooperation through a number of UNESCO institutions in the eight SAARC countries. SAF has been admitted into official relationship with the United Nations Educational, Scientific and Cultural Organization (UNESCO) and is recognized as an Apex Body of South Asian Association of Regional Cooperation

(SAARC). Its 'aims, objectives, and activities are in conformity with the spirit, purpose, and principles of the two international organizations' (SAF Website).

***India International Film Academy (IIFA)***

Bollywood also strategically places itself through the holding of annual International Indian Film Academy (IIFA) Awards in different countries, to honour both artistic and technical excellence. The first Award ceremony was held in 2000 in London (UK). So far eighteen ceremonies have taken place, with UK, USA, Malaysia, Singapore and South Africa getting the honour twice. In 2016, Spain became the new destination for the Award, as IIFA Madrid celebrated the 60$^{th}$ Anniversary of the establishment of diplomatic relations (DNA).

***Indian Art Fair***

The fifth edition of the India Art Fair was held in February 2017 in Delhi. The ownership of the Fair has passed on to the Swiss Company, MCH along with Neha Kirpal. The Swiss connection helped in bringing 'greater international interest into the fair with directors, curators, patrons and delegations from prestigious museums, including the MET, MOMA and the Guggenheim in New York, TATE, Palais de Yokyo in Paris, The Singapore Art Museum and MT in Hong Kong (Sodhi, Simran, 2017).

***Shillong Chamber Choir***

It was founded in 2001 by Neil Nongkynrih, a concert pianist who had studied at Trinity College, London and had then returned to Shillong from Europe. 25 young boys and girls of the Choir gave their first performance at Shillong, which included pieces from Khasi folk music and well known composers such as Handel, Bach, and Mozart. In 2009, it performed at Shillong and Kolkata, with the famed Vienna Orchestra. In 2010, it won Gold Awards at the World Choir Games in Shoaning, China (Shillong Chamber Choir).

It shot to fame in India after winning the reality show, 'India Got Talent' in October 2010. They crooned for the Obamas in November 2010 and performed with Amitabh Bachchan at the 'Global Indian Concert', where British rock star, Coldplay gave his first concert in India in front of over 80000 fans, which included musical rendition of the famous poem on gender equality from the movie 'Pink'. It is a blend of the East and the West, between the Northeast and the Hindi Belt of the Bollywood- a perfect picture of pluralism at work.

### *SPIC MACAY (Society for the Promotion of Indian Classical Music and Culture amongst Youth)*

It is a non-profit movement set up in 1977. It aims at increasing awareness among the youth on different aspects of India's heritage. It arranges for the artists to perform in schools and colleges. It introduced lec-dem (lecture cum demonstration) format to present Indian classical forms, as it makes it easier to generate awareness on the rich and heterogeneous cultural tapestry of India (Spic Macay). At Spic Macay's 5$^{th}$ International Convention, Prime Minister Modi talked about Indian culture, while lauding their contribution. He said, "Culture and music can play a vital role in connecting the country. It can be a big step towards realizing 'Ek Bharat Shresht Bharat" (Financial Express 2017).

### *Cross Border Cultural Exchanges*

Harsh Narayan, a Delhi based film maker has facilitated cross-border exchanges between artists, musicians youth groups and intellectuals from Pakistan for several years. These initiatives are aimed at bridging communication gap between the two peoples. A recent initiative was to organize a 10-day spiritual meditation programme in January 2016 at the Vipassana International Academy in Igatpuri with their support for a 12-member Pakistani group, hailing from Lahore, Karachi, Islamabad and Rawalpindi.

This was arranged in collaboration with 'The Society for the promotion of Indian Classical Music and Culture Amongst Youth' (SPICMACAY) and the 'Pakistani India Peoples Forum for Peace and Democracy'. During their stay here, they discussed with the representatives of SPICMACAY in Delhi as to how 'cultural exchanges can help foster peace and harmony in South Asia' (Modi, Chintan Girish). The significance of the visit was that it was taking place at a time when the Pathankot airbase was the target of attack by the terrorists from the other side of the border.

### *Routes 2 Roots: Student Exchange Programme*

It is a Delhi based non-profit organization (NGO). Its mission is to bring together people from different cultures to emphasis their commonalities and enhance peace. Under its Student Exchange Programme it has enabled students from India and Pakistan to connect through written, audio and visual recordings. In 2016, it was one of the ten grassroots organizations that were awarded the International Innovation Award, jointly by the

United Nations Alliance of Civilization (UNAOC) and BHW Graphic (Routes 2 Roots).

***Kochi Biennale Foundation: Kochi-Muzris Biennale (KMB)***

India played host to the Third Edition of this Biennale at Kochi during December 2017-February 2018. The theme of the edition was 'Forming in the pupil of an eye', which according to the curator Sudarshan Shetty 'is not an image of one reality but a reflection of multiple realities and of multiple possibilities in time'. The edition lasted for 108 days with 97 artists from 31 countries. This began in 2012 'as a government initiative', when the Department of Cultural Affairs of the Government of Kerala approached two artists to help organize an international platform for art in India.

Kochi-Muziris Biennale 2012 was 'India's first ever biennial of international contemporary art and its story is unique to India's current reality—it's political, social and artistic landscape' (KMB). This Biennale has now grown into a world acclaimed event. It now falls in the category of other internationally well known Biennales, like the Vienna Art Biennale. It is organized by the Kochi Biennale Foundation and is an example of success story of Public Private Partnership (PPP).

***Delhi Art Gallery (DAG): India's French Connection***

It is India's leading private art gallery and was established in 1993. To mark the 25th Anniversary of its existence, it held a vernissage of 'India's French Connection; Indian Artists in France' in Delhi on January 31, 2018. This brought together the work of 25 Indian artists, 'who have been influenced by French culture'. It included not only paintings, but also print-making and sculptures. The exhibition was accredited by 'Bonjour India'. The French Ambassador Ziegler described this as 'the rediscovery of the great artistic relationship between France and India' (DAG, 2018).

***The Neemrana Music Foundation***

It is a registered, national nonprofit, nonpartisan educational organisation in the field of classical music, which was set up by Francis Wazcziarg, an Indian businessman of French origin. He, along with Aman Nath, was pioneer in setting up Heritage Hotels in India. Wacziarg, who believed in the mandate to build bridges of understanding between different cultures, set up the Neemrana Music Foundation in the field of classical music. His primary interest was to promote and produce operas in India. His daughter, Priya Aude, is an accomplished opera singer and an integral part of the foundation's productions. It is considered to be 'a singular private sector example of intercultural bridge-building of special relevance to Europe' and has 'has fostered the emergence of a group of world-class Indian musicians and opera singers in India' (Isar, 2014).

### *The Foundation of SAARC Writers and Literature (FOSWAL)*

FOSWAL was set up in 1987, with its vision of 'cultural bonding among the neighbouring SAARC countries'. Its Founder President Ajeet Cour is an eminent writer. FOSWAL's primary objective is to project, nurture and strengthen 'cultural connectivity through literacy and cultural interactions among the SAARC countries'. The first SAARC Writers Conference was organized in April 2000. FOSWAL now enjoys the status of a SAARC Recognized Body, which it acquired in 2002. So far, it has organized 31 major SAARC cultural and literacy events, conferences on Buddhism and Sufism, in all the countries of the SAARC region (FOSWAL).

## The Two Punjabs Centre, Chandigarh: Connecting India and Pakistan: A Case Study

This section presents a case study on the role of Two Punjabs Centre, in connecting India and Pakistan. The Centre was set up in February 2005 at CRRID, Chandigarh, as a joint initiative of Dr. Rashpal Malhotra, Salman Haidar and the Author, playing the role of the organizing secretary. The Centre aimed at converting the prevailing 'goodwill atmospherics' (Balle-Balle spirit) between the then two Chief Ministers – Pervez Elahi (Pakistan) and Captain Amarinder Singh (India), into a meaningful programme of activities that could help in promoting connectivity between India and Pakistan, under the overall 'Peace Process' between the two countries. The purpose of the Centre was, therefore, to focus on programmes, which could promote peace and development between the two peoples and two countries, in particular, focusing on the Two Punjabs (India and Pakistan), given their contiguity.

The Centre had been charged with the responsibility of carrying out following activities:

- To promote awareness among each other at the people to people level in the areas of art, culture, media and education through the medium of Cultural Diplomacy.

- To facilitate establishment of linkages at institutional levels between academic and professional institutions in the two Punjabs, to promote students and faculty exchanges
- To promote exchange of visits among different groups, agriculturalists, business groups etc, aimed at learning from one another.
- To facilitate trade and investment linkages in conjunction with Trade Bodies/Chambers.

The Centre had undertaken a number of activities focusing on different areas and groups. These are listed below:

- Visit by delegation of Farmers Associates Pakistan (FAP), Lahore, led by Shah Mehmood Qureshi, Chairman, FAP – (January 24-29, 2006), who later became Foreign Minister.
- Visit of Journalists/Opinion Makers from Lahore (February 5-9, 2006).
- Workshop on "Socio-Economic Cooperation Between India and Pakistan – Building Infrastructural Linkages Between the Pakistan Punjab and Indian Punjab" (May 12-13, 2006), at CRRID, Chandigarh.
- Visit by delegation of Farmers Associates Pakistan (FAP), Lahore, led by the Chairman, FAP (May 11-18, 2006).
- Visit by the Indian Farmers Delegation to Pakistan led by the author (November 12-18, 2006).
- Total Agriculture-Workshop-cum-Field Visits: Farmers Connecting India and Pakistan: Through Knowledge-sharing on Agriculture, March 23-29, 2008.

Let us evaluate the success and constraints experienced. The Centre played a meaningful role in generating awareness, creating positive vibes and enlarging peace constituency. It also worked in the direction of turning the Wagah Border into not only movement for people but also of goods. Our pace had to move in tandem with the pace of the government and this was disrupted after November 2008. Later, the activities of the Centre were channelized into a broader area of South Asia and Central Asia after the November 11, 2008 Terrorist Attack, while still maintaining certain level of connectivity between the Two Punjabs.

What are the lessons and takeaways from our experience, while working at the Centre? Primarily speaking, the Centre filled the void in institutional frameworks, which could facilitate informal connectivity among peoples in the two countries. Such contacts were useful in giving a push to the peace process. We discovered that at people-to-people level there is spontaneity and a desire to have friendly relations. Both the sides exuded warmth in treating delegations and individual visitors. It helped in building peace constituency, which is still able to play a role, howsoever limited it may be. We were a drop in the ocean, but we need to enlarge the peace constituency, so that it could play a more meaningful role.

## Involving Other Cultural Bodies in a Coordinated Thrust on Cultural Diplomacy

Cultural diplomacy is no more confined to the diplomatic actors alone. In this chapter an attempt is made to provide a preliminary picture on the involvement of Other Cultural Bodies in the arena of cultural diplomacy, as the Government has provided a space for them, even though there are limitations to what a government can and should do. Involvement of Other Cultural Bodies has a positive impact, as these carry greater credibility in the absence of any official baggage.

The Akademis of Art have not made their grade, as their performance was not up to the optimum level, whatever may be their constraints, administrative or financial. The 2014 Report of the High Powered of the Ministry of Culture would like to see them playing a greater role. They need to deliver more.

It is not fathomable to understand why a limited role is being played by National Museums in India. They have to come out of their preserves and sanctuaries and find an appropriate role for themselves, befitting India's cultural heritage, as they forge partnerships with other Museums across the globe.

On the other hand, Other Bodies, have a better performance rate, although this could be improved in certain cases. IIC, however, stands out. It also has a good working relationship with ICCR, IGNCA and foreign diplomatic missions. IIC is living up to its mandate, having emerged as a 'Cultural Hub' in Delhi, as it provides space for not only Indian artists and scholars, but also diplomatic missions to showcase art and culture from their respective countries.

Private Sector is getting increasingly involved, as it has the advantage of professional expertise and technical competence. We presented a picture of some of the players in the private sector that are involved in the arena of cultural diplomacy. This list needs to be expanded and additional data collected to determine a suitable role for the private sector in the arena of cultural diplomacy. May be the government could provide a framework, under which cultural operators could function, as these supplement government's efforts.

SAARC, whose one pillar is cultural connectivity, has not fully succeeded in enthusing its processes and structures to promote cultural connectivity, given the non-cooperative attitude of Pakistan. Indian initiatives, such as South Asian University and South Asian Satellite, have not resulted in achieving desired results. A South Asian identity has yet to emerge.

We need to pay special attention to SAARC Countries. Parliamentary Committee on External Affairs would like India to "utilize cultural diplomacy to its fullest" and "expand diplomatic depth in the South Asian region" by organizing "a sufficient number of cultural activities." We have to foster will and find innovative ways to do so.

An area, where scant attention is being paid is the role of Books and how they could promote connectivity. We need to go beyond Delhi World Book Fair and aggressively promote Indian Books at regional centres also. We also need to pay greater attention to the translation of books for foreign and domestic audience, given the rich diversity of literature produced in regional languages.

We are also witnessing an initial trend in the emergence of Public Private Partnership (PPP), with increasing involvement of ICCR with the private sector as Event Managers. This ad hoc relationship needs to be converted into institutional tie-ups. We also need more institutional frameworks, like the Two Punjabs Centre, to facilitate connectivity at the people's level.

Nonetheless, all the above bodies, which could be categorised as 'Cultural Operators', have emerged as important players. The moot question is how far their activities have been coordinated with ICCR and could be dovetailed into an overall agenda and framework, so that there is a single minded and focused approach on cultural diplomacy.

**References**

Behal, Aish, 2017, 'Foreign delegates spread message of peace, patriotism', *The Hindustan Times*, October 3.

DAG, 2018, https://in.ambafrance.org/India-s-French-Connection-Indian-Artists-in-France-15233 (Accessed on December 12, 2017).

Das, Nabanita, 2016, 'Delhi International Arts Festival: Where India meets the world', *The Hindustan Times*, December 08.

Delhi Declaration, 2014, SAARC Culture Ministers' Conference, New Delhi, September 25. http://www.careerride.com/view/saarc-culture-ministers-conference-delhi-declaration-adopted-16861.aspx (Accessed on 12 December 2017).

*DNA*, http://www.dnaindia.com/entertainment/report=life-becomes bigger- and-better-thisyear. (Accessed on 12 December 2017).

*Financial Express*, 2017, 'PM Modi hails Spic Macay', says Society demonstrates how to work for benefit of society', June 5.

FOSWAL, http://www.foundationsaarcwriters.com (Accessed on September 13, 2018).

Sarkar, Bidyut (ed.), 1968, *India and Southeast Asia*: Proceedings of a Seminar, ICCR, Delhi.

ICCR, Website, www.iccr.gov.in (Accessed on 12 December 2017).

IGCNA Website, www.ignca.nic.in (Accessed on 12 December 2017).

IGNCA 2012, Inaugural Address of the President of India, November 19.

IIC 2014-15, Annual Report of the India International Centre, New Delhi.

IIC 2015-16, Annual Report of the India International Centre, New Delhi.

IIC 2016-17, Annual Report of the India International Centre, New Delhi.

IIC Diary 2017, The India International Centre diary, July-August 2017.

IIC Website, www.iicdelhi.nic.in (Accessed on 12 December 2017).

INTACH. www.intach.org.

Isar, 2014, Prof. Yudhishthir Raj Isar, India Country Report. Available at http://ec.europa.eu/assets/eac/culture/policy/international-coop -eration/ documents/country-reports/india_en.pdf (Accessed on

December 12, 2017).

Jacob, Shalini, 2016, 'A Romanian Photographer Is Capturing Beauty Around The World & She's Currently in India', January 5. https://www.scoopwhoop.com/This-Romanian-Photographer-Is-Capturing-Beauty-Around-The-World/#.77aw56hkb (Accessed on 12 December 2017).

KMB, http://www.biennialfoundation.org/biennials/kochi-muziris-biennale- india/ (Accessed on December 12, 2017).

Madhumati, D S, 2017, 'India launches South Asia Satellite', *The Hindu*, May 5. http://www.thehindu.com/sci-tech/science/india-launches-south-asia-satellite/article18391277.ece (Accessed on 12 December 2017).

Maulana Azad, 1953, Inaugural Address at the setting up of the Sangeet Natak Akademi, New Delhi, March 28, 1953.

Maulana Azad, 1954:1, Speech delivered at the first meeting of the Sahitya Akademi, New Delhi, March 12, 1954.

Maulana Azad, 1954:2, Address at the first meeting of the Lalit Kala Akademi, New Delhi, August 5.

Maulana Azad, 1951-52, *'The Selected Works of Maulana Abul Kalam Azad, Volume VI (1951-52)',* (Ed) Dr. Ravindra Kumar, 1992, Atlantic Publishers & Distributors, New Delhi.

Maulana Azad, 1953-54, *'The Selected Works of Maulana Abul Kalam Azad, Volume VII (1953-54)',* (Ed) Dr. Ravindra Kumar, Atlantic Publishers & Distributors, New Delhi, 1992.

MOC, 2013-14, Annual Report of the Ministry of Culture, Govt. of India, New Delhi.

MOC, 2014-15, Annual Report of the Ministry of Culture, Govt. of India, New Delhi.

MOC, 2015-16, Annual Report of the Ministry of Culture, Govt. of India, New Delhi.

MOC, 2016-17, Annual Report of the Ministry of Culture, Govt. of India, New Delhi.

Modi, Chintan Girish, 2016, 'A new prescription for peace from India',

*The Hindu*, January 18.

Pal, Sanchari, 2016, 'The Fascinating Story of the Talented Shillong Chamber Choir That Rocked the Stage with Coldplay', November 22. http://www.thebetterindia.com/75719/shillong-chamber-choir-neil-nongkynrih/ (Accessed on 12 December 2017).

Ramnath, Nandini, 2014, Scroll.in, *Quarts India*, December 11, 2014.

Routes 2 Roots, 2016, 'Receives International Innovative Award', Delhi Greens, April 28.

SAARC :1 , www.saarcculture.org/saarc-agenda-for-culture (Accessed on December 16, 2017).

SAARC: www.saarcculture.org (Accessed on December 16, 2017).

SAF Website, http://www.southasiafoundation.org/ (Accessed on April 2018).

Shillong Chamber Choir, https://en.wikipedia.org/wiki/Shillong_Chamber_Choir (Accessed on 12 December 2017).

Singh, Gurmukh, 2012, 'India's Soft Power Spreads', *The Tribune,* October 2.

Singh, Manpriya, 2017, 'The 12th edition of the global youth peace festival brings peace activists', *The Sunday Tribune*, October 1.

Sodhi, Simran, 2017, 'Cultural push to Swiss connection', *The Tribune*, February 20. Teamwork, Website, http://teamworkarts.com (Accessed on 12 December 2017).

Spic Macay, website: www.spicmacay.com (Accessed on 12 December 2017).

Teamwork: website, http://teamworkarts.com (Accessed on 12 December 2017).

*The Hindustan Times*, 2016, 'Delhi International Arts Festival where India meets the world', November 12.

The President, 2012, 'Inaugural Address of the President of India at the Silver Jubilee Celebrations of IGCNA', Nov. 19.

*Yuvsatta,* www.peacefestindia.in (Accessed on 12 December 2017).

# Chapter – VI

# Direction of India's Cultural Diplomacy – Case Study on Central Asia and Southeast Asia

## Introduction

In this chapter, we would look at how India's cultural diplomacy has played out in its 'Extended Neighbourhood', which is an area of priority for India's foreign policy. We have chosen these regions as the Author had been posted to some of these countries and had also been involved in the framing and implementation of cultural diplomacy. These Regions have been historically and culturally linked with India and have old civilizational ties. We will encounter both similarities and dissimilarities, as we go along in our examination.

The first striking similarity is the lack of connectivity between India and Southeast and Central Asian countries till early 1990s since India's Independence. This was for varied reasons. In the case of Central Asia, it depended upon USSR, as these territories were the constituent units of the Soviet Union and had no independent say.

In the case of Southeast Asia, the newly independent governments were wary on strengthening cultural bonds with India, as they were keen to protect their Independence in the early formative years of their existence. A certain amount of hesitancy existed in developing cultural links, because of differing political perceptions and worldview. In such an environment "a close cultural affinity then turns out to be some kind of hindrance rather than a help in forging new ties with a neighbouring country". These are now no more trammeled by such considerations, given development of multi-faceted relationship at the bilateral and regional levels (Sahai, 2009).

Interestingly for both the regions, early 1990s presented an opportunity. In the case of Central Asia, it was the break-up of the Soviet Union in 1991 that resulted in their gaining Independence, resulting in their emergence on the global scene. This led to their carving out a pattern of relationship with the international community. In the case of Southeast Asia, it was the admission of India as ASEAN's Sectoral Partner in 1992 and Dialogue Partner in 1995, that provided the real push in reviving cultural and other links.

For Central Asian countries, India emerged as the natural choice, given their historical connectivity with India. Furthermore, strong political links with the Soviet Union provided an added thrust in moving in the direction of India. India was equally keen to forge ties with the newly independent countries. India became the first destination for a foreign visit by leaders during 1991-93 and this paved the way for the establishment of diplomatic links. This resulted in the signing of a number of bilateral agreements; one of such agreement dealt with cultural cooperation. The Author was involved in facilitating the visits of dignitaries and the drafting of such agreements.

In the case of Southeast Asia, a new impetus was provided at the time of India's admission as Dialogue Partner in 1996, which was shepherded by Singapore. On this occasion, Singapore's Foreign Minister S. Jeykumar, who was ASEAN's Coordinator for India, highlighted the significance of cultural links on this occasion. He thus reiterated the strength of cultural links for building bridges on a long term basis in these words:

> "As we focus on our developing economic and political links, it is important that we continue to strengthen our cultural links. We shall reap long term gains, if we start, investing in strengthening our bridges now. This could be done through developing tourism, cultural, educational and other institutional links" (Sarkar, Bidyut, 1968).

Indian External Affairs Minister I.K. Gujral, on the other hand, underscored the need for linking culture with strengthening of commercial and political ties, as he observed that the "tremendous cultural capital that India and ASEAN have invested in each other over centuries has not been used to implement and embellish our substantive economic and political relations" (Gujral, IK, 1998).

At the same time, Gujral wanted to give a new thrust to Cultural Diplomacy by establishing more durable institutions for "continuous cultural osmosis" through setting up of Indian Centres in ASEAN Countries and ASEAN Centres in India; organizing of India-ASEAN Festivals, launching of

ASEAN-India Lecture Series, establishment of Chairs in Universities. Gujral also saw opportunity both in classical and popular culture, as he said, "We must emphasis the classical as much as the popular modern manifestation of it – in music, films and television programmes". Gujral thus gave us a blue print for a concrete action plan, some of which was implemented, while the rest is still in the works.

## CIS Focus Year 2003: Imparting a New Thrust to Central Asian Connectivity

It was in 2003 that India moved in the direction of giving contemporary colour to India's deep historical and civilizational links with Central Asia. The then External Affairs Minister Yashwant Sinha elaborated India's approach in his Keynote Address at the Third India-Central Asia Conference held in Tashkent on November 6, 2003, in these words:

> "India's connection with these splendid cities, indeed entire Central Asia, has deep roots in history. Trade between us pre-dates the Silk Road by at least three thousand years. And Aryans provide a link between Central Asia and India. Some scholars maintain that the Vedas are a blend of the adventurous 'Central Asian' spirit and the cultural genius of the Indus Valley Civilization. We in India, still use the Saka Calendar as a sort of daily reminder of the deep bonds between Central Asia and India" (Sinha, Yashwant, 2003).

President K R Narayanan saw India's Cultural Diplomacy in Central Asia as an attempt to revitalize cultural relationship "fostered by shared heritage and ideals and the geographical proximity" (President Narayanan, 2002), which had diminished during the Colonial and the Soviet Periods. For Prime Minister Vajpayee, it was a matter 'of reviving ties with new countries, but ancient nations', giving right emphasis to the nature of relationship. He captured the essence of relationship in these words:

> "The teachings and poetry of Sufi saints such as Amir Khusrau and Mir Sayyed Hamadani have forged an unbreakable bond between our cultures. From language, architecture and music to philosophy and even cuisine, there is much here which is very familiar to an Indian" (PM Vajpayee, 2003).

It was also retaining 'the cultural values of collectivism and tolerance built over centuries' with the Message of Lord Budha and Sufism's "universal concepts and the love and compassion" contained in them. Sufism represents not only a meeting point between Buddhism and Islam, but between Islam and Hinduism.

It was also an attempt to transport this relationship to its present-day context and build the same on "a shared commitment to democracy, secularism and the rule of law" and the common concerns shared between India and Central Asia. India was thus seeking to blend 'Tradition with Modernity', which was a precursor to the present-day thrust on cultural diplomacy.

The above was given concrete shape through programmes and activities, such as holding of Indian exhibitions, seminars and conducting special studies during the years 2003 and 2004, as given below:

- Visit by President Akaev of Kyrgyzstan to participate at the UNESCO sponsored 'Education for All' Summit in Delhi during 10-11 November 2003.
- Participation by the Tajikistan Minster of Culture Olimov at the 'International Conference on Dialogue amongst Civilizations' in Delhi from 9-10 July, 2003.
- Holding of a Photo Exhibition in Bishkek (Kyrgyzstan) during October 2003.
- Unveiling of Statutes of Mahatma Gandhi in Public Parks in Dushanbe (Tajikistan) and Almaty (Kazakhstan).
- Organization of a seminar on 'Amir Khusro and His Influence on Central Asia' at Dushanbe (Tajikistan) on May 15, 2003.
- Grant of support to the Shastri School in Tashkent (Uzbekistan).

Some of the important connectivity-related activities undertaken during 2003-2004 are listed below:

- Setting up of Institutes of Excellence in I.T. Education in Kyrgyzstan, Tajikistan and Uzbekistan.
- Offer of 30 full scholarships by ICCR to students from Central Asia.
- Offer of ten slots, two for each Central Asian country, at the Institute of Defence Studies and Analyses (IDSA), New Delhi.

India organized Festivals of India in three Central Asian countries, namely Kazakhstan, Kyrgyzstan and Uzbekistan during 2003-2004. A painting exhibition- 'Amrita Shergill Revisited' by contemporary artists was held as a part of the Festival activities. A Fashion Show showcasing Indian jewellery and costumes was held in Tashkent and Almaty during August 2004. A seminar on India and Central Asia was also organized at Tashkent during August 2004.

## ASEAN-India Commemorative Summit 2012 - A Forward Step in Connecting Southeast Asia

ASEAN-India Commemorative Summit held in Delhi on 20 December, 2012 represented an important milestone in India's approach on cultural diplomacy. It brought about a qualitative change in India's pursuit of cultural diplomacy, recognizing that cultural diplomacy is a two-way process of acculturation through the medium of culture; understanding of which provides connectivity with each other. It aimed at also using culture to connect into the future. This was brought out at the Conference on Civilizational Dialogue between India and ASEAN organized by ICCR 'to explore not only the history and historical dimensions linking India and Southeast Asian countries, but also the role these links will play in future world' (Goel, 2013). The thrust thus was on linking the past with the future.

The future agenda for cultural connectivity was incorporated in the ASEAN-India Summit Vision Statement, 2012 that emphasized 'socio-cultural cooperation' through 'greater people to people interaction', in practically all the fields and areas of human activity. These were spelt out as follows:

- 'To encourage the study, documentation and dissemination of knowledge about the institutional links between ASEAN and India;
- To enhance contacts between parliamentarians, media personnel and academics between Track II Institutes such as the 'Network of Think Tanks;
- To intensify efforts to preserve, protect and restore symbols and structures representing civilizational bonds between ASEAN and India' (Vision Statement, 2012).

At the practical level, it resulted in undertaking activities that enhanced this connectivity, linking tradition to modernity. Dr. Suresh Goel, the then Director General, ICCR listed out some of these, which are recapitulated in the succeeding paragraphs (Goel, Suresh)[1].

***ASEAN-India Artists Camp: Partners in Residency, Darjeeling, June 2012***

It brought together 20 painters from ASEAN countries – (Singapore, Brunei, Cambodia, Indonesia, Laos, Malaysia, Myanmar, Thailand, and Vietnam – two from each country) and 20 Indian painters, promoting acculturation of ideas.

***ASEAN-India Civilizational Dialogue, Patna, July 2012***

This seminar focused on centuries' old civilizational links between India and Southeast Asian countries, which went back to centuries in areas, such as maritime archaeology. ICCR organized this in collaboration with the Nalanda University. Dr. Karan Singh, President, ICCR viewed this as 'an important tool in the on-going effort to create a 'Pan-Asian Identity', which is assuming greater significance in the context of today's geo-politics' (Singh, Dr. Karan, 2013).

***Exhibition of Archival Material, Delhi, December 2012***

This highlighted shared heritage through photographs and manuscripts, going back to the 19th century, which included a letter from Bahadur Shah Zafar, the last Moghul King. This was organized in collaboration with the National Archives of India.

***Gala Cultural Performance at the Rashtrapati Bhawan, Delhi, December 20, 2012***

This 'spectacular display of our shared culture', where cultural troupes from India and ASEAN countries participated, represented a picture of unity in diversity.

At the popular level, ***ASEAN-India Car Rally***, a remarkable journey of 8000 kms through eight countries was completed in 22 days on 21 December, 2012. The Rally symbolized the 'Vision of an ASEAN-India Community' where people, goods, services and ideas travel freely between us' (PM, 2012). The Rally not only rekindled the 'ancient bonds of friendship between India and ASEAN', but also highlighted 'the natural strategic imperative for our relationship in contemporary times' (ibid). This again reiterated India's desire to strengthen bonds with ASEAN countries through linking tradition with modernity.

Indian also renewed its commitment at the 2012 ASEAN-India Summit for the preservation of edifices of ancient cultural heritage in Southeast Asia, given the growing recognition of the expertise and capabilities of the Archeological Survey of India. This would cover the preservation of heritage sites, such as Angkor Wat in Cambodia, Borobudur and Prambanan temples in Indonesia, Wat Phu in Laos, Bagan in Myanmar, Sukhtoi Historical Park in Thailand and My Son in Vietnam. This cooperation is viewed as an important part of the new thrust of India's cultural diplomacy (Bhattacharya, Sanjay)[2].

The launching of ASEAN-India Centre at the Resources and Information Systems (RIS) New Delhi on June 21, 2013 by the External Affairs Minister Salman Khurshid fulfilled the dream of Foreign Minister M.C. Chagla and Prime Minister I.K. Gujral. The Centre added a new dimension to the relationship, signifying that "The ASEAN-India Partnership is not only of long standing but also of great current and future strategic relevance, oriented as it is to economic growth, development, capacity building and peace and security" (EAM, 2013:1).

## Nalanda University: An Experiment in Joint Cultural Diplomacy

The setting up of the Nalanda University added another new dimension to Indian cultural diplomacy, given the fact that this is a collaborative project, enjoying the support of the Southeast and East Asian countries. Support for the establishment of this University was formalized at the 4th East Asia Summit (EAS) in Thailand on 24-25 October 2009. At the 5th East Asian Summit on 30 October 2010, Indian Prime Minister extended an invitation to EAS member states to participate in the project. The significance of the project was again highlighted at the 8th East Asian Summit Foreign Ministers Meeting on 3 July 2013, as it reiterated its character as 'a non-state, non-profit and self-governing international institution of excellence'. It is to have a Continental focus, as it brought together 'the brightest and most dedicated students from all the countries in Asia'.

This University is located at Rajgir in the State of Bihar, which has contributed land, free of cost to the University. The primary funding for the University would come from the Government of India (Misra, J N)[3]. Initial financial support for this project has been received from the Governments of China, Thailand, Laos, Australia, Japan and Singapore. The first two Schools – Historical Studies and Ecology and Environmental Studies – started functioning from the academic year 2013-14. It would be a non-Metropolitan University, with a commitment, to become a Net Zero Energy Campus, which would be one of its kind (Sabharwal, Gopa)[4].

## Thrust of India's Cultural Diplomacy in Malaysia during the 1990s

In this section, we would look at the operation of Indian Cultural Diplomacy during the late 1990s, when the Author was posted as Indian High Commissioner. The thrust of India's cultural diplomacy in Malaysia rests on the twin objectives of sustaining the existing cultural links and further generating awareness of modern India, aimed at building strong economic and political links on this cultural edifice. The presence of a large Indian Diaspora further helps in providing this connectivity.

It may be noted that some facets of Indian culture have become an integral part of Coronation and religious ceremonies. At the popular level, Bollywood now provides the connectivity. Bollywood song '*Kuch Kuch Hota Hai*' had become an integral part of local functions. Malaysia, on its part, did not fail to plug into this Bollywood magic and succeeded in projecting Malaysia as a Tourism Destination by providing facilities for the shooting of films in Malaysia. Malaysia emerged an important venue for holding Bollywood Festivals and musical concerts on a regular basis.

In the cultural arena, India provided support to existing cultural organizations as well as facilitated the visits of Indian cultural troupes. Three local organizations, which received considerable attention and support were-The Temple of Fine Arts, the Sutra Theatre and the Netaji Centre. The Sutra Dance Theatre, which is established by a renowned Malay Muslim *Odissi* Dancer, Ramli Ibrahim, has established a name for itself in promoting high quality Indian classical dances. The Temple of Fine Arts has also developed into a Centre of Excellence.

The renowned Malay choreographer and *Odissi* dancer, Ramli Ibrahim had also performed in India on many occasions and his performances had been well received, thus earning the nickname of Indian Cultural Ambassador. Later, he organized a Festival of Indian Dance 'Stirring Odissi' in December 2008 at various locations in Malaysia with the support of ICCR and the Sangeet Natak Akademi.

There was also a continuous flow of Indian Music and Dance Troupes, which supplemented local cultural shows. Exhibitions on Art and Crafts, Paintings and Photography were held periodically. Local cultural organizations were encouraged to organize cultural events that were supported by the High Commission; thereby introducing an element of Public Private Partnership (PPP).

A new salient feature of the cultural activities was to hold these activities in other State Capitals also, taking them to far off places in Sabah and Sarawak. India was also promoted as a Destination for Buddhists.

A 150-seat multipurpose Hall at the High Commission with modern stage facilities was inaugurated in 1997. This provided excellent opportunities for the holding of cultural shows, films screening, lectures and conferences. This helped in filling the void in the absence of a cultural centre and a number of cultural and other activities were organized on a regular basis. It helped in discovering local talent and provided greater connectivity with local organizations.

Netaji Subhash Chander Bose had kindled the fire for Indian independence, with his clarion call of '*Delhi Chalo*' (Charge to Delhi) in Kuala Lumpur in 1942. Netaji Centre was set up in his memory. It, however, could not function at its optimum level, because of weak financial base and poor local administrative structure. A large number of recruits for the *Jhansi Ki Rani* contingent were Malaysian girls of Indian origin; India honoured one of them- Puan Sri Janaki Nahapan- with the 'Padma Shri Award.'

Malaysian Indian Congress (MIC) was a part of the political dispensation in that country, with a number of cabinet posts reserved for MIC, being a coalition partner of the ruling party, United Malay National Organisation (UMNO). Indian Diaspora stayed connected with India and sent the largest contingent, over 100 persons, to the annual meetings of Pravasi Bharatiya Divas (PBD) since January 2003.

A significant part of the efforts had been to promote linkages among educational institutions. India had the starting advantage of being an educational hub for Malaysians, as about 30 per cent of Malaysian doctors had studied in India. Three alumni organizations – Malaysian Association of Indian University Graduates (MAIUG), the Society of Medical Graduates India Malaysia (SOMGRIM) and the Manipal Graduates Association (MGA) continue to provide connectivity with India.

Partial success was achieved in building institutional level linkages in the education sector. This resulted in an increase in the number of academicians attached to various universities, but meaningful institutional level links could not be established. India also missed boarding the education hub in Malaysia, because of slow response and dilatory procedures on the part of Indian authorities. On the other hand, Australia, Canada and UK succeeded in twining their academic institutions with Malaysian counterparts. In the case of India, a solitary success story was that of the Melaka Manipal Medical College in Malacca.

Annual Azlan Shah Hockey Tournament at Ipoh provided an opportunity for sporting links between India and Malaysia, with India lifting the trophy in 1999. Religious festivals, like 'Taipusam' provided visibility, while concerns were expressed on 'Yoga' as un-Islamic; so were on the use of the word 'Allah' in some Indian religious scriptures. Malaysian Sikh Youth Organizations promoted links with Diaspora from the ASEAN countries, in particular Singapore.

To project modern India in Malaysia, links were established with a number of think tanks, such as the Institute of Diplomacy and Foreign Relations (IDFR) and Institute of Strategic and International Studies (ISIS), Kuala Lumpur, which now holds annual conference with the Indian Council for World Affairs (ICWA). IDFA is now formally linked with the Foreign Service Institute (FSI) in the Ministry of External Affairs (MEA). A seminar on 'India and ASEAN: A Growing Partnership in the 21st Century was organized on November 12, 1997 and another on Nuclear Nonproliferation was held in 2000.

A new dimension was also added that provided interface between defence establishments and academic institutes. A new ground was covered when Admiral Bhagwat, Chief of Indian Naval Staff was invited to deliver a lecture at the Maritime Institute of Malaysia (MIMA) in 1998. Similarly, visit by Vice Admiral C de Silva, Director General, Coast Guard to Malaysia in 1999 resulted in generating goodwill. A Seminar was also organized on India-Malaysia relations in 2000 with a think tank of the then Defence Minister Najib, who later became the Prime Minister of Malaysia.

A significant development was the involvement of Indian States in promoting commercial and cultural connectivity directly with Malaysia. Chief Ministers from the States of Andhra Pradesh, Maharashtra and Tamil Nadu paid official visits. Chandrababu Naidu took some pioneering steps in turning Hyderabad into an IT City as well as facilitated the setting up of a top class Business School, taking a cue from Malaysia. These steps have become precursor of the present day thrust in involving States in cultural and commercial diplomacy

In the 1990s, Indian Diaspora in Malaysia was the largest Diaspora in the world, forming 7 % of the total population. Its political outfit, Malaysian Indian Congress (MIC), was a partner of the Ruling UMNO Party. At any given time, a number of Indians have been members of the cabinet. They played a role in providing connectivity with India. Samy Velu was the most visible face during that period. After his exit from active politics, he was designated as Special Envoy to India. He had led the over 100 strong Malaysian Delegation at the PBD for a number of years since 2003.

Indian Diaspora in Malaysia took early steps to organize itself globally under the umbrella of GOPIO (Globalised Persons of India Origin) in late 1990s. It organized the first unofficial PBD in Delhi in 2001. Simultaneously a parallel GOPIO was formed in USA. Internally also, efforts to galvanize Diaspora under one umbrella failed, as diverse groups preferred to maintain their regional or religious identities. An annual Diwali Charity Bazaar was organized at the High Commissioner's Residence with the support of the Indian Expatriates Association, called 'Bharat Club'.

The thrust of Indian Cultural Diplomacy in Malaysia was to project modern India, while continuing to retain traditional links through visiting cultural troupes. A multipronged approach was adopted, which helped in connecting with the locals and the Indian community; sending the message that India was a credible and reliable partner.

## Present Day Relationship

What is the present play of relationship between India and Southeast and Central Asian countries? We would look at these in the context of certain parameters, such as Cultural Agreements, Cultural Centres, Chairs of India Studies, Educational Links, Festivals of India, Preservation of Heritage and Partnership in Human Resource Development.

### *High Level Exchange of Visits Adding to Cultural Dimension*

A striking feature that emerges is the exchange of high level visits during 2014-16, which had a cultural component attached to these. An MOU on Culture was signed during the visit of Vice President Hamid Ansari to Indonesia during November 1-4, 2015. He also unveiled a bust of Mahatma Gandhi in Udayana University, Bali. An Agreement on Cultural Exchange Programme for the years 2015-20 was signed during the visit of Prime Minister Modi to Malaysia in November 2015 (MEA 2015-16).

MOUs on Cultural and Youth Cooperation were signed during the visit of Prime Minister of Vietnam Mr Nguyen Tan Dung to India from 27-28 October 2014. A Cultural Exchange Programme (CEP) for 2016-19 was signed during the visit of Thai PM in June 2016. A bilateral Executive Programme of Cultural Exchanges for the year 2016–2018 was signed on 14 October 2015 during the visit of Secretary of Foreign Affairs of the Philippines Albert F.Del Rosario to India (MEA 2015-16).

A new Programme of Cooperation in the field of Culture and Arts for the period 2016-18 was signed during the visit of Indian Prime Minister to Tajikistan in July 2015.

During his visit to Singapore in November 2015, Prime Minister Modi jointly released commemorative stamps depicting the Presidential Buildings of the two countries on the occasion of the 50th Anniversary of the establishment of diplomatic relations (MEA 2015-16). An Executive Programmes (EP) on cultural cooperation for the period 2015-18 was also signed during the Prime Minister's (MEA 2015-16).

### *Cultural Agreements Providing Framework for Cultural Connectivity*

India has signed Cultural Agreements with a number of countries in the region. The first Agreement was signed with Indonesia (29 December, 1965), followed by the Philippines (6 September, 1969), Vietnam (18 December, 1976), Thailand (29 April 1977), Malaysia (3 March, 1978), Laos (17 August, 1994), Cambodia (31 January, 1996) and Myanmar (25 January, 2001). India signed a Memorandum of Understanding with Singapore on 5 February, 1993, as the latter was not keen to go in for a comprehensive agreement.

India has signed Cultural Agreements with all the countries in Central Asia. Most of these were signed during 1991-92, at the time of initial visits of the Heads of these States to India. President Karimov of Uzbekistan and President Nazarbaev of Kazakhstan were the first to sign these agreements. A broad common template was used on which the Author had worked.

Cultural Exchange Programme between the Government of Turkmenistan and Government of India in the Fields of Science, Education, Culture, Art, Tourism, Sport and Mass Media, signed on 25 May 2010 in New Delhi for initial 2 years was renewed for further 2 years till 31 December 2016 under the existing terms and conditions.

Cultural Exchange Programmes (CEPs) are currently in operation with Indonesia, Laos, Malaysia, Philippines, Singapore, Thailand and Vietnam. India has also valid Cultural Exchange Programmes with the Central Asian Countries.

### *Chairs of India Studies Enhancing Academic Linkages*

India has also set up Indian Chairs of Studies at various universities in Southeast Asia. These Chairs exist at Preah Sihanouk Raja Buddhist University, Phnom Penh (Cambodia); Mahendradatta University, Bali and Gadja Madah University, Jogjakarta (Indonesia); University of Malaya,

Kuala Lumpur (Malaysia); National University of Singapore (Singapore) and University of Social Sciences and Humanities, Ho Chi Minh City (Vietnam). These Chairs are for Indian, Buddhist and Sanskrit Studies.

The Chair at the Centre for Indian Studies set up in Osh State University in Kyrgyzstan in 1997 had to be discontinued since 2010 after political unrests there. At the initiative of the Indian Embassy, an India Study Centre was established in the prestigious National Library of Kyrgyzstan in Bishkek on 14 November 2014. The Center is running with the help of volunteers and imparts training in English and Hindi languages, Yoga and Kathak dance. Another center has also been opened in Kara Balta, a city at a distance of 80 km from Bishkek.

Three Uzbek educational institutions promote studies of Hindi language, from primary to post-graduate level. Uzbek Radio completed 50 years of Hindi broadcasting in 2012. Uzbek TV channels regularly show Indian films and TV serials.

Several universities in the Philippines, such as, the University of Santo Tomas, the University of the Philippines, the University of the Visayas, Adamson University, the University of Mindanao and others have opened special 'India chapters' in their prestigious libraries, which house collection of books on India, gifted through the Public Diplomacy Division of the Ministry of External Affairs.

A number of Indian Studies Centers are operational in prestigious Thai universities. India supported construction of a new building for the Sanskrit Studies Centre at Silpakorn University, Bangkok in 2008 and has deputed a Sanskrit professor. An India Studies Centre is functioning at the Thammasat University of Bangkok since April 1993. In 2008, the Mahidol University of Bangkok started a Masters of Arts course on Indian studies. A Chair in Chulalongkorn University's India Study Centre was inaugurated by HRH Princess Maha Chakri Sirindhorn on March 6, 2012.

The Ministry of AYUSH and Rangsit University signed an MOU on establishing a Chair on Ayurveda at Rangsit University on 29 June 2015.

***Cultural Centres Projecting Traditional with Modern India***

The first Cultural Centre in Southeast Asia was opened in Jakarta in 1988 and another in 2004 in Bali, Indonesia. Among the other Southeast Asian countries, India has cultural centres in Thailand (2009), Kuala Lumpur (2010) and Myanmar (2010). In Central Asia, the first two centres were set up in Astana (Kazakhstan) and Tashkent (Uzbekistan) in 1994. Another centre was set up in Dushanbe (Tajikistan) in 2002. A Cultural Centre was set up in Hanoi in April 2017'as part of activities marking the two countries' 45 years of diplomatic ties and ten years of a strategic partnership'(Le Diem, 2017).

The Mission in Indonesia operates Jawaharlal Nehru Indian Cultural Centre (JNICC) in Jakarta (Indonesia) that conducts regular classes of Indian classical music, Indian classical dances (Kathak and Bharatnatyam), Yoga, and also teaches Hindi and Tamil languages. Cultural cooperation expanded through the activities of the Indian Cultural Centres in Jakarta and Bali. New initiatives, particularly, in the shooting of films, promoted closer people-to-people contacts.

Indian Cultural Centre (ICC), Kuala Lumpur conducts classes in Carnatic Vocal, Kathak dance, Yoga, Hindi language and Tabla by trained teachers from India and Malaysia. ICC also hosts a Library and an AYUSH Information Cell to disseminate authentic information on AYUSH systems of medicines. Indian Cultural Center was, renamed as Netaji Subhash Chandra Bose Indian Cultural Centre (NSCBICC) by Prime Minister Modi during his visit to Malaysia in November 2015.

Indian Cultural Centre in Astana is engaged in various cultural activities, including conducting of yoga and dance classes; celebration of Indian festivals; organizing of cultural performances; screening of Indian films and documentaries; organizing performances by visiting Indian cultural troupes in Kazakhstan and Kazakh cultural troupes in India; disbursement of ICCR scholarships; and organizing visits under Academic Visitors Programme.

At Dushambe (Tajikistan), the Embassy runs the Cultural Centre, where a Tabla Teacher and a Kathak Dance Teacher have been deputed by the ICCR. Hindi and yoga classes are held regularly at the Centre. There is deep-rooted liking for Indian culture and films. Indian films are routinely shown on local TV channels in Tajikstan.

Lal Bahadur Shastri Centre for Indian Culture was established in Tashkent in 1995. It has become a household name in Uzbekistan for its cultural activities. Besides organizing seminar events relating to Indian culture, the Centre also organizes regular classes for Kathak, Yoga, Tabla and Hindi language.

### *Connecting with Cities and States: Opening New Avenues for Cooperation*

This is a new development, involving cities and the states in India. Singapore has become the focus country for visits by Chief Ministers from Indian States. Singapore is developing master plan for Amravati, new capital of the Andhra State. A number of State Governments established contacts with Singapore to further strengthen bilateral ties, through concrete projects in infrastructure, skills, governance, waste management and other areas.

West Bengal Chief Minister, Ms. Mamata Banerjee visited Singapore from 18-22 August 2014; Chief Minister of Telangana K. Chandrasekhar Rao from 20–23 August 2014; Chief Minister of Rajasthan Vasundhara Raje from 12-16 October 2014 and Andhra Pradesh Chief Minister, Chandrababu Naidu from 12-14 November 2014. Delegations from Assam, Sikkim, Tamil Nadu, Uttar Pradesh, and Gujarat also visited Singapore. Closer interaction between State Governments and Singapore has 'added a new dimension in our bilateral relations' (MEA 2014-15).

Singapore has developed the master plan of the new Andhra capital Amaravati and is in discussion with the State Government for further cooperation. Minister S. Iswaran represented Prime Minister of Singapore at the foundation ceremony of Amaravati by PM Modi on 22 October 2015 (MEA 2015-16). The three-part Amaravati master plan was developed by Singapore's Surbana Jurong Private Limited and which was unveiled on 25 May 2015 by the Chief Minister. The Centre for Liveable Cities and Singapore Cooperation Enterprise is training State government officials involved in the development of Amaravati (MEA 2015-16).

Singapore is also working with the Government of Rajasthan in preparing 'Concept Plans for Townships in Udaipur and Jodhpur'. There is also cooperation in capacity building in urban planning. Singapore's Minister for Home Affairs and Law K Shanmugam attended the Resurgent Rajasthan Partnership Summit (Nov 2015) at which Singapore was Partner Country (MEA 2015-16).

A Memorandum of Understanding between Delhi Government and Singapore ITE Education Services (ITEES) was signed on 11 July 2012 to provide the necessary framework for collaboration in setting up of a Green Field World Class Skill Centre (WCSC). It started functioning from a temporary campus in 2013. Singapore is working with the Rajasthan

Government in developing the Centre of Excellence for Tourism Training in ITI Udaipur.

### *Education Emerging as a Two-way Connectivity Channel*

India is linked through educational ties with these countries. An important development is that Central Asian countries still have a sizeable Indian student population, in particular, in medicine. In Kazakhstan, about 1700 Indian students are studying in medical universities in Aktobe, Almaty, Karaganda and Semey. 500 out of more than 800 students are pursuing MBBS course at the Dushanbe Medical College. On its part, India offers generous facilities under ITEC to students and experts to pursue courses in their professional fields.

Countries in Southeast Asia are also becoming attractive centres for education for Indian students. Every year, nearly 2000 Indian students come to study in Malaysia, while nearly 1500 Malaysian students enroll themselves in Indian colleges. Out of these, more than 95% of Malaysian students join Medical and Dental courses in India. India and Malaysia also have an MOU on Higher Education since January 2010.

There are more than 4000 students studying medicine in the Philippines. India and Thailand signed a MOU on Cooperation in the field of Education in 2005. A large number of Thai students are also studying on self-financing basis. Ministry of Human Resource Development provides for secondment of eight professors every semester for the Asian Institute of Technology (AIT), Bangkok.

### *Festivals of India Adding Splash of Colour*

The years 2014-16 turned out to be significant for the organization of Festivals of India in these countries. The Ministry of Culture (MOC), in collaboration with the Indian Embassy, held Festival of India in Bishkek in October 2016 to mark the 25th year of Kyrgyzstan's Independence; 25 years of their establishing diplomatic relations with the Kyrgyz Republic and 70 years of India's Independence. The premium cultural event of the Festival of India was also dedicated to the "Year of History and Culture" of Kyrgyzstan.

In 2016, ICCR sponsored cultural troupes visited Tajikistan for celebration of 'Days of Indian Culture' in Tajikistan. From Tajikistan a 20-member art and cultural troupe visited India for participation in Surajkund Mela in February 2017 (MEA 2015-16).

The Festival of India, 'Sahabat India' in Indonesia was organized from 26 January to 15 August 2015. During the Festival of India, different events were organized, such as folk dances, dance drama, puppet show, musical shows, exhibitions, seminars, Mall promotions, screening of Bollywood films and documentaries. The shows were arranged in several prestigious locations in Jakarta, Bali, Yogyakarta, Bandung, Surabaya, Surakarta and Medan. It was a grand people to people contact program in which more than 35 different events were held across 18 different cities of Indonesia and was received positively by various segments of Indonesian society.

The First Festival of India in Malaysia was organized between March-June 2015, when 45 events were held in 100 days in all major cities of Malaysia. The Festival culminated after the holding of the first ever International Day of Yoga on 21 June 2015.

A highly successful Festival of India comprising of "Buddha Mahotsava" and Ramayana Festival was organized in Phnom Penh and Siem Reap in February 2014. An Indian food festival, Indian cinema week and "Women by Women" painting exhibition held during the year in Phnom Penh were highly appreciated (MEA 2014-15).

Cultural and people-to-people exchanges continued to grow. The yearlong Festival of India in Singapore featured a range of activities in the cultural, artistic, film, literary, theatre dimensions as well as academic seminars, business sessions and ship visits. The youth has been particularly attracted to the Festival to further strengthen the strong bonds between the two countries (MEA 2014-15).

External Affairs Minister, Smt. Sushma Swaraj visited Singapore on 15–16 August 2014 to jointly inaugurate with Singapore's Foreign Minister K Shanmugam the series of commemorative events to mark the 50th anniversary of the establishment of India - Singapore diplomatic relations.

The Embassy, in collaboration with the Ministry of Culture and several local partners, organized Festival of India in Thailand in March 2014. The second edition of the 'Festival of India in Thailand' (February – May 2015) was dedicated to the commemoration of the 60th birthday anniversary celebrations of Princess Maha Chakri Sirindhorn. Prime Minister General Prayut Chan-o-cha inaugurated the 'India through the lens of HRH Princess Maha Chakri Sirindhorn' photo exhibition and the Princess attended the concluding event of the Literary Fest, "Words on Water" on 25 May 2015.

The Embassy, in association with the Government of India Tourism Office, organized an Indian tourism promotion event in Bangkok on 8 July

2015. India and Thailand celebrated the 100th anniversary of relations between the city of Surat and SuratThani in Thailand by organizing the Southern International Trade Expo in SuratThani from 23 – 26 July 2015. A delegation of 140 business persons and exhibitors from Surat, Gujarat participated in the Expo (MEA 2015-16). In 2015, around 1 million Indian tourists visited Thailand and over 100,000 Thai tourists visited India.

The cultural component of the exchanges with Laos was facilitated by programmes, following the Festival of India, particularly on Buddhism, Ramayana, Food Festival, Film Festival and Yoga.

A photo exhibition titled "Vietnam and India – For Peace and Development" was held in August 2015 at the War Remnants Museum in Ho Chi Minh City. The Centre for Indian Studies of the University of Social Sciences and Humanities organized a seminar in October 2015 on "Indian Culture and Vietnam-India Cultural Cooperation and Development" (MEA 2015-16).

***Heritage Conservation Preserving Age Old Ties***

Conservation of Heritage Sites is an important area for India to connect with the countries in Southeast Asia. An MOU was signed with the Laotian Ministry of Information and Culture in May 2007 for the restoration of the UNESCO world heritage site at Vat Phu in Laos. The work on the project began in June 2009. India is committed to spending US$ 4.1 million on the project over an eight year period.

India is also involved in the conservation of the world famous Angkor Wat Temples in Cambodia. Various teams of Archaeological Survey of India worked from 1986 to 1993. The Project cost of around US$ 4 million was met by the Indian Government and is still appreciated by Cambodia. India has agreed to restore Ta Prohm Temple in Siem Reap and Phase II of the project was completed in July 2015 and this was to be followed up with the third phase of project (MEA 2015-16).

In Myanmar, India is working for the restoration of the Ananda Temple in Bagan. The Government of India also donated a 16 foot replica of the Sarnath Buddha Statue that was installed at the premises of Shwedagon Pagoda in Yangon.

India was appointed Co-chair of the prestigious International Coordinating Committee (ICC) on PreahVihear, a world heritage site and one of the oldest temples and pilgrimage site of Lord Shiva, in 2014. India co-chaired the 1st technical session of ICC Preah Vihear held on 6 September 2015 (MEA 2015-16).

### *International Yoga Day (IYD): India Heralding its Entry with Celebrations*

The First International Yoga Day was celebrated with great gusto, with the enthusiastic support from the local community. Our diplomatic missions went out all the way in organizing various activities, given the generous support from ICCR. Some of the important functions are briefly touched upon in the following paragraphs.

International Day of Yoga was celebrated in Kyrgyzstan on 21 June 2015, with a number of events in Bishkek and other cities of Kyrgyzstan. A Yoga Caravan was also mounted on the occasion, which covered six out of seven regions of Kyrgyzstan. A Yoga Shivir (Camp) was also organized, which trained six trainers from different regions, who would start modest Yoga training programme in their regions.

In Indonesia, the International Day of Yoga was organized on 21 June 2015. A number of events were held in Jakarta, Bali, Medan and Surabaya in Indonesia and Dili in Timor Leste and more than 10,000 people took part in them(MEA 2015-16). The Yoga event in Yogyakarta was organized in the famous Prambanan Temple complex, which is a World Heritage site.

During his visit to Malaysia in November 2015, Prime Minister Modi released a bilingual (English and Bahasa Malaysia) book on Yoga, titled "Yoga for Holistic Health" at Ramakrishna Mission, where he also unveiled a 12 ft. Bronze Statue of Swami Vivekananda.

Over 7000 people participated in the First International Day of Yoga in Bangkok on 21 June 2015. The event was covered extensively in the local media (MEA 2015-16). Over 6000 people participated in the 2nd International Yoga Day celebrations at Chulalongkorn University, Bangkok on 26 June 2016.

On 21 June, 2015 Cambodia marked the International Day of Yoga in front of Angkor Wat Temple, Siem Reap, with the participation of over 1,000 Cambodians and foreigners.The Ministry of Tourism in cooperation with the Indian Embassy in Cambodia organized the event.

In Vietnam, the 1st International Day of Yoga (IDY) was celebrated at the Quan Ngua Sports Palace in Hanoi on 21 June 2015, with the participation of about 5000 people and 900 yoga practitioners. Several dignitaries attended the event. The IYD was also celebrated in 9 other provinces (MEA 2015-16).

### *Ayurveda/Traditional Medicines*

India and Malaysia signed an MOU on cooperation in the field of Traditional Medicine in October 2010. Traditional and Complementary Medicine (TCM) Division, Ministry of Health of Malaysia has been working to popularize AYUSH systems in Malaysia. Ayurveda, Siddha, Unani and Homeopathy systems are practiced in Malaysia.

An AYUSH Information Cell has been located at the Netaji Subhash Chandra Bose Indian Cultural Centre (NSCBICC) since 2010. One Ayurveda doctor and two therapists have been deputed to Malaysia for the last 4 years. AYUSH experts (3 Ayurveda experts and two Siddha experts so far) are also being periodically deputed for short periods to deliver lectures, offer consultations, conduct seminars and periodical training to Malaysian doctors, professionals and others.

India also offers 20 scholarships for Malaysians to study Traditional medicine in Indian Institutes/ colleges. Minister of State for External Affairs, V K Singh released a book on Ayurveda in English and Bahasa Malaysia during his visit to Malaysia in August 2015.

### *India-ASEAN Eminent Persons Lecture Series*

India-ASEAN Eminent Persons Lecture Series, which commenced in 1996, provides an opportunity to share views at the leadership level. The First Lecture was delivered by the Malaysian Prime Minister Mahathir Mohamad, when the Author was High Commissioner to Malaysia. Central Information Commissioner of India Yashovardhan Azad delivered lectures in the Philippines on 1-2 December 2014 under this Series and Under Secretary for Policy in the Department of Foreign Affairs of the Philippines Mr. Evan P. Garcia visited India from 15-17 July 2015 (MEA 2014-15).

### *Media*

India has ongoing programmes with many Central Asian countries involving exchange of TV programmes, visit of journalists, participation in international film festivals, cooperation among the filmmakers of both feature films and documentaries, visit of Radio and TV personnel etc. During the visit of Prime Minister Modi to Tajikistan in July 2015, cooperation in the field of TV and Radio Broadcasting was emphasized, to promote P2P and cultural contacts.

Media exchanges are also being promoted under the ASEAN-India Exchanges Programme for the purposes of familiarisation. Four Thai journalists visited India from 14-21 June 2015 (MEA 2015-16).A delegation of 8 Indian journalists visited the Philippines from 28-31 August 2014, while India received a group of journalists from the Philippines in March 2015. Two journalists from Brunei visited India on 05-11 March 2014 to cover the Delhi Dialogue VI. A10-member Thai language media delegation visited India from 31 May-7 June 2014, while a 9-member delegation of Indian journalists visited Bangkok from August 5-8, 2014 (MEA 2014-15).

***Sports***

A 17-member team from Indian Ethnosport Confederation participated in the Second World Nomad Games held in Cholpon Ata, Issyk-Kul region of Kygyzstan in September 2016.

A 10-member Cultural troupe sponsored by ICCR, New Delhi also took part in a Cultural Park within the World Nomad Games.

***Visits by Naval Ships***

Goodwill visits by Indian Naval Ships have become a regular feature that results in connectivity at the people to people level. INS Delhi made its Maiden Visit to Malaysia in 1999, when the author was the High Commissioner. Frequency of such visits has increased over the years. Similarly, holding of Annual 'Milan' (Get Togethers) of Navies from India and ASEAN Members since 1997 provides an opportunity to build camaraderie among naval officers. Since 2012, officers from Indian armed forces have regularly attended the Royal Brunei Armed Forces Command Staff Course at Staff College, Brunei (MEA 2015-16).

Indian Naval Supply Ship "INS Shakti" paid a goodwill visit to Brunei on 08-11 August 2014 while Royal Brunei Navy's Ship "KP 80 DARUTTAQWA" also visited India (Mumbai) in August 2014 (MEA 2014-15).

The Indonesian Navy participated in MILAN 2014 and was represented by a ship and Senior Officer. The Indian Navy participated in the inaugural edition of the Multilateral Naval Exercise Komodo in Indonesia (MEA 2014-15). Indian Naval Sail Training Ship Sudarshini paid a port call at Brunei from 21-24 November 2012 and a nine-member Bruneian team participated in the ASEAN-India Car Rally.

In May 2014, an Indian Navy Submarine Delegation visited Malaysian Submarine Base in Sepanggar. INS Ranvijay made a port call to the Sepanggar Port of East Malaysia for the first time in August 2014 (MEA 2014-15).

INS 'Ranvir', a guided missile destroyer and INS 'Kamorta', an anti-submarine corvette visited Sihanoukville Port, Cambodia on a five-day goodwill visit from 23-27 June 2015, which included joint training exercises with the Royal Cambodian Navy and a medical camp for local communities. An Indian Coast Guard Ship 'Samrat' paid a goodwill visit to Sihanoukville Port, Cambodia from 07-10 November 2015, and also conducted exercises with the Royal Cambodian Navy (MEA 2015-16).

***Youth and Students Exchange***

Deputy Minister of Culture, Youth and Sports of Brunei attended the Commonwealth Youth Ministers' Meeting held in New Delhi on 27-30 July 2015.

India facilitates student exchanges under the ASEAN-India Student Exchange Programme; 12 Batches had visited India till November, 2016 (AISE 2016). 15 Bruneian youth visited India for 10 days during 2015-16, while 25 visited during November 9-18, 2014. (MEA 2015-16).

Every year, 25 Philippine students in the 17-28 age group visit India; 25 students visited India from 09-18 November 2014 and 17 students during October 25- November 3, 2015 and 24 students visited during November 20-29, 2016 (AISE 2016).

Fifteen Vietnamese youth participated in annual ASEAN-India Student Exchange Program, during January 15-18, 2017 in New Delhi (AISE 2017).

India has also offered to receive 2 Buddhist monks/scholars from Kyrgyzstan, under Distinguished Visitor's Programme.

***Initiatives/Programmes Adding New Dimensions***

Leading Artists from Central Asia are providing greater connectivity. Internationally renowned Kazakh violinist Marat Bisengaliev supported the Foundation of Symphony Orchestra of India in 2006. An ICCR alumna Ms Akmaral Kainazarova, Director, Centre for Indian Classical Dances was awarded the title of "Honoured Worker (Artist) of the Republic of Kazakhstan" in December 2015.

The Embassy organized a musical named "IssyKulskie Bollywood" (Bollywood in Issykul) in collaboration with a number of local dance and choreography schools in the prestigious National Philharmonic Hall, Bishkek (Kyrgyzstan) in March 2016.

Work on the renovation of the India-Cambodia Friendship School in Kampong Cham province was completed and a certificate was handed over by the Indian Vice President to the Cambodian Prime Minister Hun Senin September 2015 (MEA 2015-16).

Indian Embassy along with the Kyrgyz Drama Theatre organized staging of a play based on the Indian epic 'Mahabharata' in Kyrgyz language in May 2016 at the National Drama Theatre, Bishkek. Plans are afoot for the production of theatrical version of 'Ramayana' in Kyrgyz language.

The University of Philippines staged a musical adaptation of Indian epic, 'Mahabharata' in their theatre in February-March 2014 and buoyed by its success, this was staged again in July 2014.

A Festival of Traditional Crafts and Culture was held in Bishkek from 30 July to 2 August, 2016 in which India exhibited its products at the Fair.

Autobiography of Mahatma Gandhi has been translated into Kyrgyz language. The Mission is in the process of producing an anthology of Indian poems in Kyrgyz language.

The Indian Embassy in Jakarta has taken an initiative to produce You Tube videos and bring out publications on various topical issues related to education, commerce, culture and yoga in Bahasa Indonesia, in order to disseminate information to wider section of people. Three videos were produced on the Festival of India and one on the International Day of Yoga (IYD).

A well-researched Book, 'Ganga to Mekong: A Cultural Voyage through Textiles' by Hema Devare, wife of former Indian Ambassador Sudhir Devare was launched at the Museum of Fine Arts, Jakarta in June 2016.

India has been appointed Co-Chair of the prestigious International Coordinating Committee (ICC) on Preah Vihear, a world heritage site and one of the oldest temples and pilgrimage site of Lord Shiva.

An ASEAN-India Art Exhibition 'Merging Metaphors' exhibiting 4 art works of artists from ASEAN and India was organized at Waterfront Gallery, Bandar Seri Begawan (Brunei) on 6-13 December, 2012.

An 8-member cultural troupe, Rondalla Ensemble from the National Commission for Culture and the Arts (NCCA) of the Philippines participated in the Grand Finale of IIC Experience organized by the India International Centre in New Delhi from 17-24 October 2013.

A bust of Mother Teresa, gifted by the Indian Council for Cultural Relations, had been installed in the University of SantoTomas, Manila.

India also provided assistance to Myanmar to build schools in the Rakhine Province aimed at promoting communal harmony (MEA 2015-16).

The soft launch of the MGC Asian Traditional Textile Museum in Siem Reap was presided over by the Cambodian Deputy Prime Minister and Minister in charge of Council of Ministers Sok An and Secretary(East) Anil Wadhwa on 07 April 2014.

During Prime Minister Modi's visit to Kuala Lumpur in Nevember 2015, the Two Prime Ministers jointly inaugurated the Torana Gate in Brickfields, Kuala Lumpur, a gift from India to Malaysia, as 'a symbol of India-Malaysia Friendship' (MEA 2015-16).

## Cultural Links Weaving Tapestry of Multi Dimensional Relationship

Southeast Asia and Central Asia remain two main focus areas for India's Cultural Diplomacy. Southeast is more so, as old cultural linkages continue to thrive, given greater people to people connectivity, even in the present day. This is, however, missing in the case of Central Asia, in the absence of surface-to-surface connectivity and inadequate air links, at the present juncture.

The strength of India's cultural connectivity lies in the pursuit of its composite culture. It is the Hindu and the Buddhist Civilizations that sustain ties with Southeast Asia, while it is Islam that connects with Central Asia.

Cultural ties are also sustained by the presence of a large number of local cultural organizations. These need to be more actively supported, as local participation is essential for any successful cultural event and sustained cultural presence.

Presence of a large and active Diaspora community in a multicultural environment also provides the sinews for the strengthening of relationship.

Adequate framework in terms of Cultural Agreements exists. Exchange of high level visits, with a cultural component in those visits, has further spurred up cultural connectivity.

India's Cultural Diplomacy does not only serve a symbolic purpose, but is also contributing to the building of substantive relations. Holding of

Festivals of India during the years 2014-16 was a successful attempt to re-connect India with the countries in the Region.

Holding of the First International Yoga Day (IYD) on June 21, 2015 in most of these countries was a step in the direction of spiritually linking India with these countries. Holding of this function in front of Heritage Sites added splendor and grandeur to the Event, while reminding us of old civilizational links.

India stands connected with Indonesia, Malaysia and Thailand, through Indian Epics, in particular, Ramayana, which is an integral part of life of people there. Interest in Indian Epics is also growing in Central Asia.

Uzbekistan has emerged as an important centre for learning Hindi. Enhanced facilities need to be provided to keep up their interest.

India's role in the preservation of Heritage Sites was appreciated and acknowledged. There is now a growing recognition that India can continue playing a meaningful role in this regard.

Education is emerging as an area that provides two-way connectivity. Central Asian countries continue to remain Destinations for Indian students, in particular, in the study of medicine. What is more significant is the emergence of Singapore, Malaysia and the Philippines as important Destinations for our students.

India-ASEAN Programme on Students Exchange is emerging as an important initiative. This however, needs to be strengthened, as it presently involves a small student community. Similarly, there is a need for greater academic connectivity, with India-ASEAN Centre at the Research and Information Systems (RIS) playing a more active role.

India-ASEAN Lecture Series which commenced in 1996 when the Author was posted as High Commissioner, with the First Lecture delivered by the Malaysian Prime Minister Mahathir Mohamad, needs to be reinvigorated at that level, as the same had become dormant over a number of years.

An innovative approach – a friendly get-together of Naval Ships called 'Milan' (Get-together) has taken roots since 1997, which promotes camaraderie among Naval Officers from Southeast Asian countries. Regular visits by Naval Ships are also generating goodwill.

So far, Bollywood has provided connectivity at the people-to-people level in these countries. Bollywood, however, is not real India. Tourism is also picking up and this helps in promoting connectivity. We are seeing a greater flow of Indian tourists to Thailand, Singapore and Malaysia, because of their attractive tourism packages, but the same is not true for reverse tourism into India. Special efforts are needed to attract them with suitable programmes.

The missing link in our Cultural Diplomacy is the limited role played by the media. There is still lack of awareness of one another. While India story sells, yet Central and Southeast Asia does not make the grade in the Indian Media. It is absolutely essential to generate greater awareness on Southeast Asia in India and India in Southeast Asia. India-ASEAN Media and Student Exchanges are expected to bridge this information gap. These are still baby steps and need to be fostered to facilitate exchange in greater numbers.

Indian Cultural Diplomacy in Central and Southeast Asia has been a success story. It is largely on account of the existence of pluralistic societies in all the countries and secondly on the recognition that it is mutually beneficial to all the sides

In the ultimately analysis, the continued success of our Cultural Diplomacy would lie in it becoming a bridge builder through the preservation and strengthening of pluralistic societies in India and Southeast. India would like to achieve this by celebrating epical story of 'Ramayana' in all its diverse renditions and let 'Yoga' be seen, not as a form of religious manifestation, but as a spiritual experience for any secular minded person.

The five day 'India-ASEAN Ramayana Festival' in Delhi and five other cities during January 19-24, 2018 added colour and provided people-to-people connectivity to the India-ASEAN Summit, when artists from India and ASEAN countries gave their performances.

Let us strive for the above goals and fulfill the 2002 dream of the then External Affairs Minister, Jaswant Singh, who highlighted the importance of weaving Asia 'through multi-modal institutional links in a most wonderful tapestry of cooperation."

## Endnotes

1 Goel, Suresh, former Director General, ICCR, New Delhi. Interaction on May 25, 2015 in Delhi.

2 Bhattacharya, Sanjay, Joint Secretary (South), Ministry of External Affairs, New Delhi. Interaction on March 27, 2015 in Delhi.

3 Misra, JN, Additional Secretary (South), Ministry of External Affairs, New Delhi. Interaction on January 27, 2014 in Delhi.

4 Sabharwal, Gopa, Vice Chancellor, Nalanda University. Interaction on July 27, 2015 in Delhi.

## References.

AISE, 2017, *ASEAN-India Student Exchange set for Jan. 2017*, New Delhi, January 15-18. http://english.vietnamnet.vn/fms/education/168063/asean-india-student-exchange-set-forjan--2017.html (Accessed on 13 December 2017).

AISE, 2016, Embassy of Philippines, Asean-India Student Exchange Program 2016, New Delhi, https://newdelhipe.dfa.gov.ph/index.php/newsroom/embassy-news/248-asean-indian-student-exchange-program (Accessed on 13 December 2017).

Dasgupta, Arun, "Intellectual and Academic Cooperation between India and Southeast Asia" in C.Ram Prasad, *Culture and Complementarities: Implications of the Singapore – India MoU on Culture, Heritage and the Archives in Singapore-India Relations.*

EAM, 2002, Statement by Jaswant Singh, Minister of External Affairs, India at the Plenary Session of Trilateral Meeting, Yangoon, April 6.

EAM, 2013, External Affairs Minister Salman Khurshid's Speech at the launch of ASEAN-India Centre in New Delhi, June 21.

EAM, 2013, Transcript of Media Briefing by External Affairs Minister, Brunei Darussalam, July, 1.

Ghoshal, Baladas (ed.), 1996, *India and Southeast Asia: Challenges and Opportunities*, IIC, New *Delhi.*

Goel, 2013, 'Message from Dr. Suresh Goel, DG, ICCR and Special Secretary, MEA in Sharma, Anjana (ed.), *Civilizational Dialogue,*

*Asian Inter-connections and Cross-cultural Exchanges*, ICCR & Manohar.

Gujral, I K, 1998, *A Foreign Policy for India, External Publicity Division*, Ministry of External Affairs, New Delhi.

Karlekar, Hiranmay (ed.), 1998, *Independent India, The First Fifty Years*, ICCR, Oxford University Press.

Le Diem, 2017, 'Indian cultural center opens in Hanoi', *Vietnam Economic Times*, April 27. *http://vneconomictimes.com/article/society/indian-cultural-center-opens-in-hanoi* (Accessed on 13 December 2017).

MEA 2014-15, Annual Report of the Ministry of External Affairs, New Delhi.

MEA 2015-16, Annual Report of the Ministry of External Affairs, New Delhi.

Mahathir, Mohamad, 1996, First ASEAN Lecture, New Delhi, December.

Nadim, Farrukh, 2013, 'Nalanda University deserves place in World Heritage Sites: Salman Khurshid', *The Tribune*, February 13.

Narasimha Rao, P V, 1994, Singapore Lecture, 'India and the Asia Pacific: Forging a New Partnership', Institute of Southeast Asian Studies, Singapore.

Nathan, K.S. (ed.), 2000, *India and ASEAN: The Growing Partnership for the 21st Century,* IFDR.

PBD, 2009, Inaugural Address of the Prime Minister of India, Pravasi Bharatiya Divas (PBD), January, New Delhi.

PM, 2012, 'Remarks by Prime Minister, Dr. Manmohan Singh at Flag down of the ASEAN-India Car Rally', 21 December, New Delhi.

P M Vajpayee, 2003, Banquet Speech by Prime Minister in Dushanbe, Tajikistan, November 23.

President, 2000, Speech by President of India at a Banquet in Singapore, November 10.

President Narayanan, 2002, Banquet Speech by the Indian President at Almaty, February 6.

Reddy, Lakshmi, 2001, "Malaysia: Perspectives on Culture" – Paper presented at an International Conference on India Malaysia Relations, Hyderabad, December 2001.

Sahai, P S., 2002, 'Globalisation, Cultural Diplomacy and the Indian Ocean: An Indian Perspective', Paper presented at the Panjab University, Chandigarh, Nov.

Sahai, P S, 2009, 'India's Cultural Diplomacy in Southeast Asia', HCMC University, May 16-19.

Sarkar, Bidyut, (ed.) 1968, *India and Southeast Asia, Proceedings of a Seminar*, ICCR, Delhi.

Sarkar, HB, 1985, *Cultural Relations between India and Southeast Asian Countries*, ICCR and Motilal Banarsidas, Delhi.

Sharma, Anjana (ed.), 2013. *Civilizational Dialogue, Asian Inter-connections and Cross-cultural Exchanges*, ICCR & Manohar, Delhi.

Singh, Dr. Karan, 2013, Foreword in Sharma, Anjana (ed.), *Civilizational Dialogue, Asian Inter-connections and Cross-cultural Exchanges*, ICCR & Manohar, Delhi.

Sinha,Yashwant, 2003, Keynote Address by External Affairs Minister at the Third India-Central Asia Conference, Tashkent, November 6.

Suryanarayana, P.S., 2010 'India's educational diplomacy', *The Hindu*, 4pril 4.

Varma, Pavan, 2006, 'Soft Power', *The Tribune*, October 7.

Vision Statement, 2012, 'Vision Statement, ASEAN-India Commemorative Summit, December 20, New Delhi.

Yew, Lee Kuan, 1998, *The Singapore Story: Memories of Lee Kuan Yew*, Times Editions, Singapore.

# Section – IV

# Vehicles of Cultural Diplomacy

# Chapter – VII

# Education as a Vehicle of Cultural Diplomacy

## Introduction

Connectivity through education has been an important vehicle of cultural diplomacy. It serves tripartite purpose – assists in learning, facilitates exchange of ideas and helps in building friendship on a long term basis. Fulbright Scheme has been projected as the shining example of Education Diplomacy. India now operates this programme jointly with the United States through the US-India Educational Foundation (USIEF), with India providing US $ 9 million as its share of annual contributions, which caters to an exchange of 300 scholars annually. Similarly, there is the Shastri-Initiative with Canada. There is also the Erasmus Mundus plus Programme with EU.

India is not new in the arena of education diplomacy as it was a centre for learning through renowned universities – Taxila and Nalanda. India has provided a large number of scholarships primarily to developing countries. At present, India provides 3000 scholarships annually through ICCR, that include 1000 for students from Afghanistan under a Special Programme of MEA. Two recent initiatives taken by India, including the setting up of Nalanda University and South Asia University, are a pointer to India's recognition of the important role of Education Diplomacy. Other bilateral exchange programmes have been agreed to between India and many other countries.

India Study Centres are emerging and many countries are planning to set up new India Centres. There is also a move in another direction where countries like Australia, USA and UK have developed programmes to send their students to India to enable them to get a flavour of India, so that they are better prepared for a global world.

Education is also emerging as a multibillion dollar industry. India has emerged as an important source country, which is wooed by educational institutions from UK, USA, Canada, Australia and New Zealand, which compete with one another. A proposal is under consideration to allow foreign universities to operate from India and many foreign universities have shown interest and have even launched promotional efforts.

India, on its part, is also setting up educational institutions (schools, professional colleges) abroad. How has this played out and what are the prospects in the future? India is also focusing on Diaspora, as it provides educational facilities to their children at fees that are at par with its nationals. It has provided special facilities for NRIs for study at Indian educational institutions? India is scratching the surface and it has not turned into a major success story.

Against the above backdrop, it is proposed to study how effective has been India's Education Diplomacy? How the existing schemes are working? What are the expectations from the new programmes – Nalanda University and South Asian University? What further steps are required to be taken up, to enable India to reap full benefits of Education Diplomacy?

## Recognizing the Role of Education Diplomacy

Many countries are approaching education as a vehicle of cultural diplomacy from their own perspectives, which at times coalesce in some ways, but also compete in other ways. A common strand that runs through their approaches is that education is an important vehicle to connect with students, who are the likely future leaders of their respective countries. Furthermore, foreign students help in bringing about diversity in the educational institutions and promoting cultural understanding. This helps in preparing them to work successfully in any environment, be it domestic or international. They also become a source of critical funding for the universities that are facing financial crunch because of declining financial support from the governments. Resources thus generated also add to the national revenues and help in easing balance of payment situations.

It is, therefore, not surprising, to see foreign universities holding 'Education Melas' (Promotional Events) in India to attract students. India now tops the list of foreign graduates for MBA courses in the United States and has overtaken China. In many cases, these promotional events have the tacit if not open support from the respective diplomatic missions, as these are linked to the grant of assured visa and in some cases even work permit as an incentive.

What are the ways, which foreign countries use to attract students? It is largely through offer of scholarships, which help in prying open the door for others, who are prepared to pay fees. Scholarships are regularly offered by EU, USA, UK, France and many other countries. Secondly, through indirect lobbying by advertising the quality of education through a Ranking System developed by Independent Assessment Agencies. Thirdly, through offer of student-friendly visa and work permit regimes.

In the case of EU, they offer scholarships through Erasmus Plus. In the case of UK, the British Foreign and Commonwealth Office has earmarked £2.6 million (Rs.28 lakhs) for 131 fully funded scholarships/fellowships for future Indian leaders during the financial year 2017-18 under its Chevening programme (Chevening). There are more than 2300 Chevening Alumni in India. Similarly, the British Council makes offers through its 'Great Scholarships' as UK has adopted 'Great' as its Brand for Image Building. It has earmarked £1.5 million for scholarships for the financial year 2016-17. Under this scheme, it plans to offer 291 scholarships in partnership with 45 universities

India has only recently woken up to the importance of 'education diplomacy', as it seeks to engage with the world, showcasing its 'affordable excellence' in the field of higher education, given 'its vast size, competitive academic environment, cosmopolitan society and English medium education' (Indian Diaspora). This was the message that echoed from Smriti Irani, the then Human Resource Development Minister, through her inaugural address at the ICCR's 'First Conference on Higher Education in India for Foreign Students', held in Delhi on March 21-22, 2016.

Smriti Irani saw multiple advantages in hosting foreign students, who could build 'bridges between India and their respective countries in promoting mutual understanding and goodwill'. They could also add to 'cultural diversity', bring 'new perspectives and help in 'cross pollination of ideas and expand our horizons' (Irani). Not to be missed was the point that they added to the economy of the host state. These laudable objectives and goals could be achieved only, if a coordinated approach was adopted by the governmental agencies, universities and society in general, "to make India foreign students' friendly" (Rajasekhar).[1]

## Purpose of Education

Indian President Pranab Mukherjee places education at a high pedestal in this K-world. He said:

> "Education is power. It provides knowledge which provides development and in today's world, the higher educational system has great importance in building a society" (Chaba, Anju Agnihotri).

Rajika Bhandari, an eminent educationist describes, 'Higher education is about raising talents, it is about encouraging the best in students and helping them grow as responsible citizens in this global world. A cross-cultural dialogue and international dimension are doubtless crucial to achieving this objective' (Bhandari, Rajika, 2015).

In 1946, China was the first country to sign a bi-national agreement to participate in the Fulbright Fellowship Programme, followed by Burma. Many other countries have set up ambitious goals to increase international education; China aims to support 500,000 international students by 2020; Malaysia plans to attract 200,000 and Japan's target is 300,000. Allan E. Goodman, President and CEO, The Institute of International Education (IIE) opines that Governments in Asia see internationalization of their colleges and universities as a means to capitalize on rapid globalisation and remain competitive in the global market place.

International student mobility trends are becoming increasingly important to governments, business leaders and educators worldwide. Globalisation brings with it the demand for a workforce that possesses knowledge of other countries and cultures and is competent in languages other than English. IIE launched Generation Study Abroad in 2014 to address the shortfall of American students going abroad. This initiative brings together educational institutions, employers, governments, associations and others to build on current best practices and find new ways to enlist international opportunities. For Allan Goodman, studying abroad is "one of the best ways American college students can require international experience to succeed in today's global workplace".

Studying abroad is thus emerging an important trend in this globalised world. Stanford Unger, President of the Goucher College, Baltimore (USA) holds the view that benefits of 'overseas experiences are difficult to quantify, but there is little doubt that studying abroad can be beneficial for all students'. Studies by the Indiana University and the University Systems of Georgia have found concrete positive results of studying abroad as an essential element of success, a requirement to compete in the global market place and that also 'opens door for lifelong contacts and interests'.

Studying abroad is also getting important from another perspective, as it helps in widening horizons and promotes better understanding of other cultures. According to Stanford J Unger, it helped in 'broadening their perspectives and deepening their appreciation for the many different ways that other societies approach common problems'.

Another advantage is that it helps in the development of personalities that make it easier to adjust in pluralistic environment back home. Unger noted that 'coincidentally, studying overseas together sometimes improved relations among members of different ethnic, social and religious groups on campus when they returned'.

Stanford J Unger is of the view that it also helps in preparing a citizenry that understands 'America's place in the world, the security challenges it faces and the opportunities and perils confronting Americans around the world. Responding to these realities requires a massive increase in the global literacy of the typical college graduate'. It is equally true for citizenry in other countries, including India.

Indian President Pranab Mukherjee views foreign students as 'unofficial ambassadors of our country' (The Times of India, 2017). Similar was the experience of the Goucher College, Baltimore as the President of the University Stanford Unger found that 'the participants returned with new ideas, stronger personalities and a better sense of who they are as individuals and as Americans'.

US National Education Policy recognises 'the importance of international literacy and global awareness for the future of the United States' and accepted that longer programmes were preferable, as these provided for greater 'opportunities for immersion in host cultures'. Goucher College made study abroad mandatory for undergraduates, turning it into 'a laboratory for international exploration, resulting in the growth of enrolments, with 'horizons broadened and opportunities beckoned'.

Many European Countries, including Finland and Germany, with excellent universities, provide students with some tuition-free opportunities. US provides financial grants under Pell Grants and Coleman International Scholarships for Overseas Languages, if they study a language in the State Department's, 'critical need' list, such as Arabic, Chinese and Russian.

In 2011, US President Obama launched an initiative to increase slots from 90,000 to 100,000, making 'study abroad to be regarded as a key element of the US foreign policy and that more students should participate as citizen diplomats'. Under this initiative, the US State Department commits to 'supporting the next generation of diverse American leaders to gain the knowledge and skills they need to succeed in a globalizing world' as they help in building 'understanding as unofficial ambassadors for our country, defining American values and debunking stereotypes' (US Study Abroad).

## Origins of Education Diplomacy in Modern Times

The origin of modern day Education Diplomacy could be traced down to the visit of President Franklin D. Roosevelt (FDR) to Mexico in 1934. His message was on the need for 'a wider dissemination of education, of thought and of free expression'. This resulted in a modest programme of multilateral cultural exchange between USA and the nations of the Western Hemisphere (Hart, Justin, 2013). It was a partnership approach that was initiated by FDR, as he said 'give them a share' as he urged his Administration to adopt a positive attitude towards Latin America.

President Roosevelt wanted the process to be enshrined in the principles of equality, as he stated, 'They think they are just as good as we are, and many of them are' (quoted in Justin Hart, 2013). There was an overall recognition of the role of 'ideas' in changing mindset and recognition of place of academic exchanges'. Later, John Rockefeller recognised that to fight German influence in Latin America called for exchange programmes in 'culture and education to be pursued concurrently with the economic programme' (Hart, Justin, 2013).

The Office of the Coordination of Inter-American Affairs (OCIAA) created by FDR Roosevelt in August 1940, under John Rockefeller made him realize that the focus had to be on the role of image in foreign relations. It was he, who recognized that 'not only education was supposed to serve as the foundation of neighbourly good citizenship but it also held the key'. He was on the same page with the State Department, in recognizing the importance of education for ensuring 'tolerance and understanding among the peoples of all republics'.

## USA-Leader in Education Diplomacy

The United States is a major and the oldest player in running exchange programmes, which have a bearing on exchange among students, academics and leaders. Such exchanges commenced after the visit of President Roosevelt to Mexico in 1934, as he extended America's hand of friendship to the Americas as Partners. USA has devised a number of programmes over the years. The two most important exchange-programmes and among the oldest are the Fulbright and the International Visitors Leadership Programme (IVLP) (Rugh, William, 2014).

***International Visitors Leadership Programme (IVLP)***

IVLP's stated purpose is to bring 'current and emerging foreign leaders in a variety of fields' to the United States to 'experience this country first hand and cultivate lasting relationship with their American counterparts' (State Department Website). The focus is on mid-career foreign professionals for short-term visits. Since its inception in 1940, 200,000 international visitors came to the United States. It boasts of 300 former/current Heads of State or Government. Indian Prime Minister late Indira Gandhi was an invitee under this programme. A variation of IVLP is a Voluntary Visitors' Programme (VVP), which more or less follows a similar pattern, but with less financial commitment (IVLP).

***The Fulbright Programme***

Senator Fulbright was the architect of this programme, which was created in 1946. It is the one programme that 'is known the best internationally' and it has provided tens of thousands of exchanges with the United States each way (Rugh, William, 2014). China was the first country to join the Fulbright Programme, while India joined in 1950; Japan and Russia joined in 1953 and 1973 respectively. The strength of the Fulbright Programme is that it provides for two-way exchanges in a partnership mode and each country has 'a programme that is unique' (Rugh, William, 2014). Its role in providing connectivity was lauded in 2013 by the then US Secretary of State John Kerry, who described it as 'one of the great programmes that exist anywhere in the world'. It helps to break down barriers, take away ideological extremes and 'eliminate the simplistic sort of reduction to a stereotype that so many people engage in' (Fulbright Programme).

Other important programmes run by the United States include the following:

- ***Youth Exchange and Study (YES),*** which provides for one year education in American best schools, with stay with the families.
- ***Undergraduate Exchange Programme (NESA UGRAD)*** that brings in students from Near East and South Asia.
- ***Future Leaders Exchange (FLEX),*** whose focus is to bring 300 Russian high school students to US annually for two year study. "They return to Russia transformed" after 'fabulous formative

experiences' speaking "fantastic English", not only with an intimate knowledge of culture, but also networks of friends who had well past their academic year of study.

- ***Partnership for Learning Undergraduate Studies (PLUS)***, which aims at bringing non-elite gifted young men and women from Muslim countries for three junior school years. This programme started after 9/11.
- ***Youth Exchange and Study (YES)*** is One year study programme in American high schools, providing for stay with friends. This caters to Graduate students for one year non-degree programme. It provides for 10 Fellows each year. Till 2017, 205 Fellows from 80 countries have availed of facilities under this scheme.
- ***The International Writing Programme*** that brings in 25-35 authors to Iowa City for a 10 week residency.
- ***The American Council of Young Political Leaders (ACYPL),*** which aims at bringing mid-level professionals to programmes in governance for 8 to 14 days for interaction.
- ***The FORTUNE/US State Dept. Global Women's Monitoring Partnership*** is run for women leaders between 25-45 ages for one month for one-on-one internship with the most powerful women leaders, who are likely to emerge in the future.
- ***The Study of the United States Institutes for Student Leaders*** caters to undergraduate student leaders for six weeks' stay in USA.

## Some Innovative Programmes

A number of countries have initiated programmes, which would be relevant for pursuing our ideas on educational diplomacy. Some of the innovative programmes are described below:

### *Ban-Ki-Moon Global Leadership Overseas Training Programme*

This programme is named after the former UN Secretary General and is in operation since 2007 and is run at the state level by the North Chungcheong province in South Korea. The aim of the programme is 'to strengthen cultural exchange programmes for students to become global leaders' through 'experiencing various cultures overseas'. Every year, 30 sixth grade students are selected after a stiff competition, where around 100 students apply and are sent to USA for eight days. Similar programmes of cultural exchange are being initiated with Australia and France at the level of states (Hyun-Choe, Chung, 2016).

### *The Youth Ambassadors Program*

It is a youth-focused programme that brings together high school students and adult mentors from countries across Latin America and the Caribbean to the United States 'to promote mutual understanding, increase leadership skills, and prepare youth to make a difference in their communities'. Participants engage 'in workshops, community service activities, team building exercises, meetings with community leaders, and home stays with American families'. Upon their return home, the students are expected to apply their experiences to projects that serve needs in their communities (Youth Ambassadors).

### *The Global Connect Initiative (GCI)*

It is a U.S. Department of State-led multi-stakeholder effort that aims to bring 1.5 billion additional people online by 2020'. It is based 'on the notion that Internet connectivity is critical to economic development'. It aims 'to foster pro-market environments that encourage investment, innovation and job creation'. Over 40 countries and many more stakeholders have endorsed Global Connect and its connectivity principles (Global Connect).

### *Developing Languages in Multilingual Societies in ASEAN Countries*

Some ASEAN countries are pursuing policies to develop 'balanced multilingualism', to preserve diversity and richness of languages and cultural traditions, with a view to 'opening up new possibilities for cohesive society' (Kirkpatrick). A number of policy initiatives have been taken recently in Thailand, the Philippines and Myanmar to 'support local ethnic and indigenous languages; to bolster the identity and cultural life of the nation at the local level, alongside national language for unity at the citizenship level, and international languages for communication and trade relations'. Action is initiated at the state level, as UN backed research had shown the success of this bottom up process. A significant success had been achieved in some of the states in Myanmar, which had been able to successfully respond 'to local conditions while maintaining a coherent national approach'.

***New Colombo Plan***

Australia is now sending students to India under a new initiative called New Colombo Plan. This was launched by the then Australian Prime Minister Tony Abbot in India in September 2014, to promote student exchanges. One of its aims is 'to lift knowledge of the Indo-Pacific in Australia by supporting Australian undergraduates to study in India' (Deshpande, Alok). Australian Foreign Minister Julie Bishop said that 340 students were sent in 2015. Simultaneously, steps were taken to ensure that Indian students felt welcome and safe in Australia (Julie Bishop). It was a part of the Australian desire to expand strategic partnership with India (Julie Bishop).

***Global Girls' Education Initiative***

Michelle Obama, First Lady of the United States visited three countries, Liberia, Morocco and Spain under this initiative. She was accompanied, by her daughters (Malia and Sasha) and her mother, Mrs. Robinson. Actresses Meryl Streep and Friedo Pinto lent their Star Power to the 'Let Girls Learn' Initiative that was launched in March 2015. Its aim is to encourage developing nations to educate more than 62 million girls worldwide, who currently did not attend school. This Initiative had the support of the Millennium Challenge Corporation, Peace Corps and USAID (Obama, Michelle).

***Mauritius Emerging as Education Hub for Africa***

Africa has a highly mobile student population, with more than 380,000 students abroad. Mauritius has an ambitious higher education hub goal plan 'to grow its international student numbers from a current 1,000 in 2014 to 100,000, many of them from elsewhere in Africa' (Karen MacGregor).

***Emerging Leaders in the American Programme***

Canada has an active ongoing programme on educational exchanges with Mexico. Under its 'Emerging Leaders in the American Program', it offers 75 to 100 scholarships annually for post-secondary students for study or research up to six months. Since 2009, 600 Mexican students have come to Canada under government-sponsored scholarship. More than 5000 Mexican students are studying in Canada.

During the visit of the Mexican President Nieto to Canada in June 2016, both the countries launched a new programme that would promote student exchanges and industry training opportunities. Under this programme,

20 graduate students would travel each way to take part in 16-24 weeks research projects with industry partners. Prime Minister Justin Trudeau highlighted the importance of educational diplomacy in these words, 'The more we can challenge ourselves to understand different realities, different perspectives, different cultures, the more we discover about ourselves and our place in an increasingly complex world' (Canada-Mexico Exchanges).

***The Brazilian Government's 'Scientific Mobility Programme'***

Under this Programme, the government has invested US $ 2.4 billion. The Project impacts at five levels: Level One: Reach (Participators' satisfaction); Level Two: Learning (Acquisition of knowledge): Level Three (Application at community level): Level Four: Organizational Results (Impacts at the organization) and Level Five (External) at the societal level.

***Preparing for Reverse Cultural Shock***

Ohio State University Extensions 4-H International Exchange Program provides for a four or eight week summer work experience with a number of countries. It has a unique inbuilt element as it helps exchange students in preparing them to absorb reverse cultural shock, which they may experience on returning to their own state (Rohrer, D'Ann).

## Bilateral Academic Links- Some Countries

***India-Canada***

Canada and India are linked by a long history of people-to-people ties. Inter-institutional academic linkages were formalized with the founding of the Shastri Indo-Canadian Institute (SICI) in 1968 by the Governments of India and Canada to facilitate academic and other exchanges between the two countries. According to SICI over 300 bilateral instruments of cooperation exist between institutions of higher learning in Canada and India. Under the former 'Understanding Canada: Canadian Studies' program, a network of more than 25 Canadian Studies at Indian universities was established which continue to support bilateral academic relations.

Canada and India signed a Memorandum of Understanding (MOU) on Higher Education in June 2010. The MOU encourages the continued development of cooperation between institutions of higher education, based on each country's academic, scientific and educational needs (Canadian Website).

The number of Indian students choosing Canada as a study destination grew to 52738 in 2015 (MMA), representing an increase of more than 145% from 2011. This contributes to growing research collaboration and global diplomacy networks. Canada has emerged as an important destination of higher education for Indian students, with the population expected to reach 120,000.

Indian students and researchers are eligible for Vanier Canada Graduate Scholarships and Banting Postdoctoral Fellowships, as well as other federally funded awards; more information can be found at scholarships.gc.ca.

During the visit of Canadian Prime Minster Justin Trudeau to India in February 2018, both the countries renewed the Memorandum of Understanding (MOU) on Higher Education. Both the leaders 'recognized the 50th Anniversary of the Shastri Indo-Canadian Institute in promoting understanding between India and Canada through academic activities and exchanges, with the support of both governments to the institute' (India-Canada Joint Statement). Prime Minister Modi expressed a hope that the renewal of the MOU on Higher Education 'will help facilitate enhanced movement of students and teachers from both sides' (PM Modi, Press Statement, 2018).

### *India-New Zealand*

India-New Zealand Education Council was set up in October 2012, aimed at bringing together the government, academia, business and industry to further bilateral cooperation in the education sector. India and New Zealand took a new Education Cooperation Initiative in June, 2016, setting up a joint fund with US $1 million to 'promote partnerships in two key streams: higher education and research and skills and vocational education'.

During Prime Minister John Keys' visit to India in October 2016, the importance of 'the strong and growing education and migration links between the two countries were recognized'(Joint Statement, 2016).This was recognition of the linkage between higher education facilities for Indian students, while also meeting the skill demands in New Zealand. A Cultural Cooperation Agreement was signed and an amendment was carried out to the existing Sports Cooperation Agreement to provide for greater bilateral youth exchanges.

### *India-France*

During the visit of French President Macron to India in March 2018, India and France signed an Agreement on 'Mutual Recognition of Academic Qualifications', which will facilitate 'the pursuit of higher education by Indian students in France and French students in India and enhance their employability' (Joint Statement, 2018). Union Human Resource Development (HRD) Minister Prakash Javadekar termed this "historic" and more countries were expected to follow suit.

A high-level India-France Knowledge Summit, 2018 was also jointly organized, in conjunction with the signing of the Agreement on March 10. 15 MOUs, between various institutions of India and France in the areas of Higher Education, Research, Innovation, Faculty Exchange, Scientific Cooperation, were exchanged. At present, more than 5,000 Indian students are studying in France and about 1,500 French Students in India. The Minister said that the HRD Ministry planned to launch "Study in India" initiative to attract more foreign students. About 30 French Faculty members had visited India in 2017 to conduct course, under 'GIAN', an Indian initiative to facilitate faculty exchanges with foreign universities (Speed Post News Network).

## Australia Emerging as an Important Player

Australia attaches considerable importance to education diplomacy and has emerged as an important player on the global horizon. Its strong commitment was seen through the presence of six Ministers at the first meeting of the Council for International Education held in Canberra on November 23, 2016. This fully demonstrated their resolve to ensure that Australia's international education sector 'remains vibrant, competitive and sustainable', while it maintained 'its reputation for quality'. The Cabinet Ministers further noted 'the full range of economic, social and cultural benefits that international education provides to Australia' (Communiqué, 2016).

At this meeting, Minister for Foreign Affairs Julie Bishop reiterated Australian government's commitment 'to two-way mobility and exchanges for students, researchers and academics'. What is significant is that Australia projected a well coordinated approach, where the Ministers for Foreign Affairs, Education, Trade, Tourism and Development Vocational Education and Skills and Immigration and Border Protection put up a united front unlike the old players, like UK and USA, where each department plays its own tune.

The Council decided to place special focus on communicating 'the benefits arising out of international education'; opening up of increasing opportunities for international students to develop greater employability, while helping them 'to live and learn in regional Australia'. The meeting committed 'to support greater two-way mobility' through the New Colombo Plan and Australia Awards; strengthening alumni engagement through the Australia Global Alumni Engagement Strategy 2016-2020 and intensification of international research engagement and collaboration.

Australia has developed a National Strategy for International Education 2025 that is built on three pillars, with each pillar having a number of goals. Pillar 1 focuses on strengthening the fundamentals and has three goals; Pillar 2 deals with making transformative partnerships and has four goals, and Pillar 3 focuses on competing globally and has two goals. Among the goals that are relevant for international education include, developing 'World Class Education' (Goal 1); 'Strengthening Partnerships Abroad' (Goal 5) and 'Embracing Opportunities to Grow International Education' (Goal 9).

Australia and India have deepened cooperation in the education sector through the operation of the Australia-India Bridge School Partnerships Programme. This has operated since 1998; more than 290 Australian and 230 Indian teachers availed of this programme. This has resulted in expanding partnership with partner schools thereafter. Honouring the participants under the 2017 Australia-India Bridge School Partnership programme, the Australian High Commissioner Harinder Sandhu said that 'Engagement between our schools is so important for Australia-India ties'. She further added that 'By influencing our children's views of each other countries, we influence the future of our bilateral relationship and we can 'learn from each other's experience in delivering best practices to school education' (Harinder Sandhu). BRIDGE is funded by the Australian Government and operated by the Asia Education Foundation (AEF), aimed to build teacher capacity 'in developing intercultural understanding' (Harinder Sandhu).

## China and Education Diplomacy

China has adopted a four-pronged approach to Education Diplomacy. Firstly, it is through the offer of scholarships to foreign students, which are around 20000 annually. China also expects to 'win hearts and minds through such scholarships', apart from imparting knowledge to students (Shambaugh, Davis, 2015).

Secondly, China has an ambitious programme to set up 'Confucius Institutes', to teach Chinese language and culture abroad in foreign universities. These are operational in 475 centres in 120 countries and are expected to reach a target of 1000 in 2020. There is a spurt in the setting up of such institutes, since its inception in 2004. The first Confucius Institute opened on 21 November 2004 in Seoul, South Korea, after establishing a pilot institute in Tashkent, Uzbekistan in June 2004.

Thirdly, through the setting up of Cultural Centres under the Ministry of Culture, which have a different mandate to promote cultural relations, unlike that of the 'Confucius Institutes' which function under the Ministry of Education.

Fourthly, promoting linkages among think tanks and holding international conferences. The most significant being is, 'The Boa Forum for Asia', which is projected as 'China's Davos' (Smits, Yolanda, 2014).

A positive aspect to the setting up Confucius Institutes is that these are located in local institutes. On the negative side, concerns are expressed that these lack academic freedom and hence have come for criticism in some countries, such as USA. India also is not reportedly happy with their functioning.

## International Student Mobility

Governments aspiring to build their next generation of leaders continued to invest significantly in scholarship programmes that send their nationals abroad (Farrugia and Bhandari, 2014). As per OECD (2014), 4.5 million students crossed borders in 2012 and the number was expected to grow to 8 million in 2025 (OECD, 2008). The United States remained the top host country with around 1 million foreign students, representing a 20% share, although it had dropped from 28% in 2001, when the total population was 2.1 million students. U.S. is followed by U.K. (11%), China (8%), France (7%), Germany and Australia (6%), Canada (5%), Japan (3%), Spain (2%), New Zealand (2%) and others (34%).

China has also emerged as a sizeable host country, while the shares of Australia and Canada have increased substantially. Percent wise, international students make 4% of the total student population, but these form 20% in Australia and the United Kingdom. On the other hand, 30% of the world's students come from five countries; China, India, South Korea, Germany and Saudi Arabia (UNESCO, 2014). Saudi Arabia has recently joined the top ten sending countries. According to the UNESCO estimates, over 1 million students from Asia study outside their home countries.

USA, which is the largest recipient of international students, received 974926 students in 2015. 58 per cent students came from countries, such as China (31%), India (14 %), South Korea (7%), Saudi Arabia (6%), Canada (3%), and 2% each from Mexico, Japan, Brazil and Vietnam (Open Doors 2015). This resulted in the contribution of $ 30.8 billion to the US economy during 2014-15. Tuition fees were paid by personal or family (64%), US College or University (21%) and foreign governments and universities (8%) [Open Doors, 2015].

There were 132,888 students from India during 2014-15, representing an increase of 29.4% over the previous year, contributing $ 3.6 billion to the US economy. Out of these, 64% were graduate students; 12.4% were undergraduates and 22.1% formed OPT (Optional Practical Training) Group. As against this, only 4538 US students went to India during 2013-14, whereas India sent 102,673 students in that year to USA (Open Doors, 2015).

Germany is emerging as a favoured destination; in 2015, it attracted some 340,000 international students, compared to almost 450,000 in the UK. China hosted 356499 or 8% of International students. The largest contingent was from South Korea (63,029), followed by the United States (25,312), Japan (20,106), Russia (17,226), Indonesia (13,492), Vietnam (12.799), India (11,781), Kazakhstan (11,165) and Pakistan (10,941) (Open Doors 2014).

## Preferred Countries for Study by Students

The Institute of International Education (IIE) conducted a survey in 18 countries including India during 2009-2013, to ascertain country-preference perceptions of prospective students for studies. 74.2% students preferred USA, followed by UK (8.1%), Canada (4.8%), Australia (2.9%), France (1.6%), Germany (1.2%), Spain (1.2%), Japan (0.9%) and others (5.1%) [Open Doors, 2014]. The pull factors that attracted students to USA were high quality of education, wide range of schools and programmes, diversity of choices, welcoming environment and good support services.

How does the global experience transform the locals? It could take myriad forms, as described below:

- Knowledge and Learning: The beneficiary of the transformation is the individual through acquisition of job specific knowledge.

- Mutual Understanding: The more intangible impacts of international students' mobility are categorized as turning students in to 'global citizenship'. The hypothesis is that students would 'become more open to accepting other cultures, as a result of their experiences abroad' (Fulbright Programme). They thus get better prepared as participants for careers in the global market place and in building international communication.

- Impacts Beyond the Individual: Carnegie Corporation of New York's 'African Diaspora Fellowship Programme Equity' aims at equitable academic opportunities, elimination of barriers and flow of ideas and people that level the playing field of academic opportunity.

## Institute of International Education (IIE), New York (USA): A Case Study

IIE was set up in 1919 by two Nobel Prize winners – Nicholas Hurray Butler and Elihu Root and Prof. Stephen Duggan. It is one of the largest and most experienced NGO international education organizations, which highlights the significance of cultural diplomacy, both in theory and practice. They believed that 'we could not achieve lasting peace without greater understanding between nations and that international educational exchange formed the strongest basis for fostering such understanding'. International education was considered the best possible investment in making the world a less dangerous place.

IIE's three-fold Mission is to:

- Manage scholarships, training, exchange and leadership programmes.

- Conducting research and facilitating policy dialogue on global higher education.

- Protecting scholarship around the world (IIE Brochure).

IIE was born after the aftermath of World War I, as a Scholarship Rescue Fund (Mary McKey),[2] so as to prevent disruption of scholarly pursuits. This along with Emergency Students Fund and Higher Education Consortium remain the thrust areas. IIE manages 200 programmes, including the world renowned Fulbright Program since its inception in 1946, as it promotes educational exchanges across the globe. It also administers two other important programmes – Brazil Scientific Mobility Programme and the

Carnegie African Diaspora Programme. It was also involved with the setting up of the King Abdulla University of Science and Technology at Jeddah.

IIE is also involved with certain other initiative of the State Department; the most important is the Tech Women Exchange Programme, which was at the initiative of the then Secretary of State Hillary Clinton, inviting 110 women entrepreneurs from the Middle East in 2011. It now facilitates mentoring of 100 women entrepreneurs annually from Middle East, Africa and Central Asia. It also started Tech Women Development Programme and India is involved in such programmes.

IIE is also involved in a new initiative called Generation Study Abroad, aimed at doubling the number of American students studying abroad by 2020 from its current level of 300,000 students in 2014. More than 450 partners had already joined in this Initiative in 2015, the first year of its launch. It has received positive support from foreign governments, like Ireland, which have offered scholarships.

IIE has launched another initiative supporting global partnerships, called Global Innovation Initiative, a programme funded by the US & UK governments to foster multilateral research collaborations with higher education institutes in Brazil, China, India and Indonesia. IIE administers the US part of the programme.

IIE's total revenue for 2014 was ÚS $ 593 million, 36% from the US government agencies, 52% from foreign governments and international organizations, 7% from Foundations and Research Organizations, 3% from corporations and 2% from contributions. 87% of its expenditure was on international exchange of students and scholars, 5% on leadership development educational services, 2% on higher education in institutional development, 1% on Energy Student Scholarship and 5% on Management.

## Education Scenario in Asia

The following observation aptly sums up the education scenario in Asia, which describes it as conducive for building bridges of connectivity in the area of education:

> "There is no race; there is no single super power when it comes to education. What we see is greater mobility, growing interconnectedness, increased dialogue and many more bridges than barriers" (Bhandari, Rajika and Lefebure, Alessia).

What are the main trends that are emerging? Firstly, Higher Education has increasingly become a global market in the 1990s, allowing more students to select colleges outside their resident countries. Secondly, international rankings, global competition and marketing constraints also posed new challenges to the academia in Asia. Ranking Systems have transformed the research-based university and the Ivy League model into the world class university standard. Thirdly, countries like India, which otherwise has one of the largest and fastest growing college-aged cohorts in the world, had remained relatively disengaged in the international education process and the globalisation of its higher education sector. Limited higher education opportunities available in India have thus pushed a large number of domestic students abroad.

## International Student Mobility: From and To India

### *Outbound*

There is an appreciable increase in the number of Indian students going abroad. According to UNESCO data for 2012, population of internationally mobile students stood at 4 million. China took the first place, having a 17 percent share, with India having the 2nd place at 4.7 percent, with strength of 189472 students. The top four destinations for Indian students were- USA (971,200), UK (29713), Australia (11684) and Canada (8142).

As per latest information received from various diplomatic missions abroad, an estimated 553,000 Indian students were studying abroad in 86 countries in 2017 (Indian Students Abroad, 2017). 36 of these were from Asia, 32 from Europe, 8 from Africa, 6 from South America and 2 each from North America & Australia. More than 50% of the Indian students study in North America; while around 90000 Indian students study in Asia, including Australia.

In Europe, they only make up 52116 in 32 different countries. Only 3 countries have more than 50000 students each; while 5 other countries have between 10000 and 50000 students. China and Bahrain are the only two Asian countries with more than 10000 Indian students each.

### *Inbound*

As against a large outgo of Indian students, India could attract only 33156 students in 2012 from abroad. India, therefore, had a share of 0.6% of the global students' population. 19% of the students came from Nepal, followed by Bhutan (8%), Iran (6%), Malaysia (5%), Iraq (4%), Sri Lanka (3%) and USA (2%). India has not even emerged as an important hub for SAARC students, as 60.9% Sri Lankans, 59.6% Nepalese, 53.2% Bangladeshis and 49.7% Pakistanis, go to developed countries, like USA, UK, Australia, Canada.

There is, however, an appreciable increase in the growth rate, as the students figure touched 42,420 in 2014, which represented an increase of 33% percentage over the last two years. Nepal still continued to occupy the top rank, contributing 21% of the students, followed by Afghanistan (10.3%), Bhutan (6.6%), Sudan (4.8%), Nigeria (4.7%) and Malaysia (4.5%). A significant trend, however, has been the decline in the number of student's from developed countries.

India still remains a destination primarily for undergraduate students, who form around 60% of the international students' population; around 18% for postgraduate studies and only 2% for doctoral programs/research. ICCR is specifically focusing on increasing the number of postgraduate students. India has been slow in launching promotional programs. The pertinent question that is being asked by the experts is when India, which is a key source of international students, would become a destination?

***Trends in Mobility of Indian Students***

The 2016 report by MM Advisory Services makes certain interesting observations on international mobility of Indian students, based on data available for 2015 (Yojana Sharma). Some of the important trends are as follows:

- There were 340,000 internationally mobile students from India; the number from China was almost double at 450,000.
- In the US alone, nearly 45% of international students were either Chinese or Indians; Canada was heading in the same direction, with 42% in 2014.
- The number of Indian students grew faster than overall global growth rate; In case of India, it was 12% growth in 2014 and 17.8% in 2015.
- All the destinations, such as the United States, Australia, Canada, New Zealand and Germany saw a higher growth except the United Kingdom.
- Students' population in India grew by 24.3% to 11,655, given the lower cost of higher education. It overtook Russia as a destination country.

- Australia is regaining its preference as the second preferred destination of choice.
- In 2015, Indian students to China jumped by almost 23% to 16,694 – approaching the UK figure of 18,320.
- Indian student population in the UK declined by 23% between 2012 and 2014, primarily on account of stringent visa and immigration policies.

For India, UK and USA have been the two topmost destinations for Indian students. Over the years, the number of students' intake in UK had come down from 29000 in 2011-12 to 16745 in 2015-16 (Bagchi, Suvojit, 2017). Restricted visa and stay regimes in UK have led to the dwindling of students' intake.

In the case of USA, it still remains the destination for the largest number of students. Anti-immigrant feelings in USA after the ascendancy of President Trump are likely to have an impact. Educationists in UK and USA, however, have spoken on the need for 'remaining open to to-day's students and future students' (Kohli, Gauri, 2017).

Another trend is increasing student migration to other English speaking countries, such as Canada, Australia and New Zealand, which are aggressively marketing them as Destinations. India clocked 52,738 students in 2015 in Canada; the number has now touched 200,000 students. There is also an appreciable increase in the student population in Australia and New Zealand. Australia has further streamlined its admission procedures (Verma, Jatin, 2017).

Indian student population is likely to increase in destinations like Canada, Australia, New Zealand and even Germany and France, which are actively wooing foreign students. USA still remains the preferred destination and it has annual intake of around 1 million out of which around 130000 are from India. UK and USA would, therefore, have to recalibrate their policies to remain in the forefront; UK added British £ 25 billion to its economy in 2016 (UK).

## Ranking of Indian Universities

Indian institutions are making a gradual entry into the QS global ranking. Under the 2014 QS BRICS, only one institution made to BRICS top 100 for international faculty and 2 for top 100 for international students. However, 20 Indian institutions have made it into the new QS global ranking, with two in top 50 and seven in top 100. As against this, China has 71 institutions in the top 200, and six of these are within the top 10.

A total of 23 top universities in India feature in the QS Asia University Rankings 2018 including nine in the top 100. Aside from the science and technology specialists, India's highest performing comprehensive universities are Delhi University (72), Calcutta University(125), Jadavpur University (joint 125 ) and Mumbai University (181) [Rankings].

## India-Foreign Countries Linkages in Education Sector: Status and Trends

### *Bilateral Agreements*

India globally engages with the world in the education sector and has entered into arrangements through Educational Exchange Programmes (EEPs)/Memorandum of Understanding or Joint Statements with 51 countries (MHRD, 2014-15). These include 9 countries in Africa (Tanzania, Botswana, Ethiopia, South Africa, Mozambique, Burundi, Mauritius and Rwanda); 22 countries in Asia (Armenia, Israel, Australia, Myanmar, Syria, New Zealand, Thailand, Sri Lanka, Afghanistan, Saudi Arabia, China, Vietnam, Oman, Kuwait, Malaysia, , Uzbekistan, Turkmenistan, Indonesia, Yemen, Mongolia, Qatar, Tajikistan, Republic of Korea); 11 countries in Europe (Hungary, Croatia, Portugal, France, Norway, Russia, Belarus, Germany, Estonia, Czech Republic and the United Kingdom) and 8 countries in the Americas (Guyana, Mexico, Brazil, Chile, Canada, Trinidad and Tobago, Peru and USA).

Cooperation takes place under following instruments of the above arrangements:

- Exchange of students/scholars/researchers
- Holding of joint conferences/seminars/workshops.
- Developing institutional linkages
- Exchange of publications
- Working towards mutual recognition of degrees.

### *Cooperation in Higher Education*

India has also entered into arrangements with a number of countries in the area of higher education. Such cooperation has been one of the highlights of the agreements signed during VVIP bilateral visits. Some of the important and recent ones are as under:

- Launching of The Singh-Obama 21st Century Knowledge Initiative during the visit of the Indian Prime Minister to USA in November 2009, with both the governments pledging US $ 5 million to promote university linkages, faculty development and joint research. A number of joint research projects have been identified at respective institutions/universities.
- MOU in Cooperation with Germany in Higher Education and a Joint Declaration of Intent to Study German was signed in April 2013 (MHRD, 2013-14).

***UKIERI Study India Programme***

The UK India Education and Research Interaction (UKIERI) was started in 2006. It was a big step in enhancing educational relations between the two countries. UKIERI Programme is run on a five-year span basis. Announcement on UKIERI II was made in July 2010 by Prime Minister Manmohan Singh and UK Prime Minister David Cameron.

UKIERI III commenced in 2016 for the period 2016-21. The Programme is delivered by Indo-Genius, in association with Herriot-Walt University, the University of Delhi and the US-India Council. It provides for a three-week intense immersion for students into academic, business and cultural experiences.

***Erasmus Mundus Plus***

EU and India have been involved in jointly promoting higher education. The Erasmus Mundus Programme opened a new pathway for Indian students since 2008. Around 3000 Indian students and scholars have studied in European universities during the last decade, with partnership arrangements with 50 Indian universities. Erasmus Plus was launched in 2014, which opened a new chapter for studies across higher education institutions. Adequate funding is provided under the Programme for the period 2014-2020. This covers 'short term mobility and exchanges both way; joint degrees and institutional capacity building' (Dattagupta, Ishani, 2014).

***Generation UK-India Programme***

It is a British Council run project that helps young students and professionals to gain study and work experience. It helps in enhancing employability skills of participants, creating links for future collaboration and building a network. The ultimate goal 'is to build deeper, wide and stronger understanding between India and UK' (IHE website). A new internship programme, with an annual intake of 17 trainees by Tata Consultancy Services (TC) was launched in November 2015 during the visit of Prime Minister Narendra Modi to UK. So far, 250 teaching assistants, 400 young professionals and 285 students from UK have participated in various educational institutions and enterprises, to gain experience in India (IHE website).

### *The Passport to India*

This initiative was launched by the former Secretary of State Hillary Clinton in 2011 'to create a hub for U.S.-India higher education partnerships and to develop a stronger bond between the youth of both countries by increasing American student mobility'. It 'seeks to dramatically increase the number of young Americans annually learning in India on study abroad and internship programs through a sustainable philanthropic foundation'. It is a sister program to 100 Thousand Strong to China and 100 Thousand Strong in the Americas, which encourage study abroad in China and Latin America, respectively. The aims of this program are perfectly complemented by one of India's Connect India Programme (Passport to India).

### *Georgetown University's India Initiative*

The India Initiative founded at the Georgetown University in Washington DC aims at creating 'a platform for high level dialogue among American and Indian leaders from government, business, civil society and the academia'. It is expected to serve twin objectives; generate knowledge and awareness on India among future American leaders. This Initiative is expected to lead to the setting up of India-US Centre in Washington DC.

### *Joint Collaborative Research Programmes*

India has developed joint collaboration research programmes with a number of countries through Collaborative Knowledge Building Initiatives. Some of the current programmes and the funds earmarked are given in the table below (MHRD, 2013-14):

Table: Joint Research Programme with different countries

| S.No. | Country | Total Financial Commitment by India |
|---|---|---|
| 1. | U.S.A. | US $ 5.0 million for five years |
| 2. | U.K. | 2.5 million pounds per annum |
| 3. | Australia | AUD 300000 |
| 4. | New Zealand | NZD 0.5 million per annum |
| 5. | Israel | Upto US $ 2.5 million per annum |
| 6. | Germany | Euros 3.5 million for 4 years |
| 7. | Norway | Rs.8.5 crores for five years |

## Cooperation with Neighbouring Countries

### *SAARC*

The 2nd meeting of SAARC Ministers of Higher Education was held in New Delhi on October 31, 2014. At that meeting, the then HRD Minister Smriti Irani reminded the participants of the recent Declaration of the SAARC Summit which accorded importance to education and the need to work closely for a rapid change in the existing scenario (Press Release). These included harmonization of academic standards and recognition of educational qualifications, establishment of long term linkages among universities, research institutes and think tanks and institutionalizing of exchange programme among students, youth and academies.

A New Delhi Declaration on Education was adopted, identifying SAARC perspectives on the Post-2015 Education Agenda and Regional Priority Areas of Action. There was commitment to expand areas of cooperation and 'to share the best practices and achievements in education by each Member State for leveraging on mutual strengths'.

### *Nepal*

In 2014 India launched a programme, 'Bharat-Nepal Shiksha Maitri Karyakram' (Indo-Nepal Education Friendship Programme). Under this programme, 4-6 week attachment is provided to undergraduate students from Nepal. Its aim is to promote 'awareness on different facets of life in India and the progress made by the country in various fields' (MHRD,

2014-15). The first batch participated in a programme convened at the Calcutta University in November 2014.

The Government has also agreed to the establishment of the digital section of the National Library of Bhutan and the construction of Bangladesh Bhawan at the Vishwa Bharati University, Santiniketan. It was also decided to build a library at Jaffna during the visit of Prime Minister Modi to Sri Lanka in March 2015.

## New Indian Initiatives

### *Global Initiative for Academic Networks (GIAN)*

It is a new initiative undertaken by the government in 2014, to facilitate teaching by foreign scholars in educational institutions in India. GIAN aims at 'tapping the talent pool of scientists and entrepreneurs internationally, to encourage their engagement with the institutes of Higher Education in India so as to augment the country's existing academic resources, accelerate the pace of quality reform, and elevate India's scientific and technological capacity to global excellence'(GIAN) .

GIAN is envisaged to catalyse higher education institutions that initially include all IITs, IIMs, Central Universities, IISc Bangalore, IISERs, NITs and IIITs; subsequently cover good State Universities where the spinoff is vast. 1541 courses have been approved till April 2018 (GIAN: 1). It has resulted in cross-fertilization of ideas and given a push to joint academic projects.

### *Connect to India Programme*

It is a value added programme, under which around 200 undergraduate students are provided opportunities annually for a 4-6 week study programme in 15 select universities in India. The course, which is in the form of summer schools, is to familiarize students on significant developments in India. It is a win-win for all, as it is youth-focused to promote 'better understanding on contemporary India, foster closer ties and enhance their engagement with India' (Connect India). Visiting students are expected to be goodwill Ambassadors; we should consider starting similar programmes in other universities.

### *Pan-African E-network*

It is a programme that connects India with the Continent of Africa in the fields of education and health through e-networking primarily focusing on rural based communities. This project was initially announced by President Abdul Kalam at the inaugural session of the Pan-African Parliament in 2004 in Addis Ababa and an MOU was signed between the Indian Government and the African Union in October 2005. Telecommunications Consultants India Limited (TCIL) was designated the implementing agency of the project.

The project is open to participants by all the 53 African countries. At the Indian end, tele-medicine and tele-education hubs have been set up in Bangalore and Ahmedabad, while it is Addis Ababa at the African end. Initially, four countries to join were Ethiopia, South Africa, Mauritius and Ghana. This initiative was heralded by the press in Africa as the largest infrastructure project in Africa's history and 'the e-education and e-medicine programmes are particularly expected to extend ICT infrastructure to certain rural communities and under-served areas' (The Observatory).

***Nalanda University: An Experiment in Joint Cultural Diplomacy***

The setting up of the Nalanda University is a new initiative in joint cultural diplomacy, as this is a collaborative effort between India and countries in Southeast and East Asia. The idea for the revival of the University was mooted by the former President of India Dr. A.P.J. Abdul Kalam, while addressing the Bihar State Legislative Assembly, in March 2006. It was picked up by the government of the State of Bihar. The initial foreign support came from the government of Singapore. Support for the establishment of this University was formalized at the 4$^{th}$ East Asia Summit (EAS) in Thailand on 24-25 October, 2009.

At the 5$^{th}$ East Asian Summit on 30 October, 2010, Indian Prime Minister extended an invitation to EAS member states to participate in the project. To reinforce the university's international character, an inter-governmental Memorandum of Understanding came into force at the 8th East Asia Summit in October 2013. Till date 17 countries have signed the MoU, which are: Australia, Bangladesh, Bhutan, South Korea, Cambodia, China, India, Indonesia, Myanmar, New Zealand, Portugal, Singapore, Sri Lanka, Thailand, Vietnam, Lao People's Democratic Republic, Brunei Darussalam.

This University is located at Rajgir in Bihar. The Government of Bihar contributed 455 acres of land, free of cost to the University. The University became functional in 2013-14. The primary funding for the University would come from the Government of India (J N Misra).[3] The University would focus on Asia and its Unique Selling Point (USP) would be research (Sabharwal, Gopa).[4]

The President of India is the Visitor, Professor Amartya Sen was the First Chancellor, and Dr. Gopa Sabharwal was the Vice Chancellor and Dr. Anjana Sharma was the Dean of the University. The current Chancellor is Dr. Vijay Bhatkar, while the Vice Chancellor is Prof. Sunaina Singh.

The then External Affairs Minister Salman Khurshid at his media briefing at Darussalam on 1 July 2013, stated, how Nalanda University would mark 'India's soft diplomacy and engagement with Asia based on our historical and spiritual links but providing it with a new vigour and a new energy in our times in the 21st century'.

***South Asian University (SAU)***

The idea for the setting up of this University was mooted by the Indian Prime Minister Manmohan Singh at the 13th SAARC Summit in Dhaka in 2005. An Interregional Agreement was signed on April 4, 2007 at the 14th Summit held in Delhi. The University is to be a Centre of Excellence, providing world class facilities and faculty for students and researchers for the SAARC member countries (SAU Charter). The University opened its doors to students in August 2010 from a temporary location. It is expected to move to its own campus in Delhi during 2018.

The Indian Government is providing the capital cost, while the operational costs would be proportionately shared as mutually agreed upon. It is expected to have 12 post-graduate science and non-science faculties, a faculty for undergraduate studies and an Institute of South Asian Studies. SAU is expected to have 7000 students and 700 teachers, 20% of whom could be from outside the region. Degrees and certificates awarded by the University would be recognized by all the member countries. The vision of SAU is 'to enhance learning in the South Asian community that promotes an understanding of each other's perspectives and strengthen regional consciousness' (SAU VISION).

***Study in India Programme:*** On April 2018, the Minister of External Affairs Sushma Swaraj launched a Website to focus on international students. She said that this marked 'an important milestone in our efforts to bring India back to its rightful place as a global knowledge hub' (EAM 2018). It is in keeping with the recent thrust of the government to make quality education affordable, as it opened its educational institutions in higher education. India's strength lies in its ability to offer educational facilities, as it is 'one of the few places in the world, where modernity and ancient traditions coexist in harmony' (EAM, 2018). According to HRD Minister of State Satyapal Singh, the move is expected to bring 'multiculturalism and diversities in Indian universities'. India has ambitious plans to reach a target of 200,000 foreign students by 2023 (Prashant K Nanda, 2018). The primary focus areas are South Asia, Southeast Asia, West Asia and Africa. The launching of the Portal is to introduce an element of technology to smoothen admission processes to reach the projected target.

***Teaching of German in Central Schools***

India and Germany agreed to an arrangement under which students in Kendriya Vidyalaya Schools (KVS) would be able to opt for German as an additional foreign language in conformity with the National Education Policy. Max Mueller Bhavan and the Kendriya Vidyalaya Sangathan (KVS) agreed to promote teaching of German and modern Indian languages in their respective countries. This new arrangement helped in containing adverse diplomatic fallout from an earlier stand taken by the then Minister of Human Resource Development to discontinue the teaching of German at the KVS. (Ramchandran, Smriti Kak).

## India Aspiring to Reemerge as a Hub of International Education

India is not a major player in the arena of education diplomacy. It has failed to attract self-financing foreign students in any appreciable number. Even India's offer of 3000 scholarships annually to foreign students through ICCR also pales into insignificance against the global population of 4.5 million foreign students. Furthermore, it is not widespread, as 1000 scholarships are earmarked to Afghanistan, while another 1000 scholarships are meant for students from African countries.

Over the years, India has lost attraction for students from Southeast Asian countries, which have become self reliant. It is not only that but some of them, like Singapore and Malaysia, are also emerging as Destinations. We thus notice a reverse trend as Indian students are seeking admission in those countries.

India's recent major initiative on the setting up of Nalanda University has been embroiled in political controversy, as its mentor and First Chancellor Nobel Laureate Amartya Sen and the President George Yeo, former Foreign Minister of Singapore tendered their resignations, over differences with the government. Moreover, it is still at a nascent stage and has yet to fully take off. Differing political perceptions or individual preferences should not be allowed to come in the way of achieving the stated purpose and fulfilling the spirit for the setting up the University.

The other major initiative – South Asian University has not yet risen to the 'Star Status' (Murthy, Sachidananda). The major drawback has been that Pakistan is not whole heartedly involved in the process. Furthermore, it still has to acquire a South Asian character, as there is preponderance of Indian faculty and students. The government needs to stay committed on this path, as the then HRD Minister Smriti Irani spoke on the need for a joint endeavour to see that South Asian University emerged as 'an institute of excellence, which could contribute to creation of knowledge in the region through quality higher education at an affordable cost' (Irani).

Any successful education diplomacy has to project a student friendly and open environment. India's image was dented, when some African students felt that they were the victims of racial prejudices in India. We have to keep in mind that African students have become more vocal. To erase this image, there is a need to change the mindset at the societal level, as all efforts at the official and ministerial levels would not be able to easily erase that image. India cannot afford to lose its friendship with Africa and thus lose the benefits arising from education diplomacy.

There is also no clarity on India's policy on the setting up of foreign universities in India. This has put on hold a number of proposals on the opening of campuses of foreign universities in India or twining of institutions. Similarly, there are question marks on the independence of Indian universities, and this stands in the way of developing innovative research programmes, resulting in not giving a push to India's flagship programmes – Innovative and Digital India.

A positive development, however, is the initiative of foreign countries to send students to India through schemes devised by them. I would like to call this process Reverse Education Diplomacy. These include measures adopted by Australia, UK and USA etc.

India's efforts in Education Diplomacy also suffer, as it has no coherent policy on the establishment of educational institutions abroad. Our diffidence and reluctance in opening these in Malaysia in the late 90s paved the way for Australia's entry into that country.

Earlier, students from Malaysia came to India for study, now it is a reverse process for Indian students seeking admission in Malaysia or Singapore. To attract talented students, these countries are even offering scholarships.

Our one successful twining effort was the setting up of Manipal-Melaka Medical College in Malaysia. Now, Manipal Academy for Higher Education has set up educational linkages in some other countries.

Indian Universities do not rank high under the universally known and accepted grading systems. This results in India not being in the normal beat of bright foreign students. India has started a system to grade its higher educational institutes since 2016. This would help in boosting the image of good institutions, even though India has certain world renowned Brands, like the Indian Institutes of Technology (IITs) and Indian Institutes of Management (IIMs).

The increased presence of Indian Diaspora has resulted in another positive development, leading to the opening of Indian schools abroad, in particular, in the West Asian countries. Two important school chains – Kendriya Vidyalaya (KVIC) and Delhi Public Schools – are the leading groups, which have made a mark in those countries.

On the other hand, we need to review our scheme for admission of NRI students, as the interest in the same has either flagged or it has been tweaked at the stage of implementation. We need to relaunch the same by making it more attractive.

Unlike other countries, India has not promoted itself as a 'Destination for Education'. Limited efforts by the Education Consultants India (ECIL) in holding Education Melas (Fairs) have not borne any fruits. It is now only that ICCR and the Ministry of Human Resource Development (MHRD) have started selling India as an affordable quality destination for students, when ICCR held the first conference on Higher Education in India for Foreign Students on March 21-22, 2016. India has to plan its promotional strategy on a long term basis and follow it consistently.

India has also started connecting with ICCR's Alumni. ICCR held the first such Award Ceremony in 2016 when it honoured some of its important alumnus with Alumni Award. India needs to build ICCR Alumni into a powerful force like that of the Fulbright Alumni. Diplomatic Missions have to involve themselves increasingly in promoting the setting up of such Associations and engage them on a regular basis.

There is a need for recognition of equivalence of degrees, as this is the foundation on which cooperation in the field of Higher Education could be built up. The signing of an Agreement with France in March 2018, during the visit of the President of France, was a step in the right direction. We need more agreements on similar lines with other key countries.

There is also a need to promote greater twining of Indian and foreign universities, which could result in students completing some semesters in both the universities. Panjab University has such arrangements with some foreign universities. More steps, however, are needed to promote student exchanges.

*Fulbright Difference* by Arndt narrates the story of the exceptional nature of the Fulbright Programme, through the eyes of its scholars, as they gained a unique and exceptional experience (Arndt). ICCR could consider publishing a book on 'ICCR Experience' on similar lines to project India.

The government has just started its innings with Sushma Swaraj, Minister for External Affairs launching a website on 'Study in India Programme' in April 2018 to smoothen the admission process. India is set to reach a target of 200,000 foreign students by 2023. The Author lives in hope and concludes with a Bollywood song, 'Woh Subbah Kabhi to Aaye Gi' (Would see that Dawn One Day), to see India reemerge as a hub of international education and gain leadership role in education diplomacy, as per the aspirations of our leaders.

**Annexure 1**

**International Students in India**

Total international student enrolment: **42,420**

**Top 10 sending places of origin and percentage of total international student enrollment:**

| Rank | Place of Origin | Number of Students | Percent of Total |
|---|---|---|---|
| 1 | Nepal | 9,015 | 21.3% |
| 2 | Afghanistan | 4,349 | 10.3% |
| 3 | Bhutan | 2,794 | 6.6% |
| 4 | Sudan | 2,047 | 4.8% |
| 5 | Nigeria | 1,990 | 4.7% |
| 6 | Malaysia | 1,899 | 4.5% |
| 7 | Iran | 1,430 | 3.4% |
| 8 | Yemen | 1,212 | 2.9% |
| 9 | Sri Lanka | 1,121 | 2.6% |
| 10 | Iraq | 1,051 | 2.5% |
| | All Others | 15,512 | 36.6% |

**Total number of international students from all places of origin by field of study**

| Rank | Field of Study | Number of Students | Percent of Total |
|---|---|---|---|
| 1 | Health Professions | 10,662 | 25.1% |
| 2 | Business & Management | 8,509 | 20.1% |
| 3 | Engineering | 7,345 | 17.3% |
| 4 | Mathematics & Computer Sciences | 5,307 | 12.5% |
| 5 | Fine & Applied Arts | 3,516 | 8.3% |
| 6 | Physical & Life Sciences | 2,803 | 6.6% |
| 7 | Social Sciences | 1,617 | 3.8% |
| 8 | Other/Unspecified Subject Areas | 995 | 2.3% |
| 9 | Humanities | 836 | 2.0% |
| 10 | Agriculture | 592 | 1.4% |
| 11 | Education | 238 | 0.6% |

Data time reference: 2015 to 2016.

Source: Ministry of Human Resource and Development, 2016

## Endnotes

1. C Rajasekhar, Director General, ICCR, New Delhi. Interaction on March 21, 2016 in Delhi.
2. Mary McKey, Director, Institute of International Education (IIE), San Francisco, USA. Meeting on August 8, 2016 in San Francisco.
3. J N Misra, Additional Secretary, Ministry of External Affairs Meeting on January 27, 2014 at Delhi.
4. Sabharwal, Gopa, First Vice Chancellor, Nalanda University. Meeting on July 27, 2015 at Delhi.

## References:

Arndt, Richard T. and Rubin, David Lee (eds.), 1993, *The Fulbright Difference*, Transaction Publishers, New Jersey.

Bagchi, Suvojit, 2017, 'Tightening of Visa Rules impacted students', *The Hindu*, January 28.

Bhandari, Rajika and Lefebure, Alessia, 2015, 'Asia: The Next Higher Education Superpower?' https://www.linkedin.com/pulse/asia-next-higher-education-superpower-alessia-lefebure (Accessed on December 23, 2017).

Canada-Mexico Exchanges, 2016, 'Students welcome plans to boost Canada-Mexico Exchanges', *Ottawa Community News*, June 29.

Canadian Website, http://www.canadainternational.gc.ca/india-inde/academic_relations_academiques/index.aspx?lang=eng&menu_id=12, http://www.educanada.ca/index.aspx?lang=eng (Accessed on December 23, 2017).

Chaba, Anju Agnihotri, 2017, 'Mindless enhancement of educational institutes not worth pursuing: Pranab', *The Indian Express*, May 3.

Chevening, http://www.chevening.org/india/ (Accessed on December 13, 2017).

Communique, 2016, Council for International Education Meeting, Canberra, November 23.

Connect India, http://mhrd.gov.in/sites/upload_files/mhrd/files/ConnectIndiaProgramme24-06-2013.pdf (Accessed on May 4, 2018).

Dattagupta, Ishani, 'A new chapter in EU-India educational ties', *The Economic Times*, November 2.

Deshpande, Alok, 2014, 'Abbott launches New Colombo Plan for students of India, Australia', *The Hindu*, September 4. http://www.thehindu.com/features/education/abbott-launches-new-colombo-plan-for-students-of-india-australia/article6379449.ece (Accessed on Dec. 23, 2017).

Dhillon, Seerat, 2017, 'Education vs Commerce', *The Tribune*, January 6.

EAM 2018, External Affairs Minister's Remarks at Launch of Study in India Programme, April 18, New Delhi.

EdCIL 2015, EdCIL Annual Report, 2014-15, New Delhi.

Farrugia & Bhandari. 2014, 2014 – 15 Annual Report Office of International Education Beloit College, https://www.beloit.edu/oie/assets/2014.15_annual_report_.pdf (Accessed on December 23, 2017).

Fulbright Programme, https://eca.state.gov/fulbright (Accessed on December 23, 2017).

GIAN, 2015, 'Smriti Irani launches GIAN to boost higher education with international collaboration', *India Today*, December 1. http://indiatoday.intoday.in/education/story/gian-launched/1/535735.html (Accessed on December 23, 2017).

GIAN, http://www.gian.iitkgp.ac.in/cgenmenu/guidelines (Accessed on April 19, 2018).

Global Connect, https://share.america.gov/globalconnect/ (Accessed on April 26,2018).

Goodman, Allan. https://www.elsevier.com/connect/asian-research-execs-discuss-what-it-takes-to-produce-world-leading-universities (Accessed on December 23, 2017).

Goucher College, http://www.goucher.edu/learn/study-abroad/ (Accessed on December 23, 2017).

Harinder Sandhu, http://www.asiaeducation.edu.au/programmes/school-partnerships/participating-countries/india/australia-india-bridge-program-2017 (Accessed on December 23, 2017).

Hart, Justin, 2013, *Empire of Ideas*, Oxford University Press, New York.

Hyun-Choe, Chung, 2016, 'Stepping up cultural exchange program', *The Korea Times*, May 25.

IHE Website, http://www.ihe-com/index.php?option=com_content&view =article&id=12&Itemid=8 (Accessed on December 23, 2017).

IIE Brochure, https://www.iie.org/en/ (Accessed on December 23, 2017).

India-Canada Joint Statement, State Visit of Prime Minister of Canada to India, New Delhi, February 23, 2018. http://mea.gov.in/bilateral-documents.htm?dtl/29512/IndiaCanada_Joint_Statement_during_State_Visit_of_Prime_Minister_of_Canada_to_India_February_23_2018.

India-France Joint Statement, State visit of President of France to India, New Delhi, March 10, 2018. http://mea.gov.in/bilateral documents.htm?dtl/29596/IndiaFrance_Joint_Statement_during_State_visit_of_President_of_France_to_India_March_10_2018 (Accessed on May 2, 2017).

Indian Diaspora, 2016, 'Irani: Education Diplomacy: Study in India is the new Mantra', March 22.

India Initiative, https://india.georgetown.edu/ (Accessed on May 2, 2018).

Indian Students Abroad. 2017, https://factly.in/indians-students-studying-abroad-in-86-different-countries-55-in-usa-canada/ (Accessed on April 19, 2018).

Irani, 2016, 'India offers affordable excellence through education diplomacy: Irani' *The Times of India*, March 21.

IVLP, https://eca.state.gov/ivlp (Accessed on December 23, 2017).

Joint Statement, 2016, Joint Statement, Issued after the visit of Prime Minister of New Zealand to India, New Delhi, October 26.

Julie Bishop, 2015, 'We are keen on expanding our strategic partnership with India', *The Hindu*, April 20, http://www.thehindu.com/todays-paper/tp-opinion/we-are-keen-on-expanding-our-strategic-partnership-with-india/article7120265.ece (Accessed on December 23, 2017).

Karen MacGregor , 'Aiming for a slice of the African mobile student pie', University World News, 26 April 2014 Issue No:317, http://www.universityworldnews.com/ article.php? story=20140418104554993 ((Accessed on December 23, 2017).

Kirkpatrick, Andy, 2012, 'English in ASEAN: implications for regional multilingualism' www.tandfonline.com/doi/abs/10.1080/01434632.2012.661433 (Accessed on December 23, 2017).

Kohli, Gauri, 2016, 'Scholarships for Indians to study in UK', *The Hindustan Times*, September 21.

Kohli, Gauri, 2017, 'Study Abroad: US, UK have everything to lose if they look inwards', *The Hindustan Times*, Jan. 24. Aiming for a slice of the African mobile student pie', University World News, April 26. http://www.universityworldnews.com/article.php?story=20140418104554993 (Accessed on December 23, 2017).

MHRD, 2013-14, Annual Report of the Ministry of Human Resource Development, Government of India, Delhi.

MHRD, 2014-15, Annual Report of the Ministry of Human Resource Development, Government of India, Delhi.

MMA, 2016, MM Adisory Services,'Indian Students Mobility Reports.

Murthy, Sachidanand, 2017, 'Deemed Universities', *The Week*, January 22.

Obama, Michelle, 2016, 'Fact Sheet: First Lady Announces New Let Girls Learn Commitment in Liberia', The White House, June 27. https://obamawhitehouse.archives.gov/the-press-office/2016/06/27/fact-sheet-first-lady-announces-new-let-girls-learn-committment-liberia (Accessed on December 23, 2017).

Open Doors 2014, https://eca.state.gov/impact/open-doors-reports (Accessed on December 23, 2017).

Open Doors 2015, https://www.iie.org/Why-IIE/Announcements/2015-11-16-Open-Doors-Data (Accessed on December 23, 2017).

Open Doors, 2017, https://www.iie.org/Why-IIE/Announcements/2017-11-13-Open-Doors-2017-Executive-Summary (Accessed on December 23, 2017).

Passport to India, https://www.state.gov/p/sca/ci/in/passport_to_india/ (Accessed on May 2, 2018).

PM Modi, 2018, Press Statement, During State visit of Prime Minister of Canada, New Delhi, February 23, http://mea.gov.in/Speeches-Statements.htm?dtl/29638/English_Translation_of_Press_

Statement_by_Prime_Minister_during_State_visit_of_Prime_Minister_of_Canada_February_23_2018 (Accessed on May 2, 2018).

Press Release, 2014, 2nd Meeting of SAARC Education Ministers, New Delhi, October 31.

Rajasekhar, 2016, Director General, ICCR, New Delhi (Address to the Conference, March 2016).

Ramachandran, Smriti Kak, 2015, 'German to be taught again in Central Schools', *The Hindu*, October 6.

Rankings, https://www.topuniversities.com/university-rankings/asianuniversity- rankings/2018 (Accessed on April 19, 2018).

Rohrer, D'Ann, 2016, 'Returning home after an exchange year', State Coordinator Leadership and Exchange Team, June 21.

Rugh, William, 2014. *'Front Line Public Diplomacy'*, Palgrave MacMillan, New York.

SAU Charter, http://www.sau.int/downloads/accredit/Inter-Governmental-Agreement.pdf (Accessed on December 23, 2017).

SAU VISION, http://www.sau.int/about/vision.html (Accessed on December 23, 2017).

Shambaugh, David, 2015. 'China's Soft-Power Push', *The Foreign Affairs*, July-August.

Sharma, Yojana, 2016, 'Surge in growth of Indian students studying abroad' University World News, Issue No:416, June 1. http://www.universityworldnews.com/article.php?story=20160601180527213 (Accessed on December 23, 2017).

Smits, Yolanda, 2014, 'China Country Report, Culture in the EU's External Relations.

Sodhi, Simran, 2017, 'Australia allays fears over changes in its visa regimes', *The Tribune*, May 4.

Speed Post News Network, 2018, 'Javadekar hails MoU between India & France for mutual recognition of degrees', March 10, http://www.thespeedpost.com/javadekar-hails-mou-between-india-france-for-mutual-recognition-of-degrees/.

State Department Website, www.state.gov (Accessed on December 23, 2017).

State Department, www.state.gov/records/remains 2017/03 (Accessed on December 23, 2017).

The Observatory, 2006, Borderless Higher Education, June.

*The Tribune*, 2017, 'Let's work to reverse brain drain: President', May 3.

*The Times of India,* 2017, 'Reverse Trend of students' migration: Prez', May 3.

*The Times of India*, 2018, Renuka Bisht in Twinkle Twinkle, 'Books, Q & A World', January 30.

UK, http://www.universitiesuk.ac.uk/news/Pages/International-students-now-worth-25-billion-to-UK-economy---new-research.aspx#sthash.sKD7GAy2.dpbs (Accessed on December 23, 2017).

US Study Abroad, https://studyabroad.state, (Accessed on December 23, 2017).

Verma, Jatin, 2017, 'Studying in Australia, Simplified', *The Chandigarh Times*, June 5.

Yojana Sharma, 2016, 'Surge in growth of Indian students studying abroad', *University World News*, Issue No: 416, June 1. http://www.universityworldnews.com/article.php?story=20160601180527213.

Youth Ambassadors Programme, https://exchanges.state.gov/non-us/program/youth-ambassadors (Accessed on April 26, 2018).

# Chapter – VIII

# Primary Vehicles of Cultural Diplomacy

## Introduction

Each country adopts its own vehicles of cultural diplomacy and it is not even the same vehicle that is used for all the countries. For example, USA has successfully used sports as an important vehicle, when it designated Shaquille O'Neil, Basketball player and Michelin Kwan, Ice Skater, as its Sports Ambassadors to connect with other countries, using sports as a vehicle. China is using Confucius Institutes and has set up a target of 1000 such institutes by 2025. UAE is projecting its strength as a neutral venue for holding Bollywood concerts or cricket matches between India and Pakistan. The European Union (EU) resorts to holding Annual Film Festivals in India. Mexico is increasingly using its vibrant film and television industry, in particular "telenovelas" in projecting itself, while simultaneously catering to the Mexican population. Thailand is using its cuisine, as it has emerged as the Food Capital of the world. The Philippines is also resorting to Food Diplomacy, as its Embassies regularly hold Food Festivals. The United Kingdom (UK) organized a string of events to mark the 400$^{th}$ Birth Anniversary of Shakespeare in 2016.

When we talk of India, Bollywood shines. Former Minister of State for External Affairs Shashi Tharoor fully recognized the importance of this huge asset of soft power, like 'Bollywood, TV shows and the exportable products of India's culture' (Tharoor, Shashi, 2007). It is here that India ticks, says Pavan Verma, 'whether its yoga, art, music, dance, Ayurveda or Bollywood, the world is interested' (Bagchi, Indrani 2008). It was, therefore, not surprising to see the former Head of Public Diplomacy Division Dasgupta, compiling an unenviable collection of old Bollywood songs (Bagchi, Indrani, 2008). Sitar maestro, Pandit Ravi Shankar and Shenai maestro Ustad Bismillah Khan played an invaluable role for Indian cultural diplomacy; so did Qawwali singer Ustad Fateh Ali Khan for

Pakistan. Bollywood Superstars, like Amitabh Bachchan, Shah Rukh Khan and Priyanka Chopra, are now playing the role of Cultural Ambassadors for India or UN organisations.

Afghanistan's first all-girl orchestra performed a concert at the World Economic Forum, Davos on January 20, 2017, sending a message of women power. It was also Ravi Shanker's Sitar concert in New York in 1971 that according to Ambassador Ronen Sen helped in swinging the popular mood in the world towards Bangladesh, as he performed a stellar role as India's Ambassador (Bagchi, Indrani, 2012).

Similarly, music maestro Zubin Mehta's concert in Srinagar in September 2013 managed to send 'a message of oneness of humanity' demonstrating that 'Music is a universal language of peace and harmony' (The Tribune, 2013). Pakistani Sufi singer Abida Parveen has always sent the message that Sufi music "transcends all man-made boundaries. Cultural Ambassadors have managed to achieve where politicians have failed" (The Times of India, 2001).

It is not only through Bollywood, but connectivity at the people to people level, is also facilitated through sports, yoga, art and literature and music? Some of these programmes have been facilitated by bilateral exchanges, while in many other cases these have taken local routes themselves, as Yoga and Music and Dance Academies have been set up in many countries, such as USA, Singapore, Malaysia, China etc. In the past, such connectivity was largely brought about by the government. It has now also moved in to the private arena, as the commercial appetite of both the artists and organizers has been whetted.

There is a spurt in festivals, be it in the areas of dance or music; art or literature. There is both a mix of popular and classical culture; intermixing of different cultures. Literary Festivals, no longer talk about literature, but are emerging as forums for discussion on issues that impact on society. Photos are also another important tool in building images, as one photo captures one thousand words. India has regularly sent photographic exhibitions abroad. It has also successfully used these through Coffee Table Books. It looks more convincing, if a foreign photographer projects India.

Yoga has assumed the top billing in the case of India. In this Chapter, we would look at some of the vehicles, which have been used by India, both at the level of Government and cultural organizations. We would, of course, focus on Bollywood and Yoga. We would also look at the role of Music,

Literary Festivals, Cricket as a sport, Cuisine Diplomacy. We would also look at the 2015 Khushwant Singh Literary Festival, as a case study, where the Author was present.

## Bollywood

Let us start with Bollywood first, as it is not only films but also the music that attracts people. It is both, the elite and the common man who sway to the 'Bollywood Beat'. How has Bollywood acquired a preeminent place, built up an image for itself? Bollywood found its biggest supporter in the Chinese President Jinping Xi, who publicly endorsed Aamir Khan Starrer 'Dangal' in May 2017 by claiming that he was impressed by the same. It is also through its stars, who are given a place of honour, be it the placards of Amitabh Bachchan hanging alongside the Syrian President or Shah Rukh Khan honoured with a 'Datuk Title' (akin to Padma Shri) by one of the States in Malaysia. It is also the same story when an Indian journalist buys his freedom from an Iraqi soldier, as both were fans of the same film star, Shammi Kapoor (Thussu, Daya, 2013).

Indian TV Series, 'Saas Bhi Thi Kabhi Bahu' (Mother-in-Law was also Bride sometime ago) was so popular that Kabul would come to standstill, when this programme was telecast. Strangely enough or sarcastically speaking, even the thieves would thank the heroine (Tulsi) for giving them the opportunities for letting them do their job. Such examples could be multiplied to project the hold of Bollywood, which is not only on Indian Diaspora, but has also brought local persons under its charm. It is no more screening of Bollywood films in isolated theatres; the screening has become a regular feature at the multiplexes, as the number of persons who are willing to pay has increased.

How does Bollywood capture world attention? In China, it is the social themes, like empowerment in 'Dangal' or the education system in '3 Idiots' or children with special abilities in 'PK', which attract the youth. Aamir Khan, in particular, has become a hit in China, if you go by the entries in social media. Posts in Weibo reflect open admiration for him, with some comments suggesting that 'the focus is shifting on what binds the Indian and Chinese people rather than what pulls them apart' (Aneja, Atul, 2017).

Bollywood is no more considered Hollywood's poor cousin and has emerged as 'one of the strongest global cultural ambassadors of a new India. It is on way to becoming 'a global soft power to reckon with', writes Roopa Swaminathan in her latest book, 'Bollywood Boom' (The Indian Express, 2017). She writes,

> "Where earlier it was in Russia, East Europe and Africa that Raj Kapoor and Amitabh Bachchan enjoyed a devoted fan base, today the entire world is entertained by 'the three Khans and by international stars Ifran Khan, Priyanka Chopra and Deepika Padukone".

What Bollywood has achieved in diversity, Hollywood is still clamouring for the same at the Oscars or Emmy Awards.

From where does Bollywood draw its strength? It has emerged as a good revenue earner abroad. Dangal grossed US $ 11.2 million during the first weekend of its screening in China (Aneja, Atul, 2017). Bollywood's participation in film festivals across the world has increased popularity of films as well as their demand. Festivals of India abroad also give it a push, as film festivals are an important component of those Festivals. Bollywood and Indian Cinema, which include Regional Films, has emerged as a subject for study at many universities. It is also able to place itself strategically, as the International Film Festivals of India (IFFI) Awards are given abroad annually at gala shows in different countries.

Another important trend is the emergence of Indian Producers and Directors of international renown, like Ivory Merchant, Mira Nair, Gurinder Chadha. Recent addition includes filmmaker Kavery Kaul, an Indian-American, who is a name in today's documentary world. Her latest film, 'Streetcar to Kolkata' has a cross-cultural theme, where three girls negotiate their identity between 'who they are and who others think they are'. It builds 'bridges between faiths at a time when we need those bridges more than ever' (Gyatso, Kimberly, 2016).

Another trend is the joint production of films with Bollywood. Let us take the case of Morocco; it is not only Bollywood that connects with Morocco, but Morocco also is connected through Bollywood. Anurag Basu shot scenes of his movie 'Jaso Jagga' in Morocco in 2015. A Moroccon director Yassine Fennane released a movie 'Karyana Bollywood', which narrates the story of a young Moroccan who is an avid fan of Bollywood movies. Another Moroccan Director, Aahd Bensonda through his film 'Marrakech Bombay' - a love story, aims to combine the Moroccan and Indian cultures, based on a story of a Moroccan in Marrakech and an Indian in Bombay. The film would be shot in both the countries (Igrouane, Youssef).

Foreign countries, like Malaysia, New Zealand, vie with one another in providing generous facilities for the shooting of films, as it helps them in turning Bollywood into a tool of cultural diplomacy for promoting tourism in their respective countries. The shooting of the first blockbuster film, 'Chandni Chowk to China Town', shot in China, fully corroborates this point (Bagchi, Indrani, 2008). A side effect of the visit of the Turkish President Erdogan to India in April 2017 was to woo Bollywood and generate interest in shooting films in Turkey (Ray, Suchetana, 2017).

Bollywood is now providing such connectivity in many other countries. A number of films are being shot in Austria that includes Prabhudeva's Acktion Jackson and Karan Johar's 'Ae Dil Hai Mushkil'. Bollywood films are being screened at top cineplexes and the recent being 'Umrika' by Indian Director Praveen Nair. The film 'Court', India's official entry to the Oscar Awards in 2016 was screened at the famous Vienna International Film Festival. Film Weeks are being regularly held by the Film Museum, Vienna that screened films made by famous Indian Director, like Satyajit Ray and Ritwick Ghatak.

Bollywood thus provides twin benefits to India and the host country. So far, films have been shot over 51 countries; many countries vie for shooting films in their countries, as it results in promoting tourism. Another impact of Bollywood has been that many foreigners, like Sri Lankans, have started learning Hindi. Bollywood has thus emerged as an important vehicle of cultural diplomacy, as it helps in providing connectivity between India and peoples from different cultures.

Bollywood has also emerged as money spinner in foreign countries, such as China, Japan and South Korea. Bollywood continues to 'serenade Chinese, who have special love for Indian movies, soaps and songs' (The Indian Express, 2015). The Japanese go gaga over films, like English Vinglish and 3 Idiots, as the audience enjoys 'heart warming dramas' as well as those that have a message, which is also relevant to their social concerns, (Ramnath, Nandini, 2014). In South Korea, women in the 20-40 age groups, are the biggest fans and are attracted to movies that 'deal with humanism' like 'Tare Zameen Par' (Ghosh, Avijit, 2012). Ghanians are hooked to Indian TV Soap Opera, 'Kumkum Bhagya'. The visiting Ghanian U-17 football team for the World FIFA Cup in October 2017made a special request to meet film stars, when they learnt that they would be playing pre-quarter final match in Mumbai. (Judge, Shahid, 2017).

An interesting development but not well known is the entry of Cinepolis, a Mexican company, which has set up multiplexes in Mangalore and other second tier cities like Pune, Amritsar, Ludhiana, Jaipur, Surat, Ahmedabad and Bhopal. They plan to have 400 screens by 2017 with a total investment of Rs.1000 crores (US $ 150 million). Cinepolis was founded in 1947 and is the fourth largest in the world with 3400 screens in eleven countries (Ambassador Viswanathan, 2014).

India enjoys 'tremendous soft power due to cultural and linguistic similarities' in Afghanistan, with Bollywood and Hindi films being 'great Ambassadors of our culture' (Viraj Singh).[1] It was this cultural link that Prime Minister Modi tried to resurrect through 'Kabuliwala', when he visited Kabul in December 2015. Our High Commissioner in Sri Lanka would like India to enlist 'the support of Bollywood in a more organized manner as part of our soft power/cultural outreach in Sri Lanka and many other countries around the globe' (YK Sinha).[2]

**Yoga**

Yoga has also emerged as an important vehicle, given its international acceptance. It is not only an important activity in the Indian Cultural Centres, but there is also an emergence of local Yoga Centres, as more and more people feel the need for spiritualism, away from their daily materialistic lives.

The story of Yoga, however, does not start with Modi. It had made its appearance in many countries, in particular, USA and China, for their own reasons. Chinese had already taken to Yoga before the declaration of June 21, as the International Yoga Day (IYD) since 2015. BKS Iyengar visited China in March 2012 and participated in the first ever Yoga Summit. His visit led to the setting up of Yoga Centres and training of Yoga teachers (Krishnan, Ananth, 2012). Yoga Festival was launched in July 2014, which further spurred up Chinese interest before the declaration of IYD (Krishnan, Ananth: I). It is interesting to observe that in some of the Muslim countries such as Qatar, Yoga is practiced (Al Jazeera, 2016).

Prime Minister Modi gave 'Yoga' a great push at his first address at the UNGA on September 27, 2014; he sought for declaration of International Yoga Day. He highlighted its spiritual value in these words:

> "Yoga is an invaluable gift of our ancient tradition. Yoga embodies unity of mind and body; thought and action; restraint and fulfillment; harmony between man and nature; a holistic approach to health and well being. It is not about exercise but to discover the sense of oneness with yourself, the world and the nature. By our life style and creating consciousness, it can help us deal with climate change. Let us work towards adopting an International Yoga Day." (UNGA, 2014)

UNGA with 175 votes overwhelmingly endorsed June 21 to be declared as the International Yoga Day (IYD). This has resulted in the Prime Minister turning Yoga into 'India Brand'. In his speech to the Australian Parliament, Modi said, 'I know Yoga is enormously popular here; we need to connect our people more' (Wade, Matt). Dr. Murli Manohar Joshi has written on the strength of Yoga, 'where science meets spirituality' (Joshi, Murli Manohar, 2017).

After the UN declared June 21 as the International Yoga Day (IYD), full attention of the Indian government was focused on organizing multifarious activities in India and abroad. Modi himself led the celebrations in leading the show at India Gate on June 21, 2015. ICCR extended full support to the diplomatic missions in celebrating Yoga Day by sending Yoga teachers and Yoga material, apart from providing sufficient funds. ICCR is already facilitating teachings of Yoga and had placed Yoga teachers in 38 countries at Indian Cultural Centres (MEA 2015-16). ICCR has plans to depute more Yoga teachers at its Cultural Centres.

In the realm of Yoga and Traditional Medicine, two other significant developments took place; setting up Yoga Centres/Educational Institutions during the Year 2015. These are as follows:

- Setting up the first India-China Yoga College at the Yunnan Minzu University, Kunming, in May 2015. ICCR deployed two Yoga teachers for teaching as well as to provide help in preparing curriculum for the Yoga courses.
- Inauguration of the India-Turkmenistan Centre for Traditional Medicine at Ashgabat in July 2015 by Prime Minister Modi. ICCR joined hands with the Ministry of AYUSH for the deployment of Yoga and Ayurveda experts.

The offer of first master's degree in Yoga at China's Minzu University is being seen as 'a clear signal that soft power is being deployed to reactivate China-India ties in the aftermath of the tense Doklam standoff' (Aneja, Atul: 1, 2017). Perceptions can, at times, take flights of fancy.

A number of Yoga-related activities were organized by Indian diplomatic missions abroad in 2015. The Maldives emerged as a significant destination, where manifold activities were organized dealing with different aspects of Yoga. These included, 'Therapeutic Yoga Session' and 'Pregnancy Session for Women'. Nine Yoga sessions were organized at nine different venues to mark the International Yoga Day on June 21. Candle Night

Yoga Meditation was organized twice on August 17 and September 1. A Lecture-cum-Yoga demonstration was organized to generate awareness on Cancer.

Other significant events included organization of Yoga Day in front of heritage buildings in Indonesia and Cambodia. Sri Sri Ravi Shankar addressed the EU Parliament on the 'Yoga Way' on April 21, 2015. The function was attended by a number of EU Parliamentarians and Indian Ambassador (Sri Sri Ravi Shankar, 2015).

For India, Yoga has emerged as an energizer, given the boost it received from the United Nations, which declared June 21 as the International Yoga Day (IYD) since 2015. Infusion of funds by ICCR has given a further push to Yoga-related activities, which had already found a place for itself in the commercial world.

## Music

Music has always been a great connector, as it does not encounter any barriers, physical or mental. It has therapeutic or spiritual values, as it appeals to the heart. We know the power of the music of Tansen and Baiju Bawra. Language is no barrier. India has been fortunate that it has been blessed with diverse forms of music, Classical (Instrumental or Vocal); Popular (Bollywood or Regional) or Folk Music.

At SPIC MACAY's 5th International Convention in 2017, Prime Minister Modi talked about link between Indian culture and music in these words: "Culture and music can play a vital role in connecting the country. It can be a big step towards realizing 'Ek Bharat Shresht Bharat" (Financial Express, 2017). Modi said that 'Indian classical music is majestic, creates a magic and is mystics'. He further added, 'Variations in Indian classical music unifies the entire country'.

On the other hand, US Ambassador Cynthia Schneider gloated about the power of Rock and roll music in her own way:

> "Rock and roll was the Internet of the sixties and early seventies. It was the carrier of the message of freedom....... Rock and roll, culturally speaking, was a decisive element in loosening up communist societies and bringing them closer to a world of freedom" (Quoted in Ambassador Schneider).

Music's magical influence was noticed at a South Korean Group K-Pop's concert, 'Spring is Coming' held in Pyongyang on April 1, 2018. It was the first such concert attended by the North Korean President Kim Jong-un. It was highly symbolic, as it marked the ushering in of 'a spring of peace' in the relationship between the two Koreas. The North Korean leader was visibly jubilant and moved, as he saw this as an opportunity for 'his people to deepen their understanding of South Korean culture' (The Tribune, 2018).

In simpler words, I would state that 'East or West, Music is the Best for Connectivity'.

At the popular level, Cultural Diplomacy is listening to an Indian song – 'Mera Juta Hai Japani' in a restaurant at Tashkent, which I visited in 1965; or the Orchestra playing the song, "Kuch Kuch Hota Hai" at the Malaysian King's Birthday Party in July 2000 or the rendering of the number "Dukhbhare din beete re bhaiya" from the film 'Mother India' at a banquet hosted in honour of Indian President Abdul Kalam by his Sudanese counterpart on October 22, 2003 (Sri Krishna, 2003) or 'Diyas brightening the White House' in Washington DC on October 25, 2003, along with the sonorous strains of the Sanskrit prayer "asato mā sadgamaya, tamasomā jyotir gamaya" (From ignorance, lead me to truth; From darkness, lead me to light) [Rajghatta, Chidananda, 2003]. At the Indian end, it is equally being transported to a spiritual world, listening to the Sufi music of Barkat Siddhu at Chandigarh.

While renowned Pakistani Ghazal Singer Ghulam Ali was prevented from performing in Mumbai in October 2015 by the Shiv Sena supporters, yet we see India-Pakistan connectivity at a musical performance at Kuala Lumpur in Malaysia. This happened on January 21, 2016 at a musical concert called, 'Shaam-e-Dostana' (An Evening of Friendship), where two famous singers-Sonu Nigam (India) and Atif Aslaf (Pakistan) - shared the same stage. Bollywood film music is very popular in Malaysia, not only among Indians, but also among Malays, who are 'in love with South Asian music'. Look at the coverage below:

> "India-Pakistan's winning combination – Sonu Nigam & Atif Aslam – certainly did more than serenading the 2,500 strong-crowd with powerful vocals, soulful renditions and energetic performances. They made Malaysians, expatriates and tourists lose themselves in moments, a true achievement for any musicians" (Rakyatpost).

Why can't we rock in India and Pakistan, blessed as we are with music, rich in diversity?

Austrian Cultural Forum, New Delhi, set up 'the Mozart Chair of India' in 2006 at the initiative of Ravi Shankar, Gerald Wirth, Director of the Vienna Boy's Choir and the Austrian Embassy. It aims at providing Indian children with the state-of-the-art training in Western classical music and facilitates organization of public performances in India. Some years ago, ICCR sponsored 20 students to Austria, who jointly performed with the Vienna Choir Boys.

With the growth of Indian population across the United States, a number of annual music and dance events are held in different parts of the country. These primarily cater to Indians, but they attract non-Indians also, who are interested in Indian culture. In this category fall the Annual Music and Dance Festival of the Indian Fine Arts Academy of San Diego (California). Each festival has 14 events and two academic sessions. It started in 2007 for Carnatic Music but now has embraced Hindustani vocal and instrumental also in its fold. It also showcases classical dance forms like bharatnatyam, kuchipudi, kathak and odissi (Pain, Paromita, 2017).

Indian Music is also emerging as the main theme in various musical festivals. The famous Salzburg Music Festival in 2015 focused on 'Hinduism' as a theme and it included Ensemble Nepathya in Kutiyattam, Dhrupad and Khayal and Bharatnatyam. Anushka Shankar, celebrated Sitarist was 'Star Attraction' at the Edinburgh Festival in 2017.

For India, Music is also emerging as an instrument of cultural connectivity. Bollywood Music has captivated the youth across the world. We see Italian Brides and Grooms dancing to its captivating tunes at their weddings. Music also helps in sending a political and social message, as evidenced through the performance of the orchestra, conducted by Zubin Mehta in Srinagar at the initiative of the German Ambassador in India in 2013 or performance by Pakistani Musical Rock Group, 'Junoon' in Srinagar in May, 2008. In early 2000s, Pakistani Consulate at Chicago welcomed internationally renowned Sarod player, at a concert organized by the Indian Consul General Surendra Kumar, where the Author was also present. All this illustrates that Music does connect.

**Literary Festivals**

Literary Festivals are emerging as important cultural events that not only provide a venue for launching of books, but also as a forum for discussion of current societal issues of interest. These provide a good opportunity for interaction between speakers and the audience on a number of topical issues. These are also becoming avenues for connectivity. US Ambassador

Schneider highlighted the importance of literature, as it offered 'a textured, moving, thought-provoking and entertaining introduction' to any country (Ambassador Schneider, 2006).

India is also emerging as an important hub for such festivals. One such festival, the Jaipur Literary Festival (JLF, 2016) which marked its 10th year in 2016 and is held in January every year at Jaipur has grown in stature. From a conclave of local participants in 2006, it has grown into a mega conclave, attracting participation from across the globe. It is managed by Teamwork Arts. Occasionally, ICCR extends support to it. Khushwant Singh Literary Festival (KSLF) is held every year in Kasauli, which is in the vicinity of Chandigarh; the author attended it in October 2015. A copy of his article that was published then is attached at Annexure 1.

Pakistan is also actively emerging on the literary scene, as it would like to make its presence felt. The first literary festival was launched in Karachi in 2010, called the Karachi Literary Festival (KLF). Like other similar festivals, it has grown in size, numbers and stature. Lahore Cultural Festival (LLF) followed in 2012. Islamabad was not far behind, as Islamabad Literary Festival (ILF) made its appearance in 2013. These Literary Festivals have their UK and US Editions. Let us look at the Jaipur Literary Festival 2016 and the Lahore Literary Festival 2016.

***Jaipur Literary Fesrival (JLF)***

JLF 2016 was built around the themes of Privacy, Migration and Negotiating Modernity (Jaipur), but the focus remained on a number of topical issues such as growing intolerance, role of television, language, sports, identity and nationalism, and the role of Regional Literature. As expected, the issue of intolerance attracted attention with film personalities, like Karan Johar, stating, ' Freedom of expression was the biggest joke', while another actor Kajol stating that there are no dividing lines, ' No caste, no creed and no intolerance in Bollywood' (The Hindu, 2016:1).

Booker Prize Winner, the Jamaican author Marlon James said that there was a 'huge underestimation of the real reader and writer of colour', although he acknowledged that some publishers were committed to diversity and voices of colour (Fernandez, Joeanna Rebello). Marlon James also flagged the issues of identity and language when he stated that he viewed himself as a Black African while stating that Naipaul did not think himself as a Trinidadian as he 'thanked India and the UK but never thanked Trinidad' (Narayan, Manjula, 2016).

### *Lahore Literary Festival, February 2016*

Film Actress Sharmila Tagore was the star attraction. While in Pakistan, she met Prime Minister Nawaz Sharief. The other Indian speakers at the Festival included art historian B.N. Goswamy, novelist Sonia Faleiro, cinema studies expert Ranjani Mazumdar, documentary film-maker Shohini Ghosh, historian Tanika Sarkar, journalist Karan Thapar, art gallery owner Amrita Jhaveri, and cookbook writer Madhur Jaffery. LLF 2016 featured panel talks, book launches, recitals and performances, spanning fiction, film, music, poetry, history, and more.

Literary Festivals in India and Pakistan, not only connect globally, but also offer an ideal opportunity for connectivity not only among writers, but with other opinion makers in India and Pakistan. Therefore, participants get support from relevant organizations. ICCR has extended support to the Jaipur Literary Festival on certain occasions. It also supported travel by four writers to the Karachi Literary Festival in February 2017. Such participation, however, is also accident prone; as was the case of issuance of visa by Pakistan to Actor Anupam Kher or the desirability of issuance of air tickets by ICCR.

Nonetheless, both the sides view such participation positively. The organizers of LLF viewed this as an attempt 'to facilitate cultural exchange between Pakistanis and Indians.' A similar approach was taken by Amarendra Khatua, the then Director General of ICCR, who stated that, "We are working to increase India's cultural footprint across the world under the leadership of PM Narendra Modi, including in Pakistan" (Modi, Chintan Girish, 2016).

Former Indian High Commissioner to Pakistan, TCA Raghavan adopted a middle path, when he said that

> "Cultural and academic exchanges between India and Pakistan are fine but they do not have a far-reaching impact. They help but only to a certain extent. It is important to be conscious of the limited impact these initiatives have. Their impact is largely within their own circles" (ibid).

We, however, need to keep our doors open and provide facilities to the intending participants.

## Sports: Connecting Through Olympic Games and Cricket

Sports have always been a form of 'soft power in terms of promoting a national brand or identity, and which itself has been used by nations to promote their products and cultures' (Thussu, Daya, 2013). We have seen this at the time of bidding for holding Olympic Games, when countries contest for the same. This is again witnessed, when the winning country tries to weave an image for them through gala opening ceremonies, be it the Commonwealth Games in Malaysia in 1998, where the Author was present or at the Beijing Olympics in 2008 or the London Olympics in 2012 or the Commonwealth Games Delhi 2010 or the Rio Olympics in 2016.

The big story of the 2018 Winter Olympics in South Korea was the participation of North Korea and the friendly tone struck by the two countries. As the Games began in Pyeongchang in February 'the South Korean and North Korean athletes walked in the opening ceremony as a joint team' (Winter Olympics, 2018). The holding of the U-17 World Cup in India in October 2017 was a move beyond cricket as it 'puts India in a place it has not been for years on the footballing world map' (Tharoor, Kanishk, 2017). The Indian success story at the 2018 Commowealth Games in April in Australia would spur up India's interest in international and regional sports.

International sports can be seen as 'a uniquely apt strategic response to globalisation, simultaneously celebrating and promoting values of competitiveness at home, while reinforcing constructed national identities for internal and external audiences' (Black, David and Peacock, Byrin, 2013). Relationship between sports and diplomacy has not been fully appreciated. Its intensity is now being recognized, as fully expounded by Black and Peacock in these words:

> "Given the unparallel visibility, popularity, and mobilizing potential of modern sport, accompanied by intense manifestation of identity (national, regional, local, sectarian, ethnic etc), it is hardly surprising that sport teams, events and venues have been viewed as compelling vehicle for the political and diplomatic ambitions of both governments and the range of actors engaged in network diplomacy" (ibid).

India, which was not a sporting nation earlier, has started using sport as a catalyst in connecting people and nations. This is the result of commercialization of sports, which attracts players across the globe. In

2008, this phenomenon started, with the launch of Indian Premier League (IPL) – one-day cricket matches (20 Overs) among national teams, which included home and foreign players. IPL is 'the brightest example of sports uniting nations' (The Indian Express, 2018).This trend for league matches has now been picked up by other sports – Tennis, Hockey, Football (Soccer). The prize money in other sports does not match with that available to individual players in cricket.

The lure for money is so great, that many cricket players are prepared to miss national level matches in favour of the Indian Premier League. A study conducted by Super Insight said that Rs.11,000 million (US $ 106 million) was floating in the Indian sports leagues market. Foreigner's share was 64 per cent of the total market. Rafal Nadal and Roger Federer were the highest earning players, who received Rs.260 million each for playing in the International Premier Tennis League (IPTL). They earned twice that was earned by cricketers, like Dhoni and Kohli (The Hindu, 2016: 3).

For India, cricket has been in the forefront of cultural diplomacy. Cricket is the unofficial national sport in India. Interest in cricket is across the nation. Does cricket also connect India globally? The answer is positive. Cricket, whose origins in India lay in community-based teams during the 'British Raj', is now celebrated for bringing in diversity as an all-inclusive team. It is open to players from across the globe. It is, however, limited to ten countries, as cricket has not become a global sport like football (soccer). India, however, has emerged as the shining star in attracting others.

Cricket has now become a connecting bridge, as an Australian Prime Minister saw connectivity with India through 3 Cs – cricket, culture and curry. A former High Commissioner of New Zealand also underscored this connectivity with New Zealand. India has acquired strategic role in the International Cricket Control (ICC) Board, given its huge support base at the fans level. The commencement of the Indian Premier League (IPL) has resulted in infusing star power, as attractive financial package attracts players across the globe. At the last auction for the 2016 IPL matches, many players were auctioned for more than US $ 1 million.

While India has been able to connect globally, it has not succeeded in using cricket diplomacy in connecting with Pakistan. Some past attempts resulting in the presence of Pakistan leaders – General Ayub Khan and President Musharraff and Prime Minister Gilani- at cricket matches have remained only a symbolic gesture and not resulted in any diplomatic breakthrough, as all the diplomatic tete-a-tete ended in a draw. At times, cricket is tactically used, when Foreign Secretary Jaishankar launched his 'SAARC Cricket Yatra', using cricket as a prop to meet his Pakistani counterpart in May 2015. The T-20 World Cup had its moments, when it came under political pressure, when venue for a Pakistan Match had to be shifted to Kolkatta from Dharamshala.

Sports, however, have an important role in galvanizing identities as the British historian, Eric Hobsbawn, wrote that 'nations become tangible through sports that the imagined community of millions seems more real as a team of eleven named people. Indian U-17 team reflected the remarkable diversity that is India's greatest strength' (Tharoor, Kanishk). Cricket in India is 'a secular religion and the Indian fan has transformed cricket into one of the great sporting industries'. Cricket Superstars, like Tendulkar, are treated God-like.

IPL today is 'a mela, a circus, a religion and an industry' (Visvanathan, Shiv, 2015 ). Visvanathan further adds that Cricket is also "A dream, a myth, a fantasy, a fable, a norm and an ideal that has to be sustained for the next generation. Our youth live and breathe cricket."

Could we insulate it from the vagaries of political climate and let it become a bridge builder, rather than remain its handmaiden? Let the Games go on without political games being played around them.

## Cuisine Diplomacy and Food Festivals

Indian food came to 'Europe via British imperialism, labeled "curry", a generic term for any spicy dish' and it has 'become a billion dollar global industry, going beyond the diasporic constituency' (Thussu, Daya, 2013). The curry industry in UK is immense, 'worth British Pound 3.6 billion annually, with 10,000 restaurants across the country employing 80,000 people.' Commonly labeled Indian dish, 'chicken tikka masala' (Chicken Curry) has become 'an integral part of modern British culture: an indication perhaps of the fact that Indian cuisine works as an important cultural signifier and communicator in an increasingly multicultural country' (ibid).

It is, therefore, not surprising to see BBC emerging as promoter of Indian Cuisine, when it launched a BBC Series on June 21, 2016, 'India on a Plate', on the diversity and vibrancy of India food (Agarwal, Ritu, 2016). The British Prime Minister Cameron had ordered an Indian meal at the

10 Downing Street, prior to his departure in June 2016, after he quit, consequent to UK deciding to exit from EU.

Food Festivals are becoming an important feature of India's cultural diplomacy. Food Festival was an important component of Indian Festival in Madgascar in 2014-15. Cuisine diplomacy has now taken off its own, given the famous 'chicken tikka masala', which tickles the British palate and is viewed as national cuisine. Indian Food has become a normal feature at the programmes organized at the Smithsonian Institute, in connection with the exhibition 'Beyond Bollywood' and other events.

Indian Embassy in Israel organized an 'Indian Culinary Week' in collaboration with Israel's leading hotel Chain, Dan Hotels, in May 2016. A three-day programme was organized at the King David Hotel in Jerusalem with Celebrity Chef Sanjiv Kapoor joining hands with Israel's Chef David Britton. Indian food plays an important role in broadening relationship that leads to cultural interaction (Mishra, Harinder, 2016).

Cuisine diplomacy has made its appearance in another form, called 'Gastro Diplomacy', where food and culture are mixed, as diplomatic missions are organizing food festivals in their premises, to garner the universal power of food, spreading cultural awareness. The Philippines and South Korea are increasingly resorting to this practice.

Local Organizations are also resorting to 'Cuisine Diplomacy' to send a social message, as they mix it with culture. Detroit Free Press, Detroit (USA) started a monthly column 'Beyond the Plate', which generates awareness on food from foreign countries. In its column in June 2016, it reported about a new initiative that was taken by a Swedish-born Ford engineer of Iranian descent Heshmati, who set up a group, 'Peace Meal Kitchen', which is 'a pop up dining and education series that highlights cultures from different countries.' The goal is "not just to raise awareness of food and culture but to try and educate" (Gastrodiplomacy).

Another city in USA, Pittsburg has its own version, where a restaurant named 'Conflict Kitchen' serves 'food speciality from a rotating list of countries at odd with the United States' (Conflict Kitchen). Another interesting go at cuisine diplomacy was a private initiative by a group of French citizens, who tried to woo Britishers not to leave EU through supply of croissants, by way of showing their affinity, which was dubbed 'Croissants Diplomacy', but this symbolic gesture, however, failed the realty test with the Britishers deciding to exit.

Indian food is slowly gaining acceptance in practically all the corners of the world. It titillates the palates of non-Indians also. It is making its appearance as sophisticated street food in a Pondicheri restaurant in Houston (Fox, Steve) or in new India-Mexican combo form as "Burrito Chicken Masala" in 'Curry up Now' mobile food trucks in San Francisco (Yakono, Candice).

Indian food also makes its appearance in other corners of the world, as Punjabi Meal in Ghana or The 'Farzified Biryani' being served at Farzi Cafe, Dubai or 'The mishti doi cannoli' served at Indian Accent, New York or The dosa waffle at Inday at Broadway, New York, served with Indian chutneys (The Hindustan Times, 2016). What ultimately comes out is that Indian food is now available in all its diversity.

Recently, we had a glimpse of 'Indian Cuisine Diplomacy' at India-Nordic Summit in Stockholm on April 22, 2018. Prime Minister Modi and his counterparts from the Nordic countries were served a variety of Indian vegetarian dishes from all the states in India, respecting traditions of 'Diversity' in India at the Grand Hotel. The food was prepared by Dheeraj Singh, a young Indian entrepreneur from Manali (India), who runs India Foods & Co. at Stockholm (The Times of India, 2018). This is another occasion to celebrate 'Diversity', a pillar of strength on which cultural diplomacy rests.

## Photograhic Exhibitions

It is a cliché that a photograph captures a story of thousand words. How true even now, as we see this happening in our daily discourse. A photograph of Japanese Prime Minister performing 'Aarti' (Prayers) in Varanasi in December 2015 or Canadian Prime Minister Justin Trudeau attired in Indian 'Sherwani' to celebrate Diwali with Indian-Canadians in October 2017, send us a message of cultural connectivity and positivity. We all, as diplomats, have mounted photographic exhibitions abroad to covey a particular message. In this section we would look at two exhibitions organized in India- one by a Romanian Photographer Mihaela Norco, called 'Atlas of Beauty' and on 'Indian Deities in Japan' by Benoy K Behl that sent a special message of diversity and connectivity. We are diverse but are still connected.

### *Atlas of Beauty*

A Romanian photographer, Mihaela Norco's photographic project, 'The Atlas of Beauty', captured the beauty of different countries through the portraits of women. It was aimed at cultural connectivity, as she wanted to project through these photographs that diversity is something beautiful, not a reason for conflict. Through these portraits, she tried to capture the culture and history of the subjects' 'geography' (Sumeet Keswani, 2016). She visited India during November-December 2015 and her India series featured a policewoman in Pushkar, a pilgrim in Varanasi, a Rajasthani street vendor in Goa and a makeup artist in Surat. For Mihaela Noroc, a woman's beauty 'is alluring and ethereal' and beauty means 'to keep alive your origins and culture.' Her attempt was 'to show the diversity of our planet through portraits of women across countries' (Jacob, Shalini).

### *Photographic Exhibition on Hindu Deities in Japan*

The Japan Foundation and film maker and art historian Benoy K. Behl collaborated to hold an exhibition of rare photographs at the Indian Museum, Kolkata on January 11, 2016. These offered rare heart warming glimpses of the importance of India heritage in Japan (Bandyopadhyay, 2016). The exhibition helped in generating awareness on Indian photographic understanding that is most well preserved in Japan. Through this exhibition, we learn that 20 Hindu deities are still worshipped in Japan. There were hundreds of srines dedicated to Goddess Saraswati; there were innumerable representations of Lakshmi, Indra, Brahma, Ganesh, Garuda and others. The 6th century Siddham script is still preserved and Sanskrit in that script is taught in a school at Koyasan. A major milk product is called "Sujata", which is named after the girl who gave sweet rice-milk to the Buddha, when he broke his period of austerity, prior to attaining enlightenment.

## Going Beyond Bollywood

India is placed in an unenviable situation, as it is blessed with diverse vehicles to tell 'India Story' to the world. Former Canadian High Commissioner to India David Malone observes, "India "plays on its civilizational pull, the magnificence of its monuments and the majesty of its landscapes, supplementing these with occasional artistic performances" (Malone, David, 2013).

India has a rich and varied arsenal in its vehicles of cultural diplomacy. Some vehicles of cultural diplomacy are moving on their own; while in other cases, the government plays the role of a catalyst. In the first category would fall Bollywood and in the second category would fall Indian classical music and dance, which receive support, primarily from ICCR.

Despite such diversity, what clicks is not the classical culture, but popular culture. It is here that Bollywood takes the cake. At the people's level, it is Bollywood that ticks, as has been brought out in the text of this chapter. Bollywood is able to move on its own in all corners of the world, although it gets an occasional boost from the Indian government through the hosting of film festivals.

'Bollywood Films' have generated interest in Indian fashions and cuisine in many countries. Music emerges as an important vehicle of connectivity, as it can transcend physical and language barriers and can directly appeal to the heart. More than 'Bollywood Films', it is 'Bollywood Music' that ticks. We have provided numerous examples in the text, where such connectivity has been provided.

It is the performing arts that get the major support from ICCR, as it supports close to 100 such troupes every year. It is the classical culture that gets supported. What is missing from the ICCR largess is the Folk Music and Dance that needs its support.

Yoga is now at the top of the table since 2015, when UN declared June 21 as the International Yoga Day (IYD). A bulk of ICCR's funds and its energies are devoted in supporting Yoga-related activities. We now have more yoga teachers in our cultural centres.

In the above context, it was more significant to see the holding of Yoga performances in front of Heritage Monuments, like Angkor Wat in Cambodia and Borobudur Temple in Indonesia. The setting up of the Institutes for the Study of Yoga in China and Kyrgyzstan are positive developments. This framework would provide for cooperation on a long term basis.

Emphasis on supporting Yoga-related activities is also leading to the support of Ayurveda related activities. In this context, Malaysia is emerging as an important partner and an institute for the study of Ayurveda has been set up there.

A new area that is emerging is the growth of Literary Festivals. ICCR had given some initial support to the visit of four writers to the Karachi Literary Festival in February 2017, even though it invited some adverse comments from vested interests.

Participation in Literary Festivals needs to be supported. We need to provide support to, at least young and emerging writers, for participation at Literary Festivals. There is a need to connect with the writers, who are emerging as important opinion makers, beyond their literary works.

India also connects through the holding of its Festivals. Diwali has emerged as an important festival, which attracts world leaders. They see in it the message of celebration of diversity and enlightenment. It is the same picture that emerges in UK, USA, Canada, Singapore or Malaysia.

We need to take a view, as to what are the vehicles that need to be promoted by the government and what are the vehicles that could flow, like Tennyson's River, at their own speed. Yoga and Bollywood would fall in the latter category.

Sports definitely need to be promoted, till individual sports reach a take off stage, like cricket. We have to fully recognize this important area of connectivity, as sports have a direct linkage with the Youth. India's future is in the hands of the Youth, which is being projected as India's demographic advantage. It is heartening to note that the current Minister of of State for Youth and Sports, Rajyavardhan Singh Rathore, is passionately committed to promoting sports.

Finally, ICCR has to adopt, what I would call, 'Performing Arts Plus' approach, as it focuses on neglected and new areas of cultural connectivity. India is more than 'Bollywood', as the Smithsonian Institution rightly chose the theme 'Beyond Bollywood', for its Exhibition in 2015 at the Natural History Museum in Washington DC, where it celebrated the multifaceted contribution of India Diaspora in the United States.

**Annexure 1**

## 2015 Khushwant Singh Literary Festival, Kasauli-A Case Study- Connecting Indians and Pakistanis

Literary Festivals are emerging as an important rendezvous, not only for writers but also academics, diplomats, NGOs and political leaders and general public. This is natural, as literary products are a reflection of the society and reflect experiences of the writer. There is a mushrooming of such festivals over the years, both in India and abroad. Chandigarh holds an Annual Literary Festival in November. Another festival, Khushwant Singh Literary Festival (KSLF) in the vicinity of Chandigarh is held annually in October at Mussoorie, which draws a number of speakers and participants. This is dedicated to the memory of Khushwant Singh, who was a legend in himself, as a journalist, historian and a writer. His columns in the media were full of wit and humour, as these conveyed a subtle meaning.

The fourth KSLF was held on October 9-11 at Kasauli. Over the years, it has grown in size, both in the number of participants and the array of themes discussed at the festival. It has a rich mix of themes, be it on arts, books, films or contemporary political developments that are the concern of the society. Kasauli has also become a meeting ground for Pakistani journalists, writers and politicians, who have become a regular feature at this Fesival. Khushwant Singh, who was born in Pakistan, stayed connected with that country and is the author of one of the celebrated books, "The Train to Paksitan". It is, therefore, not surprising when his son Rahul Singh noted that "The KSLF is never complete without our friends from Paksitan". The Pakistani contingent included former Foreign Minister Khurshid Mahmud Kasuri; former Pakistani Ambassador to USA Abida Hussain; Pakistan Oxford University Press Managing Director Ameena Saiyid; Historian, art critic and parliamentarian Fakir Aijjazuddin and Writer-journalist Mehr Tarar.

From the perspective of cultural and public diplomacy, a number of themes were of interest, which dealt with image building and Indo-Pak relations. Some of the takeaways are as follows:

- Khushwant Singh extending support to sports, to improve bilateral ties between India and Pakistan.
- Creation of 'a salutary bond' between people through literary works.

- Settlement of the Kashmir issue through dialogue, where neither India nor Pakistan projected as victorious or felt defeated.
- Publishing of Pakistani edition of the "Train to Pakistan", which could go a long way in bridging the gulf between the two countries.
- Encouraging participation by Publishers and Writers at the Book Fairs.
- Recognizing diversity in art, music and literature, while fighting forces of intolerance and polarization.
- Avoiding nationalist slant in media coverage.
- Providing a free environment for creative artists; not confining to restricted view of Indian Culture, while continuing fight against intolerance.
- Bollywood emerging as a connectivity bridge between India and Paksitan.
- Protecting India's core values of democracy, secularism and pluralism and ensuring respect to democratic institutions.
- Facilitating people to people connectivity through liberalization of visas.

The occasion of the festival was used for the release of a number of books. Among these included "Neither a Hawk, Nor a Dove" by Kasuri, 'Resourceful Fakirs, Fifty years of Sikh Rule in Lahore' by Fakir Aijjazuddin, 'Leaves from Lahore' by MehrTarar, and 'Power Failure' by Syed Abida Hussain. There was no untoward incident, like blackening of the face of sponsors of the Festival, as happened in Mumbai. Was it the salubrious climate of Kasauli or the prevalence of liberal atmosphere there in these days of growing intolerance? Was it a celebration of the spirit of Khushwant Singh, who was renowned for his weekly column 'With Malice Towards One and All'? I travelled with Kasuri by road from Kasauli to Chandigarh, without any escort, as he was to deliver a lecture at the Centre for Research in Rural and Industrial Development (CRRID) on October 11, from where he was proceeding to Mumbai.

It is not only formal presentations or release of books, but what is more important is the opportunity that such festivals provide to the participants for an informal exchange of views and help in promoting better understanding and removing cobwebs from our minds. Dialogue is the only way out and this needs to be insulated from fluctuating political winds in India-Pakistan relations, which are accident prone.

A healthy exchange of views in an open atmosphere alone could help in bridging trust deficit and changing mindset. What we need is blue paint, which could calm our nerves and not black paint to tar the relationship. India cannot speak from high moral ground, if its image is tarnished by such untoward incidents? Hopefully, this Festival could emerge as an important venue for informal contacts between India and Pakistan and help in promoting dialogue at the people to people level. We need more of such dialogues, to widen the circle of peace constituency between the two countries. Public Diplomacy Division in the Ministry of External Affairs could consider providing some support to such events.

## Endnotes

1 Viraj Singh, Deputy Chief of Mission, Embassy of India, Kabul. Response to Questionnaire, December 1, 2015.

2 YK Sinha, Indian High Commissioner to Sri Lanka, Colombo. Response to Questionnaire, January 6, 2016.

## References

Agarwal, Ritu, 2016, 'Why India is a nation of foodies', *BBC*, June 21. http://www.bbc.com/news/world-asia-india-36415078 (Accessed on December 27, 2017).

Al Jazeera, 2016, 'International Yoga Day: Yoga in unexpected places', June 21. http://www.aljazeera.com/news/2016/06/international-yoga-day-yoga-unexpected-places-160621033833211.html (Accessed on December 23, 2017).

Ambassador Schneider, Cynthia, 2006, 'Cultural Diplomacy: Hard to Define, but You'd Know it If you Saw it', *Brown Journal of World Affairs*, Fall/Winter 2006, volume XIII, issue 1.

Ambassador Viswanathan, 2014, April 17, r.viswanathan@mea.gov.in, (Accessed on December 23, 2017).

Anand, Kunal, 2016, 'How Modi is changing global diplomacy with Bean Tacos and Dosas across the world', *Indiatimes*, June 9.

Aneja, Atul, 2017, 'Aamir Khan's soft power coup in China', *The Hindu*, May 13.

Aneja, Atul: 1, 2017, 'Post-Doklam, the healing touch of yoga', *The Hindu*, October 11.

Bagchi, Indrani, 2008, 'Bollywood to hard sell India's soft power in China', *The Tribune,* March 28.

Bagchi, Indrani, 2012, 'Shankar personified India's soft power', *The Times of India*, December 13.

Bandyopadhyay, Krishnendu, 2016, 'Hindu gods forgotten in India revered in Japan', *Times of India*, Jan 11.

Bhatia, Shyam, 2012, 'Yoga: Not in Church, Please', *The Tribune,* October 2.

Black, David and Peacock, Byrin, 2013, 'Sports and Diplomacy' in *The*

*Oxford Handbook of Modern Diplomacy*, Oxford University Press.

CJI, 2015, 'When the CJI felt like Raj Kapoor', KristnadarRajgopal, *The Hindu*, Dec, 13.

Conflict Kitchen, www.conflictkitchen.org (Accessed on December 23, 2017).

*DNA*, http://www.dnaindia.com (Accessed on December 23, 2017).

Fernandez, Joeanna Rebello, 2016, 'There is still a denial of voices of colour in literature and in films', *The Times of India*, January 24.

*Financial Express*, 2017, 'PM Modi hails Spic Macay', says Society demonstrates how to work for benefit of society', June 5.

Fox, Steve, 2017, 'Indian classics for American Palates', '*Span*', September-October.

Gastrodiplomacy, 'Start-Up Peace Meal Kitchen Launches Dinner Series' https://detroit.eater.com/2016/4/6/11380348/gastrodiplomacy-detroit-food-peace-meal-kitchen-mana-heshmati (Accessed on December 23, 2017).

Ghosh, Avijit, 2012, 'South Korea loves Bollywood dramas but wants fewer songs', *Navbharat Times*, December 3.

Gyatso, Kimberley, 2016, 'Stories that Cross Boundaries', *Span*, March-April.

Igrouanne,Youssef, 'Marrakech, Bombay..... A Love Story', Consolidates Cultural Ties between Morocco and India', http://www.morocco worldnews.com/2016/02/180254 (Accessed on December 23, 2017).

Jacob, Shalini. 'A Romanian Photographer Is Capturing Beauty Around The World & She's Currently In India', https://www.scoopwhoop.com/This-Romanian-Photographer-Is-Capturing-Beauty-Around-The-World/#.ga5d2kcqu (Accessed on December 23, 2017).

JLF, 2016, Jaipur Literary Festival, January 2016, https://jaipurliteraturefestival.org/media-post/2016-jaipur-lit-festival-privacy-migration-and-navigating-modernity-main-themes/ (Accessed on December 23, 2017).

Joshi, Murli Manohar, 2017, 'Yoga, where science meets spirituality', *The Tribune*, Mar 18.

Judge, Shahid, 2017, 'Ghana U-17 team's craze off the field: Kumkum Bhagya', *The Indian Express*, October 18.

Krishnan, Ananth, 2012, 'Indian Yoga icon finds following in China', *The Hindu*, March.

Krishnan , Ananth: 1, 2014, 'India to open yoga centre in China', *The Hindu*, July 19.

Malone, David, 2013, 'The Modern Diplomatic Mission' in *The Oxford Handbook of Modern Diplomacy*, Oxford University Press.

MEA, 2015-16, Annual Report of the Ministry of External Affairs.

Mishra, Harinder, 2016, 'India organises Indian culinary week in Israel', *India Today*, May 18, http://indiatoday.intoday.in/story/india-organises-indian-culinary-week-in-israel/1/671018.html (Accessed on December 23, 2017).

Modi, Chintan Girish, 2016, 'Sharmila Tagore is star of Lahore literary festival', *The Hindu*, February 18.

Narayan, Manjula, 2016, 'My FB posts become newspaper articles now', *The Hindustan Times*, Jan. 23.

Pari, Paromita. 2017, 'Celebrating Indian Dance and Music, '*Span*', September-October.

Rajghata, Chidanand, 2003, 'Diyas brighten White House', *The Times of India*, New Delhi, October 26.

Ramnath, Nandini, 2014, Scroll.in, *Quarts India*, December 11. http://92.com/310502/japan-is-going-gaga-over-bollywood.

Ray, Suchetana, 2017, 'Turkey to woo Bollywood to shoot its exotic locations', *The Hindustan Times*, May 10.

Rakyatpost, Surach, G, 'Concert review: India-Pakistan's winning combination rocks KL', http://www.therakyatpost.com/life/music-life/2016/01/25/india-pakistans-winning-combination-totally-rocks-kl/ (Assessed 13 December 2017).

Shillong Chamber Choir, https://en.wikipedia.org/wiki/Shillong_Chamber_Choir (Accessed on December 23, 2017).

Sri Krishna 2003, 'Hindi Song enlivens Banquet for Kalam', *The Tribune*, Chandigarh, October 23.

Sri Sri Ravi Shankar, 2015, Address to European Parliament on Yoga, April 21. http://www.huffingtonpost.in/2015/04/21/art-of-living-european-pa_n_7107412.html (Accessed on December 23, 2017).

Sumeet, Keswani, 2016, 'How beautiful is India, These photos tell you', *The Times of India*, January 11.

Tharoor, Kanishk, 2017, 'U-17 World cup puts India on the football world map', *The Hindustan Times*, October 7.

Tharoor, Shashi, 2007, 'Making the most of India's soft power', *The Times of India*, January 28.

*The Business Standard*, 2016, Israel, 'India organizes Indian culinary week in Israel', May 18.

*The Hindu*, 2016:1. 'There is no intolerance in Bollywood, says Kajol' January 24.

*The Hindu*, 2016:2, 'Khajuraho statues may soon be draped with saris', January 24.

*The Hindu*, 2016:3, 'Foreign players earn more than home-growns in Indian leagues', March 2. http://www.thehindu.com/sport/cricket/foreign-players-earn-more-than-homegrowns-in-indian-leagues/article8305215.ece (Accessed on December 23, 2017).

*The Hindustan Times,* 2016, 'An appetite for foreign shores: Offering food India eats to the world', April 4.

*The Hindustan Times*, 2017, 'KLF, Row erupts after ICCR sponsors tickets for Karachi Lit Fest', February 13. http://www.hindustantimes.com/india-news/row-erupts-after-iccr-sponsors-tickets-for-karachi-lit-fest/story-2WWR0VQxzJcUUkXUwCWKnO.html (Accessed on December 23, 2017).

*The Indian Express*, 2014, 'Afridi at home away from home', March 14.

*The Indian Express,* 2015, 'Bollywood continues to serenade Chinese audience', July 13.

*The Indian Express*, 2016, 'It's not Cricket' (Ed.), March 3.

*The Indian Express*, 2017, 'KLF, India's ICCR among sponsors at Pakistan's Karachi Literature Festival', Feb 13. http://indianexpress.com/article/india/indias-iccr-among-sponsors-at-pakistans-karachi-literature-festival-4521766/ (Accessed on December 23, 2017).

*The Indian Express*, 2017: 1, 'A window to India's rising soft pwoer – Bollywood', April 13.

*The Indian Express*, 2018, 'Closing the field' (ed.), April 24.

*The Times of India,* 2001, 'Cultural Diplomacy wins over politics', November 4.

*The Times of India*, 2018, 'Manali chef laid 220-Indian dish spread for Modi', April 23.

*The Tribune*, 2003: 'Cultural Diplomacy by ICCR', December 3.

*The Tribune,* 2013, 'Zubin concert sends positive waves', September 9.

*The Tribune*, 2015, 'Sholay, Soft power of Bollywood' (ed.), 'Welcome awaits Sholay in Pakistan', February 14.

*The Tribune*, 2016: 'Playing Pak in Dharamshala' (Ed.), March 3.

*The Tribune* 2018, 'K-Pop starts performance in Pyongyang', April 2.

Thussu, Daya, 2013, *Communicating India's Soft Power: Buddha to Bollywood*, East West Centre.

The Winter Olympics, http://www.bbc.com/news/world-asia-43063399.

UNGA, 2014, Statement by Prime Minister Modi at the 69$^{th}$ Session of UNGA, New York, September 27.

Visvanathan, Shiv, 2015, 'Pitch it right: IPL and the ethics of cricket', *The Tribune*, January 2.

Wade, Matt, 2016, 'Narendra Modi's Yoga diplomacy, or how India is winning friends and influencing people', *Western Advocate*, September 11.

Yacono, Candice, 2017, 'High Tech meets Hot Tikka', *Span*, September-October.

# Section – V

# Diaspora and Media as Connectivity Bridges

# Chapter – IX

# Diaspora: Strategic Asset on Foreign Policy

## Introduction

We live in a complex globalised world, where no phenomenon can be seen in black and white. The same is true of relationship among peoples and countries, as there are always shades of grey that define relationship. This equally holds true, in the case of Diaspora's role, in particular, in the context of foreign policy, whether it is a strategic asset or not. At one end, it is viewed as a component of 'soft power', where both the home and host states would like to use it to promote their interests. At the other end, concerns are expressed over the likely overt involvement of Diaspora in the domestic agenda of the home state or pushing the interests of the home state in the host state. Should Diaspora be involved in the foreign policy arena, which is a relatively green area for study? A lot of ground, therefore, would need to be covered, as no attention has been paid to this important aspect of Diaspora-connectivity.

In this chapter we would, therefore, look at the above critical question, as we examine Diaspora's role. Diaspora, like other pressure groups, could be a boon or bane, depending upon its size, its locale, its political involvement, its economic strength etc. This would largely depend upon the environment, in which it is allowed to operate by the host state and how open it is. How well Diaspora is politically organized? Does a framework exist in the host state that provides for channels of communication between Diaspora and policy makers in the government, both in the executive and legislative branches? What role do Diaspora legislators or executives play; are these coloured by their moorings in the home state?

Are there different rules and guidelines and approaches that permit Diaspora involvement in domestic or foreign policy issues? Furthermore, could a distinction be made between cultural, economic and strategic issues that would define or circumscribe their role? Does citizenship of Diaspora matter, with non-citizenship becoming a handicap? Would the possession of citizenship be an important prerequisite for involvement in foreign policy-related issues? Should Diaspora be involved in lobbying efforts? If so, would it need to keep in view certain guideposts? Understanding of these and other related issues would help us in defining broad reference points, which could be tested in country-specific settings.

How do the above parameters apply in the case of India? Does India have a Diaspora policy? If so, where does foreign policy fit in to this? If not, how does this work out at the operational level, with or without formal policy framework. Do the foreign policy issues get enmeshed with domestic politics? What are the structures, like cultural and public diplomacy, available in pursuing foreign policy objectives? Is Diaspora being viewed as a component of India's soft diplomacy? What are the lessons that we can draw upon policies and practices followed in other countries, in so far as these help in understanding Indian Diaspora's role in foreign policy-related issues.

## Understanding Diaspora-Foreign Policy Linkage

In this chapter, we are looking at the role of Diaspora as a foreign policy strategic asset. We would need to understand the terms, foreign policy and strategic asset. After looking at the import and meaning of these terms, we will take a view, whether Diaspora is a strategic asset or not.

Strategic Assets are 'Assets that are needed by an entity in order for it to maintain its ability to achieve future outcomes. Without such assets the future well being of the company could be in jeopardy (Strategic Assets). What applies to companies (Businesses), equally applies to various other groups/interests. Foreign Policy, on the other hand, connotes the promotion of national interests internationally. 'Soft Power' as defined by Joseph Nye Jr., connotes a situation, where the governments' aim to achieve the desired outcomes, through the use of means other than 'Hard Power'.

A holistic foreign policy would embrace all interests – political, national security, economic, commercial and cultural interests. A limited approach would focus on political and national security interests only. What would be more relevant, in the case of Diaspora- a holistic or limited approach?

Given the above definition, should Diaspora be placed in the category of a strategic asset? Could foreign policy interests be not pursued without the intervention of Diaspora? Would it be considered as the only or one of innumerable assets or pressure groups that operate in any country? Furthermore, would this construct have global application or restricted to those countries that have a regime that allows for participation by Diaspora. Do adequate structures and channels exist that facilitate participation of Diaspora? Have these been institutionalized or are of an ad hoc nature for the pursuit of the same?

This raises another question, are we talking of foreign policy interests of the host or the home state or both? What happens, if there is a conflict of interest between the two, as it is impossible to expect an identity of views in all the situations? Turkish Diaspora in Europe found itself placed in a delicate situation, as some European countries, such as Austria, Switzerland and Germany, prevented the Turkish President to reach out to its Diaspora to lobby for Referendum in April 2017, paving way for the Presidential System of Government in Turkey. This resulted in souring of Turkey's bilateral relationship with those countries (Turkish Diaspora, 2017). Mesut Ozil quitted from the German national soccer team in July 2018, citing 'racism and disrespect', because of the criticism he received to pose for a photo with the Turkish President Erdogan.

In the case of India, leaders from the State of Punjab were reportedly not allowed to promote their political agenda in Canada, resulting in the visits being called off. This, in turn, had its fall out, with Captain Amarinder Singh, Chief Minister of the State of Punjab refusing to meet the Canadian Defence Minister Harjit Singh Sajjan, during the latter's visit to India in April 2017 for his alleged sympathies with the supporters of the Khalistan Movement (Haidar, Suhasini, 2017). This created an odd and piquant situation, as a celebrated Diaspora and son of the Punjab State was not accorded official welcome in the State of his birth. This resulted in raising controversy within India and with Canada. While the visiting Canadian Defence Minister was accorded full honours as a Minister by the Government of India, yet the Chief Minister of Punjab refused to accord him State Honours and even refused to meet him (BBC, 2017).

Even if we accept that Diaspora has a role, as Diaspora engagement is emerging as an important policy plank; yet it would have to be seen, whether such involvement has taken place in the foreign policy arena. The above two cases illustrate the problems that are likely to arise in the case of Diaspora involvement in foreign policy-related issues. If so, would it be a bane or boon? This would depend upon place, issues or circumstances, as it is not possible to answer it unequivocally.

In this chapter, we, however, are starting from the premises that Diaspora engagement has taken place in some of the areas that would fall under the holistic definition of foreign policy. Diaspora has been involved in cultural, commercial and investment areas; aid, development and philanthropy-related matters. There is no paucity of information and detailed studies exist.

We would be restricting our study to the narrow construct of the foreign policy arena and thus explore an unexplored area. This would cover areas, embracing political, national security, human rights and migration related issues. Prima facie, we assume that Diaspora is an asset, but not a strategic asset for foreign policy. It is neither a traditional nor a primary channel for pursuit of forign policy-related issues. The focus in this chapter is on India, while an attempt is made to draw upon the experiences of other countries.

## Setting the Stage for Diaspora Engagement: Indian Approach

It is a fact that Diaspora's engagement with both the home and the host states is growing. For India, such an engagement was institutionalized in 2003, when India held the First Diaspora Conference, called the Pravasi Bharatiya Divas (PBD) on Jan. 9-11, 2003, to mark the return of Mahatma Gandhi to India on January 9, 1915. The then Prime Minister Atal Behari Vajpayee (PBD, 2003:1) highlighted this connectivity in these words:

> "Pravasi Bharatiya Divas itself is a celebration of the 'Jugalbandi' (mutual partnership) between the 22 million strong Indian Diaspora and your motherland; between the 'Bharatvasis' (Indians) and the 'Bharatvanshis' (Indian Diaspora)" (Atal Behari Vajpayee, Prime Minister of India, 9 January 2003).

This recognises connectivity between India and its Diaspora and between Resident and Non-Resident Indians. Such interaction had taken place every year since 2003. It is now proposed to have it on a biannual basis from 2018.To this a new infrastructure has been added, called the Mini-PBD, which is in the nature of conferences held abroad, focusing on Diaspora, but primarily on economic connectivity. So far such conferences have been held in Singapore, Mauritius, Canada and South Africa. A separate Ministry of Overseas Indian Affairs (MOIA) that engaged with Diaspora since 2004 has now been merged with the Ministry of External Affairs since 2014.

Since 2005, the Government of India, however, took a further step in opening doors for Diaspora's involvement, when it leveraged Diaspora in pursuing India's foreign policy goals in the United States, and sought its help as it negotiated India-USA Civil Nuclear Cooperation Agreement. There was an open acknowledgment to this effect regarding Diaspora's role, when the then External Affairs Minister of India stated (PBD, 2009):

> "The fact that the Diaspora can play an important role is demonstrated by the vigour and the success with which it campaigned for the India specific waiver that was granted earlier this year by the international community on the issue of civilian use of nuclear energy. I believe this was a historic achievement and one that all of us should rightly be proud of. It demonstrated the unique respect with which the international community holds India and how closely it listens to the voice of the non-resident Indian community. We are both appreciative and humbled by the gesture and would like to place on record the tremendous support that was extended to us by the Indian Diaspora". (External Affairs Minister's Address, Pravasi Bharatiya Divas, Jan 7, 2009)

India also went a stage beyond this specific case, when it envisaged a role for its Diaspora in foreign policy related issues, as stated below by the then Minister in 2009:

> "As our ambassadors abroad, your words will be heard in multiple corners of the globe. I call upon all of you to join us in playing the important role of taking forward our concerns to the world stage because these are concerns that you also share." (External Affairs Minister's Address, Pravasi Bharatiya Divas, Jan 7, 2009)

Does this constitute a formal policy statement or was it an expression of intent or wish? To the author, it appears to be the latter, as the same has not been translated in to a formal policy document on 'Diaspora Policy', which itself is non-existent. At best, it could be treated as a mini-step, taken on an ad hoc basis, which has not been translated in to a global policy. A single issue and single country approach cannot be treated as an overall policy. The statement does not also spell out, how India sees the role of foreign Diaspora in India, as a host state.

Do we see any change in the role assigned to Diaspora by the Modi government? Diaspora has emerged as a key element in Prime Minister Modi's sojourns abroad. The present government has started viewing it as an instrument of 'soft power'. Diaspora is given a larger than life role, as evidenced by Mega Events organized in USA, UK and Canada, which were attended by the local dignitaries, including prime ministers, legislators and entrepreneurs, which included a number of Indians. We are seeing an increasing and open involvement of Diaspora in elections in India, raising questions on proprietary and accounting of such funding, whether it is in compliance with the existing rules and regulations, both in the home and the host states.

## Diaspora: Setting Parameters for Involvement in Foreign Policy: Case Study

This is a green area, as suggested earlier. It would, therefore, be interesting to find out, whether a policy framework exists elsewhere that could act as a guidepost for India. A case study on Canada provides meaningful data and information and useful parameters. These could serve as yardsticks in evolving and measuring the involvement of Indian Diaspora in foreign policy-related issues.

Canada's Walter and Duncan Foundation ran a 'Canada Diaspora Programme' for a period of seven years since 2004. One of its focus areas was to determine the extent to which foreign policy 'is and should be informed and enhanced by the expertise and insights of Canada's many Diaspora communities' (Canada Study, 2013). Please note that the primary objective was on bringing about qualitative change in foreign policy. Secondly, it was to encourage 'ongoing research and capacity building in this area' (ibid).

The Foundation partnered with the Mosaic Institute to give an added dimension, as to how Canadian solutions could be advanced and peace and development promoted. The programme thus had a practical dimension, in using Diaspora to push Canada's interests; thus narrowing it to the perspective of a home state. This firmly rested on the premises that Canada's 'ever-growing diversity uniquely positions itself to play this important role, given its pluralistic and demographic character'.

The Study reached following important conclusions:

- Tapping into the Diaspora communities should 'inform and enrich both the content and the quality of Canadian foreign policy'; (ibid)
- Diaspora inputs should be consistent with Canadian multicultural policies and its diversity that could be woven into the Canadian mosaic; and
- Such participation would help in strengthening Canadian social fabric.

To this, a big caveat was attached. Diaspora involvement, however, should be subject to an empirical enquiry 'into the actual and potential role of Canada's Diaspora communities' (ibid). The ultimate objective would be to frame 'an inclusive and pluralistic foreign policy', which also reflected the views of the resident Diaspora community, besides other groups. It may be noted that Diaspora's involvement had to be within the overall governmental policy parametres.

Diaspora, however, had to be viewed as one of the special interest groups that included those who had the knowledge and the expertise on foreign affairs. It referred to Diaspora Groups that were transnational in character and took 'an interest in Canada's foreign policy with respect to their country of origin' (ibid). Were they talking of Diaspora or foreign policy experts among Diaspora? Was the emphasis on Diaspora or drawing upon the foreign policy expertise? The same was not conclusively answered; nor did it come out clearly whether involvement was restricted to Citizen-Diaspora?

The Study noted that the progress towards realizing 'the Diaspora potential for foreign policy making has been tamely slow'. While there was 'tangible Diaspora engagement' in development aid, yet Diaspora engagement in foreign policy areas 'has scarcely begun,' as seen from a narrow construct on foreign policy. It, however, noted limitations to Diaspora's involvement in policy making, requiring determination of national interest in foreign policy, ensuring its democratic involvement and to identification of its distinctive and substantive insights or values' (ibid). How would the government then engage with Diaspora, after having found answers to these pertinent aspects? Firstly, by conceptualization the policy dimension; secondly, identifying the Diaspora groups and thirdly by creating suitable conditions for participation.

Diaspora participation had to stand the test of competing interests. Would it be in the national interest or in keeping with the democratic principle of citizen inclusion and as a matter of social asset? These are debatable points, with pros and cons for each of the same. Deliberations on these aspects would help in moving the debate towards concrete action, by giving consideration to steps that would be required to facilitate Diaspora engagement. These, inter-alia, would include taking a view on a number of interrelated issues, some of which may be contentitious. These would be determining the basis for engagement – representative or complementary character of Diaspora groups and identifying a range of issues suitable for Diaspora inclusion. Diaspora engagement could then be paved through measures such as understanding the composition of Diaspora groups; taking measures in support of Diaspora initiatives; building capacities of government and Diaspora groups and creating an umbrella Diaspora organization.

The Study, however, admitted that experiences of Europe and other countries might not be relevant for Canada, affirming that there could not be one approach for all the countries or Diaspora groups. Another point that needed to be kept in view was that this Study focused on Canadian government's approach in involving Diaspora groups in formulating and promoting its foreign policy interests. It was, therefore, not from the perspective of Diaspora groups. The central thrust in this, therefore, was to engage Diaspora, as a partner in pursuing Canada's foreign policy interests.

## Diaspora and Host States: A Case Study

Here we would look at two case studies on Diaspora involvement, as an initiator and principal actor, in pushing its view in to the host state's foreign policy agenda. If so, how does it translate it into practice? Sara Kryntzki (2012) has examined this phenomenon, in her thesis for the Master's Degree. She, prima facie, accepts that Diaspora does play a role in the foreign policy agenda of the host states? She has used two research questions or hypotheses. Would it be related to Diaspora's electoral strength and hence its influence, if it has to plug in to the host state's policy framework. Secondly, would it depend upon the effectiveness of the manner in which Diaspora 'frames the issues in ways that engage and appeal to policy makers'? (Kryntzki, Sara, 2012). Having framed these questions, she looked at two case studies of Tamilian Diaspora in the United Kingdom and Canada.

Kryntzki came to the conclusion that in both the cases, what mattered was the effective manner of framing the issues in ways that would 'engage and appeal to policy makers.' She stipulated three ingredients for a successful approach – a good presentation, followed by engagement with policy makers, and finally resulting in winning them over through support on the policy front. On the other hand, the electoral strength of Diaspora did not turn out to be a sole determining factor, as there was, no uniformity in the results of the two scenarios.

In the case of the United Kingdom, support for the agenda of the Tamil separatists was inconsequential, given UK's concerns over terrorism, which had become a part of its national domestic agenda. While for

Canada, there was greater understanding to the Tamil cause, as the same was viewed through multicultural lenses, given the Canadian government's experience in finding a constitutional answer to the demand for separatists from the Quebec region. These two cases illustrate that Diaspora Groups can play a role, so long it is limited to the policy parameters determined by the host state.

It may be mentioned that the research findings could not be taken as a gospel truth, as invariably voting power does play a part. The existence of Tamil vote bank could explain the rationale for the decision of the Canadian Prime Minister Stephen Harper to boycott the Commonwealth Heads of Governments Meeting (CHOGM) held in Colombo on November 15-17, 2013. This was also relevant in the present day Indian context also, where the Centre came under pressure from residents in the Tamilnadu State, resulting in non-participation of Indian Prime Minister Manmohan Singh at the same Summit (Tuteja, Ashok, 2013). It was identity politics that led to Sri Lankan Tamilians from getting support from a large number of Tamilian Diaspora in Malaysia. In another situation, the Sikh Diaspora could also manage to get Canadian sympathies in the 1980s by stoking human rights angle.

India also encounters situations, when support for Khalistan sympathisers gets manifested through the presence of Canadian leaders at Baisakhi Celebrations or other events. Passing of a resolution on 'Sikhs Genocide' by the Ontario Legislative Assembly in April 2017 upped the ante for the Government of India, making the Indian Defence Minister Jaitley to express his concerns to the visiting Canadian Defence Minister. Apparent support to Khalistani Separatists continued at the Baisakhi Prorammes held in Surrey and Toronto during April 2017. The presence of the Canadian Prime Minister Justin Trudeau at a 'nagar kirtan' (procession) in Toronto marking the Baisakhi Festival upset the Indian government as it displayed posters of extremist leader Jarnail Singh Bhindranwale and Khalistani flags (The Hindustan Times, 2017). In his message to mark the Baisakhi Day, the Canadian Prime Minister said that it was an opportunity 'to honour the many cultures, traditions, and beliefs that make Canada such a wonderful place to live. Canada is proud to be home to one of the largest Sikh populations in the world' (Statement).

## Diaspora's Role: Policy Approach of Other Countries

How do other countries engage with its Diaspora? What is the role these see for diaspora in the formulation of foreign policy arena? There is a paucity of information in this area. **Kenya** is one of the few countries that see a direct linkage between 'Diaspora and Diplomacy'. Its draft diaspora policy states that foreign policy orientation 'rests upon four interlinked pillars: economic diplomacy, peace diplomacy, environmental diplomacy and Diaspora diplomacy' (MFA, Kenya).

**Canada** is another country, which has taken a big stride in the direction of a holistic foreign policy. In 2013, it decided to set up a new Department of Foreign Affairs, Trade and Development, merging different departments in to an integrated one. This new Department would also be focussing on Diaspora. Canada sees a role for Diaspora in 'brokering Canadian participation in the global economy'. The focus thus is on involving Diaspora in economic-related issues.

**The United States** views diaspora as a multi-dimensional asset, as it sees it playing an all-encompassing role. Hillary Clinton, the then US Secretary of State spelt out this role in 2011, in these words:

> "You have the potential to be the most powerful people-to-people asset we can bring to the world's table. Because of your familiarity with cultural norms, your own motivations, your own special skills and leadership, you are, frankly, our Peace Corps, our USAID, our OPIC, our State Department, all rolled into one". (Clinton, Hillary 2017)

She envisaged a connectivity role for Diaspora in political, economic, trade and aid-related issues, as a bridge builder for the state. What role does Trump envisage, would be anybody's guess?

A number of other countries have also high expectations from Diaspora. **China** would be prepared to use it, to broker 'a progressive relationship between China and the world;' China, therefore, sees a larger role. **New Zealand,** however, envisages a limited role; helping in promoting 'New Zealand Brand' and leveraging for investments. **The Caribbean** are candid enough, to expect Diaspora playing the role of an effective lobbyist 'on issues that affect their development' (Dewan, S, 2010). **Uganda**, on the other hand, encourages a development role, as it participates in trade and cultural promotion activities.

**For Mexico**, there is an intrinsic linkage between migration and foreign policy. A Study views how migration was catapulted into 'high politics' from 'low politics' in the foreign policy agenda between Mexico and the United States. The focus was on addressing 'the causes of emigration, economic rights in Mexico and protection of their rights in the United

States' (Delano, A, 2011). Delano noted that Diaspora had not acted as 'a unified bloc with common goals, either in relation to their political objectives in Mexico or the United States' (ibid). Immigration would be an important plank in shaping bilateral relations between USA and Mexico, as the US President Donald Trump moves in the direction of implementing his election agenda to build a wall across the border.

**The Philippines** also views Diaspora playing an important role, as an image builder in the United States. Diasporas are becoming instrumental in 'flexing soft power through mind, heart and spirit' (Gonzalez III, 2011). This has been succinctly discussed in a book on the Filipinos in the United States, whose involvement had 'a significant effect on not just economic globalisation but on averting a clash of politics and cultures' (Gonzalez III, 2011).While the role of Diaspora is increasing, yet its fragile character is noticed in the absence of it being a unified bloc.

## Indian Diaspora's Involvement: Historical Background

What are the ground realities regarding Indian Diaspora's involvement in the foreign policy related issues. Indian diaspora had cut its teeth during pre-independence days. It was the Ghaddarites in USA and Canada in the early twentieth century, who took part in the freedom movement of India from the British rule. NRIs from USA, Canada, UK, Singapore, Malaysia, Philippines and New Zealand, visited Punjab to pay homage to 'Ghadri Babas', to mark the 100th anniversary of the Movement , which fell on November 1, 2013 (The Sunday Times, 2013). Some Muslims from Singapore had also joined the Ghaddar Movement (Kamal, Neel, 2013).

Diaspora from Singapore and Malaysia also actively responded to the call of Subhas Chandra Bose and joined INA and 'Jhansi Ki Rani' outfits. In 1999, India honoured Lt. Janaki Nahappan from Malaysia with the 'Padma Shri' Award. It was again the diaspora, which fought against racially discriminatory immigration laws in Canada, consequent to the 1914 Komagata Maru Tragedy, which prevented the landing of Indians in Canada. It was again, Mahatma Gandhi, who landed in India on January 9, 1915 from South Africa and led India's freedom struggle towards its Independence on August 15, 1947. It is in recognition of the significance of this Day that the Pravasi Bharatiya Divas (PBD) is held on January 9.

Since Independence, Indian Diaspora has played a muted role in foreign policy related issues, as Indian government's policy favoured its integration with the host state. Indian Diaspora's role has been changing, in keeping with GOI's policy approaches and change in the international perspective, where Diaspora is no more required to pass the loyalty test. There has been a gradual shift, which has gone beyond meeting cultural requirements of Diaspora.

The primary focus now is on Diaspora's engagement in the promotion of economic and commercial interests and facilitating knowledge transfer. Institutional framework has been set up to achieve this objective, starting with the setting up of an independent Ministry, called the Ministry of Overseas Indian Affairs (MOIA) in 2004. MOIA has now become a Department in the Ministry of External Affairs (MEA) since 2014. MOIA had set up a number of appropriate Bodies to enhance Diaspora's involvement in a wide range of activities (Sahai, 2013).

So far, MOIA or MEA had not directly focused on Diaspora's involvement on foreign policy issues and none of the PBD's had this as an agenda item, either for the Plenary or other Sessions. It was, therefore, not surprising that the deposed Prime Minister of Fiji of Indian origin Mahendra Choudhry found himself sidelined at the first PBD, held in Delhi in January, 2003.

Over the years, Diaspora has crystallized its approach. It has become a voice for the protection of human rights and environment, grant of political rights in India (dual citizenship, voting), while it also sought personal and economic security through protection of property, for itself. At times, it has raised its voice in some countries against India's record on human rights. It has not played any significant role on issues relating to foreign policy, except lobbying for the support of India-USA Civil Nuclear Cooperation Agreement in 2008.

Regarding economic and commercial aspects, Indian Diaspora has emerged as the largest remitter (US $ 69 billion in 2017), participates in philanthropic projects, some of which are linked to development. It has also lent its hand in promoting economic and commercial links. It is in this arena that its strength lies, as it has the cultural advantage of its background to push for deals. Our focus in this chapter is on foreign policy-related issues.

There has been the other side of the story, involving Diaspora involvement. Some Diaspora groups had adopted anti-Indian policy, even prior to the Blue Star Operation in June 1984. A movement launched by Jagjit Singh Chauhan from the United Kingdom for a Sikh Homeland State, had created adverse publicity for India in UK, Europe and USA. This would be considered the beginning of Diaspora involvement in foreign policy related issues, as seen from the emergence of Diaspora groups, both for and against GOI.

Consequent to these developments, many Sikhs had resorted to seeking asylum, even though they were merely economic migrants. This dented India's bilateral relations with some of the countries. This resulted in some of them being put in the Black List and passport and visa facilities were denied to them. They are categorized as Proclaimed Offenders. With the changed situation, now there is a demand for the removal of their names from the Black List. While normalcy has resulted in Punjab, yet some Diaspora groups are still putting pressure on their host governments, Canada, USA, UK, and Australia, to declare Blue Star Operation as genocide. The latest was the passage of a Resolution in the Ontario Legislative Assembly in April 2017, declaring the anti-Sikh riots in 1984 as 'Genocide'. This caused concern to the government of India, even though the Canadian government has distanced itself from the same (Bhattacharyya, Anirudh).

An online petition to President Obama was also launched on November 15, 2012 and it got more than 25,000 signatures – threshold required for forcing a response from the While House. The White House, however, refused to declare the 1984 anti-Sikh riots as genocide, while noting these as human rights violation (The Hindustan Times, 2013). The then US President was also pressurised to raise this issue with Indian leaders (The Indian Express, 2013). Another petition was moved in 2016, which was again deflected by the White House. Attempts have also been made to file petitions at the United Nations. Cases are filed from time to time against Indian leaders and former Defence and Security Officials, who are granted visas reluctantly. This acts as a dampener to their visits.

A bizarre case was the refusal of entry to Tejinder Singh Dhillon, former Inspector General of the Central Reserve Police Force (CRPF) at the Vancouver airport in May 2017, on the alleged grounds that he had served in a force that engages in "terrorism, systematic or gross human rights violations, or genocide". This resulted in India lodging protest with the Canadian Government, stating that "such a characterization of a reputed force like the CRPF is completely unacceptable." The Canadian High Commissioner Nadir Patel expressed regret and clarified that this "does not reflect the Government of Canada's policy towards India or any particular organization, including the CRPF". Later, Mr. Dhillon was issued a ticket by the Canadian authorities, but such incidents leave an unsavoury taste and adversely impact on ties (The Indian Express, 2017).

## Indian Diaspora: Issues of Concern

What are the likely scenarios in which Indian Diaspora has got involved itself in foreign policy related issues? Its primary involvement has been in the cultural field, which is largely apolitical, even though at times it could spill into political problems, if genuine cultural needs were not met.

Let us know look at some of the recent cases, where Diaspora has been involved in foreign policy related issues:

### *Grant of Voting Rights*

Diaspora has lobbied for the grant of voting rights for general elections. GOI accepted this recommendation. Peoples Representatives Act was amended to facilitate registration of Diaspora in their home state, where they were last resident. Diaspora participation in the State elections in 2013 had been nominal. At the State Assembly Elections in 2017, Diaspora has been more vocal in its support of the AAP Party in Punjab.

### *Grant of Dual Citizenship*

Diaspora had lobbied extensively for the grant of dual citizenship. It needs to be noted that this demand was largely from Diaspora in the developed countries, which grant dual citizenship. Here there was partial success, as GOI agreed to grant only Overseas Citizenship of India (OCI), which is a half way house. OCI grants only economic rights but not political rights.

### *Reservation of Seats for Rajya Sabha*

Diaspora has clamoured for reservation of seats for itself. So far, this has not met with approval from GOI.

### *Migration Related Issues*

Migration related issues have been fought by different Diaspora groups in their respective countries, be it Immigration Bill in USA or deposit fees for visitors to UK (Menon, Parvathi) or Pakistani Hindus wanting to stay back in India.

### *Concern over Human Rights Issues*

These are raised by the Sikhs primarily in France, UK and USA (Sikhs for Justice). They are fighting their own battle in respective countries, with some amount of success.

### *Concerns over Carriage of Social Baggage*

***NRI Marriages*** like early, proxy, fraud and forced marriages and protection of children.

### *Concerns over Identity*

Indians, in particular, Muslims and Sikhs, face the identity problem. The Sikhs, however, are more vocal in their fight against identity related issues The Sikhs in New York launched a US $ 1.3 million Awareness Campaign, "We are Sikhs" to mark the Baisakhi Day on April 13 2017 to create awareness about Sikh identity and ethos. A positive message was sent, emphasizing "Sikh values are American values" and "We are Sikhs, we are Americans". April 15 was celebrated as Turban Day, when non-Sikhs lined up to tie turbans, creating a splash of colour at Times Square. Similar Awareness Campaigns were held in London and Paris (Singh, IP & Harsheen Juneja, 2017).

## Diaspora Advocacy in USA: A Case Study

In this part, we examine the role of Diaspora in 'Advocacy' in the United States. This has to be seen, as a part of the overall advocacy process that is prevalent in the country. USA is the mother of all countries in the domain of advocacy or lobbying. US system works on the principle that advocacy is a sine qua non of a democratic process, where different interests have to be given an opportunity to voice their concerns/viewpoints and be heard. It is, therefore, not surprising that the US Congress recognizes such groups.

The Diplomatic Missions also use these groups, paying heftily for their services. India has also made use of some of these groups, from time to time. The results for India have been mixed, but the practice continues. In common parlance, 'Advocacy' is euphemism for lobbying. Lobbying can be for pursuit of political, economic, commercial, social and cultural interests.

USA dubs Diaspora advocacy as 'ethnic diplomacy', where Diaspora groups pursue their own interests with the government. This has been a part of the US political and social ethos, as USA is a multicultural society, having been drawn from all the streams across the world. Ethnic Diasporas are, therefore, allowed to play their part. On the other hand, the government itself uses these Diaspora groups to promote its foreign policy interests. This largely depends upon the nature of a particular group, whether it considers itself 'Victim Diaspora' or not.

Being at the forefront, USA, which has been the home of such groups, has allowed these to operate, without much check. In the past, Polish Diaspora, Jew Diaspora, Irish Diaspora or Armenian Diaspora had fought for their perceived national interests. On the other hand, German and Japanese Diaspora found themselves throttled, as their countries were on the opposite side of the divide in World War II. In the present day context, Diaspora groups become a part of the process. They were being used for regime change, as a fall out of the 'Arab Spring' in 2011, although the 'Spring' itself has turned into a 'Fall'. Look at the situation in Iraq, Libya and Syria, where Diaspora had destabilized or are destabilizing regimes.

Despite its emphasis on 'political rather than ethnic criteria for inclusion and loyalty', USA has allowed legitimacy to 'ethnicity in public life', giving rise to hyphenated identities and thereby facilitating Diaspora's identification with the home state. It was, therefore, not surprising to receive such comments from US stalwarts like, Nathan Glazier and Daniel Patrick Moynihen, who believed that 'the ethnic influences have become 'the single most important determinant of American foreign policy.'

While accepting Diaspora advocacy, it has to be kept in view that it is not so straight forward, when it comes to foreign policy-related politically sensitive issues. What are the main focus areas of Diaspora advocacy; Kathleen Newland in a study for the USAID has classified these under four broad heads, which are as follows:

- Overseas Voting Rights and Dual Nationality.
- Caste, Ethnic and Religious Rights.
- Development and Disaster Relief.
- Commerce.

In this chapter, we are focusing on the first two areas, given the restricted construct of foreign policy, which we are using.

Diaspora groups that participate in advocacy, are those which have 'grievances, ambitions and/or agendas' (Newland, 2010); the membership in the groups is of individual choice and 'engagement in advocacy is a further choice' (Newland, 2010). Diversity and voluntary character are the hallmarks of these organizations, as these represent different interests.

Given the fact that Diaspora groups are competitive in nature, and fragmented and factitious, they have to satisfy the test of 'representation and legitimacy'. These groups could be motivated by various concerns, be it of identity, assuaging hurt feelings, acquisition of power or maintaining collective myth (Brinkerhoff, Jennifer M, 2009).

The effectiveness of Diaspora engagement is directly related to the political system prevalent in the host country. It is easier in a democratic country (UK) vis-à-vis a despotic rule (Saudi Arabia). In a democratic country also, there are shades of access; easier in a presidential system (USA) than a parliamentary system (UK), because of direct voter connectivity with the top leadership. The voting strength of a Diaspora group, its organization capabilities and financial resources would be other relevant factors. The United States, therefore, provides ample scope for advocacy by Diaspora groups, given 'its long-established system of interest group pluralism' (Newland, 2010).

Newland suggest 'an enabling framework' that donors should adopt. This would involve: listening to less well organized Diasporas; supporting the right to organize; training; evaluation; consultation and sharing of information. What is applicable to countries as donors is equally applicable to them in other foreign policy situations. She, however, adds a cautionary note that Diaspora groups should be treated as allies and not mere 'tools' in development policy. Newland concludes that 'they should neither be overlooked nor taken for granted'.

Diaspora groups therefore, would have to be handled with care. What is true of development aid, is perhaps more true of foreign policy.

## Indian Diaspora as a Foreign Policy Asset: Bane or Boon

Indian Diaspora has global presence but it is not globally organized. It is broadly divided into two categories – Persons of India Origin (PIOs) and Non Resident Indians (NRIs), the former representing foreign nationals, while the latter represent Indian nationals. Both the terms, NRIs and PIOs are used interchangeably, which adds to the confusion and complexities, as there is divergence in their agendas and views, although there would be commonality on certain aspects and in certain respects. The interests of Diaspora vary depending upon the category, to which they belong. Furthermore, Indian Diaspora would fall into two groups of migrants – permanent residents or citizens and temporary residents; the former are largely skilled persons and professionals, settled in the developed countries; while the latter are workers (semi-skilled, unskilled), who are on a contract basis.

Indian Diaspora is well adjusted and adapted in their host countries. They, however, carry their social, cultural and religious baggage with them, which they transplant in their new environment. Diaspora has sprouted in various shapes and sizes and lacks uniformity of purpose or interests. It is the economic pull that has pushed Indians abroad and therefore, they tend to maintain 'apolitical' stance in their destination countries. This is changing now; they have reached a critical mass and understand the important role of 'advocacy' to protect their interests.

Indian Diaspora is now visible in different positions, as President, Prime Minister, Governors, Legislators, Cabinet Ministers, Professionals and Entrepreneurs. This, however, has not resulted in their greater involvement in protecting Diaspora interests and the same has remained at the symbolical level.

Diaspora cannot be perceived to be openly aligning with the home state, as the appointment of Nisha Desai Biswal, as US Asstt. Secretary for South and Central Asia in October, 2013 would bear out; or Preet Bharara, US Attorney in New York, who played a significant role in the arrest of Indian Deputy Consul General Khobragade (The Guardian, 2013).

The Canadian Defence Minister Harjit Singh Sajjan, while professing love for India, was candid enough to state that he was a Canadian, during his visit to India in April 2017. Indian Diaspora Ambassadors (High Commissioners) from Canada, Australia to India also find themselves placed in a similar situation.

Given this heterogeneous character of Diaspora, it has not been possible first to represent itself in a single voice. At the global level, Globalised Organization of People of Indian Origin (GPIO) exists, but is not fully representative of Indian Diaspora. It is, however, the most visible group and two such groups (USA and Canada; Malaysia and Mauritius) formally interact annually with the Indian government at the international conference, held in January to mark the 'Pravasi Bharatiya Divas'. Simultaneously, they hold their own conferences.

The primary focus of Diaspora organizations is India-specific and is in the nature of charter of demands from India, be it their personal or property protection; meeting their cultural or educational requirements; seeking dual citizenship and political rights; issue of identity; protection of workers' human rights or social security benefits.

Diaspora involvement has been in the socio-economic areas, but largely missing in the case of foreign policy related issues. At times, some segments of Diaspora have taken cudgels for the protection of human rights of Indian Diaspora, be it in Fiji, Malaysia or Sri Lanka. However, there is no regular mechanism for Diaspora interaction with the government.

How has then Indian Diaspora performed in their host states? The result has been a mixed bag, depending upon the openness of the local systems in those countries. Here, it has presented a picture of both positivity and negativity towards India. It has been positive, when it galvanized its support for India-USA Civil Nuclear Cooperation Agreement of 2008. It has, however, to be remembered that this became possible, as both the governments were on the same page. There is also a certain amount of positivity, when the Diaspora fights for human rights or raises its voice against racialism or on curbs on religious freedom, in preventing the use of symbols, be it in UK, USA, Canada or Australia or France. Here, the success has been rather limited.

It also presents itself as a fractured community, when different Diaspora groups from Gujarat take stand on the issue of grant or denial of US visa to the then Chief Minister Narendra Modi or lobby against his participation at an event marking the 150th anniversary celebrations, connected with Swami Vivekanand (Lakshman:1, 2013).

On the other hand, in its dealings with the home state, Diaspora places itself on a collision course when it forces the government of India to change its stand on the human rights violation in Sri Lanka, being pressurized by Tamil leaders, on grounds of ethnicity. It also generates itself into a negative force, when it files cases in the United States against Indian leaders, like Prime Minister (Singh, IP, 2013), Sonia Gandhi (The Hindu, 2013), and Chief Minister Badal for violating the human rights of the Sikhs.

Diaspora also asserts itself, when it forces the government of India to remove the newly appointed Minister of MOIA in 2004. GOI also plays its own card, when it asks foreign governments to keep a watch over its Diaspora, for their involvement in extremist activities.

India's own experience in this sphere has been rather limited. On the one hand, there is the single success story of Diaspora involvement in facilitating the signing of India-USA Civil Nuclear Cooperation Agreement, as stated earlier. On the other hand, the government has seen the negative fallout of Diaspora involvement in pushing their human rights agenda, be it Kashmiris, Sikhs or Gujaratis from India. India has also found itself at the receiving end, when its foreign policy stance changed, under pressure from the Indian Tamilians, to protect the interests of Sri Lankan

Tamils. This only proves that Diaspora could be both a boon and a bane, depending upon each situation.

## Lessons Learnt from USA and Canada

What are the lessons, we can draw from the two country practices on Diaspora involvement in foreign policy related issues. In the case of USA, it is an accepted reality as Diaspora involvement in foreign policy is taken for granted. On the other hand, Canada is exploring how to use Diaspora in promoting its foreign policy interests. It is to be seen, whether we are looking at Diaspora involvement from the perspective of a home or host state. As a host state, USA is open to Diaspora involvement as an Ethnic Group, while Canada is still struggling with its policy approach. As a home state, both USA and Canada are open to their involvement. In the case of India, it is a new beginning, as it is still grappling with the reality, whether Diaspora could be a bane or boon, based on its limited experience.

USA, Canada and India, however, have some common denominators. These are multicultural societies, vibrant democracies based on the rule of law and citizenship rights that are well protected by their respective constitutions under the watchdog of the media and guaranteed by the judiciary. There is, however, a major dissimilarity on the role of ethnicity. USA accepts multiple ethno-groups, retaining their interests, as in a salad bowl as they were not able to lose their identity in a melting pot. Canada is also a multicultural society, but it has two dominant nationalities – English and French. India is also a multicultural society that respects pluralism and diversity and is based on the principle of 'Unity in Diversity'.

What are the trends? Some experts opine that 'the clout of ethnicity in US foreign affairs is likely to expand' (Shain, Yossi), as that of the professional elite goes down. Vote bank politics are also largely responsible in giving a determined voice to Diaspora, as their number increases. This outcome is also the result of 'constituency politics', which is a part of 'the institutional reality of a fragmented US foreign policy establishment, which empowers individual members of Congress' (Shain, Yossi, 1994-95).

Given their historical connectivity, Diaspora in US has kept interest in the political scene of their respective home states. The US government views Diaspora as agents of change, given their credibility in their home state and therefore fit to push US core foreign policy interests, like promoting 'human rights, democracy and good governance' (Gamage, Daya, 2012). The strength of ethnic lobbies depends upon their ability to advance a message that resonates with the American values and ideals (Shain, Yossi,

1994-95). India Diaspora groups with affiliations with political parties in India were actively involved in the US Presidential Elections in November 2016.

The same is true of Canada, where it expects Diaspora to promote its core foreign policy interests in the areas of human rights and democracy. Canada's approach, however, in using Diaspora groups, has been 'both sporadic and piecemeal'. There is, therefore, a felt need to use them 'more systematically to help strengthen the content and reach of Canada's official foreign policy' (Axworthy, Tom, Monahan, John and Brender, Natalie, 2011).

There are, however, other Canadians, who recognize that involving Diaspora is 'a dangerous game', whereby foreign Diaspora groups could be used 'to lobby or influence our leaders or bring their conflicts here' (Carment, David and Samy, Yiagadeesen, 2012). The jury is still to be out in Canada, whether to use Diaspora in pursuit of its foreign policy interests.

## Evaluating Diaspora's Role as Friendship Bridge in Foreign Policy Arena

Diaspora is celebrated as a 'Friendship Bridge', connecting the home and the host states. India has sung paeans of its glory and instituted a formal framework in 2003, called Pravasi Bharatiya Divas (PBD) to formally connect with its Diaspora. It set up a separate Ministry of Overseas Indians Affairs in May 2004, which was, however, merged as a Department in the Ministry of External Affairs in January 2016. India's engagement with its Diaspora has been broadly in the cultural and commercial arenas. Its engagement on foreign policy has been sporadic and rare and only in those countries, which are open to Diaspora involvement.

India does not have a formal Diaspora policy. Therefore, there is no foreign policy component of that policy. Furthermore, foreign policy making has been an exercise dominated by the elite and it has still not come into public domain. India's outreach efforts by the earlier Ministry of Overseas Indians Affairs (MOIA) or the Public Policy Division had not resulted in the establishment of regular flow or exchange of ideas/inputs. We cannot extrapolate Diaspora policy on one success story in USA, as 'one swallow does not make a summer.' We are faced with the Hamletian dilemma, 'To be or not to be.'

In the case of Diaspora, there is a further constraint. There is no single Diaspora group, which represents Indian Diaspora globally. Claims of

GOPIO to be the representative of Diaspora have to be taken with a pinch of salt. GOPIO, itself, is an elite club and does not represent the interests of all the groups. Could we create an umbrella Diaspora organization in the future? This does not appear to be likely, given the diversity of Indian groups and their penchant for maintaining their independence and turf. A single Diaspora organization would, therefore, remain a pipe dream, as the 'Indian Bunyan Tree' has blossomed abroad in its full diversity that fully reflects India.

We cannot think of any Diaspora involvement on a global basis, as all countries are not ready for such an intervention. It would, therefore, have to be on a country and case-by-case basis, and it could be part of such interaction with a number of diverse Diaspora groups. A beginning could be made in this regard, with GOPIO providing one such channel.

We have seen that Diaspora involvement has been largely government driven, where they have been used as a tool in promoting foreign policy interests. Could this be made Diaspora driven? If so, then would it be a bane or boon? We have seen that in the case of Indian Diaspora, it has broadly focussed on human rights issue, an area which has acquired transnational dimension, where differences based on ethnicity and not nationality are more paramount. This cuts both ways.

What are the trends and conclusions which we could draw? The United States is the only country, which openly recognizes the role of 'ethnic politics' or 'Diaspora politics' in the foreign policy arena? Canada, on its part, is still evolving its approach. Therefore, their experiences do not provide any conclusive results that could be emulated by India, as it has experienced both positivity and negativity in its involvement with Diaspora.

Does our limited experience help us in drawing out any meaningful conclusions? To this debate, we have to add the question, are we open to foreign Diaspora's involvement in promoting the foreign policy interests of their home states? India's involvement with Diaspora has still been at the fringes.

We also have to contend that views of the home and the host states may not always coalesce. A view would have to be taken, whether we are looking for an active or passive Diaspora involvement. I would, therefore, suggest a cautionary approach, as even Canada does not appear to be still ready to go full hog.

We need to contend between two incisive comments, from a former senior official and a Diaspora leader that provide different narratives in the author's conversation with them, as given below:

> "In a globalised world, India's foreign policy cannot be expected to be the same as its Diaspora policy. It can and should however, take its diaspora interests into consideration" (A. Didar Singh, Former Secretary, MOIA).

> "Developing countries are not yet confident, to engage diaspora in foreign affairs" (Selvarajoo Sundaram, GOPIO President, Malaysia).

How should then India deal with this emerging scenario with Indian diaspora, which is not only more diverse but also lacks unity? To this is added the problem of diversity of policies in the host states. Indian Diaspora's involvement in foreign policy-related issues has been marginal and sporadic and it had no strategic impact. It has, however, resulted in the creation of pressure groups, be it in the form of Caucasus of Legislators in UK or the United States. Some of these groups have supported Indian policies, while the others have opposed.

We have to finally answer the fundamental question. Should Diaspora be involved in foreign policy related issues? The Author's considered view would be that it should not be involved in hard political and national security issues. Its engagement in non-political issues, be it economy or commerce, philanthropy or development, culture or education, is legitimate and has been accepted by the home and the host states. Such has been the approach adopted by other countries, like UK, USA, Canada and EU and international organizations like World Bank, IOM etc. If we accept this approach, then we need to evolve an appropriate infrastructure for the same.

Finally, a detailed and intensive study needs to be carried out, which should focus on a number of areas – nature of Diaspora, country practices; pattern adopted by other countries; establishment of structures and creation of regular channels of communication. Diaspora involvement, however, would not be of a strategic nature, as it would be one among many voices.

## References


Agunias, D.R. and Newland K. 2012, *Developing a Road Map for Engaging Diasporas in Development*, International Organization for Migration (IOM) and Migration Policy Institute. Available at http://www.migrationpolicy.org/pubs/thediasporahandbook.pdf (Accessed on April 16, 2018).

AID (Association of Indian Diplomats), 2008, Report on Economic Diplomacy, 2008. Available at http://www.associationdiplomats.org/publications/ifaj/Vol1/ecodiplomacy.htm [accessed 16 April 2018].

Axworthy, Tom, Monahan, John and Brender.Natalie, 2011, 'Top Migrants to help shape foreign policy', *The Globe and Mail*, December, 20.

Barnard A, 2010, 'For Haitian official, mission is to mend fences with diaspora and streamline aid', *The New York Times,* March, 12.

*BBC*, 2017, 'India visit 'very productive' despite controversy, says Sajjan', April 21.

Berridge, G.R., 2005, *Diplomacy – Theory and Practice*, New York, Palgrave Macmillan.

Bhatta B., 2009, *Economic Diplomacy: How NRNs Can Contribute?* Paper presented at the 4th NRN Global Conference, Kathmandu, Nepal, October 13-15.

Bhattacharyya, Anirudh , "Ontario passes motion calling 1984 riots genocide, India says move misguided',http://www.hindustantimes.com/world-news/ontario-passes-motion-describing-1984-anti-sikh-riots-as-genocide/story-1YPs2tiMkvtW2Tp7UDyydK.html (Accessed on December 26, 2017).

Brinkerhoff. Jennifer M., 2009, *Digital Diasporas: Identity and Transnational Engagement*.

Canada Study,2013, 'Diaspora Communities and Foreign Policy', Walter and Duncan Gordon Foundation,file://G:\Chicago-June-Aug2013\Diaspora-ForeignPolicy\DiasporaCommunitiesandforeignpolicy (Accessed on December 26, 2017).

Carment, David and Samy, Yiagadeesen, 2012, 'The dangerous game of diaspora politics', *The Globe and Mail*, February, 10.

CHOGM, 2013, 'Khurshid will represent India at CHOGM', *The Hindu,*

October 27.

Chu, Henry, 2013, 'Ireland OKs abortion in some cases in blow to Catholic Church', *The Chicago Tribune*, July, 30.

Clinton Hillay, 2011, *Address of the US Secretary of State at the Global Diaspora Forum*, Washington DC, May 17.

Délano A, 2011, *Mexico and Its Diaspora in the United States: Policies of Emigration since 1848,* Cambridge University Press, New York.

Dewan S., 2010, 'Scattered emigres Haiti once shunned are now a lifeline', *The New York Times,* February 3.

Diaspora Report, 2008, Center for the Study of Democracies, Queensland University, Canada.

Diaspora, 2013, 'Modi's long shadow creates a rift in Chicago', *Business Standard,* September 22, http://www.business-standard.com/article/news-ians/modi-s-long-shadow-creates-a-rift-in-chicago-113092200449_1.html (Accessed on April 16, 2018).

Dikshit, Sandeep, 2013, 'Process under way to decide on participation in CHOGM', *Hindu,* November 1.

Diwali, 2013, 'In a first, Diwali celebrations at Capitol Hill', *The Tribune,* August 27.

Freeman, Jr., Chas. W., 2006, *The Diplomat's Dictionary,* Washington D.C.: United States Institute of Peace Press.

Gamage, Daya, 2012 'Ethnic diasporas and shaping of US foreign policy', *Asian Tribune,* August, 17.

Ghoshal, Baladas, 1996, *Diplomacy and Domestic Politics in South Asia,* Colombo, Konark Publishers Pvt. Ltd.

Gonzalez III, 2011, *Diaspora Diplomacy: Philippine Migration and Its Soft Power Influences.* Minneapolis, USA: Mill City Press.

Haidar, Suhasini. 2013, 'The Case for making it to Colombo', *The Hindu,* October 29.

Haidar, Suhasini. 2017, 'Amarinder remarks on Canadian ministers sparks row', *The Hindu,* April 12.

High Level Committee on Indian Diaspora [HLCID], 2001, Report of the High Level Committee on Indian Diaspora. http://moia.gov.in/services.aspx?ID1=63&id=m8&idp=59&mainid=23 (Accessed on April 16, 2018).

International Organization for Migration [IOM] and Migration Policy Institute [MPI], 2012 *Developing a Road Map for Engaging Diasporas in Development*.Available at http://www.migrationpolicy.org/pubs/thediasporahandbook.pdf *[accessed 26 November 2012].*

IOM, 2011, 'Migration and Development Report, 2011', International Organisation for Migration (IOM). Available at http://www.iom.int/cms/wmr (Accessed on 4 September 2013).

Kamal, Neel, 2013 'Ghadar comes alive after 100 years of its launch in US', *Times of India*, November 1.

Kissinger, Henry A, 1966, 'Domestic Structure and Foreign Policy', *Daedalus*. Vol. 95, No. 2, Spring, pp. 503-529.

Kolappan, B. 2013, 'TN house resolution calls for boycott of Colombo CHOGM' *The Hindu*, October 24. http://thehindu.com/news/national/tamil-nadu/tn-house-resolution-calls-for-boycott... (accessed on 24.10.2013).

Kryntzki, Sara. 2012, 'Diaspora and the Foreign Policy Agendas of their Host States', MA Thesis, Department of Political Science, Concordia University, Montreal, Quebec, Canada.

Lakshman, Narayan. 2013, 'Modi Links caste shadow on Vivekananda event', *The Hindu*, September, 23.

Lakshman, Narayan, 2013: 1, 'Pakistani family recounts drone strike before U.S. Congress', *Hindu*, October 30.

Mazzetti*et al*., 2011, Pakistan spies on its diaspora, spreading fear. *The New York Times*, July 23. http://www.nytimes.com/2011/07/24/world/asia/24isi.html?pagewanted=all (Accessed on January 7, 2018).

Menon, Parvathi, 2013, 'India-origin groups take protests against immigration measures to Downing Street', *The Hindu,* October 11.

MFA, Ministry of Foreign Affairs of Kenya (no date) 'Diaspora Affairs: Introduction'. Available athttp://www.mfa.go.ke/index.php?option=com_content&view=article&id=371&Itemid=116 (Accessed on January 7, 2018).

Mistry, Dinshaw, 2006, "Diplomacy, Domestic Politics and the US-India Nuclear Agreement", *Asian Survey*, Vol. 46, No. 5, Sept. pp. 675-698.

MOIA, 2011-12, Annual Report of the Ministry of Overseas Indian Affairs, Govt. of India.

Newland, Kathleen (Ed.), 2010, *Diasporas, New Partners in Global Development Policy*, USA MPI, Washington DC.

OECD, 2012, *International Migration Outlook.*

PBD Canada, 2011, http://www.pbdcanada.com. (Accessed on 18 March 2013).

PBD, 2003, Address of Yashwant Sinha, External Affairs Minister at the Pravasi Bharatiya Divas, New Delhi, January 10.

PBD, 2003:1, Inaugural Address of the Prime Minister of India, January 9.

PBD, 2009, EAM's Address at the Pravasi Bhartiya Divas, January 7.

Raj, Yashwant, 2013, 'Oak Creek Victims' son to run for US Congress', *The Hindustan Times,* October 27.

Raja Mohan, C., 2009, 'The Making of Indian Foreign Policy: The Role of Scholarship and Public Opinion', ISAS Working Paper, No. 73, July 13, pp. 1-16.

Rice, Condoleezza, 2012, *No Higher Honour*, London: Simon & Schuster.

Sahai, P.S, *et al.*, 2011, *Study of the Indian Diaspora with Particular Reference to Development and Migration from the State of Punjab*, Centre for Research in Rural and Industrial Development [CRRID], September.

Sahai, P.S., 2012, A unique study. Review of Délano A (2011) *Mexico and Its Diaspora in the United States: Policies of Emigration since 1848.* Available at http://www.diplomacy.edu/resources/books/reviews/mexico-and-its-diaspora-united-states-policies-emigration-1848 [accessed 20 November 2012].

Sahai, P.S., 2013, 'India's Engagement with Diaspora: Government Communication, Platforms and Structures' (Paper for ODI Conference, March).

Sardesai, Rajdeep, 2013, 'Confront these painful truths', *The Hindustan*

*Times*, November 1.

SGPC, 2013, 'SGPC to send books to Canada on Sikhs' role in World War', *The Tribune*, August 27.

Shain, Yossi, 1994-95, 'Ethnic Diasporas and U.S. Foreign Policy' *Political Science Quarterly*, 01. 109, No. 5, (Winter); http://www.oxfordbibliographies.com/view/document/obo-9780199756223/obo-9780199756223-0069.xml (Accessed on 16 April 2018).

Sharma, Amarinder Pal, 2013, 'Canadian Sikhs petition against 'criminal' tags', *The Times of India*, October 29.

Sheffer, G.G., 2005, 'Is the Jewish diaspora unique? Reflections on the diaspora's current situation', *Israeli Studies* 10(1). http://sino-west.org/sjtu/Is.pdf (Accessed on 16 April 2018).

Singh P, 2012, 'EcoSikh launches green drive in Amritsar', *The Tribune,* July 1. Available at http://www.tribuneindia.com/2012/20120701/punjab.htm#12 [Accessed on 26 November 2012].

Singh, I.P, & Harsheen Juneja, 2017, 'Turbans give a splash of colour to NY, London', *The Times of India*, April 17.

*Singh, I.P., 2013,* '1984 riots: justice delayed & denied', *The Times of India*, November 1.

Singh, I.P., 2013:1, 'Sikhs for Justice engages Washington firm to serve summons on Manmohan Singh, *Times of India*, October 2.

Sonwalkar, Prasun, 2013, 'Diwali: UK cops apologise for wrong Punjabi translation', *The Hindustan Times*, November 1.

Srinivasan, Krishnan, 2012, *Diplomatic Channels*, Kolkata: Manohar Publishers.

Statement, 2017, Message from the Prime Minister of Canada on Baisakhi,April. http://pm.gc.ca/eng/news/2017/04/13/statement-pime-minister-canada-vaisakhi (Accessed on 16 April 2018).

Strategic Assets, http://www.businessdictionary.com/definition/strategic-assets.html (Accessed on 30 September 2013).

Talbott, Strobe, 1998, *Engaging India: Diplomacy, Democracy and the Bomb, Penguin*, New Delhi.

Tharoor, Shashi, 2012, *PAX INDICA: India and the World of the 21st*

*Century*, New Delhi, Thomson Press India Ltd.

*The Guardian*, 2013, 'India-US row over arrest of diplomat Devyani Khobragade escalates', December 17.

*The Hindu*, 2013, 'U.S. Sikh group filing improper suits against Congress leaders', October 23.

*The Hindu, 2017,* Haider, Suhasini and Vasudeva, Vikas, 'Amarinder remarks on Canadian ministers sparks row', April 17.

*The Hindustan Times*, 2017, 'NaMo foreign policy: Bigger role for states', October 20.

*The Hindustan Times*, 2013, 'Chances bleak for PM's Lanka visit for CHOGM summit', October 30.

*The Hindustan Times*, 2013:1, 'Ex Canadian MP to help victims of fraud marriages', October 30.

*The Hindustan Times,* 2013:2, 'Sikh regiment's WW-2 veterans awarded in UK', October 13.

*The Hindustan Times,* 2013:3, 'Sikh student with Kirpan not allowed to board bus in US', October 18.

*The Hindustan Times*, 2013:4, 'US refused to declare 1984 riots as genocide', April 3.

*The Hindustan Times*, 2017, 'Canadian PM Trudeau's presence at event with Khalistani flags upsets India', May 5.

*The Indian Express*, 2013, 'Obama must raise 1984 riots at summit: Sikh rights group', September 23.http://newsindianexpress.com/nation/Obama-must-raise-1984-riots-at-summit-Sikh-rights...(Accessed on April 16, 2018).

*The Indian Express*, 2017, 'Canada refuses entry to former IG of CRPF, India lodges protest', May 24.

*The Sunday Times*, 2013, 'Visiting NRIs to pay homage to Ghadri 'Babas', October 27.

*The Sunday Times*, 2013:1, 'Muslim martyrs of Ghadar action remain unsung', October 27.

*The Times of India,* 2012, 'Mamata appeals to Bengali diaspora to pitch in for state', July 7.

*The Times of India*, 2012, 'India does not start levying proposed service tax on remittances fee paid by NRIs', July 3.

*The Times of India*, 2013, 'Pakistan Hindus seek Indian govt's support to stay back', October 17.

*The Times of India*, 2013, 'Sikh issues to figure in Conference', October 26.

*The Tribune*, 2013, 'Will oppose Canada's move to ban Sikh symbols: SGPC', August 27.

*The Tribune*, 2013:1, 'Britain decorates a Sikh Regiment WW-II veterans', October 19.

Tikku, Alike, 2013, 'No decision yet on Lanka visit of PM', *The Hindustan Times*, October 19.

Turkish Diaspora, 2017, By *Stefan Schirmer, Özlem Topcu,* 'The Fallout from the Turkish Referendum in Germany', *Handesblatt,* April 13, https://global.handelsblatt.com/politics/the-fallout-from-the-turkish-referendum-in-germany-746718 (Accessed on January 2017).

Tuteja, Ashok, 2013, 'India undecided on PM's participation, in CHOGM', *The Tribune*, October 12.

UK Africa Diaspora Programme. http://.dfid.gov.uk/work-with-us/funding-opportunities/not-for-profit-organisations/c (Accessed on 14.3.2013).

USINPAC, http://www;usinpac.com/home/our-mission (Accessed on January 7, 2018).

# Chapter – X

# Media and Foreign Policy in a Globalised World

## Introduction

Media is an essential element of cultural diplomacy, as it plays an important role in connecting people and generating awareness. Clauses on media connectivity, therefore, invariably become an integral part of Bilateral Cultural Agreements signed by the governments. Even in the absence of cultural agreements, separate arrangements are concluded to enable media play such a role. Given the sensitivities associated with media-related activities, such an arrangement is helpful. India, broadly speaking, follows this approach.

This chapter looks at the role of the media, in particular the Print Media in the foreign policy arena, covering international events in India. In the process we have to contend with terminologies associated with media-related issues. These oft-used terms that are in vogue, include, 'Images', 'Perceptions', 'Social Responsibility', 'Connectivity' and 'Understanding'. Three other terms that have emerged during the 2016 US presidential campaign are, 'Post-Truth', 'Fake News' and 'Alternative Facts'.

We live in a world of perceptions, which are at times more important than reality. Does media play a key role in creating such perceptions, which result in building public opinion that largely moulds the conduct of relations among nations? The right images, therefore, assume greater importance. This is true of the media in the national and international contexts.

How does media play such an important role in creating those images? How does it manifest itself in its triple role, as a communicator, educator and opinion maker? Its strength lies in the images that it creates that impact on the mind. The nature of this role is dependent upon the environment in which it operates. How free or independent is the media? What are the editorial policies and how are these shaped by commercial compulsions?

What is the hold of these 'Perceptions' in the international arena? Is it greater or lesser, as compared to domestic environment? Is the media confronted with the issue of 'Social Responsibility', which is becoming a 'cache' in all societies? Does or should 'Media Social Responsibility' (MSR) trigger in? Would it be on the lines of Corporate Social Responsibility (CSR), as is being legislated in some of the countries?

What role 'media images' play in providing 'connectivity' among nations and peoples? Does this 'connectivity' help in promoting 'understanding', which is the purpose of international discourse among peoples and nations? What is the ground reality on the media coverage in India?

How do the Ministries of Foreign Affairs and its Diplomatic Missions connect with the media? The moot question is how to ensure that the 'Messenger' (media) carries the 'Message' (official policy pronouncement) as it is intended, without any distortions. Has this connectivity between the 'Message and the Messenger' been a straight trajectory? How do countries resort to multipronged and diverse approaches to ensure that the message ultimately reaches the people at large, which is the ultimate destination?

Has the media made any difference in changing our mindset or do we stay transfixed to old notions? Is there a 'Media-People' or 'Media-Establishment' connectivity-deficit; if so, how could this be bridged? Could media play the role of a bridge-builder?

In this chapter it is proposed to look at all the issues and see how Media has played its role and what needs to be done to facilitate adequate coverage, without undermining its independence. It is largely based on personal experiences, both in India and abroad.

My skills were primarily honed in Moscow, during the period 1964-66, when I got an opportunity to deal with both, the media and foreign policy experts, including leaders like the prime minister and the foreign minister. The most fascinating experience for me, at the start of my diplomatic career was to act as a liaison officer to a group of senior editors, who accompanied our then Prime Minister Lal Bahadur Shastri to Moscow/ Tashkent during January 1966.

I have also drawn from my interaction with media stalwarts in India, such as S. Nihal Singh and H.K. Dua and senior journalists, Mahendra

Ved and Vijay Naik, who have been involved with foreign policy related issues. At the CRRID Chandigarh, through 'The Two Punjabs Centre', the Author has been directly involved at a practical level in encouraging visits by media personalities and opinion makers. He edited a Book, *Women Guiding the Destiny of South Asia*, which was published in 2010.

All this has provided immense insight in to the minds of journalists, as to how they interact with the 'Foreign Policy Establishments' and the likely role they play as 'Bridge Builders' or otherwise. Interaction with the visiting media personalities and opinion makers from Pakistan and other South Asian countries has further helped in understanding media's role.

## Media's Role

The reach of the media, as the Fourth Estate, is well accepted. The Media's importance as the Fourth Estate has if anything expanded and grown over the years. It has grown both in terms of power and its sweep, as it is aided by the new technology and communication revolution. The overall reach of the Media was stated by the then External Affairs Minister Pranab Mukherjee at the SAARC Editors Conference on February 10, 2007, when he said:

> "One sentence from any one of you has the potential to reach millions, it can correct a wrong: it can create an image; it can plant a seed of understanding." (EAM, 2007)

To this, I may add that it could also sow a seed of misunderstanding. The mainstream media was out of tune with the public sentiments during the US Presidential Elections in 2016.

Interrelated revolutionary changes 'in politics, international relations and mass communications have immensely expanded the media's multiple role in diplomacy' (Eytan Gilboa, 2001). This has led to growing mass participation in political processes and globalisation of the electronic media. This led to a new media-dominated governance system that was called 'Mediailsm' by Senator Richard Lugar and 'Tele-democracy' by David Gergen, Media Advisor to Presidents Reagan and Clinton. The phenomenon was nicknamed "CNN (Cable News Network) Effect", given the enormous impact that CNN was able to create.

The so called 'CNN Effect' came under strain during the US Presidential Elections in November 2016, when mainstream media found it out of sync with the majority public sentiments. To minimize this effect, President Trump gave it a new nickname 'Fake News' and tried to banish it from

White House Press Briefings. A former British Foreign Secretary Douglas Hurd observed that 'Public discourse is not run by events but the coverage of the events' (Quoted in Eytan Gilboa). This fully illustrates how important is the coverage by the Media.

Media can both be a positive and a negative force through the images it creates and the perceptions it generates on the minds of people. Media reaches out in three ways: 'News', which is merely reporting of facts; 'Opinions/Views' that reflect the views of opinion makers and 'Editorials', reflecting the views of the Editorial Board. The media thus performs a triple role – as a communicator, educator and opinion maker. It is therefore essential to use an 'adjective filter in order to restore the dividing line between news and views' (Panneerselvan, 2013:1). A newspaper, however, has to make special efforts, so as to avoid mixing facts and views.

Media has seen an exponential expansion, both in terms of variety and reach of its products and diversity in each product. It has gone beyond the print media and now embraces all forms of communication. It has been broadly categorized as 'Old and New Media'. Now a new dimension has been added, called 'Social Media', which provides direct connectivity to people and among themselves through the internet. This is a revolutionary development in terms of its outreach and instantaneousness. This also results in creating its own weaknesses, in terms of authenticity and credibility. The impact of 'Social Media' was visible during the elections for the Delhi General Assembly in December, 2013. It took centre stage during the election campaign for the 2014 General Elections in India (Chopra, Shaili, 2014) and the 2016 US Presidential Elections. We are now witnessing a similar phenomenon, prior to the 2019 General Elections.

The emergence of '24 X 7 TV News' is also both a positive and a negative development. It is positive, as developments in the world have come within easy reach on a 24-hour basis. It, however, suffers from inbuilt infirmities, as the race to become the first, at times, dents on the authenticity of the news and thus affects its credibility. Simultaneously, print media has also come under pressure and its share is declining globally. However, in the case of India, it retains its dominant presence, as mainstream and regional newspapers are still flourishing. Chief Editor of the Malayala Manorama reaffirmed his faith in the print media, when he said, 'newsprint may die, newspapers will not' (Dixit, Rekha, 2014). The mainstream papers have also brought in their own e-editions, providing a bridge with the print media (Panneerselvan, 2013: 2).

Look at the media images that touched hearts across international borders, like the washing away of the body of Aylan Kurdi, a Syrian child on the Turkish shores in September 2015, which created an instant sympathy for the refugees (Helena Smith, 2015). Similarly, the dying faces of children in Syria, who were attacked by chemical weapons, resulted in President Trump ordering air attacks in Syria, which represented a change from the earlier declared policy approach that was projected by him (NYT, 2017). It was a historic photo to see the North Korean President Kim Jung-un crossing DMZ line, as he stepped into the South Korean territory on April 27, 2018. On the same day, Prime Minister Modi was shown playing gongs at Wuhan, which symbolized the resetting of India-China ties.

We are witnessing a number of developments, as we travel from old media (print media) to new media (TV, Radio) and social media (Face book, Twitter etc.). With the emergence of social media, given its reach and speed, every person has become a journalist, who is nicknamed 'citizen journalist'. On April 14, 2017, The Times of India announced plans to encourage participation by 'citizen journalist'.

A new breed of citizen-journalists is appearing on the scene, using new instrumentalities, such as 'Blogs'. This development in itself has caused concerns among governments, which would like to control Internet in one or another form. Sometime ago, China had closed cyber cafes for a year. Efforts to block news, considered unpleasant to governments are continuing in one or another form, in different countries. Israeli Ministers approved 'Facebook Law', which if approved in Parliament, could authorize courts to ask Facebook to block/ remove messages that could cause communal disharmony (Gwen Ackerman, 2016).

The Media, however, is not primarily interested in foreign policy issues, as its focus remains on domestic agenda (Shailaja Bajpai, 2017). This opinion was also shared with the author by one of the senior Indian newspaper editors. This is not only a perception but a reality, not only in the case of India but also true all over the world. A similar perception over inadequate interest of the media was commented upon by Som Nath Chatterjee, the then Speaker of Lok Sabha (Lower House of Parliament). The Media practically omitted portions dealing with foreign policy from the Prime Minister's reply on March 8, 2007 to the Lok Sabha to the Motion of Thanks to the President's Address. This still holds true. This, therefore, presents a major challenge for the Foreign Policy Establishment.

This low priority to the coverage of international news was clearly visible in the stark coverage of the visits of the Presidents of Tajikistan and Kyrgyzstan to India during December 2016. The visits failed to make to the front pages and were barely visible in the inside pages. Media and the Foreign Policy Establishment were, therefore, not on the same page, given the importance attached to India's 'Extended Neighbourhood' policy by the Prime Minister and the Ministry of External Affairs. Similarly, the three-nation official state visit to African countries of Equatorial Guinea, Swaziland and Zambia in April, 2018 by the Indian President Ram Nath Kovind was barely noticed by the media.

Similarly, the mainstream TV channels except Door Darshan did not give live coverage to Prime Minister Modi's press conference at St. Petersburg on June 2, 2017, which was also covered by the External Channel of the Russian TV. Indian TV Channels were busy with their cacophony, dissecting domestic issues, with each participant using lung power to drown others and not winning them over through dialogue and discussion.

## Media-Foreign Policy Connectivity

We would look at the Media-Foreign Policy connectivity under different sub-heads, such as Globalised Setting; Trends in the International Media and Foreign Policy Scene; The Role of Media in Foreign Policy; Coverage of International Scene in the Indian Media; Interface between Foreign Establishment and the Media in India; and Media's Social Responsibility.

### *Globalised Setting*

The primary role of the media as a communication channel and that too as an independent and authentic conveyer of views and opinion, still remains. The Media, however, is facing new situations and challenges, to which it has adjusted in the past and is preparing to adapt to similar challenges in the future in this globalised world. What are new challenges; these are described below in the succeeding paragraphs.

In a globalised world, distinction between the local and foreign news has disappeared, as the modern means of communication and technology have bridged the distance in time and space. The coverage of the 2016 US Presidential Elections and the Terrorist Attacks in Belgium, Paris, Berlin and UK fully corroborate this point, as these could be seen across the globe instantaneously.

The Media finds itself challenged, not only from within but from outside. The Print Media is facing challenge from the TV. The TV is facing challenge from the Internet. The mushrooming of newspapers, TV Channels, Radio Channels are creating their own problems, because of cut throat competition among themselves in their respective category and between the old and the new media. Breaking News has become 'Brokering News' and the desire for better TRP Ratings have dented the credibility of the media.

Foreign Policy is no more the preserve of a select few and an elite class. It is no more conducted in secrecy and the plea of national consensus or security does not hold good, while dealing with the media. The debate on India-USA Civil Nuclear Cooperation Agreement in 2008 was reflective of this trend; so was the coverage of terrorist attacks from Pakistan at Pathankot and Uri in India during 2016.

Demand for transparency has increased and the capacity and the power of the government to either conceal facts or provide misleading information is coming under greater scrutiny. Wiki Leaks unmasks what was said in official diplomatic cables. While media censorship is losing its relevance at the national level, yet it is making its appearance in different ways, resulting in controlling the flow of news.

Media is turning into an Industry, as more Business Tycoons, like Rupert Murdoch are appearing on the scene. Such magnates are also appearing in India, as Media has now become a 'Big Business'. In India, business magnates like Birla, Goenkas have been in the media and new groups, like Reliance are entering in to the fray.

## Trends in the International Media and Foreign Policy Scene

What are the main trends, which emerge from the globalised setting, in which the 'Media and Foreign Policy' interconnect with one another? Primarily speaking, it results in breaking the barrier between the foreign and domestic news, as the news is equally accessible to foreign and domestic audiences simultaneously, given the advancement in communications technology. This has resulted in increasing the impact of the international news on national scene across the borders or vice versa. Double-speak are also not possible for foreign or domestic audiences.

The present communication technology revolution has resulted in extending the sweep of the media over a larger segment of people, irrespective of the boundaries, under which they live. This is continuation of an earlier revolution resulting from the invention of the printing press, which democratized the news and now the news has been internationalized.

Technology impact is resulting in the international news coming to the doorstep of the people, as happened in the case of the Iraq War in 1991, Terrorist's Attack on Twin Towers in New York in 2001, President Bush's Iraq War in 2003; Terrorist Attacks in Mumbai in November 2008 and Uri and Pathankot in 2016.

There is a spurt in the number of TV channels, newspapers, while it provides diversity of views, yet it is also resulting in the media acquiring a powerful influence and role, creating unhealthy competition among themselves. Foreign policy related announcements are also becoming more open and transparent, as it is no more being undertaken under the secrecy of the cables, resulting in narrowing down the gap in the perceptions of the media personnel and the diplomats, who are becoming comrades-in-arms.

This mushrooming of old and new media has also created a problem of connectivity between the 'Media and the Foreign Policy Establishments', as it is difficult to keep liaison on an individual basis with such a vast array. The increasing use of internet for communication, while it has introduced faster communication between the 'Media and the Foreign Policy Establishments', but it has reduced the relationship to an impersonal one. The warmth of personal relationship is thus missing.

Foreign Policy Establishments are now getting directly into the fray as opinion makers with columns being contributed by Foreign Ministers and Ambassadors, with a view to establishing direct connectivity with the people rather than through the intermediation of the media personnel. At times, joint messages have been sent, be it a joint column, 'Chalen Saath Saath', (Moving Together) after Prime Minister Modi's visit to USA in September 2014 or joint broadcast by Prime Minister Modi and President Obama at Modi's Weekly Radio programme, called, 'Man Ki Baat' (From the Heart) in January 2015.

The Heads of State/Government are also reaching out directly to their foreign audiences. Invariably, prior to their foreign visits, they try to directly reach out to people and opinion makers through Opeds. We have seen Opeds written by former British Prime Minister Cameron, Canadian Prime Minister Trudeau, US President Barrack Obama, Russian President Vladimir Putin and Indian Prime Minister Modi. Prime Minister Sheikh Hasina of Bangladesh started her visit to India in April 2017 with an Oped, headlined, 'Friendship is a Flowing River' (Sheikh Hasina, 2017). So did the Australian Prime Minister Turnbull during his visit to India in April

2017 and President Putin on the eve of Prime Minister Modi's visit to St. Petersburg in early June, 2017.

There is greater dependence on the media as nations are getting increasingly involved in promoting their own images. Launching of different India Brands such as 'India Shining', 'Incredible India', 'India Awakening', results in their increasing reliance on the media. Prime Minister Modi has now launched another Brand, 'New India'. On the other hand, even the media, to promote itself, is involving itself in such image building exercises, such as 'India Poised' initiative by the Times of India and holding of annual summits, 'HT Summit' by the Hindustan Times. Another initiative 'Amman ki Asha' (Quest for Peace) jointly launched by the Times of India and the Pakistani Newspaper 'The Jung' is a step in this direction.

## The Role of the Media in Foreign Policy

In this globalised world communication has become an essential component of way of life. Leaders, therefore, have a felt need to send their message to a larger audience and the media fits this bill. Media coverage, therefore, becomes an index of measuring the success or otherwise of a visit. It is also not only about column inches, but its placement, be it on the front page or not. Did it garner any editorials? Even the critics are forced to succumb to the same media (Sardesai, Rajdeep, 2014). It was, therefore, not surprising to see dignitaries succumbing to such weakness. The Chinese Prime Minister Li wanted his visit to India in March, 2013, to be covered on front pages (The Tribune, 2013).

The role of the media in foreign policy has largely remained the same and globalisation has not in any way changed that. The traditional role is that as a 'Channel of Communication/Dissemination' in conveying international news to the larger audience. This is universally recognized and no government can afford to overlook this role, except at its own cost. The relevance and the reach of the media, to a large extent, depends on the successful operation of a "Three I's" formula – flow of 'Information' from the Establishment; 'Independence' of reporting by the media; while both maintaining their respective 'Integrity'.

The media also plays other roles, as an educator, in generating greater awareness on international issues through well written and researched articles. This role is debatable, seen from the perspective of a purist, as a certain amount of editorial bias cannot be ruled out. It also performs the function of a facilitator, in becoming a vehicle for voicing the views of experts, on foreign policy issues. Debates through the media on India-USA Civil Nuclear Cooperation Agreement and India-Pakistan relations bear testimony to this trend.

Media also functions as a source of opinion through its 'Editorials and Opeds' which could serve as useful inputs in the formulation of foreign policy. It also plays the role as a 'Medium of Change'. The changes in East Europe and the breakup of the Soviet Union during late 80s and early 90s have been described as 'TV Revolution' by commentators, as TV became an instrumentality in accelerating the pace of change in those countries.

The Media thus plays an important role, as a source in providing greater connectivity at the people to people level and help in changing the mindset. India's External Affairs Minister Pranab Mukherjee and Foreign Secretary Shiv Shanker Menon, in their addresses to the SAARC Editors' Conference on February 9-10, 2007, had placed an increasing emphasis on this aspect of the role of the media.

## Coverage of International Scene in the Indian Print Media

The coverage of international news/views in the Indian Media is more extensive compared to other countries, as there is a greater interest in international affairs in the public in India. It displays much more vibrancy, diversity and independence. Its coverage of the international scene compares well with the media in any other country of the world. It provides a larger canvas, as it uses a good mix of reports, opeds, editorials, photos and cartoons.

The Media, however, still relies largely on the Western sources through tie ups with different international groups, such as The Tribune with The Washington Post and the Los Angeles Times; The Indian Express with The Independent; The Hindu with The Guardian and The Times of India with the New York Times Group.

There are, however, some tie-ups with Media Groups from other countries in the globe. The Tribune has an arrangement with 'The Dawn'; so does the Indian Express with 'The Nation' in Pakistan. This results in providing space for weekly columns.

Such collaborative arrangements with other developing countries are largely missing. This deprives the readers of getting an Asian perspective, which is essential as India enters the portals of the so-called 'Asian Century'. This reliance on the western media is also partially the result of the absence of Indian foreign correspondents in other countries.

The regional media is also paying attention to the international scene although it is largely based on similar coverage in the English edition of those Papers that exist. The international coverage is not as prominent as in the English Dailies.

## Trump's Inaugural Address and Press Coverage in India-A Case Study

Let us look at how Indian Print Media covered the Inaugural Address of US President Donald Trump on January 20, 2017. Trump did not receive complimentary coverage in the mainstream Indian Press, as there was more negativity than positivity. Headlines reporting his inaugural address and protests by women were quite uncharitable to him. These included 'Donald to be sworn in amid likely protests' or 'From Russia with love' showing Putin as the second lady (The Times of India, Jan. 20, 2017). The others were equally catchy as these projected protectionist agenda of the President, such as 'Protectionist Trump, Buy American, Hire American' (The Times of India, Jan. 21, 2017); 'US wakes up to a New Protectionist Don' (The Times of India, Jan. 21, 2017).

The Hindu, characteristic of its sobriety was sober in reporting, 'The era of Donald Trump begins in America' (Jan. 21, 2017); another headlined spoke about uncertainty about the New Don (The Hindustan Times); while another projected his commitment to fight Islamic terrorism, 'Will eradicate radical Islamic terrorism' (The Indian Express, Jan. 21, 2017). Another newspaper projected his single minded personality, with headlines like 'His ferocious efforts lead him to White House'.

Opeds and lead articles were full of scepticism and concern over the Trump Presidency, as the media greeted him with headlines, 'Build bridges, not walls', (The Tribune, Jan. 21, 2017); captioning his photograph with his fist' sign, headlined 'America's new face' (The Hindu, Jan. 21, 2017); 'Hail the Protectionist-in-chief' (The Hindustan Times, Jan. 21, 2017), 'Autumn and its discontent' (The Hindu, Jan. 21, 2017).

On the other hand, Obama got positive billing, like 'Obama ends on a note of optimism' (The Hindu, Jan. 20, 2017); 'Obama's parting words, We're going to be OK' (The Tribune, Jan. 20, 2017); 'Barak Obama calls PM Modi, thanks him for strategic partnership' (The Times of India, Jan. 20, 2017). Obama's trust in American strength in diversity was echoed in headlines, 'In future US can have Hindu prez' (The Times of India, Jan. 20, 2017), or 'One day US may have a Hindu President: Obama' (The Hindu, Jan. 20, 2017).

Concerns about the Trump presidency continued to be covered before and after the Inauguration. He received headlines in editorials 'Redefining leadership, Obama makes way for Trump and shallowness' (The Tribune, Jan. 20, 2017); 'Why Trump can't be Reagan'. Overall the coverage was mirror image of the liberal media in USA.

## Media Scene in India

What distinguishes media scene in India is its vastness, its reach and its diversity. India is 'one of the major publication hubs of the world with 94067 registered publications including 12511 newspapers and 81556 periodicals (The Hindu, 2014). Doordarshan which is in the public sector has 37 channels itself, with over 250 FM radio stations. These provide coverage in the national and regional languages, covering urban and rural areas. The media scene in India 'veers from reasoned debate, understated expression and moderation in views, to polemical overstatement, hysterical outpouring and plain misinformation' (Vice President, 2013).

What are the salient features of the media scene in India? It covers the Old Media, the New Media and the Social Media. It is both in the public and the private sector. There is growing presence of the private sector, resulting in diminishing the monopoly of the government-controlled media. It is highly professional in nature and has a good cadre of journalists, who can compete on a global basis. It adopts both traditional and investigative approaches and has largely discharged its democratic responsibilities; even though at times it has suffered from over zealousness.

Mushrooming of newspapers, radio and TV channels have introduced an element of competitiveness. This vast expanse and diversity has helped in safeguarding freedom of the press. It is largely self-regulatory in nature. There is near total freedom of press, based on the right of free speech and expression. It has simultaneously resulted in cross-media ownership, which narrows the control in a few hands.

Media coverage during January, 2014 on the issue of diplomatic immunity to Devyani Khobragade, Deputy Consul General of India at New York, is illustrative of a triple mix of news, views and editorial, as could be glanced through the following news items:

- 'Choosing goodwill over raucous', Op.ed by Prabhu Dayal, (The Hindu, 7 January 2014);
- 'Under Shadow of Devyani case, US puts off meeting'(Front Page, The Hindu, 10 January)

- 'Little to Celebrate' (editorial), (The Hindu, 12 January 2014).
- 'Diplomatic Immunity brings Devyani Home' (The Hindu, 12 January 2014).

## Media's Connectivity Role

How does media connect with the readers? As stated earlier, it does it through news and views. News, which simply means reporting, should be a neutral phenomenon. Even then, in practice, the newspapers can affect the outcome in a number of ways. This could be through the selection of the news, its placement whether on the front pages or not or keeping it alive for a longer period of time or through catchy and attractive headlines.

Visit of the Chinese Prime Minister Li to India in March, 2013 received greater attention, as it found its place on the front pages. This was, however, not the case with the visit of the General Secretary of the Communist Party of Vietnam, who paid a visit to India in November 2013, even though certain momentous decisions were taken during that visit.

An Oped headlined, 'India-Turkey relations: Turkish delight turned sour' conveyed the message that the visit of the Turkish President Erdogan to India in April 2017 was not highly successful (Rakesh Sood, 2017). On the other hand, Bangladeshi Prime Minister Sheikh Hasina's visit was positively billed in an editorial as a 'Transformative Visit' (The Hindu, 2017).

The Headlines, on the other hand, provide an opportunity to the editor, to give a slant/twist, as no headlines can be neutral, despite best efforts. The Hindu's Readers Editor Panneerselvan would like headlines writers to keep in view the golden words of Harold Evans, "The art of the headline lies in imagination and vocabulary: the craft lies in accuracy of content, attractiveness of appearance and practicality' (Panneerselvan, 2013: 3).

## Foreign Policy Establishments Connecting with the Media

The Foreign Policy Establishment – Media Connectivity has to be seen as a two-way channel, as both are required to work in tandem – the Foreign Establishments as a source of news and the Media as a communicator/ disseminator to the public at large. The Media plays an important role as a purveyor or conveyer of news, with or without comments. It also plays another role, as an original source of information.

Connectivity is integral to any media activity. This essentially involves connecting to sources of information and how reliable and diverse these are. Vice President of India, Hamid Ansari highlighted that 'what remains crucial is the credibility and commitment of the Press and Media to objectivity and to that elusive search for truth' (Vice President, 2013).

How do Foreign Policy Establishments connect with the Media? They achieve this through regular press briefings; dissemination of publicity material; arranging interviews and issuing statements of leaders, promoting exchange of journalists and publishing signed articles. In an article, British Foreign Secretary William Hague urged the Sri Lankan government to fix accountability for war crimes in the interest of long-term peace (Hague, William 2014). Earlier, the Chinese Prime Minister Li Kesiang launched his visit to India in May 2013 with a lead article written by him (Li Kesiang, 2013).

Let us now look at some situations, as these throw light on the strength and pitfalls of such connectivity. It has to be ensured that the media is not seen to be embedded with the establishment, even though the media has to rely heavily on information from official sources. It is here that the Foreign Policy Establishment faces the challenge. Let us look at coverage of some events/incidents, like 'Coverage of the Kargil War with Pakistan in 1999'; 'The Terrorist Attacks on Mumbai in November, 2008' and the 'Beheading of a Soldier across LOC in January, 2013'.

The Media-Foreign Policy Establishment connectivity was at its best at the time of the Kargil War, through daily press briefings, jointly given by the spokespersons of the Ministries of External Affairs and Defence. It was at its weakest at the time of the Mumbai Terrorist Attacks in 2008, as here media went overboard and in its zeal to provide '24x7 Coverage'; it jeopardized national security interests. Similarly, in the case of LOC skirmishes in January 2013, the same was overtaken by hysterical reporting, bordering on jingoism and thereby stifling the dialogue process.

## External Publicity and Public Diplomacy (XPD) Division Connecting with the Media

How does the Foreign Policy Establishment, the Ministry of External Affairs (MEA) in India connect with the media? India has created its own instrumentalities like the External Publicity Division and the Public Diplomacy (XPP) Division. Earlier, the External Publicity (XP) Division was the nodal point. Later, its activities were supplemented by the Public Diplomacy (PD) Division, which became the outreach arm of the MEA.

PD Division was created in 2006 with the objective of image building of India. This was broadly based on the pattern followed by the United States and the United Kingdom.

PD Division was merged with the XP Division in 2014 and now stands re-designated as External Publicity and Public Diplomacy (XPD) Division. Joint Secretary, XP Division is the official spokesperson, who maintains regular links with the media. This Division also brings out its own publications, and other publicity material, including films and books. Some of the functions of the PD Division were transferred to the Coordination Division.

The XPP Division oversees bilateral agreements on media-related issues? It has created regional institutional frameworks like the SAARC Editors Forum, BRICS Media Forum and Africa Media Forum. It facilitates media exchanges among journalists. It has created its own website, which is MEA's window to the world and was adjudged as the best in the Government of India. India, however, does not have a dedicated 24x7 TV/Radio channel to telecast and broadcast international news that are of interest to it, unlike many other countries. This idea had been broached, but so far it has not much headway.

The Ministry of External Affairs in India provides media connectivity at two levels, firstly at the Headquarters and secondly at the Diplomatic Missions abroad. At the Ministry of External Affairs, Joint Secretary (XP) is the focal point, who also acts as the official spokesperson for the Ministry of External Affairs. He provides all the connectivity with the Media. He uses standard instrumentalities, such as Press Briefings and Press Releases.

At the Headquarters, Prime Minister's Senior Media Adviser provided the necessary connectivity between the PM and the Media. Unlike other Prime Ministers, Prime Minister Modi does not have a designated Media Advisor. Senior officials and the Minister of External Affairs also provide direct briefings from time to time, as required.

Increasingly Internet is becoming the intermediary between the Joint Secretary (XP) and the Media, supplementing regular press briefings through SMS Alerts. The Ministry maintains an up-to-date website, which provides essential information on foreign policy related issues. It arranges familiarization trips for the foreign media and facilitates training of media personnel at the Foreign Service Institute. It maintains a website containing important foreign policy documents such as Speeches, Declarations, Statements, and other Background materials.

At the Diplomatic Missions, the Ambassador himself and the Press Attaché provide connectivity with the Media. In fact, Ambassador is a glorified Public Relations Officer (PRO) for his country. He has to develop an all weather relationship with the media, as a need-based approach would not suffice. Weekly Radio Broadcasts have been launched in the diplomatic missions.

The Media, on its part, plays its role also through well established channels, primarily reporting by its foreign correspondents, interviews by editors of visiting foreign dignitaries, as well as accompanying Indian dignitaries visiting abroad, writing special dispatches and providing country coverage on important occasions. The Media is expected to perform its role as a non-aligned player in its coverage of news and views.

In the case of India, the role of Indian foreign correspondents has diminished, since only a handful of them are posted abroad; either for budgetary constraints or lack of reciprocal arrangements. The Hindu is the only paper, which has a fairly good representation of foreign correspondents abroad, especially in those countries, which are of significant importance for our international relations. Their presence helps in getting the news from an Indian perspective.

External Publicity and Public Diplomacy (XPD) Division described 2015-16 as 'a year of transformational diplomacy'. It published a detailed booklet in May 2015 titled 'Transformational Diplomacy' to highlight foreign policy achievements of the government. A supplementary booklet titled, 'Diplomacy of Development: From Aspirations to Achievements', dealt with 13 key themes on the issue of diplomacy, development and national resurgence (MEA, 2015-16).

The Division's primary focus has been to work in a coordinated fashion to tell 'India story' on selected themes, reaching out directly to the media; through the medium of documentaries and publications and connecting with social media (Syed Akbaruddin). A special page was created on the MEA website on the International Day of Yoga (IDY) to mark IDY on June 21, 2015 and to mark the 125th Birth Anniversary of Dr. B.R. Ambedkar. One of the most important interactive programmes of the Division is the Distinguished Lecture Series since 2010, to allow connectivity with educational institution with former Indian Ambassadors.

XPD Division's biggest achievement is the use of social media with an aggregate following of 3.8 million, with monthly outreach crossing 17.5 million posts in Twitter and 15 million on Facebook (MEA, 2015-16).

Surya Prakash, Chairman of Prasar Bharati has mooted a proposal to set up a 24x7 Digital Platform to report on international news to a global digital audience. This apparently was in response to sharp reaction in the foreign media to the appointment of Yogi Adityanath, as Chief Minister of the State of Uttar Pradesh (Zehra Kazmi, 2017). Its aim would be tell the "India story" to challenge the anti-India narrative in foreign media (Smriti Kak Ramchandran, 2017).

## Twitter Diplomacy and MEA

Media scene is undergoing transformation, as more and more leaders are using social media, as a way of direct connectivity with people. For President Trump it is to bypass the mainstream media, which for him has come to mean only 'Fake News'. In this post-truth age, distinction between facts and fictions is disappearing, as truth is a matter of belief. 'Alternative Facts' are dished out to prove a point.

For Prime Minister Modi, it is a matter of tactical convenience, as it helps him in choosing the occasion, time and place, as he is good in communication skills in directly connecting with people and establishing rapport with them. Both the Indian President and Vice-President complimented Prime Minister for his extraordinary communication skills. The President called him as "one of the most effective communicators of the times" (The Times of India 2017).

A study conducted by Professor Joyojeet Pal at the University of Michigan came to the conclusion that Prime Minister Modi had built a powerful online brand image as a tech-savvy global leader and the social media feed has become the primary source of the Prime Minister's opinions (Financial Express, 2016). He had a following of 20 million at his Twitter handle Narendra Modi and 4 million on his institutional account @PMOIndia as in June 2016. He was one of the top ten leaders with the most Twitter followers.

It is not only PM Modi, who had a following of 30 million, but EAM Sushma Swaraj also touched a figure of 5 million followers, becoming the $10^{th}$ most followed female world leaders, as per the 2016 'Twiplomacy', a study by global communications giant Burson-Marstelle (Twiplomacy, 2016). Sushma Swaraj has established her credentials as a people-friendly minister for her prompt response in addressing the concerns of Indian diaspora. Among the foreign ministries, the US State Department was followed by 3.3 million persons as against MEA's 'Indian Diplomacy' with 1.3 million followers.

## Media and Social Responsibility

Media connectivity automatically takes us to the next stage, as to how does it relate to 'Social Responsibility'. Does or should media have 'Social Responsibility'? This issue frequently crops up, as we face the phenomenon of 'Paid News' and 'Advertorials' that are replacing Editorials, given their high revenue value. There is an erosion of demarcation of boundaries between 'journalism, public relations, advertising and entertainment' (Vice President, 2011).

The 18th Anniversary celebrations of the Chandigarh Edition of the Hindustan Times (HT) on April 18, 2018 provided an opportunity for leaders and opinion makers to voice their opinions on the role of the media and the challenges it faced. The leaders suggested the newspaper to take up 'apolitical issues', and focus on 'governments rather than personalities'. The media should also highlight socio-economic issues, such as agriculture, peace and communal harmony.

The media was also alerted 'to stay a step ahead of social media'. Equally, the media has to bear in mind public expections. HT editor-in-chief Sukumar Ranganathan acknowledged that in this age of 'instant fake news', people looked towards 'a clear, credible, sane, trustworthy voice'. He reiterated HT's goal 'to provide across platforms, an unbiased, clear-minded journalism' (The Hindustan times, 2018).

There is a strong belief that media does have social responsibility. How this can be ensured, is a debatable issue? Questions are asked, whether media needs to be regulated or allowed to self-regulate itself. The opinion in UK and India is moving in the direction of regulation, as self-regulations have failed to deliver. Whatever the steps that may be taken, it has to be ensured that the integrity and the independence of the media is maintained, through adherence of 'accepted norms of journalistic ethics and maintenance of high standards of professional conduct' (Vice President, 2012).

Media has also to vouch for a greater sense of social responsibility in the coverage of international news. This is important as such coverage directly impacts on the issues of war and peace and can affect the future discourse between peoples and nations. Should media be constrained, as this question was raised after media's coverage of the Mumbai Terrorists' Attack in November 2008? There have to be some constraints on the coverage of events, embracing national security, whether these are self imposed by the media or devised by a Media Regulatory Body. Some restrictions were placed on the coverage on the Terrorist Attack in Pathankot in January 2016.

## Media as a Bridge Builder

Finally, how do we view media's role as a bridge builder? Can we come to any firm conclusion, based on an understanding of our interests and desires and the ground realities as these exist. Media has played a dual role, as it has transmitted both negative and positive images. These images were largely a reflection of developments, although media-hypes tending to sensationalize nationalism at times had resulted in giving it a slant. Media, therefore, has played the role of not only a 'Bridge Builder' but also that of a 'Bridge Destroyer'.

Earlier, in the text of this Chapter, it had been noted how media had played this role in covering certain specific events. Let us look at some other examples, where the media had sent an unmistakable message. It played the role of a bridge builder, in reporting on Bomb Blasts in the Samjautha Express at Panipat (India) in February 2007. A cartoon captured the mood, showing the leaders standing next to the railway track, with a caption 'Track is not damaged'. On the other hand, the central message that emanated from the media coverage of the Terrorist Attacks in Mumbai, in November 2008, was that 'It's War' and the 'Nation is under Attack'. This certainly destroyed the bridge that was being built through dialogue between India and Pakistan, as the peace process got a setback.

The visit of Prime Minister Sheikh Hasina of Bangladesh to India in April 2017 was described as 'A Bridge from Kolkata to Dhaka' (HT ed. Apr. 11) and considered as a 'Transformative Visit (The Hindu, April 11). On the other hand, death sentence awarded to a former Indian Naval Officer, Kulbhushan Jadhav in April, 2017 by Pakistan allegedly charged for sedition and terrorism received strong disapprobation with editorials headlined, 'A Bizarre charade' (IE April 12), 'Judicial Murder' (TOI April 12), which echoed the statement of the External Affairs Minister Sushma Swaraj. While another newspaper headlined it 'Risky, ill-considered' (The Hindu, April 12) and yet another one headlined 'Jadhav's death sentence' (The Tribune, April 12), kept the possibility of reprieve still open. Here the media reflected the nation's mood.

Let us look at the situation from the regional perspective of SAARC. Connectivity has also emerged as an important theme at the SAARC Summits. Such meetings also result in sending a message. The warm embrace ('Jhappi') between Prime Minister Vajpayee and Prime Minister Jamali of Pakistan at the Lahore Summit in January 2004 sent positive vibes for a better relationship. On the other hand, on an earlier occasion at the SAARC Summit at Kathmandu in January 2002, a cold handshake between Musharraf and Vajpayee sent a negative message. The media, therefore, has a role to play, even though it is faithfully conveying the text. PM Modi and Nawaz Sharif just exchanged greetings, when the two came across each other at the Summit at Astana in June 2017, sending a message that all was not well between the two countries (Nikhil Agarwal, 2017).

This raises the question, what matters. Is it the 'Message' (Text) or the 'Messenger' (Media)? While it is true that it is the message that is of paramount importance, but the media has a role cut out for itself in conveying the same message. To enable it playing the role of a bridge builder, we need sync between the message and the messenger. Prime Minister Modi cautioned the leaders not to speak out of turn and give half-baked news, which provided "masala" to the media and then blame the media. While performing the role of a messenger, the leaders have to ensure that they should give that message which was in their domain (Akhilesh Singh, 2018). It is also essential that there is plurality of views and freedom of press and greater connectivity between the media and its sources, as this acts as a restraint on hyper-presentation.

## Media Evaluating Media-Foreign Policy Establishment Connectivity

In this part, we are having a critical evaluation of the role of the Media, as seen by senior editors and journalists. This is based on a response and interaction of the author with them on a set of questions.

What role does Media play? Media plays an important role in generating awareness of international affairs (S. Nihal Singh)[1]. It is considered to 'be positive, by and large' (Vijay Naik). Such a role becomes limited, as it depends upon 'what is fed by the government, especially MEA, more specifically by XP Division' (Mahendra Ved)[2]. It largely depends upon 'the dissemination of information by the Ministry of External Affairs as well as on information that media gets from informal but authoritative sources' (Vijay Naik)[3].

What importance is given to coverage of international news by the media? It depends upon the availability of space, which is a major constraint, as 'foreign affairs is not among the high priorities' and a foreign desk editor fights a losing battle, as 'politics and local issues dominate the space' (Mahendra Ved). This results in the media getting 'obsessed with Pakistan', given the troubled history of relations between India and Pakistan (Nihal Singh).

The coverage, therefore, remains 'Pakistan centric' and would remain so, given a number of historical issues between India and Pakistan, which have 'a direct impact on people' (Vijay Naik). The coverage, therefore, remains 'basically Pakistan-oriented and when there are occasional leaks from foreign media or by MEA, it is China – mostly anti-China – like border incursions' (Mahendra Ved). Availability of experts from the academia, retired diplomats and generals also helps. Jingoism is creeping in to the TV debates, which have 'lost meaning' (Vijay Naik).

Should media play connectivity role? There was diversity of views. One interlocutor held the view that media's role is 'to report honestly', but people to people connectivity could be 'a by-product' (Nihal Singh). The other interlocutor felt that media should and does help in bringing about connectivity (Mahendra Ved). To promote such connectivity, what was needed was a joint venture approach between the media, government and think tanks (Vijay Naik). South Asia Forum for Media Association (SAFMA) was involved in providing such connectivity among people and journalists. SAFMA presently was dysfunctional and even SAARC Visa had been put in cold storage. The Public Diplomacy Association under the Ministry of Foreign Affairs, Government of China had taken an initiative to invite two Indian journalists for a ten month reporting experience in 2016 (Vijay Naik).

Was 'Jingoism' creeping in the coverage of news in the media? It was becoming more visible, as this was a part of the growing divisiveness in the society, between 'us' and 'them'; of people abroad you do not like and 'us' and 'you' in the domestic arena; where people are told 'what to wear, what to eat, and what slogans to be raised to prove your patriotism' (Mahendra Ved).

Media takes the cue as 'jingoism' is promoted by political leaders, resulting in every issue and every debate degenerating into 'us' and 'them', with considerable trolling done to browbeat dissenters (Mahendra Ved). While it is true that 'nationalist and chauvinist feelings inevitably influence media', but it depended upon the nature of the media whether such feelings 'are presented soberly' (Nihal Singh). The growth of 'regional media and electronic channels has also resulted in growing nationalist or chauvinist slant' (Vijay Naik).

What triggers Media's coverage of international events? Media's presentation of international events is determined 'by readers' interests, the nature of events and the sagacity of the editorial team' (Nihal Singh). Of course, 'editorial priority is on what sells' (Mahendra Ved). 'China and Pakistan sell; so does USA and Europe. On the other hand, Southeast Asia is not on the news radar, even when there is so much interaction; whole Central Asia that is projected as extended neighbourhood, is blacked out'.

Editorial preference is also dictated 'by media preference for English speaking sources', resulting in lack of interest in Japan or South Korea, despite greater commercial connectivity and preference for cars or other electronic goods (Mahendra Ved). Terrorism related events also result in countries like Iraq, Syria, Turkey, making the grade for the coverage of news (Naik).

Should Media play the connectivity role? It is media's role to 'report honestly', 'generate awareness' but not to play the role of 'a connector' (Nihal Singh). The pragmatic view, however, is that it is a combination of factors, which prevent media to play such a role. These include, over reliance on Internet and Google, unwillingness to go beyond stereotypes and lack of interest in research. Given financial constraints, energies are directed towards marketing. While this is the case of mainstream media, 'yet dailies like Malayala Manorama, Anand Bazar Patrika, Saket, Dainik Bhaskar have shown keen interest in the coverage of international events' (Vijay Naik).

How does the Ministry of External Affairs (MEA) connect with the Media? The Ministry of External Affairs uses External Publicity Division to promote its views through domestic and international media (Nihal Singh). MEA has successfully resorted to social media, Facebook, Twitter etc and has facilitated information flow 24 x 7 to meet the requirements of media operations and needs. The long wait for XP press releases 'is over and overall approach has become upfront and transparent with JSXP fielding even inconvenient questions' (Mahendra Ved).

MEA was also playing a positive role in promoting connectivity through the media by arranging media exchange programmes over many years in most of the countries that matter to India 'in promoting better understanding and for spreading India Brand image' (Vijay Naik). It is promoting media connectivity through initiatives such as the India-Africa Editors Forum, India-China Editors Forum, which held two meeting in 2015 and the BRICS Media Forum which held meeting in Goa in November 2016.

What role does JSXP play? In any publicity efforts, 'effectiveness of the Foreign Office communicating with foreign media and people at large depends upon the person in charge. India has largely succeeded as it had very distinguished and effective men in charge' (Nihal Singh). There is an 'overall satisfaction with MEA's efforts in maintaining best relations with foreign media in India and through our Missions abroad' (Vijay Naik).

How important are the Information Advisers to the Prime Minister? They have played an important role and some of the well known stalwarts were Sharda Prasad and B.G. Varghese. The role of Information Advisor had come under strain and pressure, given the mammoth growth in the number of agencies, TV channels and journalists. Prime Minister Modi has dispensed with the office of Information Advisor as he is relying on social media for direct connectivity with people. Some concern was expressed by the media personnel over this lack of communication between the prime minister and the media, 'which is not a good sign for democracy' (Vijay Naik).

Does India need its own foreign dedicated channel? While it was felt that it was for the government to decide, whether it should have its own propaganda arm, yet the absence of a credible Indian international agency like the AP, AFP, Reuter, UPI was noted. India's focus on 'development journalism has impeded India's news outreach globally.' A need was, therefore, felt for India having an independent channel on the lines of BBC and CNN. The government should consider setting up DD's Global Channel to project India's global views, but 'to preserve and to maintain credibility, it will have to be professional to the core in its character' (Vijay Naik). India ought to have a national TV channel and one way would be to run DD on professional lines, while insulating it from political and administrative interference.

What steps should be taken by MEA to promote media's role in bridging trust deficit? Some of the suggestions made included, recreating the post of the media advisor to the Prime Minister; increasing the frequency of off and on media briefings and holding of annual press conferences by the Prime Minister.

## Media Meeting Challenges as Image and Connectivity Builder

We are witnessing a new phenomenon, where the mainstream media is being questioned and it is getting bypassed and its role challenged. It is being demonized as 'news traders', 'pressitute' and merchants of 'fake news'. This has resulted in a new lexicon 'post-truth', where fiction is fact and another new jargon 'alternative truth' is being used. The credibility of the mainstream media has come down. The Minister of Information and Broadcasting Smriti Irani struck a note for ensuring credibility, as she said that the 'journalist is not the last word on the narrative of any event' (The Hindu, 2018).

While President Donald Trump has thrown the gauntlet to the American media, yet the media in India has also come under criticism for its integrity, at the present juncture, what the Vice President Hamid Ansari called the '24x 7 agitations of television channels'. He urged the editors to withstand the pressures of breaking news in the interest of 'accurate, impartial and fair reporting' (Aditi Tandon, 2017).

Panneerselvan, the Hindu's Readers Editor would like editors to keep in view the timely advice of David Remnick, who said that 'what is most important is the integrity of what we publish and what we stand for'.

Twiplomacy has set in motion a new trend, where 'Television news has begun to feel the pressure of social media' and Twitter trends determine the content hierarchy of a news bulletin' (Burkha Dutt, 2013). Twitter Diplomacy, however, has its pitfalls as many Indian leaders have seen to their dismay.

Twitter Diplomacy also runs the risk from its inherent weakness, as it calls for briskness, speed, promptness and not well thought out remarks. It has raised concerns as to when would Trump come out of Twitter Diplomacy. What is required by diplomats and readers in this 'Age of Newspeak' are 'facts and depth, wide and varied reportage, critical analysis and insight opinion' (Salil Desai, 2016).

In his interview with Prince Harry, which was telecast on BBC on December 27, 2017, President Obama made some profound remarks on the debilitating impact of Internet in these words, "One of the dangers of the internet is that people can have entirely different realities. They can be just cocooned in information that reinforces their current biases". This is the danger in this Internet Age and Twitter Diplomacy, where we are becoming hostage to opinions of like minded persons.

Media has a role as an image builder that could promote connectivity by generating awareness and thus emerging as a bridge builder. It has not been an easy role, as images keep shifting with the changing of the text. We do not expect the 'Media' to become the mirror image of the Foreign Policy Establishment. We do, however, expect it to emerge as a player that is alive to the sensitivities and concerns of the nation and the people. Could it emerge as a promoter of peace; the views are divided?

We live in a complex and competing world. The connectivity is still not up to the desired levels. India, like other countries, would like to see 'the "India story" in a positive, accurate and focused perspective', as the then Indian President Pranab Mukherjee observed in 2014. On the other hand, concerns are expressed over broken relationship between the media and the government (The Indian Express, 2014:2). A healthy environment is essential that allows the media to operate in an independent manner; while media itself has to ensure that it maintains the highest standards of integrity.

Media should not widen the chasm that divides nations and peoples, just to score some brownie points or improve its TRP Ratings. To enable it do so, we need to provide an environment, where it can operate in an independent, free and competitive manner. We need to promote freer movement of materials and persons, as happened in 2013, when Indian media was allowed to cover the General Elections in Pakistan. This, we need to do at the bilateral and regional levels.

It is interesting that while foreign countries are outsourcing their services to Indian software industry, Indian Media is outsourcing its news sources to the Western newspapers, thereby bringing a western bias in the stories selected through arrangement with the Guardian, New York Times, Washington Post, the Independent etc. This outsourcing results in greater impact on the mind, as it is the best story that wins, where ideas score over technology.

If we dream of a pluralist world and world leaders want to play not a 'solitaire' but a bridge foursome, then the Media also has to play its role in conveying ideas from pluralist sources, which could include countries such as Russia, China, Singapore, Egypt, South Africa etc. so as to widen the horizons of its readers.

It is strange that the presence of foreign correspondents representing Indian newspapers is declining abroad, at a time when there should be a need to increase their presence, in view of the emergence of India as a global player. This weakness is noticeable, even if it is accepted that the role of foreign correspondents, per se, has declined over the years, given the technological advancement, bridging the space and time.

One blind spot, as far as Indian Media is concerned, is that it suffers from darkness in its direct coverage of the news in its neighbourhood, in particular, Pakistan because of constraint in the free flow of media personal and products. This issue has been talked about at different fora but nothing concrete has happened, despite the vigorous efforts made even by South Asia Foreign Media Association (SAFMA).

The national consensus on foreign policy is ceasing to exist, as political parties view it from their narrow and partisan agendas. This vests Media with greater responsibility in projecting competing view points and it thus places a greater responsibility on its shoulders.

Do we view Media as a passive or an active player? It is debatable and depends upon the perspective from which we view its role. Nonetheless, its primary role still remains that of a communicator and not as an educator. Can it become more pro-active, not only as an important source of information, but also as an instrument of policy formulation? Should more initiatives like 'Amman ki Asha' (Hope for Peace) be encouraged? Should it play an advocacy role?

Image building is largely about perceptions, as seen by others. The Media plays an important role in the process leading to building of images, both indirectly and at times also directly. Its coverage of news and emphasis creates a great impact.

The Guest Editor approach of the Times of India provides an interesting opportunity to tune into the views of users. A foreign policy expert becoming a Guest Editor would certainly help in focusing on foreign policy issues.

The Media also directly impacts through its own image building exercise, as being recently undertaken by the Times of India in its "India Poised" Programme or by the Hindustan Times in its Annual Summits or by India Today at its 'India Conclaves'.

Media and Foreign Policy interface is seen in different light by Media experts/diplomats. It is viewed as an adversarial relationship (Marvin Kalb, formerly of NBC, USA); as between step-sisters (Navtej Sarna, India's then Official Spokesman) or as 'pussy cats' (Anthony Lewis NYT) or as neither a foe nor a friend (Simon Serfaty). The author would, however, like to place this relationship as between two partners, who need to cooperate with each other to understand developments in proper perspective, before dressing the same in the news format.

Can Media and Foreign Policy Establishments work as partners in a notional framework of public private partnership (PPP), which helps in promoting national interest, without jeopardizing the responsibilities and functional requirements of each other? This should be possible if each one respects the independence and the professional requirements of the other. Ultimately, they both have a similar goal; to serve the broader interest of the nation, while performing their respective roles.

We may consider instituting a mechanism, whereby the External Affairs Minister can interact with the Media and the other Think Tanks prior to the budgetary session, on the pattern of Finance Minister's consultations with the financial experts and the business community.

The relationship between the Foreign Policy and the Media can be seen as between a Product and its Marketing, to use the commercial terminology. It is equally about the 'Message' and the Messenger'; the 'Text' then becomes important. If India has inherent strength, then there is bound to be acceptance of its role in the international arena, as a credible partner in managing 'evolving global, economic and political order'.

Finally there is a need for an honest relationship between the Media and the Foreign Policy Establishment. A successful modem would necessitate the Establishment playing with a straight bat and the Media avoid rebounding with 'googlies', to use the cricket terminology, especially when 2017 turned out to be the best year, with India regaining top ranking.

The Media has to play the role of blowing the wind from diverse sources and perspectives, as Mahatma Gandhi wanted to receive fresh ideas from all directions with an open mind. Does the Establishment need its own Channel for building its image or should India stand on its strength and let BBC, CNN or Fox do the rest? The latter would be a better alternative for image building, unless we are able to set up our own credible outfit, as credibility is the key to success.

The Media also has to follow the advice of the late Prime Minister Nehru, given on August 14, 1954, which still holds good and thus ultimately perform its role as a provider of news, as stated by him, "by providing a correct background, the newspapers could exercise continuous presence and bring about a change in public opinion".

The Media and Foreign Policy Establishments are not to see each other as adversaries or two step-sisters or as a hero or a villain. They have to perceive each other as partners, with each one performing its own respective functions, while serving national interest.

Annexure 1

## Cultural Diplomacy – Media Questionnaire

1. What role has media played in generating awareness in international relations?
2. What has been the focus area for coverage of news/views? Is it largely Pakistan-centric?
3. Should media help in bringing connectivity among peoples?
4. How far nationalistic/chauvinistic feelings guided the presentation of the news?
5. What is the editorial priority in covering international events?
6. What are the constraints encountered by the media, in playing its role as a connector and generating awareness?
7. How do you view the role of the Ministry of External Affairs in promoting connectivity through the media?
8. Would you like to comment upon MEA's programme on connecting with foreign media and people at large?
9. What is the role played by PM's Press Advisor?
10. Do we need a dedicated TV channel, like CCTV, Japanese or Russian channel?
11. How has the SAARC Media initiative worked? If not, then how could it be made more effective?
12. What steps should be taken by MEA to promote media's role in bridging trust deficit?

## Endnotes

1. Nihal Singh, S, Writer, Former Editor, Senior Jornalist, Columnist. Response to a Questionnaire on January 10, 2016.
2. Mahendra Ved, Columnist, President, Commonwealth Journalists Association (CJA). Response to a Questionnaire on October 19, 2016.
3. Vijay Naik, Journalist, Author, Political Commentator and Analyst. Convener - Indian Association of Foreign Affairs Correspondents. Response to a Questionnaire on March 20, 2016.

## References

Aditi Tandon, 2017, 'VP provokes editors: "24X7 agitation" putting pressures', *The Tribune*, March 2.

Akhilesh Singh, 2018,'Don't blame media for your mistakes: PM to motormouths', *The Times of India,* April 23.

Amit Dasgupta and Shaun Star, 2017, 'India and Australia are on a learning curve', *Hindustan Times*, April 12.

British DJ to hold a gig on Everest, 2017. *The Hindu*, April 11.

Barkha Dutt, 2013, 'Silence is not an option', *The Hindustan Times*, November 23.

Chopra, Shaili. 2014, 'The timeline warriors', *The Hindu*, March 20.

Dixit, Rekha, 2014, 'Celebrating Integrity', *The Week*, March 23.

EAM, 2007, Pranab Mukherjee's Address to the SAARC Editors, February 10.

Eytan Gilboa, 2001, 'Diplomacy in the Age of Global Communication' in *Global Politics: Essays in honour of David Vital*, (ed.) Ben-Zvi, Abraham & Klieman, Aaron S, Frank Cass Publishers, London/ Portland.

*Financial Express*, 2016, 'Twitter helped PM Narendra Modi emerge as techno-savvy global leader: Study', March 19.

Gwen Ackerman, 2016, 'Israeli Ministers Approve "Facebook Law" Against Web Incitement', *Bloomberg*, December 25.

Hague, William, 2014. 'Healing the wounds of a bitter war', *The Hindu*, March 17.

Haidar, Suhasini, 2014. 'Backing Bangladesh', *The Hindu*, January 11.

Helena Smith, 2015, 'Shocking images of drowned Syrian boy show tragic plight of refugees' *The Guardian*, September 2. https://www.theguardian.com/world/2015/sep/02/shocking-image-of-drowned-syrian-boy-shows-tragic-plight-of-refugees (Accessed on January 7, 2018).

*Himalayan Times,* 2014, 'PM's stress on collective effort to tackle regional challenges', February 9, https://www.bloomberg.com/news/articles/2016-12-25/israeli-ministers-approve-facebook-law-against-web-incitement (Accessed on January 7, 2018).

'Jadhav's death sentence', 2017. *The Tribune*, April 12.

Kanjilal, Pratik, 2013, 'Journalist becomes the News', *The Indian Express,* November 23.

Kanwar Yogendra, 2017, 'A Book Café run exclusively by inmates', *The Hindu*, April 13.

*Kathmandu Post,* 2014, 'Neighbourliness for Peace and Security in Asia', February 9.

Li Kesiang, 2013, 'A handshake across the Himalayas', *The Hindu*, May 20.

MEA 2015-16, Annual Report of the Ministry of External Affairs, New Delhi.

Menon, Meena, 2014, 'Like in the razor's edge', *The Hindu*, February 11.

Nikhil Agarwal, 2017, 'PM Narendra Modi says hello to Nawaz Sharif in Astana', *India Today*, June 8.

Nonika Singh, 2017, 'Pangs of Parititon', *The Tribune*, April 12.

*NYT*, 2017. Anne Barnard and Michael R. Gordon, 'Worst Chemical Attack in Years in Syria; U.S. Blames Assad', April 4 *.https://www.nytimes.com/2017/04/04/world/middleeast/syria-gas-attack.html?_r=0 https://www.nytimes.com/2017/04/04/world/middleeast/syria-gas-attack.html?_r=0* (Accessed on January 7, 2018).

Panneerselvan, A.S., 2013:1, 'The adjective filter', *The Hindu*, September

30.

Panneerselvan, A.S., 2013:2, 'The Possibility of Co-existence', *The Hindu*, April 28.

Panneerselvan, A.S., 2013:3, 'What's in headlines', *The Hindu*, February 11.

Panneerselvan, A.S., 2014:4, 'When national news dwarfs international news', *The Hindu*, March 10.

SAARC Press Release, 2011, Kathmandu, July 11, (http://saarc-sec.org/press-releases/Media-Exchange-Programme-Islamabad-5-6July-2... 2/7/2014 (Accessed on April 16, 2018).

Salil Desai, 2016, 'Why readers matter in the age of newspeak', *The Tribune*, Dec. 16.

Sardesai, Rajdeep, 2014, 'Slippery slope to crassness', *The Hindustan Times*, March 24.

Saurabh Chauthan, 2017, 'A first: Shimla gets a book café run by jail inmates', *The Hindustan Times*, April 12.

Shailaja Bajpai, 2017, 'Great Indian whitewash', *The Indian Express*, April 13.

Sheikh Hasina, 2017, 'Friendship is a flowing river', *The Hindu*, April 7.

Smriti Kak Ramachandran , 2017. 'Govt mulls digital channel to tell 'India story' to the world, counter foreign narrative', *The Hindustan Times*, New Delhi, Apr 08.

*The Hindu*, 2014, Address by Shri Pranab Mukherjee, President of India, at the Indian Newspaper Society, February 27.

*The Hindu*, 2014: 1, 'Media has kept a critical eye on government: PM', March 13.

*The Hindu*, 2014: 2, 'Yameen in India' (ed.), January 3.

*The Hindu*, 2014: 3, 'Bhutan King's visit', January 6.

*The Hindu*, 2014: 4, 'Uncertainty in Bangladesh' (ed.). January 1.

*The Hindu*, 2014: 5, 'No real winners' (ed.). January 9.

*The Hindu*, 2014: 6, 'Easing Tensions in Palk Bay' (ed.). January 17.

*The Hindu*, 2017, 'Transformative visit', April 11.

*The Hindu*, 2017:1, 'The Indo-Pak diplomatic stairwell', April 12.

*The Hindu*, 2018, 'The journalist is no more the last word, says Smriti Irani', April 28.

*The Hindustan Times*, 2013, 'Tejpal creates Tehelka', November 22.

*The Hindustan Times*, 2014:1, 'Light at the end of the Tunnel', (ed.), February 11.

*The Indian Express,* 2013: 1, 'Journalist becomes the News', November 22.

*The Indian Express*, 2014: 1, 'A PM for Nepal' (ed.), February 11.

*The Indian Express,* 2014, 'Media and government have broken relationship: Star India CEO', March 12.

*The Times of India,* 2017, 'President, Vice-President raise toast to PM's communication skills', May 27.

*The Tribune*, 2013, 'Li greets Indian audience with Namaste', May 22.

*The Tribune*, 2017, 'Jadhav's death sentence', April 12.

Twiplomacy, 2016, http://www.burson-marsteller.com/what-we-do/our-thinking/twiplomacy-2016/twiplomacy-2016-full-study/ (Accessed on January 7, 2018).

Vice President, 2011, Inaugural Address of the Vice President, World Urdu Editors Conference, 30 December.

Vice-President, 2012, Inaugural Address of the Vice President, Ramnath Goenka Excellence in Journalism Awards, January 16.

Vice President, 2013, Inaugural Address, 'National Press Day Celebrations', Press Council of India, New Delhi, 16 November.

Vidya Subramanian, 2017, 'We don't need an Indian propaganda channel', *Hindustan Times*, April 11.

Zehra Kazmi, 2017, 'Why him vs Why not: Foreign media on Adityanath's selection as UP CM', *The Hindustan Times*, Mar 20.

# Section – VI

# Cultural Diplomacy at Global and Grassroots Levels

## Chapter – XI

# Smithsonian Institution: A Global Cultural Hub and India

### Introduction

In this chapter, we would look at the role played by the Smithsonian Institution in Washington DC (USA) as a global cultural hub and how it interacts with India. Smithsonian Institution is the world's largest Museum and Research Complex, as it discharges its tripartite functions of 'dissemination of education, culture and research internationally,' either directly or through its partners. Its Office of International Relations (OIR) is charged with the responsibility of promoting 'meaningful change in the world,' as it advances Smithsonian's mission 'by leveraging the research, creativity and expertise' of this giant body.

Smithsonian has a permanent display of Indian Art Objects and Artifacts at two interconnected galleries, The Freer Gallery of Art and Arthur Sackler Gallery. Smithsonian has also been involved in organizing exhibitions to showcase modern day India, Indian life and Indian Diaspora at these galleries and its Museum of Natural History.

'Aditi' exhibition was one of the main features of the 1985-1986 Festival of India, celebrated in the United States. Its latest exhibition 'Beyond Bollywood: Indian Americans Shape the Nation' (2014-2015) at the Natural History Museum was a celebration of the role of Indian-Americans in the United States, starting from their origins in early 1900s. Another exhibition on 'Sikhs, The Legacy of Punjab' was earlier organized in 2004. The Smithsonian has also projected Indian cuisine, by organising talks on 'The Flavours of India', 'The Original Fusion Cuisine', in conjunction with the exhibition 'Beyond Bollywood'.

Smithsonian has also projected another facet of India – folk life and cultural heritage, under the aegis of the Smithsonian Center for Folk Life and Cultural Heritage. Smithsonian has also helped in capacity building and generating awareness through its various programmes/activities – Smithsonian Education, Smithsonian Channel, Smithsonian Journeys and Smithsonian Publications.

Over the years, Smithsonian has emerged as an important vehicle in promoting Indian culture through its various programmes, launched by its different galleries and centres. It has over 30,000 objects from India, including books, specimens, photographs, textiles, manuscripts and paintings under its digitalized collections. Smithsonian connects with India in diverse ways and fields, as briefly mentioned above. Details would be covered in the body of this chapter.

The Smithsonian-India connectivity is the least known in India. In this chapter we would dwell on the above and other related topics. We would look at the direction it has taken and evaluate the role and involvement of the Indian government. What needs to be done to strengthen cooperation?

## The Smithsonian Institution and its History

This Institution is based in Washington DC and is spread over the length and the breadth of the city. It has 19 museums and galleries; 9 research centres and the National Zoo under its charge (Annexure 1). It has around 200 affiliate museums in 45 states in the country. It has working relationship with over 140 countries (Liz Tunick).[1] The museums are world-class, open throughout the year and allow free entry. It has a vast global reach, not only to Americans, but also to international visitors. For visitors to Washington DC, it is the Mecca or the most important place for a visit by all domestic and foreign visitors, including Indians of all ages.

In 1826, a British scientist James Smithson willed his Estate to the United States, in case his nephew Hungerford also died without any heir, 'to found at Washington, under the name of the Smithsonian Institution, an establishment for the increase and diffusion of knowledge among men' (Founding of Smithsonian). Of course, men include women. Smithson died in 1829 and Hungerford died in 1835, without any heirs. The Estate, which was then valued at US $ 500000, was awarded to USA in 1838. Smithsonian Institution was set up in 1846, as a Trust to be administered by a Board of Regents and a Secretary of the Smithsonian, to function as CEO. Its first building, 'The Castle' was completed in 1865 and it serves as the administrative headquarters of the Institution. Each Museum has its own Director, who runs the same.

The Smithsonian's annual budget is over US $ 1 billion. Its federal appropriation for the fiscal year 2016 (Oct. 1, 2015–Sept. 30, 2016) was $840 million that included congressional appropriation and federal grants and contracts. This provides for about 60 percent funding; the rest comes from its trust funds or non-federal funds, which include contributions from private sources (endowments; donations from individuals, corporations and foundations; and memberships). It also generates revenue income from operations of the Smithsonian Enterprises (magazines, mail-order catalogue, product development, entertainment, shops, restaurants and concessions).

## The Smithsonian Mission and Areas for Cooperation

Smithsonian has 138 million objects, works of art and specimens that include 127 million specimens and artifacts at the National Museum of Natural History. It has over 6000 employees and over 6500 volunteers. It recorded 28 million visits to its various museums and galleries in 2014, to which it accords free entry. It also recorded 140 million online visitors in 2013. It also reaches audiences through all types of programme, which is closely knit through 'Smithsonian Media'. It provides multimedia connectivity through magazines, online websites and iPad Apps, television channel and signature events. Given the vastness of its global reach, it can be given the status of 'Global Cultural Hub'.

The Smithsonian's mission is 'to promote meaningful change in the world' by 'leveraging the research, creativity, and expertise of the entire Smithsonian.' It is driven by partner's 'specific request for consultancy and assistance' resulting in producing 'tangible and practical deliverables and tools' that is 'rooted in an understanding of local needs and concerns' (Smithsonian Background). The Smithsonian's Office of International Relations is the nodal point that connects with its partners, including foreign countries through diplomatic missions or directly with its counterpart institutions. So far it does not have formal MOU with ICCR or any other governmental body in India.

## The Freer Gallery of Art and Arthur Sackler Gallery

These Galleries are more in the nature of museums and not art galleries. They constitute an important part of the 19 Smithsonian Museums. Galleries fall in the category of permanent exhibitions of art objects from

India and other Asian countries. Indian art objects form an important part of the overall collections in the galleries (Debra Diamond).[2] The focus of the galleries is on the following:

- Exchange of Art Objects;
- Organization of Exhibitions;
- Conservation of Museums; and
- Training of Museum specialists.

The Galleries are largely funded by the US Government, which pays for physical infrastructure and maintenance. The US Government pays for the 2/3$^{rd}$ of the salaries of the staff and the remaining 1/3$^{rd}$ comes from the Endowment. The capacity of the galleries was doubled in 2004. On an average, 600000-700000 visitors come to the galleries every year. The galleries are involved in human resource development with other countries, but do not charge training costs. Normally they work with Foundations or Sponsors.

The galleries plan to reach out to the local communities through holding of Annual Country Festival Days. In the case of India, they now hold it on the Independence Day. This helps in generating awareness and funds. The focus is on the 2$^{nd}$ generation onwards.

The galleries are also involved in raising country specific endowments and set up a target for the same. In the case of China, it was US $ 5 million and it was successfully raised. In the case of India, they had reached a goal of US $1 million, as against a target of US $ 3 million. The Prime Minister of Japan made a donation of US $ 1 million during his last visit to USA in May 2015.

These galleries have organized a number of exhibitions on India, from time to time. Debra Diamond had created a number of India specific exhibitions: Two of the important ones were: 'Gardens and Cosmos' and 'Yoga: The Art of Transformation'. She is working on two important exhibitions that are planned for 2017-18.

Some of the other important ones were: 'Strange and Wondrous: Prints of India' (2013-14); 'Yoga: The Art of Transformation' (2013-14); 'Worlds within Worlds: Imperial Paintings from India and Iran' (2012); 'Gardens and Cosmos: The Royal Paintings of Jodhpur' (2008-2009); 'Art of Mughal India' (2004-2007); 'The Sensuous and the Sacred: Chola Bronzes from

South India' (2002-2003) and 'The Adventures of Hamza' (2002). A brief description on these exhibitions is covered below.

### *Gardens and Cosmos, 2008*

The exhibition showed Indian paintings from the royal courts of erstwhile Marwar-Jodhpur (presently in the State of Rajasthan). The focus was on gardens and cosmos leitmotif. A corpus of paintings was received from the National Museum in India. The exhibition was shown in Washington DC, Seattle and London. It was planned to take this exhibition to New Delhi, but this could not take place, because of logistic and administrative issues, even though they had budgeted for the same.

### *Strange and Wondrous*

The exhibition was a display of Prints of India from the Robert J. Del Boot's collection. This was held at the Smithsonian during 2013-14. It was a portrayal of illustrated accounts, documented by merchants, missionaries and soldiers who visited India during the 16$^{th}$ to 20$^{th}$ centuries. This reflected their fascination with Indian culture.

### *Yoga and the Art of Transformation*

This was the world's first exhibition of yogic art and was organized during 2013-14. Given worldwide interest in yoga, more for health than spiritual reasons, the exhibition attempted to reveal yoga's mysteries and illuminate its profound meanings. It depicted temple sculptures, icons, manuscripts, and court paintings created in India over 2000 years. It also included collection of early Mughal photographs, books and films. The objects were borrowed from 25 museums in India and from abroad in the United States and Europe.

The Smithsonian was not able to get material by way of murals from India, as this would have enhanced the quality of the exhibition. The exhibition was a curtain raiser on Yoga, as many people even students in the Georgetown University, who studied yoga, did not know of its origins in India. It was shown in Washington DC, San Francisco and Cleveland in USA. 180,000 persons viewed the exhibition, out of which 18,000 would be Indians.

### *Art of Mughal India*

It was held during August 2005-February 2005 and presented 31 works of art, which included manuscript paintings and luxury objects in jade and lacquered wood. These offered a glimpse into the conceptually creative and technically innovative tradition of Mughal paintings. It traced 'the origins and development of a distinct Mughal pictorial style in the 16th and 17th centuries and its artistic impact on both Rajput and Persian paintings'.

***The Sensuous and the Sacred Chola Bronzes from South India***

This was held during 2002-03. It was the first exhibition held in the United States that was solely devoted to the bronze art during the Chola period. It brought together sixty bronzes from national and European collections.

## Smithsonian's Asian Pacific Centre, Indian American Heritage Project (IAHP), National Museum of Natural History and India

This Centre was established in 1997. It is one of the three Centres; the other two being, The Latino Centre and the Folk Life Centre. It has 'created, coordinated and partnered with hundreds of Asian Pacific initiatives across the Institution'. These range from 'collections, exhibits, cultural festivals, public programs, research, fellowships and internships' (Asia Pacific Centre).

The Centre provides vision, leadership and support to present 'the history, art and culture of Asian Pacific Americans through research, exhibition, outreach and education programs'. The main objective is 'to better reflect their contributions to the American experience and world culture' (Beyond Bollywood). May is celebrated as Asian Pacific American Heritage Month and a number of cultural events are organised on a regional and country-wide basis. India falls under this Centre.

***'Beyond Bollywood: Indo-Americans Shape the Nation' Exhibition***

This was organized under the Indian American Heritage Project (IAHP), which was originally launched as the *Home Spun Project* in 2008. This was a historic initiative by the Smithsonian Asian Pacific American Centre to chronicle the experience of immigrants from India and Indian- Americans in the United States. IAHP consisted of an exhibition, public programs, a curriculum guide for youth, an interactive website, and artifacts donated to the Smithsonian's permanent collection.

This exhibition was 'the first of its kind in this series', to generate awareness on 'sense of belongingness and inclusivity as Americans' and to focus on what 'Indian-Americans have accomplished' (Sameen Piracha).[3] Young Indians became the catalysts as they provided the push factor for this exhibition. The exhibition was a part of a US $ 2 million heritage project of the National Museum of Natural History (The Hindu). It was also 'funded by more than US $ 1 million in contributions from the Indian-American Community' (Rajghatta, Chidanand).

The exhibition opened in a 5,000-square-foot space at the National Museum of Natural History on Feb 27, 2014 and ran until August, 2015. A photographic version of the exhibition was taken to other cities in the United States and to Delhi and other cities in India. It was 'the first major exhibition to chronicle Indian-American's more than 200 years of history' (Aurora de Peralta); the heritage of Indian immigrants and Indian-Americans and 'the contribution they have made to the American melting pot' (Rajghatta, Chidanand, 2014).

The exhibition covered everything 'from yoga to cuisine to hip-hop' (TOI 2014); featuring artefacts that included the trophy of the first Indian winner of the Spelling Bee Competition in 1985; gown worn by First Lady Michelle Obama designed by India-American Naeem Khan; photo of Dalip Singh Saund, the first Indian legislator and turban of Balbir Singh, the first Sikh victim after the 9/11 Attacks. The exhibition also focused on "contemporary conversations on race and immigration" (Masum Momaya);[4] while not missing the 'community's spiritual input into American consciousness' (Rajghatta, Chidanand, 2014).

The exhibition explored the heritage, daily experiences, and numerous and diverse contributions that Indian immigrants and Indian Americans had made to shaping the United States. The exhibition featured historical and contemporary images and several dozen artifacts, documenting histories of discrimination and resistance. It thus conveyed daily experiences and symbolized achievements across professions. Music and visual art works also formed a critical component and provided commentary on the Indian-American experience. The exhibition was accompanied by a website, featuring a blog, tying contemporary happenings to exhibition themes and opportunities for visitors to digitally share their stories and photographs.

The exhibition was in the nature of eulogy to Indian-Americans and celebration of their achievements over the years, since they set their foot on the American shores in 1790. The exhibition, through historical and contemporary images, photos, films and artifacts, documents, projected tales of discrimination, resistance and achievement (Rajghatta, Chidanand, 2014). The purpose of the exhibition was to go beyond stereotypes and 'to focus on cultural, political and professional contributions' that had been made by the Indian-Americans in shaping US history, as per the Smithsonian's curator Masum Momaya. The title 'Beyond Bollywood, was chosen as 'many Americans might not realize that Indian-Americans have offered more to U.S. culture than Bollywood movies' (Mayer, James, 2014).

Momaya believed that the exhibition would be a launching pad for follow up activities and she also hoped that this would be a starter of conversations—conversations that take place in all settings, between people of many backgrounds. She said, "...it's my belief that an exhibition isn't finished when it opens to the public but rather is just the beginning of an expanding and extended sharing". She further added, "We don't know where these conversations will go, but perhaps it will give people a different way in, a more heartfelt way in, and counter the popular stereotypes they see in the media" (Aurora de Peralta, 2014).

The exhibition was promoted by the US State Department 'to advance India-US relations, by focusing on Indian Diaspora; and their 200 years long history in the United States' (Masum Momaya). The curator made reference to a number of challenges faced in mounting this exhibition. These included the usual problem of inadequacy of infrastructure and challenges in projecting diversity of India Diaspora, in terms of regions, religions, gender, age and generation. Difficulties were also encountered in raising funds from local Indians, which were below expectations. The exhibition, however, succeeded in projecting the image of a vibrant community, which has become an integral part of the American dream, as it fulfils its own dream, despite facing racial discrimination and immigration challenges.

***The Smithsonian and the Festival of India, 1985***

India arrived culturally in a big way in the United States during the Festival of India 1985-86. It resulted in bringing Indian culture to the doorsteps of the Americans. The Smithsonian played an important role in this direction by mounting two important exhibitions. Both these exhibitions were curated by Rajeev Sethi. 'Aditi, A Celebration of Life' was organized at the National Museum of Natural History, while the other, 'Mela: An Indian Fair' was a part of celebrations at the Mall.

**'Mela'** is an Indian Fair that was a star attraction at the annual Folk Life Festival and celebrated the cultural heritage of India. In addition to musical presentations and lectures, the Festival featured a variety of traditional food and crafts, and demonstrations, including quilting, basketry, henna hand painting and decoy carving. Indian cuisine makes appearance at these Festivals, from time to time. 'AHAAR - A TASTE OF INDIA' brought by

Indique and Indique Heights was there to offer Indian cuisine from the South to the visitors at the 2013 Smithsonian's Folk Life Festival (Ahaar).

**'Aditi'** is about 'creative energy' that is 'abundant, joyful and unbroken', which sustains the Universe. Simulating life in a rural Indian village, it dealt with life's cycle. Each section dealt with a particular phase of life: birth, coming of age, courtship, marriage etc. The exhibition was developed in India and had earlier featured at the Indian Festival in UK in 1982. It featured more than 1500 objects; more than 40 performing artists, craftspeople and performers took part (Liz Tunick).

## The Smithsonian Centre for Folk Life and Cultural Heritage and India

This Centre aims at promoting 'the understanding and continuity of diverse, contemporary grassroots cultures in the United States and around the world'. James Early, the then Director of the Centre said that the focus was 'on "Art" rather than on "Anthropology" – to understand cultures and peoples'. The focus is on 'intangible culture' and to promote 'spiritual well being'. The objective is 'to increase and diffuse knowledge' and there would be 'no national boundaries, no national anthems, no specific faiths'. To be true to its logic, it must 'pursue scientific exploration and investigation' (Dr. James Early).[5]

The Centre, through its Annual Folk Life Festival, which began in 1967, highlights 'grassroots cultures across the nation and around the world through performances and demonstrations of living traditions' (FLCH Centre). It is an international exposition of living cultural heritage annually produced outdoors on the National Mall of the United States in Washington DC. Through its record label, 'Smithsonian Folkways', which began as 'Folkway Records' in 1948, it aims 'to document community-based music and preserve historical recordings of both music and the spoken word'.

The Centre has produced over 100 individual albums from and featuring India under its Smithsonian Folkways recording label. Some of its recent recordings were: 'Baddigeet- Songs of Baddi Community of Garhwal' (2011) and 'South India: Ranganayaki – continuity in the Karaikodi Vina Style' (2014). It had also featured Indian folk festivals, such as the Koro tribal people of Arunachal Pradesh at the Smithsonian Folk-life Festival, 'One world, Many Languages' in 2013 (Liz Tunick).

The Folk Life Festival has emerged as a model for 'Transferable Technology for Cultural Heritage Tourism'. Local governments interested in economic development through cultural tourism, while preserving their cultural diversity, see 'Smithsonian's Folk Life Festival as a way to introduce a large and diverse audience to the features that make them unique as a cultural destination'. The participant governments look to clues 'as to how to develop their own events and as a way to "learn the ropes" of cultural representation through traditions and display' (Diana Baird).

In keeping with the policies of the US State Department, the Centre 'promotes people to people connectivity'. The artists help 'in conveying American values, as seen through the power of musical genre of Black American Jazz Musicians, despite poor conditions for Black Americans'. The aim has been to 'represent the United States and not the US government, to avoid conflict of interests with US policies and to ensure independence of artists/research scholars' (James Early).

## Conservation and Capacity Building: The Smithsonian Conservation Biology Institute (SCBI) and India

The Smithsonian has partnered India in the conservation area also through this Institution. The projects include, 'Tiger Conservation Partnership and Global Tiger Initiative' (ongoing); 'Genetic Analysis of India's Leopard and Tiger Populations' (2013) and 'Asian Lion Conservation' (1994). SCBI signed an MOU with the Wildlife Institute of India (WII) to cooperate on wildlife research, academic programmes, capacity building etc. Another MOU was signed between the Smithsonian National Zoological Park (NZP) with the Indian Central Zoo Authority to provide assistance for Zoo and Wildlife training, laboratory capacity building etc.

## Smithsonian and the World's Cultural Space

The Smithsonian has worked with UNESCO and many foreign countries in this area. Some of its current projects are as follows, a study of which would be of interest to India:

- Integrating Heritage into Modern Education Systems: This aims at drawing knowledge from cultural heritage for the benefit of future generations. In a project with the Abu Dhabi Authority for Culture and Heritage, the Smithsonian has marshalled the cultural and traditional grassroots resources into more contemporary forms, for use in schools, mobile museums, and college programs.
- Looking to Culture for Inspiration: The Smithsonian is working with Oman's Ministry of Heritage and Culture to transform the Natural History Museum into a powerful educational and scientific

resource for all Omanis, tourists, and the international scientific community.

- Making Culture Relevant: The Smithsonian partnered with the National Museum of Jordan to redesign exhibits to provide a holistic experience to the visitor and also turn it into a site of cultural and intergenerational connection.
- Museum Manpower Development and Skills: The Smithsonian partnered with the National Heritage Board of Singapore to upgrade skills of museum professionals in four key areas of Curation, Exhibition Management, Preventive Conservation and Early Childhood Museum Education.

## Smithsonian and the US State Department

In 2012, The Smithsonian entered into an arrangement with the State Department to develop a project, 'American Spaces Assessment and Redesign Project'. The project was to look into the infrastructure and functional requirements of 'American Spaces', which is a general nomenclature used for all types of American Cultural Centres abroad. The overall objective has been 'to enhance the physical and programmatic environments of the State Department's public diplomacy venues abroad in support of foreign policy priorities' (American Spaces).

The project has global dimensions, as the Smithsonian interacts with diplomatic missions and helps them in providing ' infrastructure and design elements that promote and support open, flexible, and vibrant collaborative spaces'. The Smithsonian has developed a digital "Idea Book" that provides 'design concepts, furniture recommendations, Smithsonian resources, programming concepts, and digital strategies'.

Smithsonian's entering into 'a partnership programme with the US State Department, thereby results in their directly becoming a constituent part of cultural diplomacy' (Liz Tunick). It assists American Cultural Centres including American Corners, like the one located at Chandigarh. The experience of the Smithsonian would be useful for ICCR, as it is looking into the working of its Cultural Centres and how to make these better equipped to promote India's connectivity with the concerned countries.

## Smithsonian and 'Sikhs: Legacy of the Punjab' Exhibition

This exhibition opened on July 24, 2004, under the National Museum of Natural History's Sikh Heritage Project. It was on long-term display at the Museum during 2004-07. More than 5 million people had visited this

Museum in 2003 (Dr. Paul Taylor).[6] Over the years it had evolved, as it travelled to other destinations in the United States, namely Santa Barbara (California) in 2009 and San Antonio (Texas) in 2015-16. The author had an opportunity to visit the exhibition in Washington DC.

The Sikh Heritage Project was launched in 2000. The project had enormous support of the Sikh Community. It was established 'to support acquisition, conservation/restoration, and exhibitions of Sikh collections, to support research on the heritage of the Sikhs, and to support other Sikh cultural activities at the Smithsonian Institution'.

The exhibition presented more than 100 pieces of Sikh artwork and artifacts produced from the 18th century to the present, including miniature paintings; arms and armour; traditional textiles and dress; coins; musical instruments; jewellery; sacred texts; and modern works of art. It also included a scale model of the 'Darbar Sahib'(Golden Temple), a Sikh sacred space at Amritsar. Many of these objects were on loan from private collections and were on public display for the first time. The exhibition highlighted the culture and history of the Sikhs.

The Project worked on a new concept that aimed at integrating community involvement, 'both to effectively inform the general public about a culture and religion they may be unfamiliar with, as well as to involve Sikhs in decision about how their heritage can be meaningfully and productively displayed'. The project thus allowed Sikh-Americans 'to participate in the development of the exhibition, in ways that departed significantly from the traditional museum development practices' (Dr. Paul Taylor). On the other hand, the mode in which 'this exhibition was developed, within a larger framework of community development' reflected 'a changing view of the nature of museum curatorship as a social practice' (Dr. Paul Taylor).

This helped in allowing the rich cultural capital of the Sikh Community to be decoded in conveying, 'the meaningfulness and cultural contexts to a broad public' without losing the aesthetic value of the objects that were exhibited at the exhibition. This is an area that needs to be studied by us, as to how we can develop a new approach that could help 'the museum professionals with the opportunity to draw on research and collaboration with source communities to more accurately interpret and present objects in exhibitions and in other media' (Dr. Paul Taylor). This could be looked into by museum administrators in India.

The exhibition 'is one of the biggest steps in educating the United States about Sikhs' at a time in which 'discrimination and racism is at a high, particularly towards those of the Sikh and Muslim religions' (Harding, Hayli). Leaders of the Sikh Community have worked alongside the museum to educate others on Sikh Culture.

The exhibition provided information on the tenets that guide the Sikhs, such as 'justice, love, service, community and tolerance.' It depicts Sikhs as a martial race. Hayli Harding noted that 'In fact, hundreds served and died in American wars, alongside those of other faiths and beliefs, but they had been barred from serving in the US Armed Forces, as their religion requires them to keep unshorn hair and wear turbans'. The exhibition gave visitors 'a chance to learn about Sikhism through more than 100 items and interactive displays', which included hearing Punjabi music, which resonates globally. The display showed a variety of turban styles, fashions of traditional Sikh weddings as well as Sikh Art and Religion (Mariajose, Romero, 2015).

## Smithsonian's Global Thrust and India

The Smithsonian is committed to spreading knowledge in terms of its Charter. It would like to share its vast resources, drawing on opportunities that have become available 'in new media and social networking tools and technologies'. There are various ways in which it could forge partnership links with other countries and institutions. According to Nicholas Namba, Vice President, Smithsonian, which is spearheading this drive, India is one of its priority countries and should be 'a major beneficiary in its outreach efforts'.

Namba sees a natural partnership between India and Smithsonian, which is based on his experiences working as Director (Professional, Educational and Cultural Exchanges) at the US Embassy in New Delhi. He sums up beautifully in these words:

> "At its heart, the Smithsonian is an educational institution and Indians value education very highly. They have a tremendous natural curiosity, amazing universities, highly educated and highly skilled people. We have shared values. I know many Indians from my work in India, and I know that they are very interested in history and in other cultures."

The Smithsonian is willing to partner with the government, non-governmental organizations and the private sector. The aim is to bring Smithsonian's resources to those who cannot visit in person. This could take various forms, like travelling versions, more physical exhibits, expanding online access and putting Smithsonian resources into the massive open online courses (MOOC) format that many universities have developed.

## India Carving Partnership with Smithsonian and Other Global Cultural Hubs

The idea of cultural diplomacy has existed for a long time, but it is only now that 'this has acquired prominence, as everyone is now focusing on this' (Liz Tunick). More and more people are 'jellying' at it, but it is still in its infancy. The Smithsonian works as an independent institution, even though it has the support of the US Government. It is, however, 'guided by the broad American values in conceptualization and implementation of its Programmes' (Liz Tunick).

Smithsonian's primary focus is on holding exhibitions, promoting academic linkages aimed at research and human resource development and conservation of cultural heritage. It has an Advisory Programme on Museum Conservation and is associated with the Harvard University. It executed a project at the National History Museum, Oman, focusing on culture's emergence as a source of inspiration. It is also involved with the World Bank and is executing a project on cultural tourism in Uttar Pradesh (UP). It is preserving India's intangible heritage in music.

Smithsonian also assists countries in the recovery of cultural assets like Objects d' Arts. It assisted Haiti at the time of National Disaster. It is involved in a big way preparing research material under the STEM Programme. It can count on 750 Smithsonian Materials by way of publications. It helped UAE in integrating heritage into modern education systems.

What is the level and nature of connectivity with the Indian community in USA? Indian community is not fully involved in the Arts, in proportion to its strength in numbers and income levels. Indian community does get involved in those events of the Smithsonian Institution that are community specific and are about them, like the 'Beyond Bollywood', 'Sikhs, Heritage of Punjab'. Art, however, is still an area of low priority for the resident Indian community, even though it is financially strong.

Where does India meet the Freer Gallery of Art and Arthur Sackler Gallery; such cooperation takes place in the following ways:

- It is project specific as there is no MOU with India. The constraints were on their side. Now they are allowed to enter into MOUs and would be willing to consider signing one soon.

- They have cooperated with National Museums in Delhi; Prince of Wales Museums in Mumbai and Jodhpur Museum.
- They have offered training facilities free of cost, but intake from India has been very small, as compared to other countries like Japan and the Middle East. One of their trainees, Karni Singh Jasol, is now the curator at the Jodhpur Museum.
- They have received cooperation from the Indian Embassy and could count on the same. However, the nature and level of such cooperation depends upon the Ambassador. An Event at the Indian Embassy helped in raising donations for the Yoga Exhibition.

How could India enhance connectivity with the Smithsonian Institution? The following suggestions emerged from personal interaction with curators, professionals and administrators at various centres and museums of the Smithsonian Institution:

- To plan more events with Indian Museums, like Sivaji Museum, Mumbai; Mehrangarh Museum, Jodhpur.
- To increasingly involve India and the Indian Embassy in the activities of the Smithsonian Institution.
- To train Indians as curators and conservators at the Smithsonian's galleries.
- To hold another yoga exhibition, building on their past experience and taking into account UN declaring June 21 as International Yoga Day (IYD).
- To consider setting up an India-Smithsonian Institution Endowment Fund.
- To provide full cooperation to the India-related events at the Sackler and Freer Gallery.
- To work on projects in intangible heritage; INTACH, New Delhi could be an ideal partner.
- To learn from their experience with other countries, to make culture emerge as a source of inspiration and integrate heritage to modern system of education.

Smithsonian Institution is 'the single most important gift to Cultural Diplomacy' (James Early). It has no formal connectivity with ICCR. At present, no MOU with India is on its cards but it is open for considering one. It has a good working relationship with the Indian Embassy at Washington DC. Smithsonian could emerge as a good laboratory for practical ideas and a partner of ICCR for the conduct of cultural diplomacy.

Is India listening? If yes, then ICCR and other organisations could consider entering into a serious dialogue to see how we could enhance cultural connectivity with the world by partnering with the Smithsonian. A project could also be developed under Digital India Framework. Indira Gandhi National Open University (IGNOU) could also consider pooling the experience of the Smithsonian with that of theirs, in developing online courses for students.

We need to consider developing a broader canvas, which not only facilitates connectivity with the Smithsonian, but also with similar cultural hubs across the globe. To start with ICCR could identity such global cultural hubs and enter into meaningful partnership arrangements.

**Annexure 1**

## List of Smithsonian Museums

- Anacostia Community Museum
- Arts and Industries Building
- Cooper Hewitt, Smithsonian Design Museum (New York City)
- Freer Gallery of Art
- Hirshhorn Museum and Sculpture Garden
- National Air and Space Museum
- National Air and Space Museum's Steven F. Udvar-Hazy Center (Chantilly, Va.)
- National Museum of African American History and Culture
- National Museum of African Art
- National Museum of American History
- National Museum of the American Indian
- National Museum of the American Indian's George Gustav Heye Center (New York City)
- National Museum of Natural History
- National Portrait Gallery
- National Postal Museum
- Renwick Gallery
- Arthur M. Sackler Gallery
- Smithsonian American Art Museum
- Smithsonian Institution Building ("Castle")

**Annexure II**

# 'Beyond Bollywood: Indian Americans Shape the Nation' Exhibition

## Exhibit Facts

- "Beyond Bollywood" is a 5,000-square-foot exhibition in the Smithsonian's National Museum of Natural History chronicling the cultural, political and professional contributions of Indian immigrants and Indian Americans to the U.S.; it ran from Feb. 27, 2014 through Aug. 16, 2015, and a traveling version of the exhibition will tour around the country from May 2015 through 2019.
- The exhibition has seven sections: Migration; Early Immigration; Working Lives; Arts and Activism; Yoga, Religion & Spirituality; Cultural Contributions in Food, Music, Dance and Groundbreakers.
- "Beyond Bollywood" is part of the Indian American Heritage Project of the Smithsonian Asian Pacific American Center. IAHP began in 2008 and included a nationwide effort to collect stories, photographs, artifacts, art and documents.

## Highlighted Artifacts

- Dress worn by First Lady Michelle Obama to the 2012 National Governors Association Dinner, designed by Indian American Naeem Khan
- Mohini Bhardwaj's Olympic Silver Medal (gymnastics, 2004)
- Brandon Chillar's football helmet from the 2011 Superbowl-winning Green Bay Packers
- Trophy of first Indian American National Spelling Bee winner Balu Natarajan (1985)
- Campaign materials of Congressman Dalip Singh Saund (first person of Indian and Asian origin, and non-Abrahamic faith), from the collection of the National Museum of American History
- Turban of Balbir Singh Sodhi, first person of South Asian origin to be murdered in an act of retaliation after Sept. 11, 2001
- First doctor bag of Abraham Verghese, MD, author of *My Own Country*, *The Tennis Partner* and *Cutting for Stone*

## Featured Artists and Celebrities

- Artists featured in the exhibition include Chiraag Bhakta and Mark Hewko, Anjali Bhargava and Swati Khurana, Anujan Ezhikode, Ruee Gawarikar, Suraiya Nathani Hossain, Corky Lee, Annu Palakunnathu Matthew, Preston Merchant, John Merrell, Sabelo Narasimhan, Sejal Patel, Mohanpreet Singh, Vinay Srinivasan and Asha Puthli
- Celebrities featured in the exhibition include Ravi Shankar (musician), Vijay Iyer (musician), Anoushka Shankar (Musician), Karsh Kale (musician), Sarita Choudhury (actor), Kal Penn (actor), Mindy Kaling (actor), Siddhartha Mukherjee (Pulitzer Prize Winner), Nina Davuluri (Miss America 2013), Meena Alexander (poet), Shailja Patel (poet), Bharati Mukherjee (author), Floyd Cardoz (chef) and Madhur Jaffrey (chef)

(Source: Fact Sheet of the Smithsonian Institute)

**Annexure III**

## Exhibition in Texas Depicts the Legacy of Sikhs & Punjab BY MARIAJOSE ROMERO -

## Endnotes

1 Ms. Liz Tunick, International Department, Smithsonian Institution. Meeting on June 6, 2015 at Washigton DC (USA).

2 Debra Diamond, Curator, Freer Gallery, Smithsonian, Washington DC. Meeting on June 9, 2015 at Washigton DC.

3 Sameen Piracha, Asia Pacific Centre, Smithsonian, Washington DC. Meeting on August 14, 2014 at Washington DC (USA).

4 Ms. Masum Momaya, Curator, 'Beyond Bollywood' Exhibition, Washington DC. Meeting on August 19, 2014 at Washington DC (USA).

5 Dr. James Early, Director, Centre for Folk Life and Heritage, Washington DC. Meeting on August 15, 2014 at Washington DC (USA).

6 Dr. Paul Taylor, Curator, 'Sikhs: Heritage of Punjab' Exhibition, Washington DC. Meeting on August 18, 2014 at Washington DC (USA).

## References

Aurora de Peralta, 2014, 'Smithsonian "Beyond Bollywood" Exhibit Debunks Stereotypes about Indian American', *Asian Fortune*, March 14.

Diana N'Diale Baird, 2015, Smithsonian Institution, Institute of Texan Cultures, 2015 *issue of* San Antonio. *Magazine*, June.

Harding, Hayli, 2015, 'Smithsonian exhibit on Display at Texas Educates about Sikh Culture', 17 September.

Lavina Melwani, 2013, 'A chronicle of us in the U.S.', *Sunday Magazine, The Hindu,* April 6. http://www.thehindu.com/features/magazine/a-chronicleof-us-in-the-us/article4584315.ece (Accessed on December 17, 2017).

*The Hindu*, April 6, http://www.thehindu.com/features/magazine/a-chronicle-of-us-in-the-us/article4584315.ece (Accessed on December 17, 2017).

Mayer, James, 2014, 'Beyond Bollywood: Immigration, Culture, and the Indian American Experience', *The Times of India*, February, 18.

Mariajose Romero, 2015, Exhibition in Texas Depicts The Legacy Of Sikhs & Punjab, August 2. https://www.sikh24.com/2015/08/02/exhibition-in-texas-depicts-the-legacy-of-sikhs-punjab/#.V0yAjJErKhc) (Accessed on 14 December 2017).

Rajghatta, Chidanand, 2014, 'Beyond Bollywood: Indian-Americans get a call up from Smithsonian', *The Hindu*, Feb 26.

*The Hindu*, 2014, Panel Organizer, Rathje, 2014, Elizabeth Erin Panel Chair: Rathje, Elizabeth Erin Panel Title: "Reconsidering the representational frame: Nexuses between practice and theory", 'Smithsonian looks at influences of Indian Americans', Feb 27.

*The Times of India*, 2014: 'Success story or struggle? Portraying Indians in US', March 6.

## Numerous websites of the Smithsonian Institution

Smithsonian Website, https://www.si.edu/ (Accessed on December 17, 2017).

American Spaces, americanspaces@state.gov (Accessed on December 17, 2017).

American Spaces 1, https://americanspaces.state.gov/home/wp-content/uploads/2017/05/Office-of-American-Spaces-FINAL.pdf (Accessed on December 17, 2017).

Asia Pacific Centre, https://newsdesk.si.edu/factsheets/smithsonian-asian-pacific-american-center (Accessed on December 17, 2017).

Beyond Bollywood, https://www.si.edu/Exhibitions/Beyond-Bollywood-Indian-Americans-Shape-the-Nation--4689 (Accessed on December 17, 2017).

Folklife Festival, https://newsdesk.si.edu/releases/smithsonian-folklife-festival-celebrates-asian-pacific-american-culture (Accessed on December 17, 2017).

FLCH Centre, https://www.si.edu/unit/center-for-folklife-and-cultural-heritage (Accessed on December 17, 2017).

Founding of Smithsonian, https://newsdesk.si.edu/factsheets/founding-smithsonian-institution (Accessed on December 17, 2017).

Smithsonian Background, https://newsdesk.si.edu/factsheets/facts-about-smithsonian-institution-short (Accessed on December 17, 2017).

Ahaar, Taste of India, http://chefvinod.typepad.com/chef_vinod/2013/07/smithsonian-folklife-festival-2013.html (Accessed on December 17, 2017).

## Chapter – XII

# Cultural Diplomacy at the Grassroots Level: Case Study of Chandigarh and Chicago

### Introduction

Cultural diplomacy is essentially a grassroots activity as far as implementation is concerned. The role at the grassroots level is getting important with the increasing involvement of the states and cities. We are seeing a trend towards the establishment of 'city to city' relationship through the twining of cities, as that of Chicago and Delhi. It is this connectivity that manifests in India's presence at the Chicago International Airport, as Indian flag flutters with a number of flags from other foreign countries, with whom Chicago has sisterly-cities relationship.

It is now widely acknowledged that any successful diplomatic mission has a role cut out for itself, beyond the capital city of any country. It is, therefore, not surprising that many countries have set up offices in other cities, be it consulates, trade offices, tourism centres, which could facilitate connectivity at the grassroots level. Different governments adopt appropriate policies and approaches in involving the cities and the states in this direction in pursuit of their foreign policy goals.

In keeping with these functional requirements, Indian Council for Cultural Relations (ICCR) has already set up Regional Offices, including one at Chandigarh. The author is a member of the Regional Advisory Council of the Chandigarh Office. At the Indian end also, MEA is now more mindful of this requirement to have its presence in the States. The Government has set up a new Division-The States Division- in the Ministry of External Affairs. MEA also wants to set up its Branch Offices in the States, so as to ensure better coordination on foreign policy related issues between the centre and the states.

In this chapter, it is proposed to look at the working of cultural diplomacy at the Indian end – Chandigarh and also at the foreign end – Chicago in the United States. How does India connect at the grassroots level at Chandigarh and Chicago? At Chandigarh, the main focus would be on the activities of the Regional Centre of ICCR and other foreign missions. At Chicago, the focus would be on the working of the sisterly-cities relationship and its status as a cultural hub, as these should provide us with useful insights. This would help us to consider taking steps that would be relevant to involve Indian cities in cultural activities and making these more people centric.

## Policy Guidelines and Approach

The Modi Government is giving new thrust to the role of the states and cities in the pursuit of its foreign policy agenda, in keeping with its overall approach of 'Cooperative Federalism'. The External Affairs Minister Sushma Swaraj unveiled India's approach during her visit to Singapore in August, 2014 (Prashar, Sachin). This was also elaborated and stressed by Prime Minister Modi during his visit to Australia in November 2014 in these words: "We truly welcome the engagement between states and cities. That is why I am also very keen to involve states in India in our international engagements"(The Tribune, 2014).The States would be involved in the areas of 'economic cooperation, academic linkages, investment, tourism, technology transfers, exports, culture, people to people contact and community driven issues' (MEA 2015-16).

To facilitate and deepen the external linkages of the States/ Union Territories, a new Division, 'The States Division' was created in the Ministry of External Affairs in November 2014. This filled the vacuum that existed on the policy and implementation fronts, about which the author had written in an article in 2013 and suggested the need for the creation of 'suitable structures and mechanism' to provide for a role for the States in international relations (Sahai,2013). The States Division is expected to provide support in five broad areas. These include, Sister City and Sister Province Agreements, State and Provincial Leaders Forum, Humanitarian Assistance, Facilitating the Foreign Visits of Dignitaries from State Governments and implementing its Outreach Programmes. It has already taken certain laudable steps in this direction.

This Division was involved in 'the successful launch of India's first ever State/Provincial Leaders' Forum with China in the Great Hall of the People, Beijing on May 15, 2015, during the visit of Prime Minister

Modi to China. During the same visit, this Division also coordinated and facilitated the signing of a sister-state agreement between Karnataka – Sichuan, and also the signing of three sister-city agreements, namely - Chennai – Chongqing, Hyderabad – Qingdao, Aurangabad – Dunhuang. During an earlier visit of Prime Minister Modi to Japan in September 2014, Kyoto-Varanasi Partner City Agreement was signed. It aims 'to promote cooperation in the fields of water management, sewage management, waste management and urban transportation' by "drawing upon Japanese expertise and technologies" (MEA 2015-16).

## ICCR's Regional Office, Chandigarh

Chandigarh is one of the 20 Regional Offices set up across the country by ICCR to fulfil its mandate. It was established in 1990. Regional Offices are involved in looking after scholarship-related activities, arranging performances by Incoming Cultural Groups, arranging programmes for visiting dignitaries and promoting upcoming Indian artists by giving exposure to them under the ICCR's Horizon Series Programme.

This Office looked after 400 students from 21 countries during the Academic Year 2015-16. It provided all the logistical support and looked after their welfare, in coordination with the Dean, Foreign Students at the Panjab University. The students were encouraged to participate at the Annual International Students Day Function, held on November 18, 2015, to commemorate the birth anniversary of late Maulana Abul Kalam Azad, Founder President of the Council. At that function, foreign students presented cultural items, showcasing their respective countries. This occasion also provided an opportunity for networking and comradeship with the local community and fellow Indian students. The author was Honoured Guest at this occasion.

During 2015-16, the Office received two foreign dignitaries under the ICCR's Distinguished Visitors Programme and arranged suitable meetings for them. Prof. Clement K Sankat, Pro-Vice Chancellor, University of West Indies, Port of Spain, Trinidad & Tobago visited PAU, Ludhiana from 3rd to 4th November, 2015. Dr. Sam Nujoma, 'Founding President of Namibia' and 'Father of Nation' from Namibia along with a 14-Member delegation visited Chandigarh, Baddi, Solan, on 19th November, 2015.

During the FY 2015-16, the Office organized following three performances under the ICCR's Incoming Cultural Delegations Programme (Nalini Singhal)[1]:

- Folk Dance & Music by Claudio Sega Club Group from Mauritius on October 15, 2015 at the Randhawa Auditorium, Panjab Kala Bhavan. This was arranged in collaboration with the Punjab Arts Council and the Chandigarh Administration. Home-cum-Cultural Secretary Anurag Aggarwal, Chandigarh Administration was the Chief Guest.

- Folk Dance & Music by the Group from the University of Kelaniya, Sri Lanka on October 20, 2015 at the Tagore Theatre. It was arranged in collaboration with the Department of Public Relations & Cultural Affairs of the Union Territory of Chandigarh.

- Ramayana Chanting by Ballache Kali Mata Mandir Group from Mauritius on December 11, 2015 at the Tagore Theatre. It was also arranged in collaboration with the Department of Cultural Affairs, Chandigarh Administration and Home-cum-Cultural Secretary Anurag Aggarwal, was the Chief Guest.

During the Financial Year 2015-16, the Office also organized 12 cultural programmes by ICCR empanelled artistes in the region, under the Horizon Series Programme of the Council. The Programmes included Folk Songs and Dances of Punjab, Punjabi Play, Bharatnatyam, Sarod Recital, Jugulbandi, Tabla, Qawwalis, Sham-e-Ghazals and instrumental music. Most of the programmes were organized in collaboration with the Punjab Arts Council and the Pracheen Kala Kendra; while others were supported by Senior Citizens Council; Indian Society of Radiographers & Technologists and the Department of Information, Public Relations & Cultural Affairs, Haryana. All the performances were highly successful and received good publicity in the local newspapers.

The Regional Office is ICCR's focal point in Northern India and helps in the implementation of programmes sponsored by it. Regional Director has established a good working relationship with the concerned Departments of Culture of the governments of Chandigarh and Haryana and other stakeholders, like the Panjab University, Punjab Arts Council and Pracheen Kala Kendra. The major constraint that is experienced is the short lead time given for arranging performances by the Incoming Cultural Groups.

ICCR signed a Memorandum of Understanding with the State of Haryana in March 2016, making them a partner in the conduct of cultural diplomacy. No such agreement exists with the Chandigarh Administration. A Regional Advisory Committee has been set up under the Chairmanship of the President of ICCR, of which the author is a member. The meetings are infrequently held and the Committee is practically lying dormant. The Regional Office is working with the Panjab University to evolve a system of 'foster families' for foreign students; the need for this has become more urgent, given some recent attacks on African students. The Regional Director's role is largely in a support capacity, to implement ICCR's scholarship programme and other activities.

## Cultural Profile of Chandigarh and Chicago

**Chandigarh** is emerging as an important regional cultural centre, as the Union Territory is not only involved in promoting culture in this 'City Beautiful', but has also emerged as an important venue for cultural activities mounted by the States of Punjab and Haryana. Among the foreign missions, Canada and UK have set up consulates, while the US Embassy has an 'American Corner' at the State Library, Chandigarh. France has a cultural presence, through its cultural arm, Alliance Française, which has a resident centre that is fully functional.

The Union Territory at Chandigarh has an active Cultural Department. There are three fully functional and active Akademies– 'Sahitya' (Literature), 'Sangeet and Natak (Music and Dance) and Lalit Kala (Fine Arts). Besides these, many state level Arts Bodies are located at Chandigarh, like the Punjab Arts Council, Haryana Cultural Affairs Department etc. Chandigarh is also the home to a large artistic community and other cultural groups and associations.

Chandigarh earned the distinction of becoming the first city outside Delhi, where Prime Minister led the activities for the International Yoga Day (IYD) on June 21, 2016. 30,000 persons participated in performing Yoga at that venue (The Indian Express, 2016). A number of other programmees were also organized. Prime Minster highlighted the importance of Yoga for physical and mental health. He also stated that its spiritual value was invaluable, but it was not linked to any religion. It was meant to place Yoga in the secular context. He announced two Awards at the International and National levels, to recognize the contribution of persons promoting Yoga.

**Chicago**, which is a tourist friendly city, has emerged as an important cultural hub in meeting the cultural needs of its residents and foreign visitors. Through its national parks and world class museums, it provides such facilities. During summer months it organizes various festivals, in the arena of Arts and Literature; Music and Dance; Food and Fashion. These provide an opportunity for participation of groups from foreign countries.

At Chicago, India has a Consulate-General, which liaises with the Mayor of the City and the City Council and the Governor of the State of Illinois.

Chicago, being a multi-cultural city, also provides facilities for diaspora-centric programmes, including holding of street festivals and national day parades. Indian Diaspora occupies a significant place and plays an important role. July is declared the Asian Month, as it focuses on events relating to the Asian Continent. A Parade is held during August every year, to celebrate India's Independence Day, which is invariably led by a film star.

Mayor of Chicago also actively interacts with resident consulates and facilitates organization of events, connected with the national day celebrations. It has sisterly- cities relationships with many cities in the globe, including one with Delhi. It is also the seat of internationally famous educational institutions, like the University of Chicago and the Kellogg University, which have students and faculty members from India. Dr. Raghuram Rajan, former Governor of the Reserve Bank of India was the Dean at the University of Chicago.

## Chandigarh's Emergence as Regional Educational and Cultural Centre

Chandigarh has emerged as an important cultural centre, given the presence of three governments – Punjab, Haryana and the Chandigarh Administration. It is also blessed with good quality infrastructure to host these events, in particular, the Tagore Theatre in Chandigarh and the Cultural Centre in Panchkula, which is one of the tri-cities, linking Chandigarh.

Chandigarh is the seat of the Panjab University, which is one of the oldest and prestigious universities in India. The University had 205 foreign students from 19 countries on its rolls during the Academic Session of 2015-16. This represented an increase of 40 % from the previous year. 61 foreign students were doing PhD, 53 were in post-graduation courses and 91 were doing graduation. Besides this, 295 students were studying in different affiliated colleges of the PU in Chandigarh (The Tribune, 2016:1). Presence of a larger number of Postgraduate and PhD students is a welcome development.

The Department of Culture in the Chandigarh Union Territory (UT) is the nodal point for organising cultural activities. It arranges cultural functions itself and extends support to performances of local as well as out-of-state cultural troupes. The Administration also organizes Annual Chandigarh Carnival and The Festival of Gardens (The Tribune, 2016). These mega events give a festive look to the city, through various attractive competitions.

The Department also coordinates the programmes arranged by the Chandigarh Arts Council, Sangeet Natak Akademi, Lalit Kala Akademi, Sahitya Akademi and The Tagore Theatre Society and gives grants-in-aid to them to promote Art and Culture in the region (Website of Cultural Department).

The newly appointed Chairpersons of the Akademi would like to give a further push to their activities. Gulzar Singh Sandhu, Chairman of the Sahitya Akademi would like to focus on Hindi, Urdu and Punjabi literature; while Bheem Malhotra, Chairman, Lalit Kala Akademi plans to take art to the public and focus on tri-city artists; and Kamal Arora, Chairman, Sangeet Natak Akademi plans to encourage young and struggling artists (The Tribune, 2015).

Chandigarh is known for its Architecture as a planned city, designed by well known French Architect Le Corbusier. The Department of Culture in the Chandigarh Union Territory and the Haryana Government are manned by dynamic persons and the funding is adequate to hold cultural events on a regular basis. It is internationally known for its 'Rock Garden', which is unique in its creativity, by converting waste material into human faces and figures of birds and animals. It has the largest Rose Garden in Asia and the 'Sukhna Lake', whose surroundings and the water front add to the beauty of the city.

Chandigarh has also emerged as an important Tennis Centre. Chandigarh Lawn Tennis Association (CLTA) has developed a unique training programme, called the CHART (Chandigarh Academy for Rural Tennis). It picks up raw hands from rural areas at young age and grooms them into budding players. Some of its trainees have made it to the All India level. It is on the ATP circuit. It has organized some matches for the Davis Cup. CLTA has established a partnership with the Madrid Tennis Foundation (FTM) in Spain since 2013. They are working together to build excellence in tennis among deserving and talented boys and girls from villages in the States of Punjab and Haryana. They experience difficulties in getting visas and need to be helped to overcome these constraints.

## A Glimpse into Cultural Activities at Chandigarh

Some of the important events, which are organized regularly on an annual basis and some of which have also foreign participation, are covered in the following paragraphs.

### *International Puppet Festival*

This festival is organized every year during the month of February. The fourth international festival was held at Chandigarh on February 6-9, 2016 and was organized by the Department of Culture, Chandigarh, in collaboration with the Tagore Theatre Society and the Ishara Puppet Theatre Trust (IPTT). It was the 14th international festival organized by the IPTT in India and puppeteers also performed in other cities, like Delhi, Jodhpur, Jaipur, Kolkata and Pune. Puppeteers from USA, Sweden and Switzerland participated along with Aakaar Puppet Theatre from India.

Overall support came from Teamwork Arts, Delhi. Shams Jawaid of the Teamwork highlighted the significance of the shows, which was not only to fascinate the kids and the entire audience but was also to promote moral ideas in to kids through stories and poems (Kaur, Navjot, 2016). The Tagore Theatre, which has a capacity for over 1000 persons, was jam-packed with children and their parents. All the shows met with resounding success and appreciation from the audience.

The 6th International Puppet Show was held on February 25-28, 2018, with participation of Groups from Argentina, Brazil, Italy and India. The festival has been held annually since 2013, with participation of different countries. The intent is 'to preserve the art form of puppetry by using children's curiosity as a catalyst'. Kuldeep Sharma, Director of Tagore Theatre rated highly the significance of this festival in these words, "There is no festival like this exclusively for children (in Chandigarh) and puppetry is a traditional art form of India. To preserve this tradition, we started this festival" (Mehr Gill, 2018).

### *Rose Festival*

This festival has been held every year in the month of February since 1972. This is the time when the garden is in full bloom. As many as '830 varieties of roses, including hybrid teas, floribunda and polyanthus welcomed visitors at the three-day 44th Rose Festival' in 2016 (The Tribune, 2016). In conjunction with the cultural programme at the Rose Garden, a three-day Cultural Bonanza is also organized. At this function, well known Bollywood and Punjabi singers/artists perform. That year the chief guest was gardener Budh Ram, which was a departure from the standard practice of inviting VIPs.

The 46th Rose Festival was held on February 23-25, 2018. The festival is a much-awaited event in the city and a delight for travellers. Many people visited the show to not only view the beauty of roses, but also to learn about the different varieties of roses and to take part in the various activities organised. For children, it was an occasion to participate in interactive programmes, such as Rose Prince and Rose Princess competition, brass and pipe band contest, on-the-spot painting competition, quiz and more. Cultural programmes were organized in the evenings as usual.

***Theatre Festivals***

Chandigarh is host to many theatre festivals organized by the Sangeet and Natak Academy, Punjab Arts Council and many other groups. The 13th Edition of the TFT Winter Festival was organized by Theatre For Theatre (TFT) Group from January 29 to February 27, 2018. This is claimed 'to be the biggest celebration of theatre the country has seen'. Its unique feature is that the festival ushered in "thirty new colours and aspects of life in the form of stage plays, nukkad-natak among others with production being carried out by nationally acclaimed directors" (The Times of India, 2018).

***First Military Literary Festival***

Chandigarh is host to two literary festivals every year. The focus of the festivals is on promoting the work of budding writers and also to attract the youth into the art of writing.

Chandigarh, which is a home to retired defence officers, took a unique step in holding the First Military Literary Festival on December 7-9, 2017. Captain Amarinder Singh, Chief Minister of Punjab, who is also a military historian and written a number of books, gave the valedictory address. The organizers plan to hold this Festival annually.

***Pracheen Kala Kendra***

This is a private teaching institution, set up in 1956 that offers degree courses in Hindustani vocal and instrumental music, Kathak and Bharatnatyam among the Indian classical dances and also folk dances and song. Every March, it organises a week-long festival of music and dance as well as smaller programmes -baithaks- on the 11th of every month. Since its inception, it has been hosting Annual Pracheen Kala Kendra Nritya & Sangeet Sammelan, to which renowned artists are invited. Since 2005, it is also holding annual function to confer Award to a leading Indian musician or dancer. All its functions are fully packed.

The 48th edition of the All India Bhaskar Rao Nritya and Sangeet Sammelan, organised by the Pracheen Kala Kendra opened on February 20, 2018. The Haryana Governor Kaptan Singh Solanki inaugurated the programme and lauded the untiring efforts of the Kendra. On this occasion, Pracheen Kala Kendra Annual Awards of Excellence were presented to four maestros, including tabla legend Pandit Anindo Chatterjee, Vidushi Manjari Sinha, Art Critic (Delhi), and N Khosla, IAS (retd), Chandigarh (The Tribune, 2018).

### *National Crafts Mela*

Every year, this 'Mela' (Festival) is held at Kalagram, Chandigarh during the month of January. It is a display of culture, traditions, and arts and crafts of various states of India and attracts thousands of visitors. The theme for the 7th edition of Chandigarh Crafts Mela in January 2016 was Kashmir to Kohima (North to North East). Apart from stalls that sell arts and crafts items, it also has food stalls and cultural dance performances, which provide a glimpse in to cultures from different regions and provide cultural connectivity. The 8th Craft Mela was held during Nov 4-13, 2016. The Ninth Craft Mela was held on November 2-12, 2017 and the theme was 'Dadra and Nagar Haveli'.

## Other Sigificant Cultural Events

Chandigarh has also emerged as an important city for the organization of diverse types of cultural activities by local, regional and international groups. Some of the important activities that were organized during 2016 and 2018 are given below:

### *Invocation Rock Seed, Feb 8-16, 2016*

A sculpture workshop and symposium organized by the Chandigarh Lalit Kala Akademy was held at the Government Museum and Art Gallery, Sector 10, Chandigarh. The event brought together many stone carvers. The core idea was on the making of Chandigarh through art work (The Tribune 2016:2).

### *Art Festival, Feb. 2016*

This Festival was organized to present popular and folk art in India and abroad? The foreign participants were from Sweden, New Zealand,

Canada and France. This festival had foreign support from the Canada Arts Council and the New Zealand Arts Council.

### *Panchkula Art and Literary Festival (PALF), February 6-7, 2016*

PALF was an effort to bring Panchkula, which is one of the constituents of the Chandigarh Tricity, to the literary map of India. The festival focused on certain issues, like contemporary history of Punjab, Punjabi cinema and the impact of technology in daily life (*Chandigarh Times* 2016). A number of books were launched at this festival.

### *Design Festival, 2016*

The students at the Inter National Institute of Fashion Design (INIFD) imaginatively created Plaza Singapore right here at Chandigarh, as 'The Mall' was the theme of the exhibition. And once there, you cannot help but pick up memories of more than just the goodies. The spectacle was based on the concept of the Sentosa Underwater World in Singapore and showcased awe-inspiring aquatic life, including fish, and even sharks (Malik, Saurabh, 2016).

### Chandigarh Theatre Festival 2017

The Three-day Chandigarh Festival was organized by the Chandigarh Cultural Affairs Department and the Tagore Theatre during May 26-28, 2017. It aimed at providing an opportunity to the residents to view leading thespians on stage. Three well known thespians presented their performances-Himani Shivpuri (Tota Maina Ki Kahani); Liliput and Dharamvir Bharti (Anjam-e-Gulistan Kya Hoga?) and Shekhar Sen (Tulsi) [Tagore Theatre].

### *Tagore: A Musical Conversation, 2018*

Alliance Française, Chandigarh organized this function on April 25, 2018, which was recitation of Tagore's poetry in French and English interspersed with flute music. This was dubbed as three-in-one connectivity; dialogue between music and poetry; English and French languages, French artist and Indian students and India and France. Its uniqueness resulted in good response from the audience.

### *Russian Play, 2018*

Chandigarh has emerged as a centre for the organization of plays, based on stories by foreign authors, as it has adequate theatre facilities, including the Tagore Theatre. A city-based group, 'Satvik Arts' staged a play

'Khwahish' on April 16, based on a Russian story-The Shoemaker and the Devil-written by Anton Chekhov (The Times of India, 2018:1).

## Chandigarh Connecting India- Pakistan

Chandigarh is ideally located in facilitating cultural and commercial activities with Pakistan, given the similarity of culture, cuisine and clothing. It is connected with Pakistan through land border at Wagah-Atari, which is at a distance of 250 kilometers from Chandigarh. We would now focus on some of the programmes and activities, which have become an annual feature of the Chandigarh scene.

### *CRRID*

The Centre for Research in Rural and Industrial Development (CRRID), with which the Author is involved as an honorary advisor, has played an important role in facilitating this connectivity, in promoting people to people contacts among diverse groups of the academia, agriculturists, small and medium business entrepreneurs, media and opinion makers. Some of these would be covered in one of the chapters in the Book.

### *Visit by Pakistani High Commissioners: 2016 and 2018*

High Commissioner Abdul Basit visited St. Stephen's School, Chandigah on May 10, 2016 and gave a message to students, on the need for establishing communication between the youth of the two countries, as they presented 'a ray of hope' in improving the atmospherics for the development of friendly relations between the two countries. Principal Harold Carver narrated how students from India and Pakistan were holding communicative sessions. He added, "The students have been sharing letters and Skype sessions with the students overseas, breaking the barrier of mistrust and lack of communication" (Ahuja, Aastha, 2016).

It was a repeat of the same story, when the new Pakistani High Commissioner Sohail Mahmood visited Chandigarh on April 23-24, 2018. He interacted with the Vice Chancellor of the Panjab University, faculty and students; the Author was present at this meeting. Vice Chancellor Arun Grover suggested the use of soft link of Skype for video conferencing, discussions and lectures between the Panjab University and its counterpart in Lahore, before links through formal channels were established (Oindrile Mukherjee). The Pakistani High Commissioner Sohail Mahmood stressed the importance of connectivity between the universities, as he said, 'The major challenge for the two countries is the free flow of communication.

People of both the countries should be open to exchange of ideas' (The Hindustan Times, 2018).

***Panjab University Alumni Association***

At the Annual Conference of the Alumnis, International Brand Ambassador of the University, Dr. Satinder Sartaj, a famous Sufi singer and actor ('Black Prince') said that 'Art and culture can connect India and Pakistan'. He also made a proposal for the establishment of 'Shahmukhi' Centre at the University. An Indian Studies Centre has already been set up at the Punjab University, Lahore. Other distinguished alumni, Irshad Kamal, lyricist for Bollywood films, also saw positive role for the artists in the peace process between the two countries (The Tribune, 2018).

***Visits by Pakistani Journalists***

Visits by journalists from Pakistan are not uncommon, given the road linkage between the two countries. At a recent international seminar on the 'Role of Media in Promotion of Peace in South Asia', journalists from both the countries gave 'a message to spread peace among India and Pakistan through cultural ties' (The Tribune, 2016:3). It was also suggested that such cultural exchanges could take place in the form of music and celluloid art. They asked for caution on sensational reporting.

***Visit by Different Interest Groups***

Chandigarh has hosted visits of entrepreneurs, golfers, retired army officers, sports persons, teachers and advocates. A 40-member delegation of Advocates from Pakistan, led by Farah Faiz Beg, first Women Vice-Chairperson, Punjab Bar Council, Lahore, visited Chandigarh on February 7, 2016 to participate at a seminar on the 'Role of The Jurists' in strengthening democracy in the Asia Pacific Region. They echoed a message on promoting connectivity; generating greater awareness and learning from one another. The message was that greater flow of people across the border would help in clearing existing misperceptions (The Indian Express, 2016).They made a request for the relaxation of the existing visa regimes, to facilitate visits by more delegations. At the popular level, the delegates played two friendly cricket matches with the Chandigarh Bar Council.

***Visits by Theatre Groups***

The former President of the Chandigarh Sangeet and Natak Akademi G S Chani was one of the pioneers in leading a delegation of his Theatre

Group- SEWA Drama Repertory- to Pakistan in 1997, as guests of the Pirzada Foundation. They received a hearty welcome and endeared themselves to locals through their performances. Their three-day visa was extended to seven days. They were invited to family homes, which resulted in their building personal relations with people in Pakistan. From the Pakistani side, Ajoka Theatre Group has made regular appearances in Punjab; so has the Sufi Singer Abida Hussain, who has mesmerized listeners at Chandigarh.

### *Launching of the Book on 'Lost Heritage: The Sikh Legacy of Punjab'*

The Tricity Photo Art Society launched this book on March 2, 2016 at Chandigarh, written by Amardeep Singh, a Singaporean. It is a Coffee Table Book, but goes beyond capturing, not only well known historical buildings, but also others in remote places. The excellence of the Book lies in its narrative as the author captures the human aspect of the lost heritage of the Sikhs in Punjab (Pakistan). He makes out a case for the preservation of the Sikh Architecture, so as to avoid losing this heritage. Given the Modi government's interest, it would be worthwhile for the government to promote a project on the preservation of the Indian Heritage in Pakistan, as there are historical places belonging to the Hindus and other communities also. INTACH could be asked to prepare a project outline for the consideration of the government.

### *Khushwant Singh Literary Festival (KSLF)*

KSLF is held every year at Kasauli, which is in the vicinity of Chandigarh. It is emerging as an important festival for rendezvous between Indian and Pakistani writers and opinion makers. The fourth festival was held on October 9-11, 2015. From Pakistan, it attracted luminaries like former Foreign Minister Khurshid Mahmud Kasuri, Ambassador Abida Hussain, Historian and Art critic Fakir Aijjazuddin among others. From India, Farooq Abdullah, Ambassador Satinder Lambah, former Minister Mani Shankar Aiyer and former Director RAW AS Dulat made their appearances.

### *French Cultural Presence in Chandigarh*

Alliance Française de Chandigarh was set up in 1983 and 'has played a pioneering rôle in promoting French culture in the City Beautiful' (Dominique Waag).[2] It is one of the 16 such centres in India and works closely with the French Embassy. It is registered as a civil society group, like all other 'Alliance Française' establishments abroad. It is a part of Foudation AF, through which it gets 'its moral and legal sustenance'. It is self financing and the income largely comes from tuition fees for learning French. The Director of the Centre is the only one, whose salary is paid by the French government. It is centrally located and has its own premises and provides easy access to visitors. Its membership largely comes from the youth, who are also the dominant participants in its activities.

Since its inception in 1983, the Centre has been regularly organising cultural events and is one of the most active diplomatic centres in Chandigarh. Its aim is to to bring 'the disparate, yet similar cultures of India and France closer' through organizing diverse cultural events, exhibitions and interactions with visitors and artists from France and other European countries (Dominique Waag). It also organizes certain activities that mark Indian festivals, like Diwali, Holi and Lohri, apart from focusing on French activities.

The Centre's primary focus is on the teaching of the French language across all levels (beginner to the advanced) and for all age groups. It has a competent group of teachers that employs latest educational tools and uses unique methodology, which help students in getting internationally recognized DELF/DALF certificates that are provided by the French Ministry of Education. It also provides specialized courses and personalized coaching. It also provides supplementary teaching facilities to students from the Panjab University under a mutual arrangement. It's 'Campus France' Desk helps in facilitating admission of students to French universities.

The Centre offers a potpourri of cultural activities, which range from film shows, musical programmes, circus, theatre etc. It organized EU Film Festival in June 2016, although it had screened some films from individual countries in the previous years. One of the films showed the role of Sikh soldiers during World War I. What was amazing to note was that the soldiers had donned their turbans, as they fought shoulder to shoulder with the French soldiers? Now the wearing of the same turban has become an issue for French Values.

The Centre's Library has a collection of 3500 documents: books, comics, newspapers and magazines, music CDs, movies DVDs, documentary films, covering all the areas and for all ages (children and adults, Francophone and non- Francophone). The Centre has tied up with local hotels to promote certain activities, like French Gastronomic Dinner at the Taj Hotel or Musical Performances (Jazz and Black Metal) at Mountview Hotel. On its part, it also helps other diplomatic missions in providing its facilities to mount their activities, such as a photo exhibition titled 'Child and Early Forced Marriages' by Canada in March 2016 and another photo exhibition on women empowerment by the Mexican Embassy in June, 2016.

Alliance Française is also going directly to peoples at the Malls and Plaza. It organized an open door Circus Show, 'The Horsemen' by three French street theatre artists (comedians) - Jean-Luc Prevost, Olivier Rimaud and Julien Blandino - at the Plaza in Sector 17, Chandigarh. The Group 'has received international renown, as they manage to send a message, laced with humour to public at large'. The artists were able to relate to the Indian audience through their smattering knowledge of Hindi and regaled them with their pranks, which went down well with the assembled crowd that belonged to different age and gender groups (Kaur, Amarjot, 2016).

## UK's Presence in Chandigarh

The office of the Deputy High Commissioner was set up in 2013, but was officially opened in the present premises in March 2015 by the British Foreign Secretary. Earlier they had trade office since 2000. The office was set up as a part of the British Government's policy shift to connect with the developing economies like India, rather than concentrating on Europe, as a part of diversification of its focus. Under this overall policy thrust, called 'Network Shift', it is aimed to provide better networking with India and other countries (David Elliot). In 2013, UK decided to open two new offices of Deputy High Commissioner at Chandigarh and Hyderabad. Another one was established at Ahmedabad in 2015. The office at Chandigarh covers the States of Punjab, Haryana, Himachal Pradesh, Uttarakhand, Rajasthan and the Union Territory of Chandigarh.

At Chandigarh, the British focus is on two areas: Political Relations and Trade, Investment and Education. The primary focus has been on education, academic partnerships, smart cities, trade and investment and climate change. Culture-related issues are being looked after by the British Council. UK is paying special attention on establishing academic linkages. It believes that this 'serves twin objectives-generating goodwill through students and augmenting the financial resources of the institutions/ universities'. The office of the Deputy High Commissioner has organized some educational seminars to attract students from India. It has directly promoted linkages with the Panjab University and has also helped educational institutions from UK.

Some of the important academic linkages that had been established during the last three years are given below:

- Wolver Hampton University and the Jaipur University (Jan 2015).
- Birmingham and Nottingham Universities and Panjab University (March, 2013).
- Aberdeen University and the University of Petroleum and Energy, Dehradun.
- Ashton University with IIT, Ropar and the Panjab Agriculture University (PAU), Ludhiana.

Another priority area is the establishment of Smart Cities Linkages. Such linkages were facilitated between Nottingham and Chandigarh. The focus of such linkages is to promote development of business relationship and educational connectivity. The process commenced in February 2014. A delegation from Nottingham visited Chandigarh in November 2015 and had interaction with the Chandigarh Administration and the City Municipal Corporation. Another delegation visited Chandigarh in February 2016 and focused on specific areas, like transport, waste management and heritage preservation.

Chandigarh is also emerging as the venue for high level visits, which symbolically help in connecting with people. A number of important dignitaries paid visits to The Northern Region and Chandigarh. Prince of Wales visited Dehradun in November 2013. Apart from visiting IMA, Forest Research Institute, he also participated in an 'Aarti' at Rishikesh. Prime Minister David Cameron visited Amritsar in February 2013 and visited Golden Temple and Jallianwala Bagh. Baroness Verma, Minister of Environment visited Chandigarh thrice-Sept 2013, Nov 2014 and Feb 2015. Preeti Patel, Minister for Diaspora visited India twice in Jan 2014 and Jan 2016, where she along with the Minister for External Affaires Sushma Swaraj, participated in a dialogue with Diaspora.

Steps were taken to promote UK's Brand Logo, 'Great' in Chandigarh and a number of activities were organized accordingly (David Elliott).[3] UK adopted 'Great' as it's 'Brand Logo' at the time of the Commonwealth Games in London in August 2014 and Diamond Jubilee Celebrations of the Coronation of the Queen. All the promotional activities, therefore, carry the logo 'Great'. The Deputy High Commissioner uses the logo 'Great' on his visiting cards. A 'Great Week' was organized at Chandigarh during November 21-28, 2015, which focused on multiple areas, with one specific event being held on each day of the week. These are as follows:

- Media Focus on Nov 21.
- Taste of British Curry Festival at the Taj Hotel, Nov 21-29 (Four Chefs were flown from UK).
- Great Debate on Climate Change at the India Business School (IBS), Mohali.
- Visit Great Britain (Tour operators were flown from UK).
- The Great Debate at DAV College, Chandigarh.
- The Great Network Reception (Hosted by the Deputy High Commissioner).

Diplomatic Missions at Chandigarh cooperate in organizing programmes jointly. Following are some of these activities:

- August 2014: Reception for the Commonwealth Games (With Canada).
- Sept 2014: Climate Date with France and Canada.
- May 2015: Charity for Earthquake victims in Nepal
- Nov 2014: Remembrance Day with Canada

***The British Council***

The office was set up in January 2015, as a part of UK's Outreach Programme, in conjunction with the setting up of the office of the British Deputy High Commissioner. Earlier UK had a British Library since 2000, which has become an integral part of the Council. The library works under the administrative control of ICCR, although it is run by them. The Council, however, enjoys full autonomy in the selection of books (Thiara, Tanisha).[4]

At present, the Library has 2000 members. The number had come down, since they shifted to the new premises, as the earlier location was more centrally located and convenient for visitors. Library is open to members only. The Council would like to covert this in to a 'Hub' and open the same to non-members (Thiara, Tanisha). The British Council's primary focus was on Shakespeare-related activities in 2016.

The British Council runs some other programmes, which focus on women, under privileged persons and children. Some of these include:

- Word Voice Project for the Underprivileged in Himachal Pradesh.
- Training of English Teachers.
- Reading Channels: Vivek High School.

***Association of British Scholars (ABS)***

It is alumni of scholars, who have studied in the United Kingdom. There, are 24 Chapters of this Association in India, including one at Chandigarh. It helps in connecting these scholars among themselves and local residents. Each chapter also organizes their own activities, which aim at generating more awareness on UK. This is an active organization and we can learn a lot from its experiences, in bringing about connectivity at the grassroots level.

## Canadian Presence in Chandigarh

The Canadian Consul General Christopher Gibbins[5] views 'Cultural Diplomacy as the "sub-text" of Public Diplomacy, even though he accepts that it carries a large component of culture'. For Canada, Public Diplomacy is 'aligned with its strategic interests', as Canada cannot pursue an omnibus policy at the global level, given human and financial constraints. Strategic Interests could fall under various categories-political, economic or social. In the case of India, it is broadly speaking, 'social and economic; social covers people to people connectivity i.e. Diaspora' (Christopher Gibbins). It has screened a number of documentaries on Indian Diaspora, in particular from the State of Punjab, which has five cabinet ministers in the Trudeau government in 2017.

For Canada, Public Diplomacy has two broad components-Academic and Culture. Academic component involves promoting academic linkages, offer of scholarship etc. It has a 'strong Canadian Studies Programme' that promotes study of Canadian history, culture and literature. It is, however, left to the academic institutes to forge such linkages and the Consulate General plays a supporting role. The 'Cultural component' involves 'exposure of Canadian artists abroad'. This is being 'revived as more funding has become available' (Christopher Gibbins).

Canada also has an 'Advocacy component' in its programmes, which focus on promotion of Canadian values. Values that are dear to Canada are:

'Diversity, Pluralism, Human Rights', in particular, 'Women and Children and Democracy'. While promoting such values, Canada pursues these with the idea to 'promote dialogue' and 'not to preach, but to build ties' (Christopher Gibbins). In pursuing these objectives, some programmes are initiated at the Canadian end, while others are initiated by local groups with funding provided by Canada.

A Photo Exhibition, titled 'Child and Early Forced Marriages', which was held at the Alliance Françoise Centre in March 2016, was a Canadian initiative by the Consulate General. Another programme on Women's Rights was arranged during November 2015-March 2016 by the Mahar Baba Charitable Trust.

The Consulate General fully utilizes social media in reaching out to people. It achieves twin objectives-generating awareness on Canada's policies and helps it in getting feedback on how Canada and its policies are perceived. Unlike the Canadian High Commission, the Consulate General does not use 'Facebook', as it lacks a team of dedicated experts. It, however, resorts to 'Twitter' and finds it useful. The Consulate General also uses 'WhatsApp' in sending advisories to Canadian citizens.

Chandigarh does not have sister-city relationship with any city in Canada. Similarly, there is no connectivity at the State level with Punjab, despite some earlier talks to that effect. The Consulate General maintains regular contacts with the local media. It receives feedback on the ethnic media from the Canadian end and does not liaise directly with them.

## The American Corner

The American Corner was opened on December 17, 2004 at the Chandigarh Library. It was the joint initiative of the American Embassy and the State Library. Robert Blake, Deputy Chief of Mission, US Embassy, who opened the Corner, described it 'as part of a global partnership initiative to reach out to people, where no US consulates exist' (The Times of India, 2004). The Corner is expected to be 'a window on America' and offer latest information on political, cultural, educational, economic and social trends in the United States. It is the fourth such Centre established in India; the other three being located at Ahmedabad, Bengaluru and Bhubaneshwar.

The Corner is easily accessible to its members, be it students, research scholars or entrepreneurs, being located in the premises of the Chandigarh State Library. The Corner is a kind of mini-library and is expected to provide information on 'life and culture in the United State' and is expected to become the first place to visit for 'accurate and up-to-date information'. The Centre has books, magazines, CD ROMs with full text articles, videos, DVDs and internet access (American Corner Website). The Corner has arranged interactive sessions with educationists to guide students, who are seeking admission to the universities in the United States. The Centre has also been responsible in organizing Literary Meets (The Tribune, 2007).

## India Meets Chicago

India is reconnecting with Chicago, as it pays homage to Swami Vivekananda, who acquired international recognition through delivery of his historic 'Message of Acceptance of ALL Faiths' at an Inter-Faith Conference in Chicago in 1893. The Government of India signed an MOU with the Art Institute of Chicago (AIC) in 2012, placing a bronze plaque in the Hall that commemorates his Address. AIC conducted "Vivekananda Memorial Program for Museum Excellence", to impart 'a broad range of knowledge on modern operations of museums like conservation, planning of exhibitions, etc., for a four-year period'. AIC was also expected to spend a part of the $ 500,000 grant in planning 'exhibitions and conservation techniques' (Dr. Ausaf Sayeed).[6]

Under another initiative connected with Swami Vivekananda, the Ministry of Culture, Government of India agreed to provide $ 1.5 million grant to the newly established Swami Vivekanand Chair at the University of Chicago. The Chair has two components- Short Term Visiting Professorship and an Annual Public Lecture. The fields of study would include, which are more relevant 'to the teachings and philosophies of the Swami, such as Indian philosophy, politics and social movements'. This is expected to 'enrich the University's Program for the Study of the Indian Subcontinent and further promote research and teaching of India's history and culture' (Dr. Ausaf Sayeed).

Chicago is an important Centre for Study for Indian students, as it has a number of renowned universities. The University of Chicago is also known for the Study of the Indian Subcontinent. Currently, more than 60 faculty members are engaged in the study of South Asian history, culture and language. The University offers instruction in nine modern and two classical Indian languages, including advanced instruction in less commonly taught languages, such as Malayalam, Marathi and Telugu.

Chicago has emerged as one of the important destinations for the annual hosting of 'Eye on India' Festival, which is a six-week festival held during June/July at venues throughout the cultural landscape of Chicago. The

Festival is organized by Teamwork Arts, Delhi and has the overall support of our diplomatic mission and ICCR. It brings India to the Chicagoans, as they 'explore and experience Indian culture through a variety of interactive presentations and performances including literature, music, dance and food', by some of the foremost exponents of Indian literature and music (Eye on India Website).

Indian Council for Cultural Relations in association with the Consulate General of India Chicago, Punjabi Cultural Society of Chicago and Office of Governor of the State of Illinois hosted a photo exhibition on "The Sikhs – A Heritage of Valour and Devotion" at Chicago during September 9 – 13, 2013.The photo artist Sondeep Shankar had done a pioneering work that provided a glimpse of rich Sikh heritage and traditions. The exhibition showcased the valuable Sikh Heritage to devotees and admirers alike. The exhibition was also held at the Oak Creek Gurudwara in Milwaukee in Wisconsin and in the Gurudwara in Lansing in Michigan (CGI Chicago Website). There are approximately 700,000 Sikh Americans in the United States of America including thousands in the state of Illinois and they have a very active Punjabi Cultural Society.

## Chicago Meets India

Chicago meets India in diverse ways at multiple points. Chicago greets India on arrival at its International O'Hare Airport, as visitors see fluttering Indian Flag, along with flags from other countries with which Chicago has sister-city relationship. Chicago is also connected to India spiritually, as it was in this city that Swami Vivekananda gave the message of acceptance of other religions in 1893. The need for another similar message has become a top priority after recent terrorists' attacks in Paris, Brussels and Orlando.

Chicago offers opportunity for academic studies at its prestigious universities, like the University of Chicago and Kellogg University. Chicago is also home to Indian Diaspora and some of them have become a part of the 'Indian Development Story'; these include Sam Petroda, who spearheaded Information Technology and Communications (ITC) Revolution in India and Raghuram Rajan, the former Governor of the Reserve Bank of India.

India, through an artistic architectural structure, called, "Cloud' by Anish Kapur, a UK Indian, greets all visitors at the entry to the Millennium Park, the tourist and cultural spot, which is the Mecca for a visit by all the residents and foreign visitors.

Chicago also connects with India in another important way, as the City Council not only celebrates National Days, but also facilitates mounting of cultural activities, like National Day's Parade and other activities on National Day and during Heritage Week Celebrations, by cultural and diaspora associations.

Chicago is also actively involved in promoting Sister-Cities Relationships. It has such ties with 28 cities across the globe, including Delhi. This relationship is set up under an overall federal initiative taken by the US President Eisenhower in 1956, when the concept of 'Citizens Diplomacy' was evolved at a White House Conference (Salomon, Alexandra and Klocksin, Katie, 2014). The strength of the relationship is its focus on people to people connectivity. It results in student exchanges, economic cooperation, academic and language studies and cultural connectivity.

Sister Cities International marked the 60th anniversary year of Eisenhower initiative by holding the Annual Conference and Youth Leadership Summit on July 13-16, 2016 at Washington DC. The Celebration was not only 'to honor the 60 years of history behind SCI, but also its promising future of sustaining Eisenhower's original vision of fostering world peace through global people-to-people relationships' (Website SCI).

Chicago feels itself ideally placed, being a global city. An NGO called 'Sister Cities International' (SCI) oversees this relationship. SCI acts both as an advisory body and a source of funding for programmes. The criteria used to select partner cities, include its size, cultural connectivity, economic connectivity and presence of diaspora. It annually holds Chicago Sisterly Cities International Festival at Daley Plaza, which is the heart of the City. The Third Global Youth Ambassadors Leadership Summit was held in July 2018 at Chicago; the author attended it on July 27. The focus is on teenage girls emerging socially active leaders. 25 participants attended, with 15 from foreign countries and 10 from Chicago.

Chicago-Delhi Sister-City relationship was set up in 2001. There is a joint Chicago-Delhi Committee to organize various activities. Some of the latest activities organized at the Chicago end, included seminars/discussions on topics, like 'Legacy of Mahatma Gandhi', 'American Retrenchment: Implications for India and Asia' and 'Delhi: India's Defining Moment'; a fashion show, 'The Splendid Indian Closet' and social awareness events on heart diseases, 'A Red Sari Evening'.

Chicago is one among many cities in the United States that are rolling out their own smart cities initiatives. Chicago has also been selected under the 100 Resilient Cities (RC) Programme, initiated by the Rockefeller Foundation in 2013, which provides for some funding. Chicago is among the 67 cities selected so far under this programme. In June, 2016, it appointed Aaron Koch as its Chief Resilience Officer (CRO). Under this programme, cities are expected 'to connect and understand their challenges' (Husain, Nausheen, 2016). According to Navigant Research, smart cities market was expected to be US $ 12.1 billion in 2016 and is expected to rise to US $ 27.5 billion by 2023. Barcelona has been dubbed as the best smart city.

Chicago is taking a number of steps, the latest being 'Array of Things' developed at Argonne National Laboratory, in collaboration with the University of Chicago and the School of the Art Institute of Chicago. It has received a grant of US $ 3.1 million from the National Science Foundation (Bergen, Kathy, 2016). CISCO and Microsoft are involved in the implementation of smart cities projects in many countries. While smart city project is being implemented, there is an ongoing debate among experts, whether smart cities would be better cities (Bergen, Kathy, 2016). India needs to keep this in view and learn from the experiences of other cities.

Chicago is also the City that shows the way in meeting the cultural needs not only of its residents, but also of its diaspora and foreign visitors. Annual Grant Park Music Festival, which made its 82nd opening on June 16, 2016 at the Millennium Park (Rhein, John von: 1, 2016), provided an important laboratory to learn; how to use Parks for people friendly activities. It is a kind of Public Private Partnership (PPP), with the Chicago Park District providing US $ 2.9 million of the US $ 5.9 million operating budget for 2016 (Rhein, John von, 2016). The Park is a combination of Jay Pritzker Pavillion, which opens into the Great Lawn, where over ten thousand people could throng. It is a place that provides facilities for listening pleasure as well as open space for rendezvous with family and friends. It hosts not only world class American artists, but also artists from foreign countries, including India. Anoushka Shankar performed on July 19, 2018; the author attended the performance.

Chicago City is demographically multicultural in character, as it has diaspora from all over the world. The City satisfies the ethnic needs of its various components and recognizes Little India, Little Sweden, Little China and Little Italia and so on. At the same time, it provides facilities for easier integration in to the social fabric, while they realize their individual dreams.

It is in Chicago, where India and Pakistan meet at Devon Street, which is the commercial centre and has shops and restaurants run by diaspora. The street is divided in to two halves-The Gandhi Way and The Jinnah Way, where Indians and Pakistanis can mingle in harmony. The City is host to National Day Parades taken on national days and facilitates diaspora for their contributions to preserve its multicultural character.

## Making Grassroots Cultural Diplomacy: A Win-Win Phenomenon

Chandigarh is a good microcosm for the study of the working of grassroots diplomacy, as there is a growing recognition worldwide that a successful diplomatic programme/ effort has to be people-centric and has to reach out to other corners of the country rather than remaining confined to the capital city.

Opening of resident offices at Chandigarh has helped diplomatic missions 'in establishing greater connectivity at the regional level with different states', which was not possible from Delhi. There was thus a clear recognition on 'the need for such grassroots connectivity'; as they planned 'to widen networks' to bring more cities under their programmes/ activities.

Diplomatic Missions acknowledge the importance of Chandigarh, as an important regional hub. Chandigarh has all the ingredients; a growing regional educational and cultural centre; a good infrastructure, like parks, halls and theatres; presence of stakeholders, such as ICCR's Regional Office, Panjab University and Diplomatic offices of Canada, France, UK and USA.

While all stakeholders agreed on the importance of the role of Chandigarh, they played different tunes, as they conducted cultural diplomacy. The message was clear; cultural diplomacy was essential, but the thrust could vary to suit their specific interests.

For France, it is Art and Culture and the French Language, as it connected with the Youth. For UK, it is Image Building to promote its commercial interests and promote UK as an important destination for students.

For Canada, it is to stay connected with Diaspora, given its critical importance for elections. It is also to perform its 'Advocacy Role', as cultural diplomacy was getting integrated with public diplomacy. For

USA, it was still a baby step, generating awareness on America, while also using it to attract students.

ICCR has to be cognizant of the prevailing perceptions at Chandigarh on its role, as this would help it in streamlining its programmes and activities at its Regional Office. Some of these are indicated below:

- ICCR is Delhi-Centric and it should promote artists from other regions.
- ICCR should aim to go beyond 'Classical Dances" and look at other forms of performing arts, like Folk Theatre and Folk Music and Dance.
- The aim should be to project India's cultural diversity and promote rich heritage of its folk culture.
- ICCR's Regional Advisory Committee's role needs to be activated and its meetings arranged at regular intervals.
- The Regional Director should be encouraged to play the role of a Promoter also.

Where does Chicago fit in this exercise on grassroots diplomacy? It represents dual value; firstly, as a source of information and secondly to serve as a guidepost that would be ideal for connectivity with Chandigarh. It offers a fertile ground for learning about the functioning of Sister-Cities Relationship, as Chandigarh forges its own city-state relationship.

How should Chandigarh go in for a 'Smart City'? Chicago may provide some answers, as it baptizes itself through the razing fiery debate on 'Smart vs. Better Cities'. Chicago can certainly provide a good narrative and some clues on the management of diversity.

Chandigarh could also learn from Chicago on how to make its Parks people-friendly. Educational connectivity between the Panjab University and Universities at Chicago would add a new dimension to the relationship.

ICCR's Regional Office at Chandigarh should be made more pro-active and encouraged to take initiatives and should not act as a mere post office. ICCR has to consider empowering him/her and plan activities on a medium term basis. ICCR should consider entering in to an MOU with Punjab and the Chandigarh Administration, on similar lines as with Haryana.

## Endnotes

1 Nalini Singhal, Director, Regional Centre, ICCR, Chandigarh. Meeting on April 6, 2016 at Chandigarh.

2 Mr. Dominique Waag, Director, Alliance Françoise, Chandigarh. Meeting on April 18, 2016 at Chandigarh.

3 Mr. David Elliott, Deputy High Commissioner, British High Commission, Chandigarh. Meeting on March 4, 2016 at Chandigarh.

4 Ms. Thiara, Tanisha, Head, British Council, Chandigarh. Meeting on March 4, 2016 at Chandigarh.

5 Christopher Gibbins, Consul General of Canada, Chandigarh. Meeting on April 15, 2016 at Chandigarh.

6 Dr. Ausef Sayeed, Consul General of India at Chicago. Meeting on August 15, 2015 at Chicago USA).

## References

Ahuja, Aastha, 2016, 'Pak high commissioner in Chandigarh: The youth of both countries are a ray of hope', *The Tribune*, May 11.

American Corner Website, https://www.facebook.com/American-Corner-Chandigarh. (Accessed on December 19, 2017).

AR Chandigarh, 2015-16, Annual Report, Regional Office, ICCR, Chandigarh.

Bergen, Kathy, 2016, 'Will making Chicago a "smart city" make a better city', *The Chicago Tribune*, May 1.

CGI Chicago, Website, www.indianconsulate.com (Accessed on December 19, 2017).

Chandigarh State Library Website, http://cslchd.gov.in.

*Chandigarh Times*, 2016, 'Day 2: Two Book launches', February 8.

Eye on India, Website: http://eyeonindia.org/ (Accessed on December 19, 2017).

Husain, Nausheen, 2016, 'Eyeing sustainability, Chicago hiring chief resilience officer', *The Chicago Tribune*, May 1.

Kaur, Amarjot, 2016, 'No horsing around!', *The Tribune*, March 9.

Kaur, Navjot, 2016, 'Puppet show continues to delight children', *The Chandigarh Times*, February 8.

Malik, Saurabh, 2016, 'Uniquely Singapore', *The Tribune*, May 26.

MEA 2015-16, Annual Report of the Ministry of External Affairs, New Delhi.

Mehr Gill, 'International Puppet Festival to kick off on February 25 in Chandigarh', *The Indian Express*, February 2018.

Oindrile Mukherjee, 'Academia can bridge gap between two countries', *The Indian Express,* April 25, 2018.

Prashar, Sachin, 2014, 'Focus on States in Modi's diplomatic roadmap', *The Hindu*, August 17.

Rhein, John von: 1, 2016, 'Grant Park fest opens with sound relief', *The Chicago Tribune*, June 17.

Rhein, John von: 2016,: 'Late contract deal saves Grant Park Music Fest opener', *The Chicago Tribune*, June 15.

Sahai, Paramjit, 2013: 'Time to define the role of States', *Power Politics,* March.

Sahai, Paramjit, 2015: 'Connecting the neighbours', *Power Politics*, November.

Salomon, Alexandra and Klocksin, Katie, 2014. 'Sister Cities: Chicago's international family', July 15. (http://www.wbez.org/shows/curious-city/sister-cities-chicagos-international-family/6f2c3b84-a21e-40f8-a0a7-97163164e161). (Assessed on 15 December 2017).

Tagore Theatre, 2017. https://www.bookmyevent.com/EventDetail.aspx?cid=0&eid=10526&did=0&type=E (Accessed on December 15, 2017).

*The Hindustan Times*, 2018, 'Pak envoy bats for exchange programs', April 25.

*The Indian Express*, 2016: 'Special Visa to advocates can help in strengthening India-Pak ties', February 7.

*The Indian Express*, 2016, 'Yoga Day Live: PM Modi performs Yoga with 30,000 participants in Chandigarh, worldwide celebrations ensue', July 22 (updated).

*The Times of India*, 2004, 'American Corner opens at State Library', December 18.

*The Times of India*, 2018, '30-day winter theatre fest kicks off today', January 30.

*The Times of India*, 2018:1, 'Russian play staged in Hindi at Tagore Theatre', April 17.

*The Tribune*, 2007: http://www.tribuneindia.com/2007/20070114/cth2.htm (Accessed on December 19, 2017).

*The Tribune*, 2014, 'India, Australia share 'special bond', says Modi', November 16.

*The Tribune*, 2015, 'In the course of action', September 5.

*The Tribune*, 2016, Rose Festival, '44th Rose Festival to start today', January 19.

*The Tribune*, 2016: 1, 'When stories speak', February 9.

*The Tribune*, 2016: 2, 'Panjab University a hotspot for overseas students', June 12.

*The Tribune*, 2016: 3, 'Cultural ties key to promoting peace in South Asia: Scribes', April 11.

*The Tribune* 2018, 'Nritya & Sangeet Sammelan begins', February, 21.

*The Tribune*, 2018:1, 'Futile to censor songs, says Sartaj', May 4.

Website of Cultural Department, http://chandigarh.gov.in/dpr_aboutculture.asp, ( Accessed on December 19, 2017).

Website SCI, http://chicagosistercities.com/upcoming_event/sister-cities-internationals-60th-anniversary-celebration-annual-conference-and-youth-leadership-summit/ (Accessed on December 19, 2017).

# Section – VII

# Culture Diplomacy Operations at Diplomatic Missions-Indian and Foreign

# Chapter – XIII

# Cultural Diplomacy Scenario: Indian Diplomatic Missions Abroad

## Introduction

In this chapter, the focus in on the role of diplomatic missions, both as initiators of new programmes as well as facilitators in the implementation of various activities that are initiated at the headquarters by ICCR and other relevant organizations. I can think of a few initiatives taken at different assignments, such as promoting Media Linkages with Malawi; connecting with the Folk Groups and Artists and Authors in Sweden; promoting local cultural groups, like the Temple of Fine Arts and the Sutra Theatre in Malaysia; involving Indian States directly by encouraging visits of Chief Ministers to Malaysia and safeguarding the interests of Indian students in Russia, consequent to the breakup of USSR and facilitating visits of Heads of States from Central Asia, leading to the signing of cultural agreements.

A number of diplomatic missions have taken similar initiatives. A few of these come to my mind, such as sprucing up Bollywood's presence in China by Ambassador Ashok Kantha by holding a Film Festival in 2014; Ambassador Sunil Lal[1] establishing the BRIND ARC (Brazil India Association for Knowledge Network) in December 2014; Ambassador Navdeep Suri[2] launching Pat Farmer, a former Member of Parliament from Australia on a mission to promote 'Spirit of India Run' in 2016, which took him from Kanyakumari to Kashmir, as he celebrated India's diversity and pluralism or Ambassador Gurjit Singh[3] bringing out a comic on India-Indonesian relations in the 'Panchtantra' format in 2015, to coincide with the Festival of India in Indonesia; Ambassador Lalit Mansingh celebrating Indian Festivals at the Embassy Residence in USA and High Commissioner Yash Sinha celebrating Baisakhi at the UK High Commission for the first time in 2017.

There are many more such examples but the above are used by way of illustration. Indian Embassy in Washington DC has designed a cluster approach, creating five clusters featuring different set of activities in each cluster, to promote cultural diplomacy. These are 'Reading India Series' (Indian authors and writings), 'Performing India Series' (music, dance and theatre), 'Beholding India Series' (film screening, art and photo exhibitions), 'Understanding India Series' (lectures on comprehensive and cross-sectional views on India), and 'Young India Series' (catering to younger audience).

The Embassy of India adopted a novel way, not only to reach out to Nepalese, but also to involve them as participants at the programmes arranged at the Nepal-Bharat Library at Kathmandu. In association with the BP Koirala Nepal-India Foundation, it provides opportunities to local participants, aimed at promoting Nepalese art, literature, music and films. It organises a series of monthly programmes; the first of the series called 'Conversation' began in January 2013 that provided forum for writers. The second called 'Poemandu' launched a poetry recitation programme in March 2013. The third 'Cinemandu' was on screening of Nepalese films. The fourth, 'Voices' provided space for sharing of views and interaction, to young and upcoming journalists, thinkers, scholars. The above programmes are increasingly popular and have been regularly held every month and are well attended with the hall brimming to its full capacity of 100 persons. The programmes have acquired a stature of 'Brand' and have been taken to other cities in Nepal, such as Pokhra, Nepalgunj, Bigung, Biratnagar and Janakpur (Abhay K).

To determine the role played by Indian diplomatic missions in the area of cultural diplomacy, the Heads of Missions were requested to respond to a questionnaire (Annexure I) on a number of issues. These ranged from theoretical understanding of cultural diplomacy and its implementation; launching and execution of various programmes and activities. We received response from some Ambassadors and their Cultural Attachés, which was considered adequate for the purposes of our study.

Luckily for us, the response turned out to be representative in nature, as we were able to cover all the regions. In Europe, the response was from Finland, Estonia, Belgium, Germany and Austria; in Asia, the response was from Maldives, Afghanistan, Sri Lanka,[4] Qatar,[5] Pakistan, Australia, Malaysia, Mongolia and China; in the Americas, the response was from Brazil and USA (Washington DC and Chicago).

The initial response was followed by interaction with the Ambassadors/ Cultural Attaches, which helped in further clarifying important issues. All the diplomatic missions, however, did not strictly follow the questionnaire as they were given the latitude to adopt a flexible approach. The emphasis was more on the content and not the format. Based on these responses, an attempt is made to look at the picture that emerges in respect of different countries.

## Afghanistan

There is an overall acceptance that cultural diplomacy 'plays a major role in people to people contacts and improving bilateral relations' (Viraj Singh).[6] In the case of Afghanistan, the current security situation has practically diminished the prospects for organizing activities in Afghanistan, despite the fact that the Mission draws up an Annual Plan of Action for promoting culture. This became more conspicuous when ICCR was unable to send a cultural troupe to Afghanistan to join in the celebrations, when Bamayan was declared the 2015 SAARC Cultural Capital. Despite these constraints, unidirectional cultural connectivity has been maintained, with India facilitating visits of individual artists and performing groups to India. Here again, such visits had to be funded by India and thereby restricting the same to specific omnibus programmes/ festivals organized by India.

Afghanistan's participation, therefore, has been restricted to some of the special occasions, as mentioned below during 2014-15:

- SAARC Band Festival, 7-9 November 2014, New Delhi. This festival was organized by ICCR in coordination with MEA and SEHER. A four-member Morcha Musical Band participated along with bands from other SAARC countries.
- Performance by Rhubab Groupe: This group was led by a famous Rhubab player Humanyoun Sakhi and it performed at the ICCR Auditorium at Azad Bhavan on November 20, 2014. It also performed at the Rashtrapati Bhavan in the presence of the President and former Afghan President Hamid Karzai.
- Participation of Parwaz Puppet Theatre: An 8-member group participated at the 13th International Puppet Theatre Festival. The group performed at Delhi and Jaipur during February 3-12, 2015.

India signed a Cultural Agreement with Afghanistan in 1963. There is no current Cultural Exchange Programme (CEP), which is understandable. There is a Cultural Centre, which largely looks after the implementation of ICCR's Scholarship Scheme. A music teacher that was posted was withdrawn in 2014, keeping in view the prevailing security situation. This has also prevented the Centre from organizing any kind of cultural event, seminars and conferences that required public participation. The Centre, therefore, is left to look after the residual cultural activities that arise from time to time.

India enjoys 'tremendous soft power due to cultural and linguistic similarities with Bollywood and Hindi films being great Ambassadors of our culture' (Viraj Singh). Indian TV Series, 'Saas *Bhi* Thi *Kabhi Bahu*' (Mother-in-Law was also bride sometime ago) was so popular that Kabul would come to standstill, when this programme was telecast. It was this cultural link that Prime Minister Modi tried to resurrect through '*Kabuliwala*', when he visited Kabul in December 2015.The focus of Indian cultural diplomacy should be on the building of 'civilization and brotherly relations, given the commonality of social customs and traditions that exist between our two countries' (Viraj Singh).

It is in the area of education and human resource development that the relationship ticks. India provides 1000 scholarships annually to students under a Special Afghanistan Scheme that is being implemented by ICCR. These are fully utilized by Afghanistan, as students pursue their undergraduate, postgraduate and even Ph.D. programmes. However, there are no student exchanges. A small beginning in this direction was made with the visit of a five-member children group and one supervisor from Habibia School that participated at the Annual Event of the National Bal Bhavan during November 14-20, 2015.

India also offers 500 ITEC slots annually. Scholarships and ITEC slots are fully utilized. The capacity building programme has emerged as an important tool and serves to build bridges, as the same is being well appreciated by the Afghan officials. A 300-member strong dynamic Afghan Alumnae Association of India (AAAI) exists. A large number of AAAI members are on important posts in the Government of Afghanistan and are hence useful in connecting with other dignitaries.

There is still a sizeable Indian community, which now numbers around 2000-3000 of Afghan Sikhs and Hindus. Many of these have family connections, as some of their family members have moved to India and acquired Indian citizenship. This community keeps in regular touch with the Embassy and 'looks towards India as its spiritual home'. Besides this, there are a limited number of Indian citizens, who work as professionals for UN, African and International NGOs and private companies.

Despite the security hurdles, direct media contacts exist and these are working normally. The Embassy also assists in media exchanges, even though these are sporadic. Similarly, there is also a flow of Afghani experts, retired diplomats and strategic thinkers, who visit India, to attend seminars/events on regional security.

## Austria

Austria provides a unique opportunity for understanding the working of Indian cultural diplomacy in a country with which there is no cultural agreement. Cultural activities are, therefore, largely arranged by cultural organizations that exist in the private sector. Similarly, exchange programmes in the education field are also conducted directly by the educational institutions. Vienna, as one of the cultural capitals of Europe, with a full cultural calendar and openness to new forms of Art and Culture, therefore, provides a friendly environment for the India-related cultural activities. All cultural activities, therefore, result in receiving a good audience (Rajiva Misra).[7]

A number of India-specific organizations, like the Institute for South Asian, Tibetan and Buddhist Studies, University of Vienna; Austria-India Association; Austrian Indian Institute; Raga Verein; Alankara Music Society, Vienna International Centre India Club etc., therefore get involved in promoting cultural events (Pawan Bodhe).[8] The Ministry of Culture provides support to these Friendship Societies. The focus of the Mission is on holding Indian Classical Dance and Music events; promoting learning of Hindi and Sanskrit, Yoga and Ayurveda; organizing Bollywood films shows and Indian Food Festivals etc.

Cultural activities are also being arranged by a number of NRI/PIOs organizations. The Embassy organizes programmes for visiting ICCR-sponsored or private artistes. Austrian culture/art promoters also arrange performances on a commercial basis by leading Indian musicians. Over the years, well known musicians, like Pandit Ravi Shankar, Ustad Amjad Ali Khan and Zakir Hussain etc. have performed at the prestigious Vienna Concert House. Other famous names that have performed included Anushka Shankar (May 2014), Ustad Zakir Hussain, Shankar Mahadevan, Selvaganesh and John McLaughlin (November 2013). Ustad Shuzaat Hussain, Pandit Vishwa Mohan Bhatt, Rustom and Abhay Sopori had their musical concerts in 2015.

A significant feature of the Indian cultural presence is through Indian residents, who have made Vienna as their home. The most prominent of these is maestro Zubin Mehta, who had studied in Vienna and continues to give New Year Performances at the State Opera House and the prestigious golden hall of the Musikverein. The 2015 New Year's Concert was conducted by Zubin Mehta. Among other Indian origin artists of western classical music include Mr. Marialene Fernandez, Professor of Chamber Music at the University of Music and Performing Arts, who is regularly on Radio and TV Broadcasts. Another Indian composer and conductor, Vijay Upadhaya's first symphony, 'Prayer Flags', was premiered on December 1, 2014. On the other hand, a number of Indians have learned Indian classical music and dance and are settled in Vienna. Some of these include Radha Anjali (Bharatnatyam), Reena Chandra (Flute), Alokesh Chandra (Sitar) and Kaveri Sageder (Kathak).

India also connects with Austria through the study of Indology. Sanskrit began to be taught at the University of Vienna in 1845. A Chair of Sanskrit Studies that was established then was converted into the Chair of Indology. In 1955, it was transferred to a separate Institute for South Asian, Tibetan and Buddhist Studies. ICCR entered into a MOU in February 2011 for the establishment of a Short-Term Chair of South Asian Studies, which has been regularly filled up by distinguished academicians. An Austrian Professor Dr. Bettina Sharada Baumer was awarded 'Padma Shri' in 2015 for her contributions in Indology. She has acquired Indian citizenship and is now the Director, Samvidyalaya, Varanasi. Another Austrian, Prof. Dr. Ebba Koch, an art historian on Mughal and Islamic Architecture, is a renowned expert on Taj Mahal and other monuments on the banks of Yamuna River.

Austrian Cultural Forum, New Delhi, set up 'the Mozart Chair of India' in 2006 at the initiative of Ravi Shankar, Gerald Wirth, Director of the Vienna Boy's Choir and the Austrian Embassy. It aims at providing Indian children with the state-of-the-art training in Western classical music and facilitates organization of public performances in India. Some years ago, ICCR sponsored 20 students to Austria, who jointly performed with the Vienna Choir Boys.

Indian music is also emerging as the main theme in various musical festivals. The famous Salzburg Music Festival in 2015 focused on 'Hinduism' as a theme and it included Ensemble Nepathya in Kutiyattam, Dhrupad and Khayal and Bharatnatyam.

Experts on Indology have been frequently invited as Distinguished Visitors to India. From India also, experts in the field of anthropology have occupied ICCR Chair at the Vienna University. There are a number of students that travel regularly to Austria for higher studies in technical education. A significant exchange programme exists between the University of Applied Arts, Vienna and the National Museum Institute in the field of museum conservation.

A Festival of India was organized during March 14-30, 2014 in Vienna by the Indian Embassy in cooperation with the Indian Council of Cultural Relations (ICCR) and the Export Promotion Council for Handicrafts (EPCH). It had multiple components that included Film Week, Food Festival, and Seminars on Indian music, dance and information technology and an Indo-Austrian Round Table on Innovation and Technology. A three day Yoga and Ayurveda Fair is being organized annually.

Bollywood is now providing connectivity in its own way. A number of films are being shot in Austria, which include Prabhudeva's Acktion Jackson and Karan Johar's 'Ae Dil Hai Mushkil'. Bollywood films are being screened at top cineplexes and the recent being 'Umrika' by Indian Director Praveen Nair. The film 'Court', India's official entry to the Oscar Awards in 2016 was screened at the famous Vienna International Film Festival. Film Weeks are being regularly held by the Film Museum, Vienna that screened films made by famous Indian Directors, like Satyajit Ray and Ritwick Ghatak.

## Belgium

Cultural Diplomacy has played 'a key part in maintaining the momentum of bilateral relations including people to people exchanges with Belgium' (Manjeev Puri).[9] It also serves as a window to the European Union, as its headquarters are located in Brussels. It received a boost through a four month Europalia-India Festival that was inaugurated by the President of India in Brussels in October 2013. Over 500 events were hosted, with 200 Indian artists performing at 200 cultural venues in 72 cities across Belgium, France and the Netherlands.

India does not have a Cultural Agreement with Belgium. Nor does it have a Cultural Centre? All the cultural activities, therefore, are organized by the Mission with the cooperation of local organizations. Some of these included performances by the noted Sitar exponent Subrata De, Bharatnatyam dancer Aranyani Bhargav and Sitarist Subhankar Chatterjee. ICCR sponsored a six-member Madras String Quartet, led by Ms Bindu

Subramaniam. There had been no visit of cultural troupes from Belgium and Luxembourg during the last two years.

Celebrations of the first International Yoga Day on June 21, 2015 was a significant event, involving participation of Yoga Federations of Belgium and Luxembourg, Antwerp Indian Association, University of Ghent, Katholic University of Leuven, Radhadesh and the city of Enghein (Ankan Banerjee)[10]. 5000 Yoga enthusiasts from across Belgium participated. A precursor to this event was the Yoga lecture-cum-demonstration by Sri Sri Ravi Shankar of Art of Living at the European Parliament in April 2015, hosted by the Members of the European Parliament of the Delegation of Relations with India. Yoga Day celebrations are expected to become an annual feature of the activities of the Mission.

Another significant activity has been the participation of the Mission in a large number of events, organized by the Belgium government to commemorate the Centenary of the World War I in Belgium. 130,000 Indian soldiers fought the war at the Flanders Fields in Belgium, with 9000 losing their lives to save democracy. Gen. (Retd.) V. K. Singh, Minister of State attended the Celebrations and a Seminar on Indian participation was attended by the Chief of the Army Staff of Belgium.

The Mission has also held seminars on the Constitution of India at the University of Leuven on November 26, 2015. Celebrations were held to mark Gandhi Jayanti and the 125th Birthday Anniversary of Babasaheb Ambedkar. A bust of Rabindranath Tagore was presented to the Katholic University of Leuven to mark his 155th Birth Anniversary on May 7, 2015. The Mission also hosted a Book Reading Session by Javed Akhtar on his recent poems that had been translated into French.

There are two ICCR Chairs of Indian Studies: Chair of Indian Studies at the prestigious and one of the oldest European University, the Katholic University of Leuven and the Chair of Hindi Studies at the University of Ghent. Reputed Indian academicians, like Professor R. K. Jain and Professor Gulshan Sachdev from JNU, New Delhi had held the Chair of Indian Studies, while Professor Raj Kumar from Benaras Hindu University held the Hindi Chair. A Belgian was also felicitated with the Vishwa Hindi Samman at the World Hindi Conference held in Bhopal in 2015. In 2016, ICCR hosted the visit of Prof. Idesbald Goddeeris, renowned Belgian scholar on Indian Studies. Prime Minister Modi met a large number of Indologists during his visit to Brussels in March 2016.

There are no formal exchanges of students between the two countries. A large number of students are presently pursuing their studies in engineering and bio-sciences. The students also become a link of cultural connectivity with the Belgians through the organization of cultural events in their respective universities. Five MOUs on academic cooperation were signed between prominent Belgium Universities with JNU, Delhi University and the University of Hyderabad.

Indian diaspora is also actively involved in organizing cultural activities. The Antwerp Indian Association hosts an annual Diwali Reception, where a Bollywood celebrity performs for over 1500 invitees. A Food Festival in Brussels organized by the Indian Confluence was attended by over 3000 Belgian enthusiasts. Indian diaspora hosted a reception for Prime Minister Modi during his visit to Belgium in March 2016, which was attended by over 5000 members of the Indian community.

The local media has been supportive in providing adequate publicity to cultural events undertaken by the Mission. The Europalia-India Festival received huge media coverage for its entire duration of 4 months. It has generally projected a positive image of Indian Art forms, although sometimes they have attempted to delve on the negative issues confronting Indian society, like child labour etc. There is no formal programme on media exchanges, although the EU Delegation in New Delhi sponsored the visit of 8 journalists from India in 2014. The Mission is looking at the possibility of using social media to provide cultural connectivity.

## Brazil

Despite high profile partnership bilaterally and under BRICS, India-Brazil cultural connectivity has been rather low. There is a Cultural Agreement, but a Cultural Exchange Programme had been 'lying dormant on account of the economic downturn' in the country (Sunil Lal). Brazil had not been able to either sponsor cultural troupes or host Indian groups during the last two years. So far, no Cultural Festival had been held in Brazil; nor was one being planned. There is a need for sustained cultural activities, as "India's soft power is impactful and touches peoples' lives in many positive ways" (Sunil Lal). There were also limits to the tapping of the private sector, given the inadequacy of funds with ICCR.

Indian Cultural Centre, San Paulo was established on 25 May 2011 and is located in a safe place and is easily accessible. It holds regular classes on Yoga, Odissi and Bharatnatyam dances and monthly workshops on Indian culinary. It also facilitates weekly workshops and lectures, hosted by socio-cultural, educational, religious and commercial institutions. A distinct feature of this Centre is that all the teachers are from Sau Paulo, who had been trained in their respective fields in India. There is also interest in learning Hindi, but classes had to be discontinued in the absence of teaching faculty and ICCR had been requested for sending a teacher during 2016-17.

Some of the other activities that are popular and are organized by the Centre include the holding of monthly culinary workshop and Bollywood movies with Portuguese subtitles. Regular functions are held to mark national days and Indian festivals. Special activities included the celebration of the Vishwa Hindi Divas on February 11, 2016 and the first International Yoga Day that was organized in association with the Swami Sivananda Divine Life Society. There are seven reputed Yoga schools in Brazil, which is ripe for Yoga Diplomacy.

Brazil also offers a fertile ground for Ayurveda related activities. There was high level Indian participation by Dr. A. Kumar, Director of the All India Institute of Ayurveda at an international conference, held in Goiania on November 11, 2013. There are well-known Ayurvedic Institutes at Sao Paulo- Institute Dhanvantri and Naradeva Shala – which regularly organize lectures, where prominent Indians and reputed Brazilians have participated. Institutes on Wellness and Ayurveda have shown interest in the upcoming AYUSH project/chairs, as proposed by ICCR.

Indian Cultural Centre is also involved with academic institutes and collaborates with them in organising activities. Some of the important ones that were organized with the University of Sao Paulo (USP), included holding of the 'First Journey of Oriental Culture' at the campus and 'Hindi and Sanskrit Day' at the ICC. The University of Campinas (UNICAMP) held the first 'Meeting of Researchers in Indian Classical Dances'; while the 'First Cultural Evening on Indian Philosophies and Religions' was organized at the Federal University of Paraiba (UFPB). These contacts are still at a nascent stage and need to be nurtured. This connectivity has resulted in Ambassador Sunil Lal setting up Brazil-India Association for Knowledge Network (BRIND ARC), which is a network of researchers/ scholars from India and Brazil. This group, therefore, acts as a useful resource on India and Brazil.

ICC has also branched out into another direction by gearing its activities into social projects. It organized the screening of the Bollywood movie 'Taare Zamin Paar', to generate awareness on 'Children with Special

Ability' with the Brazilian Association of Dyslexia (ABD). It organized another screening of this film in association with the Hospital Emilio Ribas that helped in raising funds for the Hospital. ICC also coordinates its activities with other social organizations like Brahma Kumaris, Art of Living and Palas Athena, with which it had organized 'Gandhi Week'.

## China

In China, 'the highest importance' is accorded to 'cultural diplomacy as a means to the people- to-people aspect of the India-China' relations (Vijay Gokhale).[11] The visit of Prime Minister Modi to China in May 2015 imparted a further boost to this, as an MOU was signed to establish a Centre for Gandhian and Indian Studies at Fudan. A joint Yoga-Tai Chi event, organized at the Temple of Heaven in Beijing during the visit, symbolically highlighted the growing acceptance of Yoga in China. As a follow up to the visit, an India-China Yoga College was established in Yunan Minzu University in Kunming that was officially inaugurated in November 2015, where two yoga teachers sent by ICCR are teaching. Yoga is one of the focus areas. Classical Indian dance and music and Indian films are other vehicles of India's cultural diplomacy.

China has four Chairs of Indian Studies that are supported by ICCR; three Chairs in Hindi at Peking University (2003), Guangdong University (2012) and Shanghai International Studies University (2012) and Shanghai India Studies Chair at Fudan University.

India is specially focusing on China to provide cultural visibility. The year of 2014 was designated as the Year of India-China Friendly Exchanges, resulting in the holding of 'Glimpses of India Festival' in 14 cities, which included performance of classical dances, arranging film festival and other events on Indian Food and Yoga. Indian visibility continued in 2015, as the year was celebrated as the 'Visit India Year in China'.

What was heartening was 'the warm and encouraging response' that was received at the above Festivals. Such visibility was also maintained through participation in International Festivals and Events, with India as the 'Country of Focus' at the 2nd Silk Route International Film Festival in Fuzhou in 2015, while China was the 'Guest of Honour' at the New Delhi World Book Fair 2016.

There are regular programmes on academic and youth exchanges. There is an annual exchange for a 200 member youth delegation. Sino-India Literature Forum exists that holds annual meetings; the last such meeting took place in August 2015 in Beijing. There is a regular flow of distinguished visitors; IDSA and ICWA have regularly participated in seminars. Prof C. Raja Mohan's book '*Samudra Manthan*' was released there and he participated at a discussion at the Carneige-Tsinghua Centre for Global Policy.

India had signed a Cultural Agreement with China on May 28, 1988. The last Cultural Exchange Programme (CEP) for 2013-15 expired on 31 December 2015 and a new one was being negotiated. It was of an omnibus character, covering all areas of cultural activities including sports and provided for connectivity in the areas of education and media.

There is no Indian Cultural Centre, as China does not allow the setting up of such Centres. ICCR, however, operates a 'cultural wing' in the Embassy, which is headed by an officer at the level of a Counsellor. The auditorium located in the Chancery, becomes a multi-purpose place for conducting classes, performances and other activities. ICCR has deputed three teachers in classical vocal music, kathak dance and yoga. These are supplemented by a local Odissi dance teacher and three local Chinese staff.

The Cultural Wing arranges performances to mark National Day and other festivals like Diwali and Holi. The Cultural Wing also arranges programmes outside the Embassy premises at venues like the National Centre for Performing Arts, 798 Arts District and China India Friendship Association. As a part of its outreach activities, performances and workshops are organized at other cultural institutions, universities and schools. The Cultural Wing also plays the coordinating role for visiting Indian cultural troupes/dignitaries.

## Finland and Estonia

India signed a cultural agreement with Finland in 1983 and with Estonia in 1993. There is no Cultural Exchange Programme (CEP) with Finland. A CEP is under negotiation with Estonia since 2007 and is pending finalization at the Indian end. Cultural activities are minimal in the absence of adequate budgetary provisions and lack of staff. The Mission is slowly venturing into the cultural field by involving local organizations. No Festival of India had been organized; nor is there any Chair of Indian Studies. There is also no cultural centre. ICCR, however, had deputed a yoga teacher three years ago, but the post was discontinued, as no funds were made available for the same.

The burden of arranging cultural activities, therefore, rests on the willingness of local organizations, to shoulder such a responsibility. Such activities are, therefore, carried out by Friendship Societies, which are provided some funding by the Indian Ministry of Culture. The Mission has collaborated with some of these organizations to promote teaching of Indian classical dances and music, yoga and Hindi. Funds are made available through the publicity budget of the Mission and through donations from the local Indian community. During the last three years, only one ICCR sponsored cultural troupe visited Helsinki in 2014 and gave dance performance in an open stage located in a park.

Similarly, connectivity in the field of education is rather limited. India offers 24 ITEC slots to Estonia, but the same were not availed of, as these did not suit local requirements. Similarly, there are no student exchanges through ICCR. Privately, many Indian students come to Estonia and Finland for studies. Similarly, some Estonian and Finnish students go to India for studies. There are, however exchanges between academicians and scientists among Research Institutes and Universities, as there are ongoing programmes with Finnish Universities and the Universities of Tallinn and Tartu in Estonia.

Yoga and meditation have been 'the main elements of India's soft power in Finland and Estonia and they are likely 'to remain the focus of India's cultural diplomacy' in the ensuing years (Ashok Sharma).[12] Several Indian organizations and spiritual gurus have set up centres in both these countries. Some of the prominent ones include, Sri Sri Ravi Shankar's Art of Living; Mata Amritanandamayi (Amma); Sahaj Yoga; Brahma Kumaris and several others. The celebration of International Yoga Day (IYD) brought these organizations together, as ICCR provided funds for the holding of IYD during 2015 and 2016. Cultural Diplomacy's 'primary thrust has to be on encouraging participation by local groups and to provide adequate funding for holding future activities' (Ashok Sharma).

## Germany

India and Germany have a Cultural Agreement that was signed in 1969. The twelfth Cultural Exchange Programme was signed in October 2005, as each CEP was spread over a period of two years. Currently, there is no CEP. There is a Cultural Centre in Germany that was set up in 1994 in the Embassy, as a follow up to the success of the 'Festival of India' held in 1991 after German reunification in 1989. The Centre was formally inaugurated at Bonn on February 5, 1994 by the then Prime Minister Narasimha Rao.

In 2000, it was renamed 'The Tagore Centre' in deference to the memory of Rabindranath Tagore who visited Germany thrice after winning the Noble Prize and received overwhelming reception in Germany. The Centre aims at showcasing rich Indian heritage and its diverse culture through a broad spectrum of events like dance, music, literacy events, films, talks, podium discussions, seminars, workshops and exhibitions etc. (Cultural Attache).

The Tagore Centre was relocated to the new Embassy premises in Berlin in 2001. It is on the third floor and has a fully functional auditorium, with a capacity of 200 seats. It also has a well acquipped library, which maintains books and other material supported by ICCR and is open to general public, including students and scholars. The Centre organizes a wide spectrum of activities, presenting performing and visual art from all the regions of India. As a part of its 'conscious policy', the events are coordinated in partnership with the city administration, local German and Indo-German societies/cultural organizations all over Germany. This helps, not only 'to enhance the reach of our events but also results in improving the quality of interaction with the German audience' (Cultural Attache).[13]

The preferred course adopted by the Centre to reach out to the maximum number of Germans is through participation in local festivals and cultural events. Another deliberate effort and strategy is to reach out to the younger generation through schools/educational institutions and youth organizations. The Centre is also making extensive use of the internet, as all programmes are advertised through the website of the Embassy as well as through newsletter and social media. The Centre's annual budget of Rs. 25 million is inadequate as it leaves only 10 per cent for cultural activities, thereby making it necessary to hold joint activities with local organizations, which, however, turns into a boon as these result in the participation of locals.

The most significant feature of Indo-German cultural connectivity is the German interest in Sanskrit Studies. At present, 12 German Universities offer courses; this, however, represents a decline from the erstwhile figure of 21 universities. Declining interest in Indian Studies has resulted in these being combined with Asian Studies, as there is greater interest in Chinese, Japanese and Korean studies, given Germany's growing commercial links with these countries. There is also an on-going programme on student exchanges between Indian and German schools that is aimed at exposing German students to contemporary India.

In order to reinvigorate interest in Indology and Indian Art, the then Prime Minister Atal Behari Vajpaye announced the setting up of an Indology Chair, during his visit to Germany in 2003. The first Chair was set up at the Heidelberg University. At present, ICCR offers three Short-Term Chairs annually. Overall, this turned into 30 Rotating Chairs till 2016.

ICCR also has three Long Term Chairs in German Universities – Chair for Indian Philosophy and Intellectual History at the Heidelberg University; Chair of Corporate Responsibility at the Leipzing Graduate School of Management and Tagore Chair for Bengali Language and Culture at the Georg-August-University, Gottingen.

ICCR has also instituted two Awards – Gisela Bonn Award (GBA) and the Saraswati Sanskrit Award (SSA). GBA is awarded to a German for promoting Indo-German friendship through his/her work. The Award was instituted in 1996 and is administered by the Indo-German Society and was awarded to Ms. Anja Bolenhof in 2015. SSA is awarded every two years for promoting understanding of Sanskrit and was awarded to Mr. Rohan K. Pshipakumara from Oxford University in 2012.

Festival of India, 'Days of India in Germany' was organized in Germany from May 2012 – April 2013, to mark the 60th anniversary of the opening of diplomatic relations. It was aimed at projecting multi-faceted Indian culture. The Festival had four thematic strands – Connecting Cultures, Connecting Ideas, Connecting Minds and Connecting Capabilities. It was launched on May11, 2012 at the Harbor Birthday Celebrations in Hamburg, where India was the Partner Country.

The mainstay of the Festival was performances by cultural troupes that showcased richness of Indian culture, which included folk dances by CHINH nomadic group, classical dance forms like Kuchipudi, Odissi, Kathak and performances byTripura Theatre Group. Other features involved a series of art exhibitions, apart from Sudhir Telang's cartoon exhibition; two major film festivals at Babylon Cinema and Kino Arsenal in Berlin alongside smaller film festivals in Nuremburg, Hamburg and Frankfurt.

Academic dimension was also added to the Festival, with the holding of two events, International Conference on Rabindranath Tagore in the University of Halle and on 'Panchtantra' at the University of Leipzig. The concluding event of the Festival was 'an orchestration of Indian Dances', based on Kalidassa's classic 'Ritu Samhaara (Cycle of Seasons), choreographed by legendary dance maestro Birju Maharaj. A number of supplementary events were also organized by the Indian Embassy.

The organization of the Festival of India and other cultural events in Germany was not a cake walk. Some valuable lessons were learnt, which would be equally relevant for other developed countries. Firstly, there is a need for the involvement of Indian cultural centres of ICCR at the planning stage of such festivals. Secondly, we have to provide sufficient lead time, in order to book good venues to mount the events. There was also the problem of holding events at the prestigious venues, as the event holders preferred a dialogic approach and partnership, which made it more expensive. The festival was nonetheless a successful venture, as it helped in projecting India to a wider German audience, as many events managed to get a good footfall of attendees.

## Maldives

India has a Cultural Agreement with Maldives that was signed in 1983. Indian Cultural Centre (ICC) was set up in Male[14] in July 2011, with the primary objective of enhancing cultural relations and mutual understanding between India and Maldives. In a short time of its existence, the Centre has emerged as ‘a unique institution, enjoying a prestigious position as a place of performing arts’. It regularly organizes cultural activities at the Centre, which are largely attended by the local community. The Centre has established good working relationship with local institutions, Friendship Societies and individuals involved with cultural work.

ICC has been in the forefront in organizing cultural events related to Art and Performing Arts as well as Interactive Sessions and Academic Conferences. It conducts regular classes in Yoga, Kathak, Tabla Percussion and Hindustani Vocal by four India-based teachers; while Hindi classes are conducted by a part-time local teacher. In addition to these regular activities, the Centre has exponentially expanded its outreach programmes by organizing camps, workshops in schools in different Maldivian islands. Its activities have resulted in its achieving ‘a milestone’ in the cultural sphere in Maldives.

Some of the unique programmes/activities organized by ICC include the following:

- ‘Dosti-Ekuverkan Week’ during January 24-26, 2014. The event was inaugurated by the then Vice-President Mohamed Jameel on January 20, 2014.

- 'India-Maldives Cultural Conference' in 2015, where the Vice-President was the chief guest.
- Celebrations to mark the 4th year of the establishment of the Cultural Centre on August 7, 2015, where the Education Minister Ms Yumna Maumoon was the chief guest.
- Restoration of three Mosques -Friday Mosque and Dharumavantha Ras'gefannu Mosque in Male and Femfushi Mosque in South Ari Atoll.
- Performance by a 12-member A to Z Bollywood Dance and Music Group during February 19-22, 2015 on the occasion of the 50th Anniversary of India-Maldives Diplomatic Relations.
- A Fusion Tabla-Boduberu at Futsan Football Tournament on July 16, 2015 in collaboration with the Maldivian Film Association.
- Exhibition of 33 paintings, created by Indian, Maldivian and some young South Asian Artists, called, "Cultural Confluence – United Colours" at the National Art Gallery on January 26, 2015 in collaboration with the National Centre for the Arts. Minister for Economic Development, Mr Mohamad Saeed was the Chief Guest.

The Cultural Centre regularly holds cultural activities on dance and Bollywood music and Sufi songs, to encourage participation by local artists. Manifold Yoga activities are organized dealing with different aspects of Yoga. These include 'Therapeutic Yoga Session and Pregnancy Session for Women. Nine Yoga Sessions were organized at nine different venues to mark the International Yoga Day on June 21, 2015. Candle Night Yoga Meditation was organized twice in 2015 on August 17 and September 1. A Lecture-cum-Yoga demonstration was organized to generate awareness on Cancer. Yoga Awareness Camps are regularly organized at different locations. Yoga has become an important part of the activities, given the interest shown by the Maldivians. ICC also celebrated Hindi Day on September 14, 2014 and 2015.

Academic linkages, however, are limited. It is broadly scholarship-related; ICCR offers 41 scholarships every year under four different streams. A lecture on 'Creative Writings' by a well-known Maldivian Poet, Writer and Television Personality was organized on May 7, 2015. A seven-member delegation from the Dhivehi Language Academy visited India during March 29-April 7, 2015. The visit helped in facilitating interaction on historical, linguistic and cultural links and studying the impact of India and Dravidian languages on Dhivehi and early Maldivian languages. The Centre is also exploring the possibility of the establishment of a short-term Rotating Chair of Indian Languages at the Maldivian National University (MNU).

## Mongolia

Indian cultural diplomacy plays an important role in Mongolia as its influence has 'largely shaped the religious traditions, literary heritage, script, traditional medicine and general intellectual life in Mongolia' (Somnath Ghosh).[15] The influences flowed 'through the vehicle of Buddhism'. Former Indian Ambassador Monk Kushok Bakula Rinpoche was instrumental in reviving interest in traditional Buddhism. Several hundred monk students and scholars study in Indian Monasteries and the Central University of Tibetan Studies at Sarnath. The visit by Indian Prime Minister Modi in May 2015, the first by any Indian Prime Minister to Mongolia, further deepened cultural links.

India's primary focus has been on education and human resource development. India offers 50 ICCR scholarships and 200 ITEC slots annually to Mongolia, which is one of the highest outside SAARC and is large in relation to Mongolian population of 3 million persons. Four scholarships for the learning of Hindi are also offered every year. A new initiative was taken to establish a US $ 20 million Centre of Excellence in IT at the Department of IT of the Mongolian National University of Science and Technology. The Mission maintains a good data base on former students and ITEC alumni and maintains regular contacts with them, including Indian Diaspora, which numbers around 200.

On the cultural front, however, the connectivity is rather limited. Chairs of Hindi and Indian studies that existed earlier were not continued and no one has occupied the same for the last five years. Similarly, there had been no exchange of Distinguished Visitors for over two years. There had not been any exchange of cultural troupes during the last three years. Indian visibility is, however, there on the Mongolian TV and through articles on art, culture, science, textiles, dresses, film industry etc. that are published in local periodicals and newspapers. A Festival of India was organized in Mongolia during 2015-16 to mark the 60th Anniversary of the Establishment of Diplomatic Relations with Mongolia.

India signed a Cultural Agreement with Mongolia on February 9, 1978. Under this Agreement, a Cultural Exchange Programme (CEP) for the years 2015-2018 was signed on May 17, 2015. The CEP is divided into three parts, dealing with 'Culture and Arts', 'Information and Media' and 'Sports'. There is considerable interest on the holding of Film Weeks and joint production of documentaries/films. Five out of the 14 articles deal with information and media related areas, which would help in generating awareness on both the countries.

It is interesting to note that Indian Cultural Centre in Ulaanbaatar was set up by Mongol citizens and is housed in the Rajiv Gandhi School of Arts and Polytechnic. It is, however, inadequately funded and has no establishment budget and the post of Director is honorary. It has been supported by the Mission, through grants for specific activities, which ranged between US $ 4000-5000 annually. The Centre organizes events and seminars in partnership with government and non-governmental organizations and institutions. Budgetary constraints remain a big damper on the organization of cultural activities.

## Pakistan

In the case of Pakistan, 'cultural diplomacy is moving backwards due to the very nature of India-Pakistan relations' (Gautam Bambawale).[16] India, however, has a bilateral Cultural Agreement that was signed in 1988, but there is no Cultural Exchange Programme (CEP). On the other hand, unlike with other countries, ICCR signed an MOU with the Pakistan National Council of the Arts (PNCA) on September 8, 2012. It is lying dormant.

Cultural relationship between the two countries has to take into account the present day political realities that exist. Therefore, there are no Chairs of Indian Studies or exchange of Distinguished Visitors and students. There is no Cultural Centre. Nor was any Cultural Festival of India organized. Therefore, there is no special area of focus. Despite the above political constraints at the official level, cultural exchanges are taking place 'in the private sector, at the people-to-people level'. Our Centre, Centre for Research in Rural and Industrial Development (CRRID) has been one such institution.

Hardening of attitudes in both the countries have become a stumbling bloc, resulting in the reduction of such exchanges. This was clearly evident, when Ghulam Ali, a noted Pakistani Ghazal maestro was prevented by local groups to perform in Mumbai in October 2015.

Cultural Wing at the High Commission, however, managed to perform certain outreach activities as indicated below:

- Participation in Book Fairs: India participated at the Lahore International Book Fair in February 2015 through the joint efforts of the High Commission, National Book Trust, Children Book Trust and Sahitya Akademi, in collaboration with the local host, Idarra-e-Taleem-o-Agaahi (Pakistan, however, regularly participates at the India International Book Fair, held in Delhi during February every year).

- Assistance to Workshop on Hindi Script: The Mission provided study material and practice books to a Hindi Script Workshop held on 14-15 February 2015 at the Gurnani Centre of Languages and Literature, Lahore University Management Science, (LUMS), Lahore.

- Screening of Bollywood Films for the Diplomatic Community: Films are screened from time to time and Bollywood movie '*Bajrangi Bhaijaan*' was screened on 13 December 2015 (From time to time, Indian Films are not allowed to be screened in the local cinemas and this movie was a hit with the Pakistanis).

The High Commission has also taken an initiative to set up a Mission Museum and HCI Photo Gallery in the premises of the Mission. The Mission Museum was inaugurated on 9 October 2015 marking the IFS Day. The artifacts range from an old gramophone to a Toyota Station Wagon (Jeep) that evacuated Mission personnel from Kabul in January 1994. The Photo Gallery showcases photographs of high-level India-Pakistani Interactions since 1970s and was inaugurated on 30 December 2015. (Both these facilities apparently have no meaning for the local people, given the restricted nature of freedom of movement allowed to them).

Nonetheless, the High Commissioner envisages 'a huge role for cultural diplomacy', where 'exchanges can actually take place and need to be enhanced'. He would like culture to be utilized 'as a tool of soft diplomacy'. Bollywood could be one such area, which has a huge impact across the globe, including Pakistan. Publishing industry is another area, which offers opportunities for cooperation. Cultural cooperation could be encouraged if ICCR and PNCA could 'jump in and ensure that performing and other artists are sponsored to this area also'.

## Qatar

A Cultural Agreement, signed in April 2012, provides the broad work for cooperation in the fields of arts and culture. This replaced an earlier cultural agreement that was signed in 1980. It 'stresses the vital role of cultural cooperation in strengthening bilateral relations', through promotion of cultural activities. It aims at consolidation of cooperation between cultural and artistic institutions, exchange of exhibitions of art and literacy works and participation in international seminars.

There is no ICCR-sponsored Cultural Centre in Qatar. Normal functions of a cultural centre are performed by the so called Indian Cultural Centre (ICC), which is an official organization of the Indian expatriate community, which has the Ambassador as its patron. It also functions as 'an arm of this Mission to strengthen Indo-Qatari friendship and cultural relationship' (R.K. Singh). It has also 100 affiliated associates that are actively involved in further strengthening cultural bonds between the two countries. Events are organized to mark national days of the two countries and other important festivals. ICC is run by a 12-member Managing Committee of Indian expatriates and there are no Qataris on the Governing Board.

So far no Festival of India has been held. The government of Qatar has sent a proposal to celebrate India-Qatar Year of Culture in 2019. ICC, however, organized an Indian Community Festival called 'A Passage to India' on November 28-29, 2013. It showcased India's cultural diversity as well as achievements as a modern state in diverse fields. The Festival had usual features, like music and dance performances, multi-media presentations; display of arts and crafts and sampling of cuisine from different parts of India

The two day Festival attracted 30,000 visitors that also included artists, including several dignitaries, senior officials and member of diplomatic corps. The Festival was inaugurated by the Minister of Culture, Art and Heritage Dr. Hamad Bin Abdul-Aziz Al-Kuwaiti. Second Edition of 'A Passage to India Festival' was held on March 19-20, 2015. The highlight of the Festival was the well illuminated replica of 'India Gate', which was designed by 25 artisans of 'Viswa Kala Vedi', a socio-cultural association affiliated to ICC. The other important features were the 'Brides of India' Fashion Show, and 'A Taste of India' Food Festival.

The Mission also actively associates with several Qatari organizations in the areas of arts, culture and education. It partners with them to organize major events. Indian films/documentaries are also shown at the Annual

Film Festival of Doha Film Institute. ICC celebrated the International Day of Yoga in June 2015. Books and other publicity material were distributed on that day and also on other functions.

There is a regular flow of dignitaries from Kerala, who participate in various events organized by local cultural associations and Indian schools. Some of the important dignitaries, who visited in 2014 included the former Minister of State Dr. Shashi Tharoor, Founding Director of Delhi Metro Prof. E. Sreedharan and Dr. V.K. Saraswat, former Director of Defence Research and Development Organisation (DRDO). Here again the Kerala-connection is unmistaken.

ICCR, however, has a limited connectivity with Qatar. It sponsored a photographic exhibition on 'Islamic Monuments in India' in 2014. This exhibition of 45 photographs by renowned photographer Benoy K. Behl was held at the Cultural Village Foundation (KATARA) during September 21-October 19. ICCR also sponsored a Kathak Dance Group led by renowned artist Ms Prachee Shah, which gave performances at the KATARA Drama Theatre during August 4-7, 2015. This troupe was sent as a part of the celebrations of the 70th Indian Independence Day.

It is in the field of education that we witness a mutually beneficial cooperation. It is, however, not led by ICCR, as Qataris have not availed of scholarships or ITEC slots, as the Qatari government generously supports and funds study by its students in private institutions in Qatar and abroad. Indian participation is, however, in the form of setting up private schools in Qatar, though largely for the children of Indian expatriates. At present there are 14 such schools with a students' population of 30,000, who follow CBSE curriculum. The State of Qatar provides generous support, by way of land at nominal costs and loans at relatively lower rates for constructing buildings and other infrastructure. This in fact, is educational diplomacy in operation, where India is helping in building educational infrastructure.

## Sri Lanka

Sri Lanka offers both 'unique opportunity and challenge' for cultural diplomacy as India seeks to revitalise our abiding cultural, linguistic, religious, political and economic relations' (Y. K. Sinha). It is the civilizational ties that bind the main communities – the Sinhalese, the Tamilians and the Muslims, as they trace their origins to India. The Mission's efforts, therefore, have continued 'to cement these ancient links to the modern era' (Y.K. Sinha). The outreach programme of cultural diplomacy has, therefore, concentrated on harnessing the 'traditional mediums of classical dance forms, vocal and instrumental music, the rich tapestry of paintings, literature and philosophical exchanges'.

The visit of Prime Minister to Sri Lanka in March 2015 gave a further push to cultural diplomacy, as a number of new initiatives were taken. Cultural diplomacy is, therefore, 'assiduously nurtured' through a proactive approach by the High Commission and its consulates in Kandy, Hambantota and Jaffna.

India Cultural Centre was established in Colombo in 1998 by ICCR. The Centre is located outside the High Commission premises that facilitates easy entry for outsiders. It has a well equipped proper auditorium, with a capacity of 120 persons and a library with over 6500 titles. The special feature of the library is a 'Kids Corner', which has a sizeable number of children's books. It has a modern dance studio and satellite TV channels. The Centre regularly mounts cultural programmes to enhance cultural linkages and promote people to people relationship.

In addition to organizing cultural programmes, the Centre offers classes in Bharatnatyam and Kathak Dances, Hindustani and Carnatic music and Instruments (violin, sitar and tabla) and teaching of Hindi and yoga.

The Centre's unique feature is that it draws upon the local resources of a talented and committed group of Sri Lankan teachers in these disciplines of study. The Centre also has a long term Hindi Chair, which also guides other Hindi teachers at the Centre, apart from conducting classes for students. Interest in Bollywood films results in generating interest of Sri Lankans in learning Hindi. The Centre also organizes various educational and cultural programmes, where its students actively participate.

Education occupies an important role in Indian cultural diplomacy. India offers 800 scholarships annually to provide affordable and quality education to Sri Lankans. India is also involved in human resource development and offers 150 ITEC slots and 40 Colombo Plan slots annually. There is a short term Chair of Indian Studies at the University of Colombo. Sri Lanka has an active Alumni Association of ITEC experts and students and International Students' Day is celebrated annually in the Mission.

Some prominent Sri Lankans have visited India under ICCR's Distinguished Visitors Programme, primarily dealing with Buddhism-related sites and conferences. Former President Chandrika Bandaranaike along with other Sri Lankan dignitaries participated at a Conference, 'Samvaad: A Global Buddhist Initiative on Conflict', held in Bihar in September 2015. Earlier, another delegation participated at the International Buddhist Conclave in September 2014. President, Mahabodhi Society and Post Master General visited India in October 2014, at the time of the release of the commemorative stamp 'Angarika Dharmapala'.

A notable feature of cooperation is the presence of a number of think tanks to encourage research and collaboration. An important network, Indo-Sri Lanka Foundation (ISLF), was set up on December 29, 2015 on the basis of an MOU between the two countries. ISLF's mandate is to foster bilateral relations through enhancement of research in economic, scientific, technical and cultural fields. It provides funding for research projects, facilitates exchanges involving students, scholars and academics and publication of research work. ISLF has sponsored a number of cultural/ academic visits of Sri Lankans to India. Both the High Commissioners are the Co-Chairpersons of the Board.

Another initiative which was taken up earlier was the setting up of a Centre for Contemporary Indian Studies at the Colombo University in February, 2012, under a Memorandum of Understanding signed on July 12, 2011. The Centre is expected to emerge as 'a premier resource centre and academic hub' for studies on contemporary India (Esha Srivastava).[17]

A Festival of India in Sri Lanka was launched in November 2015, as per announcement made by Prime Minister Modi during his visit in March 2015. The theme of the Festival was 'Sangam', a Confluence of Cultures of India and Sri Lanka. The Logo of the Festival beautifully represented 'the manifestation of civilization ties that bind us' (Y.K. Sinha). A number of artistic and literacy events were held during 2015-16, which included 'Nrityarupa' – Mosaic of Indian dance forms, participation of Indian authors at the Galle Literacy Festival and an exhibition on 'Digital India'. The Festival was held in a number of cities in Sri Lanka. On its part, Sri Lanka has regularly participated at the Surajkund International Mela in 2013, 2014 and 2015.

Bollywood is emerging as an umbilical cord between India and Sri Lanka; Bollywood includes Tamil films. This has resulted in many students taking to learning Hindi at the Indian Cultural Centre. Interest in Bollywood films and songs could be gauged through the presence of dignitaries at a musical concert by Bollywood singer Shaan in August 2014, as a part of Independence Day Celebrations organized by High Commissioner Yash Sinha, in partnership with CEO's Forum in Colombo. The dignitaries included the then President Mahinda Rajapaksa, the leader of the opposition Ranil Wickeremesinghe, the then Foreign Minister G.L. Peiris and their spouses. Bollywood, therefore, does not connect us in Sri Lanka only, but also globally. This makes us think, as to how to enlist 'the support of Bollywood in a more organized manner as part of our soft power/cultural outreach in Sri Lanka and many other countries around the globe' (Y.K. Sinha).

## Diplomatic Missions Contributing to Symphony of Cultural Diplomacy

What is the picture that emerges from the operation of cultural diplomacy at the level of Indian diplomatic missions? All of them are in tandem in steadfastly holding to the importance of the role of cultural diplomacy, as it is viewed as an important instrument, in providing people-to-people connectivity. Each one has contributed in his/her unique way, keeping in view local requirements.

It also reaffirms the importance of the role that an Ambassador has to play, as a pivot and key player. It is he/she, who sets the agenda and whose interest, commitment and tenacity results in achieving the goals of cultural diplomacy. Our Ambassadors have taken a number of initiatives to keep India's flag flying, as they connect with peoples and governments. These are reflected in the text of the chapter.

The approach of each Diplomatic Mission, however, is dictated by a number of factors, like the nature and vibrancy of culture in different locales; intensity of India-connectivity; presence of strong cultural institutions and the role and profile of Indian Diaspora. Education is emerging as an important component of cultural diplomacy. We, therefore, see different picture frames, which are even different in the case of countries belonging to the same Continent. There is thus no common template.

Each country has its own story, as the narrative unfolds. India is culturally linked to Afghanistan and Sri Lanka through strong civilization links; connected to China and Mongolia through Buddhism and Bollywood; while interest in Indology binds India with Germany and Austria. On the other hand, politics emerges as a spoilsport in building cultural links with Pakistan, despite our sharing common heritage; while present security environment acts as a damper to cultural connectivity with Afghanistan.

There was recognition of the important role played by ICCR's flagship programmes, such as Festivals of India and Chairs of Indian Studies, which have helped in strengthening cultural ties. Simultaneously, some concerns were expressed over non-involvement of diplomatic missions at various stages in the selection of venues and artists and ad hoc manner in the selection of the Indian Chairs.

Indian Chairs are mainly located in the developed countries. While, there are two chairs in Austria, but there are three chairs in Germany. ICCR has also instituted two Awards – Gisela Bonn Award (GBA) and the Saraswati Sanskrit Award (SSA). GBA is awarded to a German for promoting Indo-German friendship through his/her work. There are four Chairs in China; three are for learning of Hindi. A Chair also exits in Sri Lanka. On the hand, ICCR has not been responsive to request for Chairs in Hindi from Brazil and Mongolia. There is a need for a relook at this important vehicle, so as to ensure better connectivity.

The role of the Festivals of India to enhance cultural connectivity was acknowledged; so was the desire for greater direct involvement. This was more so in the case of Germany, China, Sri Lanka, Mongolia and Belgium. Other countries, like Afghanistan, Brazil, Austria, Finland, Estonia, Pakistan and Qatar had not made the grade, as venues for holding festivals.

Europalia-India Festival that was inaugurated by the President of India in Brussels in October 2013, helped in projecting a positive image of India to the European Union. There were some local initiatives, such as organization of a festival, called 'Passage to India' by the Indian Association in Qatar, which was a unique effort. A Yoga and Ayurveda Fair is being organized in Austria.

An important trend that emerged was that India was also being accorded Partner Country status in locally organized International Fairs and Festivals, commensurate with its growing importance. Therefore, participation in International Festivals could be considered an alternate route to the Festivals of India; such an approach would be cost-effective and provide for greater outreach.

Indian basket of vehicles of cultural diplomacy had remained largely confined to its traditional ware of classical dances and music and teaching of yoga and Hindi. Yoga emerged as an important area of focus, given the boost it received from the United Nations, which declared June 21 as the International Yoga Day (IYD) since 2015. Yoga emerged as an energizer; infusion of funds by ICCR gave a further push to Yoga-related activities, which had already found a place for itself in this commercial world.

Yoga lecture-cum-demonstration by Sri Sri Ravi Shankar of Art of Living at the European Parliament in April 2015, hosted by the Members of the European Parliament of the Delegation of Relations with India, was a significant event. Brazil is ripe for Yoga Diplomacy, as there are seven reputed Yoga schools in that country. Brazil also offers a fertile ground for Ayurveda related activities. In Maldives, manifold Yoga activities were organized at nine different venues to mark the International Yoga Day on June 21, 2015. These dealt with different aspects of Yoga, which included 'Therapeutic Yoga Session and Pregnancy Session for Women and Candle Night Yoga Meditation.

Indian Cultural Centres in the countries under study in this chapter presented an interesting picture, as they narrated their own own stories. We have no cultural centres in Austria, Belgium, Estonia and Finland; and the one in Germany is inadequately funded, leaving only ten percent of its Rs 25 million budget for cultural activities. In Mongolia, it is established by local residents and relies on grants from the embassy. In Brazil, it relies upon local teachers trained in India. In Doha (Qatar), it is run by the Indian community. Our cultural centre at Colombo in Sri Lanka presents a success story, as it is well equipped and fully functional. This enormous data and information could be profitably used by ICCR in restructuring our cultural centres.

Overall, our Cultural Centres have not given us the intended dividend, as these have not emerged as vibrant hubs and have failed to attract the Youth. These lack professional expertise and funds. Indian cultural centres are not a match to the established cultural centres from countries, like USA, UK, Germany, France, which present a picture of beehive of activity that easily connects to the youth.

It is in the area of implementation of cultural agreements that we witness a dismal picture. India has cultural agreements with Austria, Estonia, Finland and Germany, but has no Cultural Exchange Programmes (CEPs). Currently, we have CEPs with Mongolia and Sri Lanka. CEPs are under negotiation with other countries. We have been lackadaisical in implementing cultural agreements, as we spend a number of years to frame Cultural Exchange Programmes. The Ministry of Culture needs to conduct a review on the status of implementation of cultural agreements and suggest remedial measures thereof.

We are seeing a new trend in the emergence of Public Private Partnership (PPP) Model in the pursuit of cultural programmes. This is largely dictated by the paucity of funds as well as the emergence of cultural operators in India and abroad, which are willing to mix culture with commerce. This has not only helped in sustaining the level of cultural activity, but has also given it a boost, as this is happening in the Western world. Such opportunities need to be tapped by ICCR to keep up the momentum.

Diaspora is also playing an important role. It is not only as a recipient of cultural products, but also as an active participant and promoter, in keeping our cultural links alive. We have seen how world renowned figures, like Zubin Mehta, Ravi Shankar, Zakir Hussain have made Indian culture popular through their versatility and high calibre performances. Well known Indian artists have established themselves in many countries and have set up Art Academies and Schools.

Bollywood has emerged as an important connector, as its charm is getting globally spread in Afghanistan, Sri Lanka, China, Qatar, Japan, Mongolia, South Korea, Africa and Middle East. Its influence as a component of Indian software was alluded to by many Ambassadors. Bollywood connects with Austria through shooting of films; results in promoting learning of Hindi in Sri Lanka and funding of local charities through screening of films in Brazil.

The role of Indian cultural diplomacy is viewed positively in all the countries. Different instrumentalities have been at play in each country, as best suited to it. The most significant lesson learnt is on the need to adopt a 'conscious policy' and prepare country-specific plans, which help in presenting cultural programmes that can better gel with local cultural ethos. The success of such programmes could be further enhanced, if the same are organized in collaboration with local partners.

The visits of Prime Minister Modi have further imparted a new synergy, as culture has become a significant component of all his visits abroad. The biggest challenge that still remains is that of ensuring 'a right mix of cultural heritage with modernity', as India struts on the world stage.

**Annexure I**

Subject: Book Project on India's Cultural Diplomacy

My dear

1. I am pleased to inform you that I have undertaken the above Book Project for the Indian Council for World Affairs (ICWA), New Delhi. My target date is to complete by October, 2016. It would be a mix of theoretical underpinnings associated with cultural diplomacy, supplemented with the practical orientation that it has received in India and abroad, reflecting the experiences of our diplomatic missions that have put this into practice. I may add that for this study 'cultural' would embrace a whole gamut of areas as defined by UNESCO and covered under our cultural agreements. Besides the Performing Arts, the focus would have to be on Education, Media, Sports and Diaspora etc.

2. I am writing this to seek your assistance in providing me with information on some of the basic points, as this would be readily available with you. I would need information on the following aspects:

- Importance assigned to cultural diplomacy in the functioning of the mission.
- What are the focus areas, which receive priority?
- Basic data for the last three years:
    - Chairs of Indian studies; the areas of specialisation.
    - Festivals of India; how successful these have been?
    - Incoming and Outgoing Cultural Delegations.
    - Exchange of Distinguished Visitors – Fields of interest.
    - Students Exchange.

3. Is there a cultural centre? If so, a brief history on its operation and the nature of activities organized. What are the focus areas and receptivity of the local population? Are these adequately funded, manned and well located; percentage of budget for programmes and staffing? Is the centre located outside the premises of the diplomatic mission and there is easy access? What is the nature and level of connectivity between the Diplomatic Mission and the Cultural Centres?

4. Do you have a bilateral culture agreement? If so, could you please e-mail me a copy of the same? Please also attach a copy of the current Cultural Exchange Programme (CEP). If not, please send a copy of the last one.

5. Apart from the above factual data, I would be happy to receive your inputs on some of these areas:

- What should be the focus of India's cultural diplomacy?
- Which should be the nodal Ministry – Ministry of External Affairs or the Ministry of Culture?
- Should culture be used as a tool for soft diplomacy?
- How effectively ICCR has discharged its responsibilities?
- Would you like to make suggestion to make it more effective?
- What are the initiatives that you have taken and their impact? These could be in the present or previous assignments.
- What should be the tools of Indian cultural diplomacy
- What role Media has played as a connecting bridge? Is there a formal programme of media exchanges?
- How are we connected in the field of Education? What role has Education Diplomacy played or can play in enhancing links between our two countries?
- Existence of local cultural organizations and their connectivity with the diplomatic mission on cultural centre.
- The nature and level of ITEC Programmes. How relevant are these in providing connectivity with India?
- Are there any Alumni Associations of ITEC experts or students? How active are these in furthering bilateral links.
- What is the nature and level of your engagement with Diaspora? What should be done to facilitate its greater engagement to promote India and if so in what areas and how? Should it be used in promoting foreign policy interests?

6. I have suggested the above to serve as a guidepost. It may appear a long laundry list, but should be easy for you, as you have the information

on your finger tips. You are most welcome to pick and choose areas of interest to you. You can also adopt your own format. To start with I would appreciate to receive basic data or note, which is readily available, along with copies of cultural agreement and cultural exchange programme. Later, you could let me have the benefit of your personal inputs and suggestions.

7. I would appreciate if you could let me know the nodal officer in your Mission, with whom I could liaise further for details or further queries. Please also let me have the contours of the Director of the Cultural Centre, with whom I could correspond, as it would be useful to have their perspective from the field.

I would be happy if you could respond to me within a month's time. I am looking forward to receiving your valuable inputs.

Yours sincerely,

Amb. (Retd.) Paramjit Sahai, IFS (1963)

1656, Sector 7-C

Chandigarh 160 019

Mob. +91-9815981656

## Endnotes

1 Sunil Lal, Ambassador of India to Brazil, Caracas. Response to a Questionnaire, April 5,2016 and subsequent interaction.

2 Navdeep Suri, High Commissioner of India to Australia, Canberra. Response to a Questionnaire, January 13, 2016 and subsequent interaction.

3 Gurjit Singh, Ambassador of India to Germany, Bonn. Response to a Questionnaire, April 5, 2016 and subsequent interaction.

4 Y.K. Sinha, High Commissioner of India to Sri Lanka, Colombo. Response to a Questionnaire, January 6, 2016 and subsequent interaction.

5 R.K. Singh, Ambassador of India to Qatar, Doha. Response to a Questionnaire on November 9, 2015 and subsequent interaction.

6 Viraj Singh, Deputy Chief of Mission, Embassy of India, Kabul. Response to a Questionnaire on December 1, 2015 and subsequent interaction.

7 Rajiva Misra, Ambassador of India to Austria, Vienna. Response to Questionnaire, December 11, 2015.

8 Pawan Bodhe, Second Secretary, Embassy of India, Vienna. Response to Questionnaire Dec. 11, 2015.

9 Manjeev Puri, Ambassador of India to EEC and Belgium, Brussels. Response to Questionnaire, May 24, 2016.

10 Ankan Banerjee, Counsellor, Embassy of India, Brussels. Response to Questionnaire, May 24, 2016.

11 Vijay Gokhale, Indian Ambassador to China, Beijing. Response to a Questionnaire, April 5, 2016 and subsequent interaction.

12 Ashok Sharma, Ambassador of India to Finland and Estonia, Helsinki. Response to a Questionnaire on April 8, 2016 and subsequent interaction.

13 Cultural Attache Manjishtha Mukherjee Bhatt, Embassy of India, Bonn.

14 Cultural Attache, Embassy of India to Maldives, Male.

15 Somnath Ghosh, Ambassador of India to Mongolia, Ulan Bator. Response to Quesionnaire, April 3, 2016 and subsequent interaction.

16 Gautam Bambawale, High Commissioner of India to Pakistan, Islamabad. Response to Quesionnaire, April 6, 2016 and subsequent interaction.

17 Esha Srivastava, Director, Indian Cultural Centre, Colombo.

## References

Abhay, K. 2013, 'Innovations in Public Diplomacy', *GPP Blog*, November 6.

# Chapter – XIV

# Conduct of Cultural Diplomacy: Foreign Diplomatic Missions in India

## Introduction

In this chapter, it is proposed to look at not only the role of well-known and major players, but also other countries that are emerging as important players in the field of cultural diplomacy. In Part I, we would look at the policies and practices of certain countries, such as the United States, Russia, China, Japan, South Korea, Mexico and South Africa. In Part II, we will peep into cultural diplomacy as practiced by some countries in India, such as the United States, Russia, South Korea and Japan, based on interaction with the representatives of diplomatic missions. This would be both in the global context, as we look at their overall outreach and also specifically in the Indian context. How could we benefit from their perspectives and experiences on the operation of cultural diplomacy in India, in formulating our policies and programmes on cultural diplomacy? Such an approach would be helpful, as cultural diplomacy is being increasingly viewed as a two-way channel. Long term relationship can only be built by introducing an element of reciprocity in cultural exchanges, albeit not in the same fields.

## Setting Parameters for Understanding Others

Our primary objective is to have a look at other countries, as they view cultural diplomacy, both in theory and practice. For this, we would keep in view certain parameters that would help us in better understanding their policies and practices that would have relevance for India. Our focus would be to look at the thrust of cultural diplomacy and the flagship programmes. How is cultural diplomacy defined and viewed? Has it been used as a component of soft power? How is cultural diplomacy connected to public diplomacy? Is there a synergy between these two? If so, how is it accomplished?

What is the administrative structure created to pursue cultural diplomacy? Is there a nodal government agency in pursuing cultural diplomacy? How does it coordinate with other key stakeholders? What role do the States play? Do they independently pursue cultural policies?

What are the thrust areas and components of cultural diplomacy that are pursued by foreign diplomatic missions in India? What are the important programmes in their cultural diplomacy armoury that are relevant and successful? What is the importance attached to the role played by cultural centres? What are the new initiatives taken in the arena of cultural diplomacy?

Could we draw any concrete suggestions from their experiences, to make India's cultural diplomacy more result oriented? How could we enhance this role; by changing our focus on programmes or by focussing on priority countries or by streamlining organizational structures? Let us now look at the experience of some countries, with a view to identifying what would be relevant for adaptation by India.

## Broad Contours of Cultural Diplomacy of Some Countries

### *China*

For China, cultural diplomacy has emerged as an important diplomatic tool. Its focus is to build its Brand Image through softening concerns over its rising economic power. China's arrival on the global stage, consequent to globalisation has given culture 'a new value and status, as a tool of China's soft power' (Smits, Yolanda, 2014). It was in 2007 that the then President Hu Jintao recognized 'the strategic importance of culture, for the image of China and its economic development' (Smits, Yolanda, 2014).

China thus signalled a new direction in its cultural diplomacy from 'cultural exchange to cultural trade'. It turned its focus on promotion of creative industries, which could be inspired by its culture. China also realized that to build its image, it had to develop its own media channels – TV and Radio and also use education, as a diplomatic tool.

Given the above objectives, China, therefore, relies upon a number of Ministries at the central government. While the Ministry of Foreign Affairs assumes key role, yet other Ministries- the Ministries of Culture,

Education and Commerce- are also involved in dealing with culture in external relations.

Another significant aspect of China's administrative structures is the role that it provides to the regional and local governments, which could directly develop their own programmes for cultural cooperation with foreign countries. Private sector is also emerging as an important stakeholder, whose role is growing.

In keeping with the UNESCO thrust on 'creative cities', to enhance local culture and creativity, China has emerged as a leading country in giving birth to creative cities at many places, which among others, include Beijing, Guangzhou, Shanghai and Qingdao. It has resulted in China taking to promoting 'sisterly-cities' relationship with other foreign countries.

The focus areas for China's cultural diplomacy are in line with its foreign policy priorities. The United States, therefore, is the primary area for focus, followed by the European Union. It is also paying attention to countries in Asia, including Japan and India.

What was started by President Hu Jintao in 2007 was further expanded by President Xi Jinping, who recognized that China's image mattered, as its global power grew (Shambaugh, David, 2015). He, therefore, in 2014 announced, 'We should increase China's soft power, give a good China narrative and better communicate China's message to the world'. The stress was, therefore, both on the narrative and equally on its communication.

Some of the steps taken by China, which are relevant from the Indian perspective, are enumerated below:

- Brand Imaging: Chinese leaders coined attractive Brand Images for itself, like 'The Chinese Dream', 'The Asia-Pacific Dream', 'The Silk Road Economic Belt', 'One Belt, One Road', and 'The Maritime Silk Road'. All these beautifully combine culture with commerce and have an in-built financial support mechanism.

- Holding of Mega Events: Some of the important image building events, included the 2008 Beijing Olympics, the 2010 Shanghai World Expo (India had a pavilion) and the 2014 Asia-Pacific Economic Cooperation Meeting.

- Launching of Dedicated Radio and TV Channels: China Radio International, with headquarters at Beijing broadcasts in 38 languages and maintains 27 overseas bureaus and it broadcasts 392 hours of programming per day. China Central Television (CCTV) went global in 2000, when it launched CCTV International, a 24-hour English Channel. In 2012, CCTV American Channel was launched, which is expected to become the global hub of its news gathering and broadcasting operations (Shambaugh, David, 2015).

- Promotion of Cultural Events: China organizes a number of events annually for international participation. Some of the important ones are, China Shanghai International Arts Festival; International Cultural Industries Fair (ICIF) in Shenzhen and Cultural Years and Art Festivals in foreign countries.

### *Japan*

Japan is, relatively speaking, a recent entrant to the arena of cultural diplomacy. It was only in the last decade that a Public Diplomacy Division was established in the Ministry of Foreign Affairs, which funds cultural and educational exchanges. The word exchange would be a misnomer, as it is largely restricted to one-way movement of Japanese Art and Artists, as Japan, culturally speaking, is still an insular country, in keeping with its physical identity as an island. At the operational level also, there is a thin line that distinguishes cultural diplomacy from public diplomacy, even though the terms 'cultural exchange' and 'cultural diplomacy' are in common usage by government as is 'public diplomacy' (Fisher, Rod, 2014).

The Japanese Foundation was set up in 1972, as an agency of the Ministry of Foreign Affairs. It now works as a quasi-independent agency since 2003 and is a principal recipient of funds from the Ministry of Foreign Affairs. It is charged with the mission 'to contribute to the improvement of a good international environment, and to the maintenance and development of harmonious foreign relationships with Japan, by the efficient and comprehensive implementation of activities for international cultural exchange' (Article 3 of 11 – Independent Administrative Institution Japan Foundation Law – quoted in Fisher, Rod, 2014).

Like other cultural bodies, the Japanese Foundation focuses on teaching of Japanese language overseas; promotion of Japanese studies, intellectual exchanges and cultural exchanges. In the arena of arts and cultural exchange, attention is paid to 'visual arts, performing arts, films and publications and culture and society' (Fisher Rod). The Foundation provides assistance in the screening of Japanese films in international and Japanese film festivals. It even funds foreign-made films on Japan. It is also involved in overseas telecasting of Japanese TV programmes; Japan even runs a dedicated NHK channel.

The Japanese Foundation is also involved in the promotion of Japanese Literature through participation in Book Fairs and translation of Japanese works. Japan participated in the International Book Fair in India in January, 2017. It held an Origami Workshop and a talk on 'Japanese Minimalism and The Art of Keeping Tidy' by Mr. Kaoru Miyamoto, Director- General. The Talk focused on Japanese way of keeping the home and workspace tidy, making the maximum use of available spaces; the essentials of how to de-clutter your surroundings. Its annual budget for the Fiscal Year 2013-14 was 113.3 million Euros, 82 per cent of which came from subsidies provided by the Ministry of Foreign Affairs (Fisher, Rod, 2014).

Japan recognizes the need for bilateral cultural agreements with foreign countries and signed many such agreements. It, however, recognizes that 'cultural engagement with other countries can be conducted without specific government-to-government agreements' (Fisher, Rod, 2014). Its policy in this regard is akin to that pursued by India. Japanese leaders also pursue the cultural agenda during exchange of such visits with foreign leaders at the bilateral and regional level. This aspect was clearly visible in Prime Minister Abe inviting Prime Minister Modi to a Japanese Tea ceremony; so was the case of Prime Minister Abe getting exposure to Indian culture at Varanasi, where he performed 'Ganga Arti' at the River Ganges during his visit to India in December 2015.

Like China, Japan is also paying special attention to the building of its image and export of Japanese cultural and creative industries products. It has thus added a commercial content to its cultural intent. This is done through the Ministry of Economy, Trade and Industry (METI) and its adoption of 'Cool Japan' Brand to develop and support talent. It is 'to promote interest in selected creative industries' and is part of a broader effort to increase 'opportunities in the international markets for 'the export of Japanese cultural goods', and 'enhance awareness of the uniqueness of Japan and increase tourism' (Fisher, Rod, 2014).

The Agency of Cultural Affairs is the principal government agency that provides funds through its office of International Culture Exchange. It is a special body of the Ministry of Education, Culture, Sports, Science and Technology (MEXT), which was set up in 1968. It is responsible for promoting and disseminating different aspects of arts and culture within Japan and internationally as well as preserving cultural properties and historical sites (Brittanica). It does this through its programmes, some of which would have relevance for India, are listed below:

- Participation in International Forums: ASEAN, ASEM etc.
- Promoting international exchange of artists and cultural specialists, such as 'the Japan Cultural Envoy' abroad and the Artists-in-Residence Programme in Japan.
- Facilitating international cultural exchange and cooperation through participation in overseas festivals, Japanese exhibitions and film festivals abroad and translation of contemporary Japanese literature into English.
- Promotion of cultural heritage conservation.

Japan has also empowered cities to play a role in cultural cooperation. Article 4 of the Basic Law for Promoting Arts and Culture and the Contents Promotion Law provides the legal basis for such participation. Japan has shown an interest in the UNESCO Creative Cities Network. It has joined hands with South Korea and China to celebrate East Asia City of Culture, in Yokohama (Japan), Quanzhan (China) and Gwangju (South Korea). Each of the cities is expected 'to host cultural events and exchange initiatives to further mutual understanding'. This initiative is considered 'significant in the context of recent territorial disputes and the difficult history between the countries' (Fisher, Rod, 2014).

India would need to have a look at the UNESCO Creative Cities Network, as Prime Minister Modi is keen to find a role for cities in cultural diplomacy, as he stated in Brisbane during his visit to Australia in November 2014, 'We truly welcome the engagement between states and cities. That is why I am also very keen to involve states in India in our international engagements' (The Hindu, 2014).

### *Mexico*

For Mexico, importance of cultural diplomacy lies in its role in building the image of 'One' or 'United' Mexico, 'instead to the hewing of a previous model of Mexico as a country of diversity, reflected by the term "mestiaze", referring to ethnic mixing and hybridity' (Mirjam Schneider). Mexican experts view culture and international cultural cooperation as 'a hidden power', because 'arts and culture are the best emissaries of a nation'. It is akin to the Indian view of looking at it as invisible Saraswati River, as propounded by Dr. Karan Singh.

The Ministry of Foreign Affairs is the nodal Ministry that oversees cultural diplomacy. It negotiates 'exchanges and agreements, and is responsible for the organisation of all cooperation in the area of culture'. All such activities are implemented by the Mexican Agency for International Cooperation for Development (AMEXCID). There is no Ministry of Culture as such, but The National Council for Culture and Arts (CONACULTA) closely resembles it.

Culture is not only an important tool in image building, but is also being used in counteracting the negative image of a violent Mexico. It is also used in stimulating economic development by providing support to 'culture and creative industries', which represent 6.7% of its GDP. Mexico places particular focus on 'the audiovisual sector and the promotion of tourism and the country's cuisine'. It was, therefore, not surprising when the President of Mexico Pena Nieto hosted Prime Minister Modi at a Mexican restaurant, to get a taste of 'Tacos', during his visit to Mexico in June, 2016.

Exhibitions and literature are considered to be two primary 'pillars of cultural diplomacy'. It is paying special attention to the translation of Mexican Books into European languages. Mexico is increasingly using its vibrant film and television industry, in particular "telenovelas" in projecting itself and generating commercial revenues, in particular in South America and USA, catering to the Mexican population. Mexico is also making its presence in the Indian market. Translation of Books is considered useful in connecting to the outside world, with increasing focus on translation of books in to European languages.

Participation in exhibitions helps Mexico in building its image, as the Country of Honour at 'MIPCOM 2014' and 'Expo Milan'. MIPCOM is a TV and Entertainment Market, which is held annually at Cannes, France. Europe is emerging as a new focus area, as Mexicans feel that 'talking to Europeans is like talking to your mother' (Schneider, Mirjam, 2013).

Mexican Diaspora, which has a sizeable presence in USA, is well connected with the home country. It also carries a considerable political weight in the United States, resulting in it being wooed or castigated to serve the interests of political leaders and parties. While meeting the cultural requirements of its Diaspora, Mexico has to perform a delicate role.

Mexico also has an arrangement with the Spanish 'Instituto Cervantes' to promote its culture, art, education, science, technology, tourism and its creative industries. India could study this model and see how this could be adapted to suit our needs.

An agreement on cultural cooperation has been in existence with India since 1975 and cooperation activities are carried out through four-yearly 'Programmes of Cultural Cooperation' under the framework of this agreement. ICCR offers four scholarships to Mexicans every year. Leading Mexican university 'Colegio de Mexico' and the 'National Autonomous University of Mexico' have important Centres of Indian Studies.

Like many other countries, Mexico interchangeably uses the words, 'cultural diplomacy' and 'cultural relations. It is also becoming cognizant of the role of 'public diplomacy'. Culture is considered an important tool in Mexico's fight against violence, under its planned programme, called 'Mexico en Paz' (Mexico in Peace).

***Russia***

There is now a renewed interest in using Russian culture and language in the international arena, by linking the same to 'Patriotism', which President Putin is using as a unifying theme. The Ministries of Foreign Affairs and Culture are the nodal Ministries for the pursuit of cultural diplomacy. It allows participation by local governments in the cultural arena and would like them to get involved in the promotion of Contemporary Art. A rigid visa regime, however, still remains an important stumbling block in connecting with people from foreign countries.

In 2012, President Putin announced the basic contours of his policy, which were as follows (Smits, Yolanda: 1, 2014):

- To build Russian image as a great and famous country.
- To promote outreach to the Russian Diaspora community.
- To disseminate the use of the Russian language.
- To promote international academic and student exchanges.
- To preserve cultural heritage.
- To promote a scheme of bilateral years with foreign countries.

The primary focus of Russian cultural diplomacy was on image building through showing its cultural strengths and building the same through the organization of country festivals on a bilateral basis. 2014 was also declared as the Year of Culture in Russia, which led to the mounting of a number of cultural activities, as Russia built its image.

Education is also an important component of Russian cultural diplomacy, as foreign students, including from India, are a source of much needed funds. Politics, however, gets injected in disrupting educational links as Russia stopped sending students to the United States, after it imposed economic sanctions after the incorporation of Crimea into Russia. Russia also stopped the adoption of children by US citizens.

The Orthodox Church also plays an important role in the implementation of policies. Russian TV and RT State-sponsored news channel has become an important tool for dissemination of news and views, which is seen by over 1 billion viewers across the world. Russia, still largely follows a top-down approach and there is a limited role for the NGOs.

Russia's primary focus still remains on Georgia and the CIS countries as The Kremlin would like to foster 'a sense of shared identity among brotherly people' (Smits, Yolanda: 1). Russian focus remains on the youth. Russia is getting more involved with India, although the people-to-people connectivity has not reached the level that existed with the Soviet Union.

### *South Africa*

There are three main players in South Africa, which directly or indirectly deal in the arena of cultural diplomacy. The Department of Arts and Culture (DAC) focuses on cultural diplomacy per se; the Department of International Relations and Cooperation (DIRCO) is concerned with foreign relations and public diplomacy; and the Department of Trade and Industries (DTI) is involved with export of cultural goods. The emphasis of DAC is on 'exchanges and mutual understanding' differs from that of DIRCO, which lays stress on 'influence for a better world'. DIRCO leaves policy formulation on cultural diplomacy to DAC, for whom cultural diplomacy is 'a tool to facilitate intercultural dialogue, enhance professionalism and encourage enthusiasm for creativity amongst the people of South Africa' (Fisher, Rod: 2, 2014).

DAC highlights the importance of cultural diplomacy in international relations. The main objectives of DAC are to strengthen relations with other countries; encourage institutional linkages and foster people to people connectivity; showcase and promote South African Arts and Culture, Arts Education and Residency; foster skills transfer and development; promote market access for cultural goods and services and promote sustainability of the sector.

The focus of DAC is on building South-South relations and promoting the African Agenda in the arts, culture and heritage arena. South Africa's cultural activities are linked to the promotion of investments and exports in the creative industries sector.

South African Constitution provides for 'both national and provincial governments oversights of cultural matters' as well as the involvement of local governments at the level of cities. The City of Johannesburg has collaboration with New Orleans in the area of Jazz music. The City of Durban hosted the $2^{nd}$ BRICS Urbanization Forum and the $3^{rd}$ Friendship Cities and Local Government Cooperation Forum on November 27-29, 2013.

South Africa, like other countries, has developed its own Signature Feature, called 'Seasons', which involves organization of multi-pronged cultural activities, under the banner of Cultural Festival. It entered such arrangements with many countries. The French 'Cultural Seasons' in South Africa was held during June-November 2012; while the South African 'Cultural Seasons' was held in France in 2013. The Russian 'Cultural Seasons' was launched in Johannesburg on November 13, 2016, while South African 'Cultural Seasons' in Russia was launched in Moscow on November 29, 2017. An Indian Festival was held in South Africa during June-August 2011; while the South African Festival was held in India in April 2013.

Other Festivals are also an important feature on the cultural horizon of South Africa. Some of these with international participation include the National Arts Festival, the Cape Town International Jazz Festival and the Standard Bank Jazz Festivals. These Festivals get their support from DAC, business groups, national cultural institutes and foreign diplomatic missions.

Music is in the DNA of every African; music and dance are an integral part of the African cultural scene. South Africa has collaborative programmes with many countries to promote African music. Under a project 'The Music in Africa', it has collaborated with the Siemens Foundation and the Goethe Institute, to establish music information and networking online portal.

Private Sector is also playing an important role in sponsoring cultural activities. Some of the prominent ones include Art Logic, which organizes Jo'burg Art Fair, which is getting increasing participation from galleries in Europe and Africa. The other is VANSA (Visual Arts Network South

Africa), which helps in generating awareness on art practices. It was involved in a project on cultural trade between South Africa and Southern Africa, which was led by the British Council.

### *South Korea*

South Korea views cultural relations and public and cultural diplomacy initiatives as distinctly different; hence two different Ministries are charged with the responsibility of overseeing these. The Ministry of Culture, Sports and Tourism (MOCST) plays the lead role in cultural exchanges. On the other hand, the Ministry of Foreign Affairs (MFA) broadly supports the public and cultural diplomacy initiatives.

The Korean Foundation (KF) is the chief instrument under the Ministry of Foreign Affairs that actively promotes academic and cultural exchanges; it funds Korean Studies programmes and broadcasts Korean TV dramas overseas.

MOCST also promotes international exchanges through its two main bodies – the Korea Arts Management Services, which assists partnerships with international festivals and cultural organizations and the Arts Council of Korea, which funds Korean input to international cultural events.

South Korea also uses cultural diplomacy, in seeking greater recognition of a Korean Brand through the international exposure of its culture and cultural industries (Fisher, Rod: 1, 2014). It is equally interested in sustaining the export income generated through the impact of the 'Korean Wave' – Korean TV dramas, pop music, films and video games (Fisher, Rod:1, 2014).

'Hallyu' or the Korean Wave, which refers to Korean cultural products, such as dance, drama and music; fashion and cosmetics and food, has put South Korea on the world map. The Korean Wave has given a spurt to export of Korean products. Korean Cultural and Information Service (KOCIS) promotes 'Hallyu' through its 29 cultural centres abroad, established in 25 countries. This, in turn, gets linked to the understanding of the Korean language; learning of this is facilitated through the Korean language institutes, called ''Sejong Hakdang' (King Sejong Institutes), which are set up under the Ministry of Culture, Sports and Tourism. As of 2016, 145 such institutes were located in 58 countries (Dhawan, Ranjit Kumar, 2017).

South Korea's main focus is on its neighbours and countries in the Asia-Pacific region. It is also actively involved with the United States, but has a limited exposure in the EU. It has 25 cultural centres abroad and more than 90 Sejong Centres for the learning of the language. It has a vibrant involvement of cities, which are networked internationally. Similarly, cultural bodies, both from the public and private sectors are actively involved.

## Operation of Cultural Diplomacy in India: Focus and Thrust Areas

This part presents a picture of how cultural diplomacy operates in India. It is largely based on interaction of the author with diplomats in India, who are involved in the area of cultural diplomacy. It is in the nature of a broad overview, while simultaneously focusing on their thrust areas. Picture that emerges in respect of some countries is discussed below.

### *Japan*

The Japanese Foundation (JF) is mandated to undertake cultural activities, as stated earlier. It works under the aegis of the Ministry of Foreign Affairs (MFA) as an independent organization. It is funded by MFA and works in close coordination with the Embassy, which is involved in the planning and evaluation of its activities. It was set up in 1990 but has functioned actively since 2006 and has its own premises. It is a non-profit organization. JF is patterned on the lines of ICCR. The Japanese Foundation has three areas of focus in India:

- Language Training
- Lectures
- Visits by Japanese scholars

Japan arranges language training through educational institutions – schools and universities. It also has special facilities for the learning of the language through courses conducted by the Mombusha Scholars Association of India (MOSAI), which is an alumni association of Indian scholars, who had studied in Japan. Presently, 20,000 Indians are studying Japanese language in India. Interest in the Japanese language is growing, as 1,200 Japanese companies are operating in India and it has a resident community of 8,000 Japanese (Mayu Hagiwara)[1].

Japan, like many other countries, is focusing on youth exchanges. It has three important programmes, which are funded by the government. JENESYS (Japan-East Asia Network of Exchange for Youth and Students) provides for one week's home stay with the Japanese families. The

Japanese government provides for airfare and local stay. This is reckoned to be a highly successful programme. During the last two years, Japan managed to send 1200 Youth from India.

The other is called, SYW (Ship for World Youth), which is an integrated programme for youth from all across the world. Here the youth mingle with one another over a period of two weeks, while they pursue their studies and learn about Japanese language and culture.

The third is visit by Japanese students on familiarization trip of India under an exchange programme with schools. The programme also provides for one day's stay with a family. Around 50 students manage to visit India. The emphasis of youth exchanges is on family orientation, as such an approach would provide for greater connectivity at the personal level, which is the main purpose of such exchanges.

Japan also promotes study by Indian students in Japan. 700 Indian students are studying in Japan, pursuing language studies and courses in other disciplines. Japan is keen to strengthen people to people linkages through promoting tourism and exchange of visits by scholars. However, visits by Japanese scholars are of an occasional nature.

Japan is also focussing on typically Japanese areas of cultural excellence, like Ikebana and Bonsai. The Lodhi Gardens have a good collection of Bonsais. Japan held the 25th Anniversary celebration of the Delhi chapter of the Ohara School of Ikebana, when its Headmaster demonstrated this art in Delhi on March 19, 2015.

***Russia***

Five Russian Cultural Centres exist in India – Delhi, Kolkata, Chennai, Mumbai and Trivandrum. All cultural centres except at Trivandrum are directly linked with the Embassy and the Consulate General. At Trivandrum, it is run by an Honorary Consul – Dr. Rakesh Nair. All the Centres have good libraries. At Delhi, the Centre is located at a Central Area – Feroze Shah Road and is, therefore, easily accessible to visitors. Not a single Centre had been closed down, after the breakup of the Soviet Union.

The Cultural Centres' primary focus is on 'people's diplomacy', to promote connectivity and friendship at people to people level, by undertaking all types of cultural activities. Russia's cultural connectivity with India goes over 70 years. This is the direct outcome of Russia's 'special privileged strategic partnership' with India. Indian friendship is 'genuine and old' (Fyodor Rozovskiy)[2].

There is a special thrust on the learning of Russian language at the Centres. There are different types of courses. At present, 700 students are learning Russian in India. Indian students still continue to go to Russia for studies. At present, 5000 students are studying in Russia, primarily in medicine, mathematics etc.

Russia is attaching great importance to reaching out to the youth. They have largely succeeded in this direction; as more young people were getting involved in cultural programmes sponsored by them. Under President Putin's direction, Russia had taken a number of initiatives to focus on the Gen Next. Some of these included, 'New Generation Programme', where Indian youth were invited to spend 10 days in Russia to get acquainted with modern Russia. Twenty youth were sent to Russia in 2014.

Another important programme was 'The Youth Innovative Forum' organized in Russia, where youth from across the globe participated. India has also participated in this programme. In 2015, they again focussed on the youth. Following activities were organized:

- Youth's Mathematics Olympiad, April 2015 (To offer 20 scholarships to Indian students from schools)
- Youth's BRICS Forum, March 2015.

2015 was declared as 'The Year of Literature', with focus on events relating to Indian and Russian literary works. Russia planned to organize a number of cultural activities to mark the 75th Anniversary, called the Patriotic Victory in the World War II. These included Film Festivals, Days of Russian Language, chess tournament etc. Other activities included a Film Festival on April 24 and a Seminar on May 9, titled "The Lessons of World War II for the 21st Century".

Festivals of India and Russia were organized, periodically. These were found to be useful as these helped in providing funds for undertaking additional activities, beyond the normal annual cultural activities.

### *South Korea*

The impact of the Korean Wave (Hallyu) is limited in India, largely on account of cultural and language barriers. Its impact is greater in Northeast India, in particular, in the States of Manipur, Mizoram and Nagaland. To promote the Korean Wave in India, the Korean Cultural Centre (KCC) was set up in 2012. The Centre's focus is on the youth; it had 59 partnership programmes with schools in India by 2016. There is also emphasis on the teaching of the language; three branches of the King Sejong Institute are operating in Chenai, Delhi and Patna.

The Embassy and KCC have been active in organizing 'quiz competitions, K-pop contests, speech contests, essay competitions and video-making contests for schools and college students and seminars on issues related to Korea in the universities and think-tanks in India'. The Academy of Korean Studies has also an MOU with the National Council of Education Research and Training (NCERT) to increase the content of Korean history in Indian textbooks (Dhawan, Ranjit Kumar, 2017). South Korea has also entered into the fast food market and the traditional Korean drink, 'Soju' is being introduced to Indian consumers. India remains an attractive but difficult market for South Korea consumer products.

### *USA*

USA conducts its cultural diplomacy under the Public Affairs Department. At the US Embassy, this department is organized under two divisions – Media and Culture. The Media Wing operates from the premises of the Embassy; while the Cultural Wing operates in separate premises that are centrally located at Kasturba Gandhi Marg. The Media Wing reaches out to the media, while the Cultural Wing connects with people at large. The American Libraries play an important role and the US Embassy operates these at five centres in India. Libraries at New Delhi and Kolkata have a membership of 1,50,000 persons. Access and smooth running of the libraries was becoming a problem on two counts – budgetary constraints and security considerations (David Mees).[3]

Cultural diplomacy with India is considered 'exceptionally important', as 'cultural connections are a big part of what brings people together'. Such connections already exist through art and literature, music, food and the films. The government's role would be to 'deepen those connections through programming' and 'recognizing peoples' achievements' and thus using 'culture as a real bridge between our two countries' (Amb. Verma).USA describes 'culture' in a broader context, which goes beyond the 'Performing Arts'. It, therefore, embraces activities that result in 'stimulating ideas' as well as those that fall under the rubric 'Arts' (Walter Douglas).[4]

In the above context, public diplomacy has acquired importance, because it interfaces with cultural diplomacy that connects with people and ensures that the programmes, 'which we do reach people directly' (Amb Verma). To do so, the United States had 'romped up' its outreach programme, so as to involve people in the dialogue process. US public diplomacy targets only foreign audiences as per its mandate.

Public diplomacy was 'messaging' through the media and building connectivity at the people to people level. The press signified 'shot gun' approach by reaching out instantaneously, while cultural diplomacy has long term gestation period. These considerations had been kept in view, when looking for results. Selection of the target audience was important for both the approaches. Media connectivity was absolutely essential and it helped in sending out 'the message publicly'. The success of this approach could be measured as they managed to get their message through leading newspapers like the New Year Times, which enjoyed credibility.

India-USA have a vibrant ongoing cooperation programme in the education sector that was built around common values of 'commitment to learn, innovation and hard work' (Amb.Verma, 2016). During 2014-15, 132888 Indian students were admitted to American educational institutes, which represented an increase of 30% over the previous year. It is not only Indian students that USA was targeting, but it would also like to see a flow of American students in to India. A new programme called, 'Passport to India', an Obama-Singh Inter-University Partnership Programme, was launched in 2012. At the US end, the Ohio State University was declared the nodal point. The Americans were now identifying universities at the Indian end, which could give a push to this programme. Similarly, American participation in India's initiative on Higher Education, called 'GIAN' (Knowledge), is slowly evolving.

It is not only higher education, but also the acquisition of required skills that community colleges could help India. This could emerge as an important area of cooperation, if it results in USA emerging an important partner in one of Modi's Missions of 'Skills India'. Another new programme that has been initiated is called, 'Internees', where internees from USA are provided with attachment in Indian companies through a consortium of Indian companies. USA was keen to be a part of the 'Start up culture and innovation in India', as per Prime Minister Modi's dream unveiled in Sillicon Valley (Amb.Verma, 2016).

Education is an important component of American's cultural diplomacy. Fulbright Scholarship Scheme was 'a largely successful story'. 18,000 Indians had been recipient of Fulbright Fellowships. In 2009, this programme was converted into a joint programme and it now operates under the aegis of US-India Education Foundation (USIEF), which operates from separate premises at the Hailey Road. While the administrative costs of the programme were still borne by the United States, but the cost on fellowships was shared by the two countries, with India contributing US $ 3.35 million annually. It was a case of 'America-Indian success story'.

Alumni Association or local cultural groups needed to be built up, as they played an important role in organizing cultural programmes. They cited one case in Pakistan, where the local cultural group stepped in to organise performance by an American Cultural Troupe, after the shooting of Bin Laden.

The US Embassy is focussing on providing connectivity to American strategic think tanks by connecting with experts other than India-country specialists. In this way, they were filling this void, as they promoted connectivity among strategic experts – an area where we should also focus, as the relationship moves in the direction of strategic partnership. The Embassy was paying attention to schools and children were invited for a day's familiarisation programme at the Embassy.

The US Embassy had also supported Literary Festivals and provided financial assistance for three years to the Jaipur Literary Festival. They had, however, left the selection of authors, who could be invited to the festival, to the organizers. The Embassy played a low key role. The US Embassy also facilitated participation at the Book Festivals also.

Diaspora has emerged as an important link that bridges cooperation between the two countries. The appointment of Ambassador Richard Verma, as the first Indian-American Ambassador to India was hailed by the then Secretary of State John Kerry as 'a homecoming of enormous consequences'. Ambassdor Verma realized the significance of this homecoming, when he received warm welcome from people in his ancestral village in the Jallandhar District in Punjab.

For USA, 2016 was an important year for cultural connectivity with India. The US Embassy had organized two important events recently – 'Beyond Bollywood' – a posters exhibition and another exhibition titled 'Kindred Nations: The United States and India: 1783-1947'. Both were held at the American Cultural Center. The first was a celebration of Indian Diaspora in the United States and was a mini version of the Exhibition held at the Smithsonian Institution in 2014. The second portrayed through photographs, India-USA connectivity that existed prior to independence and the American role in India's Independence struggle. This was built around three themes – 'Gaining Knowledge; Understanding towards Freedom' and 'Searching for Opportunities'. This was prepared by the Meridian International Center, Washington DC with which ICCR has an MOU for cooperation.

International Visitors Leadership Programme (IVLP), which was one of the core programmes of American cultural diplomacy, focussed on future leaders. Indira Gandhi had been invited under this programme. A large number of Indian leaders had been and are being invited. It is an 83 years' old programme and its 75th Anniversary was celebrated in March 2015 in India and 150 Alumni participated. It has 4000 alumni members and the Association plays an important role in providing connectivity.

The Embassy pays special attention to the selection of cultural products, to meet the taste of the local population. They averred that western classical musical programmes were not a great success, as a handful of Indians attended. Jazz Music programmes were only marginally successful. Chicago's Children's Choir in January 2013 helped in conveying a message of diversity.

America was participating as a low key partner in the preservation of Indian cultural heritage and arts. Country specific programme were needed to be organized. For example, in Cyprus, they organized activities in the 'Green Zone', which provided an opportunity for connectivity among Turkish and Greek Cypriots, who had links with USA.

## Enriching from Emerging Trends and Developments in Other Countries

What is the picture that emerges from our understanding of the policy and institutional framework of cultural diplomacy and its implementation thereof in India by some countries? There is a growing recognition of the importance of cultural diplomacy across the board. It works in tandem with public diplomacy; while it operates in two separate channels as in South Korea and South Africa, although in the case of others it stands submerged in the overall framework of public diplomacy. In the case of China and Japan, the focus is also on cultural creativity, as they would like cultural exchanges to turn into cultural trade also.

Invariably, it is the Ministry of Foreign Affairs that is charged with the overall responsibility of pursuing cultural diplomacy. It shares this responsibility with the Ministries of Culture, Economy and Trade, depending upon the areas of focus. Building Brand Image remains a key pursuit, although with varying degree of emphasis. In these efforts on nation branding, it has to be remembered that what ultimately matters is how other countries accept the brand.

Media emerges as an important vehicle for China in projecting itself. It could be, CCTV, which is doing suave projection and comes out as a polished outfit. On the other hand, its print media through the 'Global Times' makes a blatant presentation of the Chinese view and comes out adversely, as it gets in to controversy with local view point.

Cultural Centres are the primary instrumentalities used by all the countries. Of all the countries, China is the most ambitious, as it has plans to set up 1000 Confucius Centres by 2020. China's Confucius Centres are built on a partnership concept with the host universities, but are centrally controlled. The United States uses graded level of centres, from a full-fledged Cultural Centre to an American Corner, which is a mini library.

South Korea also has its own mini version of a cultural centre called, 'Sejong', which focuses on the Korean language only. Russian cultural centres are coming out of the Soviet ideology mould, as they reach out to the Youth. There is, however, a high level of professionalism in the way foreign cultural centres are manned and run their programmes. These also provide easy accessibility to local residents.

There is recognition on the need for establishing sisterly-cities relations, as seen from the steps being taken by China, Japan and South Korea. They are working jointly on 'East Asia City of Culture' Project under the aegis of UNESCO's Creative Cities Network. We need to learn from their experiences.

An overall perception was that India needed to 'punch well above its weight'. The cultural diplomacy needed to 'focus on the youth', who were more inclined to relate to modern India rather than India's cultural heritage. Lessons could be drawn out from programmes mounted by these countries.

Education, Youth Exchanges and learning of Languages emerge as the important areas of cultural connectivity between India and these countries. While efforts could be made to build on these; yet new steps could be taken to learn from their experiences in Image Building; converting cultural exchanges into cultural creativity and cultural trade and promoting linkages at the grassroots level among our cities.

## Endnotes

1 Ms. Mayu Hagiwara, First Secretary (Culture) at the Japanese Embassy. She was assisted by Bapi Raju. Interaction on April 9, 2015, Delhi.

2 Fyodor A R Rozovskiy, Counsellor and Regional Director of the Russian Centre of Science and Culture. Interaction on April 7, 2016, Delhi.

3 David Mees, Cultural Counsellor of the Embassy of the United States. Interaction on April 8, 2015, Delhi.

4 Walter Douglas, Minister Counsellor Public Affairs, US Embassy. Interaction on April 8, 2015, Delhi.

## References

Amb. Verma, 2016, US Ambassador to India: 'The Ties That Bind', *Span*, March-April.

Brittanica, https://www.britannica.com/place/Japan/The-arts#ref1036832 (Accessed on April 11, 2018).

Dhawan, Ranjit Kumar, 2017, 'Korea's Cultural Diplomacy: An analysis of the Hallyu in India', *Strategic Analysis,* Volume 41, Number 6 (Nov-Dec 2017), IDSA, New Delhi.

Fisher, Rod: *Japan Country Report*, *2014*, 'Culture in the EU's External Relations, March.

Fisher, Rod: 1, *South Korea Country Report, 2014*, Culture in the EU's External Relations.

Fisher, Rod: 2, *South Africa Report, 2014*, Culture in the EU's External Relations.

Schneider, Mirjam, *Mexico Country Report, 2013*, Culture in the EU's External Relations.

Shambaugh, David, 2015, 'China's Soft-Power Push', *The Foreign Affairs*, July-August.

Smits, Yolanda, 2014, *China Country Report*, Culture in the EU's External Relations.

Smits, Yolanda: 1, 2014, *Russia Country Report*, Culture in the EU's External Relations.

*The Hindu*, 2014, 'India, Australia share "special bond: Modi', November 17.

# Section – VIII

# Concluding Chapter

# Chapter – XV

# Concluding Observations and The Way Ahead

## Present Day Global Environment

We have come to the finishing line, but will have to return to the starting point. To determine the role of cultural diplomacy in a globalised world, we have to figure out where do we stand in the present-day world and how do we view cultural diplomacy and its place thereof? The world still remains globalised, despite concerns over globalisation.

Globalisation is resulting in 'cultural deterritorialisation' and societies are becoming 'more culturally heterogeneous'. 'Globalisation's impact on culture is viewed:

> "Both a blessing and curse: on the one hand offering unprecedented opportunities for interactive and enriching cultural exchanges and therefore increasing cultural diversity, and on the other leading to uniformity or tensions between cultures" (Kazymka, Irina, 2014).

The world is well connected through technology, as Information and Communication Technology (ICT) has shortened the distance and space by reducing communication barriers. This, however, has not resulted in greater mobility among people. We talk of Transnational Diaspora, but it cannot move on its free will, from one to another country. We witness imposition of increased physical barriers on movement and hardening of attitude, built on concerns over increasing number of immigrants, as governments attempt to strike an optimum balance between immigrants and locals.

There is an apparent desire to preserve identities, as these clash with values, real or perceived, of the host states. 'Politics of Identity' are there to stay; while voices for the strength of diversity would continue to be heard. Vinay Sahasrabuddhe, who was appointed President of ICCR in 2018, holds the view that 'culture is a unifier and while identities can't be wished away, one can't forget that smaller identities are always a part of a larger holistic identity' (cited in Hebbar, Nistula, 2018). How to harmoniously blend 'Identity' with 'Diversity'; it would be a challenge and remain one of the focus areas of cultural diplomacy?

The distinction between 'us' and 'them' is growing as it is fed on the need to protect nationalism, by invoking patriotism that borders on jingoism. We are technologically well connected; we can see our faces on Facebook, but are becoming faceless. Bonds at the personal and human level are missing. World leaders can take pride in using Twitter but that fails to connect and generates more heat than light. There is thus no human bond and love. Mutual trust is lacking. Human feelings are generated only, when we see the dead bodies of children that have washed ashore or become victims of deadly chemical weapons or are languishing on shores, deprived of food and other basic necessities.

We talk of inclusivity but refuse to 'Walk the Talk'. Instead, the seeds of divisiveness are being sown, to achieve short term political goals. It is both within national borders and outside, when immigrants are perceived as the cause of all the ills in a particular society. Even empirical studies on the positive role of immigrants have not resulted in removing blinkers from the eyes of political leadership.

Human Rights, therefore, stay confined to the national statutes or international conventions, with no benefits accruing to human beings. We see strength in diversity but stay imprisoned in our identities and would like to see acceptance of our values by the newly arrived persons. Immigrants are required to pass the test on local values, be it American, British or Australian, before they are accepted as citizens.

Even America, which is the Mecca for all persons, is losing its lure and ceasing to be a 'Dream Country'. Soul searching is taking place among foreign residents, who are asking questions, 'Do we belong here?', when confronted with taunts, like 'Go Back'. On the other hand, posters appear asking the Americans when they would return to their respective homes, as USA itself is a nation of immigrants, as American-Indians would like to regain their space as original owners.

President Clinton introduced 'Diversity Visa' in 1995 to facilitate entry of immigrants from countries from which normal migration did not take place to the United States. President Donald Trump has put 'Diversity' in the reverse gear, as he attempts to bar immigrants from certain Muslim countries. Even German Chancellor Angela Merkel is being forced to accept a lesser number of immigrants under electoral compulsions. Many other world leaders would like to follow this lead, even though, at times, remaining mute. The scandal over the targeting of 'Windrush Generation', pre-1971 migrants from the Caribbeans caused dismay, as they were targeted to produce documentary evidence of their stay in UK, leading to the resignation of the British Home Secretary in April 2018; this dented UK's image as 'an open, liberal and tolerant country'. Concerns are expressed over its likely impact on Indians immigrants (The Hindu, 2018).

Hate crimes are increasing, as we view others through the prism of colour, gender, race, caste, or religion. At times, these relate to mistaken identity. Screws are being tightened on the movement of people under trumped up political pressure to provide job security to locals. Criteria for the entry of immigrants and even admission of students are tightened by increasing threshold on minimum deposits and restrictions on post-study employment. Media depiction of The Statute of Liberty with a Blackened face or being shown holding the Torch of Liberty upside down, symbolically tells the story, if we want to hear.

We have travelled a long distance in our journey into Indian cultural diplomacy in a globalised world. The globalised world is in a flux as nationalism now dictates the agenda (Echanove & Srivastava). Joseph Nye Jr. notes the power shifts that are taking place in these words: "Two great power shifts are occurring in this century: a power transition among states and diffusion away from all states to non-state actors" (Nye Jr., Joseph 2011). The emergence of non-state actors thus further reemphasizes the need for connectivity through cross cultural conversations.

The above scenario also results in the imposition of restrictions on movement of persons, not that there was a free flow earlier. The differences between 'us' and 'them' are getting accentuated through such clarion calls, like 'America First'; UK for Britishers, not even EU citizens; 'Hungary for Hungarians'. Added to this is the requirement of passing a test on values. The latest to join the band wagon, making such formal pronouncement was the visiting Australian Prime Minister Turnbull to India in April 2017, when he also spoke of 'Australians First' (Turnbull, 2017).

An 'Inclusive Society' is becoming a pipe dream, while divisiveness rules the roost. It is not only at the international level, but also at the national level that we come across such tendencies. Perceived fears of the majority, be it in USA, UK or India, are resulting in creating feelings of insecurity among the minority groups, who feel threatened. This leads to hate crimes, which result in tearing down the social fabric.

**Cultural Diplomacy Enters Diplomatic Space**

Against this backdrop of social and cultural trends globally, there is an increasing realization on the part of governments and people that they need to connect and understand each other. For this to happen, they have to facilitate flow of people and ideas that will help them in changing their mindset. The role for cross cultural conversation, therefore, becomes essential. Culture 'provides meeting points for exposition and explanation for dialogue and debate' (Demos, 2007). This scenario results in triggering 'Cultural Diplomacy'.

The role of 'Cultural Diplomacy' thus becomes central as 'Connectivity Bridge'. Professor Justin Hart spells out in these words:

> "If cultural relations in the past have been at the periphery of foreign relations, it may be that in new situation into which the world is moving, cultural relations are at the heart" (Hart, Justin, 2013).

Yes, it is true. This results in its role being perceived to be in the genre of power, be it soft power, by writers like Joseph Nye Jr, Shashi Tharoor and Daya Thussu. In this process, they mistakenly drift themselves away from the central purpose of cultural diplomacy. It is not seeking empowerment through conversion but understanding through acceptance of 'them' as 'us', in the true African spirit of 'Ubuntu', which is 'I am because of you'(Suryakanthi Tripathi).

Xaba, a Jazz Musician, who participated at the Annual Jazz Festival in New Delhi in September 2017, had his own take on "Ubuntu". He said, "In Africa it stands for 'humanity'. That is what we want the people to feel – we are one".

Cultural diplomacy, therefore, acquires a central role, as the need for understanding assumes greater importance, by viewing humanity as one. It is, therefore, not surprising to see the US State Department flying the flag of cultural diplomacy as the 'Linchpin of Public Diplomacy'.

To find a role for cultural diplomacy would need our understanding as to the type of world, we want. Are we prepared to accept Indian ethos of 'Vasudhaiva Kutumbakam' (The Whole World is a Family), which recognize equality of all members, despite their diversities, as all the five fingers cannot be equal? If so, are we prepared to provide for freer mobility and better flow of ideas, following Mahatma Gandhi's faith in letting fresh breeze blow from all directions?

What we need is to create an environment, which could facilitate genuine dialogue rather than delving in symbolism by holding All Faiths Conferences in some countries, which remain an empty gesture only. We need to change our mindset and view all people as equal, like Maharaja Ranjit Singh, as metaphorically speaking, he had a better political and human vision, despite his handicap of one eye. Hopefully, we can see the birth of a 'Universal Man' of the dreams of Rabindranath Tagore, as described by him in his poem.

## Identity Politics

New narratives are appearing with increasing rise in populism, as the process of globalisation has failed to deliver, in particular, benefits to the lower middle class. The so-called trickledown effect has not largely reached that stratum of society. The gap between rising aspirations and fulfillment is growing. The present generation finds itself worse off than their forefathers as their standards of living are coming down. Success is measured in materialistic terms and not in terms of spiritual or other inner values. This new narrative is harking us back to the Westphalian concept of state sovereignty, stoking nationalistic chords. Vote for Brexit from EU in June 2016, was largely won through anti-immigrant campaign.

On the other hand, a recent study by the UK's New Economic Foundation came to the conclusion that the contribution of immigrants to the UK 'is hard to dispute', stating that British GDP would daily take a 4% dip, if migrant workers stopped working for a day. Many migrant workers stopped work for one day, under the banner of movement, '1daywithout us'. Will it result in a new narrative? Not likely, as UK prepares to formally exit from EU, as migration is likely to continue in some or other form in future, highlighting the role immigrants play (Ram, Vidya 2017: 1).

Politics of identity are becoming more pronounced, which is resulting in dividing societies even within nations that has its impact abroad. We have seen this happening in the United States, which is the world's oldest democracy, with likely trends appearing in India, the largest democracy in the world. Slogan mongering is increasing, as nations would like to regain their past glories or carve a new niche for themselves at the world stage.

Another new narrative that is being written is the rise of smaller local groups, which are emerging as 'judges and enforcers of identity' that cut both at the individual and societal identity (Sarukkai, Sundar, 2017). These do not help in creating conducive atmosphere for cooperation. These are not likely to result in connecting nations and people with one another. How do we then create a space for dialogue?

We are witnessing another trend, where there is increasing cultural sensitivity on the part of leaders as they would like to score a victory, based on their personal beliefs. It manifests in a variety of forms. It is the refusal by the French Far Right National Front presidential candidate Marie Le Pen to meet grand mufti Sheikh Abdul Latif Derian in Beirut, as she did not want to wear headscarf, as suggested by the latter (The Times of India 2017:1). She took the stand that on an earlier occasion she had not worn the same when she met the grand mufti of Al Azhar in Cairo in 2015 (Carraud, Simon, 2017).

On the other hand, actress Lindsay Lohan claimed that she was 'racially profiled' at the Heathrow Airport, when she was stopped because she was wearing a headscarf (The Times of India, 2017: 2). Detention of Bollywood Star Shah Rukh Khan third time by the Immigration Authorities at the New York Airport in June 2016 was viewed as a case of racial profiling by his fans (The Guardian, 2016). In another incident students at the Bhatkal College in Bangalore (India) gave vent to their cultural sensitivities by sporting saffron shawl in response to wearing of headscarf by four visiting faculty members (Raghava, M, 2017).

## Acceptance of Diversity and Celebration of Pluralism

To fight the 'Politics of Identity', 'Diversity' triggers in various ways and the same needs to be celebrated. It is the All Women Afghan Band performing at the World Economic Forum at Davos in January 2017. It is the holding of 'Immigrants' Diversity Festival' in Luxembourg in March 2017, projecting diversity of cultures. It is also the serving of 'Diversity Breakfast' on April 14, 2017 at the Sikh Gurdwara on Baisakhi Day at Dubai (UAE) to celebrate the birth of the Sikh Religion. It made it to the Guinness Book of Record as 600 persons were served from 66 nationalities.

It is also the performance of the Australian Orchestra conducted by Zubin Mehta, which had musicians from a number of foreign nationalities and included Don Bradman's daughter. It is the Pakistani Band 'Junoon' performing in the State of Jammu and Kashmir. It is an artist from

Uzbekistan regaling Indian audience in Delhi, by singing Bollywood songs of yesteryears.

It is Meryl Streep taking cudgels for the Black Actors at Hollywood in the name of 'Diversity'. It is the Indian film stars speaking for the Pakistani artists to act in Bollywood films or the West Bengal Chief Minister Mamta Banerjee saying that 'Music has no borders' or Prime Minister Modi saying , 'Culture and music can play a vital role in connecting the country. It can be a big step towards realizing Ek Bharat Shresht Bharat' (Cited in Financial Express, 2017).

It is the issuance of a poster in Canada with the picture of the First Canadian Prime Minister and Harjit Singh Sajjan, Defence Minister, showcasing that 'Diversity' (Multiculturalism) is still alive and kicking in Canada. It is the issuance of stamp in Fiji, showing the face of a Sikh among others to symbolically project that multiculturalism exists in Fiji. It is reaffirmation of commitment to diversity, when a Cabinet Minister in the State of Assam states that no ban on beef in the State was a sign of respect for other communities.

It is Foreign Minister Retno Marsud confirming Indonesia's commitment to 'Diversity' when he chooses the theme 'Celebrating Diversity, Harnessing Harmony' for its 2017 Indonesian Arts and Cultural Scholarships (IACS) programme. The programme was attended by 60 international students from 47 countries. It has been running since 2003, showcasing Indonesia's commitment to enhancing cooperation in social and cultural fields around the world. Marsud noted that IACS is 'Indonesia's flagship programme to reach out to the young generation around the world' (Indonesia, 2017).

It is Cultural Troupes from the 10 member-countries of the Association of Southeast Asian Nations (ASEAN) presenting performances based on the epic at the five-day Ramayana Festival in India during January 20-24, 2018, to celebrate 25th Anniversary of the India-ASEAN Dialogue Partnership (The Hindustan Times, 2018).

It is also about Bollywood actress Priyanka Chopra and UNESCO Goodwill Ambassador interacting with refugee Rohingya children in Bangladesh during May 2018 (Prashant Singh, 2018).

It is Hijab-Wearing Dance Group, 'We're Muslim Don't Panic' (WMDP), founded by Amirah Sackett, connecting through Hip-Hop Dance 'more people in conversation and understanding about Islam, and in the process, help bring people of all faiths together' (USC, 2016).

In the current debate on intolerance, the appointment of two women as Ministers of Happiness and Tolerance to the two newly created Ministries by Sheikh Mohammed bin Rashid al-Maktoum, Ruler of Dubai, was a welcome development (Ben Hubbard). Earlier, it was Bhutan which had announced the Gross National Happiness (GNH) Index.

It is filmstar Salman Khan being honoured with the Global Diversity Award 2017 in the British Parliament House in September 2017, for his contribution to the film industry and as a philanthropist (Deccan Chronicle, 2017). It is Bhullar guarding the Buckingham Palace in London, wearing a turban and not the usual bearskin, which was a case of showing 'glimpses into the changing face of Britain' (English, Rebecca, 2012). It is the same, when pop star Justin Beiber was offered cuisine from 29 Indian States, showcasing India's 'Diversity', during his concert in India in April 2017 (The Hindu, 2017:2).

It is also Prasar Bharti hosting the first edition of the Asia-Pacific Broadcasting Union's (ABU) International Television Dance Festival in Hyderabad during January 2017. The Festival was "conceptualized so as to bring the cultural diversities from across the world into limelight by breaking down cultural barriers".

The above Festival showcased dances from various countries, which included Afghanistan, Azerbaijan, Fiji, India, Indonesia, Malaysia, Maldives, Philippines and Uzbekistan. A total of 453 entries were received and 29 entries were chosen for the final screening. The Festival was open to participants in the age group of 28-35 years and aimed at creating 'a bridge between young people from different parts of the world through dances' (Prasar Bharti, 2017).

Diversity is the 'Mantra' for 'Cultural Diplomacy'. It is a good policy and approach, but it loses its significance and rationale if it becomes a political tool to capitalize on 'Divisiveness'. Giving the National Film Awards on May 3, 2017, President Pranab Mukherjee said that the 64th Edition represented "a microcosm of India and celebrated the diversity of languages, customs, religions and culture" (The Hindu 2017: 1).

Prime Minister Modi spoke on the strength of 'Diversity' at the celebration of the International Vesakh Day in Sri Lanka on May 12, 2017 in these words,

> "On Vesak, my hope is that India and Sri Lanka will work together to uphold the ideals of Lord Buddha and promote values of peace, accommodation, inclusiveness, and compassion in the

> policies and conduct of our governments. This is the true path to free individuals, families, societies, nations and the world at large from the three poisons of greed, hatred and ignorance".

Earlier, Modi gave a similar message at the Sufi Conference in Delhi on March 17, 2016. He said:

> "Like the strings of sitar that each produces a note, but come together to create a beautiful melody. This is the spirit of India. This is the strength of our nation. All our people, Hindus, Muslims, Sikhs, Christians, Jains, Buddhists, the micro-minority of Parsis, believers, non-believers, are an integral part of India. Just as it once came to India, today Sufism from India has spread across the world".

## Core of Indian Cultural Diplomacy

India is not new to cultural diplomacy, unlike the West, as it is a part of its ethos, since times immemorial. Indian cultural diplomacy has come a long way since its Independence. It has acquired global dimension, as India sees itself as an emerging leader. There is both a qualitative and quantitative change in the instrumentalities used by India in promoting cultural diplomacy. The creation of a new Public Diplomacy Division and a Department for Development Partnership Administration in the Ministry of External Affairs, have added a new dimension. This calls for greater coordination among various players, in keeping with the expansion and diversification of India's interests. India is placing greater reliance on cultural diplomacy, given its endeavours in connecting cultural heritage to modernity.

India views cultural diplomacy as a two-channel effort, which is the focus of ICCR, unlike the approach of cultural organizations run by other countries. In this context, it may be recalled that President Roosevelt started with the same vision of 'Two channel approach in cultural relations', when USA used this tool in its dealings with the Latin American countries, way back in the mid-1930s. It was at this time that the United States gave birth to the concept of cultural diplomacy, as a modern day concept. USA, however, now adopts a one-channel approach.

Building Brand Image remains a key pursuit with nations, although with a varying degree of emphasis and success. A Brand has to be wedded to realities, as mere crafting of it would not succeed, as many countries, including ourselves, have seen in the past. Russia harps on 'Patriotism', while China ushers in 'Chinese Dream', as it weaves the world through its 'One Belt, One Road' (OBOR) Initiative; an economic cum cultural venture. South Korea spreads its charm through culture, dubbed as 'Korea Wave'. South Africa places its emphasis on values, as it brands itself as 'A Rainbow Nation' that celebrates diversity. On the other hand, Mexico places itself at the other end, as it would like to be known as, 'One and United Mexico'. Japan is promoting its own brand image of 'Cool Japan', while UK is promoting its own 'Great' Brand.

India has its own Brand, 'Incredible India'. On September 27, 2017, marking World Tourism Day, the President of India launched 'Incredible India 2.0 Campaign' and 'Adopt a Heritage' Project. Incredible India 2.0 campaign would focus on specific promotional plans, with increased attention to social media. 'Adopt A Heritage' Project plans 'to entrust heritage sites to the public sector and private sector companies and individuals for the development of tourist amenities' (The Hindu, 2017: 2). Credibility has to be at the root of Brand Imaging.

There are two dominant narratives that we hear. Firstly, cultural diplomacy is not 'a major component of India's diplomatic outreach' and there is no GOI White Paper on Cultural Diplomacy. Secondly, India's cultural diplomacy is a component of its soft power and it gets manifested through Bollywood.

The first narrative comes from practitioners of cultural diplomacy. Cultural diplomacy has 'not become a part and parcel of national coherent policy' (Shyam Saran)[1]. India has not enunciated 'any concept of cultural diplomacy' (Niranjan Desai).[2] Cultural diplomacy has been 'under-utilized and not given the same prominence'. In India, the prevailing impression is that it is not 'recognized as an important factor' (Goel, Suresh).[3]

This invites a question. Do we need a written document, like a written constitution? In the case of India, cultural diplomacy is a living document, which it has lived throughout the ages. This is manifested through the 'Idea of India'. This is a value based concept; it rests on inclusivity, diversity, pluralism, secularism and democratic norms. None other than Vice President Venkaiah Naidu reaffirmed India's faith in secularism in these words, "Secularism is safe in India not just because of the constitution. It is part of our DNA. We inherited it from the *Vedic* days" (Vice President, 2017).

The second narrative comes from political leadership, like Shashi Tharoor and Sushma Swaraj, who would like this to be placed in the genre of 'Soft Power'. Similarly, former and present diplomats, like former Foreign

Secretaries and Director Generals of ICCR have also aspired in the same direction. Former Director General Pavan Varma views India as a 'Cultural Superpower' (Pavan Varma).

Bollywood is given the pride of place and honour as the architect of India's soft power. For India, Bollywood comes at top of the line, as a vehicle of cultural diplomacy. Bollywood is being viewed as India's Soft Power by Shashi Tharoor, Pavan Varma and Daya Thussu. Roopa Swaminathan in her book 'Bollywood Boom' comes to the conclusion that 'Bollywood is one of the strongest cultural ambassadors of a new India'. And India is on its way to becoming a global soft power' (The Indian Express, 2017).

It is true that Bollywood has spread its wings across the globe and has connected the world to India. There are various reasons for this phenomenon, which have been fully spelt out in chapter VIII of the book. Bollywood, however, does not represent core Indian values; like Hollywood, which is not about American values. Even Daya Thussu admits its limitations as a component of soft power, as 'The huge popularity of Bollywood in Pakistan has scarcely reduced anti-Indian sentiments among sections of the Pakistani establishment'. President Xi Jinping gave his personal endorsement to 'Dangal', but this did not help in softening China's posture on the border skirmishes in June 2017. Bollywood does connect and it helps in connecting India with other countries, yet it would be an over exaggeration to place it in the genre of 'Soft Power'.

## Defining Diaspora's Role

There are two other contending issues that we face. Firstly, what is the role of Diaspora and secondly, how political environment and cultural diplomacy interplay. A commonly held view now is that Diaspora plays the role of a 'Connectivity Bridge'. On the other hand, views are divided as to the level and the extent to which cultural diplomacy should be subjected to the vagaries of political clouds.

Diaspora is good for our adrenaline, as it boosts our morale and puts us on a high pedestal. It turns leaders into 'Rock Stars', as the Australian Media would like to see Prime Minister Turnbull to emerge like Modi. Diaspora has a role to play as a 'Friendship Bridge' and it does help us in making an entry and have a head start. We have, however, to also keep in view the aspect of reciprocity. To what extent, are we prepared to provide a playing field to foreign Diaspora? Certainly not; it would be a big 'No', to a large extent.

Diaspora's role has to be recognized, keeping in view inherent limitations under which it operates. We have to reckon with four types of limitations. Firstly, those that are self-imposed by the Diaspora itself. Generally speaking, it would like to align itself with the values of the host state and adopt apolitical posture, as the push factor for their migration, has been largely economic.

Secondly, we have to recognize the limits under which they work. Their role is largely dependent on the space provided to them by the host state. Diaspora can thus play ball, if the host state is willing. Thirdly, there is also no unanimity among various Diaspora groups that have varying agenda, which is reflective of India's 'Diversity'. Oneness in India represents 'Many in One'; Diaspora Policy, therefore, has to reflect this diversity.

Fourthly, the views of Diaspora and the home state cannot always coincide. We have to ultimately remember that Diaspora is like a double-edged barrel and can fire in both the directions. It can be pro-home state, but it can also be anti-India (The Hindustan Times, 2017). We have seen this happening in the past, as India's active Diaspora engagement began in early 1980s to neutralize the impact of Sikh Diaspora abroad. While wooing Indian Diaspora, the government, at times, has asked foreign governments to keep an eye on certain categories of Diaspora (The Indian Express 2017:1).

We also saw a real glimpse of Diaspora's role as perceived through their own eyes, through the statements of their luminaries. At the First Pravasi Divas held in January 2003, Bhikhu Parekh and Shridath Ramphal, were candid to state that Diaspora could not be wooed on patriotism alone. They also underscored the need for diversity in policy approaches towards Diaspora, as 'one-size fits all policy' would not work and be inadequate.

Diaspora, therefore, has to be carefully nurtured; India has to approach them in a spirit of 'Jugulbundi' (Partnership), by carefully spelling out where this partnership could work and when it should not cross red lines. Diaspora-Home State Connectivity, if it has to emerge as a "Friendship Bridge', it has to be in non-political fields of culture and commerce, while keeping it away from involvement in foreign policy or strategic issues. In this context, it may be remembered that USA, which accepts ethnic-based involvement in democratic processes, is still reluctant in getting them directly involved in foreign policy related issues (Ambrosio, 2002).

## Insulating Cultural Diplomacy from Political Winds

Insulating cultural diplomacy from political winds is a complex issue, which is faced by all the countries, in one or another form. This was stated by the then Minister of Information Venkaiah Naidu in October 2016 in these words, 'It is very simple to say art has no boundaries; but countries have boundaries' (Cited in Hebbar, Nistula, 2016) . How do we ensure that we avoid mental barriers, while we recognise physical barriers?

What matters is the extent or the level of political oversight or control, in the matters of cultural diplomacy? Each country adopts its own policies and practices, as in some countries there is greater control, while in other cases it is of a lesser nature. We have seen this happening in the case of Olympic Games, when countries are barred from participation, as bilateral proclivities creep even in International Sport Organizations (ISOs). On the other hand, we also saw how physical barriers were broken, when North Korea decided to participate in the Winter Olympics in South Korea in February 2018.

In the case of India, political involvement in cultural matters operates at different levels. It is, firstly at the level of the Union Government; secondly at the level of the State Governments and thirdly at the level of local actors. In practice, it is the local actors that have dictated whether a particular cultural event or programme should be held or not. This is so, in particular, in the case of programmes from Pakistan, where jingoistic feelings are easily aroused in the name of nationalism. We have seen this in the case of Pakistani film actors not allowed to shoot in Bollywood films; cancellation of musical performances by Pakistani singers, or visits by literary or theatre personalities or holding of sports events. The decision to hold Asia Cricket Cup in September 2018 in a neutral territory, like the United Arab Emirates (UAE), illustrates this point.

We come across a number of narratives, as views are divided among those who feel that political considerations should determine cultural flows, while others would like to insulate these from political winds. The governments have a difficult choice, as they cannot be seen to be jettisoning national interest, perceived or real. It is also not surprising to see that same persons tend to hold different views, when they are in or out of power. Should we give primacy to the relationship at the people to people level or follow the dispensation of the present day government?

Given the above dilemma, what are the main narratives that we presently encounter in India? There is the official view that terrorism and dialogue cannot go together. Dialogue is defined in a broader context, which is not only limited to official contacts at the level of governments, but also embraces civil society, including cultural, religious and sporting links.

Clarifying Government's approach at a meeting of the Standing Committee on External Affairs, External Affairs Minister Sushma Swaraj is reported to have said that increasing cross border firings did not help in setting the tone for the resumption of suspended cricket diplomacy between India and Pakistan. She hinted that 'any bilateral cricket series between India and Pakistan is unlikely unless Pakistan stops cross-border terrorism and firing' (Cited in The Hindustan Times, 2018).

The newly appointed President of ICCR, Vinay Sahasrabuddhe, has a different take. He feels that 'those with sound understanding of the importance of ethos have never allowed politics to cast its shadow over cultural concerns' (Cited in Hebbar, Nistula, 2018).

On the other hand, the Standing Committee on External Affairs, while noting that 'strained relations have always cast a shadow on cultural relations', yet it still sees merit in people-to-people connectivity, as the same is viewed as a 'robust bridge' that could 'widen peace constituency', even though such contacts in the past had not yielded 'tangible gains' (Lok Sabha Report, 2017). In its report to the Lok Sabha, the Committee opined:

"Taking a holistic picture, the committee are of the considered opinion that cultural, sporting and humanitarian exchanges need to be approached from a broader perspective as this could emerge as one potential area of creating peace constituencies in both the countries"(Cited in The Indian Express, 2017: 2).

It is interesting in this case to recall the reported statement of Sushma Swaraj as BJP leader during the visit of Pakistani Prime Minister Yousuf Raza Gilani to witness India-Pakistan match at Mohali in 2011, "Let the game be game. Dialogue diplomacy should be separated from cricket". She further reported to have made a broad statement that "games and diplomacy should be kept separate" (Cited in The Hindu, 2011).

The author would be more inclined to go along with Sushma Swaraj. We should not hold artists, writers, musicians, sportpersons, academia and students to ransom, as their interactions have the potential to emerge as bridges of understanding. We need to build a strong people-to-people constituency for peace. Any political mandate to disrupt cultural and sport links would have to stand the test that it helps in promoting the cause of peace and does not hinder people-to-people connectivity, which should be allowed to become 'a robust bridge'.

## Ground Realities

How has then Indian 'Cultural Diplomacy' worked? We need to view this at three different levels. Firstly, at the level of policy framework; secondly at the level of infrastructure for implementation and thirdly at the level of vehicles that are used.

As stated in the body of the Book, Ministries of External Affairs and Culture are involved in the area of cultural diplomacy. They, however, work in their own 'silos'. There is neither a joint approach nor a visible working level joint mechanism that could help in making these two Ministries work in tandem. The need for greater coordination between ICCR, MEA and other Line Ministries, including Ministry of Culture, was highlighted by the Parliamentary Standing Committee on External Affairs, which submitted its Thirteenth Report to Lok Sabha in November 2016.

Cultural diplomacy is now at the centre of diplomatic table. There is, however, no Policy Document. There has been no serious discussion on formulation of policy on cultural diplomacy. No conferences of cultural attaches have been held. India has taken the route of cultural agreements to promote cultural relations and had 130 such agreements by 2016. The absence of a cultural agreement has, however, not stood in the way of cultural relations. There is no common template and India has adopted a country-specific policy; this approach has worked well. Cultural diplomacy has not remained the handmaiden of government created structures, like ICCR; private sector is emerging as a partner. This is a healthy development and the trend needs to be supported by the government.

At the infrastructure level, ICCR is the nodal body charged with the implementation of cultural diplomacy. The placement of ICCR under MEA was recognition of the fact that 'Cultural Diplomacy should function as a part and parcel of Indian diplomacy' (Lalit Mansingh).[4] It has a sound structure; Foreign Secretary, being one of the three Vice Presidents in the Governing Board, also helps. What is disconcerting is the lack of attention paid to follow the existing institutional framework, as noted by various review committees?

ICCR is not an integral part of MEA and is given the status of an autonomous body, like the British Council. Such an arrangement places

ICCR in a position of arms length from the government and hence imparts it a degree of independence and its programmes are not given the official tag. It has followed the traditional path in choosing its programmes. Promotion of Yoga has emerged as the primary vehicle of cultural diplomacy since 2015, when UN declared June 21 as the International Yoga Day (IYD). Southeast Asia region remains the area of primary attention.

Despite the above advantage, ICCR has an enviable task to deliver on its mandate, given the budgetary constraints and inadequacy of staff that is not professionally trained. ICCR's present premises are also not ideally suited to serve the needs of an in-house cultural centre. No systematic review of the activities of ICCR had been undertaken (Suryakanthi Tripathi)[5]. An Audit Review of the Functioning of Cultural Centres was undertaken by the Veena Sikri Committee in 2016; the report is still not in the public domain.

Regarding the instrumentalities used by India to promote cultural diplomacy, the four most important ones are the Festivals of India, Cultural Centres, Chairs of Indian Studies and Scholarships. At the visible level of India's cultural diplomacy are the Festivals of India. At the intellectual/ academic level are the Chairs of Indian Studies. Cultural Centres play an important role, as building blocks in promoting people-to-people connectivity. Scholarships Scheme is the flagship programme of ICCR, as it focuses on the youth and is aimed at long term connectivity.

The organization of the Festivals of India is the responsibility of the Ministry of Cultural (MOC). The first Indian Festival was held in UK in 1982. Another was held in UK in 2017. We saw how the inaugural function of the 'Year of India in Great Britain' in April dazzled people, when they saw images of Indian Art and Culture splashed on the Buckingham Palace. It created greater impact, when the Queen of England was shown practising '*mudras*' (movement of hands) as shown to her by the dancer. The Independence Gala Show at Southbank Centre, London on 4 October 2017 'captured the vibrancy, richness and diversity of our cultural dialogue with the UK very well' (Sonwalkar, Prasun, 2017).

Our major festival partners are UK, France, Russia and China. We now have a mix of Mega and Mini Festivals. MOC has become pro-active since 2014, when funds were allocated on a three-yearly basis (2014-16) and 17 festivals were organized during the FY 2016-17. In 2014, MOC recreated the Festivals Cell and in 2016, it signed an MOU with ICCR, designating it as one nodal agency. Holding of 17 festivals in one year dilutes the original intent to link these to strategic considerations. No country holds festivals on such a mass scale in one year, as this dilutes their significance. Generally speaking, commercial considerations have never been part of our agenda in holding these festivals. We are seeing an increasing trend in the involvement of Private Sector in organizing these festivals. This is likely to result in the declining role of ICCR.

Cultural Centres, on the other hand, are directly operated by ICCR. These are still not adequate in numbers, commensurate with India's interests as an emerging global power. India had 36 cultural centres in 2016, which were not only woefully inadequate, but were also not evenly spread out. 2011 was the 'Year of Cultural Centres', as there was a spurt in their growth, given infusion of special funds to ICCR by the government. So far, this has remained a one-time effort only. There are plans now to set up eight more cultural centres, a proposal that has received endorsement from the Parliamentary Standing Committee on External Affairs. Administrative hurdles have delayed the setting up of the cultural centres in Washington DC and Paris. These centres, however, have not emerged as 'Hubs' for connectivity with the locals. The Youth is missing from these centres; so is the vibrancy and the vitality that is visible at the Centres run by Alliance Françoise or Max Mueller Bhawans.

Joseph Nye Jr. and Shashi Tharoor attach great importance to the winning story. Joseph Nye Jr. puts it: "In an information age, communication strategies become more important and outcomes are shaped not merely by whose army wins but by also whose story wins" (Nye , Joseph Jr. 2011). The winning story emerges from the exchange of ideas that broaden the horizons of the mind and pave way for building long lasting friendship. It is, therefore, through the Chairs of Indian Studies that we would like the world to know what India stands for. These help us in providing connectivity with the new generation for building friendship on a long-term basis. We have not still succeeded in integrating these with the local academic institutions. Our Chairs have still to weave a winning 'India Story' that is locally relevant and need to perform at an optimum level, as they have not fully succeeded in integrating with the local academia or think tanks or the Youth.

Scholarships Scheme is the biggest programme of ICCR, in terms of funding, consuming 40 % of its Indian component of budget. It is barely large enough, as it caters to 3000 scholarships annually. The spread is also limited to a small group of developing countries from Africa, Bhutan, Sri Lanka and Afghanistan. India has now only woken up on the need to emerge as a Destination for Higher Education and launched a website for 'Study in India' Programme in April 2018. India still has a long way to go and reemerge as a global hub of education. We have also not been able to successfully build exchange programmes between the academia and the students. Our star programme - Distinguished Visitors-has so far performed only a proforma role, as only a handful Distiguished Visitors have come.

## Emerging Picture

Where do 'Cultural Diplomacy' and India stand? Faith in cultural diplomacy is renewed globally, as more governments are bringing this at the centre table. It has become a regular feature with Prime Minister Modi during his visits abroad. He is paying special attention and has emerged as a catalyst in promoting cultural cooperation during his visits abroad. Cultural cooperation, therefore, emerges as an important component of Joint Statements issued during bilateral visits.

There was a large component of cultural diplomacy during the visit of President Hollande of France to India in January 2016 and again with President Macron in April 2018. The President of Cyprus during his visit to India in April 2017 highlighted the aspects of cultural connectivity between the two countries. A Cultural Exchange Programme (CEP) for the years 2017-19 was signed during his visit. Education Diplomacy was one of the focus areas, during the visit of Canadian Prime Minister Justin Trudeau to India in February, 2018.

Prime Minister Modi used Faith Diplomacy, when he inaugurated the Bus Service between historical religious sites, Janakpur (Nepal) with Ayodhya (India) during his visit on May 11-12, 2018. The relevant para in tne Joint Statement reads:

> "With a view to further strengthening the close religious and cultural ties between the two countries and peoples, the two Prime Ministers launched Nepal-India Ramayana Circuit connecting Janakpur, the birthplace of Sita, with Ayodhya and other sites associated with the epic Ramayana. In Janakpur, the two Prime Ministers flagged off the inaugural direct bus service between Janakpur and Ayodhya" (Joint Statement, 2018).

The drawback, however, is that cultural diplomacy is being seen from the paradigm of power and not as a 'Connectivity Bridge'. During the visit of the Israeli Prime Minister Benjamin Netanhayu to India in January 2018

'Shalom Bollywood' provided opportunity to interact with film stars, as he wooed Bollywood to come to Israel, as he recognised its role in promoting tourism and connectivity.

What is the Big Picture that finally emerges? India recognizes the role of cultural diplomacy, per se. The concept fits in with Indian ethos of 'Vasudhaiva Kutumbakam' and finds its manifestation through the 'Idea of India' – a vibrant secular democratic polity and an inclusive pluralistic society that respects diversity. All the governments, including the present one, have reiterated their faith in pluralism and diversity.

The focus of India's cultural diplomacy has remained on promoting 'Understanding', and it is not being used directly to promote its foreign policy interests, in keeping with the mandate of ICCR since 1950. This fact has not gone unnoticed by scholars, experts and diplomats. A New Zealand scholar on Cultural Diplomacy, Simon Mark has described it as "old fashioned" cultural diplomacy, since it 'has sought to enhance mutual understanding amongst countries and their peoples' (Simon Mark). Professor Yudhishthir Raj Isar, a well known expert on Cultural Diplomacy in an EU Country Report on India also makes this point, linking the same to India's pluralistic society, in these words:

> "This intrinsic pluralism is one of the main reasons why Indian cultural actors both governmental and non-governmental display an attachment to *the practice of international cultural relations principally as an end in itself.* They place instrumental considerations decidedly in second place" (Isar, 2014).

External Affairs Minister Sushma Swaraj reiterated this message in her Address at the International Youth Summit in February, 2015, saying, 'In India, the idea of global village is ingrained in our collective consciousness and is embedded in our DNA'. She further amplified this in these words:

> "Down the Ages, India has shown a rare receptivity and has been quick to absorb other cultures, religions and values; a relentless process of amalgamation and synthesis that has produced the rich tapestry of a pluralistic, multi-cultural and multi-religious syncretic India. In a seminal sense, India in all its vibrant diversity and receptivity is a microcosm of the world" (EAM, 2015).

At the local level, the narrative appears to be changing with non-state actors, at times, assuming the role as guardians of social and religious norms as perceived by them. Given this, the common refrain that comes from the speeches of the President, the Prime Minister and the Vice President, is to stay on course, by respecting pluralism and diversity.

In his maiden Address at the United Nations General Assembly in September 2014, Prime Minister Modi invoked the above ethos. Vice President Hamid Ansari had stated that 'Diversity is an Indian passion; we love it, tolerate it, accommodate it and relish it (Vice President, 2010). Shashi Tharoor had spoken on the need to 'preserve the precious pluralism that is such a civilizational asset in our globalizing world'.

Vice President Venkaiah Naidu also spoke in a similar vein, when he said, "One aspect of these efforts is to respect, protect, preserve and celebrate the diversity in our country" (Vice President, 2017). Vinay Sahasrabuddhe, President of ICCR finds strength for India's Diversity, 'Our diversity doesn't disintegrate us mainly because it is essentially the manifestation of our intrinsic unity' (Cited in Hebbar, Nistula, 2018).

President Pranab Mukherjee also stated that 'Diversity of our country is a fact of life. Pluralism and tolerance have been the hallmark of our civilization. This is a core philosophy that must continue undeterred. For India, strength lies in her diversity' (Cited in The Indian Express, 2016).

India is also giving due recognition to the role of 'culture', by linking modernity to cultural heritage, glorifying its past achievements, be it in the field of mathematics, medicine, science or astronomy. It, therefore, feels itself doubly blessed to play an important role. It has started on a path that cultural diplomacy could be a vehicle of soft power, as India moves in the direction of finding its seat at the high table.

Prime Minister Modi has also converted this all-inclusive approach into practical policy pronouncement, 'Sab Ka Saath, Sab Ka Vikas' (Support for Everyone, Progress for Every One). In his address at the Raisina Dialogue in January 2017, Prime Minister made a clarion call for 'Global Partnership and Development' in these words:

> 'For me, Sab Ka Saath; Sab Ka Vikas is not just a vision for India. It is a belief for the whole world. And, it manifests itself at several layers, multiple themes and different geographies' (Raisina Dialogue, 2017).

During his visit to USA in September 2014, Prime Minister Modi wrote a joint editorial with President Obama, which was captioned 'Chalen Saath Saath' (Walking, Hand-in-Hand). A cartoon by Neelabh captured similar sentiments, by showing Obama and Modi playing 'Dandia' together. Cultural diplomacy, therefore, can take us to this path towards 'Understanding' through Cultural Dialogue, resulting in the world discarding the path of hatred, which is being built on the thesis of Clash of Civilizations.

## The Way Ahead

What is the Way Ahead then? This needs to be answered at various levels. We would look at the Macro Level, Partnership Building with other Countries, Key Cultural Diplomacy Vehicles, Developing Synergy with Other Cultural Bodies and Enhancing the Functioning of ICCR.

### *At the Macro Level*

India has to abide by its belief in the 'Idea of India', which is the core of its cultural diplomacy. A strong message has to be sent continuously and regularly on the strength of pluralism and diversity; open doors and dialogue. Prime Minister Modi invoked 'Riga Veda' to make his point, 'आनोभद्रो:क्रत्वोयन्तुवश्वित: Means: "Let noble thoughts come to me from all directions" (Raisina Dialogue, 2017). This is the ultimate truth and the philosophy that guides India. It should also become the core of cultural diplomacy. There is need to ensure that cultural nationalism would not overtake us.

Cultural diplomacy has to be insulated from political winds that blow from time to time. It should remain a people-centric process. A process that could help reaching out directly to people across the borders, as Prime Minister Modi has addressed them directly on the theme of 'Joint Cooperation on Poverty Alleviation'. It is in India's interest to widen peace constituency by keeping its doors open to the academia, sportpersons and cultural groups. Let the people become a force and succeed in achieving results, where the governments have failed.

Despite the importance attached to cultural heritage, India has not enunciated a formal policy on cultural diplomacy. Is it that India did not want to find itself in a tight jacket, knowing fully well that it would be diversity in approach that would be the hallmark of its success? At the policy level, we do, however, need to give a shape to broad contours of our cultural diplomacy. We, however, have to keep in mind the golden rule that culture 'should not be allowed to become hegemonic and it should not be flaunted' (HK Dua).[6]

We need to set up a Joint Policy Mechanism that could synergize the Ministries of External Affairs and Culture, to work as strategic partners rather than working in silos. Other Ministries that have an indirect stake should be roped in to promote cultural diplomacy-related activities. These could include Ministries of Tourism, Human Resource Development, AYUSH, Textiles, Handlooms and Handicraft. Steps need to be taken to link culture with commerce.

Given India's commitment to 'Cooperative Federalism', Indian States should be encouraged to participate in activities in the arena of cultural diplomacy. States should be made to join as partners with ICCR, which has already signed MOUs with eight States. These need to be activated. Each year, ICCR could designate a Partner State and mount activities jointly with that State. This would also help in promoting India's diversity.

Our thrust on cultural diplomacy has to be to connect with the Youth. Should we adapt the Youth Ambassadors Programme of the United States or streamline our own version of the Know India Programme (KIP); we will have to take the call. Involvement of the Youth is essential for a country like India that harps on its demographic dividend. We need to go beyond Indian Diaspora, which is the focus of KIP. This would also necessitate our focusing on two primary vehicles of cultural diplomacy- Education and Sports.

***Partnership Building with other Countries***

What are the take-a-ways from other countries that would be relevant for India? Prima facie, a common strand runs among all that cultural diplomacy has an important role to play. There may be difference at the definition level, whether it is seen as an integral part of public diplomacy or a vehicle for soft power.

Each country has developed certain niche areas in cultural diplomacy, where it has succeeded and acquired expertise. India should make in-depth studies in these areas, and examine how these could be suitably adapted to serve our needs and requirements. Some illustrative areas are as follows:

- Promotion of Education Diplomacy by Australia, which has emerged as an important destination for foreign students, including from India?
- Diaspora Engagement by Mexico, which has evolved a pragmatic programme in the United States.

- Image Building by South Korea and Japan, which have been success stories through their 'Korean Wave' and 'Cool Japan' respectively.
- Linking Commerce with Culture, where Japan and South Korea stand out in promoting culturally embedded commercial products.
- Functioning of Cultural Centres by Hungary and Spain, as these would be more relevant for countries like India, with smaller budgets.
- American experience on Sister-Cities Relationship, as they have an elaborate framework at the federal and the city levels, as Grassroots diplomacy is a route for success. We need to review our existing Sister-Cities linkages, like the one between Chicago and Delhi.
- Learning from Chicago's experience as a 'Smart City', where this concept is being chiseled under a fiery debate on 'Smart vs. Better Cities'. Chicago could be a guidepost for India's Smart Cities Project.
- Replicating UNESCO's Cities Programme, as we learn from the implementation experiences of South Korea, Japan and China and aim at connecting cities in India with cities in Bangladesh, Bhutan and Nepal.
- Promoting connectivity through Cuisine Diplomacy; this is emerging as a focus area for the Philippines, Mexico and China.

***Key Cultural Diplomacy Vehicles***

What are the vehicles that are emerging as important in the pursuit of cultural diplomacy? These are: education, the youth and sports. India is deficient in these areas, even though we have separate Ministries. We need to provide greater focus in these areas. Some beginnings have been made with the Youth at the meetings with Indian Diaspora and from member states of BRICS.

India has to emerge as a Destination Country for foreign students, as at present it has a share of only 0.7 percent, while Indian students abroad form a 4.0 percent of foreign students' population. Our educational institutes have to become not only competitive, but also provide open, friendly and conducive environment. Hopefully, the new Education Policy would also focus on Education Diplomacy. We need to make a concerted drive to achieve the target of 200,000 students by 2023, under our 'Study in India Programme'.

Diaspora is turning out to be a bridge builder. We, however, have to recognize the limits under which it can work. We have to ensure that its involvement in foreign policy-related issues is within the bounds permitted by the host country. Our policies have to be pragmatic and not built around our experiences in one or two Western countries.

How to let media play the role of a friendship bridge is a multi-million-dollar question. Could it help in connecting? Do we need a government-sponsored institutional mechanism? It would be ideal to have one, provided we can ensure its independence and integrity. We need to see greater representation of Indian correspondents in foreign countries.

Festivals of India need to be strategically planned. A lot can be learned from the Australian experience, as they have developed criteria for strategic selection of countries. We need to develop guidelines to involve participation of the private sector in the Public Private Partnership (PPP) mode. It has, however, to be ensured that projection of Indian Image is not used for private commercial gains.

***Developing Synergy with Other Cultural Bodies***

There is also a need to establish greater connectivity with cultural bodies and associations abroad that could lead to the emergence of cultural institutions like the Sutra Theatre of Ramli Ibrahim and the Temple of Fine Arts in Malaysia. The Ministry of Culture's existing programme on support to Indo- Friendship Societies abroad needs to be expanded.

The Heads of Missions have an important role to play. They should be provided with 'Cultural Fund' in select countries. The success of our cultural diplomacy would lie in roping in more partners abroad.

There is a need to preserve India's tangible and intangible heritage. We need to institute a programme for the preservation of Indian Cultural Heritage, starting in South Asia. This could be developed with the support of India Diaspora.

India needs to plug into opportunities available at the Smithsonian Institution at Washington DC and consider entering into an MOU with them to learn from their programmes in some countries that focus on linking heritage to modernity. An India-Smithsonian Cultural Fund could be instituted with the support of local groups.

Indian Institutions, as indicated in the brackets, could consider establishing links with the Smithsonian in its niche areas, such as Intangible Heritage (INTACH); Online links under Digital India Framework (Indira Gandhi National Open University (IGNOU) and integrating heritage to modern system of education and making Museums people friendly (National Museum).

Indian Akademis of Fine Art have not played a meaningful role in cultural diplomacy. A serious study needs to be undertaken to look into their activities, with a view to turning these into vibrant and dynamic institutions. MOC has to ensure that its plans to make Akademis to self-generate funds result in augmentation of programmes and does not lead to diminishing of their present activities.

Indian Museums lack dynamism in connecting with other museums in foreign countries. We need to consider entering into MOUs with those Museums that hold Indian Artefacts and are actively involved in holding India-specific projects/exhibitions. They could become windows on generating awareness on Indian culture. We need to prepare a data bank on these Museums. A greater synergy needs to be built in to the existing partnerships where these already exist, while new arrangements are entered into with others.

### *Enhancing Functioning of ICCR*

At the operational level, Director General, ICCR needs to be provided with greater autonomy and security of tenure, to help him/her provide dynamic leadership. ICCR cadre needs to be strengthened and professionalized.

ICCR needs to evolve a good working arrangement with other sister Divisions in MEA, such as External Publicity and Public Diplomacy (XPP), Policy Planning and Research (PPR) and The States Division, with a view to pooling the combined resources of MEA and avoid duplication of programmes.

A Coordinating Body has to be set up with ICCR as the focal point to help in pooling the resources of other Cultural Bodies, such as India International Centre (IIC), Indira Gandhi Centre for Arts (IGNCA) and Indian National Trust for Art and Cultural Heritage (INTACH) that are involved in this arena.

ICCR also needs to review its existing arrangements with Cultural Bodies in the private sector, so as to explore optimum ways in which such relationship could be strengthened, as these are drawn into a wider network. We would have to ensure that India Focus is not missing.

ICCR has to consider planning its activities on the basis of a 'Three Years' Cycle', as the present system of a Yearly calendar has lacked dynamism and continuity.

There is lack of institutionalization of programmes, as a number of initiatives end up as one-time affairs, depending upon the interest of the Head of the Mission. Country-wise analysis and programmes have to be developed, as we cannot rely on one-size fits all policy.

Cultural tools need to be carefully developed. There is a need to organize activities of a multipronged nature, like exhibition with demonstration by craftsman or artists; lectures combined with field visits such as organizing Traditional Textiles Exhibitions in Nepal and 'Ikat' Exhibition at Sarawak in Malaysia.

We need to have a data bank on innovative and successful programmes, which need to be supported and encouraged. The role played by Other Cultural Bodies is also highlighted in chapter V. The same could become a starting point for collating information on other programmes. Our Diplomatic Missions could be involved in this exercise.

ICCR should aim at providing a more 'enriching, more dense, creative and positive ambience'. It needs to learn to move from 'Event Management' to 'Process Management' (Shyam Saran).

The Cultural Centres should be made to turn into 'Idea Exchanges' (Lalit Mansingh) or 'Cultural Hubs' (Goel, Suresh) as the fizz is missing from these centres. There is need to impart greater professionalism, either through proper selection or through imparting training. Cultural Centres in prominent cities should consider having tie-ups with leading Academies of Dance and Music, like Kalakshetra, to provide greater professionalism.

ICCR needs to link Cultural Centres with modern libraries, as the libraries have imparted great strength to cultural centres run by USA, UK, Germany and France. We could also learn from the US experience in managing these centres through their programme called 'American Spaces'.

We should consider setting up India Corners in Public Libraries abroad by donating books, as is done by many other countries. This would be more cost effective rather than having our own libraries and this would ensure better access to the readers.

ICCR has to add 'Academic Dimension' to the range of its activities. This could be easily done by expanding its existing programmes, such as 'Distiguished Visitors' Programme. There is also a need to provide greater connectivity among the academics through the holding of seminars/ conferences.

Similarly, Chairs of Indian Studies need to be better integrated with local educational institutions. Our selection process has to be improved. A feedback mechanism has to be developed, so that ICCR could derive full benefit from their presence.

## Concluding Observations and Thoughts

Cultural diplomacy has to be at the centre table, as demographically the world has become diverse, but this diversity has not resulted in harmonious living. A globalised world cannot be wished away. What has then changed? It is the players, who are pro-globalisation and those that are anti-globalisation. The whole process of globalisation is in a constant state of flux.

Borders are becoming irrelevant. We are in an IT (Information & Technology) Age where ideas shape the things to come. Cultural diplomacy is, therefore, not about crossing territorial boundaries, but it is about crossing barriers that have been created in our minds that stand partitioned. It is about the battle in our minds, as the Preamble to the Constitution of UNESCO declares that "since wars begin in the minds of men, it is in the minds of men that the defences of peace must be constructed".

What role should Cultural diplomacy play in this global scenario? It certainly is in enriching cultural relations and enhancing understanding. It is at the centre table, as cross-cultural communications have assumed greater importance for diplomatic parleys. It teaches us that it is not about toleration, but of acceptance of others as they are. It thus enthuse us with positive ethos to respect others. It is a two channel operation; its essence lies in knowing others and not only propagating oneself.

Cultural diplomacy is about openness. It is letting winds to blow from many directions, without fear of destabilization, as stated by Mahatma Gandhi. The four entry doors to the Golden Temple in Amritsar signify the same concept of openness from all directions.

Cultural diplomacy is not about losing one's identity. On the other hand, it is donning multiple identities. India exemplifies it best, as we all have more than one identity, while retaining our Indian identity.

Cultural diplomacy is 'People-centric', from where it derives its sustenance and strength. Its impact, therefore, is more lasting, as it is vested with people's power, which is the instrument of change. Its role and impact, therefore, does not diminish with the change of governments.

In this world, where strength is determined through the paradigm of power, cultural diplomacy is treated as a process of soft power by Joseph Nye Jr. Should Cultural diplomacy be placed in the same genre as 'soft power'? As it is about promoting understanding and not empowerment, we should, therefore, refrain from vesting it with the halo of power. Cultural diplomacy has to perform the role of a 'Bridge Builder' through 'Connectivity'.

Should 'Cultural Diplomacy' remain in the governmental domain? If not, whether other players have emerged and how do these connect with the government apparatus. Has this diluted or circumscribed the role of the government? Cultural diplomacy is no more confined to the pursuit of cultural relations by the diplomats alone. It has now moved to the wider public arena, as each individual/organization is perceived to be an honorary Goodwill Ambassador. Furthermore, any promotional activity by non-official bodies acquires greater credibility, since it does not carry the official tag.

The strength of cultural diplomacy lies in the intangible way it works. It opens the doors by changing mindset and creating a positive and friendly atmosphere, where diplomatic business could be conducted later. Its results are not seen immediately, as it operates slowly; its strength, however, lies in providing a stable environment.

May be India believes and rightly so, as far as I am concerned that it perceives that cultural diplomacy operates, like the invisible 'Saraswati' River, to which Karan Singh had eluded. Cultural diplomacy thus plays a better effective role, when the government is visible the least, which is the reason for its strength. It, therefore, helps it in not getting drawn into polemics.

The government, on its part, should vacate promotion of those areas, where these have already come of age and can even stand on their own. These include Films and Yoga. The government has to primarily play the role of a catalyst and a facilitator. We need to enlarge stakeholders in cultural diplomacy.

Where does cultural diplomacy finally find its place in the diplomatic architecture? Does it rest at the third place, after politics and economics, as stated by B.P. Singh, former administrator and authority on culture .Or should we believe in Arndt that cultural diplomacy is the 'First Resort of Kings' (Arndt). For the author, it occupies a pre-eminent position, as it lays the 'Foundation Stone' for all diplomatic activities. It is the 'Mother of all Diplomacies', as it helps in opening doors for the conduct of smooth diplomatic relations.

It is the best story that wins; a story that carries credibility and does not border on propaganda and is not the product of 'Sharp Power', a new terminology introduced by Joseph Nye Jr (Nye, 2018). The story has to stand on credible props. What is more important is how that story is received in the intended destination?

What matters is not the story of 'Incredible India' or the launch of 'Incredible India 2.0' by the President of India in September 2017. What is important is how credible it is and how it is listened to or perceived by the target audience. It is not about bigger or smaller nuclear button; it is about how it is received at the other end. It is not about broadcasting /telecasting, but it is about reception at the other end.

In these efforts on nation branding, it has to be remembered that what ultimately matters is how other countries perceive a brand. The core of Indian 'Cultural Diplomacy' is the 'Idea of India'; this is how India is perceived and respected. At the present juncture, there is a greater need to see how this is strengthened. It is this that gels with people abroad. It is this message that Prime Minister Modi gets, when he travels abroad and meets world leaders and feels the pulse of people at the grassroots level.

Indian cultural diplomacy, like all living organisms, has well adapted itself with times. It should, therefore, be allowed to move along at its own pace and not confined to a formal written jacket. Indian cultural footprints have withstood the ravages of history, as India had sent a message of respect for inclusivity, pluralism and diversity. India's influence was considered 'benign'. This has been the hallmark of its civilization.

This scenario begs questions. Can India give the message of 'Spiritualism' in a globalised world that is dominated by materialism? Can India lead in sending a message of diversity and pluralism, as lived by it, when the world is passing through a period of divisiveness, based on hatred? More important than this, can it retain its own "Idea of India', which is coming under strain. While achieving our political goals, we should not lose sight of our 'Big Picture' of an India, whose strength lies in 'Unity in Diversity' and which has been viewed as a benign power.

Indian leaders would like India to play the role of "Vishwa Guru", as they feel that it is endowed with spiritual and other values that could help in promoting civilizational dialogue among peoples and nations. It is a laudatory goal that needs to be pursued with all humility, selflessness and empathy.

While pursuing the above objective, India should not be seen as a 'Cultural Hegemon'. We should never move away from the legacy of the Tenth Sikh Guru Gobind Singh, who was revered by his followers, as he had abolished distinction between a teacher and a student, by following the path, "Aape Gur, Aape Chela" (He is both, a preacher and a student).

The philosophy of "One Truth, but many Paths" has guided India. This is manifested through the worship of many Gods among Hindus. This is also exemplified through harmonious living among various religious communities in India, such as Hindus, Muslims, Sikhs, Buddhists, Jains, Christians, Jews and Parsis. While we promote dialogue internationally, we cannot be perceived to have forsaken dialogic conversation in India.

We need to strengthen positive forces and further build globally on this pluralistic architecture through the core of the 'Idea of India', which has gained worldwide acceptance. While promoting Buddhist Trail to India, we need to spread his central message of love, peace and compassion. The moorings of India's cultural diplomacy have to be firmly embedded in these eternal values.

Should India use cultural diplomacy as an instrument of soft power? It has been a debatable issue among the theoreticians and practitioners of diplomacy. While some have favoured this approach, others have shunned this, as they would not like cultural diplomacy to be viewed as following government agenda, but embracing a larger canvas through connecting people. The author is inclined to go along with the latter view.

Let us, therefore, discover a bit of Swami Vivekanand, Rabindranath Tagore, Mahatma Gandhi, Nehru, Sardar Patel, Ambedkar and Maulana Azad among all of us, as we honour 'Diversity' and keep our minds open for fresh thoughts and ideas. We should not allow ourselves to be overpowered by 'Cultural Nationalism' or 'Moral Nationalism', as we should use 'Cultural Diplomacy' to connect with one another, in the true spirit of friendship and brotherhood.

We have to be true believers in the concept of 'Vasudhaiva Kutumbakam' that, prima facie, involves nurturing the diversity of the 'Kutumb' (family) and this can be achieved through celebrating ‘Pluralism’, in the benign spirit that has guided India throughout its history. The cardinal message is ‘acceptance’ and not ‘toleration’ of others and viewing relationship in a positive mould.

Can we translate the above into an Action Programme that serves humanity at large in this globalised world? Cultural diplomacy should become a force for ‘Civilizational Dialogue’, with India taking an initiative for a Global Cultural Dialogue. We may consider instituting an annual ‘Swami Vivekanand Lecture on Civilizational Dialogue’, to be held alternatively in India and abroad.

Let ‘Cultural Diplomacy’ retain its pristine form as a ‘Connectivity Bridge’, as India imparts it a spiritual hue by following and promoting its civilizational values of diversity and pluralism in this globalised world. Allowing it to move to the genre of power would be self defeating, as we would be eroding the whole concept of cultural diplomacy. Let us, therefore, celebrate Indian Cultural Diplomacy as it spreads the message of ‘Pluralism’ pivoted to the ‘Idea of India’ in this Globalised World, in keeping with its ethos of ‘Vasudhaiva Kutumbakam’.

## Endnotes

1 Shyam Saran, Former Foreign Secretary. Interaction on May 12, 2015 in Delhi.

2 Niranjan Desai, former Director General, ICCR. Interaction on December 12, 2015 in Delhi.

3 Goel, Suresh, Director General, ICCR. Interaction on September 7, 2017 in Delhi.

4 Lalit Mansingh, former Foreign Secretary and DG, ICCR. Interaction on September 7, 2017 in Delhi.

5 Suryakanthi Tripathi, former Director General, ICCR. Interaction on October 23, 2015 in Delhi.

6 H K Dua, former Member of Rajya Sabha and Distinguished Senior Jounalist, former Information Advisor to Prime.

## References

Ambrosio, Thomas, 2002, *Ethnic Identity Groups and U.S. Foreign Policy*, Greenwood Publishing Group.

Arndt, Richard M, 2005, *The First Resort of Kings, American Cultural Diplomacy in the Twentieth Century*, Potomac Books Inc., Washington DC.

*BBC*, 2017, 'India visit very productive despite controversy', says Sajjan', April 21.

Ben Hubbard, 2016, 'Conjuring happiness and tolerance, the Emirate Way', *The Hindu*, February 11 (NYT).

Benhabib, Selva, 2002, *The Claims of Culture: Equality and Diversity in the Global Era,* Princeton University Press, New Jersey (USA).

Carraud, Simon, 2017, 'Le Pen cancels cleric meet, won't wear headscarf', *The Indian Express*, February 22.

Cartoon, Jug Suraya, Ajit Ninan, 2017, 'He defended to get into the group of his Star-Spangled Banner', *The Times of India*, February 22.

Chaba, Anju Agnihotri, 2017. 'Mindless enhancement of educational institutes not worth pursuing: Pranab', *The Indian Express*, May 3.

Chidanand, Rajghatta, 2017, 'Last Night in Sweden', *The Times of India*, February 22.

Chrico, JoAnn, 2013, *Globalisation: Prospects and Problems,* Sage, London.

*Daily Mail,* 2012, 'Sikh Soldier makes history as he guards Buckingham Palace wearing turban instead of traditional bearskin', December 11. Available at http://www.dailymail.co.uk/news/article-2246410/Sikh-soldier-makes-history-guards-Buckingham-Palace-wearing-turban-instead-traditional-bearskin.html (Accessed on 15 December 2017).

*Deccan Chronicle*, 2017, 'Salman Khan honoured by British Parliament House with Global Diversity Award', September 16.

Demos, Kirsten Bound, Rachel Briggs, John Holden, Samuel Jones, 2007, *Cultural Diplomacy*, DEMOS, London.

EAM, 2015, External Affairs Minister Sushma Swaraj's Address to the International Youth Conference, New Delhi, February 20.

Echanove & Srivastava, 2017, 'Culture for a World in Flux', *The Hindu*, April 22.

English, Rebecca, 2012, 'Sikh soldier makes history as he guards Buckingham Palace wearing turban instead of traditional bearskin', *Daily Mail*, December 11.

*Financial Express*, 2017, 'PM Modi hails Spic Macay', says Society demonstrates how to work for benefit of society', June 5.

George, Varghese K, 2017, 'The Diwali stamp has added to the charm', *The Hindu*, October 18.

Ghosh, Avijit, 2017, 'Castes and faiths united against British but poll war divides them', *The Times of India*, February 22.

Hart, Justin, 2013, *Empire of Ideas*, Oxford University Press, New York.

Hebbar, Nistula, 2016, 'Art has no boundaries but countries have, says Venkaiah Naidu', *The Hindu*, October 19.

Hebbar, Nistula, 2018, 'Homogeneity is inherent to most cultural traditions: Vinay Sahasrabuddhe', *The Hindu*, Jan 7.

Heywood, Andrew, 2011, *Global Politics*, Palgrave Macmillan, New York.

Holton, Robert, 2011, *Globalisation and the Nation State*, Palgrave Macmillan, New York.

Houndmills, Basingstoke, 2011, *Globalisation and the Nation State*, Hampshire: New York: Palgrave Macmillan.

Indonesia, 2017, 'How Indonesia Promotes Diversity for Global Harmony', *National English Online*, May 12.

Isar, 2014, Prof. Yudhishthir Raj Isar, India Country Report, Available at http://ec.europa.eu/assets/eac/culture/policy/international-coop eration/documents/country-reports/india_en.pdf (Accessed on December 15, 2017).

Joseph Nye Jr., 2011, *The Future of Power*, Public Affairs. https://www.amazon.com /Future-Power-Joseph-Nye-Jr/dp/1610390695 (Assessed on 15 December 2017).

Kazymka, Irina, 2014, *The Diplomacy of Culture –The Role of UNESCO in Sustaining Cultural Diversity*, Palgrave Macnmillan.

Khurana, Suanshu, 2017, 'Pakistan students on five day peace visit sent back', *The Indian Express*, May 4.

Lok Sabha Report, 2017, 16th Report of the Standing Committee on External Affairs, August 11.

Nonika Singh, 2017, 'Stories behind the songs', *The Tribune*, Jan 23.

Nye, 2018, Joseph S. Nye, 'As democracies respond to China's 'sharp power', they must not overreact', *The Hindustan Times*, January 6, 2018.

Paul Hopper, 2007, *Understanding Cultural Globalisation,* Cambridge.

Prasar Bharti, 2017, 'Prasar Bharti hosts International Festival in Hyderabad', *Asia News International (ANS)*, January 15.

Prashant Singh, 2018, 'Priyanka takes out a week for Rohingya refugees', The Hindustan Times, May 23.

Raghava, M, 2017, 'Students protest hijab on campus, sport saffron shawls', *The Hindu*, February 22.

Raisina Dialogue, 2017, Prime Minister Modi's Inaugural Address, New Delhi, January 17.

Ram, Vidya, 2017: 1, 'Marching to be counted', *The Hindu*, February 22.

Ram, Vidya, 2017: 2, 'Kathak, qawwali and opera on the same stage', *The Hindu*, October 6.

Roy, Shubhajit, 2017, 'Small interaction during Modi US trip, no Madison Square-kind event', *The Indian Express*, June 17.

Sarukkai, Sunder, 2017,'When the unelected set the Agenda', *The Hindu*, February 22.

Saubhadra Chatterji, 2017, 'Mann Ki Baat: Don't just talk, feel India's diversity, touch it, says PM Modi', *The Hindustan Times*, Sep 24.

Simon Mark, 2008, 'A Comparative Study of the Cultural Diplomacy of Canada, New Zealand and India', The University of Auckland. Available at https://researchspace.auckland.ac.nz/bitstream/

handle/2292/2943/02whole.pdf?sequence=9 (Accessed on December 12, 2017).

Sinha, Amitabh, 2017, 'Indians' safety first, strategic partnership later: Sushma Swaraj', *The Indian Express*, March 21.

Sobi Hussain, 2017, 'No visa for Pak wrestlers: Goel justifies same', *The Tribune*, May 4, 2017.

Sodhi, Simran, 2017, 'Australia allays fears over changes in its visa regimes', *The Tribune*, May 4.

Sonwalkar, Prasun, 2017, Year of Culture: India's diversity rocks London audience', *The Hindustan Times*, Oct 05.

*The Guardian,* 2016, 'Bollywood star Shah Rukh Khan detained at US airport again, August 12. Available at https://www.theguardian.com/us-news/2016/aug/12/bollywood-star-shah-rukh-khan-detained-at-us-airport-again (Accessed on October 17, 2018).

*The Hindu,* 2011, 'Cricket and diplomacy should be kept separate: BJP', March 31.

*The Hindu* 2017, 'Film Awards celebrate India's diversity: President', May 4.

*The Hindu*, 2017: 1, 'Justin Bieber to be served cuisines representing 29 states of India', May 4.

*The Hindu,* 2017, 'President launches Incredible India 2.0 Campaign; "Adopt a Heritage" Project', September 28. Available at https://www.thehindubusinessline.com/news/variety/president-launches-incredible-ndia-20-campaign-adopt-a-heritage-project/article9876374.ece (Accessedon December 15, 2017).

*The Hindu*, 2018, 'The Windrush scandal marks another episode in Europe's hardening politics on immigration' (ed.), May 5.

*The Hindustan Times,* 2017, 'Canadian PM Trudeau's presence at event with Khalistani flags upsets India', May 5.

*The Hindustan Times,* 2018, 'Cricket between India vs Pakistan unlikely until terrorism stops: Sushma Swaraj', January 1.

*The Hindustan Times*, 2018, 'Ramayana is signature epic of eastern world: ICCR president', January 18.

*The Indian Express,* 2016, 'Pluralism and tolerance hallmarks of Indian civilization: President Pranab Mukherjee', April 10.

*The Indian Express*, 2017, 'A window to India's rising soft power – Bollywood', April 13.

*The Indian Express*, 2017: 1, 'Rijiju raises Pak lobbying with UK, seeks help to extradite Mallaya', November 7.

*The Indian Express, 2017: 2*, 'India-Pakistan cultural exchanges should not fall prey to political relations, says Parliamentary panel', August 12.

The President, 2017, 'Let's work to reverse brain drain: President', *The Tribune,* May 3.

*The Times of India*, 2017:1, 'I will not cover up: Le Pen cancels meeting, with Lebanese grand mufti over headgear', February 22.

*The Times of India*, 2017:2, 'Racially profiled at Heathrow over headscarf: LiLo', February 22.

*The Times of India*, 2017: 3, 'Break the Chains' (Ed.), May 4.

*The Times of India*, 2017:4 'Reverse trend of students migration: Prez', May 3.

*The Tribune*, 2016, 'Pluralism and tolerance hallmark of Indian civilization: President', April 10.

Turnbull, 2017, 'Australia's Turnbull seeks patriotism for citizenship', *The Tribune*, June 14.

USC, 2016, http://uscpublicdiplomacy.org/story/hijab-wearing-dance-group-brings-people-together-through-hip-hop (Accessed on December 15, 2017).

Verma, KJM, 2017, 'Devon ke Dev', Nagin & Mahabharta TV shows a big hit in China', *The Indian Express*, May 4.

Vice President, 2010, Vice President Hamid Ansari's Inaugural Address at an International Seminar on 'Indian Culture in a Globalised World', New Delhi, November 11.

Vice President, 2017, Address by Vice President M. Venkaiah Naidu at the 10th Annual Lecture on National Commission for Minorities on the theme 'Minorities in Nation Building', New Delhi, December 19.

World Sufi Forum, 2016, Text of PM's address at the World Sufi Forum, March 17.http://www.pmindia.gov.in/en/news_updates/text-of-pms-address-at-the-world-sufi-forum/ (Accessed on December 23, 2017).

# Bibliography

## Primary Sources

Address of President Clinton at the First White House Conference on Culture and Diplomacy, Washington DC, November 28, 2000.

Afghanistan, India-Afghanistan Cultural Agreement, 1963.

AID (Association of Indian Diplomats), 2008, Report on Economic Diplomacy, 2008. Available at http://www.associationdiplomats.org/publications/ifaj/Vol1/ecodiplomacy.htm [accessed 16 April 2018].

AISE, 2017, ASEAN-India Student Exchange set for Jan. 2017, New Delhi, January 15-18. http://english.vietnamnet.vn/fms/education/168063/asean-india-student-xchange-set-forjan--2017.html (Accessed on 13 December 2017).

AISE, 2016, Embassy of Philippines, Asean-India Student Exchange Program 2016, New Delhi. Available at https://newdelhipe.dfa.gov.ph/index.php/newsroom/embassy-news/248-asean-indian-student-exchangeprogram (Accessed on 13 December 2017).

Annual Report, 2015-16, Regional Office, ICCR, Chandigarh.

Australia, Address of Prime Minister Modi to the Australian Parliament, Canberra, November 18, 2014.

Bangladesh, Cultural Exchange Programme, 2015-2017, 2015, May 13. http://www.mofa.gov.bd/sites/default/files/Cultural%20Exchange%20Program%202015-2017.pdf (Accessed on 12 December 2017).

Clinton H, 2011, *Address at the Global Forum*, Washington DC, May 17. Available at https://www.marketlinks.org/library/secretary%E2%80%99s-global-diaspora-forum-opening-remarks-secretary-state-hillary-rodham-clinton

Delhi Declaration, 2014, SAARC Culture Ministers' Conference, New

Delhi. http://www.careerride.com/view/saarc-culture-ministers-conference-delhi-declaration-adopted-16861.aspx (Accessed on 12 December 2017).

EAM, 2002, Statement by Jaswant Singh, Minister of External Affairs, India at the Plenary Session of Trilateral Meeting, Yangoon, April 6.

EAM 2007, Pranab Mukherjee's Address to the SAARC Editors, February 10.

EAM 2008, Inaugural Address by Shri Pranab Mukherjee, Hon'ble Minister for External Affairs at the Seminar on "Sub-Regionalism Approach to Regional Integration in South Asia: Prospects and Opportunities" hosted by Sikkim University, Gangtok, December 19, 2008.

EAM 2013, External Minister's Speech at the launch of ASEAN-India Centre in New Delhi, June 21.

EAM 2013, Transcript of Media Briefing by External Affairs Minister Salman Khurshid, Brunei Darussalam, July 1.

EAM 2015, Address by the External Affairs Minister at International Youth Summit, February 20.

EAM 2015, Address by the External Affairs Minister at International Conference on 'Indian Diaspora and Cultural Heritage: Past and Future', New Delhi, February 22.

EAM 2015, Address by the External Affairs Minister at the Centenary Commemorative Exhibition of First World War, New Delhi, March 23.

EAM 2015, External Affairs Minister's Introductory Speech at the Session with Indian Achievers, Pravasi Bhartiya Divas 2015, Gandhinagar, Gujarat, January 8.

EAM 2015, External Affairs Minister's Remarks at the Interaction with the Indian Community in Muscat, February 17.

EAM 2015, External Affairs Minister's speech at Pravasi Bharatiya Sanman Awards Ceremony, Gandhinagar, Gujarat, January 9.

EAM 2015, External Affairs Minister's Speech at the Inauguration of 'Visit India Year 2015' in Beijing, February 2.

EAM, 2016, Address of EAM Sushma Swaraj at the Roma Conference, New Delhi, Feb 12.

EAM 2017, Address by External Affairs Minister at Inauguration of BRICS Media Forum, October 18.

EAM 2018, External Affairs Minister's Remarks at Launch of 'Study in India Programme', April 18, New Delhi.

EdCIL 2015, Annual Report of Education Consultants of India (EdCIL, 2014-15), New Delhi.

Fisher, Rod, 2014, Japan Country Report, 'Culture in the EU's External Relations, March.

Foreign Secretary, 2017, Speech by Foreign Secretary at Second Raisina Dialogue, New Delhi, January 18.

High Level Committee on Indian Diaspora [HLCID], 2001, Report of the Committee. http://moia.gov.in/services.aspx?ID1=63&id=m8&idp=59&mainid=23 (Accessed on April 16, 2018).

ICCR 1997-98, Annual Report of the Indian Council for Cultural Relations, New Delhi.

ICCR 2000-01, Annual Report of the Indian Council for Cultural Relations, New Delhi.

ICCR 2007-08, Annual Report of the Indian Council for Cultural Relations, New Delhi.

ICCR 2010-11, Annual Report of the Indian Council for Cultural Relations, New Delhi.

ICCR 2011-12, Annual Report of the Indian Council of Cultural Relations, New Delhi.

ICCR 2013-14, Annual Report of the Indian Council for Cultural Relations, New Delhi.

ICCR 2014-15, Annual Report of the Indian Council for Cultural Relations, New Delhi.

ICCR 2015-16, Annual Report of the Indian Council for Cultural Relations, New Delhi.

ICCR Pamphlet, New Delhi.

IGNCA 2012, Inaugural Address of the President of India, November 19.

Inaugural Address of M.C. Chagla, 1968, President of ICCR as quoted in Bidyut Sarkar, ed., *India and Southeast* Asia, Proceedings of a Seminar on India and Southeast Asia, ICCR.

Inaugural Address of Prime Minister Nehru in 1950 at the time of the inauguration of the Indian Council of Cultural Relations (ICCR), quoted in a *Pamphlet on ICCR*, New Delhi.

India-Pakistan Cultural Agreement, 1998.

International Organization for Migration [IOM] and Migration Policy Institute [MPI], 2012, *Developing a Road Map for Engaging Diasporas in Development*. Available at http://www.migrationpolicy.org/pubs/thediasporahandbook.pdf [Accessed 26 November 2012].

IOM, 2011, 'Migration and Development Report, 2011', International Organisation for Migration (IOM).Available at http://www.iom.int/cms/wmr (Accessed on 4 September 2013).

India-Iran Cultural Agreement, 1956.

Japan Country Report, Culture in the EU's External Relations, 2014.

Joint Statement, 2016, Issued after the visit of Prime Minister of New Zealand to India, New Delhi, October.

India-Kyrgyzstan Cultural Agreement, 2015.

*Lok Sabha Report*, 1997, Second Report, Standing Committee on External Affairs, 1996-97, Eleventh Lok Sabha, April.

*Lok Sabha Report,* 2016, Thirteenth Report of the Committee on External Affairs, November 23. 164.100.47.193/lsscommittee/External%20Affairs/16_External_Affairs_13.pdf (Accessed on December15, 2017).

MEA 1985-86, Annual Report of the Ministry of External Affairs, New Delhi.

MEA 2011-12, Annual Report of the Ministry of External Affairs, New Delhi.

MEA 2015-16, Annual Report of the Ministry of External Affairs, New Delhi.

Media Briefing, 2013, Transcript of Joint Media Interaction of External Affairs Minister and US Secretary of State Mr. John Kerry, New Delhi, 24 June.

Media Transcript, 2013, Chairman's Statement at the 3rd East Asia Foreign Ministers' Meeting, Brunei Darussalam, July 3.

MFA, Sri Lanka, 'President returns after successful visit to India: 15-18 Feb. 2015', February 18, 2015.http://www.priu.gov.lk/news_update/Current_Affairs/ca201502/20150218president_returns_after_successful_visit.

MHRD, 2013-14, Annual Report of the Ministry of Human Resource Development, Government of India, Delhi.

Milton Cummings, 2003, 'Cultural Diplomacy and the United States Government: A Survey', Centre for Arts and Culture.

Ministry of Foreign Affairs of Kenya (no date) 'Diaspora Affairs: Introduction'. Available athttp://www.mfa.go.ke/index.php?option=com_content&view=article&id=371&Itemid=116.

Mirjam Schneider, 2013, Mexico Country Report, Culture in the EU's External Relations.

MMA, 2016, MM Adisory Services,'Indian Students Mobility Report.

MOC 1985-86, Annual Report of the Ministry of Culture, New Delhi.

MOC 1986-87, Annual Report of the Ministry of Culture, New Delhi.

MOC 2011-12, Annual Report of the Ministry of Culture, New Delhi.

MOC 2014-15, Annual Report of the Ministry of Culture, New Delhi.

MOC 2015-16, Annual Report of the Ministry of Culture, New Delhi.

MOC 2016-17, Annual Report of the Ministry of Culture, New Delhi.

Modi, 2015, Media Statement by Prime Minister with Japanese Prime Minister, New Delhi, December 12.

MOIA, 2011-12, Annual Report of the Ministry of Overseas Indian Affairs, Govt. of India, New Delhi.

MOS 2017, Keynote Address by Gen. (Dr.) V.K. Singh (Retd.), Minister of State for External Affairs at the 2nd International Conference on ASEAN-India Cultural and Civilizational Links, Jakarta, January 19.

MOS 2017, Speech by M. J. Akbar, Minister of State for External Affairs at the Inauguration of the GOPIO Global Convention, Bengaluru, January 5.

MOS 2017, Address by Gen. (Dr.) V.K. Singh (Retd.), Minister of State for External Affairs at the Inaugural Session of the Youth Pravasi Bhartiya Divas, January 7.

MYS, 2013-14, Annual Report of the Ministry of Youth and Sports, New Delhi.

MYS, 2014-15, Annual Report of the Ministry of Youth and Sports, New Delhi.

OECD, 2012, International Migration Outlook.

P M Vajpayee 2003, Banquet Speech by Prime Minister in Dushanbe, Tajikistan, November 14.

PBD, 2003, Inaugural Address of the Prime Minister of India, New Delhi, January 9.

PBD, 2009, EAM's Address at the Pravasi Bhartiya Divas, January 7.

PBD, 2009, Inaugural Address of Prime Minister of India, Pravasi Bharatiya Divas (PBD), New Delhi, January 7.

PM Modi, Press Statement, During State visit of Prime Minister of Canada, New Delhi, February 23, 2018 http://mea.gov.in/Speeches-Statements.htm?dtl/29638/English_Translation_of_Press_Statement_by_Prime_Minister_during_State_visit_of_Prime_Minister_of_Canada_February_23_2018.

PM, 2012, 'Remarks by Prime Miniter, Dr. Manmohan Singh at Flag Down of the ASEAN-India Car Rally', New Delhi, December, 21.

President 2017, Speech by President at the valedictory address and conference of Pravasi Bhartiya Sanman, Bengaluru, January 9.

President 2017, Address by the President to students at Higher Educational Institutions, January 10.

President K R Narayanan, 2002, 'Banquet Speech by the Indian President at Almaty, February 6.

President, 2000, Speech by President of India at a Banquet in Singapore, November 10.

Press Release, 2014, 2nd Meeting of SAARC Education Ministers, New Delhi, October 31.

Press Statement, 2017, Prime Minister Modi's Statement during the State Visit of Prime Minister of Australia to India, April 10.

Prime Minister, 2013, Highlights of Prime Minister's Address at the Annual Conclave of Indian Ambassadors/High Commissioners abroad in New Delhi, November 4.

Prime Minister, 2015, Prime Minister's Address at the UK Parliament, November 12.

Prime Minister, 2017, Inaugural Address by Prime Minister at Second Raisina Dialogue, New Delhi, January 17.

Prime Minister 2017, Speech by Prime Minister at the Inauguration Address at the 14th Pravasi Bhartiya Divas, Convention, Bengaluru, January 8.

Raisina Dialogue, 2017, Prime Minister Modi's Inaugural Address, New Delhi, January 17.

Rajasekhar, 2016, Address of Director General, ICCR at the Higher Education Conference, New Delhi, March 21.

SAARC Press Release, 2011, Kathmandu, July 11 (http://saarc-sec.org/press-releases/Media-Exchange-Programme-Islamabad-5-6July-2... 2/7/2014.

Singapore Lecture, 1994, Address by Indian Prime Minister Narasimha Rao, 'India and the Asia Pacific: Forging a New Partnership, Institute of Southeast Asian Studies, Singapore.

South Korea Country Report, 2014, Culture in the EU's External Relations.

State Department, 2005, 'Cultural Diplomacy:The Linchpin of Public Diplomacy', Report of the Advisory Committee on Cultural Diplomacy (ACCD), US Department of State, Washington DC, September. https://www.state.gov/documents/organization/54374.pdf (Accessed on December 16, 2017).

The President, 2014, 'Address by Shri Pranab Mukherjee at the Indian Newspaper Society', February 27.

The White House Conference, 2000, Address of Madeline Albright, at the conference on 'Culture and Diplomacy', The White House, Washington DC, November 28.

Uganda, India-Uganda Cultural Agreement, 1981.

UNESCO, UNESCO Conference at Mexico, 1982.

Vajpayee, 2002, Statement by Indian Prime Minister Atal Behari Vajpayee, at the CICA Summit, Almaty (Kazakhstan), June 4.

Vice President, 2010, Inaugural Address at International Seminar on Indian Culture in a Globalised World, Delhi, November 11.

Vice President, 2011, Inaugural Address of the Vice President, World Urdu Editors Conference, Delhi, December 30.

Vice President, 2012, Inaugural Address of the Vice President at the Ramnath Goenka Excellence in Journalism Awards, Delhi, January 16.

Vice President, 2013, Speech at the Oxford Centre for Islamic Studies on 'Identity and Civilization: An Indian Perspective', November.

Vice President, 2013, Inaugural Address, National Press Day Celebrations, Press Council of India, Delhi, November, 16.

Vice President, 2016, Remarks by Vice President of India, Shri M. Hamid Ansari, at the inauguration of the Interfaith Conference at Malappuram, Kerala, January 12.

Vice President, 2017, Address by Shri M. Venkaiah Naidu at the 10th Annual Lecture on National Commission for Minorities on the theme 'Minorities in Nation Building', New Delhi, December 19, 2017.

*Vision Statement*, 2012, 'Vision Statement, ASEAN-India Commemorative Summit', New Delhi, December 20.

Yashwant Sinha, 2003, 'Keynote Address by External Affairs Minister at the Third India-Central Asia Conference, Tashkent, November 6.

## Secondary Sources

### Books

A. Didar Singh and S. Irudaya Rajan, 2016, *Politics of Migration*, New Delhi.

Akash Banerjee, 2013, *Tales from Shining Sinking India. Analyis*, New

Delhi.

Akash Kapur, 2012, *India Becoming*, Penguin.

Alexander, K. C. and K. P. Kumaran, 2013, *Culture and Development: Cultural Patterns in Areas of Uneven Development*.

Arndt, Richard M, 2005, *The First Resort of Kings, American Cultural Diplomacy in the Twentieth Century*, Potomac Books Inc., Washington DC.

Asghar Ali Engineer (Ed.), 2002, *Islam in India, The Impact of Civilizations*, Shipra, Delhi.

Asha Kaushik, Globalisation, 2002, Democracy and Culture: Situating Gandhian Alternatives, Pointer Publishers, Jaipur.

Atal, Yogesh (ed.), 1991, *Culture-Development Interface*, Vikas Publishing House.

B.P. Singh, 1998, *India's Culture, The State, The Arts and Beyond*, Oxford University Press.

Baladas Goshal, 1996, *Diplomacy and Domestic Politics in South Asia*, Konark Publishers, New Delhi.

Balmiki Prasad Singh, 2011, *India's Culture – The State, the Arts and Beyond*, OUP, New Delhi.

Bandhopadhyaya, J., 1973, *The Making of India's Foreign Policy*, Allied Publishers, New Delhi.

Banerjee, Utpal K, 1997, 'Role of Cultural Diplomacy' in *Indian Democracy: Agenda for the 21st Century*, Foreign Services Institute, New Delhi, Konark Publications Ltd., New Delhi.

Barber, Benjamin R. 1992, 'Jihad Vs McWorld', *The Atlantic Monthly*, March.

Barkha Dutt, 2016, *This Unquiet Land – Stories from India's Fault Lines*, Aleph Books, New Delhi.

Benhabib, Selva, 2002, *The Claims of Culture: Equality and Diversity in the Global Era,* Princeton University Press, New Jersey.

Berridge, G.R., 2005, *Diplomacy – Theory and Practice*, New York, Palgrave Macmillan.

Bhanu Pratap, 2015, 'India's Cultural Diplomacy: Present Dynamics, Challenges and Future Prospects', *International Journal of Arts, Humanities and Management Studies,* Vol. 1, no. 9, September.

C. Raja Mohan, 2015, *Modi's World,* Harper Collins, Noida, 2015.

Center for the Study of Democracies [CSD], 2008, *Diaspora Report*, Queensland University, Canada.

Chas. W. Freeman Jr., 2002, *Arts of Power*, USIP, Washington.

Chaulia, Sreeram, 2016, *Modi Doctrine –The Foreign Policy of India's Prime Minister*, Bloomsbury, New Delhi.

Chirico, JoAnn, 2013, *Globalisation: Prospects and Problems,* Sage, London, New York.

Cohen, Raymond, 2005, *Negotiating Across Cultures*, United States Institute of Peace Press, Washington DC, Revised Edition.

Dasgupta, Arun, 1996, "Intellectual and Academic Cooperation between India and Southeast Asia" in C.Ram Prasad, *Culture and Complementarities: Implications of the Singapore – India MoU on Culture, Heritage and the Archives in Singapore-India Relations.*

David A. Lax and James K. Sebenius, 2006, *3-D Negotiation*, IIBS Press, Harvard Business School Press, Boston.

David Black and Byron Peacock, 2013, 'Sport and Diplomacy' in *The Oxford Handbook of Modern Diplomacy*, Oxford University Press, UK.

David M Malone, 2013, The Modern Diplomatic Mission' in *The Oxford Handbook of Modern Diplomacy,* Oxford University Press, UK.

Délano A. 2011, *Mexico and Its Diaspora in the United States: Policies of Emigration since 1848,* Cambridge University Press. New York.

Demos, Kirsten Bound, Rachel Briggs, John Holden, Samuel Jones, 2007, *Cultural Diplomacy*, DEMOS, London.

Donna Gehrke-White, 2006, *The Face Behind the Veil*, Kensington Publishing Corp., New York.

Engineer, Asghar Ali (Ed.), 2002, *Islam in India: The Impact of Civilizations*, Shipra, Delhi.

Eytan Gilboa, 2001, 'Diplomacy in the Age of Global Communication' in *'Global Politics: Essays in honour of David Vital,* (ed) Ben-Zvi, Abraham & Klieman, Aaron S, Frank Cass Publishers, London/ Portland.

Freeman, Jr., Chas W, 2006, *The Diplomat's Dictionary,* United States Institute of Peace Press, Washington D.C.

Friedman, Thomas L., 1999, *The Lexus and the Olive Tree*, Farrar Straus Giroux, New York.

Ghoshal, Baladas (ed.), 1996, *India and Southeast Asia: Challenges and Opportunities*, IIC, New *Delhi.*

Ghoshal, Baldas, 1996, *Diplomacy and Domestic Politics in South Asia,* Konark Publishers Pvt. Ltd.

Gonzalez III JJ, 2012. *Diaspora Diplomacy: Philippine Migration and Its Soft Power Influences.*

Gujral, I K, 1998, *A Foreign Policy for India', External Publicity Division,* Ministry of External Affairs, New Delhi 1998.

Gurpreet Mahajan, 2002, *The Multicultural Path*, Sage Publications, New Delhi.

Hart, Justin, 2013, *Empire of Ideas*, Oxford University Press, New York.

Heywood, Andrew, 2011, *Global Politics*, *State,* Palgrave Macmillan, New York.

Hiranmay Karlekar (ed.), 1998, *Independent India: The First Fifty Years,* ICCR, Oxford University Press.

Huntington, Samuel, 1997. *The Clash of Civilization and the Remaking of the World Order*, Simon & Schuster.

Inaugural Address by M.C. Chagla, , 1968, President of ICCR as quoted in Bidyut Sarkar (ed), *India and Southeast* Asia, Proceedings of a Seminar on India and Southeast Asia, ICCR.

Irena Kozymka, 2014, *The Diplomacy of Culture*, Palgrave Macmillan, New York.

Jan England, 2013, 'Humanitarian Diplomacy' in *The Oxford Handbook of Modern Diplomacy,* Oxford University Press, UK.

Jan Hall, 2012, 'India's New Public Diplomacy: Soft Power and the Limits of Government Action', *Asian Survey*, Vol. 52, No. 6.

Jan Mellisen, 2013, 'Public Diplomacy' in *The Oxford Handbook of Modern Diplomacy*, Oxford University Press, UK.

Jayakar, Pupul, 1992, *Indira Gandhi, A Biography*, Viking, Penguin Books India (P) Ltd.

Joseph Nye Jr, 2004, 'The decline of America's Soft Power', *Foreign Affairs,* 83: 5. May-June, 16-20.

Joseph Nye Jr., 2011, *The Future of Power*, Public Affairs. https://www.amazon.com /Future-Power-Joseph-Nye-Jr/dp/1610390695 (Assessed on 15 December 2017).

Joseph S. Nye Jr., 2008, 'Public Diplomacy and Soft Power', *The Annals of American and Academy of Political and Social Science*, Vol. 616. American Academy of Political and Social Sciences, Sage.

Juan Emilo Cheyre, 2013, 'Defence Diplomacy' in *The Oxford Handbook of Modern Diplomacy*, Oxford University Press, UK.

Justin Hart, 2013, *Empire of Ideas*, Oxford University Press, New York.

Karan Singh, 2006, Remarks by Dr. Karan Singh, President, Indian Council for Cultural Relations at the Annual Dinner of the Association of Indian Diplomats', March 22.

Karan Singh, 2014, 'Valedictory Address at the Conference: The Relevance of the Traditional Cultures for the Present and the Future', India International Centre, New Delhi, March 26.

Karlekar, Hiranmay (ed.), 1998, *Independent India: The First Fifty Years*, ICCR, Oxford University Press.

Kaul, T N, 1982, *Reminiscences, Discreet and Indiscreet*, Lancers Publishers, New Delhi.

Keith Phillip Lepor (ed.), 1997, *After the Cold War: Essays on the Emerging New World Order*, University of Texas, Austin, Foreword by Gorbachev.

Kevin Avruch, 2000, *Culture and Conflict Resolution*, USIP, Washington DC.

Khosla, IP, 2006, *Economic Diplomacy*, Konark Publishers, New Delhi.

Kishan S. Rana and Vipul Chatterjee (eds.), 2016, *Economic Diplomacy: India's Experience*, CUTS International, Jaipur.

Kishan S. Rana, 2016, *Diplomacy at the Cutting Edge*, Manas Publications, New Delhi.

Krishan Chand, 2016, *Relevance of Swami Vivekananda in Contemporary India*, CRRID Chandigarh.

Lakshmi Reddy, 2001, 'Malaysia: Perspectives on Culture' – Paper presented at an International Conference on India Malaysia Relations, Hyderabad, December.

Lee Kuan Yew, 1998, *The Singapore Story: Memories of Lee Kuan Yew*, Times Edition, Singapore.

M. J. Akbar, 2011, *Tinderbox: The Past and Future of Pakistan*, Harper Collins, New Delhi.

Maharajakrishna Rasgotra, 2016, *A Life in Diplomacy*, Penguin, New Delhi.

Maulana Azad, 1992, *The Selected Works of Maulana Abul Kalam Azad*, Volume VI (1951-52)', (Ed) Dr. Ravindra Kumar, Atlantic Publishers & Distributors, New Delhi.

Mazumdar, T.K. 1969, 'Indian Development: Viewed Culturally' in *Culture-Development Interface,* (ed. Yogesh Atal).

Mehta, Vinod, 2011, *Lucknow Boy: A Memoir*, Penguin, New Delhi.

Menon, Sivshankar, 2016, *Choices inside the Making of India's Foreign Policy*, Penguin Random House, Gurgaon.

N.N. Jha and Sudhir Singh, 2016, *Modi's Foreign Policy – Challenges and Opportunities,* Pentagon Press, New Delhi.

Naima Prevots, 2001, *Dance for Export Cultural Diplomacy and the Cold War,* Wesleyan University Press, Middletown Connecticut.

Nandan Nilekani, 2008, *Imagining India – Ideas for the New Century*, Penguin Allen Lane. New Delhi.

Nathan, K.S. (ed.), 2000, *India and ASEAN: The Growing Partnership for the 21st Century,* IFDR.

Newland, Kathleen (ed.), 2010, *Diasporas, New Partners in Global*

*Development Policy: USA,* MPI, Washington DC.

Nibir K. Ghosh, 2005, *Multicultural America,* Unistar.

Noam Chomsky, 2007, *Failed States*, Allen and Unwin, Chennai.

Nye, 2018, Joseph S. Nye, 'As democracies respond to China's 'sharp power', they must not overreact', *The Hindustan Times*, January 6, 2018.

P.C. Alexander, 2001, *India in the New Millennium*, Somaiya Publication, New Delhi.

Patricia Goff, 2013 'Cultural Diplomacy' in *The Oxford Handbook of Modern Diplomacy*, Oxford University Press, UK.

Paul Hopper, 2007, *Understanding Cultural Globalisation,* Cambridge Polity.

Preben Kaarsholm (Ed.), 2004, *City Flicks– Indian Cinema and the Urban Experience,* Seagull Books, Calcutta and New Delhi.

Prem K. Budhwar*, 2016, Canada-India Partners in Progress*, Vij Books, New Delhi.

Pupul Jayakar, *Indira Gandhi, 1992, A Biography*, Viking, Penguin Books India (P) Ltd.

R. Radhakrishna, SK. Rao, S. Mahendra Dev, K. Subarao (eds), 2006, *India in a Globalising World,* Academic Publications, New Delhi.

Raja Mohan, C, 2009, 'The Making of Indian Foreign Policy: The Role of Scholarship and Public Opinion', ISAS Working Paper, No. 73, July 13.

Rajika Bhandari and Alessia Lefebure, 2015, *Asia: The Next Higher Education Superpower*.

Ramachandra Guha, 2016, *Democrats and Dissenters*, Penguin Books, New Delhi, 2016.

Rice, Condoleezza, 2012, *No Higher Honour*, London: Simon & Schuster.

Richard M. Arndt and David Lee Rubin (eds), 1996, *The Fulbright Difference,* Transaction Publishers, New Jersey.

Rod Fisher, 2014, 'US Country Report', *Culture in the EU's External Relations.*

Romila Thapar (Ed.), 2000, *India – Another Millennium*, Penguin Books, New Delhi.

Rugh, William A, 2014, *Front Line Public Diplomacy*, Palgrave Macmillan Series, New York.

Sablosky, Julient Artunes, 2003, *Recent Trends in Department of State Support for Cultural Diplomacy, 1993-2002*, Centre for Arts and Culture, Washington DC.

Saeed Naqvi, 2016, *Being the Other - The Muslim in India*, New Delhi.

Sahai P.S. et al. 2011, *Study of the Indian Diaspora with Particular Reference to Development and Migration from the State of Punjab*, Centre for Research in Rural and Industrial Development [CRRID], September.

Sahai, P S, 2002, 'Globalisation, Cultural Diplomacy and the Indian Ocean: An Indian Perspective', Paper presented at the Panjab University, Chandigarh, November.

Sahai, P S, 2009, 'India's Cultural Diplomacy in Southeast Asia', *HCMC University*, May 16-19.

Sahai, P S, 2013, 'Time to define the role of States', *Power Politics,* March.

Sahai, P S, 2011, A unique study, Review of Délano A, *Mexico and Its Diaspora in the United States: Policies of Emigration since 1848.* Available at http://www.diplomacy.edu/resources/books/reviews/mexico-and-its-diaspora-united-states-policies-emigration-1848 [accessed 20 November 2012].

Sahai, P S, 2013, 'India's Engagement with Diaspora: Government Communication, Platforms and Structures' (Paper for ODI Conference, March).

Sahai, P S, 2015, 'Connecting the neighbours', *Power Politics*, November.

Sanjay Patel, 2006, *The Little Book of Hindu Deities*, Penguin.

Sanjaya Baru, 2006, *Strategic Consequences of India's Economic Performance,* Academic Foundation, New Delhi.

Sarkar, Bidyut (ed.) 1968, *India and Southeast Asia,* Proceedings of a Seminar, ICCR.

Sarkar, H.B., 1985. *Cultural Relations between India and Southeast Asian*

*Countries*, ICCR and Motilal Banarsidas.

Shain, Yossi, 1994-95, 'Ethnic Diasporas and U.S. Foreign Policy' *Political Science Quarterly*, Volume. 109, No. 5, (Winter); Available at http://www.jstor.org/stable/21552513. https://www.psqonline.org/article.cfm?IDArticle=13388

Sharma, Anjana (ed.), 2013, *Civilizational Dialogue, Asian Inter-connections and Cross-cultural Exchanges*, ICCR & Manohar.

Shawn Power, 2013, 'Media Diplomacy and Geopolitics' in *The Oxford Handbook of Modern Diplomacy*, Oxford University Press, UK.

Sheffer, G.G., 2005, 'Is the Jewish diaspora unique? Reflections on the diaspora's current situation', *Israeli Studies* 10(1).

Simon Mark, 2008, 'A Comparative Study of Cultural Diplomacy of Canada, New Zealand and India', Thesis submitted for the Ph. D. degree for The University of Auckland.

Singh, B P, 1998, *India's Culture: The State, The Arts and Beyond,* Oxford University Press.

Singh, Dr. Karan, 2013, Foreword in Sharma, Anjana (ed.), *Civilizational Dialogue, Asian Inter-connections and Cross-cultural Exchanges*, ICCR & Manohar.

Srinivasan, Krishnan , 2012, *Diplomatic Channels*, Kolkata: Manohar Publishers.

Stephen G. Bloom, 2000. *Postville – A Clash of Cultures in Heartland America,* Harcourt, New York.

Su Changhe, 2013, 'Soft Power' in *The Oxford Handbook of Modern Diplomacy*,Oxford University Press, UK.

Surendra Kumar (Ambassador), 2013, *Beyond Diplomatic Dilemmas*, Har Anand.

Talbott, Strobe, 1998, *Engaging India: Diplomacy, Democracy and the Bomb, New Delhi*, Penguin.

Tharoor, Shashi, 2000, *From Midnight to the Millennium*, Penguin Books, New Delhi, 2000.

Tharoor, Shashi, 2012, *PAX INDICA: India and the World of the 21st Century*, New Delhi: Thomson Press India Ltd.

Thomas L. Friedman, *The Lexus and the Olive Tree*, Anchor Books, New York, 2000.

Thussu, Daya & Ellen Frost, 2013, *Communicating India's Soft Power: Budha to Bollywood*, East-West Centre, Palgrave, MacMillan.

Utpal K. Banerjee, 1997, 'Role of Cultural Democracy' in *Indian Democracy: Agenda for the 21st Century*, Foreign Service Institute, New Delhi and Konarak Publications Ltd., New Delhi.

Vatsayan, Kapila, 1997, 'Culture: The crafting of Institutions in Independent India' in *Indian Democracy: Agenda for 21st Century*, Foreign Service Institute, New Delhi.

William Rugh, 2014, *Front Line Public Diplomacy*, Palgrave MacMillan, New York.

Yogesh Atal (ed.*)*, 1991, *Culture – Development Interface,* Vikas Publishing House.

**Articles**

Aakanksha N Bhardwaj, 2017, 'I'm not your martyr's daughter, says Gurmehar in new blog post', *The Hindustan Times*, April 13.

Abhay K, 2013, 'Innovations in Public Diplomacy', *GPP Blog*, November 6.

Afan Yesvi, 2016, 'How Balochistan gave birth to the best of Bollywood', *Daily Mail*, September.

Agunias, D.R. and Newland K. 2012, *Developing a Road Map for Engaging Diasporas in Development*, International Organization for Migration (IOM) and Migration Policy Institute. Available at http://www.migrationpolicy.org/pubs/thediasporahandbook.pdf (Accessed on April 16, 2018).

Akeel Bilgrami, 2016, 'Taking back our universities', *The Hindu*, March 9, 2016.

Alok Deshpande, 2014, 'Abbott launches New Colombo Plan for students of India, Australia', *The Hindu,* September 4.

Amarjit Thind, 2013, 'Kutch farmers blame 'minority profiling' for their plight', *The Tribune,* 30 October.

Amarjot Kaur, 2016, 'No horsing around!' *The Tribune*, March 9.

Amb. Verma, 2016, Article by US Ambassador to India, 'The Ties That Bind', *Span,* March-April.

Amit Baruah, 2017, 'I misspoke, and for that I feel regret', *The Hindu*, April 11.

Amit Dasgupta and Shaun Star, 2017, 'India-Australia relations: Education as the tipping point', *The Hindustan Times*, April 12.

Amit Kumar Gupta, 2013, 'Soft Power of the United States, China and India: A Comparative Analysis', *Indian Journal of Asian Affairs,* Vol. 26, No. 1/2.

Amitabh Sinha, 2017, 'Indians safety first, strategic partnership later: Sushma Swaraj', *The Indian Express*, March 21.

Anand, Kunal, 2016, 'How Modi is changing global diplomacy with Bean Tacos and Dosas across the world', *Indiatimes*, June 9.

Ananth Krishan, 2013, 'China probes Xinjiang angle to Tiananmen clash', *The Hindu,* October 30.

Anju Agnihotri Chaba, 2017, 'Mindless enhancement of educational institutes not worth pursuing: Pranab', *The Indian Express*, May 3.

Anjuri Nayar Singh, 2017, 'Javed has never said anything romantic to me', *The Hindustan Times*, April 12.

Ankita Dwivedi Johri, 2017, 'What obscenity? What love jihad? I was targeted as I am a Muslim', *The Hindustan Times*, April 13.

Ansari, 2017, 'There is need to defend universities as free spaces', *The Tribune*, March 26.

Aseem Bassi and Usmeet Kaur, 2016, 'Ontario premier at Golden Temple today amid gay row', *The Hindustan Times*, January 31.

Aurora de Peralta, 2014, 'Smithsonian "Beyond Bollywood" Exhibit Debunks Stereotypes about Indian American', *Asian Fortune*, March.

Avijit Ghosh, 2017, 'Castes and faiths united against British poll war divides them', *The Times of India*, February 22.

Axworthy, Tom, Monahan, John and Brender.Natalie, 2011, 'Top Migrants to help shape foreign policy', *The Globe and Mail*, December 20.

Bagchi, Indrani, 2008, 'Bollywood to hard sell India's soft power in

China', *The Tribune,* March 28.

Bagchi, Indrani, 2012, 'Shankar personified India's soft power', *The Tribune*, 13 Dec.

Bandopadhyay, Krishnaidu, 2016, '*The Hindu* gods forgotten in India revered in Japan', *The Times of India*, January 11.

Barkha Dutt, 2016, 'Stand up for our rights', *The Hindustan Times*, March 12.

Barnard A, 2010, 'For Haitian official, mission is to mend fences with diaspora and streamline aid', *The New York Times,* 12 March. Available at http://query.nytimes.com/gst/fullpage.html?res=9B07E 3DA173AF931A25750C0A9669D8B63.

*BBC*, 2017, 'India visit very productive despite controversy, says Sajjan', April 21.

Ben Hubbard, 2016, 'Conjuring happiness and tolerance, the Emirate Way', *The Hindu*, February 11 (NYT).

Ben Shapiro, 2016, 'Pope Says Building Walls Is 'Not Christian.' So, What Does the Bible Say about Walls?' *Daily Wire*, February 19.

Bhatia, Shyam, 2012, 'Yoga: Not in Church, Please', *The Tribune* October 2.

Bhatta B, 2009, 'Economic Diplomacy: How NRNs Can Contribute?' Paper presented at the 4th NRN Global Conference, Kathmandu, Nepal, October 13-15.

British DJ to hold a gig on Everest, 2017, *The Hindu*, April 11.

C. Raja Mohan, 2017, 'Battling de-globalisation', *The Indian Express,* February 14.

Canada-Mexico Exchanges, 2016, 'Students welcome plans to boost Canada-Mexico Exchanges', *Ottawa Community News*, June 29.

Caroline Mortimer, 2016, 'Wine on menu ruins Rouhani – Hollande lunch', *The Times of India*, January 29.

Cartoon, Jug Suraya, Ajit Ninan, 2017, 'He defended to get into the group of his Star-Spangled Banner', *The Times of India*, February 22.

Chaba, Anju Agnihotri, 2017. 'Mindless enhancement of educational institutes not worth pursuing: Pranab', *The Indian Express*, May 3.

Charu Sudan Kasturi, 2015, 'Modi government plans Buddhism blitz in cultural diplomacy focus', *The Telegraph*, August 31.

Chidanand Rajghatta, 2014, 'Beyond Bollywood: Indian-Americans get a call up from Smithsonian', Feb 26.

Chidanand, Rajghatta, 2017, 'Last Night in Sweden', *The Times of India*, February 22.

CHOGM, 2013, 'Khurshid will represent India at CHOGM', *The Hindu,* October 27.

Chopra, Shaili, 2014, 'The timeline warriors', *The Hindu*, March 20.

Chu, Henry, 2013, 'Ireland OKs abortion in some cases is blow to Catholic Church', *The Chicago Tribune*, July 30, Available at http://articles.latimes.com/2013/jul/30/world/la-fg-wn-ireland-abortions-catholic-church-20130730.

CJI, 2015, 'When the CJI felt like Raj Kapoor', *The Hindu*, December 13.

Coomi Kapoor, 2016, 'Inside Track', *The Sunday Express*, January 31.

D'Ann Rohrer, 2016, 'Returning home after an exchange year', State Coordinator Leadership and Exchange Team, June 21.

*Daily Mail,* 2012, 'Sikh Soldier makes history, as he guards Buckingham Palace wearing turban instead of traditional bearskin', December 11. http://www.dailymail.co.uk/news/article-2246410/Sikh-soldier makes-history-guards-Buckingham-Palace-wearing-turban-insteadtraditional-bearskin.html (Accessed on 15 December 2017).

Damini Nath, 2016, 'Indian and Australian Artists collaborate for Sydney show', *The Hindu*, October 10.

*Deccan Chronicle,* 2016, 'Ghulam Ali concert can be hosted in Kolkata: Mamata Banerjee', January 10.

Deepak Yadav, 2016, '$1 billion investment every year for India, Hollande', *The Chandigarh Times,* January 25.

Deepak Yadav, 2016, 'Corbusier marvel vows Hollande', *The Times of Chandigarh*, January 25.

Delhi International Arts Festival, 2016, 'Where India meets the world',

*The Hindustan Times*, December 8.

Dewan S. Scattered, 2010, 'Emigres Haiti once shunned are now a lifeline', *The New York Times,* February 3.

Dhillon, Seerat, 2017, 'Education vs Commerce', *The Tribune*, January 6.

*Diaspora Report*, 2008, Center for the Study of Democracies, Queensland University, Canada.

Diaspora, 2013, 'Modi's long shadow creates a rift in Chicago', *Business Standard,* September 22, http://www.business-standard.com/article/news-ians/modi-s-long-shadow-creates-a-rift-in-chicago-113092200449_1.html.

Dikshit, Sandeep, 2013, 'Process under way to decide on participation in CHOGM', *The Hindu,* November 1.

Diwali, 2013, 'In a first, Diwali celebrations at Capitol Hill', *The Tribune*, August 27.

Dixit, Rekha, 2014, 'Celebrating Integrity', *The Week*, March 23.

Douglas C. McGill, 1984, 'Festival of India is set for the U.S. in 1985-86', July 12, http://www.nytimes.com/1984/07/12/arts/festival-of-india-is-set-for-the-us-in-1985-86.html (Accessed on April 16, 2018).

Dutt, Barkha 2016, 'Stand up for our rights', *The Hindustan Times*, March 12.

Dutt, Barkha, 2013, 'Silence is not an option', *The Hindustan Times*, November 23.

Echanove& Srivastava, 2017, 'Culture for a World in Flux', *The Hindu*, April 22.

Evann Potter, 2002/2003, 'Canada and the New Public Diplomacy', *International Journal*, Vol. No. 1, pp. 43-64.

Friedman, Thomas, 2002, "Globalisation, Above and Well", *New York Times,* 22 September.

Gamage, Daya, 2012, 'Ethnic diasporas and shaping of US foreign policy', *Asian Tribune*, 17 August.

Gastrodiplomacy, 2016, 'Start-Up Peace Meal Kitchen Launches Dinner Series', April 6. Available at https://detroit.eater.

com/2016/4/6/11380348/gastrodiplomacy-detroit-food-peace-mealkitchen-mana-heshm.

Gauri Kohli, 2016, 'Scholarships for Indians to study in UK', *The Hindustan Times*, September 21.

Gauri Kohli, 2017, 'Study Abroad: US, UK have everything to lose if they look inwards', *The Hindustan Times*, Jan. 24.

Gautam Chintamani, 2016, 'Why India needs to cash on Bollywood soft power', *Daily Mail*, September 3.

Geeta Sahai, 2016, 'Making India a Cultural Power', *The Hindu*, May 14.

George, Varghese K, 2017, 'The Diwali stamp has added to the charm', *The Hindu*, October 18.

Ghosh, Avijit, 2017, 'Castes and faiths united against British poll war divides them', *The Times of India*, February 22.

GIAN, 2015, 'India launches GIAN Scheme to boost higher education', *Business Times*, December 1.

Gopalkrishna Gandhi, 2016, 'Goodbye Barack', *The Hindu*, December 30.

Gupta, Vivek and Aseem Bassi, 2016, 'SGPC not to offer "Siropa" to lesbian Canadian premier', *The Hindustan Times*, January 30.

Gurmukh Singh, 2012, 'India's Soft Power Spreads', *The Tribune,* October 2.

Gwen Ackerman, 2016, 'Israeli Ministers Approve "Facebook Law" Against Web Incitement', *Bloomberg*, December 25.

Hague, William. 2014, 'Healing the wounds of a bitter war', *The Hindu*, March 17.

Haidar, Suhasini, 2014. 'Backing Bangladesh', *The Hindu*, January 11.

Haider, Suhasini, 2013, 'The Case for making it to Colombo', *The Hindu*, October 29.

Harding, Hayli, 2015, 'Smithsonian exhibit on Display at Texas Educates about Sikh Culture', September 17.

Harish V. Pant, 2015, 'India's soft-power strategy', *The Outlook India*, October.

Hasan Suroor, 2016, 'Liberal Muslims let-down', *The Tribune*, March 9.

Helena Smith, 2015, 'Shocking images of drowned Syrian boy show tragic plight of refugees' *The Guardian*, September 2.

*Himalayan Times,* 2014, 'PM's stress on collective effort to tackle regional challenges', February 9, https://www.bloomberg.com/news/articles/2016-12-25/israeli-ministers-approve-facebook-law-against-web-incitement (Accessed on January 7, 2018).

*IIC Diary* 2017, The India International Centre diary, July-August.

Indonesia, 2017, 'How Indonesia Promotes Diversity for Global Harmony', *National English Online*, May 12.

Institute of Texan Cultures, June 2015 *issue of San Antonio Magazine* (https://www.sikh24.com/2015/08/02/exhibition-in-texas-depicts-the-legacy-of-sikhs-punjab/#.V0yAjJErKhc).

IP Singh & Harsheen Juneja, 2017, 'Turbans give a splash of colour to NY, London', *The Times of India*, April 17.

IP Singh, '1984 riots: justice delayed & denied', *The Times of India*, November 1.

Ira Pande, 2012, 'Hard Power of Soft Diplomacy', *The Tribune,* July 1.

Ishani Dattagupta, 2015 'A new chapter in EU-India educational ties', *The Economic Times,* November 2.

Jaideep A. Prabhu, 2017, 'There's an Indic Way of Thinking about Foreign Policy But we are doing the Wrong Way.' *Swarajya,* January14.

James Campbell, 2017, 'Prime Minister Malcolm Turnbull shares train with India's "rock star" PM Narendra Modi', *Herald Sun*, April 10.

James Mayer, 2014, 'Beyond Bollywood: Immigration, Culture, and the Indian American Experience', *The Times of India,* February, 18.

James McAuley, 2016, 'French people are handing out croissants in London to persuade Britain to stay in the E.U' *The Washington Post*, June 22.

Jane Maulfair, 1985, 'India USA Year-long Festival to Promote Culture, Mutual Understanding'. Available at http://articles.mcall.com/1985-06-23/entertainment/2465730_1_two-largest-democracies-indian-artfestival.

Jasmine Singh, 2016, 'Punjabi Dholl, the Brazilian Way', *The Tribune,* February 15.

Jaspreet Singh Sahni, 2017, 'Snooker bigger in Pakistan than India', *Chandigarh Times*, April 11.

Jatin Verma, 2017, 'Studying in Australia, Simplified', *The Chandigarh Times*, June 5.

Jaya Row, 2017, 'Shankara's Bhaja Govindam – Seek the Spirit', *The Tribune,* March 16.

Jayant Jacob, 2016, 'Ministry criticises Airlift, says movie 'short on facts', *The Hindustan Times*, Jan. 30.

Joeanna Rebello Fernandez, 2016, 'There is a still denial of voices of colour in literature and in films', *The Times of India*, Jan 24.

Joel Brinkley and Ian Fisher, 2006, 'US says it also finds cartoons of Muhammad offensive', *The New York Times*, February 4.

John von Rhein, 2016, 'Grant Park fest opens with sound relief', *The Chicago Tribune*, June 17.

John von Rhein, 2016:1, 'Late contract deal saves Grant Park Music Fest opener', *The Chicago Tribune*, June 15.

Joseph Nye, Jr., 2004, 'You Can't Get From There', *The New York Times*, November 29.

Joseph S. Nye, Jr., 2003, 'Propaganda Isn't the Way: Soft Power', *The International Herald Tribune*, January 10.

K J M Verma, 2017, 'Top Chinese official demoted for not smoking in front Muslim leaders', *The Indian Express*, April 12.

Kadir Pethiyagoda: 'Modi deploys his cultural skills in Asia', http://www.brookings.in/in-focus/modi-deploys-his-culture-skills-in-asia.

Kaiser, Ejaz, 2016, 'Peace Unity ensure nations growth: PM', *The Hindustan Times*, January 12.

Kallol Bhattacherjee, 2017, 'Australian uranium to arrive soon', *The Hindu*, April 11.

Kanjilal, Pratik, 2013, 'Journalist becomes the News', *The Indian Express,* November 23.

Kanwar Yogendra, 2017. 'A Book Café run exclusively by inmates', *The Hindu*, April 13.

Karan Singh, 2006, 'Cultural diplomacy needs a big thrust, says Karan Singh', *The Tribune* September 24.

Karen MacGregor, 2014, 'Aiming for a slice of the African mobile student pie', University World News, April 26 http://www.universityworldnews.com/ article.php?story=20140418104554993.

Karlekar, Hiranmay. 1998, *Independence India: The First Fifty Years*, ICCR, Oxford University Press.

Kasturi, Charu Sudan, 2015, 'Modi government plans Buddhism blitz in cultural diplomacy focus', *The Telegraph*, August 31.

*Kathmandu Post*, 2014, 'Neighbourliness for Peace and Security in Asia', February 9.

Kathy Bergen, 2016, 'Will making Chicago a "smart city" make a better city', *The Chicago Tribune*, May 1.

Keerthik Sasidharan, 2017, 'Every Culture gives and receives', *The Hindu*, April 9.

Keswani Sumeet, 2016, 'How beautiful is India, These photos tell you', *The Times of India*, January 11.

Khurana, Suanshu, 2017, 'Pakistan students on five day peace visit sent back', *The Indian Express*, May 4.

Kissinger, Henry A, 1966, 'Domestic Structure and Foreign Policy', *Daedalus*. Vol. 95, No. 2, Spring, pp. 503-529.

KLF, 2017, 'India's ICCR among sponsors at Pakistan's Karachi Literature Festival', *The Indian Express*, February 13.

KLF, 2017, 'Row erupts after ICCR sponsors tickets for Karachi Lit Fest', *The Hindustan Times*, February 13.

Kohli, Gauri, 2016, 'Scholarships for Indians to study in UK', *The Hindustan Times*, September 21.

Kolappan, B., 2013, 'TN house resolution calls for boycott of Colombo CHOGM' *The Hindu*, October 24. http://the*The Hindu*.com/news/national/tamil-nadu/tn-house-resolution-calls-for-boycott... (Accessed on 24.10.2013).

Kul Bhushan, 2016, 'A more purposeful PBD: More dialogue less song and dance', *The Indian Diaspora*, January 13.

Kumar, Ankaksha, 2013, 'The wait is still on' *The Hindu*, 18 October.

Lakshman, Narayan, 2013, 'Modi links caste shadow on Vivekananda event', *The Hindu*, September 23.

Lavina Melwani, 2013, 'A chronicle of us in the U.S.', Sunday Magazine, *The Hindu*, April 6, 2013. http://www.thehindu.com/features/magazine/a-chronicle-of-us-in-the-us/article4584315.ece (Accessed on December 17, 2017).

Le Diem, 2017, Indian cultural center opens in Hanoi, *Vietnam Economic Times*, April 27.*http://vneconomictimes.com/article/society/indian-cultural-center-opens-in-hanoi* (Accessed on 13 December 2017).

Li Kesiang, 2013. 'A handshake across the Himalayas', *The Hindu*, May 20.

Luke Harding, 2006, 'Cartoons that rocked the World', *The Guardian*, London, February 6.

*Luxemburg Post*, 2017, 'Drumming diversity together –food for thought', March 5.

M. Hamid Ansari, 2016, 'Indian media in a challenging environment', *The Hindu*, July 16.

M. Raghava, 2017, 'Students protest hijab on campus, sport saffron shawls', *The Hindu*, February 22.

Madhumati D S, 2017, 'India launches satellite to help South Asian nations', *The Hindu*, May 5.

Mahathir, Mohamad, 1996, First ASEAN Lecture, New Delhi, December.

Mamata appeals to Bengali diaspora to pitch in for state, 2012, *The Times of India,* July 7. http://articles.timesofindia.indiatimes.com/2012-07-07/us-canada-news/32576834_1_amit-mitra-state-secretariat-trinamool-congress (Accessed on December 17, 2017).

Manjula Narayan, 2016 'My FB posts become newspaper articles now', *The Hindustan Times*, January 23.

Manoj C G, 2017, 'Govt authoritarian, destroying secular fabric: Oppn to tell President today', *The Indian Express*, April 12.

Mariajose Romero, 2015, 'Exhibition in Texas Depicts the Legacy of Sikhs and Punjab', *Sikh 24.com*, August 2.

Mary E. John, 2017, 'No place for scholarship', *The Hindu*, April 12.

Mazzetti *et al.*, 2011, 'Pakistan spies on its diaspora, spreading fear'. *The New York Times*, July 23. http://www.nytimes.com/2011/07/24/world/asia/24isi.html?pagewanted=all (Accessed on January 7, 2018).

Menon, Meena, 2014. 'Like in the razor's edge', *The Hindu*, February 11.

Menon, Parvathi, 2013 'India-origin groups take protests against immigration measures to Downing Street',*The Hindu,* October 11.

Mistry, Dinshaw, 2006, 'Diplomacy, Domestic Politics and the US-India Nuclear Agreement', *Asian Survey*, Vol. 46, No. 5, Sept. pp. 675-698.

Modi, Chintan Girish, 2016, 'A new prescription for peace from India', *The Hindu*, January 18.

Mona, 2016, 'In the course of action', *The Tribune*, September 5.

Monika Khanna, 2016 'When stories speak', *The Tribune*, February 9.

Moushumi Das Gupta, 2016, 'Minister says Sita's birthplace is a matter of faith, Oppn. corners govt.', *The Hindustan Times*, April 11.

Mubashir Zaidi, 2017, 'Shah Rukh Khan's 'Raees' baned in Pakistan', *The Hindu,* 7 February.

Mukesh Ranjan, 2017, 'Vijay's racist remark stalls LS', *The Tribune*, April 11.

Murli Manohar Joshi, 2017, 'Yoga, where science meets spirituality', *The Tribune*, Mar 18.

Nadim, Farrukh, 2013, 'Nalanda University deserves place in World Heritage Sites: Salman Khurshid', *The Tribune*, Feb. 13.

Namrata Joshi, 2017, 'FTII student's film makes it to Cannes', *The Hindu*, April 13.

Narasimha Rao, P.V, 1994, Singapore Lecture, 'India and the Asia Pacific:

Forging a New Partnership', *Institute of Southeast Asian Studies*, Singapore.

Narayan Lakshman, 2013, 'Pakistani family recounts drone strike before U.S. Congress', *The Hindu*, October 30.

Naresh Mitra, 2017, 'China reaction to my Arunachal visit is normal', *The Sunday Times of India*, April 2.

Nausheen Husain, 2016, 'Eyeing sustainability, Chicago hiring chief resilience officer', *The Chicago The Tribune*, May 1.

Navjot Kaur, 2016, 'Puppet show continues to delight children', *The Chandigarh Times*, February 8.

*NDTV* 2012, 'Shashi Tharoor: Soft power can make us a global power', December 4.

*NDTV, 2014,* 'Maldives Water Crisis: India Transports 1,000 Tonnes of Fresh Water to Male', Dec 7.

Neel Kamal. 2013, 'Ghadar comes alive after 100 years of its launch in US', *The Times of India*, November 1.

*New Delhi Times*, 2016, 'France mulls stripping terrorists of citizenship as Paris attack takes its toll', February 15.

Nick Cumming-Bruce and Steven Erlanger, 2009, 'Swiss Ban Building of Minarets on Mosques', *New York Times*, NOV. 29.

Nonika Singh, 2017, 'Pangs of Partition', *The Tribune*, April 12.

Nonika Singh, 2017, 'Stories behind the songs', *The Tribune*, Jan 23.

*NYT* 2017, Anne Barnard and Michael R Gordon, 'Worst Chemical Attack in Years in Syria: U.S. Blames Assad', April 4.

Obama, 'President Obama extends warmest greetings for Diwali' (www. whitehouse.gov/blog (2014 1/22).

*Odisha Sun Times*, 2016, 'Short Indian movies on Vietnam', February 21.

Omar Farooq Khan, 2016, 'Kohli's Pak fan held for hoisting Indian flag', *The Times of India*, Jan. 28.

Pal, Sanchari, 2016, 'The Fascinating Story of the Talented Shillong Chamber Choir That Rocked the Stage with Coldplay', November 22. http://www.thebetterindia.com/75719/shillong-chamber-choir-neil-nongkynrih/ (Accessed on 12 December 2017).

Pandit, Rajat, 2013, 'India begins training Vietnam sailors in submarine warfare', *The Times of India*, November 23.

Panneerselvan, AS, 2013 'The Possibility of Co-existence', *The Hindu*, April 28.

Panneerselvan, AS, 2013, 'The adjective filter', *The Hindu*, September 30.

Panneerselvan, AS, 2013, 'What's in headlines', *The Hindu*, February 11.

Panneerselvan, AS, 2014, 'When national news dwarfs international news', *The Hindu*, March 10.

Panneerselvan, AS, 2016, 'Of doctored context and vile comments', *The Hindu*, February 22.

Pant, S B, 2017, 'Carrying forward the Koirala legacy', *ECS*, January 13.

Patranobis, Sutirtho: 2016, 'India China need to strengthen people to people ties: Xi Jinping', *The Hindustan Times*, January 16.

Pavan K. Verma, 2009, 'Rs. 150 cr. to hard sell India?', *The Tribune*, November 22.

PBD, 2003, Inaugural Address of Prime Minister of India, Pravasi Bharatiya Divas (PBD), New Delhi, January 9.

PBD, Canada, 2011, http://www.pbdcanada.com. (Accessed on 18 March 2013).

*PBD*, 2009, Inaugural Address of Prime Minister of India, Pravasi Bharatiya Divas (PBD), New Delhi, January 7.

Peerzada Ashiq, 2017, 'I see India heading towards disaster', *The Hindu*, April 12.

Peter Ronald Desouza, 2017, 'India's epic dilemma', *The Hindu*, April 13.

Pillmarri, Akhilesh, 2016, '5 ways India can become a soft power', *The Diplomat*, July 6. https://thediplomat.com/2016/07/5-ways-india-can-become-a-soft-power-superpower/ (Accessed on 16 December 2017).

Prasad, S, 2016, 'Chola era idols in US custody belong to Villupuram Temple', *The Hindu*, January 23.

Prasar Bharti, 2017, 'Prasar Bharti hosts International Dance Festival in Hyderabad', *Asia News International (ANI)*, January 15.

Prasun Sonwalkar, 2013, 'Diwali: UK cops apologise for wrong Punjabi translation', *The Hindustan Tines,* November 1.

Prasun Sonwalkar, 2016, 'Fortunes Change for UK Indians as Leicester hikes Diwali budget', *The Hindustan Times*, Jan. 29.

Pratibha Prahlad, 2016, 'Making India a Cultural Power', *The Hindu*, May 15.

President, 2017, 'Argument is acceptable, but not intolerance: President', *The Sunday Tribune*, April 2.

Pulapre Balakrishan, 2017, 'At home in India', *The Hindu*, April 11.

R Sedhuraman, 2017, 'All is not well with Lalit Kala Akademi: Delhi HC', *The Tribune*, April 11.

Raj, Yashwant, 2013, 'Oak Creek Victim's son to run for US Congress', *The Hindustan Times*, October 27.

Rajdeep Sardesai, 2013, 'Confront these painful truths', *The Hindustan Times*, November 1.

Rajiv Kumar, Omita Goyal, 2015, 'Thirty Years of SAARC, *ICC Quarterly*, Winter Issue.

Ram Madhav, 2017, 'New India, different China', *Indian Express*, April 13.

Ramnath, Nandini, 2014, Scroll.in, *Quarts India*, December 11.

Ranee Kumar, 2017, 'Modernity can exist within a tradition', *The Hindu*, April 13.

Rao Jaswant Singh, 2016, 'Haryana govt to sign an MoU with ICCR to boost culture and tourism', *The Times of India*, January 29, http://timesofindia.indiatimes.com/city/gurgaon/Haryana-govt-to-sign-an-MoU-wi.

Roy, Shubhajit, 2017, 'On PM's Trump trip, a small meet, no Madison Square-kind event', *The Indian Express*, June 17.

S Ravi, 2017, 'Celebrating affinities and ties' *The Hindu*, October 23.

S. Prasad, 2016, 'Chola era idols in US custody belong to Villupuram

Temple', *The Hindu*, January 23.

S. Rama Krishna, 2017, 'Indian techies in U.S. are on alert mode', *The Sunday Guardian*, March 5.

Sachidanand Murthy, 2017, 'Deemed Universities', *The Week*, January 22.

Sachin Prashar, 2014, 'Focus on States in Modi's diplomatic road map', *The Hindu*, August 17.

Sandeep Bhardwaj, 2017, 'The Hindus Hounded from City', *The Hindu,* 6 March.

Sandeep Dikshit, 2013, 'Process under way to decide on participation in CHOGM', *The Hindu*, November 1.

Sanjoy Hazarika, 1987, 'Coming Attraction in Soviet: Festival of India', *New York Times*, June 28. Available at http://www:nytimes.com/1987/06/28/world/coming-attraction-in-soviet-festival-of-india.html

Sarabjit Dhaliwal, 2013, 'Jakhar wants issue debated in Punjab House', *The Tribune*, October 30.

Sardesai, Rajdeep, 2013, 'Confront these painful truths', *The Hindustan Times*, November 1.

Sardesai, Rajdeep, 2014, 'Slippery slope to crassness'', *The Hindustan Times*, March 24.

Sarkar, Bidyut (ed.), 1968, *India and Southeast Asia*, Proceedings of a Seminar, ICCR.

Saubhadra Chatterji, 2017, 'Mann Ki Baat: Don't just talk, feel India's diversity, touch it, says PM Modi', *The Hindustan Times*, Sep 24.

Saurabh Chauhan, 2017, 'A first: Shimla gets a book café run by jail inmates', *The Hindustan Times*, April 12.

Saurabh Malik, 2016, 'Uniquely Singapore', *The Tribune*, May 26.

Saxena, Shoban. 2009, 'How to be a cultural super power', *The Tribune*, Nov. 22

Seerat Dhillon, 2017, 'Education vs Commerce', *The Tribune*, January 6.

Serina Sandhu, 2016, 'David Bowie requested his ashes be scattered in Bali in line with Buddhist rituals', *The Independent*, January 30.

SGPC, 2013, 'SGPC to send books to Canada on Sikhs' role in World War', *The Tribune*, August 27.

Shailaja Bajpai, 2017, 'Dear Modi from Trump', *Indian Express*, March 6.

Shalini Gupta, 2017, 'Smith to take guard in Ranchi with bat made in Jalandhar', *The Hindustan Times*, March 16.

Shambaugh, David, 2015, 'China's Soft-Power Push', *The Foreign Affairs*, July-August.

Sharma, Amarinder Pal, 2013, 'Canadian Sikhs petition against 'criminal' tags', *The Times of India*, October 29.

Sharma, Yojana, 2016, 'Surge in growth of Indian students studying abroad', University World News,Issue No:416, June 1. http://www.universityworldnews.com/article.php?story=20160601180527213.

Sheffer, G.G., 2005, 'Is the Jewish diaspora unique? Reflections on the diaspora's current situation', *Israeli Studies* 10(1). http://sino-west.org/sjtu/Is.pdf (Accessed on 16 April 2018).

Shelly Bhoil, 2017, 'Indian metre, Brazilian echoes', Spectrum, *The Tribune,* December 10.

Shemina Kanwal, Vishaka Chaman, 2016, 'Rock on: French Prez was all questions', *The Times of Chandigarh,* January 25.

Shikoh, Dara, 2017, 'Conference on Dara Shikoh draws experts from 6 countries', *Business Standard*, April 25.

Shyam Bhatia, 2012, 'Yoga: Not in Church, Please', *The Tribune,* October 2.

Simon Carraud, 2017, 'Le Pen cancels cleric meet, won't wear headscarf', *Indian Express*, February 22.

Simran Sodhi, 2017, 'Australia allays fears over changes in its visa regimes', *The Tribune*, May 4.

Simran Sodhi, 2017, 'Chandigarh to host global poetic event as soft power outreach', *The Tribune*, Feb 4.

Singh P, 2012, 'EcoSikh launches green drive in Amritsar', *The Tribune,* July 1. Available at http://www.tribuneindia.com/2012/20120701/punjab.htm#12 [Accessed 26 November 2012].

Singh, Gurmukh, 2012, 'India's Soft Power Spreads', *The Tribune*, October 2.

Singh, I P, 2013, 'Sikhs for Justice engages Washington firm to serve summons on Manmohan Singh', *The Times of India*, October 2.

Singh, Karan, 2006 'Cultural diplomacy needs a big thrust, says Karan Singh', *The Tribune* September 24.

Singh, Rao Jaswant, 2016, 'Haryana govt to sign an MoU with ICCR to boost culture and tourism', *The Times of India*, January 29.

Sinha, Amitabh, 2017, 'Indians' safety first, strategic partnership later: Sushma Swaraj', *The Indian Express*, March 21.

Smriti Kak Ramachandran, 2015, 'German to be taught again in Central Schools', *The Hindu*, October 6.

Sobi Hussain, 2017, 'No visa for Pak wrestlers: Goel justifies same', *The Tribune*, May 4.

Sonwalkar, Prasun, 2013, 'Diwali: UK cops apologise for wrong Punjabi translation', *The Hindustan Times*, November 1.

Stefan Schirmer, Özlem Topcu, 'The Fallout from the Turkish Referendum in Germany', *Handesblatt*, April 13.

Steven R. Weisman, 1987, 'New Delhi Warms to Soviet Cultural Festival', *Special to the New York Times*, November 27.

*Strategic Assets*, http://www.businessdictionary.com/definition/strategic-assets.html (Accessed on 30 September 2013).

Suanshu Khurana, 2017, 'Pakistan students on five day peace visit sent back', *The Indian Express*, May 4.

*Sunday Tribune*, 2017, 'Argument is acceptable, but not intolerance: President', April 2.

Sunder Sarukkai, 2017, 'When the unelected set the Agenda', *The Hindu*, February 22.

Suryanarayana, P S, 2010, 'India's educational diplomacy', *The Hindu*, April 4.

Suryanarayana, P.S. 2006, 'Bridge chasm between the West and the Muslim World: Badawi', *The Hindu*, February 11.

Suvojit Bagchi, 2017, 'Tightening of Visa Rules impacted students', *The Hindu*, January 28.

Tagore, 2016, 'China releases first translations of Rabindranath Tagore's collective works', *Business Standard*, May 5.

Talmiz Ahmad, 2016, Book Review: Scholarship lost in hagiography, *The Asian Age,* 13 November.

Tharoor, Shashi, 2007, 'Leveraging soft power needs hard work', *The Tribune*, 18 Feb.

Tharoor, Shashi, 2011, 'Indian Strategic Power: Soft', *The Huffington Post*, May 25. (http://www.huffingtonpost.com/entry/indian-strategic-powers-so b 207785.html? section=India.

Tharoor, Shashi, 2012, 'Soft Power can make us a global power', *NDTV*, December 4.

Tharoor, Shashi, 2016, 'Iranian Islamists and *The Hindu*tavawadis', *The Week*, February 14.

*The Business Standard*, 2016, 'India organizes Indian culinary week in Israel', May 18.

*The Chicago Tribune*, 2013, 'Obama opens up about race', July 20.

The Dalai Lama, 2017, 'Secular ethics for our times', *The Indian Express*, July 1.

*The Diplomat*, 2016, Abhilesh Pillamarri, 'Ways India Can Become a Soft Power Superpower', July 6.

*The Globe and Mail*, 2012, Carment, David and Samy, Yiagadeesen, 'The dangerous game of diaspora politics', February 10.

*The Hindu*, 2005, 'Cultural Diplomacy, not a luxury: Karan Singh', Sept. 3.

*The Hindu*, 2011, 'Cricket and diplomacy should be kept separate: BJP', March 31.

*The Hindu*, 2013 'U.S. Sikh group filing improper suits against Congress leaders', October 23.

*The Hindu,* 2013, 'Engaging for a fair settlement', October *26*.

*The Hindu*, 2013, 'Indonesia gifts US a Saraswati Statue', June 10.

*The Hindu,* 2013, 'Khurshid will represent India at CHOGM', October 27.

*The Hindu*, 2014, 'Bhutan King's visit', January 6.

*The Hindu*, 2014, 'Easing Tensions in Palk Bay' (ed.), January 17.

*The Hindu*, 2014, 'India, Australia share special bond: Modi', November 16.

*The Hindu*, 2014, 'Media has kept a critical eye on government: PM', March 13.

*The Hindu,* 2014, 'Modi raises Mansarovar Yatra route with Xi', July 11.

*The Hindu*, 2014, 'No real winners' (ed.). January 9.

*The Hindu*, 2014, 'Uncertainty in Bangladesh' (ed.), January 1.

*The Hindu*, 2014, 'Yameen in India' (ed.), January 3.

*The Hindu*, 2014, Panel Organizer, Rathje, 2014, Elizabeth Erin Panel Chair: Rathje, Elizabeth Erin Panel Title: "Reconsidering the representational frame: Nexuses between practice and theory".

*The Hindu*, 2014, 'Smithsonian looks at influences of Indian Americans', Feb 27.

*The Hindu*, 2016, 'France returns head of The Hindu statue taken 130 years ago', January 22.

*The Hindu*, 2016, 'Ghulam Ali event in Mumbai cancelled', *The Hindu*, Jan. 28.

*The Hindu*, 2016, 'Khajuraho statutes may soon be draped with Saris', Jan. 24.

*The Hindu*, 2016, 'No intolerance in Bollywood says Kajol', Jan. 21.

*The Hindu,* 2016, 'Neerja banned in Pakistan', February 1.

*The Hindu,* 2017, 'Tarun Vijay's racial remarks rock House', April 11.

*The Hindu*, 2017 'The Indo-Pak diplomatic stairwell', April 12.

*The Hindu*, 2017, 'Film Awards celebrate India's diversity: President', *The Hindu,* May 4.

*The Hindu,* 2017, 'Justin Bieber to be served cuisines representing 29 states of India', May 4.

*The Hindu*, 2017, 'Transformative visit', April 11.

*The Hindu, 2017,* Haider, Suhasini and Vasudeva, Vikas, 'Amarinder remarks on Canadian ministers sparks row', April 17.

*The Hindustan Times*, 2013, 'Chances bleak for PM's Lanka visit for CHOGM summit', October 30.

*The Hindustan Times*, 2013, 'Sikh regiment's WW-2 veterans awarded in UK', October 19.

*The Hindustan Times*, 2013, 'Ex Canadian MP to help victims of fraud marriages', October 30.

*The Hindustan Times*, 2013, 'NaMo foreign policy: Bigger role for states', October 20.

*The Hindustan Times*, 2013, 'SGPC rues treatment of Sikh student in US', October 19.

*The Hindustan Times*, 2013, 'Sikh student with Kirpan not allowed to board bus in US', October 18.

*The Hindustan Times,* 2013, 'Tejpal creates Tehelka', November 22.

*The Hindustan Times*, 2013, 'US refused to declare 1984 riots as genocide', April 3.

*The Hindustan Times*, 2014, 'Light at the end of the Tunnel', (ed.), February 11.

*The Hindustan Times,* 2014, 'PM's stress on collective effort to tackle regional challenges', February 9.

*The Hindustan Times*, 2016, 'Akal Takht slams Centre for keeping Sikhs out of the parade', Jan. 30.

*The Hindustan Times*, 2016, 'Amazon faces flak in Japan for delivering monks', January 31.

*The Hindustan Times,* 2016, 'An Appetite for foreign shores: Offering food eats to the world', April 4.

*The Hindustan Times,* 2016, 'Google pays tribute to Amrita Sher-Gill', January 31.

*The Hindustan Times*, 2017, 'Pak: The Hindu women hope abductions, forced weddings will end', April 13.

*The Hindustan Times*, 2017, 'Pulitzer Prize for work on Trump, Putin', April 12.

*The Hindustan Times*, 2017, 'Canadian PM Trudeau's presence at event with Khalistani flags upsets India', May 5.

*The Hindustan Times,* 2017, 'Dutch nationals to get 5-year business, tourist visas: PM', June 29.

*The Hindustan Times*, 2017, 'I watched Dangal, and liked it: Chinese President Xi Jinping to PM Modi', June 10.

*The Hindustan Times*, 2017, 'Islamists held over attack on German football team', April 13.

*The Hindustan Times*, 2017, 'KLF, Row erupts after ICCR sponsors tickets for Karachi Lit Fest', February 13.

*The Indian Express*, 2013, 'MEA parliamentary panel talks cultural diplomacy', February 13.

*The Indian Express*, 2013, 'Anand Sharma defers meeting with Walmart's Scott Price', November 1.

*The Indian Express,* 2013, 'Journalist becomes the News', November 22.

*The Indian Express,* 2013, 'MEA parliamentary panel talks culture diplomacy', February 19.

*The Indian Express*, 2013, 'Nixon turned a blind eye to *The Hindu* genocide by Pak Army' October 17.

*The Indian Express*, 2013, 'Obama must raise 1984 riots at summit: Sikh rights group', September 23. http://newsindianexpress.com/nation/Obama-must-raise-1984-riots-at-summit-Sikh-rights.

*The Indian Express*, 2014, 'Afridi at home away from home', March 14.

*The Indian Express,* 2014, 'Media and government have broken relationship: Star India CEO'.

*The Indian Express,* 2014, 'A PM for Nepal' (ed.), February 11.

*The Indian Express,* 2015, 'Bollywood continues to serenade Chinese audience', July 13.

*The Indian Express*, 2016, 'All for better ties: China-India Tourism year launched', Jan 13.

*The Indian Express*, 2016, 'It's not Cricket' (Ed.), March 3.

*The Indian Express*, 2016, 'Pluralism and tolerance hallmark of Indian civilization: President Pranab Mukherjee', April 10.

*The Indian Express*, 2016, 'Special Visa to advocates can help in strengthening India-Pak ties, February 7.

*The Indian Express*, 2016, 'Yoga Day Live: PM Modi performs Yoga with 30,000 participants in Chandigarh, worldwide celebrations ensue', July 22.

*The Indian Express*, 2017 'Canada refuses entry to former IG of CRPF, India lodges protest', May 24,

*The Indian Express*, 2017, 'I watched Dangal, liked the actors as well as the movie: Chinese President Xi Jinping tells PM Narendra Modi', June 10.

*The Indian Express*, 2017, 'Infosys, trumped', (ed.), May 4.

The President, 2017, 'Argument is acceptable, but not intolerance: President', *The Sunday Tribune*, April 2.

The President, 2017, 'Let's work to reverse brain drain: President', *The Tribune,* May 3.

*The Sunday Times*, 2013, 'Muslim martyrs of Ghadar action remain unsung', 27 October.

*The Sunday Times*, 2013, 'Visiting NRIs to pay homage to Ghadri 'Babas', October 27.

*The Sunday Times*, 2016, 'Beyonce in desi garb stirs cultural appropriation row', January 31.

*The Times of India*, 2003, 'French-edict betrays anti-Muslim bias', December 25.

*The Times of India*, 2004 'American Corner opens at State Library', December 18.

*The Times of India,* 2012, 'Mamata appeals to Bengali diaspora to pitch in for state', July 7.

*The Times of India*, 2012, 'India does not start levying proposed service tax on remittances fee paid by NRIs', July 3.

*The Times of India*, 2013 'Rift in Chicago over Modi Shadow', September 24.

*The Times of India*, 2013, 'Af wooed Taliban to settle scores with Pak army?' October 30.

*The Times of India*, 2013, 'Pakistan Hindus seek Indian govt's support to stay back', October 17.

*The Times of India*, 2013, 'Sikh issues to figure in Conference', October 26.

*The Times of India*, 2014, 'Success story or struggle? Portraying Indians in US', March 6.

*The Times of India*, 2017, 'Abhay roasts SRK & co for fairness cream ads', April 13.

*The Times of India*, 2017, 'Break the Chains' (Ed.), May 4.

*The Times of India*, 2017, 'I will not cover up: Le Pen cancels meeting, with Lebanese grand mufti over headgear', February 22.

*The Times of India*, 2017, 'India, Oz sign 6 pacts but trade deal elusive', April 11.

*The Times of India*, 2017, 'Judicial Murder', April 12.

*The Times of India*, 2017, 'Mantri says Sita's birthplace a matter of faith, sparks row', April 13.

*The Times of India*, 2017, 'President, Vice-President raise toast to PM's communication skills', May 27.

*The Times of India*, 2017, 'Racially profiled at Heathrow over headscarf: LiLo', February 22.

*The Times of India*, 2017, 'Reverse trend of students migration: Prez', May 3.

*The Tribune*, 2001, 'Cultural diplomacy wins over politics', Nov. 4.

*The Tribune*, 2010, 'From land of snake charmers to global cultural hot spot', Nov. 12.

*The Tribune*, 2012, 'Shankar personified India's soft power', Dec. 13.

*The Tribune*, 2013 'Will oppose Canada's move to ban Sikh symbols:

SGPC', August 27.

*The Tribune*, 2013, 'SGPC to send books to Canada on Sikhs' role in World War', August 27.

*The Tribune*, 2013, 'Afghan govt 'tried to take revenge' on Pak army with help of Taliban', October 30.

*The Tribune*, 2013, 'Britain decorates a Sikh Regiment WW-II veterans', October 19.

*The Tribune*, 2013, 'In a first, Diwali celebrations at Capitol Hill', August 27.

*The Tribune*, 2013, 'India undecided on PM's participation, Ashok Tuteja in CHOGM', October 12.

*The Tribune*, 2013, 'Indian-American appointed to top', October 18.

*The Tribune*, 2013, 'Indira was wrongly advised on Bluestar: KPS Gill', November 1.

*The Tribune*, 2013, 'Li greets Indian audience with Namaste', May 22.

*The Tribune*, 2013, 'NRI can evict tenants under new law', October 30.

*The Tribune*, 2013, 'PM may skip Lanka C'wealth meet', October 17.

*The Tribune*, 2013, 'Will oppose Canada's move to ban Sikh symbols: SGPC', August 27.

*The Tribune,* 2014, 'Grateful Britain recalls valour sacrifices of Indian soldiers during World War I', October 31.

*The Tribune*, 2014, 'India sends drinking water to Maldives', December 5.

*The Tribune*, 2015, 'Sholay, Soft power of Bollywood' (ed.), 'Welcome awaits Sholay in Pakistan', February 14.

*The Tribune*, 2016 ,'Panjab University a hotspot for overseas students', Jun 12.

*The Tribune,* 2016, '44th Rose Festival to start today', January 19.

*The Tribune,* 2016, 'Cameron again says, he backs burqa ban', Jan. 20, 2016.

*The Tribune*, 2016, 'Cultural ties key to promoting peace in South Asia: Scribes', April 11,.

*The Tribune,* 2016, 'Freedom to doubt, disagree must be protected: Pranab', December 30.

*The Tribune,* 2016, 'Migrants who cannot speak English may have to leave Britain: UK PM Cameron', January 18.

The Tribune, 2016, 'Obama cites Sikhs to talk about strength of faith', February 6.

*The Tribune*, 2016, 'Playing Pak in Dharamshala' (Ed.), March 3.

*The Tribune*, 2016, 'Pluralism and tolerance hallmark of Indian civilization: President', April 10.

*The Tribune,* 2016, 'Twitter helped Modi build tech-savvy image: Study', March 20.

*The Tribune*, 2017, 'Australia's Turnbull seeks patriotism for citizenship', June 14.

*The Tribune*, 2017, 'Jadhav's death sentence', April 12.

*The Tribune*, 2017, 'Let's work to reverse brain drain: President', May 3.

*The Tribune*, 2017, 'More money for Africa, more love for Federer', April 12.

*The Tribune*, 2017, 'Nandy: Can't socialise, or discipline poetry', April 11.

*The Tribune*, 2017, 'Pakistan will now be seen as minorities' friendlily, Sharif', January 12.

*The Tribune*, 2017, 'YouTube has changed music ', April 11.

*The Times of India*, 2017, 'Reverse trend of students' migration: Prez', May 3.

Tikku, Alike 2013, 'No decision yet on Lanka visit of PM', *The Hindustan Times*, October 19.

*TNN*, 2010, 'From land of snake charmers to global hotspot', December 12.

Tunku Vardarajan, 2016, 'Europe's cultural nightmare', *The Sunday Express*, January 31.

Turnbull, 2017, 'PM calls on new citizens to become 'Australian patriots', *SBS News*.

Vandana Vijay, 2016, 'India-Iran relations: Why Bollywood is our cinema language', *BRC Hindu,* May 22.

Varma, Pavan K, 2016, 'Global Village is a Myth: Cultures still retain a stubborn opacity impenetrable to outsiders', *Times of India*, July 2.

Varma, Pavan, 2006, 'Soft Power', *The Tribune*, 7 Oct.

Vatsayan, Kapila, 2014, 'Culture: The crafting of Institutions in Independent India' in 'Indian Democracy: Agenda for 21st Century, *Foreign Service Institute*, New Delhi. Feb. 5.

Verma, KJM, 2017, 'Devon ke Dev, Nagin & Mahabharta TV shows a big hit in China', *Indian Express,* May 4.

Vidya Ram, 2017, 'Marching to be counted', *The Hindu*, February 22.

Vidya Subramanian, 2017 'We don't need an Indian propaganda channel', *Hindustan Times*, April 11.

Vishavjeet Chaudhry, 2016, 'Varsities have a pivotal role', *The Tribune*, March 9.

Vivek Gupta and Aseem Bassi, 2016, 'SGPC not to offer "Siropa" to lesbian Canadian premier', *The Hindustan Times*, Jan. 30.

Walter and Duncan Gordon Foundation, 'Diaspora Communities and Foreign Policy', file://G:\Chicago-June-Aug2013\Diaspora-ForeignPolicy\DiasporaCommunitiesandfor... (Accessed on 19.10.2013).

Walter Lacquer, 1994, 'Save Public Diplomacy: Broadcasting America's Message Matters', *Foreign Affairs,* 73: 5, September-October.

William Borders, 1982, 'London sees 'festival of India' art', *The New York Times*, March 27.

World Bank, 2011, *African Diaspora Program (ADP).* Available at http://web.worldbank.org/WBSITE/EXTERNAL/COUNTRIES/AFRICAEXT/EXTDIASPORA/0,,contentMDK:21496629~pagePK:64168427~piPK:64168435~theSitePK:4246098,00.html (Accessed on December 23, 2017).

World Bank, 2011, *Migration and Remittances Factbook 2011.* Washington DC: World Bank. http://econ.worldbank.org/WBSITE/EXTERNAL/EXTDEC/EXTDECPROSPECTS/0,,contentMDK:21352016~pagePK:64165401~piPK:64165026~theSitePK:476883,00.

html (Accessed on December 23, 2017).

World Sufi Forum, 2016, Text of PM's address at the World Sufi Forum,March17.http://www.pmindia.gov.in/en/news_updates/text-of-pms-address-at-the-world-sufi-forum/ (Accessed on December 23, 2017).

Xinhua, 2016: 'Xi congratulates on launch of 'Visit China Year' in India', Jan. 16.

Yashwant Raj, 2017, 'USL Sikh man shot at in Kent masked attacker shouted, 'go back to your country', *The Hindustan Times,* May 5.

Yaswant Raj, 2016, 'Trump dominates Trumpless debate', *The Hindustan Times*, Jan. 30.

Yojana Sharma, 2016, 'Surge in growth of Indian students studying abroad', June 01, Issue No: 416.

Youssef Igrouanne, 'Marrakech, Bombay..... A Love Story, Consolidates Cultural Ties between Morocco and India', http://www.moroccoworldnews.com/2016/02/180254.

## Key Websites

American Corner Website,http://newdelhi.usembassy.gov/libamcorners.html.

Americanspaces@state.gov or Lauren Appelbaum, Project Coordinator, Smithsonian Institution: AppelbaumL@si.edu.

Canadian Website, http://www.canadainternational.gc.ca/india-inde/academic_relations_academiques/index.aspx?lang=eng&menu_id=12.

Chandigarh State Library Website, http://cslchd.gov.in

Chevening, http://www.chevening.org/india/

DNA, http://www.dnaindia.com (Accessed on December 23, 2017).

Eye on India Website:http://eyeonindia.com/

Farrugia & Bhandari 2014, 2014 – 15 Annual Report Office of International Education Beloit College, https://www.beloit.edu/oie/assets/2014.15_annual_report_.pdf (Accessed on December 23, 2017).

Fullbright Programme, State Department Website: www.state.gov/records/remarks/2013/03206335.htm.

Goodman, Allan E, https://www.elsevier.com/connect/asian-research-execs-discuss-what-it-takes-to-produce-world-leading-universities (Accessed on December 23, 2017).

GOPIO Website, http://www.gopio.org.my/contact-us/

Goucher College, http://www.goucher.edu/learn/study-abroad/ (Accessed on December 23, 2017).

Harinder Sandhu, http://India.highcommission.gov.aus/Indi/pa0217.html.

ICCR Website, www.iccr.gov.in

ICWA Website, www.icwa.in

IGCNA Website, www.ignca.nic.in

IHE website, www.ihe-du.com/

IIC Website, www.iicdelhi.nic.in

IIE Brochure, https://www.iie.org/en/ (Accessed on December 23, 2017).

INTACH, www.intach.org

IVLP, Website: www.http://exchanges.state.gov/IVLP/evlp.htm.

MEA; www.mea.gov.in

NAPA: http://www.sikhiwiki.org/index.php/North_America_Punjabi-Associatio.

Open Doors 2014, https://www.iie.org/Why-IIE/Announcements/2014-Open-Doors-Data.

Open Doors, 2017, https://www.iie.org/Why-IIE/Announcements/2017-11-13-Open-Doors-2017-Executive-Summary (Accessed on December 23, 2017).

PBD Canada 2011.r5 http://www.pbdcanada.com. (Accessed on 18 March 2013).

SAU Charter: http://www.sau.int/about/about-sau.html.

SAU VISION: http://www.sau.int/about/vision.html.

Shillong Chamber Choir, https://en.wikipedia.org/wiki/Shillong_

Chamber_Choir (Accessed on December 23, 2017).

Smithsonian Affiliations, www.affiliations.si.edu.

Smithsonian, www.smithsonian.org

Spic Macay, website: www.spicmacay.com (Accessed on 12 December 2017).

State Department: (www.state.gov/records/remains 2017/03 (Accessed on December 23, 2017).

Strategic Assets, http://www.businessdictionary.com/definition/strategic-assets.html (Accessed on 30 September 2013).

Swami Vivekanand, http://chicagovedanta.org/1893.html

UK Africa Diaspora Programme. http://.dfid.gov.uk/work-with-us/funding-opportunities/not-for-profit-organisations/c (Accessed on 14.3.2013).

UK, http://www.universitiesuk.ac.uk/news/Pages/International-students-now-worth-25-billion-to-UK-economy---new-research.aspx#sthash.sKD7GAy2.dpbs (Accessed on December 23, 2017).

University of Southern California: http://uscpublicdiplomacy.org/story/five-global-leaders-fashion-diplomacy.

US Study Abroad, https://studyabroad.state.gov/

USC. https://uscpublicdiplomacy.org/story/five-global-leaders-fashion-diplomacy (Accessed on 29 April 2018.

USINPAC, http://www;usinpac.com/home/our-mission

USINPAC, http://www;usinpac.com/home/our-mission (Accessed on January 7, 2018).

Website of Cultural Department, Chandigarh,http://chandigarh.gov.in/dpr_aboutculture.asp.

Website SCI: http://chicagosistercities.com/upcoming_event/sister-cities-internationals-60th-anniversary-celebration-annual-conference-and-youth-leadership-summit/

# Index

## H



## I

## N



## O



## P

## T

www.ingramcontent.com/pod-product-compliance
Lightning Source LLC
Chambersburg PA
CBHW031549260326
41914CB00002B/338
* 9 7 8 9 3 8 8 1 6 1 0 7 7 *